AGE OF

Contention

AGE OF

Contention

READINGS IN CANADIAN SOCIAL HISTORY, 1900–1945

Jeffrey Keshen
UNIVERSITY OF OTTAWA

HARCOURT
BRACE
CANADA

Harcourt Brace & Company, Canada

Toronto Montreal Fort Worth New York Orlando
Philadelphia San Diego London Sydney Tokyo

Requests for permission to make copies of any part of the work should be mailed to: Permissions, College Division, Harcourt Brace & Company, Canada, 55 Horner Avenue, Toronto, Ontario M8Z 4X6.

Every reasonable effort has been made to acquire permission for copyright material used in this text, and to acknowledge all such indebtedness accurately. Any errors and omissions called to the publisher's attention will be corrected in future printings.

Canadian Cataloguing in Publication Data

Main entry under title:

Age of contention: readings in Canadian social
    history, 1900–1945

ISBN 0-7747-3522-8

1. Canada — Social conditions — 20th century.
I. Keshen, Jeffrey, 1962–   .

HN103.B54 1997   971.06   C96-930811-6

Director of Product Development: Heather McWhinney
Senior Acquisitions Editor: Christopher Carson
Projects Manager: Liz Radojkovic
Developmental Editor: Laura Paterson Pratt
Editorial Co-ordinator: Natalie Witkin
Director of Publishing Services: Jean Davies
Editorial Manager: Marcel Chiera
Supervising Editor: Semareh Al-Hillal
Production Manager: Sue-Ann Becker
Production Co-ordinator: Sheila Barry
Copy Editor: Theresa Griffin
Cover and Interior Design: Sonya V. Thursby/Opus House
Typesetting and Assembly: New Concept Complete Printing & Publishing Services Ltd.
Printing and Binding: Best Book Manufacturers, Inc.

Cover Art: Caven Atkins, *Political Discussion, Depths of Depression, Winnipeg* (1932). Mendel Art Gallery, Saskatoon. Reproduced with permission.

This book was printed in Canada.

1 2 3 4 5   01 00 99 98 97

Preface

Between the outset of the twentieth century and the end of World War II, Canada in many respects came of age constitutionally, internationally, and socio-economically. Its population grew far more diverse; its social welfare apparatus began to take shape; and its industrial and agricultural sectors matured to the point where the country served as a major supplier of food and materiel to the Allied war effort. Until recently, the vast majority of historical work focussed on the politicians and other elites held to be responsible for bringing about this progress and for fashioning a country that, leaving aside temporary glitches like the Great Depression, provided its citizens with an ever-improving standard of living.

During the last generation or so, however, historical study in Canada has undergone a revolution from the bottom up. A new army of historians, their ideas often forged by the radical politics of the late 1960s, took it upon themselves to uncover the experiences of the forgotten and frequently ill-treated masses. This mission took them, for example, from parliamentary chambers and corporate boardrooms to shop floors and urban slums, and quite often demonstrated that Canada's political and economic maturation did little to alter, and in some instances worsened, classism, racism, and sexism.

This anthology seeks to introduce students to the large body of literature that has attempted to resurrect the lives of ordinary people and their experience of those decades of "progress." Although each article is abridged so that the volume could cover as many subfields as possible of the new social history, spatial limitations made it necessary to leave out a great deal of important work (on entrepreneurial and middle-class culture, for example) and to conflate certain areas (such as the new legal history and other subfields). Articles were chosen on the basis of what issues in the 1900–1945 period, it was felt, had attracted the most attention from social historians. Moreover, while there are exceptions, an effort was made to choose articles that were of relatively recent authorship; that had not already been reprinted a number of times; that did not duplicate information; that touched on a wide range of groups and issues in locations across Canada; and that demonstrated differences in viewpoint, methodology, and kind of evidence used. The introduction seeks to provide students with some information on the rise, the branches, and the contributions of social history and on the controversies it has generated. The prefaces to each topic briefly set the articles in historical context, provide questions to help stimulate class discussion, and

furnish a short list of suggested readings, which always includes a specialized biblio-graphic guide or review article, to expedite the students' search for additional material.

ACKNOWLEDGEMENTS

I would like to thank Doug Owram, Paul Voisey, David Mills, and Rod Macleod of the University of Alberta and Wendy Mitchinson of the University of Waterloo for help-ing me choose articles. Professors Mills and Voisey were also kind enough to read the introduction and the prefaces to each topic, and Professors Owram and Macleod, as well as J.L. Granatstein of York University, generously read the article on juvenile delinquency, which was prepared for this volume. Constructive reviews were also pro-vided for Harcourt Brace by Patrick Brennan of the University of Calgary, Roger Hall of the University of Western Ontario, and John Thomas of Acadia University. Finally, my thanks go out to Chris Carson and Laura Paterson Pratt of Harcourt Brace for encouraging this project, to Semareh Al-Hillal for seeing it through to a finished book, to Theresa Griffin for her superlative editing, and, especially, to all the authors who allowed their work to appear here in abbreviated form.

A NOTE FROM THE PUBLISHER

Thank you for selecting *Age of Contention: Readings in Canadian Social History, 1900–1945*, by Jeffrey Keshen. The author and publisher have devoted considerable time to the careful development of this book. We appreciate your recognition of this effort and accomplishment.

We want to hear what you think about *Age of Contention*. Please take a few min-utes to fill in the stamped reader reply card at the back of the book. Your comments and suggestions will be valuable to us as we prepare new editions and other books.

Contents

Introduction

Survey courses of Canadian history, on reaching the twentieth century, invariably refer to Prime Minister Wilfrid Laurier's proclamation that the next hundred years would "belong to Canada." Several statistical indicators spanning the subsequent decades appear to bear out the prime minister's confidence. Between the turn of the century and the end of World War II, the country's population grew by some 110 percent to 12.1 million. Much of this growth came from immigration, which surpassed 100 000 for the first time in 1903 and played a key role in opening up 269.5 million acres (107.8 million hectares) of prairie farmland between 1900 and 1914. In the urban sphere, which by the 1920s was home to a majority of people, jobs multiplied rapidly. Manufacturing output, for instance, soared from $223 million to $1.275 billion during the first two decades of the century.[1]

Until recently, the writing and teaching of Canadian history largely reflected what seemed to be the inherent message of these facts: steady progress over time. This theme was usually given expression within a framework discussing the rise of Canada from "colony to nation." Apart from Canada's French–English division, most historians did not fully appreciate, or willfully ignored or downplayed, the country's other deep-seated regional and sociocultural cleavages. Moreover, scholars focussed on what were considered centres of power as well as on the so-called great men, primarily politicians, who were seen as responsible for securing national progress. Indeed, in the mid-1960s, Professor Stanley Mealing remarked that there seemed to prevail among historians an idea that too much "study of . . . common-place man" would lead to "common-place history."[2] This standard approach also gave rise to several "covering laws" on the subject of what had bound Canada together as a separate entity, theories that mirrored the widespread pre-occupation of twentieth-century historians with the building of the still-young country.[3]

In Europe, however, where nation-building had stretched out over centuries, there appeared, in as early as the 1920s, the intellectual seeds for a new type of history the practitioners of which came to be known as the *Annales* school. These historians talked about using both traditional documents (such as government and personal papers) and a wide range of often overlooked statistical sources (such as parish records) to write a "total history" encompassing the structure and mentality of past societies, as well as the demographic, economic, and social factors responsible for change.[4] Later, another guide for what is now called the "new social history" appeared

in the work of the Cambridge University professor E.P. Thompson, particularly in his 1963 classic *The Making of the English Working Class*. Breaking from conventional Marxism by insisting that a class had to be conscious of itself in order to exist, rather than simply bearing out economic definition, Thompson, like the *Annales* practitioners, offered a way of viewing history from the "bottom up" — that is, through the experiences and perspectives of everyday people.

Not until the last generation or so have these methods and theories exerted a notable impact on North American historical writing. For about a quarter-century after World War II, in an era dominated by the Cold War and anxieties over creeping communism, notions such as "social consensus" and themes such as the superiority of liberal democracy dominated.[5] Writing in 1965, the American historian John Higham described historical scholarship as set within a theoretical "bed of continuity" in which divisions such as class, race, ethnicity, and gender seemed irrelevant.[6] The turmoil of the late 1960s, however, shattered many people's faith in North American society. Widespread protest was spearheaded by university students, whose numbers expanded tremendously during the post–World War II era owing to the relative affluence of the period. Their castigation of the socio-economic order accordingly is ironic at one level. But the expanding university population also meant a larger, more visible constituency with time to ponder large philosophical questions (like "What is justice?") rather than being consumed by the practical concerns of working life. As well, in coming from a wider cross-section of society than had their predecessors on campus, these students developed more interest in and sensitivity to racism, sexism, and classism — a consciousness heightened by awareness of the growing, and sometimes radical, Black Civil Rights movement, which in its turn helped spawn more militant campaigns for equality among Latinos, Native Americans, and women. Focussing and intensifying the climate of protest was the role played by the so-called military-industrial complex, which was condemned for fomenting an imperialist war for profit in Indo-China. Not only did all these issues become concerns on Canadian campuses too, but they were supplemented by domestic issues pointing to a disintegrating consensus, such as the appearance of a more militant labour movement, of FLQ separatism in Quebec, and of vocal regional sentiment from the Prairies and the Maritimes.

In 1967, the year of nation-wide celebration of Canada's centenary, the presence of discordant undercurrents such as these persuaded historians Ramsay Cook and J.M.S. Careless to advise their colleagues to de-emphasize nationalist critiques of the country's past in favour of exploring what were obviously Canada's more "limited identities."[7] Enthusiastically accepting this challenge were a number of younger scholars eager to discover the roots of the social division around them. Taking advantage of increased opportunities for graduate-school training in Canada's mushrooming university system, they generated a historical revolution from the "bottom up." Whereas only two of fourteen Ph.D.s completed in Canadian history during the 1971–72 academic session fell under the umbrella of social history, twenty years later the number was 58 of 82[8] — representing research that not only found its way into many first-rate books, but also catapulted the journal *Histoire sociale/Social History* (begun in 1968) into the position of being one of the country's premier scholarly publications.

In pursuing their more inclusive approach to the past, social historians asked new questions of well-used sources; turned to a repertoire of little-used demographic, economic, oral, and material evidence; and displayed a willingness to borrow from other disciplines, such as mathematics, in order to do quantitative analysis and sociology in order to delineate power relations. In breaking so sharply from conventional historical inquiry, this new genre attracted its fair share of critics. To focus on ordinary people at the expense of politicians or other elites, insisted some scholars, was to overlook those primarily responsible for historical change. With their tendency to limit analysis more tightly in terms of time and space in order to present the unique experiences of various subgroups, social historians also found themselves attacked for "sundering" history to the point where there no longer existed any common patterns that could explain Canada as a nation.[9] On a technical level, doubts were raised as to the quality of some of the sources used by social historians: oral accounts were possibly affected by faulty memory or the tendency of individuals to embellish; material evidence like art and architecture offered too nebulous a foundation on which to build conclusions; and early statistical evidence was often non-standardized between locales and was punctuated with errors. Finally, just as social historians charged previous scholars with bias for being wedded to the notion of progress over time, they too came under fire for a supposed tendency to debunk any positive notion of capitalism and liberal democracy. But whatever social historians admit are the shortcomings of their field, almost all hold to the view that such problems pale in comparison with those of more traditional work.

Many of the scholars responsible for changing history so dramatically were drawn first into the field of urban history, since the rise of cities was connected with the growth of industrial capitalism and socio-economic division. Moreover, one could test the accuracy of previous "covering laws" through intensive local study. Over the past generation, urban history has advanced far beyond the early anecdotal community studies done by local residents, and the accounts by geographers of spatial and economic development through various stages that seemed to equate growth with progress. The new generation of scholars have produced far more analytical and critical assessments of urban development. By 1971, their work had expanded to the point of justifying a new journal, the *Urban History Review*. The fruit of their efforts has been a plethora of path-breaking studies of matters such as the shifting economic functions and social structure of communities; crime, policing, and political corruption; housing conditions, architecture, and neighbourhood divisions; leisure activities and local customs; and the idealistic, pragmatic, and/or pecuniary interests behind urban reform campaigns.

Earlier accounts of rural Canada were generally rather formulistic triumphal tales: of pioneers taming a rough wilderness who, with enough time, effort, modernization, and, in some circumstances, government assistance, ultimately achieved stupendous success both for themselves and for Canada by making it one of the world's great agricultural nations. In these accounts, tensions between rural and urban sectors over matters like tariffs and railway rates was dealt with, but compromise was eventually achieved by national political leaders, who thereby enabled the country to continue its march forward.[10] Indicative of the long-standing ignorance of the myriad groups and experiences making up "farm life" was the fact that during the first 50 years of the *Canadian Historical Review* (1920–70), less than 3 percent of the articles therein dealt with the rural sector even though as late as 1941 the single largest occupational category as revealed in the national census was "workers in agricultural pursuits."[11]

Things began to change during the 1960s and 1970s, as more works focussed on persistent regional grievances, from Western Canada, for example, and some *Annales-*

type works examined early agriculture in Quebec. Tremendous impetus to scholarship in this subfield was given by Donald Harman Akenson, a historian of Ireland, who not only wrote a brilliant study dispelling long-held notions of Canada's Irish immigrants as impoverished urban slum dwellers, but also, in 1978, started *Canadian Papers in Rural History*. To date, its nine volumes have uncovered, among other things, a rich heritage of rural protest and community co-operation; the unique lives of farm women; the effect of ethnicity on agricultural practices; the experiential and ideological similarities between landless urban and itinerant farm workers; and the possible existence of a rural culture or set of values, as well as offering more traditional work on regional economic development and rural politics.

Prior to World War II, Canadian labour history was virtually non-existent. That which emerged over the next three decades, during the Cold War, by and large focussed on the institutional growth of unions, glossed over class conflict, and applauded moderate labour leaders who worked with reasonable employers and the state to obtain a variety of concessions. The new labour history turned its attention to the rank-and-file, and, in particular, to the relationship between workplace conflict (over pay, hours, safety, shop floor control, and union recognition, for example) and the development of a separate working-class culture and consciousness. In organizations like the Canadian Committee for Labour History, formed in 1971, as well as in the pages of its journal, *Labour/Le travail*, begun five years later, scholars sparked debate on a range of matters, including the potential for radicalism among various segments of the Canadian working class; the effects of technological change and growing managerial control on the working class; and the possible hidden agenda of social welfare — to serve elites by undermining, for a small price, the potential for class conflict. In this dynamically evolving subfield, there has also appeared greater recognition of working-class divisions based on location, occupation, age, gender, ethnicity, and the effect of union leadership.

Besides attracting criticism from many consensus-style historians for emphasizing class conflict, the new labour history fostered some reservations on the part of an emerging corps of feminist scholars. These scholars pointed out that analyses focussing on class commonly glossed over the separate experience of women. A key role in creating such a perception was clearly played by the rise of the modern women's movement, which identified and attacked the stereotypes confining women to specific and usually subordinate positions in society. For generations, feminist scholars argued, the almost exclusively male authors of the history books had reinforced those stereotypes, by ignoring women or casting them as appendages of important men (in the role of political wife, for example), or, at best, by briefly mentioning such things as the success of the suffrage campaign, the implicit assumption being that it provided for equality.

In 1971, the University of Toronto created Canada's first course in women's history, and over the next twenty years 49 of Canada's 69 undergraduate history departments followed suit.[12] On the publishing front, there appeared between 1972 and 1978 *The Canadian Newsletter of Research on Women* (renamed *Resources for Feminist Research* in 1979), *Atlantis*, and *Canadian Women's Studies*.

Much of the early work in women's history portrayed women as passive victims of a patriarchal society, or else, at the other extreme, focussed on "women worthies."[13] Attention was also centred on late nineteenth- and early twentieth-century suffragism, given that it had long been represented as the single most important event of women's march towards equality — a view that many modern-day feminists regarded with considerable scepticism. In fact, there quickly emerged a readiness on the part of many early feminist scholars to dismiss the vote as relatively meaningless. Most influential among this group was Carol Bacchi, who argued that a late nineteenth-century women's movement premised upon an equal rights philosophy had been hijacked by conservative-minded middle- and upper-class women anxious to maintain social order in an urbanizing and industrializing nation. They justified their right to vote and to participate in certain moral reform campaigns on the basis of their maternal ability to purify society, a rationalization, according to Bacchi, that reinforced unequal sexual-based stereotypes.[14]

To many feminist scholars, Bacchi's thesis seemed ahistoric, revealing more about the standards of the modern-day women's movement than about the restrictive social realities with which women in previous years had had to contend.[15] With the growth of feminist scholarship has come an increasing variety of interests and opinions, and a greater willingness to accentuate previous female accomplishments[16] against the background of a past setting that in legal terms did not classify women as "persons" until 1929. The evolution of women's history can also be seen in terms of successful efforts to locate and utilize sources (such as diaries, oral testimony, and even old household appliances) that make it possible to tell stories through the eyes of women; of the development of a greater recognition of the values that united and factors that divided women; and of methodological breakthroughs like the use of "gender" as an analytical tool,[17] which argues that, leaving aside childbirth, socially rather than biologically constructed roles have largely determined the lives of both sexes.

Sometimes heard is the charge that because it cordons off the sexes for separate study, women's history constitutes an artificial scholarly construct. Its steady move towards gender analysis, however, in fact has furnished an integrative approach to historical inquiry since socially constructed notions of appropriate behaviour have been and continue to be powerful influences in the lives of men, young people, the elderly, spinsters, bachelors, and members of certain other groups. Moreover, since the social construction of gender often confined females to the domestic sphere, feminist scholarship intersected with and assumed a seminal role in promoting the recent rise of family history.[18]

Within the family, next to those of women, the experiences of children and adolescents perhaps have attracted the most attention from social historians. In addition to work deriving from inquiry into the family, considerable material has come from historians interested in social reform and the law. Several examinations have appeared, for instance, of youth groups, professional child-care services, and juvenile courts. Most to some extent explore the question of whether such groups and initiatives stemmed from untainted idealism or the desire of elites and the middle class to fashion the young into behaviour that primarily served selfish class interests. A similar debate has been joined in the related and quickly expanding field of educational history. Here, older accounts, while perhaps noting clashes in English Canada over the existence of separate French and Catholic schools,[19] still for the most part centred on the expansion of the education system as creating a level playing field for children of different social classes. But in the eyes of many social historians, the schools' professed goal of socializing children often served as a springboard for the launching of rather different aims. Among working-class youth, they say, it was translated into a program designed less to promote social mobility then to equip the students with skills and attitudes that would be useful to capitalists. Among girls, it meant to promulgate an

agenda predestining them to a life of domesticity. And among several minority groups, it often resulted in racist campaigns to suppress language, religion, and customs with the aim of forging a common Anglo-based citizenry.

The sometimes difficult experience of immigrant children within the school system, as well as their ability to adapt and thrive, also constitutes a part of the new ethnic history. Prior to its appearance over the last generation, Canadian historians, the vast majority of whom were of Anglo or French background, failed to undertake serious analysis of the various cultures making up the national mosaic. Their work, reflecting the emphasis on nation-building and a widespread belief on the part of Canadians in the superiority of their ways, usually followed a pattern in which immigrants escaped political oppression or economic deprivation for a better life in Canada, where success ultimately came as a result of "honest toil" and the desire to assimilate. Not much better were early accounts written by amateur historians belonging to various ethnic groups. Rather than demonstrating the complexity of their cultures or dwelling on the often virulent racism they faced in Canada, most chose to chronicle first achievements (the first Ukrainian doctor, and so on) in order to build collective pride and win over the host society.

Contemporary events altered the nature of the inquiry into ethnic/immigration history. In the United States, "ethnic pride" emerged as an offshoot of the Black Civil Rights movement and challenged both the "melting pot" concept and the notion of America as a land of opportunity. Such ideas spilled over into Canada. Also in Canada, a sense of separate consciousness or of grievance against the host society was raised by a more militant voice emanating from Quebec after the Quiet Revolution; it pointed to both the discrimination of francophones under the provincial Anglo elite and the need of the Québécois to promote their cultural distinctiveness. In order to prevent the development of political separatism and to demonstrate that federalism could work for Quebec, in 1963 Ottawa appointed the Royal Commission on Bilingualism and Biculturalism. Its report six years later, which resulted in the Official Languages Act, prompted complaints from other ethnic groups that they were being treated as second-class citizens. In an attempt to alleviate such protest, the federal government turned to the last book of the report, *The Cultural Contributions of Other Ethnic Groups*, as a basis for its 1971 introduction of the principle of multiculturalism.[20] Whether or not this measure was a rather meaningless political ploy on the part of the Trudeau Liberals to ease the passage of official bilingualism and garner votes from an expanding number of ethnic minorities remains debated. Less in doubt is that official multiculturalism provided further encouragement — both moral and financial — to the field of ethnic studies, which was poised to explode.

Not only did the radicalism of the late 1960s create an atmosphere conducive to the study of racism and ethnic distinctiveness, but the expansion of the country's university system during that decade brought into post-secondary education a significant number of students from non-Anglo and non-French backgrounds. A notable proportion, as might be expected, had a keen interest in ethnic studies and a superior sensitivity to the linguistic and cultural nuances of various groups. By 1969, the analysis of minorities — which had expanded markedly in sociology and anthropology as well as in history — had grown to the point of justifying the creation of the interdisciplinary journal *Canadian Ethnic Studies*; and four years later, the Canadian Ethnic Studies Association was founded. Furthering this trend was government largesse. In 1976, the new federal Directorate of Multiculturalism announced funding for the 25-volume Generations Series, which would cover the history of different ethnic groups; and among numerous provincial initiatives was the creation two years later of the Multicultural History Society of Ontario. Scores of universities established courses on the immigrant experience and, in some cases, centres for advanced study, such as the Institute for Ukrainian Studies at the University of Alberta.[21]

From some quarters have come questions as to whether the new ethnic history has been too quick to condemn earlier Canadian society for attempting to create a common nationality; too eager to support minorities who resisted assimilation; and too willing to gloss over negative features of ethnic culture.[22] Controversy has also raged over who should be considered as belonging to a particular group, for once in Canada newcomers often adapted to the point of shedding the language, religion, and customs of the old country.[23] Canada's new ethnic historians have not faltered before these challenges. They have produced ever more sophisticated work by making use of a variety of disciplinary tools and sources — to trace, for instance, settlement patterns and cultural life, interactions with the host society, divisions between and within minority groups, and socio-economic progress made by newcomers over time.

It could be said that the rise of social history has been characterized by both promise and paradox. Its practitioners set out to provide a more inclusive picture of the past, but contemporary events, such as the various crusades of the 1960s, fragmented its interests into various fiefdoms. Social historians promised broader and more balanced accounts, but they have found themselves fending off charges of advancing an agenda that champions underdogs and vilifies capitalism. Finally, with its focus on everyday people, one might have expected social history to enjoy mass appeal, but its descent not only into narrower subfields but also into finer ideological and methodological disputes has produced, according to its critics, an abundance of trivial and jargonistic work alienating history more than ever from the general reading public.[24]

As in any field of inquiry, there exists room for improvement — something most social historians would readily admit. But by no means does that qualifier lead to the conclusion arrived at by some scholars that the majority of work produced over the past quarter-century has proved an unfortunate detour for the historical profession. Many of the criticisms are overstated, narrowly constructed, or equally applicable to political history. Take the case of evidence. Certainly the state and personal papers and newspaper reports on which a great deal of political history has traditionally relied are as prone as any other kind of source to bias and (even deliberate!) inaccuracy. Moreover, even if most social history is tinted with various shades of leftist philosophy to some degree born of the political fervour of the 1960s, one would be hard pressed to deny that previous schools of analysis were value-free and divorced from the influence of contemporary events. Finally, to lament the loss of "covering laws" in history is to bemoan a unity attained by "flattening out"[25] complex patterns of human experience.

In having remained rather nebulous and self-contradictory, perhaps the new social history provides the most accurate depiction yet of past worlds no doubt as complex as our own. And its reach is still growing, as it moves into new subfields (such as medical history, consumer culture, the social role of sports, and the treatment of the elderly) and revamps so-called traditional areas such as military history (for example, by turning the focus from tactics to the experiences and culture of the common foot soldier). To suggest that social history has disconnected itself from politics is to misrepresent a field in which numerous laws and reform measures have been dissected to determine their impact on various social groups, and in which scholars are analyzing the deep significance of party rituals and rallies. Even if social history should remain rather fragmented, and confined primarily to an academic audience, therefore, the trade-offs have proved more than worthwhile. No doubt it is true that students and even professors today display more haziness over certain political and constitutional minutiae than did their predecessors. But in exchange for the need to crack an older text more often, they have received a virtual historical cornucopia of potential new sources, methods, and subjects that have sparked and will continue to spark novel questioning and analysis of still all-too-commonly accepted terms and concepts like "progress," "opportunity," "democracy," and "freedom."

NOTES

1. M.C. Urquhart and K.A.H. Buckley, eds., *Historical Statistics on Canada* (Toronto: Macmillan, 1965), series A1–19, A254–72, E202–44, K14–29.
2. S.R. Mealing, "The Concept of Social Class and the Interpretation of Canadian History," *Canadian Historical Review*, 46, 3 (1965): 207.
3. Perhaps the most influential was the Laurentian theory, which presented Canada as a natural east–west entity created by the St. Lawrence waterway system. See Donald Creighton, *The Empire of the St. Lawrence* (Toronto: Macmillan, 1956).
4. For a discussion of *Annales* theory see Michael A. Gismondi, "'The Gift of Theory': A Critique of the *Histoire des Mentalités*," *Social History*, 10, 2 (1985): 211–30. Marc Léopold Benjamin Block is considered one of the founders of the *Annales* approach. One of the most striking examples of his application of *Annales* methodology is *La Société féodale: la formation des liens de dépendance* (Paris: A. Michel, 1939). In Canada, the *Annales* first enjoyed limited application during the 1950s in Quebec, where they were used to test the thesis that the Anglo conquerors of 1760 rather than internal problems within Québécois society were to blame for ongoing socio-economic problems in the province. See Serge Gagnon, *Quebec and Its Historians: The Twentieth Century* (Montreal: Harvest House, 1985).
5. See Godfrey Hodgson, *America in Our Time* (New York: Doubleday, 1976), 67–98.
6. John Higham, *History: Professional Scholarship in America* (Baltimore: The Johns Hopkins University Press, 1983), 233.
7. J.M.S. Careless, "'Limited Identities' in Canada," *Canadian Historical Review*, 50, 1 (1969): 1.
8. *Register of Canadian Theses*, 1972, 1992.
9. See Michael Bliss, "Fragmented Past, Fragmented Future," *University of Toronto Magazine*, 19 (1991): 6–11.
10. There were, however, some angrier accounts, such as from the Western Canadian historian Vernon Fowke. See *The National Policy and the Wheat Economy* (Toronto: University of Toronto Press, 1957).
11. John Thompson, "Writing about Rural Life and Agriculture," in John Schultz, ed., *Writing about Canada: A Handbook for Modern Canadian History* (Scarborough: Prentice-Hall, 1990), 97, 100–101.

12. Ruth Roach Pierson, "International Trends in Women's History and Feminism: Colonization and Canadian Women's History," *Journal of Women's History*, 4, 2 (1992): 140–41.

13. Gerda Lerner, "Placing Women in History: A 1975 Perspective," in Bernice Carroll, ed., *Liberating Women's History: Theoretical and Critical Essays in Women's History* (Urbana: University of Illinois Press, 1976), 357.

14. Carol Bacchi, *Liberation Deferred? The Ideas of the English-Canadian Suffragists, 1877–1918* (Toronto: University of Toronto Press, 1983).

15. On this point, and for other criticisms of Bacchi, see Sylvia Van Kirk, "What Has the Feminist Perspective Done for Canadian History?" in Ursula Martius Franklin et al., eds., *Knowledge Reconsidered: A Feminist Overview* (Ottawa: Canadian Research Institute for the Advancement of Women, 1984), 51.

16. One area of study being the various religious groups through which many women, as missionaries or medical personnel, spread their influence throughout the world. See, for example, Ruth Compton Brouwer's *New Women for God: Canadian Presbyterian Women and the India Missions, 1876–1914* (Toronto: University of Toronto Press, 1991).

17. For a theoretical discussion of gender as a basis for analysis see Joan W. Scott, "Gender: A Useful Category of Historical Analysis," *American Historical Review*, 91 (1986): 1053–75.

18. For an excellent example of the integration of gender analysis and family history see Bettina Bradbury, *Working Families: Age, Gender, and Daily Survival in Industrializing Montreal* (Toronto: McClelland & Stewart, 1993).

19. See Robert Choquette, *Language and Religion: A History of English–French Conflict in Ontario* (Ottawa: University of Ottawa Press, 1975), pt 3.

20. Anthony W. Rasporich, "Ethnicity in Canadian Historical Writing, 1970–1990," in J.W. Berry and J.A. Laponce, eds., *Ethnicity and Culture in Canada: The Research Landscape* (Toronto: University of Toronto Press, 1994), 153.

21. As of 1994, there were more than twenty university chairs across Canada in ethnic studies. J.W. Berry and J.A. Laponce, "Evaluating Research on Canada's Multiethnic and Multicultural Society: An Introduction," ibid., 4.

22. See Norman Buchignani, "Canadian Ethnic Research and Multiculturalism," *Journal of Canadian Studies*, 17, 1 (1982): 23–28.

23. See Roberto Perin, "Writing about Ethnicity," in Schultz, *Writing about Canada*, 204.

24. Bryan D. Palmer, *Descent into Discourse: The Reification of Language and the Writing of Social History* (Philadelphia: Temple University Press, 1989), 204.

25. Konrad H. Jarausch, "Towards a Social History of Experience: Postmodern Predicaments in Theory and Interdisciplinarity," *Central European History*, 22, 3–4 (1989): 438.

REFERENCES

Artibise, Alan F.J., ed. *Interdisciplinary Approaches to Canadian History: A Guide to the Literature*. Montreal and Kingston: McGill-Queen's University Press, 1990.

Berger, Carl. *The Writing of Canadian History: Aspects of English-Canadian Historical Writing since 1900*. Toronto: University of Toronto Press, 1986.

Berger, Carl, ed. *Contemporary Approaches to Canadian History*. Toronto: Copp Clark Pitman, 1987.

Canadian Periodical Index.

Gilbert, A.D., C.M. Wallace, and R.M. Bray, eds. *Reappraisals in Canadian History*. Scarborough: Prentice-Hall, 1992.

Leacy, F.H., ed. *Historical Statistics on Canada*. 2d ed. Ottawa: Supply and Services, 1983.

Macleod, Laura, comp. *The Canadian Historical Review Index, 1971–1990*. Toronto: University of Toronto Press, 1993.

McKay, Ian, ed. *The Challenge of Modernity: A Reader on Post-Confederation Canada*. Toronto: McGraw-Hill Ryerson, 1992.

Owram, Doug, ed. *A Reader's Guide to Canadian History: Confederation to the Present*. Toronto: University of Toronto Press, 1994.

Taylor, Brook, ed. *A Reader's Guide to Canadian History: Beginnings to Confederation*. Toronto: University of Toronto Press, 1994.

City Life

Slum housing in Toronto, 1913. In the background stands City Hall.

Between 1901 and 1941 the number of Canadians living in areas classified by the national census as "urban" climbed from 37 to 57 percent of the population.[1] Prior to the rise of social history, this pattern was often interpreted as a sign of progress, in that it was generated by and in turn bolstered industrialization, mass retailing, the development of financial institutions, and the enhancement of cultural life. But urbanization also translated into another, less cheerful picture, one first painted by turn-of-the-century Social Gospellers, progressive reformers, and muckraking journalists, and more recently delineated by social historians.

In Article 1, Terry Copp, building on observations made by the Montreal businessman-philanthropist Herbert Brown Ames, offers a picture of turn-of-the-century Montreal, Canada's largest and wealthiest city, as containing large working-class slums characterized by dirt streets, privy pits, impure drinking water, overcrowded and dilapidated housing, astonishingly high infant mortality rates, substandard schools, and unsafe worksites. Urbanization had no shortage of advocates, however, who, as Paul Voisey argues in Article 2, came from practically all occupations and classes. Voisey examines "boosterism," that ideology obsessed with promoting rapid urban growth. During the late nineteenth and early twentieth centuries, it consumed the political agenda of several Canadian cities as well as of the small prairie towns that are Voisey's focus. Although noting that the various campaigns to attract rail and road lines as well as investment often grew out of the selfish desires of local elites and engendered disastrous development schemes, Voisey asserts that boosterism had certain positive effects, in unifying people from diverse backgrounds, creating in them a "hearty civic spirit," and encouraging them to act on the belief that, in an economically fluid environment, advancement for all was possible.

Generally, to comprehend urbanization from the "bottom up" requires bringing a relatively guarded outlook to the process. Unlike older studies centring on the physical, economic, and/or cultural evolution of cities,[2] these two articles uncover places where, along with signs of progress and prosperity, there existed class division, slums, and municipal planning sometimes premised more on avarice than common sense.

QUESTIONS TO CONSIDER

1. What, if any, action did Ames take to try to alleviate the negative effects of urbanization?
2. Why was urban density a greater problem in the early than in the late twentieth century?
3. In what ways did Western towns try to attract investment?
4. How did the booster mentality affect town planning in Western Canada?
5. Do these articles demonstrate the importance of proving the representativeness of a local study?

NOTES

1. M.C. Urquhart and K.A.H. Buckley, eds., *Historical Statistics on Canada* (Toronto: Macmillan, 1965), series A15–19.
2. See, for example, J.M.S. Careless, "Frontierism, Metropolitanism, and Canadian History," in Carl Berger, ed., *Approaches to Canadian History* (Toronto: University

of Toronto Press, 1967), 63–83, and Jacob Spelt, *Urban Development of South-Central Ontario* (Toronto: McClelland & Stewart, 1955).

SUGGESTED READINGS

Acheson, T.W. *Saint John: The Making of a Colonial Urban Community*. Toronto: University of Toronto Press, 1985.

Artibise, Alan F.J. *Winnipeg: A Social History of Urban Growth, 1874–1914*. Montreal and Kingston: McGill-Queen's University Press, 1975.

Artibise, Alan F.J., and Paul-André Linteau. *The Evolution of Urban Canada: An Analysis of Approaches and Interpretations*. Winnipeg: Institute of Urban Studies, University of Winnipeg, 1984.

Artibise, Alan F.J., and Gilbert A. Stelter, comps. *Canada's Urban Past: A Bibliography to 1980 and Guide to Canadian Urban Studies*. Vancouver: University of British Columbia Press, 1981.

Bacher, John. *Keeping to the Marketplace: The Evolution of Canadian Housing Policy*. Montreal and Kingston: McGill-Queen's University Press, 1993.

Hengen, Girard. "A Case Study in Urban Reform: Regina before the First World War." *Saskatchewan History,* 41, 10 (1988): 19–34.

Hiebert, D. "Class, Ethnicity and Residential Structure: The Social Geography of Winnipeg, 1901–1921." *Journal of Historical Geography,* 17, 1 (1991): 56–86.

Linteau, Paul-André. *The Promoters' City: Building the Industrial Town of Maisonneuve, 1883–1918*. Toronto: James Lorimer, 1985.

Stelter, Gilbert A., ed. *Cities and Urbanization: Canadian Historical Perspectives*. Toronto: Copp Clark Pitman, 1990.

Voisey, Paul. *Vulcan: The Making of a Prairie Community*. Toronto: University of Toronto Press, 1988.

ONE

The City Below the Hill

TERRY COPP

During the autumn and early winter of 1896, a young Montreal businessman, Herbert Brown Ames, employed a number of "enumerators" to undertake "A Sociological Study of a Portion of the City of Montreal, Canada." Ames assembled the results of the questionnaires into a short book called *The City Below the Hill*, which was published in 1897.[1] The district surveyed contained thirty-eight thousand people and the residents, mainly working class, were "evenly divided as to nationality, one-third

Source: Excerpted from *The Anatomy of Poverty: The Condition of the Working Class in Montreal, 1897–1929* (Toronto: McClelland & Stewart, 1974), 15–29. Copyright © 1974. Reprinted by permission of Oxford University Press Canada.

French Canadian, one-third English, and one-third Irish." It was, Ames said, an opportunity "to study a class rather than a race."

The conditions present in the very midst of the same city inhabited by "the captains of industry, the owners of real estate and those who labour with brain rather than hand" were described in minute detail with the aid of numerous maps. The section chosen by Ames for his survey was one of the older industrial quarters of Montreal. Its northwestern boundary was the C.P.R. tracks leading into Windsor Station. A block to the southeast lay the right of way of the Grand Trunk and the extensive yards of Bonaventure Station, and two blocks below that the Lachine Canal, the oldest centre of industry in the city, cut through the district. Beyond the canal, Centre Street marked the beginning of Point St. Charles. To the southwest, the still autonomous working class suburbs of Ste. Cunegonde and St. Henri marked the western limit of urbanization, but to the east the old wards of the city stretched along the river for several miles.

Rue Notre Dame bisected the City Below the Hill and was the axis of all the *quartiers* of the old city. It was paved for most of its length by 1897 with a mixture of cobblestones and wooden blocks.[2] Like most of the other main streets, it was festooned with the overhead wires of the Montreal Street Railway Company. At night the glare of arc lamps and the glow of the remaining gas lights cast dark shadows over most of the street. Notre Dame was lined with one- and two-storey structures, mainly brick, intermingled with the more substantial greystone and shanty-built wooden houses. Sewer lines served most of the area on either side of Notre Dame Street but, despite the municipal by-law that had forbidden the further construction of houses served by the "pit privy" since 1887, over five thousand privy pits remained in existence within city limits and more than half the households in the section surveyed by Ames were "dependant entirely on such accommodation." Since water service reached almost every house in the city, Ames allowed himself a rare expression of emotion in discussing "that insanitary abomination . . . that danger to public health and morals . . . the out-of-door-pit-in-the-ground privy." There is, he wrote,

> a map in my office whereon are coloured in yellow all blocks of buildings containing only proper sanitary accommodation, and whereon the presence of the privy abomination is designated by shades of purple, from violet to nearly black according to its prevalence.

This problem was general throughout the working class wards and for eight years Ames was to maintain a campaign (which earned him the title "Water Closet Ames") for the suppression of the pit privy.

The carter's waggon and the horse and carriage were the only means of transportation other than the street railway. The Haymarket was then not the name of a square but an important commercial facility. There were three thousand horse stables within city limits in 1899 as well as five hundred cow stables. The Municipal Board of Health recommended that cow stables, at least, be banned within city limits.[3]

The condition of the streets of the city occasioned much comment. Since only 27 of the 178 miles of streets were paved, "dust in the autumn is very bad and the mud wears out the streets quicker than the traffic does." According to the City Surveyor the dust also impaired the health of the city.[4] Medical officers were more explicit. Elzéar Pelletier, Secretary of the Provincial Board of Health, complained that the streets "were in an intolerable state though tolerated" and that the lanes were used as "refuse dumps."[5]

The city-owned water supply, while generally available, was of a poor quality. It was unfiltered and untreated and while it was "pure during ordinary times, it becomes dangerous during spring and fall." The main reservoir "leaked badly" and the boom which blocked floating refuse at the entrance was "in a state of decay."[6] Householders who did not pay their water tax had the supply of this dubious commodity cut off.

Little attention had been paid to city planning in Montreal and one of the most serious deficiencies of the working class wards was the lack of parks and open spaces. The thirty-eight thousand inhabitants of the western section of the lower city shared two public squares, Richmond and St. Patrick's. The twenty-six thousand residents of St. Louis possessed tiny Viger Square; in St. Laurent Ward there were the two acres of Dufferin Square; and the pattern was similar elsewhere.[7] Montreal did, of course, have its "Great Park," Mount Royal. Frederic Law Olmstead, who designed Mount Royal Park, considered it to be one of the best in North America:

> Rising in the rear of the city . . . its landscape is most captivating . . . 462 acres laid out with drives, rustic steps and seats . . . footpaths leading in every direction to wander amidst an undergrowth of ferns and flowers . . . the summit can be reached winding around the mountain side . . . on the eastern side of the mountain there is an incline railroad by which special cars carry passengers to the lookout for a small fee . . .[8]

But Mount Royal was remote from the everyday life of the city. Like St. Helen's Island, which was reached by ferry, it was a place for family outings on very special days. A newer park located just to the north of some of the more congested areas of the city had more potential as a "people's park." Logan's Farm or Lafontaine Park was being transformed in the late 1890s. The beautiful lagoons, the feature attraction, were being installed and the landscaping was largely complete. Yet the life of the majority of the population could only have been marginally affected. The playground movement, which was spreading across North America from the "sand garden" and "outdoor gymnasium" created in Boston during the 1880s, had not yet reached Montreal.

The streets of the city, however, hummed with activity. The local bar was the chief recreational facility available to adults and there was one in almost every block. Ames counted 105 licensed saloons and 87 liquor-selling groceries in the survey area and claimed that even if the ones located adjacent to railway stations were eliminated there was a "licensed liquor outlet, no one knows how many unlicensed" for every 45 families.

Herbert Ames approached the problem of the circumstances of working class life with what he felt was scientific objectivity. His purpose in writing the book was spelled out in the introduction:

> There are among the dwellers of "the city above the hill" not a few, we believe, who have the welfare of their fellow-men at heart, who realize there is no influence more elevating than the proper home, who acknowledge that there is a need for improvement in the matter of housing the working classes of the city and who would be willing to assist any movement of a semi-philanthropic character having for its object the erection of proper homes for the families of working men. These persons are business men. They are not

those who take things for granted. They require to have demonstrated to them in black and white the need for local action and the conditions — changing with every locality — to which it would be needful to conform to meet the needs of the case, and, at the same time, yield reasonable financial returns . . . "Philanthropy and five per cent" in Montreal, as elsewhere, can be combined.

Ames had spent four years at Amherst College, where he had been a contemporary of men like Robert A. Woods, the founder of Andover Settlement House in Boston, and a prominent writer and social reformer; Robert E. Ely, one of the founders of Prospect Union and the Harvard workingman's college; and a dozen other men who were active in social gospel–inspired reform.[9] Ames, like the others, had been influenced by the lectures of President Seelye of Amherst, who attacked the doctrinal individualism of Calvinism and preached an organic conception of society. He had listened to prominent social gospellers like Lyman Abbott and Henry Ward Beecher[10] and was deeply affected by the intense searching for moral purpose that marked the college. He had been taught to believe that the wealthy had special responsibilities towards their less fortunate brethren, and when, at his father's death, he succeeded to the control of the family shoe factory, he was able to resign from business activity and devote his full energies to municipal affairs. For Ames, reform was to be accomplished by demonstrating the existence of "evils" to men of good will and then working out a businesslike solution which would find support among the established classes. He accepted the wide discrepancies in income, education, and opportunity that existed in the society but believed that at least some abuses of urban-industrial society could be removed by right knowledge and right action.

As a consequence, Ames never raised fundamental questions about wage levels or working conditions. His investigation was designed to prove that the area was "eminently suitable for philanthropic investment," not to show the need for a general reform movement. In developing his case for a model tenement, Ames touched on problems of a more general kind and his statistics provide a convenient point of departure for a study of working class conditions just before the relatively static patterns of late nineteenth century life were disrupted by rapid economic growth and massive immigration to the city.

The industries located in the area surveyed represented a good cross section of Montreal's economic life. Wholesale clothing, boots and shoes, textiles, foodstuffs, cigars, iron and steel, lumber, transportation equipment as well as a host of lesser shops and service facilities provided work for 12,511 men, 3,266 women, and 460 children.[11] Approximately one-third of the labour force lived outside of the area surveyed, so Ames' sample was composed of 7,671 families who were residents. The average family income was eleven dollars per week. The range of weekly income varied from over twenty dollars (15$\frac{1}{3}$ per cent) to under five dollars (11 per cent). These groups, "the well-to-do" and "the submerged tenth," did not "properly belong to the class under study." It was the remainder, the "real industrial class," which required examination.

The average family income of the "real industrial class," $10.00 to $10.25 a week, was based on some combination of earnings from more than one wage earner, and the estimate that average weekly wages of $8.25 for a man, $4.50 for a woman, and $3.00 for a boy were "not too wide of the mark." A man able to work throughout the year could earn more than $428.00 a year according to these figures. Yet in 1901, a more prosperous year with much fuller employment, manufacturing establishments in Montreal reported average wages for men of $405.00.[12]

The figure of $10.25 a week used by Ames was the average income when the breadwinners were working. He himself noted that in addition to the "submerged tenth" the "City Below the Hill" contained "a much larger group who were on the verge of distress" because of "insufficient employment." "Few are the families" he wrote,

> where nothing is earned, although there are such subsisting more or less worthily upon charity. Almost without exception each family has its wage earner, often more than one, and upon the regularity with which the wage earner secures employment depends the scale of living of the family.

Ames' statistics showed that 23 per cent of the "real industrial class" had incomes "which could not be depended on as constant and regular throughout the year . . . the ratio of *nearly one family in four without steady work* [italics in the original] seems alarmingly high and explains much of the poverty."

Income figures have little significance unless measured against some estimate of purchasing power and minimum standard of living. Ames had no clear ideas on how to go about constructing a minimum family budget and he tried to define "the point below which comfort ends and poverty commences" in a rather curious way. "It is difficult," he wrote,

> to determine what shall constitute the low water mark of decent subsistence . . . Since a dollar a day is regarded as the minimum wage for an unskilled labourer it would seem that six dollars a week might be taken as the point below which comfort ends . . . But . . . since few are those among this class of labourers who can count upon regular work . . . we may safely fix the limit of decent subsistence at $5.00 per week.

For Ames the wage system could not possibly produce poverty; therefore, persons who worked more or less regularly for the minimum wage could not be poor. By the standards used for measuring poverty, developed in the following chapter, the vast majority of the population of the "City Below the Hill" are classified as poor.

The dimension of life in "The City Below the Hill" that Ames explored in the greatest detail was housing. He was determined to build a "model tenement" in Montreal and had commissioned the survey primarily to bolster his case for "semi-philanthropic investment." By 1897 the "model tenement" idea had been tested in a number of American cities, most successfully in Brooklyn, where Alfred T. White had conducted his experiments in "philanthropy plus five per cent." In the same year that Ames began his preparations to build "Diamond Court," a project for the accommodation of forty families, on William Street, the New York Association for Improving the Conditions of the Poor (A.I.C.P.) organized the "City and Suburban Homes Association" with a capitalization of $1,000,000 as a limited dividend corporation to build model tenements. Ames had observed the American experience closely and was determined to avoid the mistakes that had been made. In particular, he warned against building "dwellings too high priced for the neighbourhood." Though this would "benefit the locality," the mass of the people "would live as before."

Ames began by defining the housing standards he was seeking:

> I think we will agree that the ideal home is one where the front door is used by but one family, where the house faces upon a through street, where water closet accommodation is provided and where there are as many rooms allotted to a family as there are persons composing it. That this ideal is by no means obtained goes without saying.

The average house in the district was a duplex, for the lofty tenements of New York and Chicago did not exist in Montreal. Ames regarded the independence and self-reliance, which he felt these small houses promoted, as outweighing the disadvantages of "high rentals or mean accommodations" which low density housing caused. Ten per cent of the total housing stock consisted of rear tenements. "The typical rear tenement," Ames wrote,

> is either an ancient wooden cottage of the rural habitant type or a two-storey building encased in refuse bricks and reached by rickety wooden stairs or galleries. It is high time in Montreal, that the majority of these hovels were condemned as unfit for habitation . . . It is already within the power of City Council to prevent the erection of further buildings of this type . . . we must go a step further and give to civic authority, as representing the public welfare, the right to interfere with what are known as private interests and vested rights, when these latter are, as in this case, a menace to the welfare of the community. The rear tenement must go.

The average family in the area lived in a flat containing 5.02 rooms. This figure compared favourably with that for almost all industrial cities of comparable size. When broken down into segments, the statistics showed that 30 per cent shared six rooms, 40 per cent five rooms, and 30 per cent four rooms. The average rental for these flats worked out to $8.75 per month or 18 per cent of monthly income. The "poor and the well-to-do" paid from 20–25 per cent of their income for housing, the "real industrial class" closer to 16 per cent. It is fair to conclude that with the exception of a few areas such as Griffintown, where 45 per cent of the population had three rooms or less to share among a family of five, the housing was not overcrowded by contemporary standards. Equally it may be concluded that rent as a percentage of income was not out of line.

It is also evident that Montreal's low density housing kept the density per acre figure well below European and many North American urban levels. The section surveyed had a density of 94 persons to the acre. This calculation was based on excluding non-residential areas. The city's figures for density per acre did not match this calculation; its estimate for the wards, which were included in the section surveyed by Ames, were 35 and 47 persons per acre (Ste. Anne and St. Antoine Wards).

The wards to the east were much more densely populated. According to the City Surveyor, the average in St. Louis was 117 to the acre, St. James 96, St. Lawrence 67, St. Mary's 63, and St. Jean Baptiste 56.[13] Within the area surveyed by Ames, density went as high as 300 per acre and averaged 200 per acre throughout much of the district. Two hundred persons per acre in a city of small homes meant that very little open space had been left on the building lots. Ames concluded the chapter by noting that there was 5 to 7 per cent vacancy rate in the district.

A further chapter was devoted to the death rate, "the test to which cities of the civilized world, by common consent, annually submit themselves." Montreal's death rate had been steadily declining but it was still among the highest in the civilized world in the 1890s. The figure of 24.81 deaths per thousand (1895) which Ames used, compared to a rate of 20 per thousand in London and Paris, 19.4 in Rome, 18.1 in Brussels, 24.02 in Boston, and 23.52 in New York. By 1898 New York had lowered its rate to 19.0 while Montreal's rate had declined to 22.9. Toronto by comparison had a death rate of only 15.2.[14]

There was a wide variance in death rates between different parts of the city. St. Jean Baptiste Ward had 35.51 deaths per thousand, St. Mary's 33.20, and St. Gabriel 32.32 compared to 22.47 for the "City Below the Hill" and less than 13 per thousand in the upper section of St. Antoine Ward, "The City Above the Hill." Ames was able to establish a strong correlation between the death rate and housing and sanitary conditions.

One of the most obvious omissions in Ames' study was the question of infant mortality. Montreal was the most dangerous city in the civilized world to be born in. Between 1899 and 1901, 26.76 per cent of all newborn children died before they were one year old. This was more than double the figure for New York City, and it was customarily cited as being lower than that for only one large city — Calcutta.[15] The death of children under one year made up 43 per cent of the total deaths in the city in 1897. These statistics were largely the result of unsafe water, impure milk, and the limited use of vaccination against smallpox and diphtheria. The secretary of the Provincial Board of Health commented that

> . . . the thought of having little angels in heaven can only afford consolation when one is satisfied that everything possible was done . . . there should be no misconception on the subject, the use of anti-diphtheria serum has not yet become general in our province.[16]

In Montreal even smallpox vaccination had not "become general." City Health officials estimated that the 2,094 primary vaccinations they had performed on babies in 1899 represented only one-fifth of the number of births in the city. One of the schools in Ames' district was reported as having 39 per cent of its pupils without vaccinations.[17]

Ames also ignored the question of the conditions in which the wage earners earned their living. The six-day week was of course the general rule, though some employers allowed a half day off on Saturday, providing an extra hour was added on to the other five days. During the middle 1890s "short time" layoffs and plant shutdowns were normal in the winter months. The working day averaged between ten and twelve hours, though women and children in factories were not permitted to work more than ten hours a day, six days a week, unless a special permit had been obtained for a period "not exceeding six weeks."[18] This rule did not apply to women and children employed in retail shops or other establishments not covered by the Industrial Establishments Act of 1893.

In 1897 there were three factory inspectors charged with the task of enforcing the I.E.A. and the "By-laws of the Quebec Board of Health Relating to the Sanitary Conditions of Industrial Establishments (1895)," for Montreal and all of western Quebec. They were required to examine all "manufactories, works, workshops, work yards, mills of every kind and their dependencies." The main work of the inspectors was to report on the causes of industrial accidents and enforce the child labour laws, which stated that "the age of admission to work in factories not classified as dangerous or unhealthy is twelve for boys and fourteen for girls." Proof of age, in the form of a statement signed by a parent or guardian, was required in case of doubt. The factory inspectors could require that one hour be allotted for lunch. They could attempt to enforce the rule that 400 cubic feet of air per workman was available, that there were separate sanitary accommodations for men and women, that a temperature of 60 to 72 degrees Fahrenheit was maintained and that there was adequate ventilation, drainage, freedom from dirt and dust, and appropriate fire escape mechanisms. In theory, offending employers could be fined $200 for each contravention of the Act and $6 per day until the faults were remedied. In practice, since the inspector was required to institute court proceedings himself, a mixture of persuasion and threats was used to try to reform the more obvious abuses.

The improvement of working conditions and the achievement of a living wage are changes which are normally associated with successful trade union activity. For a time in the 1880s it had appeared as if the Knights of Labour might successfully organize the city's workers along industrial lines. The assemblies of the Knights broke down the barrier between linguistic groups and united skilled and unskilled labour. Their high point was reached in 1887, when there were thirty-eight assemblies or locals in the city. The failure of the Knights to achieve significant gains in a series of strikes coupled with the hard times of the later eighties led to a rapid decline in membership, and there were only four Knights of Labour locals left in 1891.

By 1897 only the craft unions with international affiliation survived as viable associations. Such union locals possessed little bargaining power and less staying power. The Department of Labour's first survey of trade unions in 1901 listed sixty locals in Montreal, one-third of which had been organized since 1897.[19] Organized labour participated in the annual Labour Day Parade and sent delegates to the Trades and Labour Council convention, but it was simply not a force to be reckoned with in the quiet times of the 1890s.

In the absence of an effective trade union movement, an alternative path to improved working class life was the universal curative of North America, education. Eighteen hundred and ninety-seven is frequently regarded as a crucial year in the history of education in the Province of Quebec. The newly formed Liberal administration of Felix-Gabriel Marchand was committed to fulfilling the *rouge* dream of a Ministry of Public Instruction. The passage of this bill in the assembly and its subsequent rejection by the *bleu*-dominated Legislative Council postponed the creation of a ministry of education for sixty-five years. For the resident of the working class sections of Montreal the great debates over public versus religious control of education must have seemed of little interest. Education was neither compulsory nor free and though the school inspectors and the Superintendent of Public Instruction insisted that the city's schools were generally excellent,[20] there is little evidence to support their view and much to contradict it. The Provincial Health Board was concerned with "the deplorable sanitary conditions of the schools," and noted that while ideal standards called for two hundred and fifty cubic feet of space per pupil and Quebec's laws demanded one hundred and fifty cubic feet, the average in Montreal was only seventy-five cubic feet. The Board reported that little attention was paid to siting, orientation to the sun, ventilation or heating and that many schools lacked fire escapes.[21] Ninety per cent of the teachers had less than eleven years of schooling[22] and their salaries were among the lowest in North America. Over 80 per cent of the total enrolment in primary schools was registered in Grades One to Three and less than 3 per cent of the students were in Grade Six.[23] Provincial government expenditure on education was at the lowest point in the province's history, having declined in absolute terms from $155,000 in 1883 to $153,000 in 1901 and from seventy-five cents per student to fifty-six cents over the same period.[24] The frequent comments of the factory inspectors on the illiteracy of children in the work force add to the picture of an educational system which had little relevance for working class children. Even the goals of the Superintendent of Public Instruction, to teach "great respect for paternal, civil and religious authority . . . warn against intemperance and extravagance that impoverish our country . . . avoid quarrels and law suits . . . show the benefits conferred by agriculture,"[25] could not have been very adequately fulfilled in such a system.

....

The typical Montreal family of 1897 was made up of a husband, wife, and three children, who lived in a five-room, cold water flat located on a narrow, densely populated side street in what is now the inner core of the city. The husband, who hoped to be able to work sixty hours a week, fifty-two weeks a year, was more likely to find himself faced with "short time" if not a layoff, especially during the winter months. Even if regular work was available, the average wage earner could not provide his family with more than a bare subsistence.

The insecurity of family finances brought enormous pressure to bear upon the children, who were expected to enter the work force at the earliest possible age. Large numbers of children were involved in part-time work as messengers, delivery boys, newsboys, and in home workshops.[26] Official statistics vastly underestimated the extent of paid child labour and did not attempt to account for the unpaid labour of hundreds of young girls who were used as full-time baby sitters. The large numbers of ten-to-fourteen-year-old girls who were not in school and are not accounted for in the labour force were often taking care of the home while their mothers worked.[27] Ames' figures indicate that one in every five adult workers was a woman. The working class woman was required to seek employment in the textile mills, tobacco companies, food processing concerns, retail stores, and in domestic service. Her wages, low as they were, often made the difference between bare subsistence and a modest "prosperity" for her family.

NOTES

....

1. Herbert Brown Ames, *The City Below the Hill* (Montreal, 1897). All quotations and statistics in this chapter are from Ames unless otherwise cited.
2. Montreal, *Report of the City Surveyor*, 1898.
3. A.R.M.B.H., 1899, p.7.
4. *Report of the City Surveyor*, 1898, p. 3.
5. A.R.Q.B.H., 1902, p. 49.
6. Montreal, *Annual Report of the Superintendent of the Montreal Water Works*, 1897, p. 2.
7. Jessie Di Paulo. "The Development of Parks and Playgrounds in Montreal: 1900–1910," Appendix B (Unpublished B.A. Honours Essay, Loyola College, 1969).
8. F.L. Olmstead, *Mount Royal* (Montreal, 1881), pp. 4–5.
9. Daniel Russell, "H.B. Ames and Municipal Reform" (Unpublished M.A. Thesis, McGill University, 1971).
10. Arthur Mann, *Yankee Reformers in the Urban Age* (New York, Harper, 1966), p. 115.

11. Ames does not define the age level that distinguished "lads" from children. Provincial law set the minimum age for boys in factories at 12, 14 for girls. This law did not apply to children employed in stores or as delivery boys.
12. Canada Census of 1901, Vol. III, pp. 232–37.
13. *Report of the City Surveyor*, 1898, p. 3.
14. A.R.M.B.H., 1898, p. 6.
15. Joseph Gauvreau, "La Goutte de Lait," *L'École Sociale Populaire*, No. 29 (Montreal, 1914), pp. 5,6.
16. A.R.Q.B.H., 1897, p. 36.
17. A.R.M.B.H., 1899, p. 23.
18. The text of key sections of the Industrial Establishments Act is contained in A.R.Q.D.L., 1896.
19. Canada, *Labour Gazette*, 1901, pp. 1–2, 243, 318, 370, 422, 488, 554.
20. By 1900 all Montreal Catholic Schools were graded "excellent" in all categories by the school inspector. See *Report of the Superintendent of Public Instruction, School Inspectors Reports 1900*.
21. Elzéar Pelletier. "Memoir on School Hygiene," A.R.Q.B.H., 1900, p. 25.
22. M.C. Urquhart and K. Buckley, eds., *Historical Statistics on Canada* (Toronto, 1965), p. 595.
23. Ibid, p. 593.
24. *Report of the Superintendent of Public Instruction*, 1901, p. xxiii.
25. Ibid, 1897, p. 383.
26. John Spargo, *The Bitter Cry of the Children* (New York, 1903).
27. See Suzanne Cross, "The Neglected Majority: The Changing Role of Women in 19th Century Montreal," *Histoire social/Social History*, VI, Nov., 1973, pp. 203–23.

TWO

Boosting the Small Prairie Town, 1904–1931: An Example from Southern Alberta

PAUL VOISEY

Boosterism — the campaign to stimulate economic and population growth by advertising, lobbying, and offering incentives to development — is now a well recognized aspect of the history of large prairie cities.[1] But George Babbitt inhabited the small town as surely as the city, and he laboured just as mightily to promote his community. Although the circumstances of prairie settlement bred the booster mentality in even the smallest places, slim resources often led to a variety of promotional

Source: Excerpted from "Boosting the Small Prairie Town, 1904–1931: An Example from Southern Alberta," in Alan F.J. Artibise, ed., *Town and City: Aspects of Western Canada Urban Development* (Regina: Canadian Plains Research Center, 1981), 147–75. Reprinted by permission of Canadian Plains Research Center.

techniques unlike those of the city. Boosterism and the messages it broadcast expressed the attitudes and aspirations of prairie settlers, and although it failed to create large cities, boosterism shaped small towns in a variety of important, if often unanticipated, ways.

To explore these themes from small town sources, the case study seems appropriate, and attention here focuses on several towns and hamlets along the Canadian Pacific Railway's Kipp–Aldersyde line in southern Alberta. These places shared major characteristics with many prairie towns. Together with a generous minority of other groups, English-speaking Protestants from Ontario and the United States planted them during the 1896–1914 settlement boom. Situated half-way between Calgary and Lethbridge, they sprouted neither in the shadow of the metropolis, nor on the isolated fringe of settlement. The vast semi-arid region of dark brown soils and gently rolling treeless plains nurtured their growth. None grew to populations greater than 1,000 by 1931.[2]

Although boosterism gripped many communities in North America, its intensity on the Canadian prairies cannot be understood without a brief description of how town founding in the area related to railways and rural settlement. In 1892 the Calgary and Edmonton Railway stretched south to Ft. Macleod, stringing new townsites together, but few settlers came until the new century. Like most pioneers, they crowded close to the railway, but by 1904 unclaimed homesteads lay ten miles east of the line. On a frontier with no pretense of self-sufficiency, the outlying settlers relied on the railway towns of High River, Nanton, and Claresholm to ship their wheat and supply goods and services for its production. The towns also provided the necessities of daily life. Since the distant trip by horse-drawn wagon was time-consuming, uncomfortable, and expensive, usually necessitating an overnight stay in a hotel, travellers to town often purchased supplies for neighbours. This practice encouraged some pioneers to open stores on their homesteads. To attract customers, they applied as postmasters, an early act of boosterism that sometimes required political connections. Country hamlets often evolved, offering specialized — if limited — services.

Hamlet formation was not always haphazard. Although scarcely a stream, the Little Bow River had cut a deep, wide ravine in the prairie skin. At one point it narrowed sharply. As a civil engineer and a speculator, C.W. Carman of Chicago reasoned that if a railway came to the area, here was the place to build a high level bridge.[3] In 1904 he bought twenty-three railway sections, launched the bonanza Carmangay Farm Company, and laid out the townsite of Carmangay. He acquired a post office, built a store, attracted merchants and tradesmen.[4] To the north, E.E. Thompson, a much travelled frontier developer, also started a huge farm in 1904; in 1905 he surveyed a townsite and built the Brant Store. He hired six men and added an implement agency, seed grain business, and a warehouse. Thompson demonstrated that a country store could make money. He reportedly earned $150,000 in ten years.[5]

Many hamlets aspired to greatness. "Our future is before us," thundered a Thigh Hill man, "watch our smoke." Another settler described Brant as a "hustling little burg."[6] A glittering future depended entirely on steel rails, and some hamlets arose solely in anticipation of the railway: ". . . it was rumoured that the Grand Trunk was to run through the Bowville district," recalled one pioneer, "consequently a village sprang up. . . ."[7] As rumours mounted, hamlet dwellers began pestering railway companies with inquiries and petitions. The companies responded with announcements and surveys; in 1909 even Premier Rutherford confirmed that four lines would traverse the area.[8] Only the CPR would actually build a line, and as usual the company intended to by-pass existing hamlets, building its own townsites on land it already owned or would acquire, and sharing real estate profits with no one. And where the new line joined the Calgary and Edmonton Railway, the CPR would infuriate High River by making the connection several miles north where a new town could rise on company lands.[9]

Carmangay proved a special case, for, as Carman hoped, the CPR wished to cross the river valley at his settlement. They agreed, however, to survey a new townsite one-half mile from the existing hamlet where both parties could participate in the sale of lots by auction.[10] Although the sale was not until July of 1909, in May merchants at the old site prepared to move; they hoisted buildings on skids and piled lumber near the townsite.[11] They learned that outsiders planned to buy lots: businessmen from the Calgary and Edmonton towns, national companies (including three banks), and speculators galore.[12] One thousand buyers swarmed to the auction and paid $79,125 for 435 lots in less than three hours. Many bought six or more lots; scarcely a soul bought only one.[13]

Manoeuvring to obtain right-of-way and townsites cheaply, the CPR gave little thought to the practical spacing of towns. Ten miles separate some; only three and one-half separate others. The company ensured Kirkcaldy's stillbirth by placing it on Vulcan's doorstep and temporarily withholding its lots from sale. While the sale of the new Brant townsite, over two miles from the old Brant settlement, triggered a three-day line-up, the close spacing of three new townsites caused the old hamlet to split in several directions. Of 216 surveyed lots, only forty-nine sold; and at nearby Ensign, only nine of ninety. Blackie, the third townsite, lured most of the buyers. Farmers later argued before the Board of Railway Commissioners that building Ensign close to Brant, but far from Vulcan, accounted for the chaotic distribution of various railway services.[14]

Why did the sale of small townsites on a mere branch line generate so much excitement? Much of western Canada experienced rapid settlement; the sudden cancellation of grazing leases — combined with a teeming multitude of newly-arrived settlers, and an expanding railway network to move them — initiated stampedes into new districts. Just as the sudden flow of settlement had sparked a boom in the Calgary and Edmonton Railway towns, so now did the new Kipp–Aldersyde line promise to launch a new land rush to the uninhabited east. Although pioneers brought along carloads of "settlers' effects," they still needed supplies and equipment to build their homesteads. In addition, the construction of the railway, a high level bridge, the giant grain elevators, a huge reservoir that would irrigate land far to the southeast, and the towns themselves, all called for legions of workmen. Those who could quickly provide the goods and services for these immense undertakings stood to reap great profits. Anticipating a boom, speculators competed with local settlers to boost land prices. CPR townsites typically featured two wide streets for commercial purposes: one parallel to the railway siding for grain elevators, warehouses, and station; and another for retail businesses. Merchants scrambled for possession of these limited properties, especially the coveted corner lots.

The boom at the new townsites between 1909 and 1913 confirmed local expectations. Established farmers realigned their trade allegiance, and new settlers poured into the area. The railway gang arrived, 150 to 250 strong. Digging commenced on the Lake McGregor reservoir; one merchant sold $40,000 worth of goods at the site in one month. Carpenters descended on the townsites. At Carmangay forty buildings rose within two weeks of the townsite sale. At Champion twenty men laboured on the new hotel alone.[15] Still there remained a shortage of workers. Speculators, merchants, and salesmen huddled in tents and shacks and packed the new hotels and boarding houses. The Carmangay hotel reported huge profits, and the first houses completed were rented at fantastic prices.[16]

Fired by a real boom, real estate speculation accelerated. Whereas lots averaged $138 each at the Vulcan townsite sale in 1910, by 1912 they fetched $400 to $700.[17] By 1914, twenty per cent of the assessed lots in Champion and Vulcan traded outside the area, some as far away as Oregon and New England.[18] At Carmangay, C.W. Carman, the CPR, and Toronto speculators built sub-divisions larger in area than the original townsite. Nearby farmers parcelled land into small acreages. Purchased on the advice of friends and relatives in the area, or through Chicago or Toronto agents, the town lots of Carmangay soon traded sight unseen in four nations, across all nine provinces, and in fourteen American states.[19] In one year, E.W. Horne of Toronto sold 199 lots throughout England, Quebec, and Ontario. By 1914 Carmangay residents owned less than eight per cent of the town lots, and the CPR less than five per cent. Seventy-three property titles found their way to England and Scotland. Ontario investors owned 840 lots, about sixty-one per cent of all town land.[20]

Given the circumstances of frontier town founding, the inspiration of a real boom, and an even greater speculative one, it is easy to understand how town residents became avid boosters. Many had just arrived from the American mid-west and east Washington state, where town promotion had always been conspicuous, and they realized the need for effective organization. The Carmangay Board of Trade actually convened before the sale of the townsite, and Boards of Trade sprang up instantly in Champion and Vulcan. Their first goal was municipal incorporation. Carmangay became a village in 1910 and pressed on to town status a year later. Vulcan attempted to by-pass village status altogether, but in early 1912 lacked the necessary population of 400.[21] The Province soon raised the requirement to 700, forcing Vulcan to wait until 1921. Champion also settled reluctantly for village status, but old Brant had been so splintered by the arrival of steel that new Brant could not attain even that lowly title. Lacking the basic device of town promotion, it soon faded into obscurity.

Limited manpower and financial impotency forced small towns to modify the promotional techniques used by cities. Town and Village Councils, for example, quickly assumed the functions normally performed by Boards of Trade.[22] Like other urban places in the West, they lobbied corporations and governments for specific facilities and tempted them with free sites and tax incentives. But because the lure of large cash subsidies lay beyond their means, Councils bargained coyly with developers.[23] A serious, but less expensive, problem was that the towns were new, small, and unknown. Hence advertising soon dominated booster activity, a preoccupation symbolized by the Board of Trade slogan "You'll Hear From Champion." Like many cities, the towns published promotional literature, mailed it across the continent, and deposited it in hotels and train stations. Occasionally, they distributed literature aggressively. Vulcan merchants once sent an automobile driver on a two-month trip to Chicago to hand out brochures, give lectures, and answer questions.[24]

Distributing literature was expensive, however, and towns often preferred to advertise in city newspapers, particularly in special editions intended for wide circulation. But local weekly newspapers soon became the most common form of printed propaganda. From inception, advertisers moulded them into instruments of town promotion, inflicting considerable injury on journalistic ideals. Indeed, special editions scarcely resembled newspapers at all. It might be supposed that such efforts fizzled; surely no one read the local press save local residents. But many distant speculators had purchased farm land and town lots in the area, and they followed land prices by subscribing to local papers. Surprisingly, acquaintances of distant land owners often wrote inquiries to the newspapers about investment opportunities. The Carmangay *Sun* (1910), the Vulcan *Review* (1912, later the *Advocate*), and the Champion *Spokesman* (1914, later the *Chronicle*) together printed about 1,200 to 1,500 copies a week throughout the 1910s; perhaps hundreds reached readers beyond the area and in many parts of the continent.[25]

The boosters also relied on distant speculators to provide free advertising. They applauded literary efforts by the Toronto-based Western Canada Real Estate Company and the Equity Trust and Loan Company to advertise Carmangay, Champion, and Kirkcaldy real estate.[26] As well, the boosters expected individual efforts by residents to advertise the area. Large land owners like C.W. Carman, with business connections in Chicago and Grand Rapids, could always be counted on to spread Carmangay's fame, but as the local press relentlessly repeated, boosterism was everyone's responsibility and everyone should write the folks back home praising their town. W.J. Morton, a photographer in Vulcan, happily designed post cards for the purpose. The newspapers back home actually published many of these letters. Rev. J.S. Ainslie, for example, promoted Carmangay real estate in articles about the Canadian West published by his home town church newspaper, the *Congregationalist and Christian World* of Chicago.[27] To impress visitors, town and village councils sponsored campaigns encouraging everyone to clean, landscape, paint, and repair their property; and local newspapers always urged residents to "talk up the town" to strangers.

Local organizations or events like sports days and fairs also served the boosters' purpose. Organizers of the 1915 Vulcan Stampede hoped to draw attention to the town by offering contestants large cash prizes, arranging for excursion trains to the event, and advertising heavily. Similarly, the Carmangay Fair sought to convince agricultural editors of the "truly wonderfully rich and teeming . . . possibilities" of the district. Circuses, chautauquas, and other spectacles also provided merchants with plenty of temporary customers, and they eagerly solicited all travelling entertainments. Promotional exhibits might also be organized at special events in other towns. Carmangay considered its Agricultural Society's participation at Dry Farming Congresses, held in various cities of the North American West in the 1910s, a model of effecting boosting.[28]

Semi-professional baseball excited the boosters most of all. Imported by American settlers, baseball became a major social activity and a popular device for gambling, but everyone recognized its potential for town promotion as well. Would Vulcan ". . . stay on the map as a real live baseball town or sink into oblivion?" fretted the editorials each spring. Some years a town might forgo a season rather than risk humiliation. To generate publicity, the teams had to be good enough to win tournaments throughout the province if not beyond. Since many western towns hoped to spread fame this way, the task was onerous.[29] Nonetheless, Carmangay, Vulcan, and especially Champion all assembled teams of sufficient quality to win many provincial tournaments and even to attract major league scouts. The teams consisted of talented local residents, some with semi-professional experience, and a core of recruited professionals. Good players could always be pirated from opposing teams, but managers cast their nets widely. Vulcan's first loss of 1919 prompted a mission to Portland, Oregon that yielded three new players.[30]

The boosters searched endlessly for any gimmick to distinguish their town from countless others. Ralph "Slim" Moorehouse, a grain hauler well known for linking horses and wagons in long caravans, arrived at the Vulcan grain elevators one day in 1922 driving a team of thirty horses pulling eight wagons of wheat. A reporter met him. ". . . we record an event," pronounced the *Advocate*, "that in type and pictures will give us publicity all over America and even in the Old Country." The newspaper printed and mailed thousands of post cards, and requests for the story poured in from magazines and calendar makers. "If you can accommodate me in this connection," wrote Robert Stead, popular novelist and publicity director for the CPR, "I think we can put over some good publicity for the Vulcan district." When he arranged the publication of photographs in twenty-six British newspapers, the *Advocate* boasted that he had "made Vulcan as well known almost as New York."[31] In the quest for recognition, no tactic was too tasteless to exploit, no straw too thin to grasp.

If the tactics of small town boosterism sometimes displayed originality, its messages did not. Typically, they emphasized agricultural opportunities. Magnified claims about rich soil producing huge yields and a balmy climate blessed with abundant rainfall and "practically immune from hail and frost" appeared with monotonous regularity. In an area of the prairies most prone to violent fluctuations in climate and weather, one literary tract boldly stated that visitors "are agreeably surprised to find that the extremes of climate to which they have been accustomed are not known here." Even an admittedly disastrous drought year like 1910 could be twisted to advantage, for as the boosters pointed out, it was a tribute to the district that Carmangay grew and prospered anyway. But while Town Council polished the image of an agricultural Eden in public, it fretted in private about the problem of soil-drifting and the embarrassing image it might present.[32]

Promoting agricultural settlement could achieve little. Most land west of the tracks had been settled before the birth of the towns, while land to the east filled in quickly. Not only was settlement almost wholly complete by the time the towns began promoting it, but the trend towards fewer and larger farms was already underway. This disturbing fact turned town boosters into fanatical advocates of mixed farming. The intensive development of small farms promised to support a great population, and a wider variety of agricultural products might stabilize town incomes, which fluctuated with the price of wheat, and would create new opportunities for food processing industries. The towns all struggled to secure irrigation systems, meat packing plants, flax mills, flour mills, and dairies.[33]

Unhappily aware of the limitations imposed on local agriculture, boosters exaggerated the importance of other resources. Small coal deposits scattered throughout the area and mined for fuel by homesteaders, became in their minds the foundation for great transportation and industrial centres. Small natural gas strikes fired local imagination more effectively than they would ever fire local industry: ". . . there is sufficient natural gas at Champion," bragged the Board of Trade, "to drive the wheels of a hundred factories." With access to cheap fuel, Carmangay expected manufacturers to flock to town to exploit "some of the finest and most valuable fire-clay, iron, stone and alluvial deposits found anywhere in Canada."[34]

Railways remained crucial to all resource and industrial development, and newspapers predicted that new lines would magically benefit their town alone. The completion of the Kipp and Aldersyde stimulated local thirst for more lines, and railway companies continually announced plans and commissioned surveys; some even secured charters and purchased right-of-way for lines that would never materialize. Each town relentlessly petitioned railways for the prize of divisional point.[35]

Increasingly, roads commanded attention too, for farmers had to be brought to town quickly and conveniently. The automobile, which farmers purchased in great numbers during the profitable war years, promised to destroy the tyranny of time and distance that horse and wagon imposed on farmers. It inspired plans in 1919 for a provincial highway between Calgary and Lethbridge, and the towns mustered as much lobbying energy as they had for railway construction. "Vulcan wants and must have this highway," protested the *Advocate* when it learned that the proposed route would by-pass the town. Council successfully solicited the support of the rural Municipal District of Royal and secured the road.[36] In addition to roads and railways, boosters also expected telephone lines to reinforce commercial ties with the countryside, and the towns raced to link the most farmers to their local exchanges.[37]

According to its own treasured yardstick, population growth, the booster campaign did not succeed. The most ambitious schemes flagrantly ignored reality. Small, politically unimportant towns on secondary transportation routes with nothing special to offer could be safely ignored by government institutions in search of a home. Thus the Province scarcely acknowledged Carmangay's bid for the southern Agricultural School.[38] Coal added almost nothing to economic or population growth because of its low quantity and poor quality. It remained a convenient source of cheap home fuel for farmers, but served no industrial purpose. By 1936 the eight mines in the M.D. of Harmony employed no more than forty-five, a figure inflated by the winter employment of local farmers. Of fifty-two mines opened up to 1967, only seventeen produced coal for more than ten years; eight had closed by 1915.[39]

Soil remained the only natural resource feasible for exploitation, and the towns remained inextricably bound to agriculture. While close analysis of economic and spatial relations with the hinterland is beyond the purpose of this paper, some special problems can be outlined briefly. Inevitably urban growth stabilized or even fell after the completion of the immense task of building facilities for agricultural production, storage, and transportation. This complex, expensive infrastructure, however, depended on numerous mixed farms supporting a densely populated countryside. Instead, in a pattern typical of the dark brown soil zone, farms specialized in wheat, grew large in size and fewer in number. This trend doomed most plans for food processing industries. Carmangay's determination to have a creamery in spite of the lack of dairy cows in the area resulted in an anemic business that operated at a loss under the ownership of private interests, then the Board of Trade, and finally the United Farmers of Alberta local before closing forever. A lack of water hindered Vulcan and Champion. No stable manufacturing enterprise that exported beyond the area appeared until a small flour mill opened at Vulcan in 1925.[40]

But the transportation network most often handcuffed towns with no resources save land. In southern Alberta its vast triangular skeleton had already hardened prior to 1900 with primary joints at Calgary, Lethbridge, and Medicine Hat. Though scarcely more than small towns themselves, without competitors they mushroomed instantly under the impact of twentieth century settlement. Filling in the transportation skeleton further benefited these centres, and it proved impossible for new railway towns to overtake them. Indeed new lines actually carved away small town hinterlands instead of expanding them. Just as the building of the Kipp and Aldersyde in 1910 robbed older Calgary and Edmonton Railway towns of trade territory, so too did its extension north strip Carmangay of its "head of steel" advantage, creating the new rivals of Vulcan and Champion. In 1914 the extension of a line from Suffield gave birth to the railhead of Lomond twenty-five miles to the east, another competitor much feared by Carmangay merchants. Further extensions of this line in 1925 and 1930 created a string of new towns that stole even more trade from the Kipp and Aldersyde line. Instead of applauding new railway construction, the towns soon waged a losing battle to retain all their own rail services.[41]

Carmangay, Champion, and Vulcan did manage to capture and hold important if shrinking trade hinterlands, but their relative influence shifted. Business services in Carmangay fell from fifty-six in 1914 to forty-five by 1928, while at Vulcan and Champion they rose from fifty-six to 114, and from thirty-six to sixty-five respectively.[42] These businesses offered farmers and townspeople a basic supply of indispensable goods and services that changed little in nature for decades, except that automobile-related businesses replaced horse-related ones. Otherwise, each townsman who moved away left a particular shop or trade that could be filled by a newcomer. In each town, businesses directly related to agriculture consistently accounted for one-third to one-half of the total. Instead of selling goods, most businesses primarily sold services, whether of an agricultural, professional, personal, or craft nature. In short, all three centres retained the status among prairie places described as "independent towns" rather than "dependent villages."[43] Although topography and transportation routes distorted somewhat the idealized pattern of central place theory, the density of the rural population, the number of services it required, the frequency of its needs, and the distances it had to travel all largely determined the size, spacing, and number of urban places in the area.[44]

Contrary to popular image, the prairie town did not settle complacently into the role of agricultural service centre following the collapse of its lofty ambitions. Of necessity, railway towns struggled constantly for the trade of the immediate hinterland. The building of the Kipp and Aldersyde had eliminated all country stores close to the line, but by stimulating new settlement further east, it ensured the viability of distant hamlets and even gave rise to new ones. All across the prairies, an expanding railway network perpetually rearranged, but failed to destroy, the constellation of country hamlets. By 1936 places with less than ten businesses still made up seventy per cent of all central places in the Prairie Provinces, a proportion they had held since 1910. Railway or not, farmers seemed reluctant to venture beyond five miles for everyday items, and as late as 1931, only thirty-one per cent of the farmers in Census Division Four (which included Vulcan, Champion, and Carmangay) lived within five miles of a railway town; thirty-five per cent actually resided more than ten miles away. The general store remained by far the most decentralized business on the prairies.[45]

As for the goods and services available only at railways, farmers were hardly the captive customers of the closest town as observers of mid-western America once claimed. Although geographers often described a "zone of indifference" where farmers equidistant from towns might patronize one as readily as another, studies of the American mid-west and the Prairie Provinces have shown that farmers often shopped at places far distant from the closest town. Vulcan farmers behaved no differently. Like other towns throughout North America, those on the Kipp and Aldersyde learned that automobiles and improved roads not only lured farmers from further afield, but also whisked customers formerly bound to the town away to other centres.[46] The highway that brought Carmangay within less than an hour of downtown Lethbridge hastened its decline, whereas Vulcan's position half-way between Calgary and Lethbridge ensured at least slow growth. After World War II, Vulcan's strategic location in terms of automobile driving time allowed it to benefit simultaneously from the centralization of local government functions and the decentralization of the provincial ones. Overlapping and shifting trade zones explain the bitter rivalry between adjacent towns. When High River published literature boasting of huge wheat yields, Vulcan accused its competitor of using "our farmers" to bolster "their claims."[47]

By shopping in different towns, farmers sought not only lower prices and greater selection but also liberal credit and convenient business hours. These issues sparked conflict between towns, and sometimes within them. Cheating repeatedly undermined agreements between merchants to restrict credit to thirty days, even in 1922 when all the merchants on the Kipp–Aldersyde line agreed to co-operate. "Cash only" policies announced by Vulcan and Carmangay merchants collapsed in 1913, and again in 1916. Since the first country merchants usually opened stores in their homes, they willingly conducted business at all hours. During the building boom, everyone remained open until nine or ten o'clock each night. The weary merchants soon pleaded for rest. During the war, merchants in most towns agreed to close at 6:30 P.M. except on Saturday, and at noon on Wednesdays in the summer. But whenever a special event brought farmers to town, many ignored the rules. The towns apparently failed to enforce by-laws in accordance with the Provincial Early Closing Act until 1930, and even then they granted exceptions at harvest time.[48]

Besides competition from country stores and neighbouring towns, places as far off as Toronto invaded Main Street. No sooner did the new towns arise than the railway that created them began delivering a wide range of mail order goods: clothing, furniture, hardware, even non-perishable foodstuffs. In harmony with small towns across the continent, local merchants cried out in protest. Throughout the "Be Loyal to Your Own Community" campaign of 1914 and the "Trade at Home" campaign of 1922, Vulcan merchants chronicled the sins of the mail order houses: they demanded cash in advance and sold inferior goods that could not be inspected beforehand, delivery took weeks and exchanges even longer, and the goods actually cost more after adding the expense of postage and handling. By contrast, local merchants offered credit and prompt service. The press depicted "Bob Simpson" and "Tim Eaton" as community wreckers. By draining money out of the small town without returning a penny in local taxes or charitable contributions, they threatened local prosperity and even land values.[49]

Pedlars also invaded the small town, from door to door salesmen to itinerant wholesalers who sold boxcars of goods at cut rate prices. Champion Council protested in 1913 that resident merchants who built the community, extended credit, and paid taxes, could not survive in the face of such unfair competition. Merchants sternly warned the public against them, and town councils begged the Province for power to tax them out of existence. Automobiles and improved roads soon gave the travelling salesman even greater mobility. In 1929 the new highway brought a tremendous increase in mobile services from Calgary and Lethbridge. When city trucking and bus companies forced local draymen out of business, the towns appealed again to the Province for protection.[50]

Although small towns failed to become cities, and scarcely averted decline after 1913, boosterism nonetheless represented more than a transparent chapter in western town history. It both shaped and revealed pioneer attitudes in a variety of ways. Most often, it expressed the unbridled optimism of frontiers generally and western Canada in particular. Once train service began, Vulcan expected to advance "with the strides of a young Chicago." Boosters predicted that Champion would "rank among the chief cities of the West."[51]

But did the boosters believe their own propaganda? Certainly in the towns' first bustling years optimism did not seem misplaced, yet many realized the boom would not last forever. By 1913 many merchants had already "made their harvest," sold out, and moved away. Of the 125 businessmen listed in directories and tax rolls along a forty-mile stretch of the Kipp and Aldersyde in 1914, seventy-four per cent were replaced by newcomers by 1920, a turnover rate that slowed significantly thereafter.[52] Just as many of the first businessmen came from towns on the Calgary and Edmonton line, they came in turn to new towns on other new lines from the Kipp and Aldersyde. The false-front store suited perfectly the mood of the western merchant; an imposing facade of stability masked transitory urges. But if optimism failed to graft itself forever to one particular town, it remained always strong; should the boom falter in one place, it would surely revive wherever railway construction created new townsites.

Promotional literature also described the kind of society pioneers hoped to create, for they naturally advertised features that they believed most likely to attract newcomers. A 1910 promotional spread emphasized the orderly character of Carmangay social life, the safety of its streets, and the sobriety of its citizens. Only a respectable population could provide the social environment necessary for progress and prosperity. "The people of Vulcan are energetic, and a splendid type of townspeople generally, and the men at the head of it are men of ability and shrewd in business," ran a typical claim. Such men would surely build a community that need not suffer from any comparison. Promotional literature never failed to exalt the progressive educational, religious, social, and recreational facilities of the towns; it linked social order and respectability with material progress to convince newcomers that their investments would be secure and their families safe and happy in a frontier town.[53] Although boosters scorned the wild west frontier in favour of civilized images, they did not wish to transplant eastern communities intact. Along the Kipp and Aldersyde, townspeople believed that entrenched interests and the inert weight of tradition handicapped the eastern town. Only on a frontier could the best features of settled communities be nurtured, while the worst might be pruned away.

The booster campaign also poses a paradox. If small communities idealized their wholesome, pastoral surroundings and decried the evils of urban life, as many claim, then why did they struggle valiantly to become large cities? The desire of the Kipp and Aldersyde towns to build an industrial base on coal mining, in particular, suggests little concern about the class and ethnic clashes, the social and moral problems, and the despoiled landscape often associated with that industry. Probably few boosters pondered the implications of their goals, but it is also possible that the anti-urban attitude of rural areas has been exaggerated and misunderstood.[54] Not until the grandest ambitions seemed doomed did the advantages of small town life creep into the promotional campaign. Rather than expressing deep-rooted anti-urban convictions, these arguments seemed designed to protect local trade or dissuade young people from leaving. Often they simply camouflaged envy and a sense of inferiority and failure. But if townspeople actually admired the city, why didn't they move there? Some did, of course, but most believed that the small community promised greater rewards to those who could only afford small investments in business and real estate.[55]

It cannot be argued that only a vocal minority supported boosterism. Merchants dominated the promotional campaign, but in farm towns without industry they constituted the largest single economic group. Furthermore, CPR town lot sales records and tax rolls indicate widespread participation in real estate speculation by independent tradesmen, professionals, and even salaried employees. Local managers of regional and national corporations also became boosters because a growing town ensured a growing business that would increase commissions or lead to promotion elsewhere. Indeed with its jubilant optimism, boosterism bolstered faith in social mobility. Was not the Ontario apprentice of yesterday a businessman in a new town today, and would not his investments in a future city make him a rich man tomorrow? Such prospects dampened social distinctions and conflicts within the towns and wedded newcomers to a common cause.

Many farmers also became boosters. A vast literature describes a rocky history of town–country relations in North America. Merchant credit, mail order catalogues, farmer-owned co-operatives, different lifestyles, goals, and attitudes, and (in Alberta) the class-consciousness of the United Farmers of Alberta have all been cited as sources of friction.[56] But boosterism along the Kipp and Aldersyde clearly blunted rather than sharpened any conflict, and long-time residents recall no special resentments by either side, in spite of the tendency of farmers to trade at more than one centre and disputes over mail order catalogues and pedlars. Too often such issues have been interpreted solely as town–country battles when townspeople themselves ordered from Eaton's or bought in the city as readily as farmers, a fact unhappily recognized by the merchants.[57] Virtually all studies of town–country conflict have focused on towns with populations far exceeding 1,000; much better relations prevailed in smaller places where town institutions could not survive without farm support and participation.[58] As with most organizations along the Kipp and Aldersyde, Boards of Trade claimed many farm members, and many merchants joined Agricultural Societies. Farmers often lived in town, especially in winter, and young people from town and country freely inter-married. On a modern frontier where literate, English-speaking farmers enjoyed the advantages of newspapers, magazines, railroads, and, very soon, automobiles, radio, telephones, and movies, the frontier merchant no longer commanded his traditional role as the transmitter and interpreter of the outside world.

Small communities bred few social differences between town and country, and even encouraged common economic interests. All the men most closely associated with town founding owned farms as well as stores: C.W. Carman of Carmangay, E.E. Thompson of Brant, Martin Clever of Cleversville and Champion, and the Elves Brothers of Vulcan. Farmers speculated in town lots as readily as merchants in farm land,

and near Vulcan alone at least seventeen farmers invested directly in stores.[59] But the vast majority who did not also discovered reasons for supporting town promotion. Boosters always emphasized the prosperity and potential of local agriculture and praised the intelligence and initiative of their farmers. Few criticized a campaign designed to raise the value of their land and flatter them at the same time. Farmers sometimes launched booster campaigns independently of townspeople. Agricultural societies and rural local governments became major instruments of promotion, publishing their own literature, organizing local fairs, and establishing promotional displays at distant events.[60]

Even people who would not gain by it economically supported town promotion, for it inspired much more than greed. Some scholars have suggested that the twentieth century invasion of the countryside by brand name advertising, chain stores, and the new cultural technology robbed the small town of its independence, its distinctive character, and its historic role in setting standards of public taste and morality.[61] Individuals derive much of their identity from where they live, and like the residents of Stephen Leacock's Mariposa, people in the small towns of the Kipp and Aldersyde cried out for recognition in a world increasingly dominated by big cities. This craving explains the pride attached to home town baseball teams, but emerged clearly in 1927 when boosters deliberately publicized an incident that could only tarnish Vulcan's image. A tornado struck. It uprooted telephone poles and drove them into the sides of homes. It tore buildings apart, demolished threshing machines, and imbedded blades of grass in fence posts. D.C. Jones, local druggist and prominent booster, photographed the tornado and gave the negative to a newspaper friend. When it received wide publication, residents forgot the destruction and basked in the fame it brought them — so much so that a local M.L.A., D.M. Galbraith, mailed Christmas cards featuring the photograph to acquaintances far and wide. The crowning triumph came when *Encyclopaedia Britannica* decided to publish Jones's photograph under its tornado entry.[62]

By harnessing strangers to a common purpose, generating optimism, instilling faith in social mobility, blunting town–country tensions, and forging local identity, boosterism instantly created a hearty civic spirit. Although cynics like Thorstein Veblen sneered that it was a device to raise real estate values, it nonetheless built sidewalks and churches and schools as well as businesses. Town pioneers organized local governments with robust enthusiasm. At Carmangay the ratepayers voted unanimously for municipal incorporation and "almost unanimously" at Vulcan.[63] Carmangay's first Village election in 1910 inspired six men to seek three Council seats, and the 157 ballots cast represented nearly every eligible voter. The following year twelve men battled for the seven positions required by the new Town status. Champion's first election attracted eight men to three Council positions, and brought out 99 voters, while the second contest produced five candidates. When 208 voters selected three of the five aspirants to Vulcan's first Council, the *Times* claimed that nearly everyone with a franchise and "many without" had voted. The next election again yielded five candidates.[64] Hence in the towns' first years many eagerly sought the challenge of building a new community and voters proved just as anxious to select the best men for the job.[65]

Boosterism also revealed its dark side, frequently imposing its narrow conformity on the thought and behaviour of small town inhabitants. Subtle intimidation accompanied such slogans as "Progress demands that there be no factions. Progress demands a unity of action. . . ." The boosters branded those who did not support promotion as "kickers and knockers," and subjected them to public abuse. When a farmer east of Carmangay told a Lethbridge reporter that crops looked poor one year, the *Sun* suggested he was a fool and a liar.[66]

Boosterism harboured other unpleasant surprises when the future refused to unfold according to plan. In ways that would erode early optimism and civic spirit, it marred the financial health of the towns, and even their physical appearance. Streets hurriedly gridded at right angles reflected only the CPR's concern for low survey costs and fast real estate sales. It planted Champion and Vulcan in soft, low-lying areas, perhaps as a precaution against runaway boxcars or in the hope of finding water easily, but both sites afforded poor water in insufficient supply. Champion sometimes hauled in drinking water, and the soft ground plagued road construction for decades, especially on Vulcan's elevator row. During the boom, merchants erected substandard buildings, and temporary shacks often became permanent structures. Only six years after Carmangay's birth, some buildings were no longer safe.[67]

Consider as well the consequences of boosterism's closest ally, real estate promotion. Townspeople applauded the far-flung sale of property in hopes that development would follow, but speculators simply wanted quick resales. Hence farm land carved into small tracts lay idle. "Around Carmangay for four miles there is little but grass growing," complained one farmer in 1913. "Who owns all this land? Why don't they do something with it? We are all tired of driving over this stretch of desert to reach town, and town people must be tired of seeing it." Similarly, Carmangay's principal business streets developed in a relatively compact manner, but homes and minor commercial buildings sprawled across the townsite interspaced by hundreds of weed-infested vacant lots. By 1921 Carmangay's incorporated area of 640 acres housed only 300 people. This dispersed pattern strained the ability of towns to provide public utilities and services.[68]

Vacant lands created other problems. Until 1916 Alberta towns employed the single tax system — taxes could be levied on land but not on improvements.[69] Hence if speculators did not pay land taxes, towns could not pay off debts acquired to finance civic improvements. These debts especially burdened frontier towns where everything had to be built from scratch. The mill rate in Carmangay spiralled from twenty in 1910 to fifty in 1917, largely to pay off debentures issued for the municipally-owned electrical and water works system. In the game of musical town lots, everyone tried to resell property before taxes came due, with the result that by 1913, sixty-one per cent of Carmangay's assessments had not been paid in full. When the recession struck western Canada that year, urban real estate values along the Kipp and Aldersyde, as elsewhere, collapsed immediately. Speculators now refused to pay back taxes because lots were suddenly worth less than the taxes owing on them. Financial disaster followed. The debenture market dried up for western local governments, and remained generally dry until the 1940s.

While failing to achieve its goals, boosterism clearly played a major role in the history of small prairie towns. The booster mentality that characterized most western settlements inspired their very founding. Spurred by the success of the subsequent boom, town promotion became the primary public preoccupation of early residents, and they utilized every technique at their disposal to stimulate urban growth. Boosterism instantly fostered identity, civic spirit, and unity of purpose in new communities made up of a variety of people lacking common traditions to guide them.

Important as this role might be, the long-term impact of boosterism often surprised its advocates. Where successful, it helped create an urban industrial society, but it could not solve its problems, and a booster mentality might even aggravate them. And where boosterism failed, as in small prairie towns, its legacy of vacant lots and financial tragedy symbolized the crushed hopes of the city builders who failed.

NOTES

Abbreviations: ALL — Alberta Legislative Library, Edmonton
GAI — Glenbow-Alberta Institute, Calgary
MDK — M.D. Keenan, privately owned archival collection, Pincher Creek, Alberta
PAA — Provincial Archives of Alberta, Edmonton
PAC — Public Archives of Canada, Ottawa.

1. See, for example, Alan F.J. Artibise, "Boosterism and the Development of Prairie Cities, 1871–1913," in Artibise, ed., *Town and City: Aspects of Western Canadian Urban Development* (Regina: Canadian Plains Research Centre, 1981), pp. 209–37.
2. Of 2,432 places in the Prairie Provinces with at least one business establishment by 1930, 2,362 or 97 per cent of them had populations under 1,000. N.L. Whetten, "The Social and Economic Structure of the Trade Centres in the Canadian Prairie Provinces, With Special References to Its Changes, 1910–1930," Ph.D. Thesis (Harvard University, 1932), p. 42.
3. Carmangay *Sun*, "Dry Farming Congress Edition," Oct. 21, 1912, MDK; and Western Canada Real Estate Company, *Some Truths of Carmangay: The Star Town of Southern Alberta* (Toronto: by author, 1912), p. 15, MDK.
4. CPR Land Sales Records, GAI, Vol. 135, pp. 56–57; *Henderson's Manitoba and North West Territories Gazetteer and Directory*, 1905; and Supt. Primrose, "Monthly Reports of D Division, Macleod, Albert," R.C.M.P. Records, PAC, Aug. 7, 1907, p. 5.
5. H.S. Parker, "Brant, Alberta," unpub. ms, n.d., GAI; High River *Times*, ALL, Aug. 1, 1906 and May 14, 1908; *Henderson's*, 1905, p. 607; H.H. Thompson, "The Thompsons in Alberta," unpub. ms, n.d., GAI; and George B. Thompson, "Memoirs of Charles H. Thompson and Dorcas L. Thompson: Their Ancestors, Their Family and Their Descendents," unpub. ms, n.d., GAI, p. 16.
6. Nanton *News*, ALL, July 22, 1909; High River *Times*, Mar. 15, 1906.
7. Carmangay and District History Book Committee, *Bridging the Years; Carmangay and District* (Carmangay: by author, 1968), p. 155.
8. Claresholm *Review*, ALL, Mar. 11, 1909. Also High River *Times*, Nov. 22, 1906 and July 30, 1908; Nanton *News*, June 8, 1905 and Jan. 18, 1906.
9. High River *Times*, Aug. 12, 1909, June 10, 1909 and Aug. 11, 1910.
10. Carmangay, *Bridging*, p. 6; Western Canada, *Some Truths*, p. 16; High River *Times*, July 1, 1909; CPR Land Sales Records, GAI, Vol. 49, pp. 62–79.
11. Claresholm *Review*, May 6, 1909; Supt. Primrose, "Monthly Reports," June 11, 1909, p. 4.
12. Claresholm *Review*, April 29, May 6, July 22, 1909; Nanton *News*, May 13, July 29, 1909.
13. Calculated from CPR Land Sales Records, GAI, Vol. 49, pp. 62–79. See also Carmangay *Sun*, Mar. 24, 1911.
14. CPR Land Sales Records, GAI, Vol. 49, pp. 111–16, 145–48, 168–73; Parker, "Brant"; High River *Times*, October 6, 1910; "Complaint of the Board of Trade of Ensign, Alberta, with Regard to the CPR Closing its Station at Brant," Board of Railway Commissioners, Transcripts of hearings, PAC, Vol. 212, file 25119 (November 26, 1914), pp. 5881–85.

15. Mrs. Folk, "A Eulogy of the Carmangay Ladies Aid From 1910 to 1935," unpub. ms, 1935?, Carmangay Pastoral Charge Papers, United Church of Canada Records, PAA; Canada, *Sessional Papers* 15, 1912, Appendix 1, p. 106; Supt. Primrose, "Monthly Reports," Aug. 24, 1910; Letter, Thos. M. Melrose to Canon Hogbin, Sept. 14, 1911, Carmangay Papers, Anglican Church of Canada Diocese of Calgary Archives, University of Calgary Library; Carmangay *Sun*, Aug. 11, 1910; Claresholm *Review*, Aug. 5, 1909; Supt. Primrose, "Monthly Reports," Nov. 15, 1910, p. 5, June 15, 1912, Dec. 12, 1912, p. 6; Carmangay *Sun*, Sept. 29, 1910, April 1, 1910, and Dec. 8, 1910.

16. High River *Times*, Nov. 30, 1911 and April 18, 1912; Carmangay *Sun*, Mar. 18, 1910; Will E. Finley, letter published in Hastings Michigan *Journal-Herald*, May, 1913 reprinted in Carmangay *Sun*, May 30, 1913; Letter, Thos. Little to Deputy Minister of Public Works, Aug. 20, 1909, Village of Carmangay Correspondence, Municipality Correspondence Files, Alberta Department of Municipal Affairs papers, PAA, Box 90, file 1177. Also Claresholm *Review*; Aug. 26, 1909.

17. Calculated from CPR Land Sales Records, GAI, Vol. 49, pp. 134–40; and High River *Times*, "Homeseekers Edition," May, 1912.

18. Calculated from Village of Champion Tax Rolls, 1914, Village Office, Champion, Alberta; and Village of Vulcan Tax Rolls, 1914, Town Office, Vulcan, Alberta.

19. Village and Town Council of Carmangay Minutes, Vol. 1, pp. 181, 134–35; Village of Carmangay Assessment and Tax Tolls, 1912–13, both in Village Office, Carmangay, Alberta; and Letter, Carmangay Board of Trade to Minister of Public Works, Nov. 9, 1909. Village of Carmangay Correspondence. Carmangay *Sun*, June 3, 1910, May 12, 1911, and May 31, 1912.

20. Calculated from Village of Carmangay Assessment and Tax Rolls, 1913–1914.

21. Letter, Carmangay Board of Trade to Deputy Minister of Public Works, June, 1909, Village of Carmangay Correspondence; Vulcan Board of Trade to Deputy Minister of Public Works, Nov. 26, 1910, Village of Vulcan Correspondence; Claresholm *Review*, June 24, 1900; and Letter, Deputy Minister of Public Works to A.A. Ballachey, July 15, 1912, Village of Vulcan Correspondence.

22. Vulcan *Review*, ALL, Mar. 19, 1913; Champion *Chronicle*, ALL, Mar. 17, 1921.

23. Village and Town Council of Carmangay Minutes, Vol. 1, pp. 177–78; and Western Canada, *Some Truths*, p. 3.

24. Vulcan *Advocate*, privately owned collection, Vulcan Advocate Office, Vulcan, Alberta, June 11 and Aug. 27, 1919.

25. "A Southern Alberta Town in the Making," in *Why Go To Canada?* (Calgary: *Herald*, June, 1910); Lethbridge *Herald*, April 2, 1910, p. 57; Carmangay *Sun*, "Dry Farming Congress Edition," Oct. 21, 1912; Vulcan *Advocate*, Oct. 22, 1913. Original subscription lists have been lost. Estimates based on Tax Rolls, incidental sources, and information in Vulcan *Review*, Dec. 17, 1912; and Calgary *Herald*, Sept. 10, 1936.

26. Carmangay *Sun*, Feb. 23, 1911; Western Canada, *Some Truths*; and Harvey Beaubier, interviewed at Champion, Alberta, June, 1978.

27. Vulcan *Advocate*, Mar. 10, 1915. A collection of post cards is located in the Vulcan Archives, Vulcan, Alberta. The Chicago article was reprinted in the Carmangay *Sun*, Mar. 24, 1911.

28. Vulcan *Advocate*, Aug. 18, 1915; *Farm and Ranch Review*, Oct. 21, 1912, p. 882; Vulcan *Advocate*, June 22, 1921 and July 7, 1920; and Village and Town Council of Carmangay Minutes, Vol. 1, p. 49.

29. Vulcan *Advocate*, April 7, 1920. For information on semi-professional baseball in the area, and its high quality, see clippings, photographs, letters, and statistical records in MDK Collection, especially Alex Allan, "Baseball Recollections," magazine clippings, n.d., Book 21M; John L. Edlund, "Baseball in Claresholm as I Remember it From 1921–1928," magazine clipping, n.d., Book 21N; "Early Years of the Champion Senior Baseball Teams in Summary," unpub. ms, n.d., Book 22L.

30. Vulcan *Advocate*, Aug. 30, 1916; Carmangay *Sun*, June 17, 1910; Newspaper clippings, MDK, Book 22A; Carmangay *Sun*, July 15, 1910; Vulcan *Advocate*, July 19, 1922, and June 11 and 18, 1919. See also "Champion Senior Baseball," Bessie Siler, interviewed in Lethbridge *Herald*, May 17, 1975; and Champion History Committee, *Cleverville-Champion 1905 to 1970: A History of Champion and Area* (Champion: by authors, 1971), pp. 531–32.

31. Vulcan *Advocate*, Nov. 29 and Dec. 20, 1922; ibid., Feb. 21, 28 and May 16, 1923. For more information see photographs in Vulcan Archives, Vulcan, Alberta; Lethbridge *Herald*, "Fortieth Anniversary Progress and Development Edition," Dec. 11, 1947, 4th sec., p. 9; Calgary *Herald*, April 27, 1963; and Vulcan and District Historical Society, *Wheat Country: A History of Vulcan and District* (Vulcan: by author, 1973), pp. 946–47.

32. Vulcan *Review*, Mar. 26, 1912; Carmangay *Sun*, "Dry Farming Congress Edition," Oct. 21, 1912, MDK; Village and Town Council of Carmangay Minutes, Vol. 1, pp. 55–56.

33. Village and Town Council of Carmangay Minutes, Vol. 2, p. 97; Carmangay *Sun*, Mar. 25, 1910; Oct. 20, 1911; Nov. 12 and 19, 1920; Vulcan *Advocate*, all issues, Sept., 1922; Claresholm *Review*, Dec. 16, 1909; and Champion Board of Trade, *Grain Golden Champion* (Champion: by author, 1912), MDK, pp. 16–17.

34. Western Canada, *Some Truths*, p. 9; Champion B. of T., *Grain Golden Champion.*, p. 15. See also Nanton *News*, July 22, 1909; Vulcan *Advocate*, July 15 and Sept. 30, 1914; and Carmangay *Sun*, July 3, 1914 and Oct. 18, 1912.

35. Claresholm *Review*, Jan. 13, 1910; Carmangay *Sun*, many issues, 1910–13; Nanton *News*, July 21, 1910; R.F.P. Bowan, *Railways in Southern Alberta* (Lethbridge: Occasional Paper No. 4, Whoop-Up Chapter, Historical Society of Alberta, 1973), p. 30; and Vulcan *Review*, July 2, 1912.

36. Vulcan *Advocate*, May 21, 1919 and Feb. 12, 1919; and Municipal District of Royal 158 Minutes, County of Vulcan No. 2 Records, PAA, Vol. 1, p. 73.

37. High River *Times*, Sept. 5, 1907; Nanton *News*, Dec. 22, 1910.

38. Carmangay *Sun*, May 12, 1911.

39. Letters, C. Rhodes to Deputy Minister of Municipal Affairs, April 3 and Sept. 9, 1936, Municipal District of Harmony 128 Correspondence, Municipality Correspondence Files, Alberta Department of Municipal Affairs Papers, PAA, Box 113, files 1339–40; Oldman River Regional Planning Commission, *Town of Vulcan, Alberta, Canada: General Plan 1967; Revised Analysis of the Survey* (Lethbridge: by author, 1967), p. 25; Alberta Department of Public Works, *Annual Reports* (Edmonton: by author, 1916), p. 153–71.

40. Carmangay *Sun*, Nov. 17, 1911; May 16 and 23, 1913; Mar. 27, Aug. 13 and 20, Nov. 26, 1914; April 24, 1915; Dec. 3, 1920; Mar. 9, 1923; and Vulcan *Advocate*, April 29, 1925.

41. Carmangay merchants worried that they would lose business to the new towns. Carmangay *Sun*, April 1, 1910 and June 5, 1914. On the rail issue see "Complaint of the Board of Trade of Ensign, Alberta, with Regard to the CPR Closing its Station at Brant," Vol. 212, Nov. 26, 1914; "Restoration of Daily Day Service on CPR Lethbridge to Calgary, via Aldersyde," Vol. 406, July 10, 1927; both in Board of Railway Commissioners Transcripts of Hearings, PAC: Village and Town Council of Carmangay Minutes, Vol. 2, p. 257; Municipal District of Royal 158 Minutes, Vol. 2, Jan. 13, 1934; and Vulcan *Advocate*, Dec. 20 and 27, 1922.

42. Most of the information for this paragraph was calculated from *Henderson's Alberta Gazetteer and Directory*, 1911, 1914, 1928–29; *Wrigley's Alberta Directory*, 1920, 1922; and R.G. Dun and Co., *Mercantile Agency Reference Book*, 1921, 1925, 1928, 1932.

43. C.C. Zimmerman, *Farm Trade Centres in Minnesota, 1905–1920* (Minneapolis: University of Minn. Agricultural Experimental Station, Bulletin 269), p. 10; and C.A. Dawson and E.R. Young, *Pioneering in the Prairie Provinces; The Social Side of the Settlement Process* (Toronto: Macmillan, 1940), pp. 48-52.

44. These problems are examined in detail by Peter Woroby, "Functional Relationship Between Farm Population and Service Centers," M.Sc. Thesis (University of Manitoba, 1957), and J.E. Lamb, "Some Aspects of the Settlement Geography of Southern Manitoba," M.A. Thesis (University of Manitoba, 1970).

45. Whetten, "Trade Centres," pp. 93–96, 42–43, 57; Carle C. Zimmerman and Garry W. Moneo, *The Prairie Community System* (Ottawa: Agricultural Economics Research Council of Canada 1970), p. 30; Canada, *Census of Canada*, 1931, Vol. 8, p. 696 and Vol. 10, pp. 876–77.

46. Thorstein Veblen, "The Country Town," in *Absentee Ownership and Business Enterprise in Recent Times: The Case of America* (first published 1923; New York: Sentry Press, 1964), pp. 147–48; Dawson, *Pioneering*, pp. 301–02; Whetten, "Trade Centres," pp. 143–46, 148–50; Lewis E. Atherton, "The Midwestern County Town — Myth and Reality," *Agricultural History*, Vol. 26 (July, 1952), pp. 73–80; Vulcan *Advocate*, Mar. 15, 1922; and many interviews, elderly farmers, County of Vulcan, 1978.

47. Vulcan *Advocate*, Dec. 3, 1913.

48. Interview, C.H. "Budd" Andrews, near Vulcan, Alberta, Jan., 1978; Vulcan *Advocate*, Jan. 25, 1922; Carmangay *Sun*, Jan. 3 and 10, 1913, Oct. 29, 1920; Vulcan *Advocate*, Dec. 1, 1913; Vulcan *Review*, Oct. 1, 1912; Canada, *Sessional Papers*, 28, 1916, p. 71; Carmangay *Sun*, Mar. 24 and June 9, 1911; Petition attached to By-law 11, Village of Champion By-laws, Village Office, Champion, Alberta; Carmangay *Sun*, May 4, 1916 and Aug. 31, 1917: Vulcan *Advocate*, May 28, 1919, May 31, 1922, and Aug. 20, 1919; Revised By-law 11, Nov. 9, 1931, Village of Champion By-laws; and By-law 53, Dec. 1, 1930, Town of Vulcan By-laws, Town Office, Vulcan, Alberta.

49. For two examples see Jean Burnet, *Next-Year Country: A Study of Rural Social Organization in Alberta* (Toronto: University of Toronto Press, 1951), p. 79; and Richard G. Bremer, *Agricultural Change in an Urban Age: The Loup Country of Nebraska, 1910–1970* (Lincoln: University of Neb. Studies, New Series 51, 1976), p. 39. See also Vulcan *Advocate*, July 12, 1922; Oct. 22, 1913; Nov. 25, 1914; Sept. 8, 1915; any issue, spring, 1922; Carmangay *Sun*, July 15, 1910.

50. Letter, Village of Champion to Deputy Minister of Municipal Affairs, Aug. 29, 1913. Village of Champion Correspondence; Carmangay *Sun*, Mar. 23, 1916; Nanton *News*, Nov. 10, 1915; Letter, Village of Champion to Deputy Minister of Municipal Affairs, April 21, 1931, Village of Champion Correspondence; and Letter, Town of Vulcan to Acting Minister of Municipal Affairs, June 1, 1931, Town of Vulcan Correspondence.

51. High River *Times*, Sept. 7, 1911; Champion Board of Trade, *Grain Golden Champion*, p. 1; Western Canada, *Some Truths*, p. 14; and Carmangay *Sun*, Mar. 31, 1911.

52. See entries for Vulcan, Champion, Carmangay, Brant, Ensign, and Kirkcaldy in *Henderson's*, 1911, 1914, 1928–29; and Wrigley's, 1920, 1922. See also Tax Rolls of Vulcan, Carmangay, and Champion, 1914, 1920, 1922, 1928.

53. Don Harrison Doyle, "Social Theory and New Communities," *Western Historical Quarterly*, Vol. 8, No. 2 (April, 1977), p. 164, notes that such appeals were also common during the settlement of the American mid-west.

54. J.F. Newman, "The Impact of Technology upon Rural Southwestern Manitoba, 1920–1930," M.A. Thesis (Queen's University, 1971), pp. 39–57, argues that small-town people believed that they could somehow accommodate a degree of industry without sacrificing the virtues of rural life.

55. Many interviews, County of Vulcan, 1978; and Vulcan *Advocate*, Sept. 2, 1914.

56. For Alberta, all these arguments can be found in Jean Burnet, "Town–Country Relations and the Problem of Rural Leadership," *Canadian Journal of Economics and Political Science*, Vol. 13 (Aug. 1947), pp. 395–410.

57. Many interviews, County of Vulcan, 1978; and Vulcan *Advocate*, Dec. 24, 1913.

58. Burnet, *Next-Year Country*, pp. 52–75.

59. Based on biographical files compiled from many sources.

60. Local Improvement District 128 Minutes, Vol. 1, p. 17, County of Vulcan No. 2 Records, PAA.

61. Veblen, "Country Town," pp. 151–56; Arthur J. Vidich and Joseph Bensman, *Small Town in Mass Society: Class, Power, and Religion in a Rural Community*, revised ed. (Princeton: Princeton University Press, 1968).

62. Calgary *Herald*, July 9, 1927; A.B. Lowe and G.A. McKay, *The Tornadoes of Western Canada* (Ottawa: Canadian Department of Transport, Meteorological Branch, 1962), p. 16; Adam Armey Papers, GAI; and D.C. Jones, interview, Calgary *Herald*, April 27, 1963.

63. Veblen, "Country Town," pp. 142–44; Village and Town Council of Carmangay Minutes, Vol. 1, p. 26; Carmangay *Sun*, Aug. 6, 1910; High River *Times*, Mar. 15, 1912; and Vulcan *Review*, Mar. 19, 1912.

64. Letter, Village of Carmangay Returning Officer to Department of Public Works, Feb. 10, 1910, Village of Carmangay Correspondence; Carmangay *Sun*, April 21, 1911; Calgary *Albertan*, April 18, 1911: Letters, Village of Champion Returning Officer to Deputy Minister of Public Works, June 2, 1911 and Jan. 22, 1912, Village of Champion Correspondence; High River *Times*, Jan. 23, 1913; Letter, Village of Vulcan Returning Officer to Deputy Minister of Municipal Affairs, Jan. 28, 1913, Village of Vulcan Correspondence; and Vulcan *Advocate*, Dec. 17, 1913.

65. This evidence seems to support the thesis advanced by Stanley Elkins and Eric McKitrick, "A Meaning for Turner's Frontier, Part 1: Democracy in the Old Northwest," *Political Science Quarterly*, Vol. 69 (Sept., 1954), pp. 321–53. They argued that the immense task of community building forced pioneers to make many decisions, resulting in widespread interest and participation in local government (pp. 321–40), especially in the American mid-west, where town promotion promised to enrich everyone (pp. 340–53).

66. Vulcan *Advocate*, Mar. 24, 1920; and Carmangay *Sun*, June 27, 1913.

67. Village of Champion Minutes, Vol. 1, pp. 93–94. Village Office, Champion, Alberta. For poor townsite selection in other areas see Bedil J. Jensen, "The County of Mountain View, 1890–1925," M.A. Thesis (University of Alberta, 1972); Carmangay *Sun*, Mar. 23, 1916; Village and Town Council of Carmangay Minutes, Vol. 2, pp. 101, 199, 315.

68. Letter to Editor, Carmangay *Sun*, Dec. 31, 1913. For other towns with the problem of vacant lands, see E.B. Mitchell, *In Western Canada Before the War: A Study of Communities* (London: John Murray, 1915), pp. 13–14; Canada, Census of Canada 1921, Vol. 1, pp. 222, 228; Village and Town Council of Carmangay Minutes, Vol. 1, p. 228.

69. Eric J. Hanson, *Local Government in Alberta* (Toronto: McClelland and Stewart, 1956), p. 40.

TOPIC TWO
Farm Life

Lethbridge, Alberta. Prairie
dust storms were rather
common; during the Great
Depression they were
devastating.

Cities may have attracted a majority of Canadians by World War II, but by no means did the rural sector stagnate. Over the course of the twentieth century, farms became more capital intensive and spatially expansive — patterns that, along with continual improvement in strains of feed and seed as well as in agricultural techniques, produced impressive results. For instance, while the number of farms in Canada increased by 39.1 percent between 1901 and 1920, the total income they generated soared by 336.1 percent.[1] But was the story simply one of progress, whereby with time, farmers overcame a harsh environment, worked through the problem of supposedly high freight rates and tariffs, successfully courted government assistance, and, as suggested in several accounts, shed their distrust of modern technology and their desire to preserve a mythical Arcadian past?[2]

The so-called "backwardness" of agriculturalists certainly receives critical scrutiny in Article 3, a quantitative analysis by Robert E. Ankli, H. Dan Helsberg, and John Herd Thompson of tractor use prior to 1940 on Canada's vast wheat farms. The use of tractors grew more slowly than the use of other machines such as threshers and combines, but the authors make clear that farmers were correct in estimating that a tractor would prove more expensive than animal power. As well as undertaking economic revisionism of this kind, rural social historians have uncovered other factors relating to people's experience of and outlook on modernization. They have shown, for instance, that some ethnic groups turned to communal block farming and refused modern technology altogether for cultural and religious reasons. And many itinerant agricultural labourers saw mechanization as constituting a threat to their prospects of employment and a barrier to their saving enough money to start farms of their own. In Article 4, Mary Kinnear focusses on the experience and outlook of farm women. Kinnear looks at a 1922 survey completed by the United Farm Women of Manitoba and an essay competition held the same year by the *Grain Growers' Guide*, both of which showed the life of the farm woman as practically untouched by modernization and therefore one of great hardship. Still, interestingly, when asked to evaluate their lives, the participants spoke favourably of their lives as farm wives. Theirs was a life, they believed, not only healthier than and morally superior to an urban-based existence, but also — images of rural conservatism notwithstanding — one that provided more opportunities for sexual equality.

While the emerging urban centre — with its industrial explosion, its starkly drawn divisions between neighbourhoods, and its class-based disturbances — initially attracted a great deal of attention from social historians, almost all scholars working in the field now realize that there exists an equally engaging and complicated story yet to be unravelled in the country's rural sector. The following articles are examples of the new rural history, which, by asking new questions, locating fresh evidence, and importing methodologies from other disciplines, is rapidly making many older studies — those preoccupied with political disputes over tariffs and railways and implicitly bound to a view of the agricultural sector as speaking with one voice — a part of the historical record themselves.

QUESTIONS TO CONSIDER

1. What is it about farming that may have led some historians to assume that farming encouraged conservativism or a clinging to traditional beliefs?

2. Why might women have seen agricultural life as promoting more sexual equality than did a city-bound existence?
3. What information, if any, does Kinnear's article add to our knowledge of the national political fight over tariffs?
4. Can you detect any problems with the sources or methods used by the authors of these articles?
5. Do these articles suggest anything about the presence of a farm "culture" or set of values?

NOTES

1. M.C. Urquhart and K.A.H. Buckley, eds., *Historical Statistics on Canada* (Toronto: Macmillan, 1965), series E202–44, L1–16.
2. For a good account of condescending views of the so-called traditionalism of farmers, see Michael Bliss, *A Living Profit: Studies in the Social History of Canadian Business, 1883–1911* (Toronto: McClelland & Stewart, 1974), chap. 6.

SUGGESTED READINGS

Akenson, Donald H., ed. *Canadian Papers in Rural History*. Vols. 1–8. Gananoque: Langdale Press, 1978–93.
Breen, David, H. *The Canadian West and the Ranching Frontier, 1874–1924*. Toronto: University of Toronto Press, 1982.
Danysk, Cecilia. *Hired Hands: Labour and the Development of Prairie Agriculture*. Toronto: McClelland & Stewart, 1995.
Friesen, Gerald. *The Canadian Prairies: A History*. Toronto: University of Toronto Press, 1984.
Hann, Russell. *Farmers Confront Industrialism: Some Historical Perspectives on Ontario Agrarian Movements*. Toronto: New Hogtown Press, 1975.
Jackel, Susan, ed. *A Flannel Shirt and Liberty: British Emigrant Gentlewomen in the Canadian West, 1880–1914*. Vancouver: University of British Columbia Press, 1982.
Jones, David C., ed. *"We'll All Be Buried Down Here": The Prairie Dryland Disaster, 1917–1926*. Calgary: Historical Records Board of Alberta, 1985.
Laycock, David. *Populism and Democratic Thought in the Canadian Prairies*. Toronto: University of Toronto Press, 1990.
MacPherson, Ian. *Each for All: A History of the Co-operative Movement in English Canada, 1900–1945*. Toronto: Macmillan, 1979.
Ryan, John T. *The Agricultural Economy of Manitoba Hutterite Colonies*. Toronto: University of Toronto Press, 1977.
Silverman, Eliane Leslau. *The Last, Best West: Women on the Alberta Frontier, 1880–1930*. Montreal: Eden Press, 1984.
Voisey, Paul. "Rural Local History and the Prairie West." *Prairie Forum*, 10, 2 (1985): 327–38.

THREE

The Adoption of the Gasoline Tractor in Western Canada

ROBERT E. ANKLI, H. DAN HELSBERG, AND JOHN HERD THOMPSON

The agricultural development of Canada's prairie west took place during a century in which agriculture itself passed through two successive technological revolutions. The first of these, the replacement of hand tools by machines, initiated by the introduction of the McCormick reaper in the 1830s, was an essential precondition to successful commercial farming in western Canada.[1] Without selfbinding reapers — "binders" as they were universally called — it would have been impossible to harvest a large grain crop before the early frosts of Manitoba and the North West Territories made it worthless. The second technological revolution, the replacement of draft animals with gasoline tractors, took place after the wheat economy of the prairie provinces was already established and stretched over three decades: from the 1920s to the 1950s.

The transformation wrought upon agriculture by the internal combustion engine has been so dramatic that from a modern perspective it seems inevitable that the tractor should have replaced the horse as the principal power source for agriculture. But if the *effects* of the tractor upon prairie agriculture have been revolutionary — a greatly decreased labour force, vastly increased farm size, a reduction by half in the number of farms — the *pace* at which the tractor was adopted was not. Prairie farmers equipped themselves with tractors at a rate which is better described as "evolution" than "revolution," and the fierce debate over the relative merits of the tractor and the horse continued for thirty years after the first gasoline tractors became available.[2] Long after the automobile had supplanted the horse for personal transportation, horses continued to provide a majority of the power for tillage and general farm work. It was not until as late as 1946 that half the farmers in Manitoba, Saskatchewan, and Alberta owned tractors. As G.P. Colman has pointed out, historians who have examined technological change in agriculture have devoted more attention to "the invention, manufacturing, distribution and capabilities of agricultural machinery" than to the actual acceptance of new technologies by farmers themselves.[3]

....

The potential of the internal combustion engine as a source of agricultural power was recognized almost as soon as the four-cycle engine was developed, but the restrictive patent rights of early inventors delayed the building of the first gasoline tractors until the 1890s. These first gas tractors varied greatly in design. Some manufacturers copied the existing steam traction engines, producing lumbering giants like Inter-

Source: Excerpted from "The Adoption of the Gasoline Tractor in Western Canada," *Canadian Papers in Rural History*, vol. 2 (Gananoque: Langdale Press, 1980), 9–39. Reprinted by permission of McGill-Queen's University Press.

national Harvester's Titan, a 45 horsepower model which weighed ten tons. Others concluded that the advantage of the gasoline engine over its steam-driven rival was that it could be made much lighter, allowing more of its power to be applied to the drawbar for pulling and less energy thereby being wasted moving the machine itself. The first decades of gasoline tractor design were marked by an uncertainty as to which line of development promised success: a heavy machine with greater absolute power or a "light" tractor with a more efficient weight-to-power ratio.

The first serious testing of gasoline tractors at the 1908 Canadian Industrial Exhibition in Winnipeg demonstrated the controversy over size. Seven tractors were entered and subjected to test of their reliability, fuel economy, and working capacity. The gold medal went to the heaviest, a seven-ton 30 horsepower Kinnard-Haines four cylinder model, while the silver medal went to the lightest tractor entered, a 9,900-pound 15 horsepower International Harvester two cylinder design.[4] Historians of tractor development cite the 1908 competition and those which followed annually until 1912 as of "undisputed importance" in creating public interest in tractors, but the contradictory conclusions which could be drawn from the results only underlined the technological unreadiness of the new machines.[5] Much of the publicity they received from the Winnipeg trials was negative, for tractors broke down, mired in the Red River gumbo of the Exhibition Grounds, or ran out of control and smashed through fences when being moved from one testing area to another.[6]

For the ordinary grain farmer, the gasoline tractor was an interesting experiment which he followed in the pages of the *Grain Growers' Guide* or the *Farmer's Advocate*, not something in which he would invest $1,700 (the price of the cheapest model entered in the 1909 Winnipeg competition). Those few who had the courage or the foolhardiness to do some of the experimenting on their own farms soon discovered that gasoline tractor engineering was still in its infancy. Primitive electrical systems meant that starting was complicated and uncertain — Hart Parr's 1910 manual listed nineteen steps for starting the engine — and a popular joke lampooned the tractor farmer who left his machine running all night during seeding rather than risk a restart the next morning.[7] Drive gears were not enclosed and were made of cast iron so that dust and dirt caused rapid wear in dry weather. Heavy steel wheels, sometimes six and eight feet in diameter, made tractor field work impossible when the weather was wet. Breakdowns were common, costly, and time-consuming. When broken crankshafts, warped clutches, dead magnetoes, burned-out bearings, or faulty plugs put a machine out of action, parts were difficult to obtain. Throughout Canada and the United States scores of independent manufacturers tried to turn out tractors for farm use and few stayed in business long enough to establish reliable parts networks.[8]

The First World War gave the gasoline tractor its first real chance to penetrate prairie agriculture. Wartime drove up demand and thus the price of grain; at the same time, farm labour became scarce and hence more expensive. It was a situation made to order for a new labour-saving source of farm power, and tractor manufacturers turned their attention to small gasoline tractors in the ten-to-twelve horsepower range in hopes of supplanting the horse on the half-section farm, then typical of prairie agriculture. The Canadian government made this attempt easier by removing the duty on all imported tractors valued under $1,400 and by arranging for the purchase and resale to farmers of the Fordson light tractor at wholesale cost — $795.[9] The Fordson, Henry Ford's venture into the tractor market, was typical of small tractors which appeared during and after the war. It was rated as a "10–20" horsepower tractor, meaning theoretically that it would deliver ten horsepower to the drawbar and double that amount when used as an auxiliary engine. It was claimed to be capable of pulling two ploughs at 2¾ miles per hour or of plowing an average of eight acres in a ten-hour day.[10] Almost 900 Fordsons were made available by the government during 1918, and when high grain prices and inflated wages for farm labour continued in 1919 and 1920, the Fordson, and similar machines, induced farmers to buy tractors in significant numbers.

This first attempt by a minority of western grain growers to adapt the tractor to their farming operations was not an overwhelming success. Tractors sold well in 1919 and 1920, but by 1921 sales had dropped dramatically. Tractor salesmen attributed the decline to agriculture's post-war recession, but this provided only a partial explanation. The real problem was that the Fordson and its competitors were not ready to replace the work horse on Canadian prairie farms: if early machines had been too heavy and cumbersome to be used for field work, the smaller tractors were too light. As one early tractor farmer remembers of his International Titan 10–20 — second in popularity to the Fordson — "it didn't have power enough to pull the hat off your head."[11] Reynold Wik's assessment of the Fordson's limitations sums up the complaints first-time tractor owners made about their small machines: they were too light, had "temperamental ignition systems," mired down easily, overheated because of inadequate cooling systems, and were expensive to maintain and to repair.[12]

Some authors have attributed the slow adoption of the gasoline tractor to the mentality of the prairie farmer, arguing that "farmers as a group have been generally conservative and slow to change their methods," refusing to recognize that "new methods were more efficient than the old."[13] Closer examination demonstrates, however, that the resistance of farmers to the overtures of tractor salesmen was based on much more than rural conservatism and that in the early 1920s there were good reasons to question if the "new" was "more efficient than the old." In addition to well-founded skepticism about the mechanical reliability and efficiency of the machines available to them, farmers recognized that the purchase of a gasoline tractor was a complicated investment decision.

Maintenance and repair of these machines was beyond the ability of the ordinary farmer, whose most complicated machine to date had been his binder. This was a problem that could not be eliminated until farmers acquired more mechanical experience — from automobile ownership, for example — or until a new generation of farmers appeared with the "mechanical skill which is absent in the earlier ones."[14] Even assuming that a farmer had the ability to put a broken-down machine back into service, he had no assurance that the parts he needed to make repairs would be available to him quickly — or, indeed, that they would be available at all. If the Ford Motor Company had an inadequate parts supply system for its Fordson during the 1920s, the problem was even more serious with models from smaller manufacturers.

Moreover, most horse-drawn equipment — plows, seeders, harrows, binders — was not adaptable to tractor operation because it could not withstand the force of acceleration or the speeds of the new machines. Equipment designed for a team's pace of 1½ miles an hour was inadequate for a sustained speed two or three times that high. The fundamental matter of hitching power source to implement presented serious engineering problems after the change from animal to tractor power.[15]

The tractor farmer of the 1920s was faced with yet another important limitation to the usefulness of his new power source: the lack of suitable support technology through which he could make himself truly independent of his horses. Although the automobile was rapidly supplanting the horse and buggy, the motorcar industry had not yet provided a reliable farm truck to replace the horse-drawn grain wagon to move grain to the elevator. C.S. Noble's experiments included trucks as well as tractors, and his conclusion was that "freighting can be done more economically with horses."[16] Clearly, most farmers agreed with Noble's outlook, as only two of every hundred farmers in Manitoba, Saskatchewan, and Alberta reported truck ownership in 1926.

It was not simply the need to retain horses for hauling that prevented the tractor and the horse from being perfectly interchangeable. During spring seeding, for example, horses could begin work before tractors, since a team could work while conditions were too wet and muddy to allow a tractor out of the barn. On the other hand, tractors provided a good portable power source of belt power for on-farm threshing, something horses could not do without elaborate treadmill systems. Asked by a farmer for an opinion on the tractor–horse controversy, Professor William Allen, an agricultural engineer at the University of Saskatchewan, pointed out that "the problem is not the elimination of the horse but the combination of horses and tractors within the farm organization."[17] Even an editorialist in *Canadian Power Farmer*, a journal that vaunted the tractor's advantages, was forced to admit that, given the conditions of the early 1920s, only "a portion" of the power on prairie farms could be provided by the tractor.[18]

Thus, for tractor manufacturers and for their sales representatives, the first half of the 1920s was a most unsatisfactory period. Throughout North America, companies that had expected large profits from tractor production ceased operation and withdrew from the tractor business or were absorbed by other companies. Giants like General Motors, long-established implement companies like the Moline Plow Company, and small manufacturers like the Bates Machine and Tractor all fell victim as sales in western Canada failed to average 3,600 units annually between 1921 and 1925.[19] The later years of the decade, however, saw a renewed interest in the gasoline tractor. Sales in 1926 reached 6,500 units, only half the 1920 figure but twice the average of the intervening years. Then, in 1927, farmers began to buy new tractors in earnest, and in a three-year period over 40,000 moved into the fields of western Canada, one for every seven farms. The sudden enthusiasm for tractors took some agricultural experts by surprise. After the failure of the tractor in the 1918–21 period, the agriculture colleges of Manitoba, Saskatchewan, and Alberta had experimented with "big teams" of twelve or sixteen horses as the most satisfactory approach to increasing drawbar power and cutting production costs.[20] The Saskatchewan College of Agriculture, in the midst of a long-term study of "The Farm Business in Saskatchewan," found very few tractors in use during its 1925 and 1926 investigations.[21]

In the years which followed, however, a dramatic increase in tractor use began to upset these earlier conclusions. In the Swift Current–Gull Lake area, for example, the percentage of field work done by tractors increased from 8.7 percent in 1927 to 39.1 percent in 1930.[22] Accompanying the increased use of tractors was the beginning of an absolute as well as relative decline in the number of horses on prairie farms.

What caused this abrupt increase in tractor use? The answer to that question is partly technological and, as the detailed comparison of horse–tractor costs in 1930 will show, partly financial. After experimenting with light and heavy tractors, as

Goldilocks did with the three bears' porridge, manufacturers had begun to concentrate on a power range that was just right. Tractors adequate for field work in the prairie provinces had to be heavier and more powerful than the Fordson, but lighter than the "lumbering, odorous, labourously groaning" monsters typical of the earliest years of gas traction engineering.[23] The new demand for tractors concentrated on machines in the 12–25 to 22–40 horsepower groups, all-purpose machines commonly known as "three-plow" or "four-plow" tractors.[24] The decade of engineering experience meant also that the new "three-plow" tractor in 1930 weighed no more than a "two-plow" model of lower horsepower had in the immediate post-war period and that fuel efficiency had increased by about 20 percent.[25]

But the single most important technical improvement was the general utilization of the power take-off. This device used shafting and universal joints to extend the drive shaft of the tractor beyond the rear axle and thus provide power to operate moving parts of an implement being towed.[26] Minor changes also helped: as George H. Daniels suggests, historians of technology have "tended to emphasize the more impressive at the expense of the run of the mill improvements," forgetting that a number of "minor modifications of detail" may be equally important.[27] During the 1920s, enclosed cooling systems, with pumps to circulate coolant, were introduced, as were oil bath air cleaners, which greatly improved operation under dusty conditions.[28] Tractor lubrication also advanced from simple "splash oiling" by agitation of oil in the crankcase to forced circulation lubrication systems, and the lubricants available reached higher standards and more uniform reliability.[29]

Grain harvesting also was being changed by new technology in the later 1920s, a factor further contributing to increased use of tractors. Whereas at one time most threshing had been done by custom threshers using large steam engines as power sources, farmers could free themselves of part of this expense by buying small separators and using the belt power of a gasoline tractor to run them. More than 6,000 of these threshers were sold in 1928, for example, each of which required a tractor to operate it.[30] More significant in the long run were the first western Canadian sales of the combine reaper thresher. The combine had been used to harvest grain in California since the 1880s, but was not used until the 1920s on the farms of the Canadian prairies because of the danger of weather damage to a crop left standing long enough to be harvested and threshed simultaneously. The introduction of swathing — cutting the grain to ripen in windrows, then combining the windrows — enabled the combine to be adapted to Canadian conditions.[31] Virtually all of the early combines were pull-type, and thus yet another reason existed for the tractor to become a practical first step in a farmer's program of mechanization. Also relevant were the high grain yields and relatively good prices of 1927 and 1928, which provided farmers either with the money to purchase equipment or the confidence to borrow funds in order to begin tractor farming.[32]

One might speculate that a further incentive to the adoption of labour-saving machinery was an increase in the wages of farm workers. Indeed, some observers argued that the farm wage bill was the principal factor inducing increased mechanization. C.W. Petersen, editor of the *Farm and Ranch Review*, took this line and explained the phenomenon as "sheer self defence . . . an act of self preservation reluctantly committed" despite "the natural unwillingness of the human being to make capital expenditure until it is forced upon him by circumstances."[33] Soaring labour costs certainly did motivate farmers in the first period of tractor purchases, 1918–20, for in those years the wages of seasonal and daily farm workers increased rapidly: in 1920 farm workers earned three times what they had in 1914. By the mid 1920s, however, wages had stabilized at much lower rates, making it difficult to accept wage increases as an immediate cause of the 1927–29 surge in tractor adoption. Nevertheless, wages in that period were consistently higher than they had been in the pre-war era, and thus represented a greater proportion of production costs.[34]

....

The increased use of tractors for field work after 1927 makes possible a realistic and systematic comparison of the cost of horse and tractor operation. Tractor and horses still were not perfectly interchangeable in 1930, but the tasks each could be called upon to perform were much more similar than they had been a decade earlier. Data for a comparison is drawn from studies done in western Canada between 1929 and 1931. The researchers reported only the costs of field work performed, without considering other jobs that horses or tractors might perform — providing a source of belt power for threshing, for example — a simplification that does not invalidate their overall conclusions. The first part of this section looks at the cost of horse operations for a prairie grain farmer in 1930, while the second looks at tractor costs for the same period, followed by a determination of the relative profitability of horses and tractors.

Comparison would be easier if we could simply base calculations on the number of horsepower a tractor claimed to deliver. In stubble plowing, for example, the accepted capacity of a draft horse was one acre for each ten-hour day, meaning that a six-horse team could plow six acres, and so on. But a 10–20 horsepower tractor did not plow ten acres a day because the actual horsepower delivered at the drawbar was usually less than its theoretical horsepower.[35] Thus, tractors were referred to by the number of plows they were capable of pulling — two, three, or four — rather than by horsepower ranges.

Whether using horses or a tractor, costs depended very much on the number of hours each source of power would be used. E.S. Hopkins et al. in a study of the *Cost of Producing Farm Crops in the Prairie Provinces*, arrived at a figure of eight cents per hour for horse operation, based on an annual expense of $64 for a work horse and a work year of 800 hours.[36] But the authors used figures obtained under experimental conditions and noted that a survey of ten private farms in 1929 produced figures of $71.34 per horse and 590 hours of work, thereby increasing costs to twelve cents per hour.

We have found two other sets of estimates. The first are from the experimental farms yearly reports. At Morden, Manitoba, in 1926, eight horses worked an average of 1,512 hours. The total cost was $167.79 per horse ($66.77 for feed) or eleven cents per hour.[37] The following year the horses worked 1,819 hours for a total cost of $155.09 per horse or 8.5 cents per hour.[38] In 1926, 1927, and 1929 the average cost of feed at Indian Head, Saskatchewan was between $76 and $78 per annum for work mares, but no other information is provided.[39] Finally, the Experimental Farm at Rosthern, Saskatchewan reported 1,053 hours per horse between June 1 and October 31, 1929. The cost per horse was $84.85 ($79.27 for feed) or eight cents per hour.[40] It is very clear that these horses were working far more than the average work horse in the prairies: thus, their fixed cost would be averaged over a relatively large number of hours, and the average cost should have been lower than on the normal private farm.

Our second source of information is a paper published in 1933, "Economic Aspects of the Horse Industry in Western Canada," by H.B. Sommerfeld.[41] This study looks at farms in the Red River Valley and the Riding Mountain Fringe area,[42] both of Manitoba, for the year 1931. The farms surveyed were divided into four groups: horse, horse–tractor, tractor–horse, and tractor farms. The division between the second and third categories was 50 percent of all drawbar work. The average number of crop acres per horse in the Red River Valley was slightly over twice the number in Riding Mountain Fringe. There were 1.09 tractors per farm in the Red River Valley, compared to only 0.46 tractors in Riding Mountain Fringe.[43] As might be expected, the more hours horses were used per farm the lower the cost per hour of using them. Costs were also almost always less on the Riding Mountain Fringe farms, probably because of feed, labour, and housing costs being lower there.[44] The cost per horse hour was slightly lower on Red River Valley farms that moved from being horse only to being horse–tractor farms, but was actually more expensive on Riding Mountain Fringe farms. Sommerfeld also reported that "As the number of crop acres per horse increases, there is a significant corresponding decrease in costs per horse hour. There is no significant correlation between cost per horse hour and yields of wheat, oats and barley. There is an appreciable increase in the work done per team unit day as the number of horses in the hitch increases."[45]

One of the controversies in the horses versus tractor literature was whether to classify horse feed as a fixed or a variable cost. The argument for designating it as a fixed cost was that the horse had to be fed, regardless of whether or not it was working. At the same time, it is recognized that beyond a certain point, a horse must be fed more if it is going to work more. Sommerfeld provided two tables which showed cost per horse hour for the lowest (and highest) twenty (and forty) farms for each region, together with information on the number of hours worked and total feed costs. Not unexpectedly, the cost per hour was lower the more the horse worked per year, but surprisingly, *total* feed cost was also lower, the more hours the horses worked.[46] This would seem to indicate that high-cost farms were overfeeding their horses, but it also meant that one can conclude that horse feed should be treated as a fixed cost.

Basic data we use to find the cost of horse operations is taken from the Hopkins et al. study, *Cost of Producing Farm Crops in the Prairie Provinces*.[47] A few notes on the data are in order: The price of horses is the 1930 price of a horse in Saskatchewan. By comparison, an average horse was worth $52 in Manitoba and $41 in Alberta.[48] An extra horse was assumed for each team, so that an injury or illness of one animal would not bring work to a halt. Interest on the investment was figured at 6 percent on half the worth of the animal or 3 percent on total worth, plus 7 percent depreciation for a total rental rate of 10 percent. This raises at least two questions: first, whether the present value of an average horse or the purchase price of the animal would be used; second, it also assumes straight-line depreciation, which is probably not accurate for any of the categories. However, more refined techniques would not add precision to our results to an extent that would justify the extra calculations, so we will be content with our estimates here. Service life for everything but horses has been taken from Hopkins[49] and is based on a 1925 questionnaire sent to prairie farmers. In all, 678 replies were received. Needless to say, these estimates may not be precise since the farmer was only guessing how long any machine might last. The service life of the horse was taken from N.P. Sargen, "Tractorization in the United States."[50] Hopkins gave prices for all implements. Feed for horses has been estimated at $40 per animal, the figure used by Sargen.[51] Sommerfeld shows feed costs of $42.51 per horse in 1931 for the Red River Valley and $31.04 for Riding Mountain Fringe for the same year.[52] Since prices were falling in the early 1930s, costs may have been above $40 for 1930, so our estimate is a conservative one. The food costs on the experimental farms also suggest this, but these animals were working far more than was usual. Labour costs per horse were figured at $27. Sommerfeld reports an average of about 110 hours of labour chores per animal, which, at 25 cents an hour, would be about $27.[53] This charge may be subject to some controversy. First, the opportunity-cost may well have been zero, so that no charge should be made. The pride of the farmer in his team may also have caused him to spend more time with his animals than he otherwise would have been required to. Nevertheless, at certain times of the year this might have slowed him down and the desire for leisure may also have led him to purchase a tractor. Therefore, the charge remains. Miscellaneous items of $6 per horse were also added. This completes our estimates of fixed costs. These costs amounted to $537 for a four-horse team, $715 for a six-horse team, and $880 for an eight-horse team. Most of the difference is due to feed and labour costs per horse.

Because feed has been considered as a fixed cost item, the only variable input is labour. This has been divided into pre-harvest, harvest, and summerfallow labour. No estimate for threshing wheat has been added to either the horse section or the tractor section. All labour was charged at 25 cents per hour or $2.50 per ten-hour day, which is the figure Hopkins et al. use. It might be argued that harvest labour should have been given a higher imputed value because there is always a need to harvest as quickly as possible, but, for practical reasons, this was not included in our calculation. Since harvest operations are faster with a tractor, using the same labour cost for both operations has biased our results slightly in favour of the tractor.

In calculating labour costs, the following pre-harvest operations were included:[54]

Spring work on stubble:	one-half ploughed
	one-half disked
	all land harrowed
	all seeded
Spring work on summer fallow (of previous year):	one cultivation (or one disking)
	all seeded

The following summerfallow operations were included where moldboard plows were used:	one-half fall disked
	one-half spring disked
	all plowed during summer
	three cultivations

Finally, the cost per acre can be determined by dividing $2.50, the cost of labour for a ten-hour day, by the number of acres covered of the particular implement used. Thus (referring to Table 3.1), the variable cost of plowing stubble would be 55 cents per acre ($2.50 + 4.5) for a four-horse team. Since different types of operations were used, depending on whether the land was summerfallowed or cropped the year before, it was decided to make the acre the basic unit. Notionally, this means that one-third of an acre was seeded to wheat on land where wheat was grown the year before,

TABLE 3.1 *Acreage Covered per Ten-Hour Day*

| Operation | Horses | | | | Tractor | |
	4-horse team	6-horse team	8-horse team	2-plough	3-plough	4-plough
Plowing stubble	4.5	4.8	7.6	8.1	12.6	15.7
Plowing sod	1.9	3.6	4.6	5.7	7.6	8.9
One way disking	—	—	10.0	—	26.6	32.2
Disking — single	13.7	20.3	30.5	33.1	62.1	72.9
Disking — tandem	8.2	14.9	16.8	27.9	34.4	35.7
Cultivating	13.1	16.5	20.1	30.0	35.0	37.5
Rod weeding	—	23.0	28.0	35.0	47.5	64.4
Harrowing	31.8	42.5	63.0	66.5	98.7	123.0
Seeding	19.2	25.4	33.5	33.0	42.0	55.2
Binding	17.4	—	—	26.8	30.3	31.6

Source: E.S. Hopkins, J.M. Armstrong, and H.D. Mitchell, *Cost of Producing Farm Crops in the Prairie Provinces,* Dominion of Canada, Dept. of Agriculture, Bulletin no. 159 (New Series, Ottawa, 1932), 55.

one-third of an acre was seeded to wheat on summerfallowed ground, and one-third of an acre was summerfallowed. The total variable cost of 82.7 cents an acre, there-fore, includes all operations, and the variable cost for any size farm can be calculated, assuming the division by thirds.

The results indicate that a six-horse team would never have been the cheapest to operate. From the data given above, one can calculate that the threshold point for a four-horse and eight-horse team would be at 1,149 cultivated acres, while "threshold" for a four-horse and six-horse team would be 1,495 acres. But this, of course, does not consider the timeliness of operations. A four-horse team could never get a thou-sand acres ready for seeding and still permit enough growing time to elapse before a killing frost. Assuming the numbers of Table 3.1, it would take 35.4 days to sow 300 acres with a four-horse team, 29.3 days with a six-horse team (Hopkins et al. say 31),[55] and about 20.8 days with an eight-horse team. Hopkins et al. seemed to have been operating with about a 30-day period as desirable. Saskatchewan has an average of 110 to 125 days between killing frosts, so there was little time to waste.[56] But the plowing, harrowing, disking, and cultivating could be done before the last spring frost, and even seeding could be done, although any frost would certainly lower the yield. The real constraint seems to have been how soon the land became dry enough to be worked, a situation which varies greatly from year to year; so we will accept 30 days as the length of preparation and seeding as a reasonable estimate. This means that a four-horse team could have handled about 250 acres, a six-horse team 300 acres, and an eight-horse team 430 acres. Acreages beyond any of these estimates would have required two teams.

Let us now turn to tractors. We face the same problems here that we faced with horses. The more hours a tractor is used, the cheaper the average cost of running it, so we must be careful of any historical cost figure which did not specify how much the tractor was being used. Table 3.2 shows the cost per hour of using a tractor cal-culated from data collected from 256 farms in Alberta and Saskatchewan in 1931,

TABLE 3.2 *Hours Operated per Year as Related to Total Cost of Operating Tractors per Hour*

		Size of Tractor				
	Three-plow				**Four-plow**	
Hours operated per year	*Number*	*Average hours operated*	*Power cost per hour*	*Number*	*Average hours operated*	*Power cost per hour*
1–199	34	117	$2.31	8	148	$2.45
200–399	47	305	1.59	25	324	1.76
400–599	33	484	1.30	24	507	1.52
600 and over	35	794	1.17	20	781	1.47
All tractors	149	417	$1.38	77	482	$1.58

Source: E.G. Grest, "Cost of Tractor Operations on Prairie Farms in Western Canada," *Scientific Agriculture*, 14 (October, 1933): 84.

when fuel costs averaged 27 cents per gallon. As Table 3.2 shows, the hourly cost varied by a large amount, and the study in fact concluded that a tractor was not a wise investment unless it could be used at least 500 hours each year.[57]

At this point, our study divides tractor costs into fixed and variable costs, following the same procedure that was employed for horses. Repairs were figured at 2.5 percent of cost and shelter at $12 per year.[58] Labour costs for repairs were taken from the Hopkins et al. prairie farm survey. Variable costs were calculated the same way as they were for horses, except that we added fuel costs to labour cost.[59]

The results indicate that a four-plow tractor was always inefficient as compared to a three-plow tractor. The reason for this seems to be that four-plow tractors were commonly pulling implements designed for three-plow tractors. E.G. Grest's "Cost of Tractor Operations on Prairie Farms in Western Canada" reported that tractors of all sizes were commonly underloaded, thus resulting in inefficient use of power.[60] We find that the threshold for a three-plow tractor compared to a two-plow tractor was about 300 acres. A two-plow tractor could prepare and seed 300 acres in 18.5 days, a three-plow tractor in 13.5 days,[61] and a four-plow tractor in 11.0 days.

A tractor also permitted some change in soil preparation practices because a one-way disk could be substituted for plowing. If this were done, operations would have been as follows:[62]

Spring work on stubble:	all one-way disk
	all seed
Spring work on summerfallow (of previous year):	all cultivated
	all seeded
Summerfallow:	all one-way disk
	(3 cultivations) or 1 cultivation
	and 2 rod-weedings

And, if this were done, the variable cost for a three-plow tractor would have been 85.9 cents per acre and 85.3 cents per acre for a four-plow tractor. A three-plow tractor

could have prepared and seeded 300 acres in 11.5 days,[63] and a four-plow tractor would have taken 9.4 days for 300 acres.

....

Only now can we turn to the central focus of our study — the cost of using horses as opposed to the cost of using a tractor. We notice first that the fixed cost of using horses was greater than the fixed cost of using a tractor, but that the variable cost per acre of a tractor was greater. This means that, if we did not consider any acreage constraints, the larger the operation, the relatively cheaper it became to use horses. For example, if we compare a two-plow tractor with a four-horse team, it was cheaper to use a tractor up to 430 acres, but thereafter the four-horse team was cheaper. Table 3.3 shows the maximum feasible acreage, assuming a 30-day period in the spring. For any feasible range of horse operations, it always would have been cheaper to use a tractor, assuming 1930 conditions.

One might think of the horse–tractor decision as a "putty–clay" capital decision. The farmer had horses — how fast could he or should he convert his field operations to a tractor? If he were a very large farmer, with, say, two or more sections and four or five six-horse teams, he could sell perhaps half his horses and buy a tractor. This would yield a fixed cost saving. At the same time, he would only use his tractor in the spring, when there was some urgency to getting the seed in the ground, and also at harvest, when again he was in a hurry: he could continue to use his animals for summerfallow work, when there was no rush. This practice would provide a variable cost saving. Thus, initially the farmer might use both horses and a tractor for peak-load times. Some such process actually seems to have taken place during this period.

....

The calculation of horse and tractor costs clearly demonstrates that, by the end of the 1920s, operating with tractors cost less than continuing to farm with horses at almost all acreage levels. This suggests that had the 1930s been normal years for western grain growers, the switch to tractors would have continued. Drought and depressed grain prices completely changed this pattern. Not only did the dramatic decline in farm incomes produce an equally dramatic decline in tractor sales, but farmers who had been farming with tractors returned to their horses as the cost of feed and labour fell much more than did the cost of tractor repairs and gasoline. The *cash* costs of horse farming were much lower than those of tractor operation, since farmers could care for their own horses and raise their own feed grains. A study completed in 1934–35 by Andrew Stewart of the Manitoba Agricultural College found that "since 1930 the decline in tractor use has been substantial" and that "numbers of horses have tended to increase and more work is being done with horses."[64]

Paradoxically, the two most important improvements in tractor design were made at precisely this period, demonstrating the delicate relationship among tractor technology, operating costs, and farm incomes as determinants of tractor adoption. The introduction of pneumatic rubber tires, begun by Allis-Chambers in 1932, meant that tractors could operate at higher speeds and travel on public roads. The second innovation, the Ferguson three-point hydraulic hitch, became available in 1935. It was "a revolution in implement control," which permitted implements to be raised or lowered from the driver's seat and to be operated at different depths in varying soil conditions.[65]

TABLE 3.3 *Maximum Feasible Crop Acreage*

4-horse team	2-plow tractor	
250 a	486 a	
6-horse team	3-plow tractor	3-plow tractor
300 a	666 a	(one-way disk)
		782 a
8-horse team	4-plow tractor	4-plow tractor
430 a	818 a	(one-way disk)
		957 a

Source: Calculated from data in H.B. Sommerfeld, "Economic Aspects of the Horse Industry in Western Canada," *Proceedings of the Fifth Annual Meeting of the Canadian Society of Agricultural Economics* (Regina, 1933): 84–85, assuming 30-day maximum for preparation and seeding.

World War II had ambivalent effects on the rate of tractor adoption. Because of the need to produce tanks, trucks, and planes, production quotas of 84 percent of 1940 production were imposed in 1941 and permitted to increase at only 5 percent a year from 1943 to 1945. But wartime regulation also controlled prices, keeping tractors within affordable ranges, and tractors were exempted from tariffs as they had been during World War I.[66] Grain prices increased slowly between 1942 and 1945, never reaching the levels of 1917–19, but farm incomes were higher than the rock-bottom levels of the 1930s. Improved employment opportunities in urban areas during wartime combined with enlistment to produce an outmigration of 250,000 people from Manitoba, Saskatchewan, and Alberta between 1941 and 1946, and the resulting decrease in the farm labour supply was an incentive to tractor purchase.[67]

At the war's end, tractor sales exploded upwards, until by 1951, almost all serious commercial farms were operating with tractors. The continued use of compulsory wheat marketing through the Canada Wheat Board, which used a quota for wheat deliveries based on absolute acreage, encouraged farmers to farm as many acres as possible. If, for example, the Wheat Board established a delivery quota of five bushels to the acre, a farmer could not profit from an increase in yield, but only from producing the first five bushels on a greater number of acres. This stimulated tractor use by encouraging investment in any technology which permitted cheap, extensive operations — tractors and combines — rather than in things such as agricultural chemicals, which would increase output per acre.[68]

The prairie farmer's decision to replace his horses with a gasoline tractor was not made quickly and thus cannot be attributed to any one particular technological development or to the change in price of any one of the many elements which determined production costs of grain growing. A number of conditions had to exist simultaneously before the tractor could be universally adopted. First, the technological development of the tractor itself and the availability of suitable auxiliary equipment for tillage, harvesting, and hauling was necessary. Second, the costs of the tractor had to be significantly lower than those of horse operation. Finally, farm incomes had to be high enough to make the heavy capital investment necessary, possible, and desirable. During the 1918–21 period, the tractor simply was not ready to fulfill the first condition. From 1927 to 1930, all three conditions were fulfilled, but falling incomes and

reduced costs for feed and labour swung the advantage back in favour of the horse. In the 1940s, all three conditions coincided, banishing Dobbin to old timers' reunions at summer fairs and changing forever the shape of prairie agriculture.[69]

NOTES

1. For a discussion of the concept of agricultural "revolution," see R.W. Murchie, *Agricultural Progress on the Prairie Frontier* (Toronto, 1936), p. 293; E.D. Ross and R.L. Tontz, "The Term Agricultural Revolution as used by Economic Historians," *Agricultural History* (Jan. 1948): 32–39; and W.D. Rasmussen, "The Impact of Technological Changes on American Agriculture," *Journal of Economic History* (Dec. 1962): 578–99.
2. For this reason, Earle D. Ross argues against the use of the concept of an agricultural revolution, describing the changes machinery and tractors have brought to farming as a "gradual, relatively belated response to the demands of an industrialized age" which, although "truly remarkable," is nonetheless not "revolutionary." Ross, "Retardation in Farm Technology Before the Power Age," *Agricultural History* (Jan. 1956): 18.
3. G.P. Coleman, "Innovation and Diffusion in Agriculture," *Agricultural History* (July 1968): 173.
4. Score sheets from the Winnipeg trials are reproduced in R.B. Gray, *The Agricultural Tractor* (St. Joseph, Michigan, 1975), Part I, pp. 19–22. Gray's book is the most detailed survey of the tractor's technical development.
5. Grant MacEwan, *Power for Prairie Plows* (Saskatoon, 1974), p. 63.
6. See, for example, University of Saskatchewan Archives (hereafter USA) College of Agriculture Collection I B 1, A.R. Greig to Dean Rutherford, 29 Aug. 1912.
7. R.M. Wik, *Steam Power on the American Farm* (Philadelphia, 1953), p. 204.
8. W.G. Phillips estimates that by 1916 over 200 different tractors had been placed on the Canadian Market. Phillips, *The Agricultural Implement Industry in Canada* (Toronto, 1956), p. 26.
9. See John Herd Thompson, *The Harvests of War: the Prairie West 1914–1918* (Toronto, 1978), pp. 59–72.
10. *The Canadian Grower's Guide*, 20 Feb. 1918.
11. Interview with Roy Huffman, Bozeman, Montana, 25 June 1976.
12. R.M. Wik, *Henry Ford and Grassroots America* (Ann Arbor, 1972), pp. 94–95.
13. A.W. Wood, "A Study of Labour Productivity in Saskatchewan Agriculture" (M.Sc. thesis, University of Saskatchewan, 1955): 8. Evans and Irwin in "Government Tractors in Ontario," p. 100, make the same type of statement about Ontario farmers.
14. Archives of Saskatchewan (hereafter AS), C.M. Hamilton Papers, W. Allen to E.A. Updike, 16 Mar. 1928.
15. Merrill Denison, *Harvest Triumphant: the Story of Massey Harris* (Toronto, 1948), p. 236.
16. *Grain Growers' Guide*, 16 June 1920.
17. A.S., C.M. Hamilton Papers, Allen to Updike, 16 Mar. 1928.
18. *Canadian Power Farmer*, March 1922, p. 6.
19. For a description of the industry's problems in this period, see Gray, *Agricultural Tractor*, Part II, pp. 4–10, and Canada, *Report of the Royal Commission on Farm Machinery* (Ottawa, 1971), pp. 38–39.
20. The best-known advocate of the "big hitches" was M.L. Wilson of Montana State University. Wilson's book, *Big Teams in Montana* (Bozeman, Montana, 1925), went into a second edition and circulated widely in western Canada.
21. University of Saskatchewan, College of Agriculture, *Extension Bulletin no. 37*, 1927, 45–48; *Bulletin no. 43*, 1928, 34–41; *Bulletin no. 46*, 40–41.
22. Ibid., *Bulletin no. 52*, 57–58, 110.
23. The quotation is from *The Farmer's Advocate*, 6 Nov. 1910.

24. Phillips, *Implement Industry*, p. 175.
25. United States Department of Agriculture, *Power and Machinery in Agriculture*, Misc. Pub. no. 15, 1931, 28.
26. Denison, *Harvest Triumphant*, pp. 269–70.
27. G.H. Daniels, "The Big Questions in the History of American Technology," *Technology and Culture* (Jan. 1970): 10.
28. E.M. Dieffenbach and R.B. Gray, "The Development of the Tractor" in USDA, *Power to Produce* (Washington, 1960): 34–35.
29. Bruce Narstead, "Tractor Technical Development" in Alex Vicas, *Research and Development in Farm Machinery*, vol. 7 of the *Royal Commission on Farm Machinery*, pp. 80–82.
30. AS, Agricultural Machinery Administration Records, Ag 12 I file 2.
31. H.H. Hanson, *History of Swathing and Swath Threshing* (Saskatoon, 1967), pp. 1–18.
32. H.G. Strange, *A Short History of Prairie Agriculture* (Winnipeg, 1954), Appendix II. M.C. Urquhart and K.A.H. Buckley, *Historical Statistics on Canada* (Toronto, 1965), Series L98.
33. C.W. Petersen, *Wheat: the Riddle of Markets* (Calgary, 1930), p. 75.
34. A wage table for harvest hands, who were paid by the day, can be found in John Herd Thompson, "The Harvest Excursionists, 1890–1929," *Canadian Historical Review* (Dec. 1978): 482.
35. Using data from the Nebraska tractor tests, 1920–30, the weighted average of actual horsepower as a percentage of claimed theoretical horsepower is 83 percent. See also Naum Jasny, *Research Methods on Farm Use of Tractors* (New York, 1938), pp. 32–33.
36. E.S. Hopkins et al., *Cost of Producing Farm Crops in the Prairie Provinces*, Canada, Department of Agriculture, Bulletin no. 159 (Ottawa, 1932), p. 5.
37. Experimental Farm, Morden, Manitoba, *Report of the Superintendent*, 1926, p. 4.
38. Ibid., 1927, p. 4.
39. Experimental Farm, Indian Head, Saskatchewan, *Report of the Superintendent*, 1926, p. 5; 1927, p. 4; 1929, p. 6.
40. Experimental Farm, Rosthern, Saskatchewan, *Report of the Superintendent*, 1929, p. 5.
41. In *Proceedings of the Fifth Annual Meeting of the Canadian Society of Agricultural Economics* (Regina, 1933): 82–95.
42. An area comprising all of Shoal Lake, and parts of Strathclair, Harrison, Saskatchewan, Blanchard, and Hamiota municipalities. The 157 Red River Valley farms averaged 529 acres with 81.5 percent under cultivation. The 229 Riding Mountain Fringe farms averaged 462 acres with 51 percent under cultivation. Ibid., p. 82.
43. Ibid., p. 84.
44. Ibid., p. 86.
45. Ibid., p. 89.
46. Ibid., pp. 87–88.
47. Hopkins et al., *Cost*, pp. 35–37.
48. Canada, Dominion Bureau of Statistics, *Handbook: Livestock and Animal Products Statistics*, p. 101.
49. Hopkins et al., *Cost*, p. 45.
50. Nicholas P. Sargen, "Tractorization in the United States and Its Relevance for the Developing Countries" (Ph.D. thesis, Stanford University, 1975), p. 97.
51. Ibid.
52. Sommerfeld, "Horse Industry," pp. 87–88.
53. Ibid.
54. Hopkins et al., *Cost*, p. 34.
55. Ibid., p. 37.
56. W. Burton Hurd and T.W. Grindley, *Agriculture, Climate and Population of the Prairie Provinces of Canada*, DBS (Ottawa, 1931), pp. 18–20.

57. E.G. Grest, "Cost of Tractor Operations on Prairie Farms in Western Canada," *Scientific Agriculture* (October 1933), p. 84

58. Experimental Farm, Morden, Manitoba, *Report of the Superintendent*, 1926, p. 4.

59. Grest's study ("Tractor Operations," p. 84) of 1931 farms used fuel costs of 27 cents per gallon. A three-plow tractor used 24.1 gallons of gasoline per 10-hour day.

60. Ibid., p. 85.

61. Hopkins et al., *Cost*, p. 39.

62. Ibid., p. 34.

63. Ibid., p. 39.

64. Andrew Stewart, "Trends in Farm Power and their Influence on Agricultural Development," Appendix A of Murchie, *Agricultural Progress*, p. 304.

65. Dieffenbach and Gray, "Power to Produce," p. 36; Gray, *Agricultural Tractor*, Part II, pp. 36–38.

66. This information is from the Britnell Papers, 95/3 V, file d4. Britnell, an economist at the University of Saskatchewan, was a member of the Wartime Prices and Trade Board, so that his papers contain several valuable letters about the effect of the war on agricultural mechanization.

67. USA, V.C. Fowke Papers, "Agriculture in the Canadian Economy," mimeographed lecture. See also Britnell and Fowke, *Canadian Agriculture in War and Peace* (Stanford, 1962).

68. For a detailed discussion of this question, see W.H. Furtan and George E. Lee, "Economic Development of the Saskatchewan Wheat Economy," *Canadian Journal of Agricultural Economics* (Nov. 1977): 15–28.

69. For a consideration of the effects of increased mechanization, see Saskatchewan, *Royal Commission on Agricultural and Rural Life*, vol. 2, *Mechanization* and Canada, *Royal Commission on Farm Machinery*, vol. 1, "The Mechanization of Agriculture," pp. 395–502.

FOUR

"Do You Want Your Daughter to Marry a Farmer?": Women's Work on the Farm, 1922

MARY KINNEAR

This article uses two main sources to examine farm women's work in Manitoba in 1922, before mechanization completely transformed the agricultural economy. The first is a quantitative source: a survey of the work of members of the United Farm Women of Manitoba. The second is qualitative evidence of farm women's attitudes towards their work, provided by an essay competition run by the *Grain Growers' Guide*. Both were produced in the summer of 1922.[1] Placed in the context furnished

Source: Excerpted from " 'Do you want your daughter to marry a farmer?': Women's Work on the Farm, 1922," *Canadian Papers in Rural History*, vol. 6 (Gananoque: Langdale Press, 1988), 137–53. Reprinted by permission of McGill-Queen's University Press.

by the census and other indices of rural living, this material expands our knowledge of a livelihood more common than industrial or service work to Canadian women before the Second World War.

More of the Canadian population was rural than urban until the 1921 census, "rural" being defined as all those not living in incorporated villages, towns and cities, regardless of size.[2] In the province of Manitoba there was still a rural majority until 1951, and in the 1921 census, 57 percent of the total population of 610,118 was rural.[3] As Gerald Friesen noted, between 1880 and 1930 "the farm had become the paramount institution in the prairie west," and in his book on prairie history, he cited graphic descriptions of women's daily rounds on farms, given him by a pioneer and also by a farm woman in the next, more stable and prosperous generation.[4] Eliane Leslau Silverman discerned the need for a general analysis of the contribution of women to western agricultural society and has herself placed women in the history of the frontier in *The Last, Best West*.[5]

The value of this 1922 survey material is that it sharpens the impression created by individual recollections and provides a broader framework to help distinguish the typical from the unusual. Also, the emergent model of women's farm work in 1922 can be compared with information on the same livelihood in other pre-industrial western societies. The most significant feature of women's farm work then was in its essential productive contribution to the farm economy. Women were producers as well as reproducers. This article demonstrates that farm women in 1922 made a major contribution to the farm's productivity, both directly by "outside" work and indirectly, by catering to the needs of the other workers on the farm.

Early surveys of women's work in western Canada were produced primarily for propaganda purposes. "What Women Say of the Canadian North West" was a pamphlet published by the Canadian Pacific Railway (CPR) in 1886 to help would-be immigrants decide to make a new home in the Canadian West. The pamphlet printed answers to questions which the company had sent to "as many women throughout the Canadian North West as could be addressed with accuracy." Two further pamphlets, "Words from the Women of Western Canada" and "Women's Work in Western Canada," published, respectively, in 1905 and 1906, were also issued by the CPR and were probably based on the same questionnaires.[6] The pamphlets chronicled women's material aid in "developing the Canadian West and transforming a wilderness into a great and prosperous Homeland."[7]

Two surveys conducted just before the First World War, in the summer of 1914, served as more practical models for the farm women's survey of 1922. Turtle Mountain, in the southwest of the province, a community which had already been established for a generation, and Swan River, on the Saskatchewan border, more recently settled, towards the northern edge of grain growing country, each instituted a rural survey under the jurisdiction of a joint committee of the local Methodist and Presbyterian churches. The aim of these surveys of the "agricultural, educational, social and religious life" of the community was to provide "a broad basis in knowledge for constructive work in rural betterment," an amelioration to be directed towards the two institutions of the school and the church. Five schedules, or questionnaires, were constructed. One gave a comprehensive view of the population of each township; another obtained information regarding religious organizations; a third dealt with the vocational influence of the schools; and the last two concerned the farmer and the farm household. Detailed results of the surveys were not published, but their reports included several tables as well as descriptive summaries. The 1922 survey used the Rural Report questions about the size of farms, whether they were owned or rented, and several parts of the schedule on the farm household.[8]

The 1922 survey conducted by the United Farm Women of Manitoba (UFWM) was not their first foray into social science. In 1920 they surveyed forty-eight rural homes to show "the effect of the tariff on homes" for the Tariff Commission at its Brandon session. This "revealed such alarming conditions" that the following year they conducted a more extensive survey, receiving reports from 225 homes.[9] The 1920 conditions which so disturbed the UFWM Executive were the heavy and unrelenting physical work demanded of the farm wife, coupled with the lack of labour-saving devices in the farm household. The 1920 survey singled out the tariff as being responsible for the high price of labour savers and came to the dramatic conclusion that of the women polled, "every one" would gladly quit the farm. "They had not enough money to live, [they were] too old to enter new fields of labour [and were] thoroughly dissatisfied with conditions in the country."[10]

Such findings were a challenge to the UFWM. Their constituency was the women and girls of the rural communities and their constitution had ten particular objectives over and above the "social and general progress in the rural community" which was the aim of their partner organization, the United Farmers of Manitoba (UFM).[11] The UFWM's own objectives stressed "the finer things of life — 'the things that are more excellent,'" as shown in practical efforts to reduce drudgery in the household and enhance the social, cultural and educational amenities in the community.[12]

Organizationally, they were in a strong position to exert influence. Membership in 1922 was 2,151. This figure was composed of 1,183 in women's locals, and 968 in mixed locals, for each local could have either separate or integrated membership with the UFM.[13] The women's membership was not as large as the men's, who at the end of 1922 reported a 50 percent increase over 1921, for a total of 15,701, reflecting the keen interest and participation brought by a provincial general election in which the farmers fielded their own candidates in the new Progressive Party.[14] No other provincial women's organization of the time approached the UFWM in membership. It had a lively and socially concerned board and employed a full-time paid secretary in Winnipeg. The UFWM had representation on the women's section of the Canadian Council of Agriculture, a national pressure group promoting farmers' interests, on the Social Service Council of Manitoba, and on the provincial Temperance Board. The UFWM Board worked with the Extension Service of the Department of Agriculture and individuals had close connection with the *Grain Growers' Guide*, the farmers' weekly newspaper with the largest circulation.[15]

At the UFWM local level, Mabel Finch, provincial secretary, described a typical women's section in her Report to the 1923 Convention:

> Their work is carried on in a systematic manner. The majority call meetings regularly once a month, the average of meetings in all sections reporting being nine this year, with an attendance of ten members. . . . [they] map out definite programs of activity, and . . . the subjects usually include some of the special UFWM topics, such as public health, social service, young people, education and the marketing of the by-products of the farm. Forty-five percent include debating in their programs, 70 percent have community or travelling libraries, which later, in every instance reported, are filling a long-felt need.[16]

In an article entitled "Woman as Organised Force," the associate editor of the *Grain Growers' Guide*, Mary P. McCallum, credited the Women's Grain Growers' Association (the UFWM's name before it was changed in 1920) with achieving "better medical facilities for rural districts," the establishment of free child welfare clinics, "the betterment of the rural schools," rest rooms in towns for the benefit of rural women, travelling libraries, and well-appointed cemeteries, as well as campaigns for a higher standard of citizenship and greater use of the franchise.[17] The board member responsible for the surveys, Mrs. James Elliott of Cardale, claimed credit on behalf of the UFWM for "that splendid light and water power display of the Government" put on at the Brandon summer agricultural fair of 1922.[18]

Mrs. Elliott was an old hand at surveys and in 1922 confident that the work that went into administering them was worthwhile. An "Official Circular" of June 1922 described how the board wanted cooperation from the membership "so that we, as farm women, can work for the things most needed" in farm homes. "It may seem trivial," wrote Mabel Finch to the secretaries of locals, "to ask about the kitchen sink, and vacation, too, may seem ridiculous," but the UFWM wished to document the heavy burden under which farm women were labouring and wished to agitate in order to bring about conditions in which they could take a rest each year for the sake of their "strength, happiness, and contentment of mind." Local secretaries were asked to call a meeting for the purpose of filling out the questionnaire. Miss Finch alternatively suggested that the secretary could give the questionnaires to individuals, who would complete them at home and then mail them to Winnipeg directly or through the local secretary. Yet a third way was suggested: "a group of women might canvass for membership and fill out the questionnaire at the same time."[19]

These three ways of submitting completed questionnaires contribute to certain difficulties in their interpretation. Not all the questions were unambiguous; some were clearly open ended; and, from the occasional mix of handwriting on a single questionnaire, one suspects that a local secretary sometimes considered she knew better than the respondent what the latter's replies should have been. At least one local would have nothing to do with the survey. "Our section did not take very kindly to the rural home survey," wrote an officer from Manson on 24 July 1922.[20] In her presidential address to the 1923 Convention, Mrs. Elliott alluded to the "antipathy shown by many of our women to the survey."[21] There is a hint of disappointment, too, in the response rate: "Our objective this year was 1000 homes, but . . . we received only 307 surveys in time for inclusion in this report."[22] Nevertheless, altogether 364 completed questionnaires eventually found their way into the UFWM files and served as a valuable repository of information on farm women's work in 1922.

There are in the 1922 survey four main areas of enquiry. First, questions on the size and tenure of farm, and the number of rooms in the house, give an indication of socio-economic standing. A second section establishes the size of household: how many children there were at home, and whether the farm wife took responsibility for looking after hired help. Third, distance from social and community services, together with the possession of a car or telephone, show the women's relative geographical isolation. Most of the questionnaire, however, in a fourth section, is concerned with indices of labour inside the farm house and in its immediate vicinity. Facilities for heat, light, and water are described; a single question which says so much about the daily round is, "Distance from well?" There is a section on power appliances; on the "outside work" performed and its significance in the household budget; on sewing and canning for the family; and on recreation and leisure: the length, or existence, of vacations, the number and names of incoming newspapers and magazines, and the sort of musical instruments possessed. This elementary quantification provided by the survey is then augmented by the testimony of farm women who responded, the same summer, to an essay competition in the *Grain Growers' Guide* on the topic, "Should My Daughter Marry a Farmer?"

The survey respondents had higher socio-economic standing than the rural population as a whole. A high proportion, 87 percent, owned their own farms, compared with 78 percent in the province. More of the survey respondents owned larger farms: 65 percent of their farms were 320 acres or bigger, compared with 41 percent of the farms in the province.[23] Also, the survey respondents tended to live in larger houses — 80 percent of them lived in houses of more than 4 rooms, compared with only 55 percent of the rural population as a whole.[24] Most of the respondents had a cellar, and in the survey occasionally embellished their answers with expressions of irritation. These were echoed by Mrs. Elliott when she asked whether the cellars were "labour and health savers, or are they not? Usually, we see a chair dropped down and the woman swings herself down, and strains herself up."[25]

These UFWM respondents came from the more prosperous parts of the farm population, and this is borne out by analysis of where they lived. Was the population of the survey distributed in the same areas as the population of the province? The answer is no. The survey population was underrepresented in the east, southeast, and northern areas of the province — the poorer and more recently settled parts. It was overrepresented in the western and southwestern areas, those more prosperous places of longer settlement with Ontario-origin communities.[26]

The size and composition of the household were directly relevant to the farm wife's workload. Babies, old people and invalids demanded more care than teenage children, who could be expected to help with chores. While more children could provide more labour, they also had to be fed, clothed and cared for — all primary responsibilities of the mother.

The survey gave no clue to the structure of the farm household, but three questions bore on its size. "How many children at home?" was the most direct of these. Fifty-nine respondents said either "none" or left the space blank. The remaining 73 percent were fairly evenly distributed among households and the average number of children at home was three.

A second source of information on workload was the response to "Have you domestic help?" Only 14 answered "yes." The third set of questions on the size of household was, "Have you a separate home for hired man?," "Do you do his washing?" and "Do you do his mending?" There was no direct question asking if they had a hired man at all, but 46 percent said they did the hired man's washing, and 25 percent did his mending. The implication followed that at least 46 percent had a hired man, at least sometimes. Ten percent said they had a separate home for a hired man.

By 1922, the geographic isolation of many of these UFWM members could partly be overcome by telephone conversations. A large proportion, 70 percent, had a telephone. Fewer, 62 percent, had a car — but the survey did not ask whether "car" could be interpreted as "truck." Only 22 percent said they drove the car themselves. Only the small proportion of 14 percent had companionship of a sort provided by paid domestic help, and in most of those cases, the help was seasonal and for less than six months of the year.

When Mrs. Elliott composed her report on the 1922 survey, she showed an understandable distaste for the heating arrangements disclosed by the majority of respondents. Sixty percent reported homes heated by stoves, which required cleaning, "wood to carry in, ashes to carry out, and the never-ending muss to sweep up." Only 25 percent said they heated by furnace, clearly preferred by Mrs. Elliott: "furnaces . . . enable [the women] to perform those tasks easily and at the same time provide the homes with a more even temperature."[27]

The simple question, "How lighted?" evoked a multitude of responses. A small minority specified electric light — not surprising when widespread rural electrification was still twenty years in the future. It seems that the vast majority lit their homes by coal oil lamps.

Water in the home was a matter of grave concern. Mrs. Elliott was proud to take responsibility on behalf of the UFWM for the water exhibition at the 1921 Brandon summer fair. She herself was fully aware of the connection between cleanliness and health and averred that baths were essential on farms because of the strenuous manual labour and consequent unavoidable perspiration. She also drew attention to the hard physical labour demanded "of often weak or delicate women" by the use of the pail and dipper at an outside well. Her indignation was well-placed. Two-thirds of the respondents said they had no water in the kitchen. More, 82 percent, had no bath. Only 27 percent had an indoor toilet. The survey was silent on whether the bath was a freestanding tub, or the toilet unconnected to a water tank. The information gathered under "distance from well" suggests severe hardship for many families. Seventeen percent had to go over 300 feet to get daily water, and the largest cluster of respondents, 18 percent, walked between 51 and 100 feet. The average distance was 217 feet.

The majority, 56 percent, answered "no" to the question, "Have you machine power?" Even of those who said they did, some interpreted the power to apply to a farm yard workshop rather than to the home. Nevertheless, even if power was not available for home appliances, it reduced a woman's muscle power and drudgery in jobs like separating the cream, or milking, or pumping water. Forty percent said that they did have power, and when asked what it was used for, the majority described a washing machine, but few other labour-savers were listed.

Since the cataloguing of labour savers was to a large extent the whole object of this exercise, Mrs. Elliott permitted herself a few didactic comments. "With a little thought and a minimum of expense," she wrote in her summary report, could those homes that had power "not extend it a little further and do a few more of the woman-killing chores?" She called for willing hands and urged the consideration of such practical ideas as those described in the *Grain Growers' Guide* columns. With the earnestness of a crusader she overlooked the humour of one respondent, who wrote, in the space beside "Other labour savers," "a well trained husband." Mrs. Elliott took this woman to task and demanded to know, "What is going on outside while this man is in the house?" She went on to preach about the "fine distinction between economy and extravagance which women should learn to realise."[28]

The UFWM Board was prevailed on to accord great significance to this survey. The board's report to the 1923 Conference mentioned a desire that it "will be but a stepping stone to a much more comprehensive governmental survey." Mrs. Rinn from

Lisgar said the United States government had done surveys which "awakened the public to the need of providing more labour savers and better conditions for the farm women in order that they might be encouraged to remain on the farm."[29] At the very least, the board asked all UFWM locals to study "labour savers" in their 1923 program.[30]

While the question, "What outside work do you do?" was doubtless clear enough to the UFWM membership, to other observers it is not without ambiguity. Respondents interpreted it to mean work outside the house but more or less in the yard or its vicinity. Only 16 percent declared "none." The sort of outside work mentioned were poultry or eggs (51 percent), milking (40 percent), gardening (39 percent), and calves (4 percent). The questionnaire additionally asked, "Do dairy and poultry nearly finance home?" A judgment call was needed in the reply. Sixteen left this question blank, 53 percent said "no," and 42 percent said "yes." Regrettably, it is not clear whether "financing home" meant providing the housekeeping money, or whether it also included house maintenance or indeed purchase.

"How much family sewing do you do?" allowed respondents to be less than precise in their replies. The three responses most favoured were "all" 33 percent, "some" 30 percent, and "nearly all" 27 percent. Since only fifteen women (4 percent) had mentioned a sewing machine in the labour-saver category, this sewing must have been a time-consuming chore.

Canning similarly evoked a variety of responses. Some people replied with quantitative nouns, as with the sewing, but many elaborated on this by saying what produce they canned. Over half mentioned fruit, 38 percent mentioned vegetables, 10 percent said pickles, and the same number said meat.

The majority, 57 percent, answered "none" to the question, "How long a vacation do you take in a year?" Only a quarter declared that they took a vacation of any sort.

Newspapers and magazines were more than entertainment. They provided educational information of the household hint sort and also news of women's activities, a conduit to the wider world for women who were either isolated or living in very small communities. The questions in this section differentiated between newspapers, magazines, and farm papers, but from the answers it is apparent that respondents were not sure which publications fitted into which category. Only 2 percent said they took no newspapers. An overwhelming number took one newspaper (53 percent) or two (25 percent). Fewer took magazines: 39 percent said they took one and 11 percent took two. More answered positively to the farm papers question: only 9 percent either said "none" or left this space blank. *The Grain Growers' Guide* was mentioned more than any other publication, 64 percent to the 43 percent who mentioned the other most commonly read paper, the *Norwest Farmer*.

Musical instruments were more directly related to leisure. The question was, "What musical instruments have you?" Fifty percent had one, 23 percent had two, and 5 percent had three. Only 14 percent declared "none." In specifying which instruments they had, a piano was most frequently mentioned, by a third, but a quarter had an organ, 15 percent a violin, and 34 percent a gramophone, variously described as phonograph or victrola, as well as by other brand names. One respondent wrote "baby."

The 1922 UFWM survey can inform us, as it informed the organization's board at the time, of the paucity of "labour savers." It can also reveal to us much of what was taken for granted by the UFWM: that farm women expected to do large amounts of manual labour, that they habitually hauled water from an outside well, and that relative isolation was part of the job. How the women actually considered these facts of life is revealed in a remarkable contest run by the *Grain Growers' Guide*, then claiming a weekly circulation of 79,000. In March the *Guide* offered $30 in prizes for the best twelve letters on the question, "If you had a daughter of marriageable age, would you, in the light of your experience as a farm woman, want her to marry a farmer and make her future life on the farm? If so, why? If not, why not?" The *Guide* received 440 entries, and reported that "never before, as far as we know, have such a large number of Canadian farm women endeavoured to express in writing in their own words their opinions as to whether or not farm life is satisfying." 360, or 82 percent, of the contestants answered "yes," showing their "faith and hope in the calling of agriculture." The forty negative replies showed "there are still very serious obstacles in the road to the ideal rural life."[31]

The prize winning positive letters favourably contrasted the "higher moral tone of the country" with that of the town. City life, wrote "Mother of one," "might keep her hands soft and her skin unwrinkled" but Mother would "Fear for flabby soul muscles as well." A "moral" environment for raising children was frequently mentioned, as was the observation that the farm wife "knows where her children are." "Plenty of wholesome food and pure air were good for all country dwellers, young and old," wrote "Ex-Teacher." Altogether, the physical and moral superiority of the country was repeatedly stressed. "Country Life Ideology" had a grip on these contestants.[32]

However, the critical entries scorned the idea that farm life promoted "morality and its kindred virtues." There was "not much encouragement for the growth of any of the virtues except it be patience." And "Patience" herself asked, "when the soul is starving, can one be satisfied with a fat body?" "Disillusioned" saw a darker side. "Something too in farm life seems to blunt the fine edge of a man's scruples, and one finds many farmers sailing very close to the wind in their moral dealings with others." Nor did the healthy physical environment go unchallenged. Sanitation was a "hit or miss affair" said "One of Many," and several noted the deplorable lack of facilities or support for women in childbirth. The quality of the schools, too, was criticized: a child's educational future was "oftimes in the hands of a young, inexperienced and inefficient teacher."[33]

Some proud feminist claims were made on the pro-farmer side. A farm wife and her husband were "real partners," wrote "Topsy Turvey." The average farmer, asserted Anne Whyte, "does not mind getting ready a meal occasionally, will lend a hand with the washer or anything that threatens to be a stress" in genuine "team work." The business opportunities for the farm wife to contribute to the household income through dairy work were often mentioned, not least her ability to earn money "without losing social position." An egalitarian community was also appreciated. "We do not worry over class distinctions" declared "Farm Woman," author of the fourth prize letter.[34]

The main drawbacks seen by critics were overwork, monotony, loneliness, and financial pressure. Unfortunately, the letters were printed with no clue to the material well-being of their writers, and it would be unjustifiable to conclude that the happy, confident entries came from the prosperous farm wives and the more miserable contributions from the poorer families. At least "Ellen" drew attention to prevalent economic conditions, which, in the summer of 1922, were the subject of intense reforming zeal: "markets are more uncertain; and what with the present hopeless credit system, the disproportionate freight rates, the low price of his produce, and the high price of all he has to buy, [the farmer] is faced with bankruptcy no matter how he turns. . . . We are headed straight toward the condition of the peasantry of Europe."[35] "One of Many" said she loved work, "but not slavery." Another described "too much of soul-sickening monotonous drudgery, unbroken by recreation." Against these sombre assessments, it is hard to judge the brisk dismissal of the farm wife who wrote, "Much twaddle has been written about the toilworn hand of the farmer's wife and the weary monotony of her days. Most of the farm women I know are healthy, happy and contented."[36]

The 1922 UFWM survey and the *Guide* essays reveal more than just farm women's working conditions. Many of the survey questions relate to more general issues of isolation, shared culture, and recreational facilities. They touch, too, on community services in health, education, and religion. Several essays reveal an awareness of a perceived threat to farming traditions posed by current economic and political conditions of 1922, and Mrs. Elliott herself was a committed partisan of Progressive anti-tariff policy. However, the main purpose of the surveys was to demonstrate a need for labour savers on the farm. Mrs. Elliott wanted to show that the farm wives' work load was exorbitant, and that labour savers — by which she meant household machines — should be made more readily available. This could be accomplished in two ways. First, the women themselves must demand labour savers and persuade husbands that money spent inside the farmhouse was in the interests of overall farm efficiency. Second, the plumbing and heating systems and household implements must be made more attractive by lower prices, to be achieved mainly be reducing or removing the tariff. The information generated by the surveys was intended to make the case for alleviation of the women's workload. The second part of the argument, the means by which the workload might best be reduced, was part of the stock-in-trade anti-tariff stance of the United Farmers of Manitoba.[37]

The Elliott survey had a single major purpose geared to a specific objective. Sixty years later, its value for the historian lies in the wealth of detail it reveals in its descriptions of the main features of a farm wife's expected work. The very assumptions informing the questions tell us what the expectations were, and the responses give us much more than generalities. Benefitting from the questionnaires already utilized by the church rural surveys, the UFWM had a fairly clear model of a farm wife. She was responsible for the farm house water supply, and for food processing, preserving, and storage. She did sewing for family members, and, if the farm had a hired man, serviced his clothes by washing and mending them. She kept the household accounts and she rarely enjoyed domestic help, either full-time or seasonal. While taking prime responsibility for inside work, cleaning and maintaining the house, caring for children and farm workers, she was expected to do some outside work too, particularly that connected with poultry and dairy animals. She would market any surplus from their produce. Both the surveys and the essays stress the interdependence of family members, who, while accepting a rough sexual division of labour, were not immutably constrained by it. Frances Shaver's contention that women "played and continue to play a major productive role [in addition to their work in the home] . . . as unpaid family labour" is amply borne out in this 1922 agricultural survey.[38]

The picture of farm women's work painted in 1922 carries conviction not only because of its contemporary corroboration in statistics and literary sources but also because it is consistent with the descriptions of women's farm work in other pre-industrial western societies. The work of Lillian Knowles and two of her London School of Economics students, Alice Clark and Ivy Pinchbeck, published between 1919 and 1930, described the full range of productive, as well as reproductive, labour undertaken as a matter of course by the vast majority of British women before industrialization.[39] As Joan Thirsk remarked, this economic contribution to a business partnership gave women "more dignity and status than was granted them after the industrial revolution" — a sentiment echoed in the 1922 essays.[40] "A woman in the country counts for so much. In the city she is only one of thousands."[41]

The overall level of satisfaction which actuated the majority of the essay writers did not erase the need for improvement in 1922. While Mrs. Elliott's passion did not lead her to the extravagant claims she had made before, that "every one" of forty-eight farm wives canvassed in 1920 would gladly quit the farm, she nevertheless voiced an appreciation of the difficulties of farm women's work and a desire to recognize their importance in productivity by a reallocation of farm resources:

> If a woman were allowed the sale price of the half-worn, discarded, and need-never-have-been-bought machinery on the ordinary farm, she would be able to instal a convenient water system in the home, which would tend to preserve her strength and the health of not only herself, but the whole family.[42]

The importance of her survey lies primarily in that it furnished evidence of farm women's productive labour. The survey methodology cannot be considered rigorous. We have insufficient information to conclude that participants in either the survey or the essay competition were "typical." The existing clues suggest that the UFWM respondents had greater capital assets than the average farm family. Such investment nevertheless required unrelenting labour from the women as well as the men, work which we can now begin to evaluate in a more informed way.

NOTES

1. United Farm Women of Manitoba (UFWM), 1922 Rural Survey Questionnaires and Report, *United Farmers of Manitoba* (UFM), Provincial Archives of Manitoba (PAM); *Grain Growers' Guide*, June, July, and August 1922.
2. Tables A67–69 in M.C. Urquhart and K.A.H. Buckley, *Historical Statistics on Canada* 2nd ed. (Ottawa, 1893); John Herd Thompson with Allen Seager, *Canada 1922–1939: Decades of Discord* (Toronto, 1985), p. 3.
3. Census of Canada, 1951, I, Table 13.
4. Gerald Friesen, *The Canadian Prairies: A History* (Toronto, 1984), pp. 301, 305–308.
5. Eliane Leslau Silverman, "Writing Canadian Women's History, 1970–82: an Historiographical Analysis," *Canadian Historical Review* LXIII, 4 (1982): 515; Eliane Leslau Silverman, *The Last, Best West* (Montreal, 1984), p. x.
6. *What Women Say of the Canadian North West* (Canadian Pacific Railway Company, 1886), p. 3. See extracts in Susan Jackel, *A Flannel Shirt and Liberty: British Emigrant Gentlewomen in the Canadian West, 1880–1914* (Vancouver, 1982), pp. 31–65; *Words from the Women of Western Canada* (Canadian Pacific Railway Company, 1905).
7. *Women's Work in Western Canada* (Canadian Pacific Railway Company, 1906), p. 3.
8. *Swan River Survey Committee Report on a Rural Survey* August–September 1914; *Turtle Mountain Survey Committee Report on a Rural Survey* June–July 1914. Manitoba and Northwest Ontario Conference Archives, United Church of Canada.

9. *Statement submitted to the Tariff Commission* by the Executive of the UFWM, 13 October 1920, UFWM 1922 Rural Survey Report. UFM.

10. *Statement submitted to the Tariff Commission* by the Executive of the UFWM, 13 October 1920, p. 3. UFM.

11. *Constitution* of the United Farmers of Manitoba and of the United Farm Women of Manitoba, as revised and adopted at the Annual Convention, January 1921. UFM.

12. *Constitution* of the UFM and UFWM, p. 24. UFM.

13. UFWM Secretary's *Report* to the 1923 Annual Convention, 13; UFM *Handbook of Practical Work* (n.d. but compiled 1920–1921), p. 8. UFM.

14. UFWM Secretary's *Report* to the 1923 Annual Convention, p. 8. UFM. These figures are higher than the approximations in Louis Aubrey Wood, *A History of Farmers' Movements in Canada* (1924), F.J.K. Greizic intr. (Toronto, 1975), p. xii, and in W.L. Morton, *The Progressive Party in Canada* (Toronto, 1950), p. 212.

15. UFWM Board of Director's *Report* to the 1923 Annual Convention, p. 23. UFM.

16. UFWM Secretary's *Report* to the 1923 Annual Convention, 14. UFM.

17. *Grain Growers' Guide*, January 1920.

18. UFWM 1922 Rural Survey *Report*, p. 2. UFM.

19. UFWM *Official Circular No. 4*, 14 June 1922. UFM.

20. Elizabeth Benson to Miss Finch, 24 July 1922. Included in the surveys, UFM.

21. UFWM President's *Address* to the 1923 Annual Convention, 4. UFM.

22. UFWM 1922 Rural Survey *Report*, p. 1. UFM.

23. *Sixth Census of Canada*, 1921, V, Table 79, pp. 118–20.

24. *Sixth Census of Canada*, 1921, III, Table 13, p. 49.

25. UFWM 1922 Rural Survey *Report*, p. 4. UFM.

26. *Sixth Census of Canada*, 1921, V, Table 81, pp. 250–54.

27. UFWM Rural Survey *Report*, p. 4. UFM.

28. Ibid, p. 3.

29. UFWM Board of Directors' *Report* to the 1923 Annual Convention, p. 12. UFM.

30. UFWM *Official Circular No. 1*, 16 February 1923, p. 2. UFM.

31. *Grain Growers' Guide*, 14 June 1922.

32. Gerald Friesen, "The Western Canadian Identity," Canadian Historical Association Annual *Report* (1973), p. 15; David C. Jones, "'There is Some Power About the Land' — The Western Agrarian Press and Country Life Ideology," *Journal of Canadian Studies*, 17, 3 (1982): 106.

33. *Grain Growers' Guide*, 14 June 1922, 9 August 1922.

34. Ibid., 14 June 1922, 9 August 1922.

35. Ibid., 14 June 1922.

36. Ibid., 12 July 1922, 9 August 1922.

37. Gerald Friesen, *The Canadian Prairies: A History* (Toronto, 1984), pp. 329, 370.

38. Frances M. Shaver, "Women in North American Agriculture," *Resources for Feminist Research II*, 1 (1982): 3–4; Joyce K. Lapping and Mark B. Lapping, "Rural Women's Work: A Note on the Canadian Council on Rural Development Study on Canadian Rural Women," Ibid., pp. 54–55.

39. Lillian Knowles, *The Industrial and Commercial Revolutions in Great Britain during the Nineteenth Century* (London, 1921); Alice Clark, *Working Life of Women in the Seventeenth Century* (1919) new ed., London, 1982; Ivy Pinchbeck, *Women Workers and the Industrial Revolution, 1750–1850* (1930) new ed., London 1977.

40. Joan Thirsk, Foreword, in Mary Prior, ed., *Women in English Society 1500–1800* (London, 1985), p. 8.

41. *Grain Growers' Guide*, 12 July 1922.

42. UFWM Rural Survey *Report*, p. 3. UFM.

TOPIC THREE
Paid Employment

Mounties crush the General
Strike in Winnipeg, 21 June
1919.

Canada's paid workforce, aged 14 and older, roughly doubled to just over eight million during the first four decades of the twentieth century. The most spectacular growth occurred in urban-based manufacturing, retailing, and various administrative and professional spheres. More employment, however, did not automatically translate into greater social contentment; often the nature of work underwent significant, and unsettling, changes. As factories and firms enlarged, became more capital intensive, and were more rigorously managed, often lost was a personal and relatively relaxed relationship between workers and employers. In order to increase productivity, profits, and control over the working class, many companies broke down jobs into small tasks that could be performed by the less skilled. From the perspective of labour, therefore, Canada's drive towards advanced capitalism was often accompanied by increasingly repetitive and monotonous work, as well as an ongoing battle with ever more hegemonic employers whose desire to maximize returns commonly resulted in paltry pay, derelict safety standards, and a refusal to recognize unions — factors that generated approximately 30 million strike days between 1901 and 1945.[1]

In Article 5, in which they analyze the causes of over 400 industrial disputes in ten southern Ontario communities between 1901 and 1914, Craig Heron and Bryan D. Palmer assert that even among supposedly elitist and relatively conservative craft unionists, there developed a class "consciousness" in response to the innovations of employers who turned to mass mechanization, scientific management techniques, court injunctions, the use of industrial spies, and collusion with fellow employers in the interests of corporate well-being. As social historians have expanded their scope, academic debate over the prevalence of working-class "consciousness" or unity has continued to grow more complicated. The question of the degree to which workers forged links across region, ethnicity, occupational levels, union structure, or even the ideological proclivities of their leadership has resulted in copious and often contradictory work. Also a focus of greater attention have been women workers, a group that, like ethnic minorities, often faced a double dose of exploitation. Here, social historians have usually dwelt on the failure of the working class to establish cross-gender solidarity because of a patriarchal belief within the male proletariat that women's work was unimportant and merited little remuneration — most women, it was assumed, would leave the employment market once married, or would continue to work only to supplement the husband's income. Furthermore, though the number of women workers climbed nearly 300 percent from 1901 to 1941, to reach a figure of 1 248 575,[2] women remained overwhelmingly confined to the lowest-paid jobs and to areas associated with the "household" sphere or the so-called feminine attributes — such as domestic work, the textile trade, the nurturing professions like teaching and nursing, and the retail and clerical sectors, where their "pleasant disposition" and "nimble fingers" could be utilized.

The importance of gender in determining the separate and unequal roles played by women workers is made clear in Article 6, Robin John Anderson's study of Vancouver women's employment agencies. Motivated by a quasi-religious social preoccupation with protecting female virtue and the desire to satisfy the need of that city's middle class for domestic help, YWCA employment counsellors directed women away from newer kinds of jobs becoming available within the urban sphere, such as waitressing, and towards domestic service. Yet with its long hours, strenuous chores, low pay, and the little it offered in the way of freedom or protection from employers, domestic service remained unpopular. Despite the Y's benevolent image, therefore, by the time of the Great War, numerous women seeking employment had turned away from that organization to commercial employment houses. Motivated primarily by the desire to make a profit, commerical houses responded to the changing demands of the job market and thus offered at least a modicum of opportunity to women in a domain where the gendered division of labour always remained as much a harsh reality as any injustice based on social class.

QUESTIONS TO CONSIDER

1. Do Heron and Palmer offer a convincing portrait of the strike as demonstrating class consciousness?
2. What factors do you think might prove the existence of a separate working-class culture or consciousness?
3. What does Anderson's article suggest about the potential for unity and strength in the early women's movement?
4. Does Anderson provide any indication of how the social construction of appropriate gender roles and behaviour affected women's lives outside the workplace?
5. How might ethnicity, regional background, and gender contribute to or detract from working-class unity?

NOTES

1. M.C. Urquhart and K.A.H. Buckley, eds., *Historical Statistics on Canada* (Toronto: Macmillan, 1965), series C1–7, D426–33.
2. Urquhart and Buckley, *Historical Statistics*, series C8–35.

SUGGESTED READINGS

Acton, Janice, ed. *Women at Work: Ontario, 1850–1930*. Toronto: Women's Press, 1974.

Bercuson, David J., ed. *Canadian Labour History: Selected Readings*. Toronto: Copp Clark Pitman, 1987.

Heron, Craig. *The Canadian Labour Movement: A Short History*. Toronto: James Lorimer, 1989.

Lowe, Graham. *Women in the Administrative Revolution: The Feminization of Clerical Work*. Toronto: University of Toronto Press, 1987.

MacDowell, Laurel Sefton, and Ian Radforth, eds. *Canadian Working Class History: Selected Readings*. Toronto: Canadian Scholars Press, 1992.

McCormack, A. Ross. *Reformers, Rebels, and Revolutionaries: The Western Canadian Radical Movement, 1899–1919*. Toronto: University of Toronto Press, 1977.

Naylor, James. *The New Democracy: Challenging the Social Order in Industrial Ontario, 1914–1925*. Toronto: University of Toronto Press, 1991.

Palmer, Bryan D. *Working Class Experience: Rise and Reconstitution of Canadian Labour, 1800–1980*. Toronto: Butterworths, 1983.

Piva, Michael. *The Condition of the Working Class in Toronto, 1900–1921*. Ottawa: University of Ottawa Press, 1979.

Radforth, Ian. *Bushworkers and Bosses: Logging in Northern Ontario, 1900–1980*. Toronto: University of Toronto Press, 1987.

Rouillard, Jacques. *Les Syndicats nationaux au Québec de 1900 à 1930*. Québec: Les presses de l'Université Laval, 1979.

Vaisey, Douglas, comp. *The Labour Companion: A Bibliography of Canadian Labour History Based on Materials Printed from 1950 to 1975*. Halifax: Committee on Canadian Labour History, 1980.

FIVE

Through the Prism of the Strike: Industrial Conflict in Southern Ontario, 1901–1914

CRAIG HERON AND BRYAN D. PALMER

The trouble with the heads of many industries is that they become money mad and drunk with the power that money brings. They think that they can do anything and everything in a high-handed and ruthless manner just because they have a fat bank account and gilt-edged securities lying in some safety deposit vault.[1]

This outburst from the *Bobcaygeon Independent* in 1913 reflected a marked upswing in industrial conflict which accompanied the massive economic expansion in early twentieth-century Ontario. In Berlin, Brantford, Guelph, Hamilton, London, Niagara Falls, Oshawa, Peterborough, St. Catharines, and Toronto, the "toilers" and the "greedy, grasping, and gloating galoots" clashed frequently after the turn of the century. What emerges clearly from even the most superficial glance at strike activity in the years 1901–14 is the magnitude of the conflict between labour and capital: the ten cities under discussion experienced the trauma of 421 strikes and lockouts in this fourteen-year period and approximately 60,000 working men and women participated in these battles.

The pattern of this strike activity buttresses the classic contention that industrial unrest follows closely upon the heels of economic cycles of contraction and expansion. In the boom years prior to 1904 an unusually tight labour market brought about a sharp increase in the incidence of strikes. As years of economic retrenchment, 1904 and 1905 saw the pace of unrest slacken; a resurgence of strikes in 1906 and the early months of 1907 told of the return of more prosperous times. But with the economic downturn of 1908 strike activity came to a virtual standstill, and the severe depression year, 1908, witnessed the least number of conflicts in the entire period. Only in 1910 did the number of strikes begin to rise again significantly, reaching a peak in the early part of 1913. The prewar recession quickly stifled the growing conflict, however,

Source: Excerpted from "Through the Prism of the Strike: Industrial Conflict in Southern Ontario, 1901–14," *Canadian Historical Review*, 58, 4 (1977): 423–57. Reprinted by permission of University of Toronto Press Incorporated.

and by 1914 strikes were once again quite uncommon. Strikes, then, were commonly resorted to in times of prosperity, when concessions were more easily wrung from recalcitrant employers, and were more sparingly employed in years of recession, most prominently 1908 and 1913–14, when labour's chances of even the most marginal victories were slim indeed.[2]

Finally, the contours of industrial strife in these years reveal important patterns of geographical and industrial concentration. Predictably, the geographical locus of strike activity coincided with the concentration of population. Toronto and Hamilton, the largest urban centres under consideration, far outstripped the other cities in terms of the number of strikes and workers involved: Toronto sustained 198 strikes or lock-outs in the years 1901–14, in which 38,903 workers participated, while Hamilton experienced 92 such conflicts, involving 11,249 working men and women. Oshawa, in contrast, saw only 263 workers strike on a single occasion in the entire period, in February 1903. Workers in the building and metal trades were clearly in the vanguard of this industrial upheaval, leading fully half of the total number of strikes in the ten cities. Trailing them, but playing a major role, were workers in the clothing, food, liquor and tobacco, and woodworking trades. More generally, it was the skilled that provided the cutting edge of opposition: unskilled labour participated in less than 6 per cent of the total number of strikes in the ten southern Ontario cities.

Perhaps the fundamental feature of the context of industrial strife in southern Ontario between 1901 and 1914 was the accelerating pace of industrial capitalist development. After more than thirty years of economic expansion, the first decade and a half of the twentieth century saw the pace of industrialization quickened and pushed to new heights. Penelope Hartland has argued that the years 1900 to 1914 represented the most rapid growth in the Canadian economy since the decade preceding Confederation, and the 1911 census noted "the gratifying movement of the country's industrial prosperity during the last decade."[3] Finally, the period witnessed the acceleration of the process of concentration and consolidation of business enterprises initiated in the late 1880s. In his study of the Canadian "merger movement," H.G. Stapells documented fifty-six major consolidations in manufacturing industries in the years 1900–12.[4] As a result more and more southern Ontario workers found themselves working in large factories: in Hamilton, for example, 135 firms employed 18,695 of the city's 21,149 industrial workers in 1911.[5]

While this economic development was undoubtedly a national phenomenon, southern Ontario seemed destined to play a leading role: the area offered easy importation of raw materials, especially the coal and iron vital to the development of heavy industry; efficient and lucrative marketing facilities and transportation networks were close at hand; skilled and unskilled labour was long established in the area; cheap hydro, particularly after the turn of the century, was easily obtainable; and local politicians eagerly enticed firms, notably branches of large American corporations, with lucrative bonuses and tax exemptions. Under these conditions southern Ontario cities attracted industry and capital with relative ease, and new factories mushroomed while older concerns expanded.

The impact of the expansion of these years, of course, transcended the figures of aggregate growth and gross output compiled by statisticians and economists. As E.P. Thompson has stressed, "the transition to mature industrial society entailed a severe restructuring of working habits — new disciplines, new incentives, and a new human nature upon which these incentives could bite effectively . . ."[6] Two such disciplines and incentives, mechanization and new conceptions of managerial authority or industrial efficiency, were of particular relevance in capital's quest for "the restructuring of work habits" and the creation of a new, more pliable, human nature. Although set in motion a century earlier in the first throes of the Industrial Revolution, this process was accelerating rapidly by the early twentieth century.

The disruptive impact of technology and mechanized production on the skilled crafts of the late nineteenth century in advanced capitalist countries is an often told tale, although the Canadian experience has only just begun to receive attention. What has recently been stressed, however, is the other side of the historical coin: the degree to which skilled workers retained much of their craft status, pride, and economic security through a thorough organization and control of the productive process. Gregory S. Kealey has recently demonstrated the lasting power of iron moulders and printers in the face of the mechanization of Toronto's skilled trades,[7] while David Montgomery's study of craft workers in the late nineteenth century in the United States regards skilled workers' control of the productive process as the touchstone of their self-conception of manhood: "Technical knowledge acquired on the job was embodied in a mutualistic ethical code, also acquired on the job, and together these attributes provided skilled workers with considerable autonomy at their work and powers of resistance to the wishes of their employers."[8] In many trades, as George Barnett early demonstrated in the case of the printers, mechanization had little disruptive impact, for craft unions were able to "keep tabs" on the new machines by forcing employers to hire only skilled journeymen to run them.[9] Craft workers, as Benson Soffer has argued, cultivated a rich and varied collection of shop-floor control mechanisms throughout the course of the nineteenth century. Such devices, assuring skilled workers a degree of autonomy at the work place, exercised a tenuous hold over work relationships in many nineteenth-century trades.[10] Underpinning these mechanisms was a resilient consciousness of pride and self-confidence in their social worth that would carry these workers through many struggles.

Yet, even granting the significant degrees of control over the work processes exercised by many craftsmen to the end of the nineteenth century, by the early twentieth century technology had made real strides in diluting skill and transforming the workers' status on the shop floor. Complementing this propensity of modern machinery, moreover, was another development. Aware of the impediments that the autonomy of the skilled worker had raised against productivity and authority, employers turned to an array of managerial innovations and efficiency schemes after the turn of the century. Ranging from the employment of autocratic foremen, pledged to drive men and women harder and faster, to the utilization of complex systems of task simplification, job standardization, time and motion study, cost accountancy, and piece and bonus systems of wage payment, this amalgam of tactics became known as "scientific management." This pervasive thrust for efficiency, coupled with the impact of mechanization, constituted a concerted assault upon the control mechanisms and customs of the trade embedded within the consciousness and shop practices of the skilled worker.[11]

While the drive to rationalize and intensify the productive process through the agency of scientific management and industrial efficiency had its greatest impact in the United States, the movement's presence was felt to some degree in all industrial capitalist countries. Canada, and particularly southern Ontario, did not escape this generalized experience. Much of the efficiency zeal undoubtedly became transferred to Canadian settings via the introduction of branch plants, while the increasing size of corporate holdings, accentuated after 1907 by the accelerating merger movement, lent a logic to the introduction of managers and shop-floor planners. In Hamilton, for instance, where by 1913 forty-five companies attested to US parentage — including such major employers as Canadian Westinghouse, International Harvester, and the Imperial Cotton Company — it is unlikely that managerial personnel were unaware of recent conceptions of techniques gaining such widespread currency south of the border. But the case of Canadian manufacturers' adoption of the new "science of management" does not rest on inference alone.

Frederick Winslow Taylor, the proclaimed "father of scientific management," received an enthusiastic endorsement from the *Hamilton Spectator* as early as 1906.[12] By 1908 Taylor's hand-picked disciple, Henry L. Gantt, was introducing a sophisticated piece-work system on a number of North American railroad lines, including the Canadian Pacific.[13] Moreover, in the spring of 1913 the journal of the Canadian Manufacturers' Association, *Industrial Canada*, printed three articles by Taylor, outlining the essence of his system of job standardization, task simplification, and wage payment; on 18 January of the same year Taylor himself had addressed the Canadian Club of Ottawa on "the principles of scientific management."[14]

With the potential of innovative managerial techniques laid clearly before them, it is not surprising southern Ontario employers made tangible efforts to jump aboard the efficiency band-wagon. As early as 1906 H.L.C. Hall, a member of the International Accountants' Society, introduced a system of cost accountancy at the B. Greening Wire Company of Hamilton. Involving the transfer of authority from skilled workmen to foremen, job standardization, efforts to eliminate all lost time and motion, a record of the minutes required to complete each job, strict tabulation of all materials and tools employed, and the adoption of piece rates and premium plans, Hall's system exemplified the exactitude introduced on the shop floor by the new managers. Also characteristic was Hall's purpose: "First to induce economy by the elimination of waste and second to induce economy by intensifying production."[15]

The showplace of Canadian "efficiency in production methods," however, came to be the Lumen Bearing Company of Toronto. In 1911 *Industrial Canada* approvingly described the role of experts and the resulting jump in productivity:

Practical assistance to the workmen must be given by an expert. In the Lumen Bearing Co.'s shop a man is placed on the floor in an advisory capacity to the foreman. His is not the work of administration or management. He is there to assist the workmen, to suggest short cuts, to evolve economical methods, to save time for the workman, and for the manager, to the material advantage of both . . .

It is the place of the "staff boss," the "expert adviser," to show workmen where these minutes may be saved. He is on the floor all the time; he is corrective to slovenly practices. The stop watch is his gauge. By careful and accurate observations a basis is arrived at for piece work prices . . .

In the Lumen Bearing Co.'s foundry a certain class of castings was formerly made at the rate of twenty-eight a day. That was in the day work era. To-day the average production per man of the same casting is sixty-five. The history of the change in output from

twenty-eight to sixty-five daily is the story in concentrated form of efficiency management. It was accomplished by showing the moulders how this, that and the other operation could be accomplished with greater speed and with less labor. It is the story of
economy of time and energy; of making the head serve the hand; the story of developing more efficient workmen.[16]

Southern Ontario craftsmen lost no time in pointing to the destructive impact of the
twin processes of mechanization and modern management upon their callings: spe-
cialization, simplification, payment by the piece or on the bonus, the utter disregard
of apprenticeship training, and the flooding of the labour market with unskilled,
uninformed, "green hands" all contributed to the demise of their skill and the erosion of their craft pride. James Simpson, a prominent trade unionist long associated
with Toronto Typographical Union No 91, wrote in 1907 of the "extension of the
principle of the division of labour," in which Canadian workingmen were required
to specialize ever more narrowly in one small aspect of production. The Royal Commission on Industrial Training and Technical Education, on which Simpson served,
received numerous letters from disgruntled workers and stressed in its report the
degradation of skilled workers occasioned by modern methods of production.[17]

Most trades, of course, by this late date accepted mechanized production as
inevitable and attempted to control its ill effects through staunch enforcement of
union rules, the introduction of training programmes, petitions for the establishment
of technical schools, and, above all else, the thorough organization of their craft. Some
workers, however, reacted bitterly when employers sought to utilize machinery to dis-
place skilled labour. Such was obviously the case at the International Harvester plant
in Hamilton in 1904, when 125 machinists led a three-month struggle against efforts
to mechanize their craft.[18] Similarly, thirty-two stone masons left their Toronto work
place for five days in October of 1905, protesting the introduction of a planing machine. Upon their return they found their places filled by other workers — prompting a sympathetic strike of seventy-two of their brothers employed at six other stone-
cutting firms.[19]

Most often skilled workers rallied to the defence of their unions as a bulwark
against a loss of their shop-floor power. Throughout the period thirty-two strikes were
fought for union recognition; a further seventy-three involved victimization of trade
unionists, employment of non-union labour, and various violations of trade standards; and on at least fourteen occasions workers struck in sympathy with fellow
trade unionists already on strike. It was this defiant trade unionism, attempting to
consolidate and expand its range of influence in Ontario's industry in the opening
years of this century, that raised the hackles of employers.

Moreover, the question of apprenticeship, which had raged during the late nineteenth century, continued to exert its presence in the years 1901–14. Indeed, in a least
a dozen instances, as employers sought to introduce unlimited numbers of apprentices into the mechanized shops and factories of southern Ontario, this issue became
the apex of a violent labour–capital clash.

Toronto early became the focal point of this battle over apprenticeship. In September and October 1903, 150 bookbinders struck because an apprentice was doing
a journeyman's work. On 20 July 1904 twenty woodworkers at the Adamson Mould-
ing Company engaged in a similar job action and, like the bookbinders, reached a satisfactory settlement with their employer. Bookmakers, wall-paper printers, and bakers

waged summer-long fights to limit the number of apprentices in their respective trades in 1905, although their efforts were apparently unsuccessful. The following year saw sheet-metal workers victorious in a strike aimed at preventing helpers from doing skilled work. And, finally, in the autumn months of 1906, 600 employees of eight Toronto piano manufacturers staged a significant last-ditch attempt to prevent the flooding of their shops with "green hands." Their demands included the limitation of the number of apprentices to one for every five mechanics, and the extension of the term of apprenticeship to five years of service.[20]

Strikes were frequently resorted to in order to curb the "autocratic" and "tyrannical" practices and attitudes of managers, foremen, and superintendents, many of whom had been imported from the United States. Garment workers and iron moulders in London in 1901 and 1905, for instance, refused to work under supervisors they considered intolerable.[21] In February 1908, "when an officious foreman in the Morlock Brothers establishment, Guelph," informed a committee of upholsterers that they could either accept a cut in wages "or get to h . . . out of the shop," the furniture coverers, objecting to "the ungentlemanly conduct of foreman Webber," obliged their supervisor and abruptly left work.[22] In all we found eighteen strikes where the issue was clearly the workers' disapproval of a particular company employee, usually supervisory staff.

Beyond this hostile reception afforded "crushers" and "drivers" lay even more blatant rejections of the "new management." Hamilton's *Labour News* struck hard at the introduction of efficiency measures in many Canadian machine shops: "The 'one man two machines,' the 'Taylor,' 'Scientific,' 'Premium,' 'piece work' and other systems introduced in the metal shops are making of men what men are supposed to make of metals: machines."[23] In many southern Ontario cities this distaste for efficiency systems resulted in the cessation of work.

Hamilton, for instance, witnessed a number of conflicts that appeared to have had their roots in working-class dissatisfaction with various modes of "shop management." Late in 1902 several hundred female employees of the Eagle Knitting Mill objected to a new system of cutting and work classification. Leaving their benches, they claimed the innovations would result in a wage reduction of upwards of $2 a week. The dispute was ultimately "amicably adjusted," management claiming the cutters would soon be doing more work and collecting larger wages. Forty hands at the Chapman-Holton Knitting Mills struck in 1910 against a system of deductions levelled against spoiled work. And in May 1911 one hundred coatmakers at the Coppley, Noyes, and Randall Company successfully blocked the introduction of a piece-work system. Finally, in 1913, workers at the Canadian Westinghouse Company left the plant in an unsuccessful display of opposition to the introduction of time clocks. Like the machinists at the Watertown Arsenal in the United States, these electricians refused to be "put under the clock."[24]

But perhaps the most vivid example of the impact of efficiency-conscious managers upon work processes, and the working-class distaste for such developments, was the 1907 Bell Telephone strike, involving women operators. In 1903, in an attempt to undercut unnecessary and inefficient work techniques, the company installed new equipment, demanded the completion of routine tasks in drastically reduced time periods, and cut the hours of work from eight to five per day. Two shifts of women catered to the needs of an "overexacting public." For many the severe nervous tension, heightened by the company's absolute refusal to consider work breaks and the constant flashing of lights and clicking of receivers attendant upon the work, proved unbearable. Maud Orton, Minnie Hanun, Aria Strong, and Laura Rochall later testified that their employment at Toronto's Bell offices had brought about nervous breakdowns and frequent mental discomfort. Shocks from the switchboards were everyday occurrences and the women's seating apparatus, lacking back supports, produced constant irritation. Medical authorities were quick to condemn the unhealthy working conditions prevailing in the offices. Nor was this all that rendered the operatives' work oppressive. Lady supervisors paraded the aisles, making sure the working women violated no rules; talking was strictly forbidden; and a monitoring system, which management deemed essential, intensified the strain and tension seemingly inherent in the job.[25]

Yet from 1903 through 1906 the women at Bell Telephone endured their lot, albeit begrudgingly. Lacking the traditions and practices of control so embedded within the craft consciousness, existing outside the pale of trade unionism and only recently injected into modern work settings, these women had few benchmarks to guide them in their orientation towards an increasingly burdensome and exploitative job situation. If their dissatisfaction grew too great, they left, a frequent occurrence if we are to believe management's complaints of high turnovers in personnel; this process simply exacerbated the problem of inefficiency since trained staff did not always stay on the job long enough.[26] But the women's relatively passive acquiescence was not to last forever.

In March 1906 the company decided to assess the relative merits of the innovative five-hour day. Two studies were commissioned, one by James T. Baldwin and another by Hammond V. Hayes, both employees of the American Telephone and Telegraph Company. Completed late in 1906, the reports concurred in their findings. Through elaborate analyses of the speed and quality of service and minute calculations of the number of seconds allotted per call, as well as the number of calls handled in one hour, both agreed that the eight-hour system, then in effect in Montreal, surpassed Toronto's five-hour plan in the efficient and effective utilization of labour.[27]

From these conclusions the company proceeded quickly. Overly confident of the pliability of its work force, Bell acted as it had in the past, reintroducing the eight-hour day as it had all previous changes in technical and organizational operations: without warning, the women at Bell were told that they should once again work eight-hour shifts. Aware of the intensity of work under the old system, and with no assurance that they would receive increased relief or lessened pressures, the employees rightly feared that their new work load would become even heavier. Like their employer, the Bell women acted promptly, striking in January 1907 and soon after joining the International Electrical Workers Union. Within the city the strike was widely reported and discussed, and a Royal Commission consisting of deputy minister of labour William Lyon Mackenzie King and Judge John Winchester conducted a thorough investigation of the issues involved. Although the delay created by the investigation diffused the momentum of the women's protest and ultimately led to defeat for them, the strike serves to remind us that it was not only the skilled who suffered the consequences of managerial drives to perfect human efficiency.[28]

Struggles such as these — built around fundamental changes in the way work was to be organized and carried out — must be seen as efforts by the working class, especially the more skilled sectors, to secure or retain control over their job settings. Although tabulating precise statistics on the issues in dispute in prewar strikes is extremely difficult owing to the sketchiness of much of the Department of Labour's reporting, and although the analysis is further clouded by those strikes involving two or more clearly discernible issues, we have concluded that probably more than two hundred strikes involved conflict over some aspect of control of the work place.

Just how critical and contentious control struggles could become was illustrated in London.[29] In July and August of 1901 cigarmakers were locked out of one shop for refusing to make expensive, high-quality cigars at the same rates paid for cheaper variants. Twelve days later they returned to work under their own conditions. In 1913, with the prewar recession already well underway, fifty members of the same trade struck a local establishment for the right to control practices of hiring and firing. While their walk-out was waged in vain, the stogie-makers' proposal that a committee of workmen regulate employment during the coming recession spoke of their deeply embedded conception of their rights as craftsmen.[30] Moulders, too, saw control of their trade as a vital issue. In a strike at McClary's in the summer of 1905, the firm's "sand artists" presented a list of demands to the superintendent which included the establishment of a shop committee, selected by the workers, to be the sole determinant of pricing work done in the foundry.[31] Two years earlier 263 carriage workers had raised a similar demand in Oshawa's McLaughlin Carriage Company.[32] The Toronto garment industry saw even bolder efforts. During the summer of 1911 thirty-five workers waged a lengthy, unsuccessful strike against the Puritan Skirt Factory for the right to appoint committees to adjust all prices, to control hiring and firing, and to distribute all available work evenly in order to avoid layoffs. Another sixty cloakmakers, twenty-five of them women, walked out of M. Pullan & Sons the following January demanding a similar price control committee and the right to appoint a shop chairman with wide powers.[33]

Finally, our discussion of control struggles must make brief mention of working-class attempts to shorten the working day, a demand with a long and rich history. Fifty-eight of the 421 strikes and lockouts in the years 1901–14 involved this issue. At the beginning of our period a Toronto labour publication noted that in certain kinds of work, becoming increasingly common, "workers cannot stand as many hours of toil as they used to stand. The man who tends a never slackening machine in a well-equipped factory works at a higher tension than did the man who hammered out the article to be produced on the anvil, or shaped at the bench . . . This growing tension ought to be accompanied with shorter hours, or the heavy strain will be too much for the men who have to stand it." In the face of technological and managerial innovation many workers undoubtedly invested energy previously devoted to "soldiering" and other forms of restrictive control in the struggle for the eight- or nine-hour day.[34]

Not all conflicts centred directly on the issues of control of the work place. Of the 421 strikes and lockouts examined, 212 involved the question of higher wages, and twenty-eight more were the consequence of resistance to wage reductions. Behind this activity undoubtedly lay, in large part, the widely discussed issue of the soaring cost of living in the two prewar decades. In an 1100-page statistical survey of this problem in the period under study, Robert Coats of the federal Department of Labour revealed increases in prices of food, fuel, and lighting in southern Ontario cities of 43 to 58 per cent and in rents of 35 to 90 per cent. Wages, he concluded, seldom kept pace.[35] Small wonder, then, that so many workers were prepared to strike over conditions that were eroding their real wages.

Yet it is these struggles which are the most difficult to classify, for as Knowles has argued, wage strikes "tend to be symbolic of wider grievances"; to view them as simply conflicts over the size of a pay packet would be overly reductionist. Certainly disputes which pitted a working-class notion of "a fair wage" against the employer's criteria of efficiency and productivity epitomized fundamentally opposed views of labour in the productive process. Moreover, many of these strikes for higher wages also involved issues that fell more clearly within the sphere of control struggles. And in the case of those conflicts arising out of efforts to impose wage cuts it is clear that many unionists saw such struggles as a defence of their unions, for employers were not above using wage reductions to destroy entrenched craft organizations. Then, too, we have no way of knowing how many workers, conscious of the loss of autonomy occasioned by the drift of modern industry, sought recompense in a higher wage. Nevertheless, it can not be denied that in the context of rampant inflation and declining real wages, which, to many workers, became the encompassing reality of everyday life in the modern world, strikes over wage issues were an important feature of industrial unrest in the years 1901–14.[36]

However, if many of these strikes fought to win increased rates of remuneration, resist the rising tide of inflation, or forestall attempts to reduce wages were not concerted attacks upon managerial prerogatives, neither were they passively accepted by capital as mere "bread and butter" skirmishes. Rather, as Louis S. Reed long ago argued, strikes for higher wages often bit deeply into narrowing profit margins. To the employer, also feeling the pinch of inflation, such conflicts were viewed as the straw aimed at breaking the camel's back, and it is not surprising that capital soon organized a retaliatory assault.[37]

Labour upsurge prompted an increasingly hostile reception on the part of employers. Most businessmen viewed with distinct displeasure, for example, the phenomenal growth of the American Federation of Labor in Canada — the association with which most of the skilled workers involved in our 421 strikes and lockouts were affiliated — in the years 1896–1904.[38] Capital's consternation, like that of labour, was to be an organized force, utilizing a plethora of sophisticated techniques that ranged from the open-shop drive to the development of subtle forms of paternalistic manipulation of working-class needs and aspirations.

Southern Ontario employers early learned the value of organization and collective, as opposed to individual, action. In October 1903 the National Association of Manufacturers in the United States, an organization which was to provide the cutting edge of a nation-wide open-shop drive, held a special convention in Chicago where a national federation of employers' associations was born, the Citizens' Industrial Association of America; representatives from Toronto were present at the proceedings.[39] Many Canadian firms were connected to the American open-shop campaign through affiliations with American associations: the National Founders' Association, the National Metal Trades Association, and the United Typothetae of America, for instance, all had a Canadian membership.[40] Skilled workers, it seems, were not the only beneficiaries of international connections.

Canadian employers quickly learned important lessons in anti-union practices from their American confrères; strikebreaking in the years 1901–14 became something of an art, involving intricate infiltrations of plants and factories by spies, detectives, and "spotters," as well as massive influxes of often notorious "blacklegs."[41] In a strike at the Canada Foundry Company in Toronto in 1903, a local officer of the moulders' union reported that the company was employing twenty-four to twenty-eight roving professional strikebreakers supplied by the National Founders' Association at $1.50 a day over and above regular moulder's wages; these men had been sent from Duluth and were encamped on company property.[42] The National Metal Trades Association also advised members in the handling of industrial disputes, furnished men and money to break strikes and troublesome unions, and operated an immense labour bureau where the records of hundreds of thousands of men were kept, allowing employers to determine the potential loyalty of prospective employees.[43] Moreover, the resources and expertise of American businessmen often proved quite useful, as in February 1903, when a prominent figure in the American open-shop drive, John Kirby of Dayton, Ohio, visited Toronto to help employers launch their anti-union offensive.[44]

While the American presence and example was thus critical in the origins of the southern Ontario employers' offensive, it was soon outstripped by indigenous developments. Canadian employers' associations mushroomed in the post-1901 years: the *Labour Gazette* found over sixty such organizations in 1905 in the ten cities under consideration. It was from these locally based bodies, as well as the newly reorganized CMA, predominantly an Ontario concern in its early years, that capital's counterattack was initiated.[45]

In October 1902 two hundred Toronto manufacturers were invited to attend a meeting on 14 October to discuss the "placing of business on a more stable and permanent basis by preventing strikes and providing means of arbitration upon an equitable footing in all matters of dispute between capital and labour . . ."[46] From this gathering emerged the Employers' Association of Toronto, led by men who had recently experienced some of the city's most bitter strikes and lockouts: James P. Murray of the Toronto Carpet Company, a prominent figure in the CMA; W.H. Carrick of the Gurney Foundry Works; and Frank Polson, a well-known local foundryman. In a clear rejection of the principle of collective bargaining, Murray's presidential address revealed the impetus behind the group's formation: "The growth of industry and of transportation facilities had so increased competition that stable prices, unreliable deliveries, and imperfect goods were now fatal to trade. The strike was the most productive agent of these conditions . . ." The artisan, according to the president, had no right to interfere with the prices another artisan might demand for his labour. Labour organizations, he urged, by fixing a uniform price under which unionists must work, "brought it about that the quality and quantity of work plays no part in relation to what is paid for it." In their stated aim of assuring "their rights to manage their respective businesses in such lawful manner as they deem proper," the Toronto employers left no doubt as to where they thought control of the work place should reside.[47] To the CMA the group was attempting "to meet union with union"; after four years' experience with the Toronto body, the *Tribune*, organ of the Toronto Trades and Labour Council, saw it as one more effort aimed at "dragging down and crushing the working people."[48]

Simultaneously, pressure was being exerted within the CMA for a more militant opposition to organized labour. "Why should one body of men," complained a committee set up in 1902 to consider the employers' relationship to organized labour, "be permitted to unionize the shop or factory of their employer? In every trade or community there are many who are opposed to unionism and who stand for freedom of contract. This is their right. Yet the demand for unionism is to compel a man to join their organization or leave the shop."[49] In their conclusions the committee struck sharply at working-class initiatives to control production, especially criticizing the growing numbers of struggles around the issue of apprentice limitation. Like the monumental US Special Report of the Commissioner of Labor, the employers were scathing in their indictment of "soldiering," "ca'canny," and other modes of restricting "the output of our factories": "Labour unions in general refuse to work 'by the piece' and the daily output in many lines notwithstanding the introduction of labour-saving machinery is not more than two-thirds of what it was a few years ago. No man, nor any body of men, have the right to retard so unreasonably the growth of our national trade and commerce."[50] Out of the committee's dissatisfaction flowed a "Declaration of Principles" regarding "the labour question," subsequently adopted by the association. In language similar to that used by proponents of the open shop in the United States, all the major arguments against the aggressive craft unionism of the early twentieth century were transferred to Canadian settings.[51]

These developments added fuel to the anti-union fires burning in the breasts of many local employers. The most typical response of industrial capital, it seems, was to precipitate strikes, often in periods of economic crisis when labour could ill afford costly work stoppages, in the hope of ridding itself of the irksome presence of the trade unions. The employers' assault had begun to check the growth of trade unionism by 1905, but they never managed to drive the unions completely from the field. In March 1908 the *Industrial Banner* reported on what it considered to be the dismal record of one open-shop campaigner:

> The Toronto Employers' Association, which has deliberately forced two-thirds of all the strikes occurring in Toronto during the last three years, is apparently disappointed with the results of that struggle. Despite the loss of thousands of dollars in these unnecessary battles, and the further loss of additional thousands in profits as a result of demoralization in business, they have not succeeded in destroying a single union; in fact, the contest has had a directly opposite effect. The machinists and plumbers, who have both borne the especial brunt of the attack, are as confident and determined as they were months ago.[52]

It was in this context of stalemate on the economic front, then, that capital was forced to adopt other, more indirect, means of repression.

For decades legislation had been a bone of contention between workingman and employer. *Industrial Canada* insisted that it was essential that "no legislation should be adopted which will place our Canadian manufacturers at a disadvantage."[53] From this premise the CMA consistently lobbied to roll back all pieces of legislation that appeared to grant concessions to organized labour. In 1901 the Alien Labour bill was amended so "that nothing in this Act should be taken to prevent the importation of skilled labour requisite to the development of . . . industry in Canada."[54] Labour representatives, in their attempts to introduce legislation aimed at bettering the lot of their constituencies, also met the stern resistance of the CMA. The legalization of the union label was successfully blocked, while attempts to introduce eight-hour bills in the House of Commons were persistently deflected.[55] Employers also sought to promote legislation useful to their cause, bills prohibiting American labour officials from operating in Canada, restraining the activities of striking workmen, and attacking "foreign agitators," all gaining unqualified support from the CMA and local employers.[56]

The courts, too, became transformed into arenas of the growing conflict. It was the injunction, the tried and true method of legalized opposition to labour's demands and actions, and the suit for damages which were perhaps the most useful tools in capital's legal struggle to stifle opposition. Probably taking its cue from the famous Taff Vale case in Britain, the Metallic Roofing Company of Toronto, owned and operated by J.O. Thorn, chairman of the Toronto branch of the CMA, launched the systematic use of the weapon in 1902.[57] After prolonged attempts to secure the union shop in the Thorn concern, Local No 30 of the Amalgamated Sheet Metal Workers International Association abandoned negotiations, informing workers in the trade that "on or after August 20, your men refuse to handle any products of the Metallic Roofing Company of Toronto, as they are unfair to organized labour."[58] The company immediately secured an injunction restraining the boycott and brought a suit of damages against the union. In 1905 Thorn was awarded $7500, but the union stalled payment by appeals to higher courts. Both capital and labour recognized the importance of the case, *Industrial Canada* stressing that it was of "the greatest importance to every manufacturer in Canada," and the *Toiler* contending that it was "the battle of all trade union organizations." Not until 1909 was the dispute resolved, plaintiff and defendant calling off the feud with a quiet, undisclosed agreement.[59] In the meantime, however, other employers were quick to follow Thorn's pioneering example. Two of the better known cases, the H. Krug Furniture Company's action of 1903 and the Gurney campaigns of 1903 and 1905 against prominent members of various metal trades unions, the Toronto Trades and Labour Council, and the *Toiler*, siphoned the strength of picketing and boycotting as union tactics and severely hampered the effectiveness of many strikes. Just how heavy-handed the courts could be was revealed in orders given to that labour council during the Gurney boycott of 1903, restraining it "from interfering with or intimidating the company's workmen; from wrongfully interfering with the company's customers; from boycotting its goods and from publishing wrongful statements that they are made by incompetent workmen; and from wrongfully and maliciously conspiring against the company"; the council also had to pay for "damages for having already committed these acts."[60]

Employers supplemented these organizational, legislative, and judicial efforts with a drive to flood southern Ontario cities with foreign workmen. Such a tactic served the purposes of employers well, for immigrant workers could often be used to break strikes and, in generally increasing the supply of labour, they undermined the strength of craft bodies, whose power traditionally resided in their ability to restrict labour's availability. But, because the unions were most often entrenched in the more highly skilled trades, recruitment necessarily had to attract a like class of workmen; unskilled labour posed a relatively minor threat to the trade unions.

In their attempts to import such labour, Canadian industrialists and manufacturers were somewhat restricted by the Alien Labour Act, originally passed in 1897 in retaliation against American alien labour legislation. Although amended in 1901 in the employers' favour, the act retained some force in this period. James E. Merrick, secretary of the Toronto Employers' Association, was twice taken to court for his pains to secure contract labour from New York to work in two lithographing plants experiencing strikes for union recognition. In one instance the charges were dismissed, while his conviction in the second case brought a minimal $50 fine. A year later the same individual was acquitted on similar charges.[61] In 1906 four Toronto-based companies — the Toronto Carpet Company, run by the president of the CMA, the Freysburgh Cork Company, the Menzie Wall Paper Company, and the Gerhard Heintzman Company — were charged with similar offenses; each company was in the midst of a strike at the time of the transgression.[62] Thus, while the law was never rigorously enforced, the machinery for instituting criminal proceedings was clearly open to unions and their members, and for this reason employers tended to concentrate their efforts on the more distant, but less awkward, British labour market.

The CMA, *Industrial Canada*, and W.T.R. Preston, Canada's commissioner of emigration in Britain, openly encouraged the immigration of skilled English mechanics to Canada.[63] As early as June 1903 the Toronto District Labour Council felt compelled to publish an "Open Letter to the Workmen of the United Kingdom," in which the CMA's portrayal and promise of employment opportunities in Ontario was curtly dismissed as a sham. The letter apparently did little to stop the rising tide of foreign workmen, and the CMA's initiatives met with success after success, culminating that same year in the formation of a privately-run "Canadian Labour Bureau" in England which promised employment in Ontario's rolling mills, machine shops, foundries, building trades, stove works, and agricultural implements plants. Three years later the operation of this bureau, functioning with Preston's complete co-operation, created a minor scandal for the Canadian government.[64]

The stick, however, was not the only means employed by capital to stifle opposition and siphon working-class discontent. A more subtle tactic slowly developed and involved pre-empting the humanitarian appeal of the labour movement by offering employees numerous social amenities associated with the health, safety, recreational, and security requirements of working people. In an article entitled "How about your Factory," *Industrial Canada* argued that "pleasant surroundings are conducive to the economic production of good work, while at the same time they attract a better class of working people."[65] At the Berlin firm of Williams, Greene and Rome, manufacturers of shirts, collars, and cuffs, the "Right Idea," featuring employee dining-rooms, women's rest-rooms, a relief fund, athletic and benefit associations, a complaint department, and dramatic and literary societies, gained province-wide acclaim. The Frost Wire Fence Company, about to locate in Hamilton's East End in 1904, claimed that in its construction plans, "Space has been set apart for a recreation room, which will be fitted up with pool tables and will be nicely furnished. Current literature will be kept on file for those of a more serious turn of mind. Some vacant property adjoining has been acquired, which will be turned into grounds for out-of-door sports, and the company will encourage their employees to enter a team in local hockey, football and baseball leagues."[66]

Behind provisions like these the *Labour Gazette* perceived a conscious purpose: "The officials of the company anticipate that they will get a return for their expenditure in better service from the man."[67] *Industrial Canada* was even more blunt, arguing in a 1912 article, "Homes for Workmen," that "Workmen who have comfortable homes are more efficient, contented and reliable than those who have not . . . Out of the slums stalk the Socialist with his red flag, the Union agitator with the auctioneer's voice, and the Anarchist with his torch."[68] To men like the efficiency-conscious H.L.C. Hall, efforts to alleviate the drudgery of modern work settings made good business sense, and he chastized Canadian manufacturers: "You will spend money every time to increase the efficiency of your machinery. Then why not spend a little time and effort to increase the efficiency of your human machines? It will pay and pay handsomely. It is in some localities quite the fashion to beautify factory buildings and grounds. Civic pride you say. Not a bit of it. Certain wise ones have discovered that it pays to spend a little something on the comfort of the worker. It is a cold business proposition. You get more out of them."[69]

Employer-sponsored welfare schemes for industrial workers were as old as the Industrial Revolution itself, but in the prewar years a new, more sophisticated form of welfare capitalism was emerging throughout southern Ontario.[70] It is crucial to see the development of paternal modes of management as part of a continuum embracing force as well as manipulative coercion. In January 1904 the *Toiler* commented on welfare programmes in an article appropriately entitled "The Wrong Idea": "It can safely be said that the majority of them are designed to protect the firm in a systematic way by keeping the deluded employees under their special care so that they can be more easily robbed of what is their just dues as a return for their labour. These schemes are designed to keep out the trade union or if it is already in to bring about its destruction."[71] For the workingman, welfare capitalism was simply one more chapter in a lengthy book written by capital in which other, preceding sections had been formulated around the themes of mechanization, "scientific management," strikebreaking, and the open shop.

The years 1901–14, then, are an important chapter in the history of Canadian industrial relations. Much of what transpired in this period was, of course, rooted in the nineteenth century. Conflicts which arose in response to mechanization or the abuse of apprenticeship regulations had been common since the 1860s, and often seem strangely archaic in the world of the twentieth century. Yet we should not be surprised that skilled workers continued to resist the encroachments of industrial capitalism, for their adaptation to the new disciplines of the factory had always been uneven and far from complete.[72] And when startlingly new developments were thrust upon them — such as the innovative techniques of an efficiency-conscious management, or the militantly collectivist response of Canadian manufacturers to craft unionism — skilled workers naturally took refuge in the control mechanisms of the past. It is in this context that we have come to regard control as a vital issue in these years, linking the nineteenth and early twentieth century experience of skilled workingmen. From this perspective it would seem that the strike was *not* simply a battle over the division of the economic pie. Like Edward Shorter and Charles Tilly, whose massive compilation of data on strikes in France also stresses the role of craftsmen in pre–World War I industrial conflict, we have come to regard the strike as an implicitly political event, a clash over the distribution of power on the shop or factory floor flowing directly from the desire and ability of working people to act collectively.[73]

NOTES

1. *Bobcaygeon Independent*, 16 May 1913, 2, from an article "One of the Causes of Strikes," reprinted from *The Windsor Record*.
2. Thirty-one strikes occurred in 1901, 48 in 1902, 53 in 1903, 35 in 1904, 24 in 1905, 47 in 1906, 43 in 1907, 7 in 1908, 10 in 1909, 20 in 1910, 24 in 1911, 30 in 1912, 36 in 1913, and 12 in 1914.
3. Penelope Hartland, "Factors in the Economic Growth of Canada," *Journal of Economic History*, XV, 1955, 13; Census of Canada, 1911, III (Ottawa 1913), v. Cf. Gordon D. Bertram, "Historical Statistics on Growth and Structure in Manufacturing in Canada, 1867–1957," in J. Henripin and A. Asimakopulas, eds., Canadian Political Science Association Conference on Statistics, 1962–3, *Papers* (Toronto 1964), 93–146.

4. H.G. Stapells, "The Recent Consolidation Movement in Canadian Industry" (unpublished MA Thesis, University of Toronto, 1922).
5. *Census*, 1911, III, 331.
6. E.P. Thompson, "Time, Work-Discipline and Industrial Capitalism," *Past & Present*, XXXVIII, 1967, 57. Cf Herbert Gutman, "Work, Culture and Society in Industrializing America, 1815–1919," *American Historical Review*, LXXVIII, 1973, 531–88; Sidney Pollard, "Factory Discipline in the Industrial Revolution," *Economic History Review*, XVI, 1963, 254–71.
7. Gregory S. Kealey, "'The Honest Workingman' and Workers' Control: The Experience of Toronto Skilled Workers, 1860–1892," *Labour/Le Travailleur*, 1, 1976, 32–68.
8. David Montgomery, "Workers' Control of Machine Production in the Nineteenth Century," *Labor History*, XVII, 1976, 485–509.
9. George F. Barnett, *Chapters on Machinery and Labor* (Carbondale 1969), 1–29; Barnett, "The Printers: A Study in American Trade Unionism," *American Economic Association Quarterly*, X (Cambridge 1909), 182–208. Cf Wayne Roberts, "The Last Artisans: Toronto Printers, 1896–1914," in Gregory S. Kealey and Peter Warrian, eds., *Essays in Canadian Working Class History* (Toronto 1976), 125–42.
10. Benson Soffer, "A Theory of Trade Union Development: The Role of the 'Autonomous Workman,'" *Labor History*, I, 1960, 141–63.
11. This paragraph draws on material in Bryan Palmer, "Class, Conception and Conflict: The Thrust for Efficiency, Managerial Views of Labor and Working Class Rebellion, 1903–1922," *Review of Radical Political Economy*, VII, 1975, 31–49; David Montgomery, "The 'New Unionism' and the Transformation in Workers' Consciousness, 1909–1922," *Journal of Social History*, VII, 1974, 509–29.
12. *Hamilton Spectator*, 5 Dec. 1906, 1.
13. US Congress, *Final Report and Testimony Submitted to Congress By the Commission on Industrial Relations*, 64th Congress, Senate Document 415 (Washington 1916), X, 9761.
14. *Industrial Canada*, March 1913, 1105–6; April 1913, 1219–23; May 1913, 1349–50; Frederick Winslow Taylor, "The Principles of Scientific Management," in Canadian Club of Ottawa, *Yearbook, 1912–1913* (Ottawa 1913), 115–43.
15. *Industrial Canada*, June 1906, 732–5.
16. *Industrial Canada*, May 1911, 1073–4.
17. Toronto District Labour Council, *Labour Day Souvenir, 1907* (Toronto 1907); Commission on Industrial Training and Technical Education, *Report*, I, 63; II, 173; IV, 2125.
18. Canada, Department of Labour, *Report on Strikes and Lockouts, 1901–1912* (Ottawa 1913), 189.
19. *Labour Gazette*, VI, 1905–6, 673.
20. *Report on Strikes and Lockouts, 1901–12*, 173, 184, 195; *Labour Gazette*, VI, 1905–6, 207; VII, 1906–7, 440, 612. Cf *Labour Gazette*, V, 1904–5, 85; *Report on Strikes and Lockouts, 1901–1912*, 184, 188; *Industrial Banner*, Dec. 1901, 1; Feb. 1903, 1; March 1905, 3; Sept. 1905, 3, on further apprenticeship struggles in Guelph, St. Catharines, and London, where moulders, smithers, painters, and carpet weavers were active.
21. *Labour Gazette*, I, 1900–1, 250, 308; VI, 1905–6, 207, 398; *Industrial Banner*, Sept. 1905, i; Nov. 1905, 3; Jan. 1906, 1; April 1906, 1.
22. *Industrial Banner*, Feb. 1908, 1.
23. *Labor News*, 1 March 1912, 1; 26 July 1912, 1; 2 Jan. 1914, 1.
24. *Labour Gazette*, III, 1902–3, 479, 566; X, 1909–10, 1441; XIII, 1912–13, 1000; *Report on Strikes and Lockouts, 1901–12*, 224; Hugh G.J. Aitken, *Taylorism at Watertown Arsenal* (Cambridge 1960), 15.
25. See *Industrial Banner*, May 1903, 2; Royal Commission on a Dispute Respecting Hours of Employment between the Bell Telephone Company of Canada and Operators at Toronto, Ontario, *Report* (Ottawa, 1907), 7, 13, 55–60, 98.

26. Royal Commission on Bell Dispute, *Report*, 13.
27. Ibid., 5–7.
28. Cf accounts on the strike in *Labour Gazette*, VII, 1906–7, 922; Alice Klein and Wayne Roberts, "Beseiged Innocence: The 'Problem' and the Problems of Working Women — Toronto, 1896–1914," in *Women at Work: Ontario, 1850–1930* (Toronto 1974), 244–51; R. MacGregor Dawson, *William Lyon Mackenzie King: A Political Biography*, I: *1874–1923* (Toronto 1958), 144–6.
29. For background on these developments see Bryan D. Palmer, "'Give us the road and we will run it': The Social and Cultural Matrix of an Emerging Labour Movement: The Case of London, 1867–1914," in Kealey and Warrian, eds., *Essays in Canadian Working Class History*, 106–24.
30. *Labour Gazette*, II, 1901–2, 127, 144; XIII, 1912–13, 895.
31. *Industrial Banner*, Sept. 1905, I. Cf *Labour Gazette*, I, 1900–1, 517, 590; IV, 1903–4, 86, 119–20, 308–9, 350; V, 1904–5, 150; VII, 1906–7, 139, 621; VIII, 1907–8, 234–7; XIII, 1912–13, 557–9, for similar control struggles waged by other London skilled workers.
32. *The Toiler*, 27 Feb. 1903, 1.
33. *Labour Gazette*, XII, 1911–12, 196, 784.
34. F.S. Spence, "The Shorter Hours Movement," Toronto Trades and Labour Council, *Labour Day Souvenir, 1900* (Toronto 1900), 13.
35. On the inflationary surge of these years in southern Ontario see Canada, Department of Labour, Board of Inquiry into the Cost of Living, *Report* (Ottawa 1915), II, 3, 76, 80, 381; *Labour Gazette*, III, 1902–3, 308; V, 1904–5, 308, 437, 556, 689; VI, 1905–6, 388; VII, 1906–7, 689, 1082; XVIII, 1907–8, 271; X, 1909–10, 864; XI, 1910–11, 49, 53; XIV, 1913–14, 770; *Industrial Banner*, Feb. 1912, 4.
36. K.G.J.C. Knowles, *Strikes — A Study in Industrial Conflict* (Oxford 1952), 219.
37. Louis C. Reed, *The Labour Philosophy of Samuel Gompers* (New York 1930), 30.
38. On the rise of the AFL in Canada see Robert Babcock, *Gompers in Canada: A Study in American Continentalism Before the First World War* (Toronto 1974).
39. J. Castell Hopkins, *The Canadian Annual Review of Public Affairs, 1903* (Toronto 1904), 559; *Industrial Canada*, Jan. 1905, 379.
40. Clarence E. Bonnett, *Employers' Associations in the United States* (New York 1922), esp. 63; *The Toiler*, 2 Dec. 1904, 3, which noted the case of the National Metal Trades Council, on whose executive sat G.W. Watts of Toronto and J.M. Taylor of Guelph.
41. On the proliferation of these practices see *The Toiler*, 9 April 1903, 3; *Industrial Banner*, Dec. 1903, 3; Jan. 1904, 1; Oct. 1905, 1; May 1906, 2; Sept. 1906, 1; May 1908, 1; Aug. 1908, 1; July 1911, 1.
42. *The Toiler*, 10 July 1903, 1.
43. Bonnett, *Employers' Associations*, 109, 117–18.
44. On Kirby's visit and the working-class response to it see *The Toiler*, 6 Feb. 1903, 3; 15 May 1903, 1; *Industrial Banner*, Feb. 1903, 1; May 1903, 1.
45. *Labour Gazette*, VI, 1905–6, 279–88.
46. Ibid., III, 1902–3, 374.
47. Ibid., 375–6.
48. Quoted in Michael J. Piva, "The Decline of the Trade Union Movement in Toronto, 1900–1915" (paper delivered before the Canadian Historical Association Meetings, 1975), 8.
49. *Industrial Canada*, Oct. 1903, 133; Nov. 1905, 280.
50. Ibid., Oct. 1903, 133–4.
51. Ibid., 134.
52. *Industrial Banner*, March 1908, 1.
53. *Industrial Canada*, 20 Nov. 1900, 107.
54. Ibid., 22 April 1901, 233.

55. Ibid., 22 April 1901, 233; Sept. 1902, 90; Oct. 1903, 131; July 1904, 586.

56. Trades and Labour Congress of Canada, *Proceedings of the Annual Convention, 1909* (Toronto 1909), 58; Trades and Labour Congress of Canada, *Proceedings, 1910* (Toronto 1910), 54; *Industrial Canada*, Oct. 1903, 131; Aug. 1903, 13.

57. See John Saville, "Trade Unions and Free Labour: The Background to the Taff Vale Decision," in Asa Briggs and John Saville, ed., *Essays in Labour History* (London 1960), 317–50. The case of Metallic Roofing is also discussed in Wayne Roberts, "Artisans, Aristocrats, and Handymen: Politics and Trade Unionism among Toronto Skilled Building Trade Workers, 1896–1914," *Labour/Le Travailleur*, I, 1976, 92–121.

58. Ontario, Bureau of Labour, *Annual Report*, 1905, 180.

59. *Industrial Canada*, Oct. 1903, 205; *The Toiler*, 3 April 1903, 4; Trades and Labour Congress of Canada, *Proceedings, 1906*, 76.

60. Ontario, Bureau of Labour, *Annual Report*, 1903, 179, 195; *The Toiler*, 19 June 1903, 2; Ontario, Bureau of Labour, *Annual Report*, 1905, 169, 180; *Industrial Canada*, Dec. 1903, 288; Trades and Labour Congress of Canada, *Proceedings, 1906*, 9–10; *Proceedings, 1905*, 16, on the use of the injunction and the union response.

61. Ontario, Bureau of Labour, *Annual Report*, 1905, 178–83; *Annual Report*, 1906, 138.

62. Canada, Department of Labour, *Annual Report, 1906–1907* (Ottawa 1908), 111–12, *Labour Gazette*, VII, 1906–7, 612.

63. *Industrial Canada*, May 1903, 436; June 1903, 480; May 1912, 1158–61; Hopkins, *Canadian Annual Review*, 1903, 556.

64. On the successful importation of foreign workmen see *Industrial Canada*, Oct. 1903, 129; Oct. 1907, 208–9; Oct. 1908, 235; S.D. Clark, *The Canadian Manufacturers' Association* (Toronto 1939), 47; *Labour Gazette*, IV, 1903–4, 150; *The Toiler*, 19 June 1903, 1; *The Tribune*, 26 May 1906, 1, 4; 7 April 1906, 1; May 1906, 1. The scandal, which revealed the government's involvement in the importation of strikebreakers, Preston's corrupt acceptance of large sums of money, and bonuses and subsidies to firms engaged in the increasingly lucrative promotion of immigration, is chronicled in *The Tribune*, 26 May 1906, 4.

65. *Industrial Canada*, 2 June 1902, 354. Cf *Industrial Canada*, April 1901, 205; March 1909, 664.

66. Canada, Department of Labour, *Annual Report, 1907–1908* (Ottawa 1908), 26; *Industrial Canada*, Dec. 1904, 327.

67. *Labour Gazette*, V, 1904–5, 466.

68. *Industrial Canada*, May 1912, 1064.

69. Ibid., Sept. 1906, 105.

70. See the accounts of various welfare schemes in *Labour Gazette*, V, 1904–5, 136; IX, 1908–9, 744; XI, 1910–11, 1056, 1352; III, 1902–3, 83; XIV, 1913–14, 757.

71. *The Toiler*, 22 Jan. 1904, 1. For an analysis of the management thinking behind welfare capitalism at International Harvester (whose Hamilton plant was one of the city's largest) see Robert Ozanne, *A Century of Labour–Management Relations at McCormick and International Harvester* (Madison 1967), 71–95.

72. See Gutman, "Work, Culture, and Society," 531–88; Thompson, "Time, Work-Discipline, and Industrial Capitalism," 56–97; Frank Thistlethwaite, "Atlantic Migration of the Pottery Industry," *Economic History Review*, X, 1957–8, 264–73; Sidney Pollard, *The Genesis of Modern Management* (Cambridge 1965), 160–200; Peter Stearns, *Lives of Labour: Work in a Maturing Industrial Society* (London 1975), 342–3; Stearns, "Adaptation to Industrialization: German Workers as a Test Case," *Central European History*, IV, 1970, 303–31.

73. Edward Shorter and Charles Tilly, *Strikes in France, 1830–1968* (London 1974). Cf Charles Tilly, Louise Tilly, Richard Tilly, *The Rebellious Century, 1830–1930* (Cambridge 1975); and a brilliant local study, Peter Friedlander, *The Emergence of U.A.W. Local 229, Hamtrack, Michigan: A Study in Class and Culture* (Pittsburgh 1975). Our conclusions,

then, stand counterposed to those of Peter Stearns, who regards the main impetus behind strikes as the struggle for economic gain,realized in higher wages. See Stearns, *Revolutionary Syndicalism and French Labor: A Cause without Rebels* (New Brunswick 1971).

SIX

Domestic Service: The YWCA and Women's Employment Agencies in Vancouver, 1898–1915

ROBIN JOHN ANDERSON

Anyone familiar with the moral economy of the progressive era knows the awful reputation of commercial employment agencies before the First World War. Employment agents were accused of a litany of humanitarian and economic transgressions, including fraud, theft, moral degradation and the stimulation of unemployment. The issue of the employment "shark" became so heated that an international movement calling for the abolition of private job agencies and their replacement by labour exchanges emerged before World War One. This movement offered a "scientific" alternative to commercial agencies, a language of criticism and an impressive cadre of British, American and Canadian experts to carry the message. While these labour exchange theorists and their followers recognized unemployment as an inevitable feature of the capitalist system, the labour exchange was never meant to interfere with industry; rather, the exchange system was a preventative overlay which was meant to assist industry and workers, while preserving, to varying degrees, ideals of self-initiative and personal responsibility.[1] Commercial agencies, North American relics of an unorganized and inefficient world of competitive capitalism, stood in the way of the labour exchange movement and were therefore attacked by American and Canadian reformers after 1910.

Historians have done little to test the negative stereotype of employment agencies constructed by reformers. One immediate problem with the traditional critique is its almost complete disregard of women's employment agencies. The stereotypical agent was male, and his clients were invariably presented as transient male labourers working in casual urban employment or on railway construction. Yet in most Canadian and American cities, up to one-third of commercial agencies were for women workers. This study examines the rise of Vancouver employment agencies for women

Source: Excerpted from "Domestic Service: The YWCA and Women's Employment Agencies in Vancouver, 1898–1915," *Histoire sociale/Social History*, 25, 50 (November 1992): 307–32. Reprinted by permission of *Histoire sociale/Social History*.

in the two decades before World War One. At the centre of this discussion is the issue of abuse of workers by employment agents. The evidence presented in this paper, however, suggests that the positive functions of women's employment agencies far outweighed the abuses attributed to them by social reformers. Commercial agencies proliferated, not because they tricked or defrauded workers, but because they served a practical function in the labour market.

The job-find process was not the sole preserve of commercial agents. In Vancouver, the Young Women's Christian Association played an important role in importing and distributing paid household immigrant workers. The YWCA also operated an employment bureau for domestics, and consequently there developed a tension between the YWCA and commercial agencies over the securing of these women workers. It is argued here that the directors of the YWCA were more closely connected to the domestic employers than the household servants with whom they worked. The stories of commercial agency abuse in fact had more to do with the self-serving motives of reformers and employers, and less to with the actions of women's employment agents.

THE STRUCTURE OF THE VANCOUVER EMPLOYMENT BUSINESS

Commercial employment agencies had existed in Vancouver since the city's founding in 1886, but these multiplied in number between 1898 and 1915 in response to local and regional labour demands associated with the rapid growth in resource industries, railway building, city construction, women's domestic service and "new" service work outside the home. In all, some 138 agencies opened and (often quickly) closed their doors between 1898 and 1915.[2] These agencies reflected the racial and sexual divisions within Vancouver's regional labour market and the contours of that market over time. As a result, three distinct agency sectors emerged before World War One: a large group of agencies for white males and two smaller groups for Asian males and white women. Each of these groups was more or less distinct; each tended to locate in different commercial neighbourhoods in order to attract its particular clientele.

Commercial employment agencies also reflected sectoral or occupational structures as these changed over time. Thus, as the importance of Asian male domestic labour declined in the new century because of an increase of white women and increased racial exclusion, the women's domestic agency emerged. The economic downturn in 1907–1908 severely hampered the activities of men's agencies, but did not affect women's domestic agencies since household servants were hired mostly by middle-class employers. The 1913–1916 depression, however, forced many employment offices for women out of business, when the slight occupational expansion for women into service and clerical jobs outside the home came to a sudden end. After the autumn of 1913, the remaining women's agencies offered little work other than domestic service. Each employment business sector responded to seasonal labour market demands as well. For white and Asian males in resource industries, construction, agriculture or railway building, this activity was fairly predictable: a strong spring, an active summer, fall slowdowns and a dead winter. Women's agencies followed the seasonal rhythms of the home, child-care and the city's social calendar. Thus, in December, when men's agencies were depressed, desperate or dead, women's agencies were bustling with activity as Vancouver's middle class hired on help for the holiday season.

Employment agencies for women also marked the fundamental segregation of women's and men's work. Employers contributed to and profited from this division by encouraging the recruitment of low-waged women workers into socially-defined women's jobs. Women workers typically earned, on average, between one-half and two-thirds of men's earnings. The average weekly wage for women in Vancouver was sixty-three percent of the male rate in 1911.[3] Segregation was bound, however, not simply by employer avarice but by an ideology of gender that stressed the domestic role for women as proper, natural and subordinate to the male experience.[4] As a result, women's wage labour confirmed women's role as primary domestic workers dependent on men — women were not expected or encouraged to be breadwinners. Areas of paid work consequently deemed appropriate for women before the war were in domestic or servile occupations, including household help, service work in stores, restaurants, hotels and hospitals and, increasingly, clerical-professional jobs as stenographers, typists and teachers.[5] Women working outside these areas were the exceptions. Women's employment agencies, most of which were run by women, profited from the segregated labour market by bringing together working women and appropriate jobs. Yet within the confines of proper women's work was a changing women's labour force. At the turn of the century, a majority of women previously employed as household workers were moving into new service occupations outside the home.[6] Women's agencies also reflected this transition, as the jobs offered women by agents kept pace with labour market changes. In this sense, employment agencies performed a function in the labour market by remaining responsive and flexible to employment conditions.

DOMESTIC SERVICE AND THE RISE OF EMPLOYMENT AGENCIES

While women's occupations expanded slowly within socially-defined limits, a mainstay of employment continued to be paid household labour. Women wage workers made up a minority of the city's total workforce, but their employment agencies took a disproportionately large share of the city's employment business. In 1910, only one out of eight workers living in Vancouver was a woman. However, in 1912, employment agencies dedicated to women's work comprised one-third of all active agencies.[7] The number of women's agencies therefore was related only indirectly to the number of women workers. Agency totals were determined instead by the nature of domestic labour, the structure of its labour market and the special demands of Vancouver households before World War One.

Employment agencies in general were attracted to areas of casual and seasonal labour where turnover was high, and paid household labour was particularly transient. While space limits a full discussion of the hardships of domestics, British, American and Canadian studies have identified those problems which were universal to household wage work. These included the negative association of housework with woman's work, the often-difficult employer–servant relationship due to an atomized and unregulated workplace, and the gruelling nature of household work itself.[8] As well, many young women used domestic service as an initial point of entry to the workforce before taking up other kinds of work; others left domestic service to get married. For these reasons, domestic service was chronically plagued by labour shortages and high turnover from New York to Toronto to Vancouver. To make matters even more volatile, the supply of domestics was always higher in the East than the West. With European immigrants filling the domestic ranks, disembarking ports such as Halifax and Montreal had a supply advantage over western cities. The wider gap between supply and demand was reflected in higher wage-rates received by domestics on the West coast.[9]

The severe shortage of domestic help overwhelmed most middle-class women in Vancouver before the First World War. In 1907, the National Council of Women of Canada (NCWC) held its annual meeting in Vancouver and local women used the opportunity to vent their domestic concerns in a passionately expressed resolution: "That in view of the present difficulties surrounding domestic life in Canada, the impossibility of procuring women to help in housekeeping, causing a situation that threatens to entirely annihilate our homes, the National Council appoint a Committee" to increase the numbers of domestic workers.[10] Because domestics also left service due to its poor status, women's groups tried to raise the profile of household work by introducing the element of professionalization offered by domestic science or training. The NCWC's 1907 *Annual Report* claimed that importing servants from "all over the world" would not solve the servant shortage; rather, "things will not be right until our Canadian Women learn to glory in homemaking instead of despising it."[11] Vancouver's Women's Council was less convinced of the merits of domestic training, fearing that proper training would only raise already "exorbitant" domestic wages.[12]

The domestic's awareness of constant servant shortages probably contributed more to high turnover than anything else. As Lacelle notes, quitting was the most frequent method used by household workers to express job dissatisfaction. "People in service," she writes, "had a sovereign remedy when ill-treated — they changed employers."[13] With the knowledge of a labour market tipped in their favour, domestics might change jobs four or five times a year.[14]

High turnover and publicized domestic shortages drew employment agents into the domestic placement business. This was as true for Vancouver as it was for New York. However, we know very little about Vancouver's labour market for paid household servants before the First World War. Was there, for instance, something particular about domestic work or any other women's work in Vancouver that contributed to the success of women's employment agencies? In an effort to answer this question, a study was made of some 1,500 newspaper want ads for women workers over three years, 1911–1913. These years were chosen for a number of reasons. First, they include both boom and depression years and, thus, provide a fuller view of domestic service's changing demands through good and bad economic times. Secondly, these years reflect changes in the wider labour market for women, as clerical, retail and industrial work increased its share of women's employment at domestic service's expense. Of course, the pre-war depression, which made itself felt in the women's service job market by the summer of 1913, reversed this trend until the war economy geared up in 1916; unemployed clerical, retail and industrial women workers threw themselves into the domestic labour market, creating, it would appear for the first time, a surplus of household servants.[15]

Of the 1,483 advertisements for female workers recorded between January 1911 and December 1913, 685 (46 percent) asked for domestic servants of one form or another. Of these 685 requests, 437 (64 percent) gave no information other than that a "servant" or "help" was required and the address or telephone of the employer. The remaining 248 ads, however, specified duties and these were separated into 7 types:

general, general/nanny, nanny/nurse, mother's help, cook, cook/general and washer-woman (laundress). Employment related to children — 178 (26 percent) of all jobs — comprised the largest specified group. The second largest grouping — cooks and cook/generals — was specified 55 times. Washerwomen were sought only 14 times. Other than outlining duties, over 200 of the ads contained specific requests or discrete bits of information meant either as inducements or as warnings to applicants. Thirty-seven ads, for instance, asked specifically for "live-out" servants. Twenty-six wanted half-day workers, 24 asked for half-week duties or less, and 7 wanted to hire full-time domestics for a specific but temporary length of time — from one week to a couple of months. Other key requests were for specific ethnic (20) or religious (6) preferences, that no washing (21) or care of children (20) was required, or warnings that the employers were single men (19). The most frequent information offered, however, was the admission of a "small family." Whether this was meant as an inducement or as a warning against children is unclear.

This survey of employer requests supports many of the conclusions drawn elsewhere about domestic service. That less than half (46 percent) of the "Help Wanted" ads were for paid domestic workers, for example, reflects the growth of retail, manufacturing and clerical jobs for women; a similar browse through classified ads at the turn of the century reveals a women's employment market dominated by paid household work.[16] That so many employers specifically asked for "live-out" workers, rather than resident servants, mirrors the change found elsewhere from live-in to outside help — a change symbolized by the semantic shift from the live-in "servant" to the live-out "housekeeper."[17] Vancouver, however, might have always had a higher proportion of live-out domestic help; a good deal of the requests came from areas of the city — East and South Vancouver — where smaller houses, less suited for live-in help, were common. Thirty-nine ads, for instance, were placed by apartment dwellers. The oft-made request for a "young girl" or a "middle-aged woman" might have reflected more than a concern over wages, susceptibility to training, or steadiness: both might have had homes to return to in the evening. Finally, the low number of laundresses requested, coupled with the frequent inducement of "no washing," was a testament to the growth of steam laundries in the city.

Employer requests showed, above all, the extent to which domestic service in Vancouver was linked to the birth and care of children, and the service's dependence on child-care encouraged labour turnover. Nurses, nannies and mother's helps made up the overwhelming majority of specified ads (72 percent) and a significant percentage of the total domestics requested (26 percent). A healthy portion of the 437 unspecified requests undoubtedly would have been child-related as well. The fact that some ads took space to inform applicants that "no children" were in the home emphasizes the extent to which child-care dominated paid household work. Most of the child-related requests appear to have been meant as half-time or temporary positions. Many, for instance, required help only mornings, evenings or a couple of days per week. "Nursegirls" were often requested for a "maternity period" only — as were some nannies. Some child-related positions were meant to be long term, but most were not.

Thus, Vancouver's job market for domestic workers was active because of the nature of household work. Perhaps half of all domestic workers were employed to serve half-time, short-term, often child-related demands in middle-class homes. This encouraged turnover, not simply because jobs were task-specific, but because child-care was a difficult task. The frequency within the sample of the warnings "small family" and "no children" testifies to an overt tension between domestics and employers' children. How many servants quit their jobs because of the trials of child-care, however, is unknown.

Domestic service, like logging and railroad construction, had its own seasonal patterns. The annual expansions and contractions were perceptible in Vancouver's employment market and they helped to increase turnover. In the three-year period covered by the want ad survey, employment opportunities for household workers were strongest in the spring (a traditional period of housecleaning), declined in the summer and fell even further in the fall to a low usually in November. Bi-monthly reports on labour market conditions produced by the Department of Labour reinforce this conclusion.[18] As well as following annual rhythms, domestic employment expanded during seasonal high points, such as Christmas, Easter and summer outings, when temporary help was engaged. Ads for household help, for instance, reached annual lows in November and early December, but by the middle of December, requests would double. Many of these Christmas requests were for cooks and "dining room girls" in larger West end homes. Thus, along with the very nature of domestic work, seasonal patterns helped to stimulate even further the turnover of paid household servants. The result was a domestic labour market full of motion and, needless to say, an irresistible lure to employment middlemen — or in this case, middle-women.

THE YWCA AND DOMESTIC EMPLOYMENT

We do not know how most domestics in Vancouver found work. Many probably found jobs through informal means — through friends, relatives or word-of-mouth. The survey of Vancouver domestic "Help Wanted" advertisements indicates the importance of direct contacts between mistress and servant through newspapers. Yet the atomized domestic workplace meant that the job market for women domestic workers was managed by commercial and philanthropic agencies to an extent unmatched by any other form of men's or women's work. High labour turnover drew self-interested agents into the domestic employment business, while chronic labour shortages brought in the YWCA and other middle-class organizations. In one sense, the voluntary and commercial forces never competed for the patronage of workers or employers. The YWCA helped to promote and receive single immigrant women into the city, provide them with secure lodging, a morally-uplifting environment, and, eventually, place them in an employer's home. After this initial introduction to the local domestic market, however, the role of the YWCA declined and that of the commercial agency grew for women who needed intermediaries to find employment. Commercial agents offered a wider range of jobs, in and out of domestic service, and did so without overt moral aims or the same degree of employer influence.

In another sense, the YWCA and commercial agencies were incompatible. Middle-class protectors of young women argued that commercial agencies could not be expected to shield working women from "emissaries of evil."[19] Employment agencies were widely-held to be uncritical exploiters of young women at best and, at worst, fronts for prostitution and white-slavery. "Many of the female employment agencies in the United States are but agencies for the recruiting of the white slave traffic," declared the *Western Clarion* in 1912; "in Vancouver similar agencies have been established."[20] Fraudulent job advertisements placed by "bogus agencies" were the greatest danger, according to the National Council of Women of Canada. "The insertion in newspapers of misleading and criminal advertisements which lure young girls, looking for honourable employment, into lives of sin and shame, should be suppressed," demanded the NCWC Committee on the White Slave Traffic in 1907.[21] The NCWC joined the YWCA in 1911 to combat white slavery by placing articles in local newspapers warning women against using employment agencies and/or replying to their want ads.[22] For these moral reasons, the YWCA was the first choice of many employers looking for household help, but the association was unable to fill these needs adequately. The huge demand, coupled with the structure of domestic service already mentioned, contributed to the dramatic growth of women's commercial agencies after 1909. The YWCA was more dedicated to the interests of employers than were employment agents; employment agents were dedicated to none but themselves.

In a recent study of English Canadian moral reform before World War One, Mariana Valverde examines the moral panic surrounding the alleged white slave trade. Valverde admits that the trade was likely illusory but necessarily "constructed" as an ideological site upon which real social and moral fears were expressed and discussed: "The fears that underlay the white slavery panic — young women moving to cities and taking up new occupations, urban anonymity, immigration, the breakdown of traditional networks of support and social control — were the fears of a large sector of the Canadian population. Anglo-Saxon middle-class Protestants were somewhat uncertain about their ability to manage the drastic changes in social, economic and cultural relations taking place in turn-of-the-century Canada in such a way as to preserve their newly won economic superiority and cultural hegemony."[23] Valverde goes beyond this sociological explanation to offer a discourse analysis of white slavery rhetoric and an explanation for its mass acceptance. She shows, for instance, that published tales of slavery followed similar narrative forms, and these often included deception by familiar or apparently benevolent characters, such as matronly women and widows. The women's employment agent fit the stereotype rather nicely; the employment agency — a place of outward opportunity — became a deceptive trap when placed in the gothic tale of female abduction.[24] Stories of white slavery commonly were critical of women's new wage work outside of the home, and included restaurants, shops and department stores as sites of procurement and abduction. Reformist studies of white slavery were less subtle, identifying most non-domestic urban experiences as causes of the traffic. Not surprisingly, stories of rescue invariably included domestic training as a means of moral purification.[25] The employment agent who offered jobs outside the home did not fare well in this moral economy.

Valverde's presentation of white slavery as a symbolic experience knowable at the level of language is original and revealing, yet there may be, at the individual or community level, a host of supporting material motives that better explain the phenomenon's specific success. For instance, when a commonly-conceived material need and powerful ideological support met, as they did in Vancouver with shortages of domestic servants and tales of white slavery, the marriage between self-service and ideology was inevitable. Much of the strength of the white slavery myth in Vancouver was related to middle-class concerns about domestic servants. The YWCA in particular tried to use this potent myth to overcome unfavourable household conditions.

From the time of the YWCA's arrival in Vancouver in 1897, the organization wedded its traditional material and spiritual concerns with the housekeeping demands of the city's middle-class women. Most pressing of these was the shortage of competent,

reliable domestic help. Many of the local Y's efforts therefore were taken up with channelling newly-arrived women immigrants into local homes. In 1899, the organization
opened the city's first employment bureau to deal exclusively with female domestic
servants.[26] The bureau promised employers "competent, reliable and trustworthy"
servants, and set about recruiting "efficient, desirable help" from abroad.[27] The organization worked closely in its immigration efforts with the British Women's Emigration Association (BWEA) to bring out parties of young women under matrons'
care. The BWEA was created to solve the sex ratio imbalance in urban Britain and its
colonies by encouraging British working women to emigrate. The British organization
would sponsor groups only if the entire route were fully escorted and the travellers
were housed in secure hostels at their final destination.[28] The Vancouver chapter of
the YWCA satisfied these BWEA demands. In fact, the two organizations were joined
in Vancouver: local Y President Annie Skinner was also the long-time regional secretary of the BWEA.[29] Just how many women entered Vancouver under joint BWEA–
YWCA sponsorship is unknown because of inconsistent record-keeping. However, we
do know that the annual number of individual BWEA sponsored parties increased
from 7 in 1906 to 17 in 1913. Approximately 10 girls comprised a party, and most of
these groups arrived between April and October.[30] As well as these fully sponsored
parties, BWEA agents also recruited domestic workers on behalf of the Vancouver
YWCA at immigrant centres in eastern Canada. In 1912, for instance, hundreds of
women travelling without BWEA sponsorship were intercepted by BWEA/YWCA
agents in Quebec: "Many of these women," writes Skinner, "were advised and
helped to obtain suitable positions in Vancouver."[31] In 1906 (a year for which we
have figures), some 350 immigrant women were recruited into household work in
this way.

The Vancouver YWCA was also allied with the Traveller's Aid society, another
British women's organization out of London. "The object of this work," Skinner spoke
of the Society, "is to guard young women, when travelling alone, whether in search of
employment or otherwise, from the dangers to which young girls are exposed."[32] The
local YWCA sent, on behalf of the Traveller's Aid Society, two uniformed women to
meet every incoming train. From there, both sponsored and unexpected travellers,
"young and attractive and utterly unconscious of any danger," were scurried off to the
YWCA annex, where it was "impossible for any evil influence to lead them astray."[33]
Like BWEA recruitment work, the local YWCA presidents personally supervised the
work of the Traveller's Aid Society, considering it "the most important part of our work
here."[34] According to Y directors, Vancouver's "special function" in the worldwide
YWCA family was the care of strangers.[35] YWCA officials linked the work of the
Traveller's Aid with the dangers of white slavery. Before the advent of the Traveller's
Aid, writes Skinner, "there were few lodging places at reasonable rates in desirable
localities, and young girls were often compelled to go to cheap hotels, where they
were thrown in the way of undesirable acquaintances, often with disastrous results."[36]
For this reason, the Traveller's Aid Society came to an arrangement with the CPR to
have a permanent office at the train station and to placard the building with notices
warning of white slavers.[37] Although the total number of travellers met by Traveller's
Aid is unknown, it would appear that the agents were kept extremely busy, especially
during the summer months. In 1907, for instance, the Society assisted over 500 travellers; this had increased to 600 in 1908 and, in 1909, close to 2,000 women were
met by Traveller's Aid.[38]

Whether immigrants or travellers, the women brought to the YWCA annex were encouraged to seek work through the Y's domestic employment bureau or to upgrade their household skills through the Y's Education Department. The bureau was under some pressure by employers to perform its placement function. Part of this pressure was financial. The operating expenses of the Immigration and Employment Department — brought together to co-ordinate the work of the BWEA, the Traveller's Aid and the Employment Bureau — were heavily subsidized by civic and provincial government grants. YWCA directors, always proud of the self-supporting character of virtually all of the organization's other services, were repeatedly irritated by the rising costs of the Immigration and Employment Department. Vancouver YWCA President Peter complained in 1912 that the department had "taxed our finances far more than we had anticipated," and that the government grants of $500 from the province and $1,500 from the city had been entirely gobbled up by the Immigration and Employment Department.[39] Government grants, in fact, did not pay for all of the department's expenses; fees charged to women immigrants, including transportation, accommodation and employment fees, made up anywhere from one-third to three-quarters of the department's annual revenues between 1908 and 1915.[40] The government grants nonetheless ensured a certain degree of accountability, which the directors took very seriously — the organization's success or failure was often publicly measured in terms of domestic labour recruitment and placement.

President Peter claimed that the local Y employment bureau was "one of the largest in Canada," and consistently stressed the close connection between the bureau, immigration work and the placement of domestic workers. But job placement was no easy task. Writes Skinner in 1909: "It has been our great endeavour to find suitable positions for all. I know that many will think of the numerous vacant places here, where help in the home is so badly needed and will say, surely there is no difficulty here. But I can assure you that this, though one of the most important branches of our work, is often the most difficult and perplexing."[41] One of the chronic problems, according to YWCA directors, was the high expectations of women workers who visited the employment bureau. The wages demanded by newly-arrived domestics were always deemed too high, and conditions within homes were never what the women had expected. As a result, YWCA officials warned that "courage, determination and adaptability" would be needed by immigrant women coming to Vancouver.[42]

To ensure that its domestic recruits had a minimum of household skills, Vancouver's YWCA offered a wide range of primarily domestic education courses between 1906 and 1915. Various forms of sewing, cooking, first aid and home nursing dominated YWCA vocational offerings for young women, while very little was done to promote job education outside household skills.[43] Courses of a non-vocational character were common as well, such as bible study, literature, choral singing, expression, foreign language (French and German), china painting and physical training. These courses were available for all women who could pay the fees, but were specifically tailored for "business women" — that is, women who worked in shops or offices. In this sense, Vancouver's YWCA catered quite effectively to the intellectual and recreational needs of non-household workers, but made no efforts to increase their numbers through job education. For example, shorthand — the sole business course offered — was given only in 1906 and 1912. Indeed, the two thrusts of the Y's Education Department were towards leisure activities for business women and domestic training for young wives and paid domestic workers. And this "streaming" was maintained until the middle of World War One. When money was raised to build a new kitchen for domestic science instruction in 1910, directors of the YWCA also lobbied for a "literary club for business women."[44]

It is unclear from the YWCA records who actually enrolled in the courses. Class sizes increased steadily from 1906 onwards, when 150 women registered, to 1913 when enrolment peaked at 400. Fees were charged for all classes; the directors of the YWCA were proud that the Education Department was "on a self-supporting basis." In 1915, however, the Vancouver YWCA abandoned its leisure education classes for business women entirely, citing competition from commercial and municipal night school programmes.[45] Those few courses offered after 1915 — home nursing, first aid and "plain cooking" — were of a domestic bent. The Education Department of the Vancouver YWCA never undermined its fundamental aim of securing an adequate supply and raising the talents of paid household workers. There was nothing in the streaming approach to the classes to encourage non-domestic employment; in fact, courses in household skills would have worked to promote domestic jobs for business women.

The Vancouver YWCA was unable to adequately satisfy employers' needs for paid household help or working women's demands for employment. In terms of employer satisfaction, the household placement rate (number of employer applications compared to number of employers satisfied) began at a high of thirty-seven percent and declined to twenty-five percent thereafter.[46] The YWCA was somewhat embarrassed by this failure to live up to its civic responsibility — a twenty-five percent employer satisfaction rate was difficult to defend. Skinner blamed other cities (Seattle and San Francisco) for luring potential help away from her city. Certainly, the sponsored trainloads of immigrant domestics from the east offset this imbalance somewhat (although it is unclear from the records the degree to which imported workers were incorporated into the statistics). Even so, such obvious failure at a time of extreme domestic labour scarcity pushed the YWCA on the defensive. From 1910 onwards, therefore, statistics on numbers of employers applying for help and those supplied with workers were not made public. The Vancouver YWCA avoided the issue of employer satisfaction with the employment bureau and, instead, defended the institution as a service to women workers.

The Vancouver YWCA also failed over half of the women workers who applied for work at the bureau. Presumably because the rates were more attractive, the records of workers applying and those placed were far more complete than those dealing with employers.[47] Between 1906 and 1915, this placement rate steadily declined from a high of sixty-six percent in 1906 to less than thirty percent in 1915. The 1913–1915 depression helps to explain the low placement rate for those years, but the poor rates during the boom years (1908–1912) point away from the wider economic context and directly at the shortcomings of domestic work and the YWCA itself. Skinner was frank in explaining this failure; women were simply turning down the domestic work offered by the YWCA.[48] By 1909, alternatives to paid household labour were drawing women out of domestic service, and employers and working women were turning to the "emissaries of evil" for help with child-care and housework.[49]

Workers increasingly were ill-served by the YWCA's style of labour distribution as well. Part of this failure was ideological. The high moral tone, class condescension and simple interference in the workers' personal lives were likely stifling for many women workers. When Janet Smith became homesick, an employer suggested she visit one of the counselors at the YWCA; when Janet expressed her fear of a Chinese co-worker (later charged with her murder), the counselor at the Girl's Friendly Society listened, but did not suggest changing employers or occupations.[50] Newly-arrived women under YWCA care had little choice but to accept Y control; the veterans of the domestic wars, however, were more apt to exercise their independence, and apparently they did. Women workers were also ill-served by the YWCA in a vocational sense as well. Vancouver's YWCA training courses and job referrals pointed towards paid household work at a time when working women were rejecting domestic service for ideological and material reasons. That only one-half of those women who applied to the YWCA bureau accepted the work it offered underlined the shortcomings of available domestic work. As women's work changed before World War One, the YWCA was slow to follow. The directors of the YWCA, in particular, remained devoted to the promotion of domestic service, but commercial agents were more pragmatic.

WOMEN'S COMMERCIAL EMPLOYMENT AGENCIES

The story of women's commercial agencies must be told in terms of the history of changing women's work in Vancouver. Agencies reflected the expansions and contractions of acceptable vocational roles for women. Elsewhere, especially in large eastern American cities, women's agencies acquired a loathsome reputation for raising the cost and lowering the efficiency of help, for encouraging labour turnover and shortages, and for being fronts for prostitution and white slavery.[51] Whatever reputation preceded agents, it was ignored by employers and women workers in Vancouver. After the 1907–1908 recession, women's agencies grew rapidly in response to the rising demand for women workers. Most offered a wide range of then-acceptable vocations and were very sensitive to their change. Unlike the YWCA, commercial agencies for women were less concerned with their clients' respectability. The extreme imbalance between the demand for domestic workers and their supply also meant that women's agencies supported their worker-clients even more than men's agencies did. Finally, commercial agencies offered working women a measure of independence that the YWCA did not. If the YWCA was interested in converting working women into loyal, hardworking Christian servants, the "emissaries of evil" simply wanted to increase their own profits — and this often depended upon the freedom of working women to choose.

Women's agencies were slow to develop in Vancouver in part because of the early influence the YWCA had on the recruitment and distribution of domestic servants. An early attempt, The Ladies' Exchange, opened and closed its doors in 1898. Men's agencies would, from time to time, advertise for domestics, but these skid-row agents were badly situated to attract employers. The first agency to specialize in domestics was the Elite Intelligence Bureau, which began business in 1904. The Elite was located on the West side to serve middle-class employers, and dealt almost exclusively in household workers. Women ran the majority of women's agencies; Sadie Stone ran the Elite. The shortage of domestic help hurt the agency, as Stone was always in need of women to fill positions. In 1905, she began to advertise for Chinese male household help in order to satisfy demand, but this was short-lived. Stone also advertised to fill non-household jobs, all of which were service occupations in restaurants and hotels.[52]

The women's employment business mushroomed after 1908 in response to city residential growth. Of the 21 women's agencies that appeared before the war, 17 opened in 1909 or later. These agencies opened to meet the demand for household workers, but advertised non-domestic work as well. Some even became specialists in certain types of new women's work. The Germaine Agency (1912) and The Dominion Employment Bureau (1911–1912), for instance, exclusively dealt in hotel and restaurant help. Germaine's claim, that it was "not here for the short term, but expected to make Vancouver home for a good many years," was not enough to ensure a sustained trade; the agency closed in the same year that it opened. Other offices specialized in what would replace domestic service as the mainstay of women's wage work: clerical and office jobs. Most of these agencies were office equipment companies that ran employment offices on the side. Clarke and Stuart was an early example; in 1904, the typewriter sales and service company promised to furnish women stenographers without charge.[53] After 1908, a handful of other typewriter firms opened employment offices. The Remington Typewriter Company foreshadowed the modern "temp" agencies in the summer of 1911 when it claimed it "pays to do substitute stenographic work during the vacation season."[54] A year later, United Typewriter and The Vancouver Typewriter Company both opened employment bureaus. None of these companies charged employers for the service (it is unclear whether the stenographers paid fees), all promised to "screen" applicants, and all probably offered the employment service as a way of selling more typewriters. For these reasons, The Remington Typewriter Company called itself a "public service company."[55] Commercial colleges in American cities are known to have placed their graduates in clerical positions. The only example of this in Vancouver before World War One was Vogel Commercial College, which ran such ads between 1902 and 1904.[56]

The most active, numerous and enduring women's employment agencies were not specialists, outside of their dependence on domestic workers. Twelve such companies operated between 1909 and 1915. Eight of these were run by women, as were all of the most durable; six were open for three or more years. Little is known about these agencies. The owners' backgrounds, for instance, are unclear, but we do know that the proprietors tended to be widowed, divorced (or separated) or single, and that many came from working-class families. The majority lived on the city's poorer East side. Like the owners of white male agencies, most women agents were newcomers to the city. Even so, some became so well known that their own names preceded that of the company's in promotional advertisements: Alberta Crawford, Bertha Kirk, Sadie Stone, Emma Smith and Emily Brown. Women's agents were most likely working-class women like their working clients.

One of the most successful of these agents was Katherine Maloney of the Universal Female Employment Office. Maloney's activities tell us about the changing nature of women's work, how those changes were accommodated by the employment agents, and to what extent agents served the interests of women wage earners or employers. The Universal bureau was one of the most enduring employment agencies — men's or women's — in the city's early history. Maloney began business in 1910, closed in 1919, and in the interim, moved her office only twice. The Universal was indeed a fixture in Vancouver's employment scene.[57] Maloney arrived in Vancouver in 1909 with her husband John H. Maloney (a machinist who died the following year) and her son, who worked as a janitor at Sam Sell's "Canadian Pacific Employment Agency" (for loggers). Universal was located adjacent to the financial district for the comfort of middle-class employers and women applicants. In 1912, perhaps buoyant times or ill-health forced Maloney to take on a clerk, Alberta Crawford, and a year later, Crawford left Universal to set up her own agency, Central Female Employment. From then on, Maloney ran the office alone until she retired in 1919.

Because Maloney regularly advertised in newspapers, we can begin to chart the long-range patterns of her business. Universal began in 1910–1911 by placing domestics, then expanded its business beyond household help in 1912–1913 and, with the depression of 1913, returned to the domestic trade until Maloney's retirement. Maloney's business roughly mirrored the changing labour market for women until the wartime economy accelerated in 1916. The domestic jobs Maloney offered in 1910–1911 were often related to children, and many required temporary (either daily or weekly) rather than permanent help to reflect the structures of household work.[58] During the 1912–1913 period, Universal expanded to place non-household workers: waitresses, dishwashers and restaurant cooks, hotel chambermaids and hospital workers, seamstresses and tailoresses, and stenographers, bookkeepers and office help.[59] Maloney's business was not limited to Vancouver during this expansive period. She sent restaurant cooks to Victoria, cannery workers up the coast and, on one occasion, teachers to Australia.[60] Maloney's business clearly profited from the apparent expansion of women's employment.

By the fall of 1913, Universal's diversification ended. The depression squeezed Maloney's business and forced her to take some desperate measures. In August 1913, she experimented with commissioned salesmen roaming the city to drum up new employers. At the beginning of September, Maloney tried placing men, and changed her name to reflect this new venture. This was unsuccessful. The Universal's advertisements began to reflect desperation: "AT ONCE" read a September entry: "Thanking my numerous patrons for past favours — hope for the continuance of same."[61] Domestic service was the only work available for women after the summer of 1913, and Maloney slowly realized this. In October, she abandoned the scheme to place men and changed her name to Universal "Domestic" Employment Office.[62] Virtually all of Maloney's itemized advertisements after October 1913 were for household workers.

We may never know how women workers or employers were treated by Katherine Maloney, Alberta Crawford, Emma Smith or the other owners of Vancouver's women's employment offices. There are no records of their correspondence, few comments were made by them or about them in the press, and they were totally ignored by the 1912 BC Commission on Labour — the same body which had investigated at length the activities of men's employment agencies.[63] What records we do have of these agents suggest they performed a needed service for women workers and, because profits and not morality motivated them, they did so without the degree of interference that characterized charity agencies such as the YWCA. That these agencies provided a needed service is unquestionable. Domestics looking for new homes and better positions found a welcome seat in Maloney's waiting room. While the YWCA stressed permanence, Maloney and the other agents thrived on turnover; agent and domestic both gained from the servant's drive for improvement. As well, women wanting to escape the trials of domestic service could never do so at charity agencies. New employment choices, however, did exist at the Universal as long as those jobs were offered in the labour market. The employment office provided a glimpse of change for domestic workers seeking non-domestic work.

Evidence also suggests that Maloney and the other women's agents were more apt to support their worker-clients than the employers who entered their offices. Certainly, American employers thought so. Historian Carol Lasser stresses the positive role of the employment agency in the domestic's manipulation of the labour market in nineteenth-century Boston. Employers were increasingly resentful of being at the mercy of the seller's market for servants; women's agencies, argued employers, conspired against "domestic peace" and the "unity of interest between mistress and maid."[64] Domestic agencies in New York City in the 1880s were blamed for recirculating women unfit for employment: the independent, poor, unhealthy, aged, dishonest or inefficient. American employers also believed that agencies persuaded applicants to demand high wages in an attempt to gain better commissions from employers.

Canadian evidence, while sketchy, supports this favourable view of women's agencies as well. Finnish domestic agencies in eastern Canada, argues Lindstrom-Best, "were the key to the domestic's flexibility. They were quick to advise the women not to accept intolerable conditions [and] they kept close watch on the 'greenhorns' who were most vulnerable to exploitation."[65] While Vancouver's domestic–agent relationship lacked the ethnic connections and motives of the Finnish women's community, there is reason to believe, given labour market conditions, that Vancouver's agencies were also supportive of their worker-clients as long as their pocketbooks and the economy would allow. When the labour market for women reversed itself in the fall of 1913, for instance, some commercial agencies were forced to drum up business for themselves and their domestic clients. In mid-December 1913, the Universal urged employers to take on temporary help: "Mrs. Maloney," ran the ad, "will furnish on short notice reliable women to keep house where parties going to theater or otherwise require house and children taken care of. Employers call me up for Christmas catering, cooking, waiting and dinner parties."[66] Another agency asked homeowners to hire part-time help after the Christmas season. Of course, domestic agencies were not selfless in these efforts. Profits and service sometimes merged in the worker–agent relationship. Significantly, the YWCA bureau was silenced by the 1913 depression. The glutted market for domestics aptly demonstrated the extent to which the YWCA was employer-controlled; the Y's employment bureau advertisements for help, now unnecessary, were pulled in the fall of 1913. Nonetheless, the YWCA and women's employment agencies could not create work for the unemployed; both proved useless to working women during bad economic times.

Women's employment agencies provided a needed service to women workers before the First World War. At times the agent's drive for profits inadvertently complemented the worker's needs for security and occupational flexibility. This service, however, only proceeded as far as society or the economy would allow. An expansion, change or redefinition of women's occupational roles could be facilitated, but never initiated, by women's agents. Commercial agents were interested in money, not reform. This was not true of organizations like the local YWCA, which manipulated working women for specific moral and material reasons. Because women's agencies did not actively serve the interests of employers, moreover, most were condemned by the YWCA.

When studied at all, employment agents have been cast as the arch miscreants of the progressive era. This article, it is hoped, has shed some new light on these "villains" by looking closely at one sector of the employment business in one community before World War One. The structure of women's agencies, the motives of their agents and the demands placed on them complicate the prevalent, simplistic, and largely masculine image of the omnipotent employment "shark." There clearly was a gap between the experiences of employment agencies and the criticisms raised against them.

NOTES

1. For a general discussion of the rise of the international labour exchange movement, see Robin John Anderson, "Sharks and White Slavers? The Vancouver Employment Business, 1898–1925" (MA thesis, Simon Fraser University, 1991), 9–25; Udo Sautter, "North American Government Labor Agencies before World War One: A Cure for Unemployment?" *Labor History*, 24 (1983), 366–393; John Garraty, *Unemployment in History: Economic Thought and Public Policy* (New York: Harper and Row Publishers, 1978); Tomas Martinez, *The Human Marketplace: An Examination of Private Employment Agencies* (New Brunswick, N.J.: Transaction Books, 1976); and Bryce M. Stewart, "The Employment Service of Canada," *Queen's Quarterly*, 27, 1 (July 1919), 37–61.

2. Information on the numbers, names and activities of Vancouver employment agencies has been drawn from a number of primary sources. Since employment agencies were such marginal endeavours, no business or personal records are available. However, agents did use classified advertisements in newspapers, and this study is based on an extensive newspaper search over a twenty-year period (1898–1918). Three Vancouver dailies were used: the *Vancouver Daily World*, the *News Advertiser* and the *Province*. Information from these sources was correlated with an exhaustive name and street search drawn from two city directories, *Wrigleys and Hendersons*, over the same period.

3. See Gillian Creese, "Exclusion or Solidarity? Vancouver Workers Confront the 'Oriental Problem,'" *BC Studies 80* (Winter 1989), 24–51.

4. Ibid.

5. *Census of Canada* 1911, Volume VI, Table 5. See also Star Rosenthal, "Union Maids: Organized Women Workers in Vancouver, 1900–1915," *BC Studies* 41 (Spring), 39–41; Gillian Creese, "Working Class Politics, Racism, and Sexism: The Making of a Politically Divided Working Class in Vancouver, 1900–1939" (Ph.D. dissertation, Carleton University, 1986), 124; and Marjorie Griffin Cohen, *Women's Work, Markets, and Economic Development in Nineteenth-Century Ontario* (Toronto: University of Toronto Press, 1988), 135–151.

6. Veronica Strong-Boag, *The New Day Recalled: Lives of Girls and Women in English Canada, 1919–1939* (Markham, Ontario: Penguin Books, 1988), 50–56.

7. *Census of Canada* 1911, Volume VI, Table 6. Of the 50,628 working people over 10 years of age listed in the census, 6,452 were women.

8. On the experience of paid domestic workers in Canada, see Genevieve Leslie, "Domestic Service in Canada, 1880–1920," in Janice Acton, Penny Goldsmith and Bonnie Shepard, eds., *Women at Work: Ontario, 1850–1930* (Toronto: Women's Press, 1974); Marilyn Barber, "The Women Ontario Welcomed: Immigrant Domestics for Ontario Homes, 1870–1930," *Ontario History* 62:3 (September 1980), 148–172; Varpu Lindstrom-Best, "'I Won't Be a Slave!' — Finnish Domestics in Canada, 1911–30," in Robert Harney and Jim Albert, eds., *Gathering Place: Peoples and Neighbourhoods of Toronto, 1834–1945* (Toronto: Multicultural History Society of Ontario, 1985); Claudette Lacelle, *Urban Domestic Servants in 19th-Century Canada* (Ottawa: Environment Canada — Parks, 1987); and Strong-Boag, *The New Day Recalled*, 54–55. For discussions of the nature of unpaid housework, see Veronica Strong-Boag, "Keeping House in God's Country: Canadian Women at Work in the Home," in Craig Heron and Robert Storey, eds., *On the Job: Confronting the Labour Process in Canada*

(Montreal: McGill-Queen's University Press, 1986), 124–141 and *The New Day Recalled*, 113–144; and Cohen, *Women's Work*, 118–151.

9. For American evidence, see David M. Katzman, *Seven Days a Week: Women and Domestic Service in Industrializing America* (New York: Oxford University Press, 1978), 56.
10. National Council of Women of Canada, *Annual Report* (Toronto, 1907), 66.
11. Ibid., 68
12. Ibid., 77.
13. Lacelle, *Urban Domestic*, 131.
14. Ibid., 98.
15. For a review of labour market conditions for women from boom to bust, see the bi-monthly reports on Vancouver's women's employment conditions in *Labour Gazette*, July 1913 to March 1914.
16. Over 70% of help wanted ads for women in 1899–1902 asked for domestic servants.
17. See Katzman, *Seven Days*, 87–94.
18. *Labour Gazette*, 1913–1914.
19. From a speech delivered by Vancouver YWCA President Annie Skinner in 1909. See *News Advertiser* June 15, 1909.
20. *Western Clarion*, March 16, 1912, 1.
21. NCWC, *Annual Report* (Toronto 1907), 83–84.
22. NCWC, *Annual Report* (Toronto 1911), 28.
23. Mariana Valverde, *The Age of Light, Soap, and Water: Moral Reform in English Canada, 1885–1925* (Toronto: McClelland & Stewart, 1991), 103.
24. Ibid., 96–97.
25. Ibid., 102.
26. *News Advertiser*, August 1, 1899.
27. On the central importance of domestic placement activities in Vancouver's YWCA work, see *World*, February 5, 1901, 2; February 21, 1908, 7; and Vancouver YWCA, *Annual Report*, 1907, 6; 1909, 4; and 1914, 18.
28. Barber, "The Women Ontario Welcomed," 154–158. See also Desmond Glynn, "'Exporting Outcast London': Assisted Emigration to Canada, 1886–1914," *Histoire sociale/Social History*, 15:29 (May 1982), 209–238.
29. *News Advertiser,* February 23, 1910.
30. Vancouver YWCA, *Annual Report*, 1906–1913.
31. Vancouver YWCA, *Annual Report*, 1913, 12.
32. *News Advertiser*, June 15, 1909.
33. Ibid., February 23, 1910.
34. Vancouver YWCA, *Annual Report*, 1905, 10.
35. Ibid., 8.
36. Ibid., 1909, 3.
37. Ibid., 1907, 7.
38. *News Advertiser*, February 23, 1910. See also *World*, February 21, 1908.
39. Vancouver YWCA, *Annual Report*, 1912, 12–13.
40. Vancouver YWCA, *Annual Report* and Treasurer's Report: 1909–1916. See also the reports on civic grants, *News Advertiser*, March 13, 1906.
41. Vancouver YWCA, *Annual Report*, 1909, 6.
42. Ibid., 1914, 16.
43. Information on classes was taken from Vancouver YWCA *Annual Report*, 1906–1918.
44. Ibid., 1909, 12 and 1910, 11.
45. Ibid., 1915, 5.
46. Vancouver YWCA, *Annual Report*, 1907, 1909–1910.
47. Vancouver YWCA, *Annual Report*, 1907–1916.
48. *News Advertiser*, June 15, 1909.
49. Ibid., February 23, 1910.

50. Edward Starkins, *Who Killed Janet Smith* (Toronto: Macmillan, 1984), 82–83.

51. See Martinez, *Human Marketplace*, 25–31. The classic study of women's agencies in the United States is Frances A. Kellor's *Out of Work: A Study of Employment Agencies, Their Treatment of the Unemployed and Their Influence upon Homes and Business* (New York: Knickerbocker, 1905).

52. See *News Advertiser*, November 15, 1904 and May 15, 1905.

53. Ibid., December 1, 1904.

54. Ibid., July 15, 1911.

55. Ibid.

56. For instance, see *News Advertiser*, October 18, 1903.

57. See Henderson's, *Greater Vancouver Directory* (Vancouver: Henderson Directory Ltd.), 1911–1920.

58. See *News Advertiser*, May 7, 1911.

59. For instance, see ibid., October 16, 1912, November 15, 1912, and February 1, 1913.

60. Ibid., June 17, 1913.

61. Ibid., September 2, 1913.

62. The emphasis is mine.

63. The 1912 British Columbia Commission on Labour was originally constituted to look into general labour conditions in the province, and the activities of men's employment agencies were a key focus. For information on the Commission, see Anderson, "Sharks," 64–75.

64. Carol Lasser, "The Domestic Balance of Power: Relations Between Mistress and Maid in Nineteenth-Century New England," *Labor History*, 28:1 (Winter 1987), 17–20.

65. Lindstrom-Best, "I Won't Be a Slave," 44–45.

66. *News Advertiser*, December 15, 1913.

TOPIC FOUR
Religion and Reform

McGill University versus the University of Toronto, 1909. Later that year, U of T won the first Grey Cup — a sign of the new popularity of "rough sports" in several urban centres.

Clearly, urbanization and industrialization presented Canada with problems as well as opportunities. People not only celebrated economic growth, but also fretted over what they perceived as rapidly rising, if not already rampant, crime, intemperance, disease, vagrancy, and class conflict. Some called for the state to alleviate such conditions through social welfare. Prior to World War II, however, the conventional wisdom rejected big government and deficit financing out of an awareness that state revenue was scarce, a belief that the laissez-faire approach was essential for economic vibrancy, and a conviction that public assistance would encourage indolence.

One consequence of governmental parsimony was that most early welfare was administered privately, by churches or philanthropic groups. But many organizations — constrained by limited finances, fearful of promoting laziness, and, in some instances, more concerned with maintaining social order than securing social justice — imposed stringent, often heavy-handed moral guidelines when it came to the distribution of assistance. By examining the background and rhetoric of different actors as well as the application and impact of their many reform initiatives, social historians have generated considerable debate over the motivation behind a range of supposedly benevolent measures. Did they derive from a true religious commitment to uplifting society; a sense of *noblesse oblige* on the part of the upper class; a belief among an emerging corps of professionals that they could engineer an efficient and harmonious environment; or the desire of the economically and socially dominant to retain their privileged position in a society seen as vulnerable to upheaval?

The motivation behind the various reform measures and movements appearing in Canada during the formative stages of urban and industrial growth will undoubtedly continue to generate lively scholarship. For E.R. Forbes in Article 7, a sincere adherence to the new Social Gospel prompted many Maritime churches to further the cause of prohibition. Seeing intemperance as linked with a slew of social problems, they presented prohibition as a key ingredient in a wide-ranging reform program that would regenerate a society they perceived as threatened by the negative manifestations of modernization. According to Morris Mott in Article 8, another important reform campaign was the promotion of "manly sports." Mott, who sets his study in early twentieth-century Winnipeg, argues that organized sport was seen by many as providing a means of offsetting the debilitating effects of the modern urban environment. Those participating in sports, it was thought, would be both better able to resist the diseases that festered in grimy, overcrowded cities and — since the prevailing wisdom of the day linked physically unhealthy bodies with mental illness and aberrant behaviour — more likely to keep away from crime and other kinds of misconduct. Nor was it lost on the advocates of participation that sport could ease class tensions by teaching lessons such as that "'success' went to those who 'earned' it through determination and disciplined skill."

QUESTIONS TO CONSIDER

1. Why was the Nova Scotia government reluctant to impose prohibition?
2. For what reasons did prohibition ultimately fail? Why does Forbes see irony in its decline?
3. Was there any class-based opposition to prohibition? If so, why?
4. For what reasons did organized sport increase in popularity during the early twentieth century?

5. Why was sport encouraged among women and newcomers to Canada? What type of society did the leading advocates of organized sport seek to create?

SUGGESTED READINGS

Blake, Raymond, and Jeffrey Keshen, eds. *Social Welfare Policy in Canada: Historical Readings*. Toronto: Copp Clark Longman, 1995.

Cook, Ramsay. *The Regenerators: Social Criticism and Reform in Late Victorian English-Speaking Canada*. Toronto: University of Toronto Press, 1985.

Craven, Paul. *"An Impartial Umpire": Industrial Relations and the Canadian State, 1900–1911*. Toronto: University of Toronto Press, 1980.

Howell, Colin. *Northern Sandlots: A Social History of Maritime Baseball*. Toronto: University of Toronto Press, 1995.

McLaren, Angus. *Our Own Master Race: Eugenics in Canada, 1885–1945*. Toronto: McClelland & Stewart, 1990.

Morton, Desmond, and Glenn Wright. *Winning the Second Battle: Canadian Veterans and the Return to Civilian Life, 1915–1930*. Toronto: University of Toronto Press, 1987.

Owram, Doug. *The Government Generation: Canadian Intellectuals and the State, 1900–1945*. Toronto: University of Toronto Press, 1986.

Rooke, Patricia, and R.L. Schnell. *Discarding the Asylum: From Child Rescue to the Welfare State in English Canada, 1800–1950*. Lanham, Mo.: University Press of America, 1983.

Shore, Marlene. *The Science of Social Redemption: McGill, the Chicago School, and the Origins of Social Research in Canada*. Toronto: University of Toronto Press, 1987.

Shortt, S.E.D., ed. *Medicine in Canadian Society: Historical Perspectives*. Montreal and Kingston: McGill-Queen's University Press, 1992.

Struthers, James. *No Fault of Their Own: Unemployment and the Canadian State, 1914–1941*. Toronto: University of Toronto Press, 1983.

Valverde, Mariana. *Age of Light, Soap, and Water: Moral Reform in English Canada, 1885–1925*. Toronto: McClelland & Stewart, 1991.

SEVEN

Prohibition and the Social Gospel in Nova Scotia

E.R. FORBES

The success of the prohibition movement in Nova Scotia in 1921 was a result of the transformation of a narrow nineteenth century temperance crusade, based

Source: Excerpted from "Prohibition and the Social Gospel in Nova Scotia," *Acadiensis*, 1, 1 (Autumn 1971): 11–36. Reprinted by permission of *Acadiensis*.

upon rural values and ideas of personal salvation, into a broad campaign for progressive reform. Armed with a new idealism, leadership and greatly expanded institutional support, prohibition became politically irresistible. The change was brought about largely through the churches, in which development of a collectivist, reform theology accompanied the rise of progressive ideology in secular thought. As influential elements among the clergy became committed to the social gospel, as the new theology was called, they provided both an agency for the propagation of reform ideas and the leadership for their implementation.

Viewed in this context, the popular image of the prohibitionists as frustrated puritanical zealots bent on suppressing the pleasures of others rapidly breaks down. A detailed examination of the prohibition movement in Nova Scotia suggests that the prohibitionists were motivated primarily by a desire to eliminate the roots of human unhappiness. They wanted to create a new society in which crime, disease and social injustice would be virtually eliminated. Their success in committing society to these goals would be reflected both in the victory of prohibition in Nova Scotia and in its ultimate defeat.

The agitation for prohibition dated from the mid-nineteenth century. It seems to have been spearheaded by the fraternal groups and actively supported by the evangelical churches. By the end of the century the movement had made some progress towards regulating and restricting the sale of alcoholic beverages. The *Report of the Dominion Royal Commission on the Liquor Traffic* in 1895 described Nova Scotia as "a strong temperance province."[1] It noted that liquor could be legally sold only in Halifax City and the two counties of Halifax and Richmond. Of the remaining sixteen "dry" counties, sales were prohibited in twelve under the Canada Temperance Act (Scott Act) of 1878 and in the other four by a stringent provincial act which required an annual petition by two-thirds of the local electorate to permit the renewal of liquor licences. Strong popular support for prohibition appeared to be indicated by the plebiscites of 1894 and 1898, which yielded majorities of more than three to one in favour.[2]

Yet one could easily exaggerate both the extent of prohibition and the sentiment supporting it in Nova Scotia before 1900. Certainly the people had never experienced, nor, perhaps, did many of them yet envision, the "bone dry" legislation which would later be attempted. While it is true that the saloon had largely disappeared from rural Nova Scotia, there was nothing in the existing legislation to prevent an individual from ordering liquor from legal outlets. Shipments were regularly sent out by mail coach or train, frequently under the guise of groceries and other merchandise. To facilitate matters, the Halifax merchants deployed agents to take orders and make deliveries. In several towns, sales persisted as local councils, which were responsible for enforcing the Scott and License Acts, arranged "deals" with retailers by which certain periodic fines served to replace the inconvenience of the licensing system.

It is clear that the prohibitionists of the nineteenth century had, to some degree, persuaded governments to regulate and remove the more blatant features of the liquor traffic. By the end of the century, however, it became evident that the politicians were unwilling to go farther. Both federal parties, after stalling by means of royal commissions and plebiscites, made it clear that action could not be expected from them. The Liberal government of Nova Scotia, under the leadership of George Murray, not only rejected any further extension of prohibition but in 1905 appeared to move in the other direction. In that year the government legalized the on-the-premises consumption of liquor in Halifax hotels and extended the hours of sale for that city. It is doubtful if the prohibition movement would have had any greater impact on Nova Scotia had there not been in motion at this time a fundamental change in the social theology of the churches which directly affected their attitude towards prohibition.

In broad terms this change might be seen as part of the growth of a collectivist trend in social thought. In the 1870s, Herbert Spencer's widely publicized portrayal of society as an evolutionary organism governed by the law of the "survival of the fittest" was initially employed as a doctrine justifying poverty and laissez-faire capitalism. But it soon produced a strong progressive response. Henry George in *Progress and Poverty* and Edward Bellamy in *Looking Backwards*, for example, both accepted organic and evolutionary concepts, but made them the basis for an optimistic projection of social progress and reform.[3]

Collectivism in secular thought was closely paralleled in theology by a similar movement which became known as the social gospel. In the United States, Washington Gladden, Richard Ely and Walter Rauchenbush developed theories of an organic and dynamic society.[4] It was a society which might ultimately be perfected on the principles of the fatherhood of God and the brotherhood of man as expressed by Jesus in the "Sermon on the Mount" and elsewhere. Such a belief transformed the social attitude of many churches. No longer could the primary emphasis be placed on individual salvation. If "Christ . . . came to save society" as the Nova Scotia Methodist Conference claimed in 1907,[5] the churches were obligated to follow his example.

Both the secular and the religious movements for reform owed much of their popular appeal to the serious social problems which confronted the people. In Canada the rapid industrialization and urbanization of the Laurier era created or threw into sharp relief a host of social ills. Red light districts abounded in the towns and cities, alcoholism increased sharply, the exploitation of workers became blatant and the failure of traditional institutions to provide security for the less fortunate was increasingly manifest.[6] Rural residents were alarmed not only by the moral and social problems of the cities and towns but also by the depopulation of their own communities. Nova Scotians, who were noted for their strong church allegiance,[7] tended to look to the clergy for leadership in solving their problems. The latter proposed as a general solution implementation of the social gospel — a fundamental reform of society on the basis of Christian principles.

The acceptance of the new theology by the churches had profound implications for the prohibition movement. Firstly, the social gospel tended to justify or even compel a church's interference in politics. If society were capable of regeneration along Christian lines, a heavy responsibility rested with the churches to employ every means in bringing this about. To those firmly imbued with the reforming vision, traditional methods of teaching and preaching appeared too slow. Legislation and government activity represented the obvious method of implementing large scale reform. Secondly, the social gospel changed the emphasis and strengthened the motivation in the churches' advocacy of prohibition. It was understandable that progressive churchmen, as they surveyed the ills of their society, should emphasize the problem of intemperance. Not only was alcoholism a serious social problem in itself, but it was thought to be an important contributory cause to a host of other ills, including poverty, disease, the disintegration of the family, and traffic and industrial accidents. Prohibition thus became an integral part of a sweeping programme for social reform.

If the social gospel contributed to prohibition, the question of prohibition played a key role in the transition of the churches to the social gospel. This was one issue on which religious conservatives and progressives could readily unite. It was thus no accident that the social gospel made its initial appearance in the churches by way of the temperance committees. These in fact served as useful agencies through which the social gospel ethic might be spread in each church.

The Methodists appear to have been among the first in Canada to accept formally the implications of the new ideas. A move in that direction was indicated by the change in name of the Committee on Temperance to that of Temperance, Prohibition and Moral Reform at the Canadian Conference of 1898. This committee became a permanent board in 1902 and Dr. S.D. Chown was appointed its full time secretary. In the Nova Scotia Conference, the change in name of the committee was accompanied in 1903 by what appeared to be a general acceptance of the social gospel. The report of the committee which was adopted by the 1903 Conference declared in its opening sentence that it was the "intention of the Lord that . . . through his faithful ones the principles of the gospel of Christ are to be made supreme in all departments of human activity."[8] The report went on to discuss tactics for the defeat of intemperance, cigarette smoking by the young, commercial dishonesty, social vice and political corruption. In the next three years, other abuses singled out for attack included the opium traffic, race track gambling, prize fighting, and in 1906 the committee expressed its wish to investigate "any forms of commercial or industrial oppression affecting our people."[9] As part of their programme for social reform, the members of the Conference in 1905 endorsed the policy of provincial prohibition and pledged themselves to vote only for men who would support this measure in the Legislature.[10]

More dramatic was the simultaneous adoption of the cause of prohibition and the social gospel by the Maritime Synod of the Presbyterian Church. The convener of the Temperance Committee which proposed the acceptance of the social gospel was H.R. Grant, the man who would dominate the prohibition movement in Nova Scotia for the next thirty years. A native of Pictou County, Grant had undertaken his theological studies at Queen's University, where the new theological trends appear to have received full consideration under the principalship of George Monro Grant.[11] After further study at Edinburgh and experience in mission work in Manitoba and New Brunswick, H.R. Grant returned to take charge of the congregation of Trenton in his home county. Keenly interested in temperance and social reform, he served as convener of the Temperance Committee of the Maritime Synod from 1902 to 1907. In 1904 he resigned his charge in Trenton to undertake full time the task of temperance organization in Pictou County. In 1906 Grant participated in the formation of the Nova Scotia Temperance Alliance, of which he became general secretary in 1907. He held his post until 1917, when he assumed a similar position in the Social Service Council of Nova Scotia.

The Baptists seem to have pursued a similar course in the direction of the social gospel. In 1903 the Temperance Committee of the Maritime Baptist Convention under the chairmanship of W.H. Jenkins submitted a report which clearly viewed the temperance problem in terms of the social gospel. Christ's "mission," it stated, was both "to save souls" and "to save society." Christ was "the greatest social reformer that the world has ever seen." "Loyal hearts" were needed "to battle boldly with that monster iniquity, the liquor traffic which . . . gathering under its banner all the supreme ills that afflict the people . . . stalks forth to challenge Christianity to mortal combat."[12] In 1908, a resolution of the Convention urged Baptists to "rise above party in voting on questions of temperance and moral reform" and denounced the idea of government control as "complicity with the drink traffic."[13]

The Church of England, lacking a strong temperance tradition and proud of its conservative stance, responded more slowly to the new ideas. Yet respond it did. Some Anglicans seemed prepared to accept them on the grounds that if members did not find them being implemented in their own church, they might go elsewhere. This was the argument used by the Temperance Committee of 1902 in urging the need for a temperance organization in every parish.[14] Others, such as Rev. D.V. Warner of Shelburne, advocated the acceptance of a new social ethic on theoretical grounds and pointed to a social gospel tradition within the Church of England itself. Warner in 1909 published a pamphlet entitled *The Church and Modern Socialism* in which he referred specifically to the tradition of "Christian Socialism" set forth in the writings of the nineteenth century English cleric Charles Kingsley. By analyzing Christ's teachings as illustrated in the "Sermon on the Mount," the "Lord's Prayer" and other selections from the New Testament, he sought to prove that socialism was closer to "practical Christianity" than was the practice of the Church.[15]

The Anglican debate on the social gospel appeared to reach a climax in the Nova Scotia Synod of 1912. The conservative position was strongly stated in the opening address of Bishop C.L. Worrell. Worrell expressed his alarm that "some of the clergy . . . have endeavored to take up the socialistic tendency of the time" and cautioned against "undue playing with this dynamic force." While it might be proper for individual churchmen to take the lead in movements which tended to the "purity, sobriety and thrift" of the people, it was not the Church's duty to devote its attention to the social problems of the day "except through the general instruction of Christian principles." In conclusion he quoted the dictum of Dean Inge that "political agitation is not the business of the clergy."[16] The Synod disagreed. Its "Report of the Bishops Charge" opened with a reference to the "Sermon on the Mount" and argued that "The Church of God exists for his glory and the true happiness and well being of his children, the sons of men, and therefore anything which emphasizes this aspect of his kingdom is to be fostered and strengthened."[17] By 1914 this creed had been translated into practical action with the formation of a Diocesan Commission of Social Service. A year later the Synod passed a resolution calling for the "fullest possible measures" by Dominion and provincial legislatures to prevent the sale and use of intoxicating beverages in Nova Scotia.[18]

The Roman Catholic Church in Nova Scotia also reacted favourably to the new ideas. The papal encyclical *Rerum Novarum* of 1891 had paved the way by its rejection of economic liberalism and condemnation of the exploitation of workers by employers. The Antigonish *Casket*, a spokesman for Celtic Roman Catholicism in the eastern half of the province, displayed an increasing interest in the problems of labour, particularly in the mining areas.[19] The Roman Catholic view of prohibition seemed ambiguous. The Antigonish *Casket* conceded that the liquor traffic should be suppressed, but argued that public opinion was opposed and advocated a generous licensing law providing for "drinking on the premises" but limiting licenses to 1 per 750 of population.[20] The *Casket* also suggested that the activities of the League of the Cross, the Roman Catholic temperance organization, should be limited to converting people to temperance through teaching. Yet as early as 1903 the League was reported to be nominating candidates in the municipal elections and in 1907 was campaigning for the repeal of the Scott Act so that the more stringent License Act might apply in Cape Breton County. In that year its president reported a membership of 2108 in 29 branches.[21] While the motivation of the League is unclear, from its actions it would appear that at least some of its leaders were fired by the reform spirit of the age.

Against this background of changing opinion and demand for reform by the churches, a political agitation was building up which would make the passage of prohibition almost unavoidable. But the Liberal administration of Premier George Murray did everything it could to keep from having to act on the question. In fact the story of the struggle for prohibition between 1904 and 1916 is largely the story of a political duel between the temperance forces led by H.R. Grant and the provincial government led by George Murray. On one side were the churches, leading moulders of public opinion in the province, on the other the Liberal Party, holding every seat but two in the Assembly and having as its leader one of the wiliest politicians in the country.

The object of the struggle soon became clear. The Liberals wanted to avoid taking a definite stand on the controversial issue of prohibition. The prohibitionists were determined to manoeuvre the government into a position where it would be compelled to act or publicly demonstrate its disdain for the stated wishes of a large element of the population.

Each year between 1902 and 1905, a bill was introduced to prohibit or render more difficult the sale and shipment of liquor into the dry areas of the province.[22] For the first three years, these were debated briefly and unceremoniously rejected. The churches voiced their anger in unmistakable terms. In the Presbyterian Synod, the Temperance Committee condemned the Legislature for its encouragement of the liquor traffic and called for "more definite, united and aggressive action."[23] The report adopted by the Methodist Conference pledged its members to secure "by voice, influence, and vote the defeat of that portion of the Legislature that stood for the liquor traffic against the moral and material welfare of our people."[24]

With an election planned for June of 1906 and the Conservatives committed to a promise of provincial prohibition,[25] Murray decided that an appropriate gesture to the churches would be in order. In the 1906 session, the government introduced a bill prohibiting the shipment of liquor from "wet" to "dry" areas of the province. In general, the bill was similar to those advocated by prohibitionists in previous years. But a large "joker" had been added by the phrase restricting the application of the bill to liquor "to be paid for on delivery."[26] The effect of the bill was merely to require people in rural areas to order their liquor prepaid rather than C.O.D. The Conservatives strove valiantly to make this fact clear, while demonstrating their own championship of prohibition with an amendment designed to restore the restrictive intent of the legislation. Government members replied by strongly denouncing those who would make the "sacred" cause of prohibition a party issue. Only two Liberals broke party lines on the amendment, which was defeated eighteen to four.[27]

In the election campaign which immediately followed, prohibition played a prominent role. The Conservatives included in their platform a promise of provincial prohibition within a year of a successful plebiscite on the question. At Pictou, Conservative leader Charles Tanner issued a reform manifesto which called for prohibition, purity in elections, public interest as opposed to corporate power and betterment of the working classes.[28] But the government's last minute "prohibition" bill had helped to blur party divisions on the question and in the constituencies candidates adopted positions which were locally popular. In rural areas where temperance sentiment was strong, such as Yarmouth County for example, all candidates pledged themselves to support prohibition.[29] In Halifax, with its military and seafaring traditions, opposition to prohibition was predominant. Here local Conservative newspapers left the prohibition plank out of the party platform, while Liberal premier Murray promised the inhabitants that his government would not impose prohibition upon the city without their consent.[30] Thirty-two Liberals, five Conservatives and one "Methodist" Independent were elected.

The Liberals had apparently suffered little on the issue, but the prohibitionists had gained in the election a solid corps of M.L.A.s pledged to support their demands. Meanwhile, the temperance groups of the province co-ordinated their efforts in the formation of the Nova Scotia Temperance Alliance. As secretary of the new organization, Grant stationed himself in the gallery of the Legislature to direct the strategy of the temperance forces. The first step was the introduction of a prohibition bill by E.H. Armstrong of Yarmouth, a young Liberal M.L.A. pledged to the cause in the election. Armstrong made clear that he was serving as the mouthpiece of the Alliance and that he himself had nothing to do with the drafting of the measure.[31] The bill called for the prohibition of the sale of liquor throughout the province and enforcement by provincial inspectors.

The bill was immediately rejected as unconstitutional by the Premier on the grounds that only the government could introduce bills which encroached upon the revenue of the crown. Armstrong was prepared for this development and at once gave notice of a resolution requiring the introduction of the bill by the government.[32] Obviously Grant had manoeuvred the government into the position he wanted. The resolution could only be debated on the open floor of the House. Members would have to take a definite stand which could be identified by their constituents.[33]

Armstrong's speech in introducing his resolution clearly reflected the characteristic social gospel approach to prohibition. The measure was necessary as a basic social reform. Problems of poverty, neglect of wives and children, disease, and accidents could be traced in large measure to intemperance. Its influence was both direct, as people on "sprees" caught pneumonia or were injured, and indirect, since in spending their money on "drink," men failed to provide the care and nourishment for themselves and their families necessary to ward off diseases such as typhoid fever or tuberculosis. Armstrong quoted a Dr. Reid who estimated that "90% of the cases in our hospitals are directly or indirectly due to the evil effects of intemperance" and suggested that prohibition might even put the hospitals out of business.[34]

Armstrong went on to deal with the constitutional argument, which had hitherto been one of the government's favourite means of escape. Reviewing the ancient controversy over whether Dominion or provincial governments had the power to impose prohibition, he cited various decisions of the Judicial Committee of the Privy Council to establish the limits of each level's authority. While it was true that only the federal government had the power to prohibit the shipment of liquor from outside of a province, provincial governments, as had been clearly determined in 1901 in the case of Manitoba, could legally prohibit the sale or shipment of liquor within the province. It was this and no more that the Alliance's bill proposed to do.

But once again, the members of the Legislature were saved from having to declare themselves unequivocally on the issue. Liberal M.L.A. C.F. Cooper, Baptist clergyman from Queens County, proposed an amendment calling for an address to the Dominion Parliament to request legislation banning the importation of liquor into "dry" counties from other provinces. When this was achieved, provincial legislation could then be secured to prevent its importation from areas of the province where liquor was legally sold. This, according to Cooper, was a much greater step towards prohibition than the measure proposed by the Alliance.[35]

Certainly Premier Murray was much happier with the latter proposal. The imposition of prohibition in Halifax would be in Murray's words "a dangerous experiment." Nova Scotia was already far in advance of other provinces in temperance legislation and "fully up [to], if not in advance of what public opinion demands."[36] Nevertheless, Murray quite agreed with Cooper's idea of an address to the federal parliament. To Murray the ideal solution was Dominion legislation enforced by municipal authorities.

After a long and tedious debate which filled nearly one hundred pages in the official record, the amendment was carried twenty-two to twelve. The Liberal strategy had worked; the members of the party who wished could still pose as champions of prohibition. Nevertheless, the vote did reveal the friends of the Alliance, as in addition to the Conservative opposition, five Liberals and the independent member opposed the amendment.[37]

At its annual meeting of 1908, the Alliance outlined more clearly the goals which genuine prohibitionists would be expected to support. It wanted to replace the existing jungle of temperance legislation with a federal measure outlawing the importation and manufacture of alcoholic beverages, and a provincial law prohibiting their sale. Both would be enforced by provincial officers. These proposals were presented to an unsympathetic Premier Murray by a delegation from the Alliance led by H.R. Grant. Murray explained that it was government policy to seek an amendment to the Scott Act which would prevent the importation of liquor into the province. Grant refused to be associated with any such legislation, which would apply only to areas where the Scott Act was in effect and merely serve to increase the confusion.[38] In the Legislature in 1909 Premier Murray described as "incomprehensible" the Alliance's repudiation of the government's proposal and suggested that this could only arouse "suspicions" as to the motives of the organization. In a remarkable reversal E.H. Armstrong opposed the prohibition measure introduced by Independent M.L.A. C.A. Campbell, and suggested that the Alliance was plotting with the Tories.[39]

The Liberal concern was understandable. Far from keeping the "sacred" cause of temperance out of politics, prohibitionists appeared to be using every opportunity to embarrass the government politically and force them to adopt the Alliance programme. Speakers imported from other regions added their testimony to the failure of the government. For example, Dr. J.G. Shearer, secretary of the Committee on Temperance and Moral and Social Reform of the General Assembly of the Presbyterian Church, denounced the lack of law enforcement in Halifax, claiming that "sixty-four bar-rooms, with shop licenses which expressly forbid selling for consumption on the premises, are doing business in direct violation of section 63 of the Licence Act."[40]

The prohibition forces were operating from an ever-expanding base. In January of 1909, H.R. Grant represented the Alliance in the creation of the Social Service Council of Nova Scotia, which included representatives of all the major churches, the farmers' associations, organized labour and boards of trade. The provincial organization was to be supplemented by similar councils in the municipalities. Intemperance was listed as one of the primary social problems with which the council proposed to deal and the solution advocated was education and prohibitory legislation.[41]

In 1909 and 1910, by-elections were fought in five counties. In two, Queens and Hants, Conservatives were elected on platforms including provincial prohibition.[42] With a general election approaching, the worried Liberals introduced a bill in the session of 1910 providing for provincial prohibition. The bill forbade the sale of intoxicating beverages (those containing more than 3% alcohol) in the province outside the city of Halifax. The only exception was for medicinal, sacramental, art trade and manufacturing purposes. "Spirits" for these uses would be supplied by specially authorized vendors. Liquor might not be shipped from Halifax to any other part of the province unless actually purchased in the city for personal or family use. In the capital city, the number of licenses was reduced from 90 to 70 with further reductions promised. The act was to be enforced by municipal officers under the supervision of a provincial inspector-in-chief. Early in 1911, with an election still pending, the Act was tightened to include all beverages containing alcohol, to prevent societies and clubs from keeping such beverages on their premises and to provide mandatory sentences of three months' imprisonment for second offenders. At the same time the Legislature passed a resolution urging the federal government to prohibit the transportation of liquor into the province.[43]

The Alliance had attained a large portion of its demands. The obvious reason for its success was political. The Liberal government was acting to satisfy an aroused public opinion before the election — a public opinion which had been largely moulded by the influence of the churches under the impact of the social gospel. The weight of this opinion was responsible not only for prohibition. In fact the latter was only one item in a broad slate of reform legislation passed by the Murray government in 1909 and 1910. Other measures included workmen's compensation, factory legislation, stricter limitations on child labour and a system of contributory old age pensions. In a relatively prosperous economy the vision of a transformed society was yielding practical results. The churches expressed their appreciation to the government,[44] and in the election of 1911, the Liberals were returned by a comfortable majority of sixteen seats.

The Alliance's pressure on the government was not eased for long. H.R. Grant soon declared that prohibition must be extended to Halifax, both to save the young men of that city from destruction and to cut off a major source of supplies for illicit sale in the rest of the province.[45] In 1912 the Liberals sought to divert attention from this issue by "packing" the annual meeting of the Alliance with government supporters. E.R. Armstrong, by this time a member of the Cabinet, requested several M.L.A.s to have their friends attend the meeting of the Alliance to block "unsound" proposals and the efforts of those who would "complicate the situation as far as the local government is concerned."[46] This attempt was a failure. The following year, Conservative leader C.E. Tanner openly championed the Alliance's cause by introducing an amendment to the Nova Scotia Temperance Act to extend the application of its prohibitory clauses to Halifax. This was defeated eighteen to thirteen. In May of 1914 a similar proposal was lost fourteen to thirteen and in 1915 the measure was defeated only by the vote of the speaker. Early in 1916, with another election just months away, a similar amendment by Conservative H.W. Corning passed with only the three members from Halifax in opposition.[47]

The War was an obvious factor in overcoming resistance. In the final debate, several of the members mentioned the endorsement of prohibition by the Nova Scotia Synod of the Church of England as influencing their decision on the question.[48] Although a prohibition resolution had been submitted to the Synod before the outbreak of war, the matter had been referred to the Social Service Commission for further study. Canon C.W. Vernon, who moved the resolution of 1915, was quoted as saying that he himself had been converted to prohibition by the needs of the war effort and that without the War his motion would never have passed.[49] The need for conservation created by the War was mentioned by some speakers and the need for sacrifice by others. Premier Murray, still very sceptical of the measure, called it "experimental legislation" which the province might afford in "days of strain and stress . . . as we perhaps could not do under more normal conditions."[50] The emotional climate in which the bill was passed was further illustrated in Corning's concluding speech, in which he appealed for a moral regeneration of the Empire and quoted Admiral Beatty on the need for a religious revival as a necessary prelude to victory.[51] Amid this climate of idealism and sacrifice the standard objections to prohibition as an infringement of personal liberty appeared to carry little weight.

In 1916 the Dominion Temperance Alliance called for prohibition for the duration of the War and a three year reconstruction period thereafter. In January, H.R. Grant was a member of a delegation that called upon Robert Borden to press for Dominion prohibitory legislation. In March, the so-called Doherty Bill banned the importation of intoxicating beverages into provinces where provincial legislation was in effect. Since they still might be imported for personal use, this had little effect in Nova Scotia. In December, 1917, as a part of the war effort, the importation of intoxicating beverages was prohibited for the whole country. This still left the door open for Nova Scotians to order, legally, in unlimited quantities, liquor for personal use from Quebec.[52] Finally in March of 1918, by an Order-in-Council under the War Measures Act, the manufacture and sale of intoxicating beverages was prohibited throughout the whole country. Thus "bone-dry" prohibition came to Nova Scotia for the first time.

Thereafter attention shifted to the problem of enforcement. In 1917 the temperance forces of Sydney organized a citizen's league, which campaigned in the municipal elections and overturned a council which it claimed had failed to enforce the Act.[53] Inspector-in-chief J.A. Knight stated that "on the whole" prohibition in Halifax had been a success.[54] On this occasion Knight's opinion appeared to be supported by statistics, as the number of arrests for drunkenness in the province, which had reached 3614 in 1916, dropped to 2546 in 1917.[55] Evidence of improvement in restricting consumption of alcoholic beverages came from other sources as well. Sixty-nine per cent of the Anglican clergy of Nova Scotia who responded to a poll by the Council for Social Service of the Church of England in 1919, testified to the success of prohibition in their province.[56]

On December 31, 1919, the Orders-in-Council prohibiting the importation of liquor were repealed in favour of an amendment to the Canada Temperance Act, providing for provincial plebiscites on the question. A simple majority vote in favour of prohibition would result in the extension of the necessary federal legislation to the province concerned. In Nova Scotia the plebiscite was scheduled for October 25, 1920, after the provincial election of that year. Meanwhile, the people quenched their thirst and stocked up for the dry years to come.

By the time of the plebiscite, prohibition had acquired new enemies and friends. Organized labour made unsuccessful representations to the legislature to plead for the exemption of beer from prohibitory legislation and thereafter became increasingly hostile.[57] Organized farmers took the opposite view and in 1920 the newly formed United Farmers' Party campaigned on a platform advocating "bone-dry" liquor legislation.[58]

The most important accession to the temperance forces was the direct support of the Roman Catholic Church, the largest denomination in the province. During the campaign for the plebiscite, the Antigonish *Casket* came out strongly for prohibition, claiming it "has done wonders but it has not yet had time to do its best."[59] In the plebiscite, Nova Scotians declared for prohibition 82,573 to 23,953, the largest support for prohibition ever recorded in the province.[60] Every county yielded a majority except Halifax, whose people still appeared to resent the fiat imposed upon them in 1916.

The prohibition movement had reached its zenith by 1921 and thereafter began a gradual decline. The social gospel ideology on which it was based was approaching a crisis which would undermine its position of influence within the churches. Already it had been compromised to some extent by the Russian Revolution. In urging a fundamental reconstruction of society most social gospel reformers were forced to distinguish after 1917 between the right and wrong kinds of revolution. Many clergymen apparently judged from the newspaper reports available in Nova Scotia that the Winnipeg General Strike of 1919 was a dangerous experiment of the wrong kind. The focus of Communist activity in Cape Breton in the early 1920s — especially the activities of J.B. McLachlan, leader of the largest union in the province (District 26 United Mine Workers), in promoting "Bolshevist" doctrines and attempting to affiliate his union with the Red International[61] — tended to confirm their fears and strengthened the conservative element in the churches. The dilemma of the social gospel wing was reflected in the churches' initial failure to support labour in its critical struggle with the British Empire Steel Corporation. Not until international president John L. Lewis dismissed McLachlan and his radical executive in 1923 did the assistance materialize which one might expect from a socially committed clergy.[62]

The re-imposition of Federal prohibitory legislation on Nova Scotia in February of 1921 did mark the beginning of a "new era" in the province, but it turned out to be the era of the "rum-runner." In January, 1920, the Volstead Act prohibited the importation of liquor into the United States. An elaborate system of smuggling quickly evolved in which the Nova Scotian fisherman and ship owners came to play a prominent role. With the return of prohibition to Nova Scotia the new techniques were applied at home.

Attempts to enforce the legislation led to co-operation between the Customs officers attempting to prevent smuggling, the Department of Revenue officers hunting for stills and the Temperance inspectors trying to suppress bootlegging. Assisting all three were the prohibitionists, operating on their own initiative in an attempt to make effective the legislation for which they had worked so hard. Thus in 1921, these groups began a game of "cops and robbers" with the smugglers, bootleggers and moonshiners which would continue until the end of the decade.

It was a game which before long the ill-equipped, untrained and quite inadequate municipal and provincial officers were obviously losing. In 1925, a discouraged inspector-in-chief, J.A. Knight, gave the following assessment:

So much liquor is now smuggled and distributed throughout the Province in motor cars and by bootleggers that the closing of bars and blind pigs does not have much effect on the total consumption. It is beyond the power of local inspectors to control smuggling or even check it to any appreciable extent. Dominion Officers, whose duty it is to deal with smuggling, are few in number and quite unable to keep an effective watch on all parts of the coast where liquor may be landed . . . Owing to the prevalence of home manufacture, the consumption of intoxicating beer in some country districts, probably, has been greater in recent years than it was under the old licence law.[63]

In July of 1925 a Conservative government came to power in Nova Scotia. Murray had retired from politics in 1923, leaving the reins of government to the one-time prohibition advocate E.H. Armstrong. The luckless Armstrong was left to face a critical depression, disastrous strikes in the major coal and steel industries, mounting costs of government and dwindling revenues. The result of the election of June 25, 1925, was almost a foregone conclusion, as the Conservatives under the leadership of E.N. Rhodes won 40 of the 43 seats in the Assembly.[64]

Rhodes appeared to have viewed the termination of prohibition as a potential solution to the critical problem of government deficits. By 1925 the four Western Provinces and Quebec had abandoned prohibition for a system of so-called "government control," that is, government sale of liquor. It was proving an extremely lucrative business for the provinces involved. British Columbia, for example, in 1923 realized a net profit from liquor sales of over three million dollars,[65] an amount equal to three-fifths of the entire Nova Scotia budget. In 1926, Rhodes reported to Sir Robert Borden that he detected "a marked swing towards Government control of liquor. This will probably be accelerated by our financial position as we are faced during the current year with a deficit of $1,050,000."[66]

Nevertheless, Rhodes was in no position to abandon prohibition. Temperance sentiment was still strong and well organized. Rhodes was also cognizant that a large element of his party's support in the election of 1925 had come from the reform element in the province. Within the first six months of coming to office his government was presented with petitions supporting prohibition from nearly five hundred organizations in the province — temperance societies, church groups, women's institutes and agricultural clubs. In September, 1925, the Maritime Conference of the newly created United Church endorsed prohibition by an "unanimous standing vote."[67] Early in 1926, Rhodes adopted a policy intended to reassure reform elements of his sincerity in enforcing prohibition while leaving the door open for its subsequent abandonment. He pledged his government to a determined effort to enforce the prohibition laws, but if, after a reasonable time, this proved impossible he would introduce a program for government control. Lest any should doubt his sincerity in enforcing prohibition he appointed as his inspector-in-chief Rev. D.K. Grant, a lawyer, clergyman and prohibitionist. It was an appointment which won the immediate and grateful approval of the United Church.[68]

Grant set to work in a burst of energy to increase the size of the provincial force, raise the wages of the municipal inspectors and propose fresh amendments to the Nova Scotia Temperance Act. Assisted by the newly created Dominion Preventive Force of the Department of Customs and Excise, Grant and his inspectors launched a determined assault upon illicit liquor traffic. During his first year in office, arrests, seizures and convictions by provincial inspectors more than doubled, while successful prosecutions by both provincial and municipal inspectors increased from 716 for 1926 to 938 for 1927.[69] This increased activity was far from appreciated by influential elements in both political parties. The Conservative Halifax *Herald* began a campaign against Grant for his "arbitrary" methods of prosecuting offenders.[70] Some Liberals indicated their displeasure by securing the dismissal of the federal preventive officer at Glace Bay for being "too active in his duties."[71]

In fact, despite Grant's best efforts at enforcement there was evidence of a gradual decline in support for prohibition and an increase in the consumption of alcohol. In 1926 there were 1898 arrests for drunkenness, 2053 in 1927 and 2176 in 1928.[72] There also appeared to be an increased reluctance on the part of juries to convict bootleggers, especially in the case of second offenders, for whom jail terms were mandatory.[73] The resistance to prohibition as usual was strongest in Halifax. The Conservative M.L.A.s from the city found it expedient to show their opposition by resolutions in the House.

The pressure upon the provincial administration to resort to government control was substantially increased in 1926 by the federal government's announcement of an old age pension scheme, the costs of which were to be shared equally by the provinces and the Dominion. While such a plan might be within the reach of the Western Provinces and their relatively young population, it was totally beyond the resources of the Nova Scotia government, with its much larger percentage of potentially eligible recipients.[74] In 1928, Rhodes appointed a Royal Commission to explore methods of financing old age pensions and called an election before the Commission was due to report. During the campaign he reiterated his promise not to abandon prohibition without a plebiscite but gave no indication when such a referendum would be held.[75]

The election nearly proved disastrous for the Conservatives as their majority shrank from 37 to 3. Both prohibition and old age pensions were issues in the campaign. Discontent over the former was probably a factor in Halifax, where Conservative majorities of over 7000 in 1925 melted away and three of the five Conservative candidates were defeated.

After the election the Royal Commission presented its report. To the surprise of no one, it recommended government control of liquor sales as a possible source of revenue for old age pensions.[76] Shortly thereafter, Rhodes scheduled a plebiscite, on the question of prohibition versus government control, for October, 1929. Armed with the ammunition supplied by the Commission and with the tacit encouragement of the provincial government, a new Temperance Reform Association was organized in Halifax in September, 1929.

As the campaign increased in intensity, it became evident that the prohibitionists had lost many of their allies of 1920. The Anglican *Church Work* was conspicuously silent before the plebiscite and expressed its "relief" when it was over. The *Casket* went to considerable pains to explain that the Roman Catholic Church had never endorsed more than personal abstinence and that membership in the League of the Cross did not convey any obligation to vote for prohibition.[77]

Government control won a decisive victory in the plebiscite, 87,647 to 58,082. It received a majority in every county but six. Only in the rural counties of Shelburne, Queens, Kings, Hants, Colchester and Annapolis — counties in which the Baptist and United Churches were predominant — did prohibition retain a majority.[78]

The government lost no time in implementing the wishes of the people. The old Act was quickly repealed and a Liquor Commission was set up with a complete monopoly of liquor outlets in the province. Sale by the glass was to be limited by local option; otherwise Commission sales would be unrestricted. Within less than a year the Commission had established a store in every town and city in the province plus a special mail-order agency in Halifax for the convenience of rural customers.

A number of obvious factors might be mentioned in explaining the defeat of prohibition in Nova Scotia. The *United Churchman* claimed that the lack of enforcement discredited the movement among its friends and led to the desire to experiment with government control.[79] This raises the question of whether enforcement was possible, given the opposition to the law by such a determined minority. The answer would appear to hinge on the goal desired. Even with the relatively lax enforcement of the early 1920s, the arrests for drunkenness had been halved throughout the period from 1922 to 1926. Still it is doubtful if even the most rigorous enforcement would have ended the accounts of smuggling, illegal manufacture and related crimes which filled the press of the period. And it was these which made many Nova Scotians wonder if the prohibition cure were not worse than the disease. Such doubts must have become more acute as the prohibitionists saw their cause abandoned by every other province but Prince Edward Island. Then came a positive factor in the province's need for additional revenue, which the demand for other reforms made crucial. This was certainly the main consideration for the Rhodes government, and after the report of the Royal Commission on old age pensions, the issue apparently achieved a similar clarity for the people of Nova Scotia. They were given a choice between prohibition and old age pensions and opted decisively for the latter.

There were more fundamental reasons for the rejection of prohibition in 1929. In the early twentieth century, the movement had rapidly increased in strength, rising upon the tide of optimistic, idealistic reform which accompanied the churches' conversion to the social gospel. As the tide began to ebb, prohibition suffered accordingly. The reform movement of the social gospel reached a climax in Nova Scotia immediately following the World War. People had confidently prepared to create the new and better society which they expected would be within their reach. But conditions in Nova Scotia in the 1920s were conductive neither to optimism nor to reforms. Instead of the anticipated triumph of humanitarian justice, there came a critical and lingering depression, bankruptcy, wage-cuts, strikes, violence and emigration. In the industrial sphere, proposals for social reform were blocked by the financial difficulties of the corporations on one side, and compromised by the strident voice of radical Marxism on the other.

The decline of prohibition to some extent paralleled that of the general reform movement. As partially a utopian reform, it had suffered on implementation from the inevitable reaction. It did not yield the results predicted by its proponents. There was apparently no spectacular decline in disease, mental illness, poverty or crime in the province. On the contrary, prohibition was blamed by its opponents for much of the crime which did occur. For a time, many of its supporters maintained faith in their programme by attributing its deficiencies to the obvious lack of enforcement by the Murray-Armstrong administration. Then came the expected transition in government and with it the ultimate disillusionment of the prohibitionists, as one of their own number was no more successful in securing the desired results from prohibition than his predecessors.

There was a note of irony in the defeat of prohibition in 1929. Prohibition had acted as mid-wife at the birth of the social gospel in Canadian churches. The two had been closely linked in the flowering of the reform movement. But the latter, in creating the public demand for social welfare legislation, contributed significantly to the economic pressure providing the immediate cause for the defeat of the former. It was a measure of the success of the social gospel that as one dream was being destroyed, others, perhaps more realistic, were gaining a hold on public opinion. J.S. Woodsworth's victory in forcing the Mackenzie King government to adopt old age pensions had contributed to the fall of prohibition in Nova Scotia. Yet it also symbolized a future victory of the social gospel ideals in secular society, the ultimate goal of the leaders of the prohibition movement in Nova Scotia.

NOTES

1. *Report of the Royal Commission on Liquor Traffic* (Ottawa, Queen's Printer, 1895), p. 661.
2. *Debates and Proceedings of House of Assembly of Nova Scotia*, 1907, pp. 308–309, and R. Elizabeth Spence, *Prohibition in Canada* (The Ontario Branch of the Dominion Alliance, 1919), p. 218. In 1894 the vote was 42,756 to 12,355 in favour; in 1898, it was 34,678 to 5370.
3. See Richard Hofstadter, *Social Darwinism in American Thought* (rev. ed., New York, 1959), pp. 42, 108 and 112–113, and Daniel Aaron, *Men of Good Hope* (New York, 1961), pp. 72, 103.
4. For a discussion of the origin and nature of the social gospel in the United States see Charles H. Hopkins, *The Rise of the Social Gospel in American Protestantism, 1865–1915* (New Haven, 1940) and P.A. Carter, *The Decline and Revival of the Social Gospel* (Ithaca, 1956).
5. *Minutes of the Nova Scotia Conference of the Methodist Church* (hereafter cited as *Minutes, Methodist*), 1907, p. 78; from the Report of the Committee on Temperance and Moral Reform as adopted by the Conference.
6. For a brief description of conditions in one Nova Scotian city see *Sydney, Nova Scotia: The Report of a Brief Investigation of Social Conditions by the Board of Temperance and Moral Reform of the Methodist Church and the Board of Social Service and Evangelism of the Presbyterian Church* (n.p., 1913).
7. W.S. Learned and K.C.M. Sills, *Education in the Maritime Provinces of Canada* (New York, 1922), p. 14.
8. *Minutes, Methodist*, 1903, pp. 80–81.
9. Ibid., 1906, p. 83.
10. Ibid., 1905, pp. 76–77.
11. H.H. Walsh, *The Christian Church in Canada* (Toronto, 1956), p. 330. See also A. Richard Allen, "Salem Bland and the Social Gospel in Canada" (unpublished M.A. thesis, University of Saskatchewan, 1961), pp. 30–32.
12. *Year Book Maritime Baptist Convention,* 1903, p. 22. Jenkins later became a staunch supporter of J.S. Woodsworth's Labour Party.
13. *Wesleyan* (Methodist), Halifax, 23 September 1908, p. 1. Taken from the *Maritime Baptist*.
14. *Journals of Nova Scotia Synod, Church of England,* Appendix N, printed in the *Year Book* (hereafter cited as *Year Book, Church of England*), 1901–1902, p. xxxi.
15. D.V. Warner, *The Church and Modern Socialism* (Truro, N.S., 1909).
16. *Year Book, Church of England*, 1911–1912, pp. 111–113.
17. Ibid., Appendix Q, pp. xxvi–xxvii.
18. Ibid., 1914–1915, pp. 149 and 320.
19. *Casket*, 12 August 1909.
20. Ibid., 29 August 1907, p. 4.
21. Ibid., 31 January 1907, p. 6; 15 January 1903, p. 4; 8 August 1907, p. 2; and 12 September 1907, p. 2.
22. For a brief sketch of these early attempts see E. Spence, op. cit., pp. 330–333.

23. *Minutes of the Maritime Synod of the Presbyterian Church of Canada* (hereafter cited as *Minutes, Presbyterian*), 1905, p. 31.
24. *Minutes, Methodist*, 1905, p. 78
25. See below, n. 27.
26. *Debates*, 1906, p. 309.
27. Ibid., pp. 312, 330–331.
28. J. Castell Hopkins, *The Canadian Annual Review* (hereafter cited as *C.A.R.*), 1905, p. 331 and 1906, p. 393.
29. *Debates*, 1907, pp. 313 and 372.
30. Ibid., pp. 313 and 400.
31. Ibid., p. 301.
32. Ibid., pp. 224, 227.
33. Nova Scotia, *Journals of the House of Assembly* (hereafter cited as *J.H.A.*), 1907, various references pp. 45–154 and *Debates*, 1907, p. 310.
34. *Debates*, 1907, p. 304.
35. Ibid., p. 317.
36. Ibid., p. 385.
37. Ibid., p. 400.
38. *C.A.R.*, 1908, pp. 426–427, 108.
39. *Debates*, 1908, pp. 334, 374.
40. *C.A.R.*, 1908, p. 427.
41. *Halifax Herald*, 22 January 1909, p. 6.
42. E. Spence, op. cit., p. 339; *C.A.R.*, 1909, p. 432, and 1910, p. 459. In the latter constituency this was reputed to be the first election of a Conservative in thirty years.
43. *C.A.R.*, 1911, p. 551.
44. *Minutes, Presbyterian*, 1910, p. 29. *Minutes, Methodist*, 1910, p. 89.
45. E. Spence, op. cit., pp. 341–342.
46. Armstrong to Dr. J.W. Reid, 15 February 1912 and Armstrong to W.M. Kelly, 15 February 1912, E.R. Armstrong Papers, P.A.N.S.
47. *Presbyterian Witness*, 4 March 1916, p. 5 and *Debates* 1916, p. 225.
48. *Debates*, 1916, p. 176.
49. Ibid., p. 143.
50. Ibid., p. 206.
51. Ibid., p. 258.
52. See Report of the Inspector-in-chief for 1919, *J.H.A.*, 1920, Appendix 26, p. 1.
53. *Year Book, Church of England*, 1916–1917, p. 146.
54. Report of Inspector-in-chief, 1917, *J.H.A.*, 1918, Appendix 26, p. 1.
55. *The Control and Sale of Liquor in Canada* (Ottawa, Dominion Bureau of Statistics, 1933), p. 9, Table 5.
56. Compared with only 48.3% who were of a similar opinion in 1917. See *Prohibition II* (Kingston, 1919), p. 9, and *Prohibition I* (Kingston, 1917), p. 6. (Bulletins of the Council for Social Service of the Church of England).
57. *C.A.R.*, 1919, p. 703; Halifax *Citizen*, 30 May and 22 August 1923.
58. *C.A.R.*, 1920, p. 678.
59. *Casket*, 14 October 1920, pp. 1 and 6.
60. *Presbyterian Witness*, 20 November 1920.
61. See William Rodney, *Soldiers of the International* (Toronto, 1968), p. 111.
62. *Wesleyan*, 1 April 1925, p. 4.
63. Report of Inspector-in-chief, 1925, *J.H.A.*, 1926, Appendix 18, pp. 5–8.
64. See E.R. Forbes, "The Rise and Fall of the Conservative Party in the Provincial Politics of Nova Scotia, 1922–1933" (unpublished M.A. thesis, Dalhousie University, 1967), chapter 2.

65. *The Control and Sale of Liquor in Canada*, p. 8.
66. Rhodes to Borden, 1926, Rhodes Papers, P.A.N.S.
67. Rhodes Papers, P.A.N.S., vol. 81 and *Minutes of the Maritime Conference of the United Church of Canada*, 1925, p. 23.
68. *Minutes, United Church*, 1927, p. 27.
69. *J.H.A.*, 1927, pp. 5, 12; 1928, pp. 6, 15.
70. Halifax *Herald*, 1 March 1928.
71. "Memorandum Re: N.S. Affairs," 1927, vol. 7, Col. J.L. Ralston Papers, P.A.C.
72. *Control and Sale of Liquor in Canada*, p. 9, Table 5.
73. Report of Inspector-in-chief, 1927, *J.H.A.*, 1928, Appendix 8, p. 10.
74. 4.7% of Nova Scotia's population was over 70 years of age compared with 1.2% to 1.8% for the four Western provinces. *Report of the Royal Commission on Old Age Pensions, J.H.A.*, appendix No. 29, p. 43.
75. Copy of speech delivered at Windsor, 8 September 1928, Rhodes Papers, P.A.N.S.
76. *Report of the Royal Commission on Old Age Pensions*, p. 41.
77. *Church Work*, December 1929, p. 3 and *Casket*, 16 May 1929.
78. *J.H.A.*, 1929, Appendix 27, p. 38.
79. *United Churchman*, 6 November 1929.

EIGHT

One Solution to the Urban Crisis: Manly Sports and Winnipeggers, 1900–1914

MORRIS MOTT

In the first fifteen years of the twentieth century the people of Winnipeg began to realize that their city possessed urban problems that were not unlike those faced by residents of many large centres. They responded by advocating and initiating reforms similar to those introduced in several Canadian cities in the years 1880–1920. Urban and social historians have written extensively about both the widespread consciousness of urban difficulties and the reform movement that grew out of it in the late nineteenth and (especially in the case of Winnipeg and other Western Canadian cities) the early twentieth centuries. However, unless what occurred in Manitoba's capital was unusual, they have neglected to reveal the way in which the growing awareness of urban troubles, on the part of both "reformers" and others, resulted in the energetic promotion of organized "manly" sports.[1] At the same time, although several Canadian sports historians have shown that the era of widespread urban reform featured a remarkable growth of athletic activity, they have failed to provide information that adequately links the growth of sport to developments in society as a whole.

Source: Excerpted from "One Solution to the Urban Crisis: Manly Sports and Winnipeggers, 1900–1914," *Urban History Review*, 12, 2 (1983): 57–70. Reprinted by permission of *Urban History Review*.

....

Students of Western Canadian history are familiar with the process by which a large number of British Protestant immigrants, primarily from Ontario, moved into Winnipeg and Manitoba in the last three decades of the nineteenth century and, acting upon the assumption that they were bringing "progress" to a semi-wilderness, quickly began to establish their institutions, values and ways of life in the community. Less well known are the facts that these people were remarkably fond of a vast number of games and that, in their new province and city, they were only slightly less anxious to reproduce their best sporting practices than they were to reinstitute their best political, economic, legal, educational and religious ones.[2] They particularly wanted to ensure that they reestablished the games they referred to as "manly."

"Manly" games were those that seemed to test, and therefore dramatize and inculcate, that quality of character that late nineteenth century British Protestants, in the Canadian West and all over the English-speaking world, called "manliness." "Manliness" was the ultimate masculine quality, the attribute of the ideal male. Major components were not only physical vitality and courage, but also decisiveness, clear-headedness, loyalty, determination, discipline, a sense of charity, and especially the moral strength that ensured that courage would be used in the service of God and of Right.[3] The several manly sports, like the various integrants of manliness, were never written down, but if Manitobans and Winnipeggers did not designate explicitly the competitions they considered manly they did so implicitly.

Ruled out of the manly category were the sedentary games of chance or strategy, including all the card and board games, and sports, such as horse racing, where the competition was essentially between animals. Sometimes referred to as manly, especially when played by those who were past their physical prime, were tennis, bowling, golf and other competitive activities in which physical attributes were tested, but wherein the hardiness that was often associated with manliness was not usually required. Two groups of sports were almost invariably called manly. The first, exemplified by snowshoeing and the various track and field events, were the relatively straightforward, strenuous trials of speed, strength or other physical qualities. The second, generally more highly regarded than the first because they seemed to test a greater variety of the manly attributes, were games that were more complex than the straightforward sports but which, like them, required a good deal of vigour. The most important of those were the team ball games, especially cricket, baseball, lacrosse, football (in both the "rugby" and "soccer" forms), curling and hockey.

Because they appeared to inculcate manliness, because they symbolically revealed that genuine success came only to those who possessed it, and because they seemed peculiarly "British" and therefore necessary in a truly British and Canadian part of the world, manly sports had been well established in Winnipeg and the prairie West by the end of the nineteenth century. Then, especially in Winnipeg, in the years between the turn of the century and the outbreak of World War I, the degree of participation in manly sports simply exploded.

....

In the Manitoba capital in the early twentieth century, a significant number of individuals began to take part in a few sports that were new to the city. Among those sports were field hockey, skiing, squash, volleyball, badminton, indoor baseball and basketball. Basketball, played regularly by several hundred people by 1914, was the most popular of the "new" sports. The overall increase in activity, however, was not attributable so much to the rise in the popularity of unfamiliar games, as it was to the increased popularity of sports that had been present for several years before 1900.

Canoeing was one of these sports. Although competitive canoeing was introduced in the 1880s it was a minor sport until 1910, when the Winnipeg Canoe Club, founded in 1893, moved its headquarters from the foot of the Norwood Bridge, up the Red River to the big bend opposite Elm Park. When in 1913, the Club moved again about one mile further upstream, its present location, membership increased substantially.[4] Snowshoeing, a sport that had been popular in the 1870s and early 1880s, had a revival during the decade before the Great War.[5] The enhanced attractiveness of other well-established sports is obvious when the number of clubs in the city at the turn of the century is compared to the number ten to fifteen years later. There was one swimming club in the city in 1900, and five by 1913. During the intervening years swimming and water polo became two of the most popular sports at the Winnipeg Y.M.C.A.[6] Four lawn-bowling clubs were present in 1910, while there had been only one in 1900.[7] Three or four "Canadian" rugby clubs existed at the turn of the century, but by 1912 there were a dozen; in addition, in the years after 1908, anywhere from three to five teams played a series of games in what was advertised as Canada's largest "English Code" rugby league.[8] In 1914 there were at least twenty-six cricket clubs in Winnipeg; fifteen years earlier there had been about five.[9] The Winnipeg Golf Club, formed in 1894, was the only one in the city until 1905, when the exclusive St. Charles Country Club was formed. By 1914 there were five clubs, all of which joined the Manitoba Golf Association, an association formed in the same year.[10]

Probably the most sizeable gains in popularity occurred in tennis, curling and pin bowling. The number of new tennis clubs and new tennis players was a constant source of amazement to observers of the Winnipeg sports scene after the turn of the century. Whereas before 1900 there had never been more than two private clubs, and in most years only one, by 1914 there were five or six, and individuals who did not want or could not afford to join one of these could play in church leagues or on the many public courts built in schoolyards or parks.[11] In 1900 there were three curling clubs in Winnipeg, with 218 members, but by 1914 there were ten clubs in the city proper and one in St. Vital, with a total membership of 1,230. In addition, during these years the city clubs began to rent their ice to hundreds of non-members, who curled periodically in small leagues or bonspiels.[12] Pin bowling was evidently played by a few devotees from as far back as the early 1870s; in the decade before the War the sport's popularity increased so rapidly that there may have been close to a thousand regular Winnipeg bowlers by 1914.[13]

Generally all the sports mentioned so far either were introduced to Winnipeg in the early twentieth century or enjoyed a noteworthy increase in appeal. A host of others were consistently popular. Included among these were rowing, rifling, trapshooting, boxing, wrestling, polo, handball, competitive skating, track and field and lacrosse. Included as well were the three games that had been the most popular for a decade — hockey, baseball and soccer. In 1914 it was estimated that there were 4,500 soccer players in Winnipeg.[14] The number of participants in baseball and hockey must have been comparable because the organizational structure for the three sports was very similar. For each sport there was a huge entity, such as the Winnipeg Amateur

Hockey League, the Winnipeg and District Football League or the Winnipeg Amateur Baseball Association, that arranged games for players of "senior," "intermediate," "junior" and even "juvenile" age or caliber. Those same players, and thousands of other less serious ones, might join dozens of teams in a host of leagues: intercollegiate leagues (except in baseball); church and Sunday School leagues; lodge leagues; "occupational" leagues such as bankers', mercantilers', wholesalers', printers' or building tradesmen's leagues; and the remarkably active "company" leagues, such as the 1908 soccer league for Eaton's employees, that had no fewer than sixteen teams.[15]

....

There were several reasons for the increase in sports participation in the early twentieth century. A major one was certainly population growth; between 1900 and 1914 Winnipeg's population jumped from about 40,000 to probably more than 150,000.[16] However, the figures previously cited on the number of clubs and athletes indicate that the growth in participation was much greater than the increased population alone can explain. A decrease in the number of hours per week that many men were required to work was an additional reason in the sports explosion, although it cannot be advanced as the major one, as people could have spent their increased leisure time in any number of ways.[17] Two other reasons were much more important. The first — one that will be discussed only briefly here — was that games were "fun" to play, perhaps more so than they had been before. The second was that people were rewarded by others for playing and promoting them.

In attempting to explain why people participate or have participated in games, one can never overlook the fact that games are structured activities, and that one thing they are designed to do, and normally succeed in doing, is to produce a state of being in which "awareness merges with action," a feeling that we refer to when we say we are "having fun" or "playing."[18] What can be said with certainty is that the pleasure of participating in games, enhanced by the pleasure of interacting with others who were also participating in them, was something that many Winnipeggers experienced in the early twentieth century; and that they were therefore motivated to take part in these activities again and again.[19] What can be suggested, furthermore, is that although manly games had provided enjoyment for the people of Winnipeg since the city's earliest days, after the turn of the century they offered more fun for more individuals than ever before, in large part because of the greater availability of recently developed standardized, improved, moderately priced sports equipment that could produce more kinesthetic and competitive pleasure than the equipment available in previous years.[20] And what seems beyond doubt is that the growing enjoyment of manly games complemented the second important reason for the explosion of sporting activity after 1900, which was that those who participated in and promoted these activities were rewarded for doing so.

For a few highly proficient sportsmen, the reward was money or a "soft" job. For many more individuals the reward was a trophy, a medal or a locket. And for everyone who took part in sport the reward was incessant, repeated praise especially from leading or very respectable members of the city's British Protestant charter group, particularly clergymen, educators, businessmen and journalists. These people believed, as they had for decades, that manly games tested, inculcated, and brought into focus the many qualities of character that, taken together, constituted manliness. They felt that now, more than ever before, those qualities needed to be developed and highlighted. The reason for the new emphasis on both manliness and the games that tested this quality was that now the charter group, and especially the most articulate members of it, was conscious of what could be called the "problem of progress" or the "problem of modern civilization." Of course members of the group were still proud of being part of the "British" or "Anglo-Saxon" race, proud that their ancestors had built what they regarded as the greatest, most progressive civilization in the history of man. Nevertheless, like many others in the English-speaking world, they were now more aware of the detrimental effects of progress, and especially of those things that most symbolized "British" or "Anglo-Saxon" paramountcy — wealth, technological expertise, and large urban centres.[21]

The major modern problem seemed to be declining "health." The age of "super-civilization," as the *Winnipeg Saturday Post* called the contemporary period, was characterized by excessive, leisure-creating wealth for a few and, in the cities, overcrowded living conditions and sedentary, technologically sophisticated occupations for many. All of this was contributing to a degeneration of physical well-being, and since it was assumed that body and soul were indissolubly connected, the physical decline was necessarily contributing to a moral one. In fact, some people argued that the signs of physical deterioration revealed moral decay that had already reached an advanced state.[22] Winnipeggers were especially conscious of and bothered by these problems. Over the years they had expressed confidence that their city would be the metropolis of a region occupied by healthy individuals whose physical and moral strength would provide the backbone for Canada and the British Empire. Now there was growing evidence that residents of the city, especially the young, had physical problems similar to those affecting people who had grown up in large British or Eastern North American centres.[23] Even more disconcerting were the seemingly widespread moral problems. Juvenile delinquency, prostitution and violent behaviour all seemed to be increasingly prevalent and, in the age of the "great barbeque," it appeared that Winnipeggers and Western Canadians had forgotten that men could not be measured solely by their ability to make money. Therefore, the attributes that had made Canada, the Empire and the Anglo-Saxon race so powerful and influential — the manly qualities of self-discipline, will-power, devotion to fair play and equality, and above all that sense of loyalty and duty to a side that was the essence of patriotism — had to be reemphasized.[24]

Modern inadequacies might be remedied, it seemed, if among other things people participated more extensively in manly games. Therefore, in addition to recommending such things as restructured city government, public ownership of utilities and environmental planning, and with more unanimity among themselves and more support from the general public than they received when advocating these and other reforms, Winnipeggers who were conscious of urban problems made greater efforts to encourage sport. Those greater efforts were marked by new means of promoting games, by an especially aggressive endeavour to make sure that young men played *organized* sport forms, and by the encouragement of wider participation patterns than previously had been in evidence.

....

Since at least the 1880s, almost all sporting activity in Winnipeg had consisted of forms of "pick-up" contests or games arranged through sports clubs, and the facilities used had been either vacant lots or fields and structures provided by clubs or joint-stock companies. After the turn of the century, however, many Winnipeggers began to believe that "pick-up" games and clubs either did not supply enough sport or did not supply it in the right atmosphere. They also began to recognize that, because of the rapidly expanding population and the escalating value of real estate, vacant lots were becoming very scarce, and clubs and joint-stock companies could not furnish accommodations that most people could afford to use.[25] A large number of citizens chose to seek out new means of accommodating games after considering the detrimental consequences that seemed likely to result from relying on traditional means of instigating and accommodating games.

Probably the most striking new departure was the use of public money to provide facilities. In the nineteenth century, fields, rinks, gymnasia, stadia, clubhouses and other facilities could have been built or maintained only indirectly at public expense.[26] In 1902, however, the City made its first move to directly finance athletic facilities when it began to provide dressing rooms and attendants for a few outdoor skating rinks,[27] and over the next dozen years a host of new sports grounds and buildings were built and maintained through taxpayers' money. By 1913, for example, a Playgrounds Association had been in existence for four years, and it was equipping and providing supervisory personnel for seven winter outdoor skating rinks and at least sixteen summer playgrounds where games such as soccer and baseball were encouraged.[28] Meanwhile, one indoor swimming pool had been built, a second was under construction, and the practice of playing supervised floating swimming "tanks" in the rivers in summer had become commonplace.[29] Furthermore, the role and budget of the City of Winnipeg Public Parks Board had been expanded to enable it to provide several major sport facilities. The board had been established in 1893, and until the first decade of the twentieth century, its energy and money had been devoted primarily to the construction and upkeep of "relaxation" parks characterized by an abundance of gardens, flowers, shrubs and trees. In 1907 the board began, wherever feasible, to set up tennis courts in its parks, and by 1915 it had not only taken the initial steps that would result in the opening in 1921 of Winnipeg's first public golf course, but constructed or taken over four huge sports-oriented parks that helped to reduce the "overloading" of facilities. As it happens, they are still in use in the 1980s: the Old Exhibition Grounds, off McPhillips Avenue in the north end, responsibility for which was assumed by the Parks Board in 1908 and which soon became an important site for baseball, football and tennis; and Assiniboine, Sargent and Kildonan Parks, built by the City and opened in 1909, 1913 and 1915 respectively, all of which contained tennis courts, huge fields for the summer team games, and sometimes skating rinks and lawn bowling greens.[30]

A less dramatic departure than the use of public money for facilities, but still a very important new means of providing sport, was the use of institutions that previously had not been utilized. One of these was the business firm. In the nineteenth century, employees of certain establishments frequently had formed teams, especially to play baseball, and occasionally different companies had held picnics at which employees and their families participated in athletic events.[31] Emerging after 1900 was the company athletic association, set up for employees by or through the assistance of managerial personnel. Normally these entities sponsored baseball, soccer and hockey teams, some curling games and perhaps other sports activities as well. In the years between 1900 and 1915, the Canadian Pacific Railway, Ashdown's Hardware, Robinson and Company (department store), the Hudson's Bay Company and other institutions formed such associations. The T. Eaton Company even went as far as to build a ten acre athletic ground, Eaton Park, situated close to what is now the Polo Park Shopping Centre, where, after 1910, their employees could enjoy baseball, soccer, cricket, basketball, tennis and track and field. The objective of these firms was outlined in 1913 by a spokesman for the Grand Trunk Pacific Railway Company, who described the purpose of the recently formed Grand Trunk Pacific Athletic Association as the development of the physical and mental "faculties" of employees, with a view to allowing them to enjoy better health and, as a result, give "better service and satisfaction" to both the company and those whom it served.[32] The church was the second institution that members of the charter group really only began to use in the early twentieth century for fostering sport. Prominent members and clergymen of Protestant churches had endorsed and abetted manly games since the city's earliest days, but in the nineteenth century it had really only been through the annual picnic that they had used the churches, as institutions, to promote them. However, between the 1890s and the beginning of the Great War, more and more of Winnipeg's religious leaders, like those in other cities throughout the English-speaking world, became convinced that the churches should directly sponsor sport. Their feeling was that this would not only draw to the church people who might not otherwise be interested, but also contribute to a more "wholesome," less commercial and vulgar sporting atmosphere.[33] Acting on these assumptions, by the turn of the century the leaders of many Winnipeg Protestant churches were arranging recreational cycling for members of their congregations, and by 1914 they were facilitating dozens of teams, clubs and events in tennis, basketball, baseball, soccer, hockey, track and field, and other sports.[34]

....

These new methods of promoting and facilitating sport emerged, in large part, because of the prevailing early twentieth century assumption that adolescent and pre-adolescent boys did not weigh up to the physical and moral standards of previous generations, and they represented part of a diligent attempt to promote *organized* forms of the manly games among male youths. Of course, a good deal of the game-playing of boys between the ages of about nine and seventeen remained unsupervised and impulsive, as it always had been,[35] but there is no denying that there was an intensified and relatively successful effort to have church leaders, social workers, school teachers or other responsible adults arrange and govern their play activities. Wherever possible the attempt was made to replace "aimless," unorganized play with structured games that had "constructive tendencies" and "educative value," especially the manly ones. The supposition was that youngsters would receive just as much exercise and enjoyment from these supervised activities as they could from less organized forms of play and, without being conscious of it, would also absorb valuable lessons about life that manly sports could teach — especially that rules must be obeyed and that "right," not might, should always triumph.[36]

One aspect of this effort to provide organized games for young men was arranging sport through Protestant churches; the majority of the leagues, teams and events that, as we have mentioned, these institutions sponsored, were designed to help churches "regain and maintain" their hold on teenaged boys.[37] The construction and maintenance of most of the publicly financed facilities previously referred to, notably the playgrounds, skating rinks and swimming pools, was a second feature of the effort to reach young men; these accommodations were expected to be used primarily by youngsters, particularly those who, because they had careless or less well-to-do parents, learned about life "on the street" instead of in respectable homes, churches or schools, and who would quite likely become juvenile delinquents and adult criminals if they were not exposed to "uplifting" influences such as properly supervised manly sports.[38] There were several other indications of the new commitment to organized sport for male youths. One of them was the intensified promotion of games by the Winnipeg Branch of the Young Men's Christian Association. Like other early branches of the Y.M.C.A. around the world, the first Winnipeg chapters had attempted to develop morally upright young men through programmes of prayers, Bible study, recitations, readings and singing, but from the mid-1880s "Y" leaders, in Winnipeg as elsewhere, had begun to concentrate on developing the "whole" man, and in order to do so the local branch had fostered a number of summer sports.[39] In the early twentieth century the emphasis on sport at the "Y" was amplified, especially once the branch moved into new headquarters that enabled it to accommodate such winter activities as basketball, volleyball, swimming, amateur boxing and wrestling.[40] Still another development that signified the enhanced appreciation of organized sport for young males was the formation of several youth organizations that consciously used games to inculcate proper values and attitudes. One such institution was the Winnipeg Boys' Club, founded in 1904 and financed by contributions from businessmen and the City; it sponsored annual field days and a host of teams in several ball games in an effort to make sure that "working" boys, especially newsboys, became "strong, healthy, upright" young Canadians.[41] Finally, the new emphasis on organized sport for young men was revealed by what took place in the city's schools.

In the latter decades of the nineteenth century educators in Winnipeg, like educators throughout most of the English-speaking world, had become "athleticists" and had encouraged male students to participate in manly games. In the twentieth century they emphasized sport even more than they had in the nineteenth. At Winnipeg's three Protestant denominational colleges, for example, the authorities seemed to feel guilty that they had hitherto turned out too many effeminate individuals who were, as one writer put it, "sentimental, scholarly, speculative . . . and soon winded on the race-track of practical life."[42] In order to enhance the ratio of virile graduates, the colleges built new or improved rinks, gymnasia, and other facilities.[43] They also accelerated their athletic programmes. For example, they maintained the existing intercollegiate football and hockey leagues and organized a new intercollegiate basketball league.[44] Furthermore, with a new enthusiasm, they fostered intercollegiate field days and matches in those sports, such as baseball and cricket, for which no association existed.[45] Above all, they created or gave new life to intramural sports organizations that provided tennis, rugby, curling, soccer, hockey and basketball for hundreds of students who, for the most part, were not good enough to play on teams representing their institution. In 1910, one hundred and fifty young men took part in such an intramural rugby league at St. John's College School.[46]

In the public school system, as well, there was a new emphasis on sport. After about 1905 the province's educational authorities, and the public in general, began to regret that they had not been sufficiently conscious of students' physical development and sense of discipline. Suddenly, new importance was attached to nutrition, hygiene and especially physical exercise.[47] One consequence, all across the province but especially in Winnipeg, was that supervised periods of military drill became common; this was true especially after 1911, when provincial authorities negotiated an acceptable arrangement with the trustees of the Strathcona Trust, through which the Department of Education received a share of money that had been set aside by Donald A. Smith, now Lord Strathcona, to supply schools with exercise equipment and to train teachers in "physical education."[48] But because the prevalent assumption was that organized manly games could inculcate health and discipline in young people just as well as, if not better than, formal drill, more emphasis was placed on them as well.[49] As a result, many schools inaugurated inter-class leagues in some of the team ball games, and the Schools Football League and Schools Lacrosse League, established in 1900 and 1901 respectively, grew year-by-year until, by 1914, each entity provided competition for well over five hundred boys of twelve to sixteen years of age.[50]

....

The explosion of sports activity in the early twentieth century not only featured, and in part resulted from, the new means of arranging sport and the heightened emphasis on providing organized games for young males. It was also marked, and in part caused, by greater participation than in the nineteenth century on the part of certain recognizable groups that were responding positively to the encouragement they received from leading and respected Winnipeggers. In a way that was not as paradoxical as it might seem. Women were also urged to become more active in many sports. Members of non-British Protestant minority cultures also became more involved, partly because they were praised for doing so by members of the charter group. Finally, people of the lower or working "classes" participated in a greater variety of sports and were, in general, much more active than in earlier years.

In the early twentieth century, as in the nineteenth, Winnipeg women were encouraged primarily to watch manly games, but after 1900 they were more often praised, by articulate males, for participating. Along with the realization that Winnipeg was beset with many modern urban problems, came an appreciation of the facts that only healthy mothers could bear healthy children, and that there would be more such mothers if more women played invigorating sports. This was especially obvious and important to the many people who believed that the British "race" had a mission to civilize the world and that, if something were not done soon to curb the detrimental effects of modern living, they might not have the strength to carry it out. When W.J. Sisler, the famous Winnipeg educator, went to London in 1910 he was appalled, as were other Canadians who visited the heart of the Empire in this era, by the living conditions of England's poor, and especially by the number of drunken, devitalized women. He did not have very much confidence in the "kind of race" that would emerge from these conditions.[51] Winnipeggers should remember, said a writer in the Wesley College student newspaper Vox Wesleyana, something that the ancient Greeks had known but which had evidently been forgotten over the centuries, namely that "healthful recreation for women" was "essential" to the "physical perfection of the race."[52]

Partly as a result of the prodding they received from males, after the turn of the century Winnipeg women played more manly sports more often than ever before. They could now be seen, regularly engaging in rather strenuous sports such as hockey, baseball, curling, competitive snowshoeing and basketball. They also became much more active than they had been in other, more familiar sports such as tennis, golf and track and field.[53] There is no denying that much of the increased female participation in sport resulted from greater desire on the part of many of the gentler sex to become involved; not only did they find the games kinesthetically satisfying, but by playing them they could announce to themselves and others that they were "modern" women, not "swooning" females whose type was out of fashion.[54] But the encouragement they received from influential males also stimulated them, and their response contributed more than a little to the explosion of activity in the manly sports.

Another group of Winnipeggers who helped cause the increase in sport by participating more extensively than before was the city's non-British Protestants. From the 1870s until the late 1890s British Protestants had formed the vast majority of the population, and they had been much more involved in sport than members of other culture groups. Icelanders, English-speaking Roman Catholics, and Franco-Manitobans from across the Red River in St. Boniface had not been completely inactive of course, but they had taken part in manly games to a considerably less extent than had members of the charter group. In the 1890s, however, Icelanders, Anglo and Irish Catholics and Franco-Manitobans began to become more prominent. They especially exhibited greater participation in team ball games such as baseball and hockey, which previously had been played essentially by British Protestants, while at the same time they kept their interest in certain individual sports, such as foot-racing and wrestling, that are and have been played nearly universally and that had been handed down to them, in some form, by their own ancestors.[55] In the early twentieth century, the number and frequency of games played by these people expanded still further,[56] and joining in now, though not to the same degree, were members of the Central and Eastern European culture groups who entered Winnipeg in such huge numbers in the decade and a half preceding the Great War. Most of these Germans, Russians, Ukrainians, Poles, Jews and other immigrants came from peasant backgrounds, and sport seems to have been only a minor aspect of their traditional cultures.[57] Nevertheless, by the years just before the War, a significant number of most of the minorities had become very attached to the manly games that were historically so much more a part of the majority group's culture than of their own.

One reason why members of the minorities became more involved in games was that, just like British Protestants, they often discovered that, especially when good friends were fellow-participants, these activities provided pleasurable experiences that were almost irresistibly attractive.[58] A second reason was that a few leaders of many of the ethnic groups themselves began to foster sport, in the hopes that adult members of a minority would thereby be able to maintain contact with and influence over younger members and even, in some cases, develop in them the strength and discipline that might be used in future to "free" a homeland.[59] But certainly an important cause of the augmented participation by non-British Protestants was the encouragement it received from members of the charter group.

Since the pioneer years British Protestants, in Winnipeg and throughout the prairie West, had assumed that their part of the world was and should be a "British and Canadian" one, and that minorities should accommodate themselves to and adopt British-Canadian institutions, values and customs. Because of the physical, mental and moral training and benefits that manly games provided, and especially because these activities seemed capable of bestowing upon others the celebrated British sense of "fair play," in the nineteenth century participation in sports had often been recommended by members of the majority to non-British Protestants, especially to native peoples.[60] In the early twentieth century there was a greater awareness of the role that games could play in inculcating proper values to members of minority groups. The reason, of course, was that "foreign" Europeans were moving into the city and the region by the thousands, and especially in the city their presence was associated with the apparently increasing incidence of drunkenness, disease, crime, prostitution and violence, as well as with the perceived erosion of commitment to traditional British Protestant customs and values.[61]

Although some people believed that foreigners should be excluded from the country, most Winnipeggers were "assimilationists" — that is, they believed that through constant effort and, especially, through concentration on the "Canadianization" of the younger generation, "foreigners" could be taught to behave and even to think like the majority.[62] One important instrument of assimilation was manly games. "The play world leads to the heart of the foreign child as readily [as that of] the British born," was the way one writer put it.[63] Through participation in sport, non-British people would not only develop healthy bodies, but unconsciously become familiar with such things as the acceptable "Canadian" ways of reacting to victory or defeat, and the appropriate attitudes toward rules and the individuals empowered to enforce them.[64] Therefore, the people in charge of Winnipeg's public playgrounds made a special effort to reach "foreign" children through sport, and the immigrant youngsters who attended institutions such as W.J. Sisler's Strathcona School found that they were virtually forced to play "Canadian" games such as soccer.[65]

Finally, the sports explosion was characterized by, and in large part attributable to, certain games becoming less exclusive, in terms of their "class" appeal, than before. Ever since several manly sports had been established in the city some of them had been primarily played by and associated with particular "classes" of people. In the early twentieth century a number of games that had been previously the preserve of the "upper" or the "solid and respectable middle" classes were becoming popular among the "working" class. Coupled with the phenomenal rise of unexclusive new or formerly unpopular sports such as indoor baseball, basketball and pin bowling,[66] this brought about a significant "democratization" of the manly sports as a whole in the first decade and a half of the twentieth century.

This does not negate the fact that, in the early twentieth century, some sports remained "upper" class recreations; polo and golf, for example, were still played, as they always had been, almost exclusively by the rich, and the types of individuals, who, in 1912, could afford the St. Charles Country Club's initial membership fee of $750.00 or the Winnipeg Golf Club's $400.00.[67] It was also true that, although "upper" class or "very respectable" people applauded the involvement of their socio-economic "inferiors" in sports such as tennis, curling and cricket, they evidently preferred to see these people, who of course were often "foreign" as well as "working" class, use public facilities or form their own clubs rather than try to become members of such distinguished entities as the Winnipeg Lawn Tennis Club, the Winnipeg Cricket Club or the Assiniboine Curling Club. In 1914 "working" class people still could not afford to play all games, and they were evidently not encouraged to play others in the particular surroundings associated with "better" people, but they were much more involved in the manly sports than they had been in 1900.

No doubt an important reason for this process was that "working" class people wanted to play new games. They now enjoyed tennis, curling and cricket, just as men of their station in Winnipeg had for many years been fond of, and still enjoyed, such sports as hockey, baseball, soccer, lacrosse, boxing and track and field.[68] They were also attracted to the prospect of fraternizing with the kind of individuals they could expect to be around when participating in these games. But certainly a further reason was the encouragement of wider participation patterns by the solidly established "middle" and "upper" class members of the charter group. These people knew that it was members of the "working" or "lower" class who usually lived in crowded, unsanitary conditions, and who were therefore particularly in need of the physical exercise that manly games provided. "Middle" and "upper" class people also knew that "working" or "lower" class individuals, because they often lived in unattractive surroundings, were apt to ignore, or even to challenge, some facts of life that games could teach or reconfirm. Among those facts, the most important were that "success" went to those who "earned" it through determination and disciplined skill, and that "failure" could ultimately lead to "success," especially if, rather than prompting angry or violent outbursts, it resulted in a calm resolve to improve upon the weaknesses that had just been revealed.[69] It was in large part because respectable Winnipeggers assumed that participation in sport would be very beneficial, both physically and morally, for the less well-to-do, that they provided public facilities, arranged "business" or "church" leagues and events, and used their control of the newspapers, the pulpit and the school system to publicize the value of games. The positive response of the "working" class contributed immensely to the early twentieth century explosion of activity.

....

In the years between the turn of the century and the beginning of the Great War, then, organized sport was very popular among and important to Winnipeggers, especially those who realized that their city was beset with urban problems. The new departures they used in this era, to help encourage greater involvement in sport by more people, evidently had a permanent impact on the city's sporting culture. If one task of historians is to intelligibly reconstruct the circumstances and ideas of people living at a certain time and in a certain place, then what happened in Winnipeg indicates that historians of Canada's period of urban reform, like historians of so many other eras, should become more aware of how important and highly valued sport has been to the citizens of this country. If a second task of historians is to help explain the present by noting ways in which it has evolved out of the past, then the Winnipeg experience suggests that they might look to the early twentieth century as the seminal period in the development of current Canadian sports attitudes and practices.

NOTES

....

1. The way in which sport was promoted in the urban reform period has been suggested, but never discussed at length. See Paul Rutherford, "Introduction," in *Saving the Canadian City: The First Phase, 1880–1902*, ed. Rutherford (Toronto: University of Toronto Press, 1974), xx; Alan F.J. Artibise, *Winnipeg: A Social History of Urban Growth, 1874–1914* (Montreal: McGill-Queen's University Press, 1975), 193.
2. On this, see Morris K. Mott, "Manly Sports and Manitobans, Settlement Days to World War One" (unpublished Ph.D. thesis, Queen's University, 1980), chapters 2–3.
3. David Newsome, *Godliness and Good Learning, Four Studies on a Victorian Ideal* (London: John Murray, 1961), 207–211; Norman Vance, "The Ideal of Manliness," in *The Victorian Public School, Studies in the Development of an Educational Institution*, ed. Brian Simon and Ian Bradley (Dublin: Gill and Macmillan Ltd., 1975), 115–117.

4. *Manitoba Free Press*, hereafter referred to as *MFP*: 14 May, 1910, 5 of sports section; 22 August, 1910, 14; 23 March, 1911, 5; *Winnipeg Saturday Post*, hereafter referred to as *Sat. Post*: 14 September, 1912, 4; 8 March, 1913, 5; 21 March, 1914, 5.

5. *MFP*: 9 February, 1895, 5; 10 November, 1905, 5; 18 February, 1911, 33; 21 November, 1991, 6.

6. Ibid: 12 June, 1909, 1 of sports section; 11 October, 1913, 22; 14 February, 1914, 1 of Y.M.C.A. section.

7. Ibid: 11 July, 1908, 1 of sports section; 21 July, 1910, 7.

8. Ibid: 24 October, 1908, 2 of sports section; 10 May, 1910, 6; 10 September, 1913, 7; *Sat. Post*, 3 January, 1914, 5.

9. *MFP*: 5 June, 1900, 5; 16 May, 1914, 19; 19 May, 1914, 6; 21 May, 1914, 6.

10. Ibid: 5 September, 1908, 1, 3 of sports section; *Sat. Post*, 11 April, 1914, 5.

11. *Western Sportsman*, July 1906, 201; *Sat. Post*, 3 July, 1909, 11; *MFP*: 24 April, 1909, 6; 18 July, 1914, 6.

12. See "List of Clubs," *Annual, Manitoba Branch, Royal Caledonian Curling Club*, 12 (1900–01): 65–118; "List of Clubs," *Annual, Manitoba Curling Association*, 26 (1914–15): 106–161; *MFP*: 6 January, 1914, 6; 27 January, 1914, 6; 17 March, 1914, 6.

13. *MFP*: 26 September, 1908, 1 of sports section; 24 December, 1910, 34; *Sat. Post*, 3 January, 1914, 5.

14. *MFP*, 25 April, 1914, 20.

15. On the Eaton's league, see *Sat. Post*, 15 August, 1908, 10.

16. Artibise, *Winnipeg*, 130–131.

17. The decrease in hours of labour in this period is documented in "Wages and Hours of Labour in Canada, 1901–1920," Supplement, *Labour Gazette*, March 1921, 447–480.

18. I am drawing here on the following: Bernard Suits, *The Grasshopper: Games, Life and Utopia* (Toronto: University of Toronto Press, 1978), 34; Marshall McLuhan, "Games: The Extensions of Man," in *Understanding Media*, ed. McLuhan (New York: McGraw-Hill Book Company, 1964), especially 215; Mihaly Csikszentmihalyi and Stith Bennett, "An Exploratory Model of Play," *American Anthropologist*, vol. 73 (1971): especially 46; Mihaly Czikszentmihalyi, "Play and Intrinsic Rewards," *Journal of Humanistic Psychology*, vol. 15 (1975): especially 55–60.

19. See Conrad S. Riley, *Rowing Memories* (Winnipeg: Conrad S. Riley, 1934), 110; James H. Gray, *The Boy from Winnipeg* (Toronto: Macmillan Company Ltd., 1970), 16, 45–50, 55, 182; *Annual, Manitoba Curling Association*, 22 (1910–11): 111–119.

20. On the improvements in sporting equipment in the later decades of the nineteenth century, see Ian F. Jobling, "Sport in Nineteenth Century Canada: The Effects of Technological Change on its Development" (unpublished Ph.D. thesis, University of Alberta, 1970), chapter 4.

21. On others in the English-speaking world that possessed similar anxieties, see Bernard Semmel, *Imperialism and Social Reform: English Social-Imperial Thought, 1895–1914* (Cambridge, Mass.: Harvard University Press, 1960), chapters 2 and 9; Geoffrey Harpham, "Time Running Out: The Edwardian Sense of Cultural Degeneration," *Clio*, vol. 5 (1976): 283–301.

22. *Sat. Post*, 6 July, 1912, 7; A.E. Garland, M.D., "Why the City Man Needs Gymnasium Exercise," *Western Sportsman* (Dec. 1906): 318; *MFP*: 7 April, 1908, 7; 7 November, 1908, 1 of sports section.

23. See *Winnipeg Tribune*, 15 February, 1895, 1.

24. *MFP*, 7 November, 1908, 1 of sports section; *Western School Journal*, June 1909, 209–210.

25. *MFP*: 19 November, 1903, 5; 24 August, 1905, 6; 24 March, 1906, 29; 28 November, 1908, 1 of sports section; 2 April, 1910, 19; *Sat. Post*, 19 November, 1910, 11; *Western Sportsman*, August 1906, 224.

26. "Indirectly" through property tax exemptions or deductions that were occasionally granted to sports organizations, or through the taxes that financed school sporting facilities.

27. City of Winnipeg, *Minutes of City Council*, 1902, 262; *MFP*: 18 November, 1902, 6; 19 December, 1902, 5.

28. *Sat. Post*, 7 December, 1912, 3; *MFP*, 30 December, 1913, 6. The establishment of public playgrounds had been suggested to Winnipeggers by the example of "advanced" American cities. See *Sat. Post*, 15 August, 1908, 10; *Western Sportsman:* August 1906, 224; March 1907, 34; *Western School Journal*, September 1910, 226–229.

29. *MFP*, 18 May, 1912, 19; City of Winnipeg Archives, Library and Public Baths Committee Communications, file #565, 588, 809.

30. J. Norman Wiebe, "The Historical Development of the Winnipeg Parks System 1892–1945, and a brief description of the major parks of the period" (unpublished paper in possession of J.E. Rea, University of Manitoba, n.d.), 7–9, 25, 45; City of Winnipeg, *By-Laws of the City of Winnipeg*, 1908, By-law #5490; City of Winnipeg, *Annual Reports of the Public Parks Board: 1907*, 5–6, 14; 1910, 5; 1913, 5, 7, 19; 1914, 19–32; *Sat. Post*, 9 May, 1914, 5.

31. *MFP*: 19 July, 1897, 5; 18 August, 1897, 3.

32. *Sat. Post*: 18 July, 1914, 5; 4 June, 1910, 19; 24 August, 1912, 4; *MFP*: 23 March, 1908, 6; 28 November, 1908, 1 of sports section.

33. *MFP*: 31 May, 1902, 20; 4 November, 1908, 6; D.C. Coleman, "The Church and Wild Olive," *Western Sportsman*, September 1906, 246–247.

34. *MFP*, 24 April, 1914, 19–20.

35. See Gray, *The Boy from Winnipeg*, 50, 55.

36. *MFP*: 20 October, 1903, 5; 21 November, 1908, 1 of sports section; *Sat. Post*, 14 June, 1913, 5; *Western School Journal*: December 1906, 19–20; June 1909, 201–203; September 1910, 226–229; April 1913, 135–138; *Western Sportsman*, February 1907, 16.

37. Coleman, "The Church and Wild Olive," 247; *MFP*, 25 April, 1914, 19–20.

38. *MFP*: 21 November, 1908, 1 of sports section; 28 November, 1908, 1 of sports section, 22 May, 1909, 3 of sports section; *Western School Journal*, September 1910, 228–229.

39. Murray G. Ross, *The Y.M.C.A. in Canada, The Chronicle of a Century* (Toronto: The Ryerson Press, 1951), 22–28, 89–90, 169, 177, 189–192; H.E. Meller, *Leisure and the Changing City, 1870–1914* (London: Routledge and Kegan Paul Ltd., 1976), 145–146; *Young Men's Christian Association of Metropolitan Winnipeg, Layman's Handbook, 1975* (Winnipeg: Y.M.C.A., 1975), 10; *MFP*: 10 November, 1874, 3; 7 December, 1874, 3; 12 May, 1888, 4; 13 April, 1895, 5.

40. *MFP*: 18 January, 1901, 6–7; 8 April, 1902, 5; 12 June 1909, 1–2 of sports section; 14 February, 1914, 1–4 of Y.M.C.A. section.

41. Public Archives of Manitoba, Winnipeg Boys' Club File, "Fifth Annual Report of Winnipeg Boys Club," 1909, especially 7–10; *MFP*: 4 January, 1908, 6; 18 January, 1908, 6; 27 September, 1909, 6; 13 February, 1914, 7; 17 April, 1914, 7.

42. Rev. T.E. Holling, "The Gymnasium of Christ," *Vox Wesleyana*, June 1910, 49. See also *St. John's College Magazine*, June 1914, 232.

43. *Manitoba College Journal*, January 1912, 17; *St. John's College Magazine*: Easter 1911, 71; November 1912, 1–2, 25, 47; *Vox Wesleyana*, December 1903, 69.

44. *Manitoba College Journal*, April 1907, 21–22.

45. *St. John's College Magazine*, April 1910, 44–45; *Vox Wesleyana*, June 1910, 55.

46. *MFP*, 15 November, 1910, 6.

47. See *Western School Journal*: February 1907, 38; April 1907, 114–117.

48. *MFP*, 24 June, 1905, 7; *Western School Journal*, November 1906, 7–9, 11–12; David A. Downie, "Physical Education in the Public Schools of Manitoba" (unpublished M.Ed.

thesis, University of Manitoba, 1961), 66–68, 95; L.C. Green, "The History of School Cadets in the City of Winnipeg" (unpublished M.Ed. thesis, University of Manitoba, 1950), especially chapter 3.

49. See the remarks of H.R. Hadcock of the Winnipeg Y.M.C.A. in *Western School Journal*, April 1907, 117.

50. *MFP*: 20 September, 1900, 5; 13 April, 1901, 5; 16 April, 1901, 5; 3 October, 1911, 7; 10 October, 1913, 7; 11 July, 1908, 3 of sports section; 6 March, 1914, 6; 4 April, 1914, 8; *Sat. Post*, 1 April, 1911, 8.

51. Public Archives of Manitoba, W.J. Sisler Papers, "Diary of a Trip to Europe, July and August 1910," entry for July 31.

52. *Vox Wesleyana*, March 1908, 107. On the concern with healthy mothers around the English-speaking world in these years, see Stephanie Lee Twin, "Jock and Jill: Aspects of Women's Sports History in America, 1870–1940" (unpublished Ph.D. thesis, Rutgers University, 1978), 115–127.

53. This is an impression gained from reading most issues of the *MFP* between 1872 and 1914. For specific references to women engaging in rather vigorous sports, see *MFP*: 3 March, 1906, 6; 4 January, 1912, 6; 9 February, 1914, 7.

54. *Vox Wesleyana*, July 1902, 153.

55. *Northwest Review*: 17 October, 1885, 4; 22 June, 1892, 4; *MFP*: 27 May, 1884, 4; 28 May, 1884, 4; 5 November, 1886, 4; 13 June, 1894, 5; 20 November 1901, 5; *Le Manitoba*: 24 May, 1888, 3; 20 May, 1891, 3; 7 December, 1898, 3; W. Kristjanson, *The Icelandic People in Manitoba, A Manitoba Saga* (Winnipeg: Wallingford Press, 1965), 259–263, 286, 455, 461.

56. See *MFP*, 3 April, 1914, 6; *Le Manitoba*: 10 June, 1908, 3; 11 October, 1911, 4; 8 November, 1911, 4; *La Liberté*, 30 May, 1913, 8; Fred Thordanson, "The Romance of the Falcons" (unpublished article in Icelandic Collection, Elizabeth Dafoe Library, University of Manitoba, Winnipeg), no pagination.

57. See Victor Turek, *Poles in Manitoba* (Toronto: Canadian Polish Congress, 1967), 2; Arthur Grenke, "The Formation and Early Development of an Urban Ethnic Community: A Case Study of the Germans in Winnipeg, 1892–1919" (unpublished Ph.D. thesis, University of Manitoba, 1975), 81, 95; Arthur A. Chiel, *The Jews in Manitoba: A Social History* (Toronto: University of Toronto Press, 1961), 109; Paul Yuzyk, *The Ukrainians in Manitoba, A Social History* (Toronto: University of Toronto Press, 1953), 160–163; Helen Potrebenko, *No Streets of Gold, A Social History of Ukrainians in Alberta* (Vancouver: New Star Books, 1977), 88; Leible Hershfield, *The Jewish Athlete: A Nostalgic View* (Winnipeg: Leible Hershfield, 1980), 20.

58. Chiel, *Jews in Manitoba*, 109–110; *Le Manitoba*, 27 June, 1889, 3; Peter Humeniuk, *Hardships and Progress of Ukrainian Pioneers, Memoirs from Stuartburn Colony and Other Parts* (Steinbach, Man.: Derksen Printers Ltd., 1977), 87; W.J. Sisler, *Peaceful Invasion* (Winnipeg: W.J. Sisler, 1944), 35–40.

59. See Chiel, *Jews in Manitoba*, 155; Turek, *Poles in Manitoba*, 191, 206–208, 234; Grenke, "Germans in Winnipeg," 233–235; *Der Nordwesten*, 8 June, 1910, 5.

60. *MFP*: 16 July, 1883, 8; 12 February, 1895, 5; 23 February, 1895, 5.

61. Alan F.J. Artibise, "Divided City: The Immigrant in Winnipeg Society, 1874–1921," in *The Canadian City, Essays in Urban History*, ed. Gilbert A. Stelter and Artibise (Toronto: McClelland & Stewart Ltd., 1977), 312–314; G.F. Chipman, "Winnipeg: The Melting Pot," *Canadian Magazine*, 33 (1909), 413–416; J.S. Woodsworth, *Strangers Within Our Gates or Coming Canadians* (Toronto: The Missionary Society of the Methodist Church of Canada, 1909), 125, 134–137, 139–141; *Vox Wesleyana*, November 1907, 63–66.

62. Artibise, "Divided City," 314; Woodsworth, *Strangers Within Our Gates*, chapters 9–12, passim; G.F. Chipman, "The Refining Process," *Canadian Magazine*, 33 (1909): 548–554.

63. *Western School Journal*, April 1913, 137.

64. *MFP*: 22 May, 1909, 3 of sports section; 31 August, 1909, 7.

65. Ibid., 22 May, 1909, 3 of sports section; Sisler, *Peaceful Invasion*, 35, 40.

66. The fact that these games were popular among all "classes" of people is supported by the names of teams given in *MFP*: 14 October, 1913, 7; 20 February, 1912, 7; 20 November, 1913, 6; 6 November, 1913, 6; 3 January, 1914, 6; 6 January, 1914, 6, as well as by an analysis of occupations of individual participants given in the same references.

67. See *MFP*, 6 June, 1903, 17; *Sat. Post*, 28 December, 1912, 6. An occupational analysis has been made of polo players and golfers mentioned in *MFP*: 6 June, 1903, 17, 23; 9 September, 1913, 6.

68. This statement is supported by an occupational analysis of 400–500 participants in these sports mentioned in about two dozen different newspaper reports.

69. See *MFP*: 15 February, 1894, 2 of special bonspiel edition; 14 February, 1896, 1; 21 January, 1909, 6; *Sat. Post*, 30 May, 1908, 10. Note especially Prof. R.O. Joliffe, "On Sport," *Vox Wesleyana*, December 1908, 25–26.

TOPIC FIVE
Women and the Household

Presentation of a petition by the Winnipeg Political Equality League for the Enfranchisement of Women, 23 December 1915.

Today, many scholars who write women's history refer to the "social construction of gender" — that is, how some of the roles assigned to women in the public and private domains are determined by social mores rather than biological factors. Perhaps the most powerful images that have shaped and limited the experiences of women have been those of "caregiver" and "preserver of the family." Often, these images have dictated what jobs are suitable for women — that of nurse, elementary-school teacher, textile worker, seamstress, for example. But such stereotypes have also generated opportunities. Numerous women during the late nineteenth and early twentieth centuries rationalized their participation in reform crusades and, in part, their demand for the vote as prompted by a desire to care for society as for an extended family.

The role played by the state in the social construction of gender is the focus of Article 9, Margaret Hobbs and Ruth Roach Pierson's analysis of the federal government's 1937 Home Improvement Plan. Hobbs and Pierson show that the Plan's near sanctification of the home, family life, and a domestic role for women derived from a perception of each as contributing to economic buoyancy, social stability, and cultural progress. While attempting to help women perform certain functions as efficiently as possible with such improvements as the modern "scientific kitchen," the Plan fortified an unequal and gendered division of labour.

The degree to which the family defined and dominated the experiences of women is also made painfully apparent in Article 10, Andrée Lévesque's account of the consequences that befell women who impugned the family's morally normative place in society by giving birth out of wedlock. In the Church-dominated Quebec of the 1930s, such women were treated as moral lepers (though in other parts of Canada, the situation was not much better as "unwed mothers," unless deserted or widowed, were denied assistance from provincial governments and most private agencies, on the ground that to assist them would be to condone promiscuity). In order to hide away their shame, many of those destined to have "illegitimate" children availed themselves of Montreal's Hôpital de la Miséricorde, where the nuns held them in virtual isolation, assigned them new names to conceal their identities, and — as a means of bringing about their moral reform and enabling them to pay for their board and care — required them to perform arduous and often humiliating chores. So powerful was societal disapproval of these "fallen women" and their children that few mothers took their babies with them when they were discharged, recognizing that discovery would result in lifelong stigmatization of mother and child.

QUESTIONS TO CONSIDER

1. Why was housing viewed as the cornerstone of economic growth?
2. Did the Home Improvement Plan harden or alleviate class divisions and the social construction of gender? Did it impart any other values?
3. Did the Home Improvement Plan increase home ownership in Canada? Why or why not?
4. Describe the values and goals behind the program provided for unwed mothers at the Hôpital de la Miséricorde.
5. Does Lévesque's article shed any light on medical history, religious history, or the history of youth?

SUGGESTED READINGS

Bacchi, Carol. *Liberation Deferred? The Ideas of the English-Canadian Suffragists, 1877–1918*. Toronto: University of Toronto Press, 1983.

Bradbury, Bettina. *Canadian Family History: Selected Readings*. Toronto: Copp Clark Pitman, 1992.

Le Collectif Clio. *L'histoire des femmes au Québec depuis quatre siècles*. Montréal: Quinze, 1982. Trans., *Quebec Women: A History*. Toronto: Women's Press, 1987.

Comacchio, Cynthia. *Nations Are Built of Babies: Saving Ontario's Mothers and Children, 1900–1940*. Montreal and Kingston: McGill-Queen's University Press, 1993.

Danylewycz, Marta. *Taking the Veil: An Alternative to Marriage, Motherhood, and Spinsterhood in Quebec*. Toronto: McClelland & Stewart, 1987.

Gagan, Rosemary. *A Sensitive Independence: Canadian Methodist Women Missionaries in Canada and the Orient, 1881–1925*. Montreal and Kingston: McGill-Queen's University Press, 1992.

Iacovetta, Franca, and Mariana Valverde, eds. *Gender Conflicts: New Essays in Women's History*. Toronto: University of Toronto Press, 1992.

Parr, Joy. *The Gender of Breadwinners: Women, Men, and Change in Two Industrial Towns, 1880–1950*. Toronto: University of Toronto Press, 1990.

Pederson, Diana, comp. *Changing Women, Changing History: A Bibliography of the History of Women in Canada*. Toronto: Green Dragon Press, 1992.

Prentice, Alison, Paula Bourne, Gail Cuthbert Brandt, Beth Light, Wendy Mitchinson, and Naomi Black. *Canadian Women: A History*, 2nd ed. Toronto: Harcourt Brace, 1996.

Sangster, Joan. *Dreams of Equality: Women on the Canadian Left, 1920–1950*. Toronto: McClelland & Stewart, 1989.

Snell, James. *In the Shadow of the Law: Divorce in Canada*. Toronto: University of Toronto Press, 1991.

Strong-Boag, Veronica. *The New Day Recalled: Lives of Girls and Women in English Canada, 1919–1939*. Toronto: University of Toronto Press, 1988.

Strong-Boag, Veronica, and Anita Clair Fellman, eds. *Rethinking Canada: The Promise of Women's History*. Toronto: Copp Clark Pitman, 1992.

NINE

"A Kitchen That Wastes No Steps...": Gender, Class and the Home Improvement Plan, 1936–1940

MARGARET HOBBS AND RUTH ROACH PIERSON

"When is a kitchen not a kitchen?" was a question posed in January 1937 by a press release for Canada's Home Improvement Plan (HIP). Women were told that the "old-fashioned" and "inefficient" kitchens which most of them used were "not worthy of the name."[1] Advertisements such as this aimed to enlist the support of women for the federal government's major job creation project during the late years of the Depression. The Home Improvement Plan, one of the few recommendations of the National Employment Commission (NEC) to be implemented by the federal government, was designed to relieve unemployment through a nation-wide scheme of residential renovation and repair.[2] Clearly intended to defuse radicalism among the jobless, the policy, in its media presentation to the public, operated to blur class distinctions; in actuality it may have helped to redraw and harden class lines. Paraded as a boon to the "average" home-owner, the Plan was an attempt to win over the property-owning stratum of the working class to the existing social and economic order. By the provision of low interest loans the securely employed male wage earner could modernize his house and thus also protect his investment. In addition, the Home Improvement Plan presupposed and worked to further entrench existing gender divisions in Canadian society. In the context of social attitudes and policies that discriminated against all women in relief provisions and against married women in paid work other than domestic labour,[3] it is no coincidence that the HIP planners considered women only in their capacity as dependent home workers. The plan represents one facet of the state's increasing involvement in defining what constitutes a proper home as well as in designating the proper roles and relations between and among family members. Formulated in a climate of opinion which scapegoated women for unemployment, especially married women,[4] the Plan is also an example of the way governments have attempted to ameliorate economic dislocation at the expense of women's autonomy in the family and the work force.[5]

Modelled on Title One of the U.S. Federal Housing Act of 1934 and building on many local initiatives to general employment by stimulating the building trades, the Canadian Home Improvement scheme offered loans on favourable terms to property owners for the modernization and repair of their homes. Although intended above all

Source: Excerpted from "'A kitchen that wastes no steps...': Gender, Class and the Home Improvement Plan, 1936–40," *Histoire sociale/Social History*, 21, 41 (May 1988): 9–37. Reprinted by permission of *Histoire sociale/Social History*.

for urban single-family homes, farm houses, duplexes and small apartment buildings also qualified. The interest on repayment was set at only 6.32 percent, a rate lower than that offered through the American plan and considerably lower than the average charged by Canadian finance companies of the time (12 and 14 percent for purchases bought on the instalment plan). The money was to be repaid within three years for a loan of $1,000 or less and within five for larger amounts up to a fixed maximum of $2,000 (later $3,000). Improvements possible under the Plan included surface changes like wall papering; repainting (interior and exterior); refacing clapboard with brick, stone or stucco, and plaster walls with wood panelling; replacing or repairing roofs and eavestroughing; repointing chimneys; and laying new floors. Loan recipients could also make structural changes like enlarging rooms; reclaiming unused basements; converting attics into bedrooms; building in cupboards, closets, bookcases and kitchen counters; installing new piping, wiring, heating and air conditioning systems, and insulation; erecting garages or fences; and altering windows. Under the Plan appliances could be purchased only if they constituted permanent not moveable fixtures, i.e., toilets but not shower curtains, kitchen sinks but not refrigerators, flooring but not rugs.[6] The fears of home-owners that utilizing the Plan would cause property taxes to skyrocket were put to rest by municipalities' agreeing not to increase assessments on HIP-improved houses.[7] The Plan did not speak to the basic need for shelter of the destitute homeless or of those in want of low-rental housing. These housing concerns were addressed, albeit inadequately, by the other major federal government housing initiatives of the Depression, the Dominion Housing Act (DHA) of 1935 and the National Housing Act (NHA) of 1938.[8]

Co-operative agreements between Canadian financial institutions and the Dominion government underwrote both the HIP and the DHA/NHA. Fifty million dollars were made available for HIP loans in exchange for the federal government's promise to guarantee chartered banks and other approved lending institutions against losses of up to 15 percent of the aggregate amount. The total for which the Canadian government might be out of pocket was thus set at $7,500,000.[9] Certain lending institutions, like Heating and Plumbing Finance, Limited, which were affiliated with building supply firms, gained government approval to operate alongside the banks as lending institutions under the Home Improvement scheme.[10] In addition, some building and plumbing suppliers developed their own instalment buying plans, like Crane's "New Budget Plan," which promised "the same low rates of interest as the Government Plan."[11] Necessarily, loans negotiated directly with a building firm could not be "squandered" on "luxuries" and other items that did not qualify under the Plan, as some conservatives, suspicious of the spending habits of government aid recipients, feared might happen with money borrowed from banks.[12]

The Home Improvement Plan was billed as the saviour of the building trades, which, as one early HIP press release stated, "have tossed helplessly in the doldrums"[13] for over six years. Moreover, regarding the building trades as a pivotal industry, policy makers assumed that recovery in this sector would stimulate economic recovery more generally.[14] Many shared that belief. Indeed, Gordon S. Harrington of the NEC announced in his February 1937 radio address to the nation that "when the building trades are busy the benefits spread very widely throughout the whole country."[15] The Trades and Labour Congress agreed that stimulating the building trades would act as a stimulus to the economy generally.[16] According to Maclean's, "activity in the building trades" would mean "an increased demand for a long list of materials with consequent benefit to those engaged in their manufacture and production."[17] The list included the lumber industry, paint companies, building trades suppliers, the manufacturers of bathroom fixtures and linoleum and the makers of air conditioning units. Employment would also be generated for electricians, plumbers, carpenters, house painters, roofers, masons and bricklayers, as well as certain professionals like domestic architects and engineers.[18] Furthermore, its benefits would not be limited to one locale. As the NEC boasted, "the beauty of the Plan is that it creates opportunities for employment in every nook and corner of the country."[19]

The expected boost to employment was tied to the further expectation that the Plan would create an atmosphere of business confidence in which lending institutions would free up credit to the general public, and the general public would be encouraged to spend. U.S. studies estimated that total expenditures on home improvement could exceed amounts borrowed by as much as 3 or 4 to 1.[20] Armed with this information, Harrington assured his radio audience that in the U.S. "for every $1.00 borrowed from the Banks there were some $3.00 used for the same purpose by persons who did not have to borrow."[21] The NEC assured businessmen that the Home Improvement Plan was not primarily extended "to get people to borrow money," but "to SPEND money."[22] HIP was expected to stimulate the circulation of money as "idle men in the building industry are returned to work and renew their lost purchasing power."[23] The NEC relied on the momentum of friendly neighbourhood competition and a "keeping up with the Joneses" mentality to spark a frenzy of clean-up and repair. Commissioners expected that home improvements financed by one homeowner through the HIP would trigger a chain reaction down the street as one neighbour after another compared his or her house to the renovated one next door.[24]

The Home Improvement Plan was to straighten out a tangle of related problems: unemployment, tight credit, consumer parsimony and deteriorating property. Windsor, the site of the HIP pilot project, had been very hard hit by the Depression. Because of the collapse of the automotive industry, unemployment there was so severe that residents defaulted on their taxes and the city in turn "defaulted on its bond interest." Lending institutions and insurance companies refused to loan; credit dried up; and house construction, repair and renovation ground to a halt. While extremely acute in Windsor, the adverse effects of unemployment and tight credit on residential property could be seen in many other localities across Canada. "For six years," the National Employment Commission advised, "Canadians, thousands of them, have been living in rundown, drab, shabby homes," having to watch "their property deteriorate . . . because they could not, or in some cases would not . . . finance needed repairs and improvements."[25]

In the minds of the National Employment Commissioners and members of the federal government more generally, the state of the nation's homes was a measure of the prosperity of the nation: rundown homes reflected a rundown economy. This view derived from an underlying commitment to private property and property owners. Implicitly the NEC and government subscribed to the opinion advanced by one spokesman for the building trades "that the best type of citizen is the one who owns his own home."[26] Certainly the Commission regarded the individually-owned home as the cornerstone of the nation. In the words of Arthur B. Purvis, NEC chairman, the home was "the beginning of the nation," and "the national structure" was "erected on homes."[27]

Having come to power in 1935 on the heels of the Bennett government, Prime Minister Mackenzie King was under considerable pressure both to appease the unemployed and to allay property owners' fears of social unrest. One of the first acts of the new government was the appointment of the National Employment Commission, whose mandate was to investigate unemployment and make recommendations to the Prime Minister. King, reluctant to further the federal government's involvement in direct relief, willingly embraced the NEC's proposal for job creation through the Home Improvement scheme.[28] On 9 September 1936, King announced that the necessary legislation would be passed at the next session of Parliament. In the meantime, a pre-legislation agreement was worked out with lending institutions allowing the Plan to be launched by November, five months ahead of the passage of the Home Improvement Loans Guarantee Act, which did not receive royal assent until 31 March 1937.[29] It was believed that urgent action was required in order to avoid the violence and disruption of previous winters, especially that of 1933–34. The government felt that mere word of the Plan could act as "a barrage against [winter] riots."[30] A special effort was made to put announcements into the foreign-language press, "in view of the possibility of riots which may arise through non-English speaking people, or at least with their cooperation."[31] Indeed, officials were particularly fearful of the activities and influence of certain ethnic groups, such as the Finns and the Ukrainians, who were known to be well represented in the Communist Party of Canada.[32]

The Home Improvement Plan was especially appealing to King because it rested on a philosophy of "voluntary corporatism."[33] In reaction to the radical left's advocacy of class struggle as the vehicle for social change, the corporatist vision assumed that competing segments of society — identified by King as capital, labour, management and the community — could and should pull together for the common good. In the post-war decades, not just government, but businessmen, conservative labour unions and social organizations commonly subscribed to this "co-operative" philosophy. In his endorsement of the HIP, for instance, the President of the Trades and Labour Congress of Canada acclaimed it as "non-partisan" and "confined to no class or calling."[34] Also engaged in the corporatist discourse, the anti-Left *Labour Leader* of Toronto urged labour organizations to support the HIP in order to demonstrate that all "legitimate trade unions can and do participate in constructive and practical work for the general welfare of all."[35]

No doubt King and his Party were also pleased by the knowledge that the Plan required few direct government expenditures, beyond its promise to cover a portion of the banks' losses in case of loan default. According to E.J. Young of the NEC, clearly a pre-Keynesian, government spending could not possibly solve the problem of unemployment anyway, because governments did not have any money apart from what they collected from the people.[36] Leonard C. Marsh, the democratic socialist Director of the McGill Social Science Research Project, astutely faulted the National Employment Commission Reports for only appearing to be Keynesian in their encouragement of pump priming while, in fact, prescribing stimulation to the economy that was dependent on private not public investment, as in the case of the Home Improvement Plan.[37] In addition to those of pre-Keynesian convictions, the Plan was also attractive to members of government and their advisors who were opposed on principle to giving money directly to the poor, lest it foster a dependency mentality or outright irresponsibility. Furthermore, the scheme had the added advantage of channelling "relief" to the unemployed through the respectable, responsible, propertied segment of society. It located the potential for economic recovery within the property-owning class. Perhaps alluding to the limited success of the Dominion Housing

Act of 1935,[38] Young asserted that to "build new houses for all who need them is out of the question. The country cannot afford it."[39] Instead, the HIP would prompt people to spend their own money directly. One advertising notice spoke of "bringing together the houses that needed repair and the men who are anxious to repair them."[40] "It would be possible," observed Young, "for the Government to put all the men in Canada to work at some useless task — such, for instance, as bailing the water out of Lake Ontario and pouring it back in again."[41] The Home Improvement Plan, in contrast, would involve the unemployed in work that was socially valuable.

While the propertyless and the jobless were to benefit from increased employment opportunities, they were not eligible for loans. Indeed, as over half of urban householders were not home-owners, they were ruled out from the start. Moreover, from the first press release, issued on 17 October 1936, it was made clear that those without a steady and substantial income were not invited to apply.[42] Officials and loan companies further specified that applicants must demonstrate "moral worth."[43] Sometimes referred to as "character loans,"[44] they were advertised as requiring no other security "behind the note" than "the man's character and his earning capacity."[45] Although good character in the first instance was defined in terms of financial security and responsibility, bank forms generally extended the concept to include conformity with prevailing norms of marriage and the family. The premium placed on stability in marital relations, employment and residency was intended to weed out the unmarried and the transient.[46]

Just as the poverty-stricken were not to be the direct beneficiaries of the Plan, neither were the nation's wealthy.[47] In fact the Plan was seldom mentioned, either by writers or advertisers, in upper-class magazines like *Canadian Homes and Gardens*. In a radio address of early 1937, Purvis identified the main target group as "ordinary credit-worthy owner[s] of residential property."[48] A broad middle class was included in this category, but so was a portion of the working class. In a move to attract the stable upper-working-class home-owner, HIP advertising strategists spoke of using the image of "the humble cottage," rather than that of the baronial mansion, and of showing what a difference a few low-cost home improvements could make.[49] Fully 37.6 percent of urban working-class households in 1931 owned their own homes — although in decline by 1937, still a sizeable group of potential HIP borrowers.[50] How many of these could have afforded going into debt to improve their houses is another question. At a strategy meeting of government and industry representatives in December 1936, it was suggested that some proportion of the ads should appeal to those making between $1,200 and $1,400 a year.[51] Most working-class families were situated well below this income bracket and would therefore not have qualified financially for HIP loans. Moreover, some contemporary critics, like Alan Dunlop in the *Canadian Forum*, argued that HIP would be affordable only to those who earned enough to pay income tax, that is, single persons earning over $1,000 per annum and married couples with incomes over $2,000. Dunlop estimated that only 7.5 percent of all Canadian households would fall into that category.[52] As no statistics are available to show the distribution of loans by income, it is impossible to determine the number of loans made to working-class home-owners. We do know, however, that before the Plan expired on 30 October 1940, the 125,652 loans approved comprised only about 10 percent of the total number of owner-occupied households.[53] Clearly, only the highest echelons of the working class could have been represented among them.

In Parliament when the HIP bill was debated, several members attacked the Plan's exclusionary nature.[54] Moreover, J.R. MacNicol worried that many working-class families who were eligible would nonetheless find it impossible to pay back the money. He was thinking of a particular worker, thrifty and steadily employed for ten months of the year at $28 a week, who was hoping to borrow $750. How, MacNicol challenged, could this ordinary working-class home-owner possibly afford to repay an annual total of $250 for three years, as required, on his yearly income of $1,120?[55] In fact, the majority of loans would turn out to be considerably smaller, except in the wealthier communities such as St. Hyacinthe and Outremont, where, by the end of 1937, loans were not numerous but their average size was $1,013 and $799 respectively.[56] Throughout the duration of the Plan, amounts borrowed averaged under $400 in most provinces, about $500 in Quebec.[57] Nevertheless, MacNicol's concern was not unwarranted. Studies estimated the cost of living (which dropped significantly during the Depression) at varying amounts, generally ranging from $910 to $1,456 a year.[58] Allowing for the fact that many working-class families had more than one breadwinner, it is still apparent that none but the wealthiest workers could afford to repay even an average sized loan. In implicit recognition of this, the National Employment Commission placed an HIP advertisement in the *Canadian Congress Journal*, urging members of the Trades and Labour Council of Canada:

> If you have a steady job and own your own home which needs repairs or alterations, negotiate a loan yourself and help spread prosperity among less fortunate workers.[59]

In various ways, then, the HIP worked to differentiate between strata of the working class: between the respectable and the unrespectable, the stable and the unstable, those who owned property and earned a solid income and those who did not, those who found repayment affordable and those who found it difficult or impossible.

The Plan also worked to differentiate between the sexes. "Canada is a land of many home owners," proclaimed one NEC press release. The 1931 census had recorded close to one and a half million — almost all of whom were assumed by HIP promoters and bankers to be male.[60] Very rarely did a press release even acknowledge the existence of a female home-owner.[61] For all intents and purposes, a basic characteristic of the "credit-worthy home-owner" was a male identity. Advertisers typically referred to "Mr. Home-Owner and his wife."[62] Women were thus situated, by and large, in an indirect relation to the Plan; it was chiefly as dependants of men, not as home-owners or labour force participants, that they were to benefit. After all, the loans themselves were to go to men and the employment to be generated was located in male-dominated job sectors.

Nonetheless, women were cast as central to the Plan's successful functioning. Mary Sutherland, the only woman member of the NEC, acclaimed the Plan as "one occasion when a government has legislated right into women's hands along [the] lines of women's most serious interest."[63] That statement was premised on the relegation of women to the roles of homemaker and consumer. As production moved from home to factory, the work of housewives shifted from production to consumption. The 1920s witnessed the triumph of the mass media and capitalism's investment in mass consumerism, promoted through mass advertising, as the basis for the mass production of new domestic technologies.[64] Concomitantly, consumer credit institutions emerged to encourage buying on the instalment plan. By the late 1920s U.S. and

Canadian advertisers were basing their marketing techniques on studies which claimed that women were responsible for 80–85 percent of a family's household expenditures.[65] Convinced that women were the managers of most household finances, consumer credit companies, like the Central Finance Corporation of Toronto, produced a series of "Better Buymanship" booklets advising women on how and what to buy.[66] So influential a role were women seen to play in the spending of the family dollars, that each local advisory committee — established to publicize and implement Canada's Home Improvement Plan — was urged either to strike a women's sub-committee or to include representatives from local women's organizations on the other sub-committees, i.e., publicity, finance and trouble-shooting.[67]

While the first step to introducing the Plan had been to win the co-operation of banks and other lending institutions, its implementation also depended on the involvement of those businesses and unions whose interests would be served and on utilization of the most up-to-date advertising techniques. The Plan would operate as an example of voluntary corporatism in action. The National Employment Commission hired Cockfield, Brown and Company, a prestigious Canadian ad agency, to coordinate the advertising campaign.[68] Finance Minister Charles Dunning explained to Parliament that HIP publicity costs would be financed not by the government "but by private funds raised from public-spirited citizens and business interests who expect to benefit from the expenditure involved."[69] To raise contributions from private industry for an estimated advertising budget of $466,000, Cockfield, Brown and Company contacted large corporations, like Imperial Oil, Canadian General Electric, Westinghouse, and Dominion Oilcloth & Linoleum, the major department stores, and four large banks and six smaller lending institutions, as well as a long list of suppliers for the building trades.[70] From these funds, Cockfield, Brown and Company produced a run of over one hundred press releases, issued to all major media, as well as a series of NEC-sponsored ads trumpeting the features of the HIP, for placement in newspapers, magazines, and special-interest journals.[71]

According to the HIP organizational chart drawn up by Cockfield, Brown and Company, the network for promotion and implementation would stretch out from the NEC in Ottawa, east and west across the country through nation-wide businesses, lending institutions, and HIP provincial chairmen appointed by the NEC, down to the local participating businesses and the local HIP advisory committees and sub-committees in individual towns and communities. The advertising campaign would thereby hit Canadians at every turn, making use of urban and rural newspapers, including the foreign-language press, magazines, farm publications, booklets, billboards, posters, radio spots, window displays, street car signs, and movie trailers.[72] In co-operation with the NEC's bid for support from the housewives of Canada, *Chatelaine*, for example, declared "1937 — HOME IMPROVEMENT YEAR" on the cover of its January issue and announced a $25 prize every month beginning in March "for the best example of home improvements submitted" to *Chatelaine's* "Home Improvement Contest."[73]

The "Outline of Plan for Promoting and Popularizing the Home Improvement Plan" urged the adoption of an aggressive advertising campaign which was to become "the weapon with which each member of our organization is armed."[74] Two months after the Plan was put into operation some manufacturers were praised for their initiative in sending their employees "around the city, making notes of homes that need improvements," and then "approaching these prospects with suggestions."[75] Later a special press release, aimed at contractors, chastised them for being too passive in their approach. The techniques of the car salesman were held up for emulation.[76]

The potential of photography was exploited in much of the publicity. By the late 1920s and early 1930s, photography was replacing drawings and paintings for advertising illustration, partly because it was cheaper, but also because it was thought to convey "a literal matter-of-fact realism." Photographers, however, like other illustrators and the advertisers who hired them, were aware of their role as manipulators of images and, through those, the public.[77] One manipulatory technique in photography's bag of tricks was the capacity for taking "before" and "after" shots and displaying them side by side. Much favoured by advertisers in general,[78] the tactic was seized upon by HIP promoters.[79]

Building on the 1920s love affair with the concept of modernity and its elevation by advertisers to the status of a supreme value, HIP promoters held up modernization as the path of escape from the Depression. "Modernization" became the synonym for home improvement. HIP loans were called "modernization loans."[80] For economy's sake, Canadians were advised to write away to the Canadian Institute of Plumbing and Heating for the free-of-charge booklets *How to Modernize Your Heating Equipment* and *How to Modernize Your Plumbing Equipment*.[81] One ad, sporting the HIP logo, asked " . . . have you MONEY TO BURN?" and warned "Don't let the worn-out FURNACE keep you poor!"[82] A link was made between increasing the property value of one's home, putting men to work, and keeping up-to-date. Warning that the market value of "a down-at-heel property" was "considerably lessened," Gertrude Crawford's 1936 *Maclean's* article "It Pays to Modernize" gave advice on how best to make use of HIP loans. Instructing readers that "pride of ownership dictates that the house should be brought into line with modern times," she plugged the government's Home Improvement Plan by shaming readers for being old-fashioned. "The fact is," Crawford pronounced, "that the world has moved on — industrially, architecturally and decoratively — leaving many old houses old-fashioned or even obsolete, according to present standards."[83] To boost its Home Improvement Contest, *Chatelaine* of March 1937 featured a "dramatized presentation" of a "modernized" Winnipeg house. The "almost unbelievable changes" to the exterior were achieved by removing "a dark old veranda,"[84] a bay window and an "ugly oversized dormer," and adding a "new finish of brick veneer."[85] In another *Chatelaine* article, architect Richard A. Fisher condemned the "clumsy front porch" for having "outlived its usefulness" since, with the increased privatization of the home, the backyard had superseded the veranda as the preferred place to sit outside. "So off with the porch!" Fisher decreed.[86] In general, HIP ads advocated the elimination of all Victorian decorative detail. "Trimming may brand the house as of the 'Gingerbread Period,'" warned one press release. Home-owners were advised to remove exterior trimming if possible, or, if not, to camouflage it by painting it the same colour as the main part of the house.[87] To our contemporary eye, the execution of many of these schemes resulted in the desecration of Canada's architectural heritage.

Interiors were also to be "stream-lined" and brightened. Above all, the principle of less is more was to guide renovation. "Dressing up a room in this day of simple lines," said an HIP publicity statement, "frequently means dressing it down."[88] The living room of the Winnipeg house was completely done over with floor to ceiling drapes, blond maple furniture, indirect lighting, and "soft greys and tones of red." One of the original "absurdly small windows" on either side of the fireplace had been taken out and the other enlarged.[89] Throughout the house "dark, massive and drab" were outdated; fashionable were bright or off-white walls, "cheery" furniture, and light woodwork.[90]

Although Home Improvement Plan promoters made efforts to draw in the upper working class with assurances that striking alterations need not be costly,[91] most of the suggestions featured here were way beyond the budget of ordinary Canadians. Moreover, the total transformation of a house could not even be accomplished within the $2,000 limit first established by the HIP Act, as *Chatelaine* admitted in reference to the Winnipeg house.[92] Despite the NEC's intent to woo the upper working class to the existing system, and in startling contrast to the realities faced by most Canadian urban dwellers, the Winnipeg house, like much HIP promotion, presumed an ideal nuclear family (occasionally compromised by the addition of one grandparent) that was WASP, middle to upper middle class, and composed of "Mr. Home-Owner," his wife "Mrs. Consumer," and their two children, a boy and a girl. Similarly the cost-of-living index prepared by the federal Department of Labour posited a standard five person nuclear family. This ideal was also consistently invoked by advocates of a "family wage" which would allow a male breadwinner to support a dependent wife and three children. The extended family was implicitly excluded from these calculations and arguments. Idealization of the isolated nuclear family, with money to spare, was being marketed at a time when many married women were making ends meet by taking in lodgers[93] and recent immigrants were still living in extended family households.[94] Although the low prices of the Depression enabled a comfortable few to consume on a scale heretofore unimaginable, and some to afford their first washing machine and live-in hired help, the idealized picture projected by HIP ads ignored the existence of the thousands of Canadians "who lived in shacks, and patched their clothes, and hung around the relief offices, and went to bed hungry."[95]

Nevertheless, HIP appeals were made to the patriotism and social duty of *all* Canadians. These were predicated on the corporatist belief in the principle of enlightened self-interest, the notion that people, "in helping themselves, . . . are helping others."[96] The President of the Canadian Manufacturers' Association, for example, saw the very success of the Plan as dependent on harnessing self-interest to patriotism. "National and patriotic motives, as well as self-interest," he was reported to have said, "should prompt Canadians from coast to coast to support the Home Improvement Plan."[97] Its merchandising compared to the Victory Loan Campaigns of the First World War,[98] the HIP was hailed as "a genuine national community effort," the largest co-operative endeavour known in Canada during peace time.[99] "It is said you can't pull yourself up by your own bootstraps. Perhaps not," Purvis conceded. "But Canada can pull herself out of this swamp of unemployment and depression by her own co-operative effort."[100] "Co-operation" became another catchword of HIP publicity.[101] With government, financial institutions, municipalities, chambers of commerce, women's organizations, service clubs, building associations, "and other social agencies" all working together, King said that the Plan was guaranteed to succeed.[102] This ideological manipulation of the term "co-operation" papered over the very social rifts that the Plan served to reinforce.

Although many HIP ads were aimed at a female audience, appeals were also made to men. The National Employment Commission, for example, placed several full-page ads in the *Canadian Congress Journal*, organ of the Trades and Labour Congress of Canada, advising the male worker, employed or unemployed, that "HIP means work for YOU."[103] Other ads focussed on the man as home-owner, appealing to his pride of ownership, his concern to lower house maintenance costs yet protect his property investment, and his commitment to fulfilling his familial responsibilities. The President of the Canadian Chamber of Commerce clearly had men in mind when he said in his endorsement of the HIP: "Unemployment is definitely the responsibility of every citizen, and when *he* improves *his* home, he is contributing at least something of benefit to unemployed men."[104]

The NEC and the business community, however, approached men and women very differently. For instance, a Royal Bank ad for Home Improvement loans, run in the labour and general interest press, showed a young boy gripping an ice cream cone and cheering "Dad's got a job again!" Stressing the national service performed by HIP borrowers to the alleviation of "Canada's unemployment problem," this ad was clearly set up to tug at the heart strings of readers. Attention is drawn to the ice cream cone, a small luxury, perhaps, but only affordable after the boy's father was given work by the Plan.[105] The appeal here was to the sentiment of women and the instrumentality of men, for it was men, not women, who were identified as the patriotic, home-owning citizens.

In contrast, appeals to the distaff side were always made to women in their various homemaking capacities — as mothers, wives, and housekeepers as well as consumers. Backers of the Home Improvement Plan, like the National Council of Women, assumed that it was not as business women, home-owners, or paid labourers, but as "home workers" that women "must accept our full share of the responsibility of the success of this venture."[106] Recalling proudly the "instinct for Mothering" out of which the NCWC was born, the organization's President, Edith (Mrs. George) Spencer, endorsed women's involvement in the Plan as combining self-interest with a socially nurturant maternalism:

> Every improvement made, every dollar spent in providing your family with prettier, more convenient, comfortable home surroundings is turning in another dividend for you. You are putting people to work. You are helping to solve that pressing problem of unemployment. You are giving other women, perhaps less fortunate homemakers, their chance to live and be happy.[107]

In keeping with an advertising trend that developed in North America in the 1920s and 1930s, Home Improvement ads marshalled the opinion of "scientific experts." Ads were peppered with the advice of psychologists and home economists, as well as home decorators and architects.[108] Invocation of the experts was integral to the advertisers' strategy of playing on the fears and insecurities of the public by reinforcing consumers' "suspicions of their own inadequacies."[109] Home economists who doubled as advertising consultants, like Lillian Gilbreth and Christine Frederick in the U.S., helped "ad men" zero in on the special susceptibilities of the female market. Frederick's 1928 book *Selling Mrs. Consumer*, for instance, advocated the manipulation of "what she called women's suggestibility, passivity, and their 'inferiority complexes.'"[110] HIP publicity exploited women's anxieties about their appearance, about their home-making talents and about the state of their homes. In an attempt to persuade Canadian housewives of the need to install a combination of medicine cabinet and dressing table in their kitchens, one ad suggested the importance of having hand lotion and a mirror at the ready "to make those few adjustments sometimes required when the door-bell rings unexpectedly."[111]

Christine Frederick and other home economists also championed the extension of Frederick Taylor's "scientific management" principles from the industrial work place into the privatized home. In the name of efficiency, household labour was to be broken down into specialized processes along the same lines as factory production, despite the fact that in the home the woman was the sole worker.[112] Many of the renovation tips contained in HIP ads were inspired by pseudo-scientific management theory and infused with its rhetoric and imagery.

The kitchen above all became the focus of "scientific" planning for efficiency, simplicity and convenience. "A kitchen that wastes no steps but has all the necessary equipment is the aim of nearly every housewife," claimed one HIP press release.[113] Such HIP ads received reinforcement from "experts" writing in the popular press on how best to make use of the Home Improvement loans. In a *Maclean's* article entitled "Replanning the Kitchen," design consultant John Alexander warned that HIP beneficiaries had been making costly errors through insufficient attention to "scientific kitchen planning." While HIP loans were available only for permanent equipment (i.e., bath tubs, toilets, fixtures and flooring), whether one bought a sink or a refrigerator, its installation required the reconceptualization of the room and its contents as a well-ordered space.[114] A proper arrangement could well necessitate both rewiring and replumbing, themselves costly ventures but justifiable as "short term pain for long term gain."

Achieving the new ideal of a "laboratory-like kitchen"[115] involved not simply the introduction of new appliances but their positioning in a work environment of maximum efficiency. The "kitchen that was not a kitchen" was "hard to work in,"[116] with appliances and work surfaces scattered haphazardly throughout the room in no logical relation to one another. In many older houses, kitchens were so large and badly arranged that "a woman had to be a marathon walker to prepare one meal."[117] In general, design experts applauded the collaboration of "Home Economists, Architects, and Kitchen Specialists . . . to make the kitchen sanitary, pleasant and efficient."[118] Time/motion studies and diagrammatic floor plans were produced to contrast the poorly laid out kitchen of the past with the convenient modern one. Spurious quantification was cleverly utilized to lend an aura of scientific authority to the efficiency claims. In the diagram reproduced in the Alexander article, flow arrows emphasized that the orderly modern kitchen cut out "much needless walking," reducing, by as much as 50 percent, the time and energy involved in meal preparation.[119] Those spearheading the "planned kitchen" answered the question "How many steps make a Pie?" with the reply "more than 100" in an old-fashioned kitchen as compared with a mere 22 in a modernized one. Leisure was held up as "THE REWARD OF KITCHEN EFFICIENCY."[120] In an HIP press release the Canadian husband was promised that the well-planned kitchen would sweeten his wife's disposition and improve her cooking.[121] Another HIP statement predicted that "the housewife will find that she is not as tired at the end of the day if she has less space to walk around in to locate the mixing bowl, the flour or a clean dish towel."[122]

Experts generally divided the kitchen into separate work stations, ranging in number from three to five, laid out in a U-shaped pattern.[123] Where possible, work surfaces and appliances were to be continuous and at a uniform height (normally 36 inches from the floor) "to eliminate tiresome bending," "stooping and consequent backaches."[124] Work stations were to have their own drawers and cupboard space for utensils and dishes in compliance with the scientific management axiom that "each tool should be located near the work process of which it forms a part." Recommended was the replacement of free-standing pieces of furniture, like large Victorian wooden hutches, by built-in cabinets extending across the wall on either side of the sink and along other available wall space.[125] The kitchen without adequate cupboard space, an HIP press release admonished, kept the housewife "continuously on the run."[126]

While the tone of many of these appeals tended to trivialize housework, and their gender-specific pitch contributed to the perpetuation of an inequitable distribution of domestic labour, there is another side to the "scientific" redesign of kitchen space. Indisputably the installation of counters at uniform heights minimized bending, and the layout of cupboards, utensils and appliances in a convenient, work-related pattern eliminated at least some waste motion. But in the process of abandoning the large, less efficient kitchen of the past that had served as the hub of the household's activities, the modern housewife was left isolated within a small, well-ordered, and tidy kitchen, stripped of its social functions and designed solely as a site of work.[127]

Manufacturers of kitchen equipment did not hesitate to capitalize on these HIP modernization schemes. Canadian General Electric, for example, sold appliances in a coordinated ensemble around which a total kitchen would be created. So closely were these companies tied in to the promotion of the HIP that one ad for the "General Electric Kitchen" used the "before" and "after" photographs of the first Canadian kitchen to have been "scientifically" modernized under the Home Improvement Plan, in Valois, Quebec. The CGE ad promised the Canadian housewife that "For a few dollars a month" she could "own a General Electric kitchen — under the new Home Improvement Plan," and thereby fulfill her dreams for a kitchen that is "trim and compact . . . clean and cool." Emphasizing the magically transformative power of electricity when joined with the ingenuity of CGE-designed appliances, this ad tantalized women with the vision of "A kitchen where a score of tedious tasks are done quickly and economically, merely by turning electric switches!"[128]

Ads like these were aimed most pointedly at an urban and fairly well-to-do market. While approximately two-thirds of Canadian households were electrified by the early 1930s, most of these were located in cities and towns. In Ontario in 1935, for example, 90 percent of urban households were wired with electricity as compared with only 16 percent of those in farm regions and hamlets. Moreover, of the urban electrified homes few were equipped with the full array of kitchen appliances available: only 12.6 percent owned refrigerators, only 27.3 percent had ranges, and only 53.5 percent had toasters. The average farm wife was still hauling wood to stoke a wood-fired stove, lighting her kitchen with difficult-to-clean gas or kerosene lamps, and storing fresh fruit and vegetables in root cellars, not refrigerators. CGE certainly hoped through its ads to increase electrification in rural areas and to capture more dollars from the urban working-class family budget, but realistically the CGE "total kitchen" was affordable only to the well-off.[129]

While CGE flogged "packaged" kitchens, the Crane company, manufacturers of plumbing and heating supplies, spoke of three "vital points" in a house — kitchen, bathroom and furnace room — where home improvement should start. In an ad bearing the HIP emblem, Crane singled out its "Sunnydale Cabinet Sink" as the place to begin modernizing the kitchen. Crane's "Cabinet Sink" was guaranteed to meet the scientific management requirements for "generous storage space" beneath the basin for utensils used in food preparation, cleaning agents and a garbage disposal unit.[130] Crane paid even more attention to the bathroom, where it could supply a complete line of toilets, bath tubs, sinks, and plumbing.[131] Yet, while HIP promoters were declaring "the day of the prosaic bathroom is gone forever,"[132] many rural households lacked even the simplest indoor plumbing, let alone the sophisticated hardware advertised here.

In their appeal to "Mrs. Consumer," ads conveyed conflicting messages. On the one hand, the woman was represented as a responsible "purchasing agent"[133] with a careful "eye on her budget."[134] She was the one who could exercise a restraining influence, "persuading the family to spend" its money "for the improvement of the home rather than for an automobile or a radio."[135] One HIP press release told the story of a man who saved enough to take his family on a trip to Europe. His wife, however, "being wiser than he, thought they would do better to renovate their home."[136] While the HIP programme in general promoted spending over saving, it also sought to channel that spending into modernization rather than holiday flings or other "frills." Here, the *thrifty* "Mrs. Consumer" was to the fore.

On the other hand, women were portrayed as spendthrifts and compulsive shoppers. Universalizing the upper-middle-class woman with considerable spending power, one HIP ad opened with the claim: "Every woman has hoped some time or other for a cupboard just for her hats." The suggested design featured separate drawers for makeup and gloves and pocketbooks and scarves.[137] In the corporation of the family the woman may have been the "purchasing agent," but, through her economic dependency, she remained accountable to her husband, the "president."[138] One woman wrote in to *Chatelaine's* "Kitchen Idea Contest": "I hope to win a prize and coax my husband to modernize my kitchen."[139] Built into this relationship, because of her need to account for every penny spent, was the wife's vulnerability to her husband's criticism of her performance as financial manager. Even the thriftiest housewife could be made to appear wasteful or frivolous from the man's perspective. Women were seen as waging a constant assault on the wallets of their husbands, an image that certain comic strips, like "Dagwood and Blondie," have helped keep alive for decades. Ten-Test, an insulation company that advertised its product in conjunction with both the Dominion Housing Act and the Home Improvement Plan, exploited this potential for creating guilt in women. One ad invited the reader to eavesdrop on a domestic squabble in which the husband reprimanded his wife for poor consumer decision making with the charge: "Women Think money grows on Trees!" "Discouraged" and guilt-ridden, the wife sought out a woman friend for consolation and was told that the advice of an architect could solve her problems.[140]

Appeals to women as homemakers also contained contradictory images. At the same time that the "average" Canadian housewife was being proletarianized into a home worker, she was also being elevated to the status of a chatelaine. Although some HIP ads left it open as to whether "a housewife does her own work or leaves it to a maid,"[141] most press releases as well as scientific management schemes presupposed a maidless house. So also did domestic appliance manufacturers. Despite the fact that the percentage of gainfully-employed women in domestic service increased during the Depression,[142] Canadian General Electric continued to trumpet the advantages of replacing hired help with "modern electric servants." In the imagination of CGE advertisers, the mistress of a General Electric home, modernized under the HIP, would possess "Lovely Hands . . . free from toil."[143] Similarly, while HIP modernization literature recognized the home, especially the kitchen, as a site of work for women, they were pressured to conceal the evidence of their household labour. Promoting the HIP in the pages of *Chatelaine*, architectural consultant Evan Parry claimed to know that "the

average woman is not keen on having the next door neighbour or the casual trades-
man see her when engaged upon the family wash."[144] Just as HIP press releases
reflected the modern design requirement for concealment of the functional apparatus
of the home (like plumbing fixtures, radiators, even telephones),[145] the modern housewife was repeatedly enjoined to hide "unsightly" utensils, pots and pans.[146]

In the HIP appeals to women as homemakers, women were identified so closely
with the home that they were encouraged to express the essence of their personalities
through the rooms and furnishings of their houses, particularly the kitchen. HIP press
statements typically sought to instill in women the desire to stand out from all their
neighbours through unique home decoration. "Every once in a while," one ad posited,

> the average home-maker wants a kitchen that is entirely individual and doesn't resemble
> in the slightest the yellow and blue, or the red and white or the pink and brown work-
> shops of her friends.[147]

Some ads recognized that women's confinement to the home might be a source of
depression or restlessness. Paradoxically, these same ads urged women to undertake
home decoration as a cure for discontent. "One of the surest antidotes for a home-
minded woman with a discouraged feeling is redecoration," one HIP ad prescribed.
"The redecorating of one room or an entire house can do more to soothe the troubled
spirit of the true housewife than a trip to the Canary Islands," this ad maintained, as
though the average home-owner in Depression Canada could have contemplated such
an extravagant vacation.[148] Another HIP press release told those suffering from *Wan-
derlust*, "One way to appease your desire for a change is to rearrange completely the
furniture in your house and, if possible, redecorate."[149] Thus women's feelings of
entrapment and their yearnings for independence were subverted and channelled
back into domesticity.

Indeed, women were so home-identified in Home Improvement Plan advertising
that woman and dwelling became one, and the house took on a feminine persona.
The homemaker was encouraged to empathize in a very personal way with the feelings of her house. "Did you ever look at your house as you approached it and think
it looked dispirited and dejected?" one HIP press release queried the Canadian housewife. "Remember how a facial or a wave will raise your own morale and let the house
profit accordingly," the ad continued knowingly.[150] Renovating the facade of a house
was made analogous to giving a woman a face lift.[151] In contrast to women's personal-
ized identification with their homes, men were assumed to objectify their houses, viewing them simply as pieces of real estate.

Despite the extent to which HIP ads promoted the coalescence of woman with
home, some expressed the worry that women might make the home too feminine an
environment for the male head of household and his son. Excessive accommodation
to the feminine taste for ruffles and frills threatened to overthrow the "natural" order
of the patriarchal family. In a thinly disguised reference to the wife's economic dependence on her husband and consequent fear of losing him, one press release warned
that "only a foolish woman plans a totally feminine house in which a man will feel out
of place." Accordingly, this ad instructed the woman to go easy on the "dainty," "lady-
like" touches, for such decor would "hardly . . . make a man want to stay around and
read the evening newspaper and spill ashes."[152] Elsewhere, a wise housewife was com-
mended for having turned part of the basement into a game room with boxing ring

to entice her husband and two sons to stay at home evenings instead of "always going off to the club for a few rounds of fun."[153] While it was not all right for the living room to be overly feminine, it was quite proper for it to evoke male overlordship. One HIP redecoration tip recommended panelled walls and beamed ceilings "reminiscent of the days of turrets and towers," and suggesting "to the mind of its owner the fact that 'every man's home is his castle.'"[154] Not only were women to cater to masculine tastes, they were also to create if possible a "man's room," where he could "read, write or play cards" and not worry about having it tidied by his wife before the arrival of company. A room such as this, women were told, "should be the aim of every housewife who wants to see her husband happy and contented."[155] The female persona of the house notwithstanding, man's privileged place in it was to be protected and confirmed.

In general, the spatial ordering of the house and the gender identity embodied in rooms and their furnishings expressed and reinforced the sexual division of labour. The mother/wife was to give priority to the spatial needs of other family members before her own. Only after the husband got his den, the son a club room, and the daughter an attic bedroom, could the wife expect a space of her own, perhaps a sewing room.[156] "The housewife who enjoys sewing will find a room specially planned for this purpose a great joy," crooned one HIP ad.[157] Ironically, like the other rooms considered woman's domain, the laundry or utility room and the kitchen, the sewing room was a site of work. The reality of the home as a place of leisure for men and work for women was thereby preserved.

As mothers responsible for the upbringing of their children, women were charged with implanting and enforcing gender divisions. Although HIP ads held sex-role differentiation to be innate, they also gave instructions to the mother on how to preside over the proper gender development of her children.[158] Women were advised that "the home-making instincts of a little girl may be fostered or stunted by the kind of room she lives in." The responsible mother would furnish her daughter's room with "a dressing table, a desk, a comfortable chair for reading" and maybe "a coffee table from which she might dispense cocoa or orange juice to her young friends." It was expected that "the pride of the child's heart" would be "her draped dressing table, 'like Mother's.'"[159] In contrast, a boy's room might use "ships, dogs, hockey, football or soldiers" as the decorative theme.[160]

The Home Improvement Plan's intent to generate male employment by the salvaging of rundown homes was in keeping with Depression values. "Use it up, wear it out, make it do, or do without" was an oft-repeated saying of the 1930s.[161] At the same time, the encouragement that the HIP gave to loosening credit and stimulating consumerism heralded an end to the period of "telling ourselves that self-denial is good."[162] The injunction to lift self-restraint on spending was directed, it should be noted, at the more affluent of Canadian society, the group of middle-income home-owners truly targeted by the Plan. While some ads focussed on the practical importance of certain structural repairs and upgrading fire prevention standards, a much greater number featured such luxuries as breakfast nooks, a second living room, a thoroughly modernized kitchen and "rumpus room conversions" for the well-off.[163] The class bias underlying the Plan did not go entirely unnoticed. While the right-leaning *Labour Leader* and the TLC's middle-of-the-road *Canadian Congress Journal* jumped on the HIP bandwagon, the radical press was unimpressed. Although somewhat hopeful of the Plan's job creation potential, the Communist *Clarion* reminded readers that the HIP was designed to benefit the banks, not just workers, and chastised policy makers for once again "overlooking the slums" and their inhabitants.[164] Opposition parliamentarians also voiced serious doubts about the social benefits that would accrue to the least fortunate of Canada's working class. "The industrial workers of Canada will wait until doomsday before they get any relief from this Bill," T.L. Church, Conservative M.P., charged in the House.[165] It was not designed to help them cope with high taxes or to fend off foreclosures. As CCF member J.S. Woodsworth pointed out, "it simply does not touch the great problem of housing that faces the country at the present time." In fact, he warned, "it may become a substitute for a more comprehensive scheme."[166] Despite increasing public awareness of the wretched housing conditions endured by the nation's poor,[167] the HIP was never intended to tackle this problem. Ironically, those most in need of home improvement were therefore left to fend for themselves in their inadequate and often overcrowded, ramshackle dwellings. Moreover, despite the "great hullabaloo" surrounding the promotion of the Plan, the job creation it promised was limited to a small and specialized group of workers in the building and allied trades. Nor was the job creation distributed evenly throughout the country. Indeed, between 1937 and 1940, 48 percent of the loans and almost half the total number of dollars borrowed under the Plan were located in Ontario. Other provinces trailed far behind, beginning with Quebec, which captured about 15 percent of the loans and 19 percent of the dollars, and ending with Prince Edward Island, which received less than 1 percent of the loans. Woodsworth was clearly right when he warned early on that the HIP would not "begin to touch the great mass of unemployed people of this country."[168] Furthermore, in keeping with the corporatist philosophy so dear to the heart of Arthur Purvis, Chairman of the National Employment Commission and head of the Dupont dynasty, the planners made sure that benefits would accrue to Canadian business, both large and small.

While criticism of the class implications of the Act were raised on the floor of the House and elsewhere, rarely if ever did anyone question its gender implications. This silence indicates the depth to which the priority of the male and ensuing gender divisions were unquestioningly entrenched in Canadian society. Despite evidence of widespread female joblessness, women's unemployment was simply not addressed by the Plan. Indeed, the Plan's clear assignment of women to domesticity reflected the strong opposition during the Depression to the gainful employment of the married woman and the prevailing assumption that her right to work should be sacrificed to the needs of the male breadwinner. In addition, the Plan became another arm of the state's intervention in the home to establish norms of familial constitution and gender roles. While other kinds of familial size and arrangement existed in Canada in the 1930s, the HIP consistently represented a male-headed household with a stay-at-home wife and two to three children occupying a single-family dwelling. Respect was paid to the "proper" hierarchical relationship between husband and wife. Granted, the wife was regarded as the financial manager; but she was to remain answerable to her husband, the boss. The housewife's freedom to transform the environment to which she was confined was always to be limited by her prior duty to safeguard her husband's comfort and authority. Her home decorating activities were also to serve the proper gender development of her children, a task with which she, as mother, was entrusted. The imagery and rhetoric with which the privatized home was endorsed contributed to the domestic oppression of women by ideologically reinforcing their confinement to domesticity and by adding new features to the oppressive nature of unpaid household labour. Women, isolated from other home workers, were caught in a cross fire of contradictory images while their domestic labour was rendered both more monotonous and invisible. The scientific management blueprints for reordering the housewife's work space and breaking down her work into a series of discrete, repetitive tasks, not to be varied, recognized the homemaker as worker. At the same time, however, the chatelaine image which she was to project required a masking of her household labour.

The Home Improvement Plan, therefore, stands as an example of the Canadian state's role as an important agent in the social construction of class and gender relations. Furthermore, critical response to the Plan demonstrates the extent to which, in this period of economic distress, class inequities were visible and challenged, however feebly, while the patriarchal structuring of gender inequities was not only accepted as given but viewed as crucial to economic recovery by all but a small minority of vocal women.[169] For most Canadians, the problem of men's unemployment took priority over women's. Indeed the belief was strong that women, particularly married women, were holding down jobs that properly belonged to men. Women's attachment to the home was perceived as precarious. Thus, in the minds of policy makers, reinforcing the ideal of women at home and out of the paid work force went hand in hand with creating jobs for males in order to redress the "genuinely" problematic unemployment, that of men.

NOTES

1. Public Archives of Canada [PAC], Record Group 27, Department of Labour Records, Vol. 3347, file 5, [HIP] Press Release #20; Vol. 3355, file 3, [HIP] Press Release, 15 January 1937.
2. For a detailed discussion of the formulation and administration of the housing policy dimension of the Home Improvement Plan, see John C. Bacher, "Keeping to the Private Market: The Evolution of Canadian Housing Policy: 1900–1949" (Ph.D. Thesis, McMaster University, 1985), pp. 181–202.
3. See Marjorie Cohen, "Women at Work in Canada During the Depression," unpublished paper presented at the Blue Collar Workers' Conference, University of Windsor, May 1979; and Veronica Strong-Boag, *The New Day Recalled: Lives of Girls and Women in English Canada, 1919–1939* (Toronto: Copp Clark Pitman Ltd., 1988), pp. 46–47.
4. See, for example, the anonymous letter to R.B. Bennett dated 8 November 1934, PAC, Bennett Papers, MG 26 K, Vol. 790, Reel M-1447, pp. 486574–77, and the mention of Montreal Mayor Houde's discriminatory solution to male unemployment in PAC, Montreal Council of Women Papers, MG 28 I 164, Vol. 5, file: Annual Reports, *Forty-First Year Book and Annual Report 1934–35*, p. 23.
5. Ruth Roach Pierson with Marjorie Cohen, "Government Job-Training Programs for Women, 1937–1947," in Ruth Roach Pierson, *"They're Still Women After All": The Second World War and Canadian Womanhood* (Toronto: McClelland & Stewart, 1986), pp. 62–94.
6. H.R. Robinson, "Fifty Millions for Modernization," *Canadian Homes and Gardens*, December 1935, p. 17; Canada, House of Commons, *Debates*, 18 January 1937, p. 20; *Labour Gazette*, May 1937, p. 502; Canada Statutes, *An Act to increase Employment by encouraging the Repair of rural and urban Homes*, 1 Geo. VI (1937), chap. 11.
7. Canada, House of Commons, Debates, 1 February 1937, pp. 467–68: "The Home Improvement Plan," editorial, *The Labour Leader* (Toronto), 23 April 1937, p. 2.
8. J. David Hulchanski, "The 1935 Dominion Housing Act: Setting the Stage for a Permanent Federal Presence in Canada's Housing Sector," *Urban History Review/Revue d'histoire urbaine* XV, 1 (June/juin 1986): 19–39; Wm. L. Best, "National Housing Act,"

Canadian Congress Journal XVII, 11 (November 1938): 18–20; John C. Bacher, "Canadian Housing 'Policy' in Perspective," *Urban History Review/Revue d'histoire urbaine* XV, 1 (June/juin 1986): 3–18.

9. *Profit for You from the Home Improvement Plan* (Ottawa: National Employment Commission, December 1936), p. 7. Copy at PAC, RG 27, Vol. 3364, file 1.

10. "Is yours a 1918 1928 1938 home?" *Canadian Homes and Gardens*, June 1938, p. 11; Canada, House of Commons, *Debates*, 2 February 1937, pp. 484–85.

11. *Maclean's*, 15 January 1937, p. 35.

12. Canada, House of Commons, *Debates*, 2 February 1937, pp. 496–97.

13. PAC, RG 27, Vol. 3347, file 4, Press Release #5, "Statement by Arthur B. Purvis, Chairman, National Employment Commission, on the Improvement Plan," 2 November 1936.

14. PAC, RG 27, Vol. 3354, file 13, "A British Building Society for Canada, 1936": Vol. 3347, file 4, Press Release #10, 12 November 1937; Vol. 3366, file 10, Press Release #156, "A Year of the Home Improvement Plan."

15. PAC, RG 27, Vol. 3347, file 5, Radio Address by Hon. Gordon S. Harrington, 12 February 1937.

16. "The Home Improvement Plan — A National Co-operative Effort," *Canadian Congress Journal* XV, 11 (November 1936): 27.

17. "A Job in Your Home," *Maclean's*, 15 November 1936, p. 4.

18. PAC, RG 27, Vol. 3355, file 3, "Address of H.A. McLarty," 17 October 1936; Vol. 3347, file 4, Press Release #10, 12 November 1936.

19. PAC, RG 27, Vol. 3354, file 10, Press Release #68, Speech by E.J. Young (NEC) at Opening of HIP Exhibition, Toronto, 4 May 1937.

20. PAC, RG 27, Vol. 3347, file 4, Press Release #1, "House Renovation Scheme," for release in the morning papers on Saturday 17 October 1936; file 4, Press Release #10, 12 November 1936.

21. PAC, RG 27, Vol. 3347, file 5, Radio Address by Hon. Gordon S. Harrington, 12 February 1937.

22. *Profit for You*, p. 7.

23. Ibid., p. 4.

24. PAC, RG 27, Vol. 3347, file 4, Press Release #10, 12 November 1936.

25. PAC, RG 27, Vol. 3347, file 4, Press Release #5, "Statement by Arthur B. Purvis," 2 November 1936; Press Release #10, 12 November 1936.

26. PAC, RG 27, Vol. 3354, file 13, "A British Building Society for Canada, 1936."

27. PAC, RG 27, Vol. 3347, file 5, "Speech of Arthur B. Purvis . . . Over a National Network, March 25th, 1937."

28. James Struthers, *No Fault of Their Own: Unemployment and the Canadian Welfare State, 1914–1941* (Toronto: University of Toronto Press, 1983), p. 157.

29. Canada, House of Commons, *Debates*, 29 January 1937, p. 388; "Labour Legislation Enacted by the Parliament of Canada and the Legislatures of Ontario and Manitoba in 1937," *Labour Gazette*, May 1937, p. 502.

30. PAC, RG 27, Vol. 3355, file 3, HIP Press Release, "For Release in Morning Papers of Saturday, 17 October 1936"; file 3, "Outline of Plan for Promoting and Popularizing the Home Improvement Plan," p. 1.

31. PAC, RG 27, Vol. 3355, file 3, "Outline of Plan for Promoting and Popularizing the Home Improvement Plan."

32. Ivan Avakumovic, *The Communist Party in Canada: A History* (Toronto: McClelland and Stewart, 1975), p. 35; William Rodney, *Soldiers of the International : A History of the Communist Party of Canada, 1919–29* (Toronto: University of Toronto Press, 1968), pp. 35, 41, 68, 81, 85.

33. Bacher, pp. 179–80, 184, 185, 187, 199. On King's liberal corporatist thought as articulated in his 1918 work *Industry and Humanity*, see Reginald Whitaker, "The Liberal Corporatist Ideas of Mackenzie King," *Labour/Le Travailleur* 2 (1977): 164–69.

34. PAC, RG 27, Vol. 3347, file 5, Press Release #37.

35. "Get it Done Now!" *Labour Leader* (Toronto), 12 March 1937, p. 1.

36. PAC, RG 27, Vol. 3354, file 10, Press Release #68, Speech by E.J. Young, 4 May 1937, p. 1.

37. Leonard C. Marsh, "Reports of the National Employment Commission," *Canadian Journal of Economics & Political Science* 5 (1939): 83.

38. PAC, RG 27, Vol. 3347, file 5. Speech of Arthur B. Purvis, 25 March 1937, p. 2. The DHA assisted only 2.7 percent of housing starts in 1937 and 4.5 percent in 1938, according to Michael Audain, "Transforming Housing into Social Service," *Plan Canada* 13, 2 (August 1973): 95.

39. PAC, RG 27, Vol. 3354, file 10, Press Release #68, Speech by E.J. Young, 4 May 1937, p. 1.

40. Ibid., p. 2.

41. Ibid., p.1

42. PAC, RG 27, Vol. 3347, file 4, Press Release #1.

43. Canada, House of Commons, *Debates*, 29 January 1937, p. 394.

44. *Maclean's*, 15 November 1936, p. 4.

45. PAC, RG 27, Vol. 3354, file 10. Press Release #68, Speech by E.J. Young, p. 2.

46. PAC, RG 27, Vol. 3355, file 7, "Applications for Home Improvement Loan."

47. PAC, RG 27, Vol. 3347, file 5, Press Release #23; Canada, House of Commons, *Debates*, 2 February 1937, p. 497.

48. PAC, RG 27, Vol. 3347, file 5, Speech of Arthur B. Purvis, 25 March 1937, p. 2.

49. PAC, RG 27, Vol. 3354, file 10, Press Release #120; Vol. 3355, file 3, Minutes of Meeting at Cockfield, Brown & Co. Ltd., 8 December 1936, p. 4.

50. In comparison, approximately 51.7 percent of urban middle- and upper-class households owned their own homes in 1931. Calculated from Richard Harris, "Home Ownership and Class in Modern Canada," *International Journal of Urban and Regional Research* 10, 1 (1986), Table 5. See above, note 36.

51. PAC, RG 27, Vol. 3355, file 3, Minutes of Meeting at Cockfield, Brown & Co. Ltd., 8 December 1936.

52. Alan Dunlop, "Home Improvement Plan — a Mouse?" *Canadian Forum* XVI, 192 (January 1937): 21.

53. Calculated from *Canada Year Book*, 1941, p. 371, and 1936, pp. 138–39.

54. Canada, House of Commons, *Debates*, 2 February 1937, pp. 469–76.

55. Ibid., p. 472.

56. PAC, RG 27, Vol. 3370, Press Release #178.

57. Calculated from *Canada Year Book*, 1941, p. 371.

58. The $910 figure was an "emergency budget" determined by the Montreal Council of Social Agencies in 1933, while the $1,456 estimate was worked out by a Toronto study on relief allowances. Struthers, p. 122.

59. *Canadian Congress Journal* XVI, 4 & 5 (April and May 1937): 1.

60. PAC, RG 27, Vol. 3347, file 5, Press Release #23.

61. PAC, RG 27, Vol. 3354, file 10, Press Release #83.

62. PAC, RG 27, Vol. 3347, file 5, Unnumbered Press Release.

63. PAC, RG 27, Vol. 3354, file 10, Press Release #27, 22 February [1937].

64. Dolores Hayden, *The Grand Domestic Revolution: A History of Feminist Designs for American Homes, Neighborhoods and Cities* (Cambridge, Mass.: M.I.T. Press, 1982), Part VI.

65. Stuart Ewen, *Captains of Consciousness: Advertising and the Social Roots of the Consumer Culture* (New York: McGraw Hill, 1976), p. 167; Roland Marchand, *Advertising the*

American Dream: Making Way for Modernity, 1920–1940 (Berkeley: University of California Press, 1985), p. 167.

66. Six titles were available by 1936: 1. *Eggs, Meat and Poultry;* 2. *Silk, Synthetic Fibres and Silk Stockings;* 3. *Fruit and Vegetables, Canned and Fresh;* 4. *Sheets, Flannelette Blankets, Table Linen and Towels;* 5. *Floor Coverings;* 6. *Dairy Products.* Listed in *Money Management* (Toronto: Central Finance Corporation, 1936), copy at PAC, RG 27, Vol. 3350, file 18.

67. PAC, RG 27, Vol. 3355, file 3, "Local Advisory Committees. Some suggestions for their Organization."

68. PAC, RG 27, Vol. 3355, file 3., Minutes of Meeting at Cockfield, Brown & Co. Ltd., 8 December 1936, p. 5.

69. Canada, House of Commons, *Debates,* 2 February 1937, p. 467.

70. Bacher, "Keeping to the Private Market," p. 189.

71. See, for example, "H.I.P. means work for YOU," *Canadian Congress Journal* XVI, 4 & 5 (April and May 1937), 1; "Magic! . . . The Home Improvement Plan," *Maclean's,* 1 October 1937, p. 31, and *Chatelaine,* October 1937, p. 72; "Magic! with the Home Improvement Plan," *Canadian Congress Journal* XVI, 11 (October 1937), 1; "Magie! . . . quelques dollars suffisent à transformer votre maison!" *La Revue Populaire,* octobre 1937, p. 62.

72. PAC, RG 27, Vol. 3355, file 3, "Outline of Plan for Promoting and Popularizing the Home Improvement Plan."

73. *Chatelaine,* January 1937, front cover and p. 35.

74. PAC, RG 27, Vol. 3355, file 3, "Outline of Plan for Promoting and Popularizing the Home Improvement Plan," p. 6.

75. PAC, RG 27, Vol. 3355, file 3, Minutes of Meeting at Cockfield, Brown & Co. Ltd., 8 December 1936, p. 5.

76. PAC, RG 27, Vol. 3347, file 5, Press Release #59.

77. Marchand, p. 149.

78. See, for example, "You'd Never Know the Old Place NOW!" *Canadian Homes and Gardens,* August 1938, p. 45.

79. Richard A. Fisher, "Before/After," *Chatelaine,* March 1937, p. 20; the General Electric ad "The Same Kitchen But What a Difference!" *Chatelaine,* March 1937, p. 3; and the Crane ad, "Avant et après," *La Revue Populaire,* September 1937, p. 33.

80. PAC, RG 27, Vol. 3354, file 10, Press Release #111.

81. *Maclean's,* 15 September 1937, p. 29.

82. Ibid.

83. *Maclean's,* 1 December 1936, p. 61.

84. Richard A. Fisher, "Modernizing an Old House," *Chatelaine,* February 1937, p. 72.

85. Fisher, "Before/After," p. 20.

86. Richard A. Fisher, "Modernizing the Small House," *Chatelaine,* April 1937, p. 22.

87. PAC, RG 27, Vol. 3354, file 10, Press Release #120.

88. PAC, RG 27, Vol. 3354, file 10, Press Release #130.

89. Fisher, "Before/After," p. 20.

90. PAC, RG 27, Vol. 3347, file 5, Press Release #40; Vol. 3354, file 10, Press Releases #130, #148, and #154; *Maclean's,* 15 May 1938, inside front cover.

91. PAC, RG 27, Vol. 3354, file 10, Press Releases #120 and #128.

92. Fisher, "Before/After," p. 20.

93. A crude estimate for the proportion of households with lodgers is one out of five, as in 1931 there were 84,738 lodgers and 417,702 urban households with husband and wife living in owned homes. Calculated from Canada, *Census* 1931, Vol. V, Table 73, p. 1061.

94. Lillian Petroff, "Sojourner and Settler: The Macedonian Presence in the City, 1903–1940," in Robert F. Harney, ed., *Gathering Place: Peoples and Neighbourhoods of Toronto, 1834–1945* (Toronto: Multicultural History Society of Ontario, 1985), pp. 177–203;

Franc Sturino, "The Role of Women in Italian Immigration to the New World," in Jean Burnet, ed., *Looking into My Sister's Eyes: an Exploration in Women's History* (Toronto: Multicultural History Society of Ontario, 1986), p. 26.

95. L.M. Grayson and Michael Bliss, "Introduction," *The Wretched of Canada*, edited by Grayson and Bliss (Toronto: University of Toronto Press, 1971), p. vi.

96. PAC, RG 27, Vol. 3355, file 3, "Outline of Plan for Promoting and Popularizing the Home Improvement Plan."

97. PAC, RG 27, Vol. 3354, file 10, Press Release #45.

98. Bacher, "Keeping to the Private Market," p. 186.

99. Canada, House of Commons, *Debates,* 2 February 1937, p. 468; PAC, RG 27, Vol. 3366, file 15, "The Work of Rehabilitation," Address by Arthur Purvis before the Canadian Club, Toronto, 29 November 1937.

100. PAC, RG 27, Vol. 3347, file 4, Press Release #5, "Statement by Arthur B. Purvis."

101. PAC, RG 27, Vol. 3347, file 5, Press Release #37; Bacher, "Keeping to the Private Market," p. 192.

102. Bacher, "Keeping to the Private Market," pp. 192–93.

103. *Canadian Congress Journal* XVI, 4 & 5 (April and May 1937): 1.

104. Our emphasis, PAC, RG 27, Vol. 3354, file 10, Press Release #30.

105. *Maclean's*, 1 October 1937, p. 53; *Canadian Congress Journal* XVII, 4 & 5 (April & May 1938): 13.

106. PAC, MG 28 I 25, National Council of Women of Canada Papers, Vol. 71, Edith Spencer [President of NCWC] to Ray Brown [Director of Publicity, NEC], 29 April 1937.

107. PAC, MG 28 I 25, Vol. 71, correspondence between Ray Brown and Mrs. George Spencer, May 1937.

108. PAC, RG 27, Vol. 3354, file 10, Press Release #106; Vol. 3366, file 8, Press Release #70; Gertrude Crawford, "It Pays to Modernize," *Maclean's*, 1 December 1936, p. 61; 1 March 1937, p. 57.

109. Marchand, p. 352; see also Ewen, pp. 97–99.

110. Hayden, p. 285.

111. PAC, RG 27, Vol. 3354, file 10, Press Release #179.

112. Hayden, p. 285. Christine Frederick's book, *Household Engineering: Scientific Management for the Home*, was published in 1920.

113. PAC, RG 27, Vol. 3354, file 10, Press Release #85.

114. John Alexander, "Replanning the Kitchen," *Maclean's*, 15 April 1937, pp. 72–73.

115. "Planning for a Maidless House," *Chatelaine*, November 1940, p. 55. On new household technologies and designs see also Veronica Strong-Boag, "Discovering the Home: The Last 150 Years of Domestic Work in Canada," in Paula Bourne, ed., *Women's Paid and Unpaid Work: Historical and Contemporary Perspectives* (Toronto: New Hogtown Press, 1985), pp. 44–48.

116. PAC, RG 27, Vol. 3355, file 3, HIP Press Release, 15 January 1937.

117. Alexander, "Replanning the Kitchen," p. 72.

118. "Planning the Kitchen: Ignored Yesterday — A Necessity Today," *Maclean Building Reports Annual* (1936): 26; and Léonard Knott, "Ayez, vous aussi, une Cuisine Systématisée," *La Revue Populaire*, May 1937, pp. 28, 67.

119. Alexander, "Replanning the Kitchen," p. 72.

120. "Why Planned Kitchens?" *Maclean Building Reports Annual* (1937): 58.

121. PAC, RG 27, Vol. 3354, file 10, Press Release #104.

122. PAC, RG 27, Vol. 3354, file 10, Press Release #85.

123. Alexander, "Replanning the Kitchen," pp. 72–73; "Why Planned Kitchens?" *Maclean Building Reports Annual* (1937): 58, 60; "Is a Pantry Necessary?" *Maclean Building Reports Annual* (1937): 62.

124. "Is a Pantry Necessary?" p. 62; "Planning the Kitchen," p. 26.

125. Alexander, "Replanning the Kitchen," p. 72.

126. PAC, RG 27, Vol. 3354, file 10, Press Release #175.

127. Glenna Matthews, *"Just a Housewife": The Rise and Fall of Domesticity in America* (New York: Oxford University Press, 1987), pp. 169–70.

128. PAC, RG 27, Vol. 3355, file 3, HIP Press Release, 15 January 1937; *Maclean's*, 1 March 1937, p. 27.

129. Calculations are based on statistics from *Canada Year Book,* 1936, p. 139, along with figures from *The Bulletin of Ontario Hydro* in the 1930s and other sources used by Dianne Dodd in "Delivering Electrical Technology to the Ontario Housewife, 1920–1939: An Alliance of Professional Women, Advertisers and the Electrical Industry" (Ph.D. thesis, Carleton University, 1988), Figure 8, p. 163.

130. *Maclean's*, 15 June 1937, p. 37.

131. *Maclean's*, 18 January 1937, p. 35; and *La Revue Populaire*, May 1937, p. 5.

132. PAC, RG 27, Vol. 3354, file 10, Press Release #84.

133. Marchand, p. 170.

134. PAC, RG 27, Vol. 3354, file 10, Press Release #76.

135. PAC, RG 27, Vol. 3355, file 3, "Local Advisory Committees. Some Suggestions for their Organization."

136. PAC, RG 27, Vol. 3354, file 10, Press Release #68, Speech by E.J. Young, 4 May 1937.

137. PAC, RG 27, Vol. 3354, file 10, Press Release #151.

138. Marchand, pp. 169–70.

139. Helen G. Campbell, "Paging the Winners in Chatelaine's Kitchen Idea Contest," *Chatelaine*, February 1937, p. 77.

140. *Maclean's*, 15 May 1938, p. 1.

141. PAC, RG 27, Vol. 3366, file 9, Press Release #113.

142. Cohen, "Women at Work in Canada During the Depression," pp. 7–8.

143. *Maclean's*, 1 May 1937, p. 25.

144. Evan Parry, "The Utility Room," *Chatelaine*, March 1939, p. 55.

145. PAC, RG 27, Vol. 3354, file 10, Press Releases #84, #101, and #91; Vol. 3366, file 8, Press Release #64.

146. PAC, RG 27, Vol. 3355, file 3, HIP Press Release, 15 January 1937.

147. PAC, RG 27, Vol. 3354, file 10, Press Release #48.

148. PAC, RG 27, Vol. 3354, file 10, Press Release #92.

149. PAC, RG 27, Vol. 3354, file 10, Press Release #135.

150. PAC, RG 27, Vol. 3354, file 10, Press Release #111.

151. "1937 Home Improvement Year," *Chatelaine*, January 1937, p. 49.

152. PAC, RG 27, Vol. 3354, file 10, Press Release #136.

153. PAC, RG 27, Vol. 3347, file 5, Press Release #57.

154. PAC, RG 27, Vol. 3366, file 8, Press Release #88.

155. PAC, RG 27, Vol. 3347, file 5, Press Release #44.

156. PAC, RG 27, Vol. 3354, file 10, Press Releases #43 and #177; PAC, RG 27, Vol. 3347, file 5, Press Releases #57 and #44. *Maclean's*, 15 March 1937, p. 1.

157. PAC, RG 27, Vol. 3354, file 10, Press Release #177.

158. PAC, RG 27, Vol. 3354, file 10, Press Releases #116 and #96.

159. PAC, RG 27, Vol. 3354, file 10, Press Release #96.

160. Ibid.

161. Susan Ware, *Holding Their Own: American Women in the 1930s* (Boston: Twayne Publishers, 1982), p. 2.

162. "1937 Home Improvement Year," *Chatelaine*, January 1937, p. 41.

163. Bacher uses this phrase to characterize the use made of loans approved in the 1950s under a similar plan created by the 1944 National Housing Act but not put into opera-

tion until 1955. The term is also applicable, however, to many of the HIP ads of the 1930s. John Bacher, "Canadian Housing 'Policy' in Perspective," p. 10.

164. "Overlooking the Slums," Editorial, *The Daily Clarion* (Toronto) 4 February 1937, p. 4.
165. Canada, House of Commons, *Debates*, 2 February 1937, p. 468.
166. Ibid., p. 476.
167. Hulchanski, "The 1935 Dominion Housing Act," p. 22.
168. Ibid., p. 475.
169. See the CP and CCF women of the 1935 Canadian League against War and Fascism and the 1936 CCF Toronto women discussed by John Manley, "Women and the Left in the 1930s: The Case of the Toronto CCF Women's Joint Committee," *Atlantis* 5, 2 (Spring 1980): 100–19.

TEN

Wages of Sin: Unwed Mothers

ANDRÉE LÉVESQUE

Premarital sex and the birth of a fatherless, hence nameless, child threatened to overturn the patriarchal family, a cornerstone of Quebec society. An irregular pregnancy of this sort was proof positive of the failure to guard one's daughters and evidence of their freedom in an area where they were not supposed to be free. It created a drama in which the actresses were not permitted a role in the family play. It furthermore made all too evident a lapse that might otherwise have passed unnoticed. Only if every trace of the transgression were erased could the sinner be reintegrated into her normal society. The women who were either unable or unwilling to obliterate the consequences of their sexual activity, activity to which they may or may not have consented, entered the ranks of those who had long been termed unwed mothers.

There are no exact data on the frequency of extramarital pregnancy, but it must have been far more common than the figures indicate, if one considers how often abortion or miscarriage must have intervened before a pregnancy was brought to term. The "illegitimate" birth rate in Quebec ranged between .03 and .07 per cent, less than the national average and lower than that in most Western countries. According to official statistics, which probably underestimate the facts, 2.9 to 3.4 per cent of live births were to unwed mothers.[1] Close to 40 per cent of these births took place at either the Hôpital de la Miséricorde in Montreal or the one in Quebec City, 560 a year on average in Montreal and 457 in Quebec.[2] Some women who were rather more fortunate gave birth in private maternity clinics, typically far away from home, or at the home of distant relatives or, more unusually, under the familial roof, which had often hidden the young woman's condition for a number of months. The women who gave birth at the two Miséricorde hospitals comprise a group quite representative of the majority of unmarried mothers and, thanks to the archives and medical files, one that is easier to analyse.

Source: *Making and Breaking the Rules: Women in Quebec, 1919–1939*, Yvonne M. Klein, trans. (Toronto: McClelland & Stewart, 1989), 101–16. © 1994 Andrée Lévesque. Translation © 1994 Yvonne M. Klein. Reprinted by permission of Oxford University Press Canada.

TABLE 10.1 *Illegitimate Births, Quebec, 1926–1939*

1926	2,055	1933	2,433
1927	2,319	1934	2,335
1928	2,419	1935	2,506
1929	2,359	1936	2,469
1930	2,519	1937	2,451
1931	2,450	1938	2,525
1932	2,433	1939	2,668

Source: Quebec, *Annual Report of the Minister of Health and Welfare*, 1927–40.

The Hôpital de la Miséricorde had been performing a service for single mothers and "illegitimate" children since the mid-nineteenth century. In 1840, Bishop Bourget asked the widow Rosalie Cadron-Jetté to take a young, unmarried pregnant woman into her home. This request was followed by others until finally he asked her to leave her own home and children, rent a house, and manage it as a home for unwed mothers. This was the beginning of the Refuge Ste-Pélagie in 1845. Three years later, Rosalie Cadron-Jetté and seven other women founded the Congregation of the Soeurs de Miséricorde to care for women who "needed to hide."[3] The babies were then looked after by the Grey Nuns. This arrangement lasted until 1889, when the Soeurs de Miséricorde established their own crèches. By 1920 the hospital had a school of nursing and was used by students at the University of Montreal medical school for their obstetrical training.[4]

It is difficult to establish whether or not the rise in the number of "illegitimate" births reflects the economic difficulties of the twenties and thirties. Admissions remained stable, limited as they were by the number of available beds. Yet we know that the total number of births by single women in Quebec rose from 2.9 per cent of live births in 1931 to 3.4 per cent in 1939.[5] In 1933, the Miséricorde Hospital in Montreal and the one in Quebec City were full and were turning women away. In Montreal, the Hôpital de la Miséricorde began to restrict admission to women who were residents of the city and in their seventh month or later. We ought not to conclude too hastily, however, that illicit sex was on the rise. The illegitimacy rate rose only from 3 per cent in 1930 to 3.2 per cent in 1933; the pressure on the two Miséricorde hospitals came about because private maternity hospitals were closing as a result of the depression.[6]

The archives, registers, and medical files of the Hôpital de la Miséricorde in Montreal permit us to construct a profile of the woman who came to the Dorchester Street institution. As we might expect, she was usually French-Canadian and Catholic; only occasionally was an Irish, Italian, or Lithuanian woman admitted, but Anglophone women were usually directed to other agencies, like the Salvation Army. Even if she came from outside Montreal, a close female relative — a mother, an aunt, or a cousin — was likely to accompany her on admission. But the mother was the least likely to be present, not merely because she was being kept in ignorance of her daughter's condition but because 27.7 per cent of single mothers had lost their own mothers (and 25.8 per cent their fathers).[7] She was usually a young domestic servant. Sixty per cent of the women were between eighteen and twenty-two years old, 47 per cent of them were domestic servants, and 31 per cent lived with their families. Only 5.7 per cent worked in factories or offices. Now and then a schoolgirl, a nurse, or a teacher sought admission.[8]

The occupations recorded in the register may give us a false impression of the number of domestic servants. The women may have come to Montreal to disguise their condition once they had become pregnant and then taken a job in a private household while waiting to be admitted to Miséricorde. Similarly, it is difficult to determine their true place of residence. Of the women who gave a Montreal address, some had been there only a very short time.

The occupation and address of the patients allow us partly to infer their social origins; their fathers' occupations allow us a slightly greater precision. As an institution supported by the state, where the inmates were able to work off the cost of their confinement, the hospital accepted a very large number of women who could not have afforded private care. Among them there were some daughters of lower-middle-class fathers or tradesmen, but the fathers of most were farmers and labourers, when they were not actually unemployed. All in all, patients at the Miséricorde represented the broad lower levels of Quebec society; the narrow upper ranges were altogether absent.

Coming as they did from deprived circumstances, the women presented the kind of medical problems associated with poor nutrition and inadequate living conditions. They received a medical examination upon admission and had access to care in case of complications. The medical records do not tell us very much about their state of health. This was not the first pregnancy for 16 per cent of the women. As an indication of their general health, their recorded weight is meaningless, as it represents their weight when pregnant and their usual weight is not indicated.[9] A large number had bad teeth that had to be extracted in the hospital. Venereal disease was common. In 1928 the provincial health service treated more than half, or 344 patients, for VD at the Miséricorde.[10] According to the medical records, 38 per cent suffered from gonorrhea and 3.7 per cent had positive Wasserman tests for syphilis. There was, however, an improvement in the syphilis rate, which exceeded 8 per cent of admissions in 1930 but never went above 6 per cent after 1936.[11] It is difficult to measure the effect of the anti-venereal campaign on the infection rate since the Bennett government cut federal funding for the campaign in 1931 as an austerity measure. More refined studies are needed to connect education and screening campaigns with the decreasing rate of syphilitic infection in a particular group. More fortunate than most of the women of their social background, the Miséricorde patients obtained diagnosis and treatment that they might otherwise have been denied. Their stay in the hospital was not necessarily more attractive on this account, however.

Although the women had certainly not become pregnant single-handedly, they were extremely reluctant to furnish any information, however vague, about the fathers of their children. The fathers' listed occupations lend little support for the staple of romance fiction — the seduction and betrayal of the young domestic worker. If the woman sometimes suggested that the father was a manager or a student, it may be assumed that her employer or his son was to blame. But most of the time, the partner belonged to the same social class as the woman herself — he was a chauffeur, a delivery man, a farm worker. The hospital wanted to know if the father drank or smoked, but the significance of positive responses is unclear. After December, 1937, information regarding the nationality and height of the father was demanded, but the data are irregular and imprecise. The image of the father, whom the nuns liked to call the accomplice,[12] is shrouded in a vagueness that arises out of indifference, unfamiliarity, or simply a desire to protect one's privacy.

During her isolation at Miséricorde, which could last for months or even a year, the boarder was provided with a new identity. On registration, she received an "imposed name" drawn from an existing stock of names bestowed on generations of single mothers since the nineteenth century. These names were not in common use but were highly unusual, like Héraïs, Calithène, Potamie, Rogata, Macédonie, Gemelle, Nymphodore, Extasie, and Symphorose. If these names were not peculiar enough, others were fraught with meaning, like Humiliane and Fructeuse.[13] The names were assigned in alphabetical order and when, after many months, the list was exhausted, it started all over again from the beginning. Along with her new identity, which assured her anonymity among her fellow inmates, the boarder acquired a uniform. The two dollars it cost represented the first of her debts. In exceptional cases, some paying boarders occupying private rooms would wear a veil for the entire length of their stay to assure absolute secrecy. From the moment she registered until the day she left, the unwed mother, or penitent (repentante) as the nuns called her, would be cut off from the world and could count on the vigilance of the sisters to protect her secret.

Except during Lent and Advent, she could receive visitors in the parlour once a week, but visitors were confined to close relatives who were provided with a card with the boarder's "imposed name" on it. No card, no visit, as the mother of a young woman from out of town learned to her sorrow. Having left her card at home, she could hardly afford the fare for a return visit. Discretion was assured even in the case of a mother inquiring whether her thirty-four-year-old daughter was a patient. The director, Sister Tharcisius, answered, "If your daughter was always a good girl, what are you worried about?"[14]

This anonymity was extended to the child from the moment of birth. The mother evidently had little say in the name given her child. All the babies born in a month bore the same surname; it might be that of a nurse or intern on duty. First names were assigned in alphabetical order. To a mother who wanted a note so that she could visit her child in the crèche at Trois-Rivières and who asked about the names of the child's godparents, Sister Tharcisius wrote that the names were not necessary and, in any event, the godparents were absolute strangers, being "a nurse and one of our interns."[15] Assigned godparents and names chosen at random both contributed to a depersonalization of the connection between mother and child. Frequently, baptismal certificates indicate the child was born of "no known parentage," as if the existence of the mother herself was a mystery.[16]

The Miséricorde was a peculiar institution in that boarders usually entered voluntarily, if we leave social pressures aside for the moment, but were subjected to strict isolation and strong discipline once inside. A brief one-page prospectus described the terms of admission, the cost for single or double rooms or wards ($90, $60, and $8 a month), and a fee of $155, $130, or $120 for the cost of the delivery and adoption fees. The new boarder was told that she would have to give six months of service to the hospital starting two weeks after the birth of her child in order to repay the cost of her care and the adoption fees. Any time spent working at the hospital before delivery could be credited against the six months. Death of the child either at birth or afterwards did not change the terms; in fact, a burial charge of $25 was added to the bill.[17] Even though these terms were laid out in the prospectus, the length of time to be served surprised many women, especially when the baby died.

Although 53 per cent of the inmates were over twenty-one, all were considered minors regardless of their age. Visits were controlled and correspondence censored. Letters could only be written on Sundays, and not at all during Lent and Advent. If a patient tried to escape, she was promptly retrieved by a detective. The pregnant single woman was viewed not only as equivalent to a child but also as a criminal. If the father was termed an "accomplice," then the mother was his partner in crime.

As a matter of fact, although these women were seen as criminals, many of them were themselves victims of crime. About 3 per cent of the women were under the age of sixteen. If they were of "previously chaste character," according to section 210 of the Criminal Code, the father of the child would be guilty of seduction and subject to five years in jail. If the woman was between sixteen and seventeen, as 11 per cent were, "and of previously chaste character," he was liable to two years in prison. If he was over twenty-one and she under that age, and he had promised to marry her, he was still guilty of seduction and liable to a year's sentence.[18] Very few of the seduction cases tried in court each year resulted in conviction.[19] To seduce a feeble-minded woman or an employee was also a criminal act, but it is impossible to estimate the number of single women who were victims of these crimes or of incest.

Whatever the circumstances surrounding the single mother's pregnancy, great care was taken to shield the world at large from her presence. Once inside the institution, it was very difficult to escape its walls. In vain did the mothers of some of the inmates implore the hospital to release their daughters before the six months were up because "people were beginning to talk" about their long absence. In another case, a mother wrote of her fear that her husband would suspect the cause of his daughter's being away so long when he returned from the logging camp and found her not at home.[20] Sister Tharcisius refused the request. The nuns argued that the younger members of the family had to be protected from the scandal their older sister had caused.[21] A father wrote that he could not telephone the hospital, nor did he want the nuns to call him about the birth of his grandchild, since people listened in on the party line he shared with twenty families. He also asked that all letters come in a plain envelope, since the post office workers would recognize the Dorchester Street address and "find out."[22] The requirement for secrecy explains why one young woman fled the hospital when she recognized a new boarder.[23]

While the world was being protected from her presence, the single mother found herself reduced to the status of a child. Depending on her behaviour, she could earn good conduct marks, which could shorten her stay by two weeks, or demerits, which had the opposite effect. Trying to smuggle out a letter, for example, resulted in a black mark.[24] One patient had to serve an extra month for striking a child and keeping a pacifier for her own baby.[25] Two parents who arrived to pick up their daughter discovered that she had to serve an additional fortnight.[26] On the other hand, merit points were given to women for donating their blood to their own babies or for nursing several children.[27] Good behaviour resulted in being allowed to perform certain duties, like supervising a dormitory, which could also earn merit points and an earlier release.

This treatment was justified by the view taken of the single mother in Quebec society. If she was not strong-minded and wicked, she was seen as weak and ignorant or perhaps feeble-minded. Perhaps because mentally handicapped women were more subject to abuse, single mothers were often believed to be dull-witted. A doctor writing in a Quebec medical journal in 1932 stated that "natural [i.e., illegitimate] children seem particularly vulnerable to madness. . . . It is probable, in fact, that the parents of a natural child are themselves often abnormal."[28] The nuns sometimes termed the inmates "stupid" or "idiots" in their written comments. A patient who was slow in finishing her tasks, for example, might be considered stupid. Of course, we cannot rule out passive resistance on the part of women who wanted to be expelled before their time was up or, if they had been brought in against their will by their parents, before the birth of the child. In any event, the letters intercepted by the nuns and preserved in the files seem coherent and not lacking in intelligence.

Regardless of their intelligence, a good number of the women found themselves in the Miséricorde as a result of sexual abuse, sometimes on the part of a relative. The parish priest might write a letter of recommendation observing that the young woman came from a poor but honest family and had been taken advantage of.[29] Abused or not, they were seen as in need of repentance — they had fallen and now must atone for their sin. The inmates' mothers sometimes shared this sentiment. One wrote that she hoped her daughter's stay of one year and three months would be a good lesson for her.[30] In a few cases, the parents or the parish priest wrote to ask that a young woman be kept after her six months, until she turned twenty-one, or even longer, working in return for her room and board and being protected from the outside world and her own weakness. A parish priest wrote to Sister Tharcisius that he would be "happy for both the parents and for their daughter Y. if you could decide to keep her with you, like another of the sisters, among the penitent girls. I am convinced that only thus will she be protected from further misfortunes which await her at home."[31] These cases were referred to the Soeurs du Bon-Pasteur d'Angers, who had a home for young delinquent women. Many were most reluctant to go, for transferring to the reform school meant entering an even more restrictive atmosphere.[32]

The women at the Miséricorde were confined both to avoid scandal and to encourage them to reform. The rules were intended to form good habits. They rose very early, performed domestic tasks under close supervision, and were required to attend chapel three times a day. They were enveloped in an atmosphere of humility, repentance, and atonement. As Sister Tharcisius wrote to a woman who was coming back for a second stay, "Poor lamb, wounded by the thorns along the path, no one will reproach you if you are repentant, submissive, and humble."[33]

The work performed by the women at the Hôpital de la Miséricorde had both a moral and an economic intention. The stated purpose of the six months of service was to pay for the costs of delivery and medical treatment and the care of the child who was to be left behind. If the baby was placed for adoption, then the term of service was reduced to three months. If the baby died, the mother was still liable for six months of work to pay for the cost of the burial. Leaving a baby at the crèche cost a dollar a day for board, while labour was rated at being worth $20 a month. Days lost to illness did not count.[34] But economic considerations alone did not dictate the length of stay — those conduct marks, good or bad, also played a part. In addition, external considerations also had an effect — in 1933 a shortage of beds meant that some residents were allowed to leave a month early.

Not surprisingly, an examination of the correspondence reveals considerable confusion about the period of service that was to be exacted. Inmates wrote notes to Sister Tharcisius asking how long they still had to serve, relatives were uncertain about the release date, and many parents begged the administration to let their daughters out early because they were needed at home to help their mothers or to nurse sick members of the family. There were several cases in which families attempted to raise the money to pay off a sister's or a daughter's debt. One woman begged the nuns to release her daughter and asked if the government could not help. "I understand," she wrote, "that it is neither your fault nor that of the government," and offered to pay $75 a month. Sister Tharcisius replied that the young woman could not leave until her account had been reduced to the last $75 and "that it should not be forgotten that this is her child, not the government's nor ours although we will keep him for six years."[35] A letter from the parish priest, if it could be obtained, provided the likeliest route to an early release. Women who had nowhere else to turn went on working at the hospital for months, even years, in return for room and board. In this way they received the spiritual and material benefits of life in a religious community without being bound by vows.

Although there were women who took refuge in an institution that offered them shelter and spiritual comfort, others were forced to remain against their will to work off a non-existent debt. Someone who was interested in the welfare of the inmate, a priest or a nun from her home town, might send money for her keep but ask that she not be told, so that her stay could be prolonged to assure "as complete a recovery as possible."[36] It appears to have been a moral rather than a physical recovery that was at issue here. When the father of a patient was successful in suing the father of the baby, the hospital got $300, but the family was not reimbursed for the work the woman had done: $126.50 for her board before delivery; $50 for abandoning the child; $44 for doctor's fees and treatment.[37]

Whether its purpose was to atone for sin or to pay off a debt, the service required consisted largely of general housework, like washing furniture, or work in the scullery, in the laundry, where washing diapers was the hardest task, or in the nursery or crèche, feeding, supervising, or changing the babies and children. One mother breast-fed three or four children until, exhausted, she developed anemia and then was discharged because she was incapable of continuing to work. A few days before giving birth, wrote one boarder, "I spent the entire day ironing."[38] In 1938, a twenty-year-old English-speaking Lithuanian woman was allowed to leave after four months as a wet-nurse. She wrote to Sister Tharcisius, "My mother thinks I only do six babies, she doesn't know I have been doing thirteen of them for three months, washing them, feeding them and cleaning them."[39] One wonders how many of these thirteen she actually nursed. In another case, a doctor intervened to ask that a woman who had developed a skin rash washing furniture be permitted to stop work for forty days. She was then given damp clothes to fold and told by the doctor to stop if she felt weak and to take a tonic three times a day.[40] It is difficult to argue that this sort of work was intended solely for moral reform, since the private patients were exempt from all work before their delivery, except for "fancy needlework for their own use, and reading," and did not, of course, work afterward because they had paid the fees.[41] On the other hand, a Protestant was sent on her way after three months of service because, "as a Protestant, she will not be able to derive any spiritual benefit."[42]

Faced with the prospect of having to work for many months after the birth that would relieve her of the evidence of her sin, many an inmate rebelled and sought to shorten her term of service. Comments by the nuns in the files give glimpses of cases of passive resistance, if not tacit sabotage. The severe limitations on contact with the outside world stimulated more revolt. Desperate women threw letters out of the windows or tried to sneak them out with visitors or fellow inmates leaving the institution. We only know about those who got caught and whose letters were intercepted.[43]

Supervisors reported the breaches of the rules they observed, but how many did they miss? The best way to get expelled quickly was to be insubordinate, to use vulgar language, or to talk about shocking subjects, yet only 4 per cent were discharged for these reasons.[44] A tiny minority managed to escape without being returned. A detective brought in by the authorities usually managed to retrieve those who tried to get away. When a rebellious boarder threatened to escape in August, 1938, a detective accompanied her as she was being transferred to another institution run by the same order in Sault-aux-Récollets in suburban Montreal.[45] In the case of minors the nuns were acting *in loco parentis*, but in the case of adults they were abusing their authority, as a lawyer for one of the inmates successfully argued in securing her release.[46] But very few had the education, the contacts, or the financial resources to seek judicial relief. Closely guarded, often unfamiliar with the city, lacking sympathetic relatives to turn to, and threatened with a police pursuit and a longer sentence if they tried to escape, even rebellious women were reluctant to act.

Open revolt, in the form of an escape attempt that involved considerable risk, was the most overt manifestation of rebellion. For most boarders, even passive resistance was out of the question. Women who were depressed, frequently abandoned by their lovers, cast out from the family setting, and working hard all day despite the discomforts of pregnancy had little energy left for defiance. Like their mothers, most of them would have internalized the traditional patriarchal religious values that justified their punishment. They and their sexual partners had violated society's rules and they and, in time, their children would have to pay.

Confronted with an unwanted pregnancy, many of the women had attempted some kind of abortive procedure, from taking hot mustard baths to inserting an implement into the cervix. Not everyone admitted it, but this information appears on 5.1 per cent of their medical records.[47] Short of abortion, the surest way of evading the social consequences of an out-of-wedlock pregnancy was to marry the father. Canada and Quebec do not keep statistics on births occurring within six months of marriage and, except by consulting parish records, we cannot estimate the incidence of premarital pregnancies. The letters retained by the hospital indicate that a certain number of men claimed they intended to marry the mother when their financial situation improved, after they found a job, for example. Some, in fact, did keep their word and the child was recovered by its natural parents. Some parents prohibited their daughter from keeping in touch with her lover, and their correspondence ended up in her file, without ever reaching its destination, even though she was no longer a minor.[48] The nuns observed on at least one occasion that the mother had married a drunk whom she did not love in order to give her baby a name.[49] A few times a year marriages took place in the hospital chapel either before the baby's birth or, more often, when the woman was about to leave with her child. If the father was acceptable, both the parents and the nuns considered marriage the best solution, as it permitted the woman to be reintegrated into society in the approved role of married mother.[50] As Sister Tharcisius explained to the mother of a boarder, "The best advice is to let her get married if the young man is agreeable. . . . It's the best solution because she is not drawn to the religious life and work is hard to find."[51] The ideal solution often remained entering a convent.

The complete rehabilitation of the penitent sometimes required a permanent rejection of the world and its temptations. The most pious could enter the Madelon, named for Saint Mary Magdalene, and become Oblates. According to Sister Tharcisius, the conditions of admission were good health and good will. After spending a few months as a Daughter of Saint Marguerite, patron saint of new mothers, the candidate was issued a habit and a new name; she then entered the order on July 22, the feast day of Saint Mary Magdalene. The Oblates did not observe the strict discipline of other religious orders. They were not required to fast, but they could receive visitors only once a month and were not allowed to go out at will. They worked for the nuns, the stronger ones in the kitchen, the others doing sewing or housework.[52] In this way they could atone for their sins for the rest of their lives. At least one mother wrote her daughter recommending she expiate her fault by renouncing her life and entering this subordinate order, which would be happy to welcome her.[53]

A very small number entered the Madelon. Those who did not have a religious vocation had to deal with their immediate responsibility for the children they had borne and who were neither wanted nor "legitimate." Single mothers were generally encouraged to keep their children. As early as 1915, the Women's Directory of Montreal, which was involved in reforms for single mothers, sought to keep mother and child together to encourage breast-feeding, which had the further advantage of reducing infant mortality.[54] In 1931, the feminist Idola Saint-Jean recommended to the Royal Commission on Social Services (Monpetit Commission) that the single mother keep her child as a "safeguard" for her. She argued that not only the mother but the child would benefit from the warmth and maternal care that no institution could provide.[55] While experts encouraged single mothers to keep their children either for their own or the child's benefit, only one in eight of the patients actually left the Miséricorde with the baby. The "illegitimate" child was the legal responsibility of the mother; it was a crime to neglect or abandon it. She was required to take care of it, though the law allowed for easy adoption.[56] Many nevertheless refused to sign the papers that would permit their children to be put up for adoption. They hoped to marry or even to save enough so that one day they could retrieve their babies. This hope proved an idle dream for most, who sooner or later resigned themselves to signing the necessary documents.

For over a third of the mothers, however, long-term care for their babies did not become an issue, since the children did not survive their first year. At the beginning of the 1930s, Montreal had the unfortunate reputation of having one of the highest infant mortality rates in Canada, if not in the Western world: it fell from 125 per 1,000 in 1931 to 72 per 1,000 in 1938.[57] At the Miséricorde, 37.7 per cent of the infants born between 1929 and 1939 died in their first year, primarily of preventable diseases such as gastro-enteritis or pulmonary complaints.[58] In the hospital, the deaths of infants under one year of age underwent a marked decline in the decade, falling from 43 per cent in 1930 to 27 per cent in 1939, which mirrors the trend in Quebec and in Canada. Since the physical conditions inside the institution changed hardly at all in the period, the decrease can only be attributed to the causes commonly identified by physicians and social historians — better nutrition and an improvement in standards of sanitation.[59]

For the sisters, and even for some mothers, the death of a child was almost an occasion to rejoice. To a mother who wrote that she could not forget her child and wanted to know his whole name, Sister Tharcisius wrote, "Our Mother in Heaven has herself taken care of little Adrien. She came and got him last May. He is now a little angel up there in heaven, watching over his *maman*."[60] This was written in November, six months after Adrien's death. In the same spirit, the director wrote to a grandfather,

"Dear Sir: We regret to say that the baby born to E.C. is dead. Thank God for this great favour."[61] Conscious of the weight of a life of poverty and shame, the mothers wanted their children to be spared such an end. A nineteen-year-old, who had left the hospital just two weeks after giving birth, provides an eloquent expression of this sentiment in a letter she wrote to Sister Tharcisius: "If the Good Lord would come to take her away and make her a little angel in heaven, I would be happy because who can say that she will not be miserable later on. I know that she will maybe curse me some day, but I have to accept my fate, because I wanted to do what I did." She did not need to fear her daughter's curse, since the baby died when it was nineteen days old.[62]

Even if it was less painful for some mothers to forget their infants and wish them an easy death or a generous adoptive family, others continued to write the nuns, even after they had signed the adoption papers, for news about the weight, behaviour, and health of their babies. The information provided was not always accurate, perhaps to allay fears, perhaps because it referred to the wrong child. One mother wrote to ask if her child was dead so she could stop worrying about her. In April, she was informed that "she was well and always amiable"; shortly thereafter, she was informed that the child had died the previous December.[63]

While Sister Tharcisius herself encouraged women to keep their children, most could not and, after leaving the hospital, a large number took up positions as domestic servants. The "luckiest" were picked by a doctor to serve his family.[64] Most of them tried to start a new life far from their home town, hoping that their past would remain buried.

But if the woman were to take up her life as if nothing had happened, she could not keep her child, whereas the law, the child-care specialists, and the Church itself made the mother primarily responsible for its welfare. Thus she was caught in a contradiction that could only generate profound feelings of guilt and incompetence. As an example, there are the parents who, seventeen years later, wrote to ask about their child and acknowledged that "The older we get, the more we think about him — it doesn't go away."[65]

To survive economically and socially, the single mother rarely had the choice of whether or not to abandon her child. Jobs were hard to find during the Great Depression and domestic service remained the principal employment for single women in Quebec. Few would employ a single woman with a child. In 1937 the city of Montreal, on orders from the provincial government, cut single mothers from the welfare rolls.[66] Economic conditions forced many women to place their children in institutions and offer them for adoption. They were perhaps unaware that the number of adoptions was falling during the depression and that children placed with the nuns were very likely to remain in their care until adolescence. The social stigma of illegitimacy would pursue the child for its entire life. The label appeared in the parish registers and some religious orders did not accept bastard children, cutting them off from the highest aspiration of the believing Catholic. A mother could well feel guilty for condemning her child to a life of discrimination by putting her own welfare first. In this context, the expressions of relief at the death of a child are not surprising. As one grandmother wrote to Sister Tharcisius, "We are satisfied. The baby is dead, the past erased."[67]

Hidden, punished, perhaps rehabilitated, the women who sought refuge at the Hôpital de la Miséricorde were taking advantage of a service that prevailing social attitudes had made invaluable. Whatever the intentions of the nuns may have been, how did the hospital inmates view the period they spent washing diapers, peeling pota-toes, and scrubbing floors? The letters that were intercepted and kept in the files may not tell the whole story of how the boarders lived, since they were written by the dis-satisfied. Some letters, written by the genuinely repentant, expressed gratitude to Sister Tharcisius. Others, more common, talk of tears, exhaustion, depression, and even thoughts of suicide. Unhappiness was to be expected and the authorities viewed it as a sign of repentance. Sister Tharcisius wrote to a former patient with whom she had kept up a warm correspondence and who planned to come to Montreal for a visit, "You will certainly be happy to see once again the chapel where you prayed so often and shed so many tears."[68]

Except for the wholly destitute who had nowhere to turn and for whom the hos-pital represented a refuge from a cruel world, we may assume that the majority of young women within its walls hoped to leave as soon as possible. Since they had accepted the conditions on admission, they had little choice but to resign themselves, perhaps trying to earn good marks to speed their release or begging their parents or boyfriend to find the money to pay off their debt. But the nuns, of course, had no intention of merely providing a pleasant haven safe from prying eyes.

As a refuge, the hospital guaranteed concealment. The protection it offered ex-tended beyond the women who sought asylum there to their families and to the larger society that was shielded from the scandal that the presence of a pregnant single mother generated. Once she had lost her virginity, whether willingly or not, a woman became, according to the popular expression, "debauched." Few young men could be expected to choose such a woman as a wife and mother of his children. Concealing both the pregnancy and the child was the only way in which she might hope to resume a "normal" life, to marry and to become a mother once again, but this time in the only approved fashion. In addition, the austerities of the spiritual regime reflected the hopes of the nuns for a genuine reformation.

The means adopted to assure anonymity and to produce rehabilitation indicate the degree of social intolerance of a kind of behaviour that was hardly uncommon but that remained insupportable. Society dealt severely with those who had failed to observe the approved sexual codes. These single women may have accomplished their maternal destiny, but by doing so outside of marriage they were seen to have per-verted the ideal of motherhood. In a society where the patriarchal family was absolutely fundamental, this perversion of the "natural" female function appeared as a potent assault on the very foundations of society itself.

NOTES

1. M.E. Fleming and M. MacGillivray, *Fécondité de la femme canadienne, Septième Recensement du Canada*, 1931, 12 (Ottawa, 1936), p. 262.
2. Statistics compiled from the registers of the Hôpital de la Miséricorde, in the Archives of the Hôpital de la Miséricorde, Jacques Viger Hospital (AHM). For the Hôpital de la Miséricorde of Quebec City, run by the Sisters of the Good Shepherd, see Albert Jobin, "Hôpitaux de la Miséricorde et de la Crèche St-Vincent-de-Paul," *Bulletin de la Société Médicale des Hôpitaux Universitaires de Québec* (1934), p. 304.
3. Sr. Saint-Jean Vianney, SM, MSS, "Un peu d'histoire," paper presented at the Journée d'étude held on the occasion of the 10th anniversary of the incorporation of the Miséricorde social services (17 November 1955), pp. 4–5.

4. J.E. Dubé, "Nos hôpitaux. Leur passé, leur évolution, le présent," *L'Union médicale*, 61, 2 (February, 1932), pp. 179–80. In Quebec City, the Hôpital de la Miséricorde, under the direction of the Soeurs du Bon Pasteur, performed the same function as the hospital in Montreal and recorded an average of 457 deliveries a year between 1929 and 1933. See Jobin, "Hôpitaux de la Miséricorde," p. 304.

5. *Rapport annuel du Ministère de la Santé et du Bien-être social pour les années 1935 à 1941* (Quebec, 1944), p. 204.

6. AHM, C. Joncas to Sr. Tharcisius (20 February 1933); Sr. Tharcisius to Fr. B. (January, 1933).

7. AHM, 1929–1939.

8. AHM. Given the small percentage of factory workers who entered the Hôpital de la Miséricorde, it does not seem that illegitimacy was linked to industrial work, except to the degree that the industrial development of the towns encouraged an influx of young, unmarried women into the urban milieu. For a discussion of modernization and illegitimacy, see Edward Shorter, "Illegitimacy, Sexual Revolution, and Social Change in Modern Europe," *Journal of Interdisciplinary History*, 2, 2 (Autumn, 1971), pp. 237–72; J.W. Scott and L.A. Tilley, "Women's Work and the Family in Nineteenth Century Europe," *Comparative Studies in Society and History*, 17, 1 (January, 1975), pp. 36–64; J.R. Gillis, "Servants, Sexual Relations, and the Risks of Illegitimacy in London, 1800–1900," *Feminist Studies*, 5, 1 (Spring, 1979), pp. 142–73.

9. AHM. Mothers' and babies' weights are of little use in establishing the state of health of these patients because they are rarely given. This lack of information prevents us from comparing our findings with those of Patricia Ward and Peter Ward in "Infant Birth Weight and Nutrition in Industrializing Montreal," *American Historical Review* (April, 1984).

10. Québec, Service provincial d'hygiène, *Rapport annuel,* 1928.

11. AHM.

12. AHM. The examples drawn from AHM are identified by the patient's file number, or the date, and if possible by both: #32653; #32771.

13. AHM.

14. AHM, 1932.

15. AHM. Sr. Tharcisius to A., #12637.

16. Arthur Prévost, *Toute la vérité sur la fille-mère et son enfant* (Montréal: Princeps, 1961), p. 46.

17. AHM, Sr. Tharcisius (30 September 1935; 21 October 1935; 7 November 1935).

18. NAC, Charlotte Whitton Papers, MG 30, E 256, Vol. 20, John Kerry, "The Legal Status of the Unmarried Mother and Her Child in the Province of Quebec" (1926).

19. Montreal, Judicial Archives, Sessions Court, Court of the King's Bench, 1929–39.

20. AHM (24 July 1937).

21. AHM (1933).

22. AHM (20 June 1936). A mother also wrote (2 March 1933) that as she had "relatives who were priests, cousins in religious orders in many Montreal communities," information must be given out to no one, "even a priest or a nun."

23. AHM, #35181 (10 May 1937).

24. AHM. A patient caught trying to send an uncensored letter had to serve an additional month, making a total of seven months after her confinement. #334502 (30 March 1936).

25. AHM. #32542 (1933).

26. AHM. As one mother from St. Hyacinthe wrote, "I wouldn't want to travel for nothing the time is too hard." #32000 (1933)

27. AHM. A blood transfusion was worth $20 or a month of service. #32357.

28. C.A. Décarie, "Malades mentales," *Annales Médico-chirurgicales de l'Hôpital Ste-Justine*, 1, 3 (May, 1932), p. 126.

29. AHM.
30. AHM (1939).
31. AHM, #32760 (17 October 1933). Similar requests on the part of patients' mothers may be found in #32357 (17 October 1933); #32578 (19 November 1933).
32. A seventeen-year-old "made a scene to avoid going and had to be taken by force." #35209 (May, 1937).
33. AHM, Sr. Tharcisius (18 August 1938).
34. AHM, Sr. Tharcisius (30 September 1935; 21 October 1935; 15 October 1937).
35. AHM (22 July 1938).
36. AHM (3 November 1937). Even a woman over the age of twenty-one might be kept against her will. To a hotel-keeper, who had brought his twenty-seven-year-old employee, an orphan, to the hospital, Sister Tharcisius wrote, "She wants to leave the hospital at all costs . . . she believes she is in prison. . . . If we keep her here it is only because of your clearly expressed desire." (#31557, 12 April 1932).
37. AHM, #32460 and #35175 (May, 1937). The woman still owed $97.
38. AHM, #32662 (1932).
39. #35436 (1935).
40. AHM (1932).
41. AHM. Sr. Tharcisius to the parish priest of Ste-Justine-de-Dorchester (18 April 1939).
42. AHM, #33660 (2 October 1935).
43. AHM. For having tried to send a clandestine letter, #34502 had to work an extra month at the crèche, serving a total of seven months after her confinement. Others punished for the same reason were #32771; #35217 (29 May 1937); #35840 (14 May 1938).
44. AHM, #33275 (1934); (May, 1939). Statistics compiled from the AHM registers.
45. AHM, #30621.
46. AHM. According to the records, she owed $97 to the hospital (#35175). In October, 1935, the police were called to put #34168 to bed.
47. Statistics compiled from AHM registers.
48. AHM, #36523 (9 October 1939). Gillis has shown that in nineteenth-century London, men who might have considered taking care of their girl friends and their children were often prevented by circumstances from doing so. Gillis, "Servants, Sexual Relations," pp. 157–163.
49. AHM, #30377 (18 February 1930).
50. AHM.
51. AHM, #32578 (19 November 1933).
52. AHM, Sr. Tharcisius to E.P. (15 July 1937).
53. AHM (2 March 1933).
54. First Annual Report of the Women's Directory of Montreal (Montreal, 1915).
55. La Presse, 13 January 1931.
56. Kerry, "Legal Status," pp. 9–10.
57. Quebec, Department of Municipal Affairs, Industry and Commerce, Annuaire statistique du Québec, 1930–1940 (Quebec: King's Printer, 1931–1941).
58. Statistics compiled from AHM registers, 1929–39.
59. AHM. Statistics compiled from the registers of 1929–39. The crèches were extremely dangerous places to the lives of the babies. Dr. A. Jobin complained of the crowded conditions and unhealthiness of the crèche at the Hôpital de la Miséricorde in Quebec City. There, contagious diseases were devastating. In 1929, two-thirds of the 186 children taken there from Sacré Coeur Hospital in Quebec City were dead in a few months of whooping cough or measles. A. Jobin, "Historique d'une épidémie de rougeole à la crèche," Bulletin médical de Québec, 32 (1931), pp. 108–09. Venereal diseases transmitted by parents also claimed their victims. In 1928, there were eighty-seven children affected with syphilis and 516 with gonorrhea. Provincial Health Service, Rapport annuel, 1928.

60. AHM, 27 November 1939.
61. AHM, 1934. This type of comment appears more than once. For example, "Little Jeannine is dead. The Lord has been good enough to come and take her away, thanks be to God." 16 October 1935.
62. AHM, #35065.
63. AHM, #32364 (April, 1934, and 9 September 1934). The nuns were very aware of the rumours circulating regarding mistakes in identity at the crèche. In 1936, following a scandal in the United States, *La Revue moderne* printed a laudatory article about the Hôpital de la Miséricorde with the subtitle "Some babies switched in American maternity wards. Precautions taken to avoid these mistakes." See "A visit to the maternity ward," *La Revue moderne*, 15, 5 (March, 1936), pp. 30–31. All the same, the hero of *Soeur ou fiancée* is saved from an incestuous relationship because of a misunderstanding about his birth. de Cotret, *Soeur ou fiancée,* p. 56.
64. AHM, #32192 (April, 1933).
65. AHM (17 December 1956).
66. *Le Devoir,* 18 May 1937.
67. AHM, #31541 (April, 1932).
68. AHM, #34378. The woman had spent a year and a half at the Miséricorde.

TOPIC SIX
Youth and Education

Child labour in the mines of
Cape Breton, 1903.

To explain the initial rise of student protest during the 1960s, the American psychologist Kenneth Keniston identified the phenomenon of "extended adolescence."[1] More widespread affluence during the post–World War II period, he asserted, permitted a record proportion of young people to finish secondary school and attend college. There they enjoyed the luxury of indulging in broad moral and philosophical speculation that, in part, led them to denounce signs of inequality and repression in society. By contrast, only a quarter-century earlier almost all older teens would have been engrossed in the more practical business of surviving or getting ahead in the working world.

That the experience of young people changed dramatically over the course of the twentieth century is made clear by a reading of Article 11, in which Rebecca Coulter chronicles the tendency of Edmonton youth during the 1920s to take low-paying and dead-end full-time work. Some young Edmontonians were required to supplement the family income from an early age; others were seeking the shortest route to financial independence and a place of their own in the world. Among many young people and even their parents, moreover, there prevailed a view of formal education (particularly in rural areas, where school facilities often were dilapidated and teachers frequently unqualified, and where the curriculum commonly did not proceed beyond Grade 8) as being of marginal value in teaching the skills essential for "real life."

A low opinion of the school system, according to Neil Sutherland in Article 12, rallied educational reformers into action during the early years of the twentieth century. Focussing on the Macdonald-Robertson plan, a privately funded venture that sparked significant government action, Sutherland outlines the inauguration and development of manual training and domestic science, nature study and agricultural science, physical education and cadet training as components of the curriculum, along with the steps taken towards school consolidation and improved teacher training. Sutherland seems to accept the educational reformers about whom he writes as idealists dedicated to the amelioration of Canada via the creation of a better school system. Yet just as social historians have often questioned the general perception of economic growth as implying progress, so some scholars have cast such educational reforms — including the moves on behalf of mass public education during the mid-nineteenth century — as geared primarily towards establishing social control over the masses rather than towards providing them with new opportunities. Such schemes, they have argued, were furthered by elites, business and manufacturing interests, and the middle class as a way of removing children from the temptations and disorder of the streets and instilling in them the skills and attitudes that would promote economic growth (particularly in the emerging industrial economy), social tranquillity, a common nationality, and the patriarchal construction of society.[2]

QUESTIONS TO CONSIDER

1. For what reasons did Edmontonians fret over the tendency of youth to seek employment?
2. Did employers adopt a compassionate or a paternalistic attitude towards their younger workers?
3. What proof is there that idealism lay behind the Macdonald-Robertson educational program?

4. In what ways did early twentieth-century educational reform serve industrialists? the national economy? the patriarchal construction of society? the maintenance of social order in a class-divided community?
5. To what extent did the Macdonald-Robertson plan attain its goals?

NOTES

1. See Kenneth Keniston, *The Uncommitted: Alienated Youth in American Society* (New York: Harcourt, Brace & World, 1965) and *Youth and Dissent: The Rise of a New Opposition* (New York: Harcourt Brace Jovanovich, 1971).
2. One of the clearest statements of this view is contained in Alison Prentice, *The School Promoters: Education and Social Class in Mid-Nineteenth Century Upper Canada* (Toronto: McClelland & Stewart, 1977).

SUGGESTED READINGS

Axelrod, Paul. *Making of a Middle Class: Student Life in English Canada during the Thirties.* Montreal and Kingston: McGill-Queen's University Press, 1990.

Barman, Jean. *Growing Up in British Columbia: Boys in Private Schools.* Vancouver: University of British Columbia Press, 1984.

Barman, Jean, and Yvonne Hébert, eds. *Indian Education in Canada.* Vancouver: University of British Columbia Press, 1986.

Jones, Andrew, and Leonard Rutman. *For the Children's Sake: J.J. Kelso and Child Welfare in Ontario.* Toronto: University of Toronto Press, 1981.

Parr, Joy. *Labouring Children: British Immigrant Apprentices to Canada, 1868–1924.* Montreal and Kingston: McGill-Queen's University Press, 1980.

Raymond, Joycelyn Motyer. *The Nursery World of Dr. Blatz.* Toronto: University of Toronto Press, 1991.

Rooke, Patricia T., and R.L. Schnell, eds. *Studies in Childhood History: A Canadian Perspective.* Calgary: Detselig, 1982.

Sheehan, Nancy M., J. Donald Wilson, and David C. Jones, eds. *Schools in the West: Essays in Canadian Educational History.* Calgary: Detselig, 1986.

Stamp, Robert. *Schools of Ontario, 1876–1976.* Toronto: University of Toronto Press, 1980.

Sutherland, Neil, Jean Barman, and Linda L. Hale, comps. *Contemporary Canadian Childhood and Youth: A Bibliography.* Westport, Conn.: Greenwood Press, 1992.

ELEVEN

The Working Young of Edmonton, 1921–1931

REBECCA COULTER

In the early months of 1929, the good citizens of Edmonton were shocked to learn that teen-age prostitutes were plying their trade in the downtown area of the city. The daily papers announced the arrest of one "Miss X" (as they delicately put it) on charges of vagrancy and then proceeded to unfold the sorry story of her young life.[1] At the age of fourteen she had left home and come to the city in search of work. The only employment she had been able to secure was in the cafeteria of Ramsey's Department Store, the second largest store of its kind in Edmonton. As Miss X pointed out in her court testimony, the $7.50 per week she earned there was not enough to pay for her room and board, let alone buy clothes. She took to wandering the streets as the only form of recreation available to a poor and lonely girl and shortly fell in with a taxi-driver. She began to share lodgings with him and he asked her to "hustle for him" though she claimed that she "didn't really know what it meant then." In the course of several months, Miss X moved from pimp to pimp. These men fed, clothed, and sheltered her and to some extent, at least, met her emotional needs. By the time of her arrest she had joined forces with a young man who was in the process of taking her home to marry. Thus, in the course of a few short months, she experienced the three options most often available to the poor working girl — low-paying, unskilled menial work, prostitution, and marriage.[2]

That her case was not exceptional is reflected both in police testimony and in the evidence of many other girls who were picked up as part of the "vice ring clean-up" that occurred after Miss X's arrest. One girl poignantly explained her situation. She had absolutely no money; she could not find work of any kind; she felt that she could not return home so in her desperation she simply approached a likely looking male prospect and asked him to look after her.[3]

Of course, not all teen-age girls were forced into this mode of survival, and there is no evidence to suggest that young males had similar arrangements. Nonetheless, the experiences of Miss X and the other teen-age prostitutes serve to illustrate significant aspects of the lives of the working young of Edmonton from 1921 to 1931. They did not enjoy the "invented" adolescence of which historians speak or a prolonged, dependent, and protected childhood. Rather, in large numbers, they faced the harsh realities of the work world at an early age.

Edmonton in 1921 was a small city with a population of 58,821. Seventeen per cent or 10,271 of these people were between the ages of ten and nineteen. By 1931 this age group had grown to 20 per cent of the population or 16,353 persons. The

Source: Excerpted from "The Working Young of Edmonton, 1921–1931," in Joy Parr, ed., *Childhood and Family in Canadian History* (Toronto: McClelland & Stewart, 1982), 143–59. Reprinted by permission of the author.

majority of these young people had been born in Canada and most of the others had begun life in the British Isles or the United States. Despite the frequent emphasis of social reformers on "the problem of the foreign-born," the fact is that most children had experienced a dominant English-speaking culture from the time of birth. Indeed, Edmonton in 1926 was a city in which over 90 per cent of the inhabitants had been born in Canada, the British Isles, or the United States.[4]

Through the twenties, while the ratio of males to females in the 10–14 age group remained about equal in any given year, the 15–19 age group showed a marked drop in the proportion of males to females. During their later teens, more girls were entering than leaving the city; for boys this pattern was reversed.

Where were the males going and why was the female population growing? It appears that urban boys were leaving the city to find jobs on farms or in the primary resource industries. And, while historical sources are silent on the exact ages of the groups of single men who drifted in and out of the western cities in the first four decades of this century, young men of fifteen to nineteen were likely part of this migratory pattern. On the other hand, the newspapers and youth workers often commented on the fact that young rural girls flocked to the cities to find work in the service, clerical, and manufacturing sectors. Miss X is a case in point. Once in the city, girls were more likely to stay because job opportunities for females were scarce in the countryside. As well, their freedom of movement was restricted by their sex. Only occasionally do girls appear to have "ridden the rails" and then only after dressing as men.[5]

In Edmonton, teen-agers made up 8 per cent of the male and 26 per cent of the female work force in 1921 though by 1931 these figures had dropped to 6 per cent and 20 per cent respectively. Only a negligible number, fewer than one per cent, of young people in their early teens were recorded as working either in 1921 or 1931. But 42 per cent of fifteen- to nineteen-year-olds were earning wages in 1921 while 19 per cent of sixteen- and seventeen-year-olds and 51 per cent of eighteen- and nineteen-year-olds were similarly engaged. A further small proportion of young people was listed in the census as "gainfully occupied," that is, they were materially helping their parents with work (other than housework) at home or at their place of business.

Predictably, many young people outside the labour force were full-time students. In 1921, of the 9,760 children aged seven to fourteen years, 93 per cent were at school. Of the 669 youngsters not at school, a few likely did not attend because of illness or other infirmities. Many others were probably working undetected in the street trades or in home industries. George Donnolly, Edmonton's attendance officer, found at least ninety-eight children working illegally and returned them to school. Donnolly also granted attendance exemptions to thirteen others that year under the provisions of The School Attendance Act.[6] By 1931, however, 99 per cent of seven- to fourteen-year-olds attended school full-time as did 57 per cent of the fifteen- to nineteen-year-olds.

These figures distort the total contribution of the young to the labour market for, by definition, the census did not count work before or after school hours, on weekends, or during vacation periods. Nor is any account made of the work done by truant children, many of whom were kept at home to work or deliver messages as the need arose. Even young people who spent the major portion of their time at home in the full-time performance of household duties were specifically excluded from among the "gainfully employed."[7] This would be the case for the 145 girls in 1921 and the 201 in 1931 who married while still in their teens if they worked only in the home.

Census methodology also masks the problem of youth unemployment. In 1921, 606 youths between fifteen and nineteen, 13 per cent of the total, were neither at work nor at school. In 1931 these figures were 1,030 and 12 percent respectively. Most of these young people were likely unemployed but because they had never worked full-time they were not recorded in wage-earner statistics. As well, the increase in school enrolments between 1921 and 1931 is partly a reflection of the tightening job market for teen-agers. Young people, unable to secure employment, reluctantly stayed on at school. High school inspectors, in particular, frequently commented on the direct relationship between economic stagnation and sudden substantial increases in secondary school enrolments.[8]

The problems of youth unemployment did not go unnoticed, however. In 1920 the federal government established a juvenile division within the Employment Service of Canada. This junior employment service was designed to replace the informal and "inefficient" methods by which work had been found previously. Alberta quickly followed the federal lead by establishing a Juvenile Department of the Alberta Government Employment Bureau. Theoretically the juvenile employment service was to refer back to school young people not ready for employment. Juvenile employment agents were to conduct home visits to establish that youngsters sought work of necessity. They were to talk to school officials, youth club leaders, medical people, and local librarians, who might provide "valuable placement information." Placement officers would screen prospective workers to match their special abilities and ambitions with positions in industry. Once a job had been secured, agents were to encourage individuals to "stick to the job," to become mature and stable workers. Finally, young workers would be urged to "develop greater efficiency" in their work by taking advantage of educational resources and recreational facilities. This benevolent care was to continue until young workers could "mark out" their progress for themselves.

In practice, in Alberta at least, the Juvenile Department had little impact. The Employment Bureau hired no extra staff for youth work. The procedure followed was simple. School principals were asked to advise the Bureau of school-leaving dates. The Bureau then wrote to the parents or guardians offering its service and asking for an interview with the youth seeking work. The Bureau also provided employment information, but this was the extent of its work. Financial considerations severely curtailed the elaborate scheme proposed at the federal level. Perhaps, too, local officials had more confidence in the old methods of job-seeking. Young people continued to find work through their parents, relatives or friends, private employment agencies, informal job registries such as the one for office workers at the United Typewriter Company, and classified ads in local newspapers.[9]

Patterns of employment for the working young of Edmonton in the 1920s appear to resemble those found in the United States, Britain, and elsewhere in Canada. In 1921, 80 per cent of the employed young men found jobs in the manufacturing, transportation, trade, service, and clerical sectors of the economy. Ten years later these were still high employment areas for boys along with an additional area termed "other," a category which collected in one place labourers and unskilled workers. Within these broad occupational groups, youth tended to be restricted to work as labourers, messengers, deliverymen, truck drivers or teamsters, salesmen, bookkeepers, and office clerks. These jobs occupied 58 per cent of teen-age males in 1921 and 64 per cent in 1931.

Opportunities for females were even more narrow. In 1921, 98 per cent of all the employed girls between the ages of ten and nineteen were found in the manufacturing, trade, service, and clerical sectors. By 1931, few were employed in manufacturing and most found work as domestics, waitresses, saleswomen, stenographers, and typists. In fact, out of a total work force of 1,235 females in this age group, 940 or 76 per cent were employed in those five occupations.[10]

The 1931 census allows for some comparisons of average earnings and numbers of weeks worked in the year prior to census day in 1921 and 1931. With few exceptions, the young had less job security and lower wages than the rest of the working population. Between 1921 and 1931 they experienced a drop in both wages and amount of time worked. This was part of a drop experienced by all workers, but for the young whose earnings were low to begin with this decrease must have been particularly difficult to manage, especially for those not living with their families. Young females received a lower average annual income than young males, even in cases where the women were employed for more weeks in the year than the men.

Certain areas of employment offered more weeks of work and better wages than others. In general, clerical work was the most financially rewarding for both boys and girls, while domestic work for girls and labouring or messenger jobs for boys paid the least. By 1931 salaries in all areas of employment had dropped substantially. Decreased weekly wages account for part of the drop in annual salaries from 1921 to 1931, but young people also found themselves employed for fewer weeks during the year. The drop in weeks at work was particularly large for female office workers and saleswomen and male labourers and salesmen.[11]

Because both 1921 and 1931 were troubled years economically in Edmonton, these statistics may not correctly reflect the earnings and weeks of work achieved through the decade, and flat rates of pay are not alone a reliable guide to changes in the standard of living. But both current writings and contemporary evidence suggest that at no point in the 1920s did the material welfare of working people improve. Michiel Horn is correct. "The Twenties had not roared" for the more than half of the Canadian people who were "never anything but poor between the wars."

In 1935, the League for Social Reconstruction had concluded that the majority of Canadian families in 1930, and probably 1929 (the year of peak prosperity), lived "below the bare standard of decent livelihood." This family poverty clearly had adverse effects on the young. Charles William Bolton, a statistician with the Department of Labour appearing before the Select Standing Committee on Industrial and International Relations in 1926, specifically mentioned the ill effect of poverty-induced malnutrition on school performance and the tendency for the young of the poor to leave school early to supplement family incomes. This led teen-agers into "blind-alley occupations" or dead-end jobs — work with low wages, no job security, and little chance for promotion or improvement.[12] Since workers, especially the unskilled and non-unionized, appear to have made few real monetary gains in the 1920s, it is unlikely that juvenile workers, most often unskilled, inexperienced, and non-unionized, ever did much better than the figures for 1921 and 1931 indicate.

While it is always difficult to learn much about the qualitative aspects of the lives of the working young, some documentation is available as a result of the debate on the minimum wage, which continued in the province throughout the 1920s. In 1920 an advisory committee which would deal with wages and hours of work for women and young persons was provided by legislative amendments, and an official Minimum Wage Board was established in 1922.

To set a minimum wage, the board examined annual budgets of working girls. Certain elements of the business community later accused board members of "fixing" the accounts, for many of the budgets were "estimates" drawn up by the Commissioner of Labour and the female factory inspector. However, an actual record kept by one informant for a nine-month period in 1922 shows that the board was not overly generous in its final award. Of the $762.55 spent by this young woman over the nine months, the largest expenditures were on room and board and clothing. She also sent $196.70 home to her family. If we consider this last amount an unnecessary expense, we find that $14.51 per week was needed to meet her budget. With the addition of a payment to the family, the weekly rate would go up to $19.55, a figure very close to the $20 per week base rate suggested by the Employed Girls' Council of Regina and adopted by the Women's Labour Conference held in Edmonton in 1929.[13] The Minimum Wage Board, however, established a $14 per week wage as being fair to both business interests and working girls. It is unlikely that a higher minimum could have been ordered because the business community was extremely persistent in its lobby against any regulation at all. The board, caught between labour and business and accountable to both the government and the community, set the wage at a level it thought defensible.

Few girls under twenty received anything like $14 per week or even the $12.50 minimum established for female employees in manufacturing plants, shops, stores, and mail-order houses. Girls just starting out were especially ill-paid. As Walter Smitten, the Commissioner of Labour, wrote in 1929, the board "recognized that during the period of learning it was absolutely impossible to fix a rate that would provide full maintenance for a self-supporting girl." How, then, was such a girl to live, wondered the local members of the Canadian Brotherhood of Railroad Employees, if she had to pay for room and board and "dress decent, to have work at all." It would be unfortunate, they suggested, if girls felt "compelled by force of circumstances, to take a step that is neither a credit to themselves, nor the City."[14]

For some young women like Miss X, taking this step seemed the only way to survive. Nineteen-year-old Olive V. explained that she worked as a waitress when she could but turned to prostitution when she was out of work. Others were able to manage without recourse to prostitution and eked out a meagre but "respectable" existence. Those who lived at home and only contributed part of their pay package to family maintenance were, by most accounts, better off than the self-supporting girls. Girls at home at least had the assurance of regular shelter. But young women coming to the city or those wishing to live alone had difficulty finding lodging. A YWCA survey in 1929 discovered only 209 rooms in established institutions and fifty in private homes for females to rent. The real problem, said Eunice Whidden, General Secretary of the YWCA, was low wages. Girls had less than $7.50 per week to spend for room and board and housewives simply could not provide rooms and meals for that amount. Thus, many working girls lived in small, shabby rooms in poor neighbourhoods and went without sufficient food.[15]

Employment was no easier to find than lodging. In 1921 the Local Council of Women reported that unemployment was on the increase for girls and women. The YWCA found a similar situation in 1929 — there were too few jobs for all the girls wanting to work. In 1930 the files of the United Typewriter Company, the unofficial job registry for stenographers, listed more than 100 young, inexperienced girls looking for work. The Retail Clerks' Association estimated that 400 girls were looking for jobs. In 1931 the YWCA began registering unemployed girls and on the first day more than 100 girls came forward.[16] We can only imagine the despair and desperation these figures hide.

Closely allied to the problem of unemployment was the issue of part-time work. The Royal Commission on Price Spreads and Mass Buying found that chain stores were evading minimum wage legislation by making wide use of part-time help. The situation of Miss X is a case in point. After she testified about her $7.50 weekly earnings, J.H. Ashcraft, the former manager of Ramsey's Department Store, rebutted. She had not been paid below the minimum wage; she had only worked part-time and hence had been paid on a pro-rated basis. Girls employed in the millinery work room of the Hudson's Bay store experienced part-time work of another sort. Their jobs were divided into two seasons each year, the first lasting from February 15 to June 15 and the second from August 15 to December 15. Despite these two annual periods of layoff, their weekly salaries while working were no larger than those paid full-time employees.[17]

In addition to part-time work and routine lay-offs, employers used the idea of apprenticeship to escape paying the minimum wage. The provision in The Factories Act that specified a minimum wage for apprentices of $1 per shift was easily broken. Employers paid apprentices $6, but required the return of as much as $4 for "tuition fees," leaving a true weekly wage of $2. Department stores were accused of circumventing minimum wage regulations through serial apprenticeships. A girl would be hired on as an apprentice with one department in the store at $7.50 or $9.50 a week. At the end of the apprenticeship period, rather than receiving the full minimum wage, she would be transferred to another department to begin a new period of apprenticeship at the learner's wage. This problem was seen as particularly acute in larger stores with many departments, where girls could thus spend several years working as apprentices for less than the minimum wage.[18]

Neither the Alberta government nor the Minimum Wage Board accepted arguments for lengthy apprenticeships in retail sales. Accordingly girls were entitled to receive a weekly wage of $7.50, $9, $10, and $11 for the first, second, third, and fourth quarter respectively of their learning year and then were to be placed on the $12.50 per week minimum wage.[19]

Domestic servants were even more vulnerable than other young female employees because they did not come under the auspices of any labour legislation. Their salaries were notoriously low, their working hours long, their days off few, and their lives subject to the constant scrutiny of their employers. Girls avoided domestic employment if at all possible and tolerated it only as a stop-gap until they found other jobs. Nonetheless, domestic service claimed a larger percentage of female workers in 1931 than it had in 1921.[20] Young women were forced into the most confining, unrewarding work of all as the depression deepened.

Like others of their age, these young females found the opportunities available to them severely curtailed by circumstances beyond their control. For many teen-agers, early entry into the labour market was an essential part of a family strategy for economic survival. In both 1921 and 1931 children's earnings were an important part of total family income. Among families headed by men in unskilled, semi-skilled, or seasonal jobs, the contributions of children were particularly large.

Because of their class position, many teen-agers had to choose earning over learning. This was a significant decision with life-long implications because throughout the 1920s the nexus between schooling and employment possibilities tightened. The better paying, more secure, and more comfortable jobs available to teen-agers required skills such as typewriting, shorthand, and accounting. After a suitable academic preparation, the young were expected to learn these skills in a commercial high school or a business college. By 1930 parents were urged to keep their girls in school until they had completed grade nine or ten before sending them into commercial courses. Unemployment among young office workers was blamed on their inexperience, immaturity, and lack of schooling.[21]

Working-class parents were aware of the value of a good education for their children. But, as E.J. Thompson of the Edmonton Local of the Grand Trunk Pacific Carmen pointed out, the training provided by the state was often beyond a working man's means. Low wages and the high cost of living meant that the breadwinner needed the help of other wage-earners to balance the family budget.

Organized labour repeatedly demanded reforms that would offset the educational disadvantages of working-class youth. For example, the Alberta Federation of Labour called for evening continuation classes for those "compelled to leave school at an early age" but who wanted "a second chance in life." Throughout the 1920s, the AFL and labour candidates in Edmonton's municipal elections called for "free and full educational opportunity for the children of all the people," free school books and supplies, and adequate health policies in the schools.[22]

Interest in the academic and vocational preparation available through the schools increased in the 1920s because alternatives to moribund apprenticeship programs were required. The Royal Commission on Industrial Relations, visiting Alberta in 1919, heard from A. Farmilo, Secretary of the Edmonton Trades and Labour Council, about the "half-educated workmen" being produced by the city's apprenticeship system. By 1928 little had changed. T.J. Thornton, the business agent for the Edmonton Local of the United Brotherhood of Carpenters and Joiners of America, complained that employers and managers neglected the training of the young and showed more concern for short-term gains than for craftsmanship. Thornton argued for a well-directed apprenticeship plan modelled on Ontario's Construction Apprenticeship Council.[23]

The Carpenters and Joiners Local did organize an apprenticeship program for young men between ages seventeen and twenty-two, specifying the number of apprentices an employer could hire, the training an apprentice would receive, and the wages to be paid over the four years of service. Despite elaborate plans, only fourteen apprentices had been indentured between 1927 and 1930, four of these had been suspended, and one had withdrawn. The Brotherhood's failures emphasize the frailty of organized apprenticeship schemes in Edmonton in the 1920s. In most cases the term "apprentice" became simply a synonym for "learner" and, as some surviving collective agreements show, "learners" were usually people under twenty who were paid lower wages for longer periods of time just because they were young.[24]

Contemporary evidence from other localities shows similar developments. The loss of the old and meaningful form of apprenticeship was clearly part of the more complex changes in industrial organization that went along with new technologies, "scientific" management, and the transformation of the labour process.[25] Control over the learning process in the skilled trades passed from workers to a tripartite arrangement that included state regulation and technical school training. This transition signalled a significant change in the way the young would be prepared for work. One union leader at least recognized some of the implications of state intervention in vocational training. T.J. Thornton of the Carpenters and Joiners Local criticized technical schools for creating false distinctions between mental and manual workers and argued for programs that would emphasize the continuity of mental and manual craftsmanship. He wanted young people to understand the totality of their work and not just one specialized aspect of it.[26]

Thornton's concern for the quality and nature of the educational experience and his understanding of the "hidden" curriculum is particularly insightful. Many other union leaders uncritically favoured the use of the school for vocational training as they saw the state as a neutral power operating in the interests of all citizens. Their demands for change were limited to specific reforms, such as the abolition of military drill in the schools or the provision of school health services. Only the Labour Women's Social and Economic Conference shared Thornton's concerns about what was happening in the hearts and minds of working-class youth. These women organized a young people's group which was consciously designed to counteract the influence of the high schools, the sports world, and youth groups such as the Boy Scouts. These existing organizations were thought to turn the young against the labour movement and were accused of failing to assist teen-agers in the resolution of "the real problem facing the world today, that of bringing about a new social order. . . ." Like the early Kibbo Kift Kindred in Britain and the Pioneer Youth for Democracy in the United States, the Labour Women's youth group tried to provide a class-conscious alternative for the offspring of the labouring class. In this they achieved no lasting success.[27]

The experiences of the young in the work world reflected the realities of a capitalist labour market. In many respects they shared with their older comrades a first-hand knowledge of unemployment, menial work, job insecurity, and poverty. On the other hand, the taint of their age and their status as beginners, as untried and inexperienced commodities, meant that they were even more vulnerable to exploitation than were their elders. Unlike other teen-agers who knew a "modern" adolescence marked by dependency, protection, prolonged schooling, and an experience of what is loosely termed "youth culture," the working young entered the adult world early and had to face that world on its own terms.

NOTES

1. "Whirlwind Cleanup of Vice Rings . . . ," *Edmonton Journal*, 1 February 1929; "Case for Crown Tightened . . . ," *Edmonton Journal*, 5 February 1929; "Four Convictions," *Edmonton Journal*, 6 February 1929; Provincial Archives of Alberta (hereafter PAA), Alberta Provincial Police, Acc. No. 72.370, Item 2d, "A" Division Annual Report, 1929.

2. For a discussion of the choices open to poor working girls, see Ruth Rosen, "Introduction," in Rosen and Sue Davidson (eds.), *The Maimie Papers* (New York: The Feminist Press, 1977), xxv.

3. "New Drive Against Vice," *Edmonton Journal*, 7 February 1929. For information about working girls and prostitution in Toronto, see "Report of the Social Survey Commission, Toronto" (Toronto: n.p., 1915). Portions of this report are reprinted in Irving Abella and David Millar (eds.), *The Canadian Worker in the Twentieth Century* (Toronto: Oxford University Press, 1978), 114–19.

4. *Census of Canada*, 1921, 1931; *Census of the Prairie Provinces*, 1926, 622.

5. On drifting single men, see, for example, Stuart Marshall Jamieson, *Times of Trouble: Labour Unrest and Industrial Conflict in Canada, 1900–66* (Ottawa, 1968), 235; H.M. Cassidy, "Relief and Other Social Services for Transients," in L. Richter (ed.), *Canada's Unemployment Problem* (Toronto: Macmillan of Canada, 1939), 172–221. On rural girls in the city, see, for example, Alberta Department of Neglected Children, *Annual Report, 1912*, 36; "Report of Women Probation Officers for the City of Edmonton," in Alberta Department of Neglected Children, *Annual Report, 1918*, 42; "Whirlwind Cleanup of Vice Rings . . . ," *Edmonton Journal*, 1 February 1929. On transient girls, see "Calgary Girls Don Men's Attire to Beat Their Way to Coast," *Edmonton Bulletin*, 16 November 1921.

6. Minutes of the Edmonton Public School Board, 1921, 1922. The Annual Reports of Alberta's Department of Neglected Children, 1909–1919, provide hints about the street trades and home industries. Canada Department of Labour, *The Employment of Children and Young Persons in Canada* (Ottawa, 1930), 11. In 1921, of the 4,660 youths between fifteen and nineteen, 1,998 were in school.

7. *Department of Labour, Employment of Children*, 11–12; Census of Canada, 1921, IV, x.

8. On the relationship between the job market and school attendance see, for example, Alberta Department of Education, *Annual Report 1922*, p. 15, *AR1930*, p. 14, *AR1931*, p. 14.

9. PAA, Alberta Employment Service Papers, Acc. No. 65.118, Box 16, File 33, "Proceedings of the Second Annual Meeting of the Employment Service of Canada, 1920"; "Junior Employment Service in Canada," *The Labour Gazette* (December, 1920), 1613–17; PAA, Alberta Sessional Papers, Acc. No. 70.414, Box 11, 1921 Sessional Paper No. 23, 2nd Annual Report, Alberta Government Employment Bureau. On job-seeking, see Leonard C. Marsh, *Employment Research* (Toronto: Oxford University Press, 1935), 112–15; and "Enquiry Made Into Unemployment Among Local Business Girls," *Alberta Labor News*, 18 October 1930.

10. Based on the *Census of Canada*, 1921, III, Table 40, and *Census of Canada*, 1931, V, Table 36.

11. *Census of Canada*, 1931, V, Tables 11, 12.

12. Michiel Horn (ed.), *The Dirty Thirties* (Toronto: Copp Clark, 1972), 14; League for Social Reconstruction, Research Committee, *Social Planning for Canada* (Toronto: T. Nelson, 1935; University of Toronto Press, 1975), 7; Canada, Select Standing Committee on Industrial and International Relations, *Minutes of Proceedings and Evidence, Session 1926* (Ottawa, 1926), 20–1. See also Leonard C. Marsh, *Canadians In and Out of Work* (Toronto: Oxford University Press, 1940), 197–9.

13. Examples of the budgets are found in PAA Premiers' Papers, Acc. No. 69.289, File 505. Reports on the Women's Labour Conference and the $20 budget are found in "The Alberta Labour Women," *Alberta Labor News*, 30 March 1929; and "Women's Labour Conference, Edmonton," *The Labour Gazette* (April, 1929), 407.

14. PAA, Premiers' Papers, Acc. No. 69.289, File 505, Walter Smitten to Premier J.E. Brownlee, 4 March 1929; PAA, Premiers' Papers, Acc. No. 69.289, File 505, J. Wintersgill to Edmonton City Council, 14 February 1929.

15. The testimony of Olive V. can be found in PAA, Criminal Case Files, Acc. No. 72.26, File 3864/C, 1921. "Edmonton Totally Unfitted to Meet Needs of Girl Worker," PAA, YWCA Clipping Book, Acc. No. 68.301, Box 1, Item 12 (clipping dated 12 March 1929).

16. "Local Council of Women Reviews Activities of Year," *Edmonton Journal*, 28 January 1921; PAA, YWCA Clipping Book, Acc. No. 68.301, Box 1, Item 12 (clipping dated 23 April 1929); "Enquiry Made Into Unemployment Among Local Business Girls," *Alberta Labor News*, 18 October 1930; "The Alberta Labour Woman," *Alberta Labor News*, 3 October 1931.

17. Canada Royal Commission on Price Spreads and Mass Buying, *Minutes of Proceedings and Evidence*, vol. III (Ottawa, 1934); "Deny Statement on Store Wage," *Edmonton Journal*, 7 February 1929; PAA, Premiers' Papers, Acc. No. 69.289, File 505, P.J. Parker to Premier H. Greenfield, 24 December 1924.

18. "Factories Act Does Not Fulfill Requirements," *Edmonton Free Press*, 8 November 1919; "The Alberta Labour Woman," *Alberta Labor News*, 30 March 1929.

19. PAA, Premiers' Papers, Acc. No. 69.289, File 505, P.J. Parker to Premier H. Greenfield, 24 December 1924. See Harry Braverman, *Labor and Monopoly Capital* (New York: Monthly Review Press, 1974), 371, on fractionalization of retail labour. PAA, Premiers' Papers, Acc. No. 69.289, File 505, Alex Ross to H. Greenfield, 31 December 1924, and Minimum Wage Board Order No. 6.

20. "Problems of Girls in Industry Before Local Council of Women," *Edmonton Journal*, 25 May 1929; "The Girl of Today," *Edmonton Journal*, 23 April 1929; *Census of Canada*, 1921, III, Table 40; and *Census of Canada*, 1931, V, Table 36.

21. Marsh, *Canadians In and Out of Work*, 218, discusses learning versus earning. "Enquiry Made Into Unemployment Among Local Business Girls," *Alberta Labor News*, 18 October 1930.

22. Thompson's observation is found in "Industrial Commission Receives Suggestions," *Edmonton Free Press*, 10 May 1919. Demands of organized labour can be found, for example, in "Representatives of Alberta Fed. of Labor Submit Proposed Legislation to Prov. Cabinet for Consideration," *Edmonton Free Press*, 31 January 1920. "Platform of Labor Candidates," *Alberta Labor News*, 10 December 1927.

23. For material on the state of apprenticeship training, see Canada Royal Commission on Industrial Training and Technical Education, *Report* (Ottawa, 1913); "Apprenticeship in Canada," *The Labour Gazette* (July, 1921), 892–9; "The Decline of Apprenticeship," *The Labour Gazette* (May, 1927), 532–3. Farmilo's remarks reported in *Edmonton Free Press*, 10 May 1919; Thornton letter in *Alberta Labor News*, 3 November 1928.

24. PAA, United Brotherhood of Carpenters and Joiners Local 1325 (Edmonton) Correspondence Files, 1929–34, Acc. No. 67.88, File 142, "Report on Apprentices," 28 November 1930.

25. See Jamieson, *Times of Trouble*, 196; Braverman, *Labor and Monopoly Capital*; "The Decline of Apprenticeship," *The Labour Gazette* (May, 1927), 532–3; "Apprenticeship in Canada," *The Labour Gazette* (July, 1921), 892–9.

26. *Alberta Labor News*, 3 November 1928. Thornton's argument foreshadows much of what Braverman, *Labor and Monopoly Capital*, says about the degradation of work.

27. References to the specific reforms proposed or supported by the A.F.L. and the Edmonton Trades and Labor Council can be found in the *Alberta Labor News* for 1920–1931 and in PAA, Edmonton Trades and Labour Council Minute Books 1920–1932, Acc. No. 74.57. On the Labour Women's Youth Group, see Isabel Ringwood, "Organizing Our Young People," *Alberta Labor News*, 31 May 1930. On the Kibbo Kift Kindred, see John Springhall, *Youth, Empire and Society* (London: Croom Helm, 1977).

TWELVE

"The Common Centre from Which Radiated Plans and Labours": The Macdonald-Robertson Movement Demonstrates the New Education to Canadians, 1900–1913

NEIL SUTHERLAND

As a product of his growing concern for the learning of farm children and of the difficulties he found in teaching their parents, in 1899 James W. Robertson organized a contest for youngsters to select choice heads of grain from one year's crop to be used as seed in the next. Robertson later explained to the National Education Association that, as commissioner of dairying and agriculture, he had discovered that farm families often failed to appreciate the advantages "of a plan or scheme set out in a written statement." He therefore designed the contest to counter this lack of understanding and to help improve Canadian crops through the use of better seeds. In the task of selecting choice heads of grain for seed "was something," Robertson explained, "which would be so helpful and instructive to boys and girls that they would go on with it, and the habits of observation and thought and study would remain with them."[2]

In this modest effort at "leavening the system," Robertson embarked on a course of action which, more than any other event, changed turn-of-the-century school reform in English Canada from a heterogeneous collection of people and ideas into an organized movement. As a result of the seed contest, Robertson teamed up with the Canadian tobacco merchant and philanthropist Sir William Macdonald. Over the 1890s Macdonald had made generous donations to McGill University. He shared with Robertson a desire to improve the quality of rural life in Canada, especially in the English-speaking parts of Quebec and in his native Prince Edward Island.[3] To broaden the scope of the seed-growing contest and keep it going for a three-year term, Macdonald therefore provided $10,000 for prizes. The two men then went on to conduct a campaign, called the "Macdonald" or the "Macdonald-Robertson Movement," which formed a core around which many others worked to improve Canadian schooling. Except for the seed-growing contest, neither Robertson nor Macdonald invented

Source: Excerpted from *Children in English-Canadian Society: Framing the Twentieth-Century Consensus* (Toronto: University of Toronto Press, 1976), 182–201. Reprinted by permission of the author.

the educational ideas which they incorporated into their movement. Gradually and eclectically, they put together a program out of public discussion of education over the 1890s, work going on elsewhere, and their growing experience with what they were doing. Over the first decade of the twentieth century they gave Canadians practical demonstrations of such elements of the "new" education as manual training, school gardening, nature study, domestic science, consolidated schools, and better methods of training teachers.[4] They also incorporated into their demonstration schools the results of separate efforts to introduce kindergartens and systematic physical training into Canadian education. The Macdonald-Robertson movement culminated in 1910 when the federal government named Robertson as chairman of its Royal Commission on Industrial Training and Technical Education.

After the seed contest was under way, their quest for a means to improve rural life through rural schooling led Robertson and Macdonald to the subject of manual training. While it did not have exactly the effect which its two sponsors had in mind, their effort to introduce manual training into Canadian schools was remarkably successful. Reasoning that all educational movements "begin in cities and spread into the country districts," Robertson decided that the place to start encouraging manual training was in the schools of the cities and towns "in places where newspapers were published and to which the country people looked for guidance."[5] The man in the country, went one of Robertson's more dubious judgments, was "not willing to take a lower grade of education for his boy than the town or city man."[6]

They followed a model developed by James Huff Stout to improve the schools of Menominie, Wisconsin. Macdonald offered to "pay for the equipment required for educational manual training in one place in every province in the Dominion, and also to meet the expenses of qualified teachers, and of maintenance for three years in all those places."[7] The response to the offer was so overwhelming that Macdonald eventually agreed to finance demonstrations in seventeen centres. Robertson travelled to England to visit various institutions offering manual training and to hire instructors. By the summer of 1900 he had recruited a band of twenty-four; one from Sweden, one from the United States, and the other twenty-two from the British Isles. After a summer's indoctrination into the principles of the movement, these men spread out across Canada to set up twenty-four manual training centres for the autumn term.[8] Before the period of Macdonald maintenance ceased in 1903, there were forty-five fully qualified manual training teachers in Canada, half of them native Canadians, receiving assistance from the Macdonald funds and training over 700 boys each week.[9]

In the next few years the manual training idea spread rapidly. In 1904, Ontario made manual training an option in the elementary school curriculum and appointed the Macdonald fund director for that province, Albert H. Leake, as provincial inspector of technical education.[10] In 1908, the province made it possible for those teachers-in-training who passed their examinations at Easter to attend a special course at Guelph, with travel, room, and board paid for by the Department of Education. Significantly, the course was directed at potential city teachers who would be able "to give such instruction in drawing and woodwork" as would lay "a proper foundation for real industrial training." By 1911, manual training was taught in 26 of Ontario's 279 urban municipalities and in one township.[11] By 1909, Robertson estimated that over twenty thousand Canadian boys and girls annually received "the benefits of Manual Training Education."[12]

While the new subject was more popular in central and western Canada than in the Maritimes, Orville H. White's careful calculations show that there was some growth in manual training all across the nation. From four manual training teachers in 1900–1, British Columbia expanded its force to sixteen in 1909–10 and to fifty-eight in 1918–19. Saskatchewan had one such teacher in 1901, one in 1910, and twelve in 1917. Ontario extended its initial seven manual training centres in 1900 to sixty in 1910 and to one hundred in 1919. New Brunswick's centres increased from three in 1900 to eighteen in 1910 and to twenty-one by 1917.

Canadian educational reformers also sorted out the various elements of practical education. They came to define more sharply what they meant by what they variously called manual training (in the wide sense in which they used the term), hand work, hand-and-eye training, constructive work, and industrial education. By 1910, they had divided the broad territory of practical education into five relatively distinct areas: "manual arts" for younger children, manual training in the narrower sense of the term, vocational and technical education for adolescents and young adults, domestic science, and nature study and school gardening.[13]

For kindergarten and younger elementary pupils, both practical and child-centred reformers called for handicrafts, plasticene modelling, needlework, raffia crafting, scissor work, basketry, clay modelling, and cardboard work.[14] These "manual arts," their proponents argued, were a "means of developing the sense organs and of training faculties and powers to meet the things and forces of the outer world with intelligent discriminations."[15] As such, they were both pre-vocational and part of general education.[16] They also accorded with the active practices developed by the proponents of kindergartens, the child study movement, and other pioneers in teaching methods.[17]

By 1910, most English Canadians had narrowed their use of the term "manual training" to refer to a one-, two-, or three-year course taught to boys in the upper grades of the eight-year elementary program. Reflecting the English, American, Swedish, and Canadian origins of its early teachers and their freedom to develop their own courses, what boys did under this heading initially varied from teacher to teacher and region to region. As local and provincial authorities made the subject compulsory, included it in teacher education, and added special directors and inspectors to help practising teachers, the context became quite astonishingly uniform and was to remain unchanged for a generation or even longer. This standard curriculum, which was roughly based on English and Swedish models, combined mechanical drawing, introduction to hand tools, and the making of such useful objects out of wood as watch holders and plant stands.[18] By this time, too, both groups of proponents of manual training had come together in the view that it could both be pre-vocational and serve general educational purposes.[19] In order to assuage the fears of trade unions that it was a device to undermine tradesmen and mechanics, the subject's supporters were careful to downplay the practical side of the work. The aims of the manual training teacher, explained T.B. Kidner, Macdonald fund supervisor in Nova Scotia and then manual training supervisor in New Brunswick, were "quite different from those of a craftsman." While the latter's goal was to produce an article, the teacher's was that of "training and developing a human being"; in this task the article was "simply the *means* and not the *end*."[20] Through such rhetoric, and the rudimentary level of skills built into the course, the advocates of manual training were eventually able to persuade organized labour to give wary support for its introduction in the schools.[21]

In its Canadian form, however, manual training failed to fulfil its promised role of integrator of the curriculum. While Robertson had assured the sceptical that manual training was not another subject but a means of integrating what youngsters did in school, in practice specialist teachers, mostly with a craft rather than a teaching background, taught batches of boys for a half a day a week in a manual training centre.[22] In consequence, the subject turned into a sterile, mechanical progression which, White argues, even boys failed to enjoy.[23] Despite these facts — and expert critics like Albert Leake forcefully pointed them out — advocates of the new education continued to promote manual training vigorously.[24] Putman and Weir also noted a characteristic of both manual training and domestic science that would have dismayed Macdonald and Robertson: outside of the large urban centres, the subjects had "precarious standing."[25] Rural parents were, apparently, slower in demanding urban-style schooling for their youngsters than Robertson had expected.

In the third phase of their joint effort, school gardening, Macdonald and Robertson turned more directly to the problems of rural education. In their most original contribution to the movement they supported a scheme whereby one or two children tended and experimented with a small plot of land on or near the school ground. Macdonald movement school gardening was a blend of three separate educational ideas: nature study, manual training for rural pupils, and agricultural education for elementary pupils.[26] Nature study, which began in a small way in Canada in the late nineteenth century, was the result of an effort to introduce some elementary principles of science into the school curriculum. In nature study, teachers were supposed to conduct field studies on local plants, animals, and minerals with their classes. Until it was combined with the school garden, however, nature study in the lower grades often consisted of planting a tree or a flower bed on Arbor Day or taking a class walk to the woods on a fine spring day. In the upper grades it frequently emphasized "committing to memory a mass of terms descriptive of the various modifications which the organs of plants" underwent, a practice that provincial curricula encouraged.[27] Most teachers, observed a Manitoba school inspector in 1905, ignored nature study; of those who attempted it, most went no further than "reading such books as 'Wild Animals I Have Known' or futile little stories about flowers."[28] When, however, school gardening was coordinated with nature study teachers took their charges outside regularly to give them a systematic course.

The Macdonald-Robertson movement gave its characteristic practical demonstration of school gardening. Robertson recruited eight teachers with wide experience in rural schooling and in 1903–4 sent them on a year's study tour of Chicago, Cornell, Columbia, and Clark universities in the United States and to the Ontario Agricultural College. These teachers then established twenty-five "object lesson" school gardens, five each in Ontario, Quebec, New Brunswick, Nova Scotia, and Prince Edward Island. In Carleton County, Ontario, J.W. Gibson set up gardens at the schools at Carp, Galetta, Richmond, North Gower, and Bowesville.[29] At the end of the first year, one of the teachers reported that because the school garden had "relieved much of the drudgery of the school work" it had been his "pleasantest year" of teaching.[30]

School gardening gradually became an important aspect of rural education in Canada. For the minority of rural children who received any benefits from the new education, it was more likely to take this form than any other. After adding the subject to the school curriculum in 1904, three years later Ontario began to make special grants to schools and teachers for conducting school gardening. In 1910, fifteen schools qualified for the grant and the next year thirty-three schools did so. At this time, the province appointed S.B. McCready of the Ontario Agricultural College as director of elementary agricultural education.[31] In 1904, McCready had begun a series of special courses at the Macdonald Institute in nature study which gave great emphasis to school gardening.[32] In the first nine years, over eight hundred teachers took this course.[33] Not all of these teachers, however, actually taught their new specialty. In the spring of 1909, McCready had ninety-seven teachers in his class. When he polled them all a year later only sixteen had started school gardens and, because sometimes trustees and even inspectors were "not favourable," many were not doing any sort of nature study at all.[34]

Nevertheless, the growing concern for the quality of rural life continued to have some effect on schooling. In an address to a New York YMCA gathering in 1911, Robertson expressed the naive belief which characterized many of those who talked about what they called the "rural problem" in Canada: "our vast areas of good lands," he said, "could and should carry happy homes for millions more people and not have them huddled into big towns where the children cannot play."[35] Efforts to improve rural schooling through agricultural education, school gardening, nature study, and school consolidation were one result of this interest. Another was that, under the pressure of representations from farm organizations, Women's Institutes, church organizations, and members of Parliament for rural ridings, the federal government began to take a financial interest in rural improvement.[36] In 1912, Parliament passed the Agricultural Aid Act, which distributed half a million dollars to the provinces for the general improvement of rural economic, social, and educational conditions.[37] The next year it enacted the Agricultural Instruction Act, which provided provincial departments of agriculture and education with ten million dollars to be spent over a ten-year period, some of which could be spent on the "amelioration of the conditions of rural life, particularly in so far as women and children are concerned."[38] Research sponsored by the Commission of Conservation provided information of great value to provincial departments planning programs under the act. In the summer of 1916, the commission's Committee on Lands, which Robertson chaired, conducted a detailed survey of 400 farms in Dundas County, Ontario, that discovered that 98 per cent of farmers and 92 per cent of their wives had attended only elementary school. To F.C. Nunnick, an agriculturalist on the staff of the commission, these figures indicated "the wisdom and advisability" of making rural elementary schooling "as efficient, adequate and suitable as possible to prepare the young men and young women for real life in the country."[39]

Each province, however, had sole authority to decide how it would spend its annual share of the federal funds. In Prince Edward Island, the government increased the number of school inspectors, provided a summer school in agricultural education at Prince of Wales College, and bonuses for teachers who developed school gardens and provided agricultural instruction to their pupils.[40] British Columbia hired J.W. Gibson from the Ottawa Normal School as provincial director of agricultural education. Gibson taught agricultural education and school gardening at summer schools, supervised school gardening and distributed grants to teachers, and organized agricultural courses in high schools.[41] By 1924, about one-third of the public and separate schools in Ontario gave instruction in elementary agriculture. About two-fifths of them had school gardens and four-fifths had home gardens.[42]

School gardening and agriculture varied greatly in quantity and quality. Its chairman, Sir Clifford Sifton, proudly reported to the Commission of Conservation that its work in Dundas, the illustration county in Ontario, was having some remarkable effects. Harold Foght found great variation in school gardening and agricultural teaching in Saskatchewan, as did Gibson in British Columbia.[43] An Alberta inspector noted that there were "too many cases" where little mounds of earth served "but to mark the grave of the seed or of the early-departed plants."[44] Some teachers did only barely enough work to collect their grants, provincial departments were slow in adapting courses to local conditions, frequent changes of teachers broke the continuity of the work, and teachers encountered great difficulties in pruning needless repetition from the course and bringing it to bear on the local district and its possibilities.[45]

Although Macdonald and Robertson incorporated domestic science as a major strain in their movement, others were more central in demonstrating its effectiveness. Throughout the 1890s, a growing band of influential and mostly urban women, many associated with the YWCA, the Local Councils of Women, the WCTU, and Women's Institutes, conducted a campaign for girls to receive this kind of manual training. While their ranks included Lady Aberdeen and Mrs Lillian Massey-Treble of Toronto, Adelaide Hoodless was undoubtedly the most effective campaigner for domestic science in Canada. Working through the Hamilton YWCA, of which she was president from 1890 to 1900, the National Council of Women, of which she was treasurer for ten years, and the Women's Institutes, which she helped to found, Mrs Hoodless preached what she sometimes called the "message" of domestic science.[46]

Domestic science found favour amongst both child-centred and practical educational reformers. The subject was not, explained Mrs Hoodless, "Cookery" but "the application of scientific principles to the management of a Home, or briefly — correct living."[47] Like other manual training enthusiasts, those who favoured domestic science believed that it served "a general educational purpose" in that "the cultivation of manual dexterity" reacted "advantageously upon the intellectual faculties" and might even "act as a stimulant in the pursuit of other studies."[48] Others argued its practical merits. To some, domestic science had a two-fold function: to teach housewifely duties to those in "humbler homes" and to provide proper vocational training for potential domestic servants.[49] The most widely used argument for domestic science, however, was that in a time of rapid change and consequent social stress, society had to come to the support of the home.[50] The "influence of the home on the children," explained the report of the Royal Commission on Industrial Training and Technical Education in its advocacy of domestic science, was "direct and continuous." Good homes ministered to the welfare of the people "by ensuring conditions under which the children may be healthy, wholesome and happy." Since the effect of the home was "like the influence of the moon on the level of the sea," good homes kept "the tide of life high for the whole community and the state."[51]

Whatever wider educational implications other saw in it, however, domestic science teachers quickly made the subject a practical experience for the girls who took it. In her domestic science classes in Winnipeg in 1908–9, Dora Dibney learned about such matters as air in relation to life and fire, cleaning with powders, brooms, and dishcloths, general rules for canning and preserving, and she made baked apples, bread, salads, and ice cream.[52] Although Mrs Hoodless always argued the wider case for domestic science, her own textbook focused on practical and useful information.[53] By 1920, British Columbia's thirty-nine domestic science teachers and forty-nine domestic science centres provided a three-year course that began in grade six. Visiting a centre for a half-day each week, girls studied and practised household sewing, home management, personal hygiene, laundry work, and theoretical and practical cooking. The province required that girls able to take the course had to complete it satisfactorily in order to be eligible to write the high school entrance examinations.[54]

Growing concern for the physical condition of school pupils produced another constituent of the prewar "new" education.[55] Physical activity, body training, physical training, physical culture, calisthenics, and physical education — to cite some of the names which Canadians used when they talked about this topic — had a variety of roots. As a part of preventive medicine, public health workers insisted that hygiene teaching and fitness exercises be included in the school program. Others believed that regular exercise helped in maintaining good school discipline. The "proper use of drill and calisthenic exercises" argued James L. Hughes, gave "an erect, graceful figure and easy carriage," benefitted the health, and aided "in securing effective discipline."[56] Canadians also shared the growing public interest in the western world in physical fitness, games, and other sports. This development, which was related to contemporary attitudes to sex, produced an almost mystical aura about games and play. In turn, it shifted the YMCA and, to a lesser extent, the YWCA to their characteristic concern with fitness as an element in the development of Christian character.[57] Play, explained the director of physical training for the Montreal YMCA, was "the spirit of immortality made manifest."[58] Finally, as an expression of contemporary militarism, some Canadians called for general fitness, military drill, and cadet corps to be included in the school program.[59] What he wanted, explained the minister of militia and defence, Sir Frederick Borden, was "not only the bodily development of children of all classes and both sexes" but also that all boys acquire "an elementary knowledge of military drill and rifle practice," so that they could if necessary "take part in the defence of their homes and country."[60]

Despite official encouragement, few turn-of-the-century Canadian teachers followed any systematic program of physical activity with their charges.[61] After 1900, however, some urban youngsters were able to use a growing number of supervised and unsupervised playgrounds.[62] Nevertheless, the combined efforts of schools, voluntary associations, and playgrounds reached only a small proportion of Canadian children. To remedy this situation, Borden's Militia Department began in 1907 to assist provincial departments of education by providing some drill instruction in schools and courses for interested teachers.[63] Capitalizing on Lord Strathcona's long interest in military affairs and preparedness training, Borden persuaded him in 1909 to establish a fund to support physical and military training in the schools. Its constitution stated the two aims of the Strathcona Trust: "to improve the physical and intellectual capabilities of the children, by inculcating habits of alertness, orderliness and prompt obedience" and "to bring up the boys to patriotism."[64]

Not all Canadians approved of the militaristic trend in physical education. "True patriotism" did not consist "in presenting a warlike front to other nations" wrote a Saskatchewan school inspector, "but in maintaining a spirit of justice, fairness and kindliness towards our fellow citizens." Patriotism, he argued, could be taught better through literature, history, civics, and geography.[65] Despite such opposition, most provincial departments of education, in accepting Strathcona grants, cast their physical education programs in a "preparedness" mould.[66] In response to what it described as an often expressed need for a graded program of exercises that could be performed with little or no equipment under the direction of someone with little or no training in the subject, the Trust prepared a Canadian edition of a British syllabus of exercises.

Based on a Swedish system of gymnastics, the exercises in the *Syllabus*, claimed its preface, had "been most admirably selected and arranged in proper progression with a view to the promotion of the harmonious development of all parts of the body, and their suitability for children." Further, it included "games and dancing steps" to ensure some "freedom of movement and a certain degree of exhilaration" that were essentials "of all true physical education."[67]

In another phase of their movement Macdonald and Robertson established four "object-lesson" consolidated rural schools. Unlike their other activities, these schools were more means than ends, a way to demonstrate that rural children could partake in all aspects of the new education. Under this scheme, which was modelled on some already under way in Iowa, Ohio, and Indiana, a number of weak local rural schools were consolidated into one strong district school.[68] "Placed in some central locality," the new schools could "employ efficient, well-paid teachers, and increase the value of the educational system in many other ways."[69] Consolidated schools could make manual training, domestic science, nature study, school gardening, and physical education integral parts of their curriculum. This improved quality of education in turn would arouse the interest of pupils so much that the "attractiveness" of consolidated schools would itself become "a form of compulsory education."[70]

Robertson set up the schools in the characteristic fashion of the movement. Macdonald offered to buy the land, provide and equip the buildings and vans, and pay the teachers' salaries and other expenses above current tax rates for a period of three years. On sites selected by the provincial departments of education, the Macdonald Funds built a Macdonald Consolidated School at Middleton, Nova Scotia, which opened in September 1903, at Kingston, New Brunswick, which opened in September 1904, at Guelph, Ontario (next to the Agricultural College), which opened in November 1904, and at Hillsborough, Prince Edward Island, which opened in May 1905. To staff the schools, Robertson recruited competent teachers and principals, sent them to various places in Canada and the United States for training, and paid them well.[71] To draw public attention to their merits, Robertson surrounded them with as much publicity and fanfare as possible.[72]

Macdonald schools were amongst the best in their day. They were housed in fine buildings, staffed by young, capable, and enthusiastic teachers, and incorporated all the latest ideas in curriculum and methods. In addition to the regular range of school subjects taught along the lines of a first-class urban school of the time, Hillsborough had a kindergarten, taught manual arts in the lower grades, music and drawing to all pupils, and manual training, domestic science, nature study, and physical drill to the upper grades. Each pupil had his or her own garden and, as well, the girls shared a kitchen garden and the boys experimental farm crop plots.[73] In 1910, the school added a special high school course in agriculture for farmers. Each attracted fee-paying children from other districts. At each, when compared to the schools they replaced, enrolment of school-aged children was more complete, they attended more regularly, and stayed in school longer.[74]

Nonetheless, while each accomplished with its pupils what its proponents had promised it would, the four consolidated schools were the least successful ventures of the Macdonald-Robertson movement. Although transportation costs and the poor conditions of rural roads were factors in their failure, the principal cause was the extreme reluctance of rural ratepayers to bear the extra costs of consolidation. As Albert Leake later explained, despite some initial arguments that consolidation might reduce costs, experience in both Canada and the United States generally showed that the gross costs of consolidated schools were higher than those of the small district schools they replaced. Although, due to their much better attendance records, the cost per pupil per month was often lower in consolidated schools, the actual taxes paid by the local ratepayers were considerably higher.[75] Before consolidation and over the three-year experimental period, the tax rate in the Hillsborough district was eleven cents per $100 of valuation, with individual school taxes in the area ranging from twenty cents to $5.20 per year. After the experiment was over and three of the six districts withdrew from the arrangement, the rate became forty cents per $100 and individual taxes ranged from eighty cents to $20.80.[76]

The most important permanent monuments to the Macdonald-Robertson movement were the Macdonald Institute at Guelph, Ontario, and Macdonald College of McGill University at Ste-Anne-de-Bellevue, Quebec.[77] As Robertson explained, as a product of the school garden, consolidated schools, manual training, and domestic science movements, Macdonald established these institutions to train leaders needed for rural regeneration and educational reform.[78] More than anyone else, Adelaide Hoodless encouraged Macdonald to put up the money for the institute at Guelph. In 1900, she had persuaded Lord Strathcona and the Ontario provincial government to help transform the YWCA domestic science operation in Hamilton into the Normal School of Domestic Science and Art.[79] Mrs Hoodless was convinced, however, that because of its excellent laboratory and other facilities, the Ontario Agriculture College in Guelph was the most appropriate permanent location for such a school. After she had persuaded Macdonald and Robertson of the merits of this arrangement, the latter conducted the necessary negotiations with the college and the Ontario government.[80] At a cost of $182,500, Macdonald built and equipped the institute, which was formally opened in December 1904.[81] In addition to teaching manual training and household science teachers, most of whom went to urban schools, the institute conducted short courses for farmers' daughters and other women in cooking, sewing, and "domestic art" and courses in nature study and school gardens, without fees, for rural school teachers. Unlike Macdonald College, however, the institute did not offer a full training program for teachers. Macdonald and some provincial governments provided scholarships for teachers to attend. In 1904, the institute held its first summer school for teachers and that fall it conducted its first inter-provincial teachers class. By 1908, Mrs Hoodless was able to claim, "without fear of contradiction," that the Macdonald Institute stood "at the top of the list for practical, earnest effort in organizing and placing the study of Home Economics on a solid basis."[82]

Although Macdonald College — "Sir William's greatest yeast cake [and] . . . the supreme illustration of Dr. Robertson's methods of leavening" — was a much more substantial project than the Macdonald Institute, its aims were similar.[83] Robertson, who organized the college, supervised its building, and became its first principal, declared that its instruction was to be "vocational for the three fundamental, mothering occupations" which nurtured the race: first, farming, where man became "a partner with the Almighty"; second, "the making of homes"; and third, "the teaching of children." Together "the homes, the schools, and the farms" were finding the "common centre from which radiated plans and labours; 'A little child shall lead them.'"[84] The project was announced in November 1904, work began in 1905, and the college opened in November 1907. At a cost of about a million and a half dollars, Macdonald bought the site and erected and equipped the buildings. In 1906, he turned over the site, the buildings, and a two million dollar endowment to McGill.[85] The provincial government then amalgamated the McGill Normal School with the new college.[86] In addition to its schools of agriculture, household science, and teacher education, the college included facilities for short courses of the sort which had been initiated at the Macdonald Institute. In 1914, Macdonald increased the endowment by a further one million dollars, and, on his death in 1917, he left the college a similar amount.[87]

Graduates of the two MacDonald institutions quickly spread out across the nation, training their new colleagues in the principles of the movement. In the nature study course at the institute which ended in June 1905, there were four teachers from Prince Edward Island, nine from Nova Scotia, seven from New Brunswick, twelve from Quebec, and nineteen from Ontario.[88] Vancouver appointed Miss Elizabeth Berry, a graduate of the institute, as its first teacher and supervisor of domestic science.[89] Abigail DeLury went from the institute to the staff of Macdonald College to · Moose Jaw to teach domestic science and then to the faculty of the University of Saskatchewan.[90] Henry MacLean went from the institute to be a teacher at and then principal of the Hillsborough school, to Victoria, BC, as a school principal and an instructor at the Provincial Summer School for Teachers and, finally, to the Provincial Normal School in Vancouver.[91]

Partly as a product of Macdonald-Robertson and other activities, Canadian interest in education rose sharply over the first decade of the new century. In 1898 and 1899, the Ottawa and Toronto boards of trade appointed committees to consider ways and means of establishing technical education in Canada.[92] In 1902, Nova Scotia's Legislative Committee on Education reported that the schools, in seeking "to train memory only," failed "to fit the pupil for skilled labour or practical life."[93] In 1904, Ontario introduced a new elementary school curriculum that included nature study, art, music, and physical education and listed manual training, domestic science, and agriculture as optional subjects. The same year, the Montreal convention of the Canadian Manufacturers Association set up a committee on technical education.[94] In 1906, Ontario sent Albert H. Leake to examine industrial education in the United States.[95] In 1907, the National Council of Women set up a permanent committee on education.[96] In 1908, Prince Edward Island appointed a royal commission on education that recommended nature study, school gardens, manual training, and rural school consolidation.[97] In the same year, Alberta established a committee to revise the curriculum in that province which strongly supported the introduction and extension of music, art, physical education, manual training, domestic science, and other elements of modern education.[98] At their triennial meeting in Victoria in July 1909, over 400 members of the Dominion Educational Association discussed the "new" education and elected James W. Robertson as their new president.[99] Manitoba set up a royal commission in 1910 to study technical education for agriculture and industry in the province that recommended technical schools, "hand-and-eye" work in the elementary grades, and better training of teachers for the "new" education.[100] While each of these events had important regional implications, the federal Royal Commission on Industrial Training and Technical Education had the greatest national influence.[101]

On the first of June 1910, Sir Wilfrid Laurier's government passed an Order-in-Council establishing a royal commission to enquire into the "needs and present equipment of . . . Canada respecting industrial training and technical education, and into the systems and methods of technical instruction obtaining in other countries."[102] While business, labour, and educational interests had promoted the idea, the ambitious minister of labour, W.L. Mackenzie King, deserved the major credit for persuading a reluctant cabinet to venture into territory which was constitutionally reserved to the provinces.[103] Although King reassured the provincial premiers that the commission was "solely for the purpose of gathering information . . . to be at the disposal of the provinces and available for general distribution," provincial response ranged from grudging to enthusiastic.[104] To chair the royal commission the government selected James W. Robertson.

Robertson wasted no time in getting to work. On 6 July 1910, the commissioners met with Mackenzie King in Ottawa. By 18 July they were in the Maritimes on the beginning of a nation-wide tour which lasted until February 1911. The commission travelled extensively in Canada, the United States, and Europe, visited over one hundred places, held 174 sessions to hear testimony, took transcripts of evidence from 1470 men and women, and requested 180 written memoranda. In March 1911, they submitted a preliminary statement to the minister.[105] The final report of the commission, in four volumes, was published in 1913 and 1914.

Since the commissioners stretched their terms of reference to the very limit, their report was far more than a narrow study of industrial training and technical education. It was, first of all, a thorough account of the current state of Canadian education at the time. In addition, its comments and recommendations made the report into a blueprint for the implementation in Canada of the "new" education. The commissioners opened their report with a survey of "the present Equipment" for industrial training and technical education. They reported on universities, technical and trade schools, agricultural colleges and extension work, normal schools, high schools, elementary schools, evening classes, correspondence courses, apprenticeship programs, playgrounds, and physical culture and drill.

The commissioners then discussed "Elementary education in relation to industrial training and technical education." The tenor of their recommendations for this level of schooling was well summarized in their comment that the "experience of the school should tend more directly towards the inculcation and conservation of a love of productive, constructive and conserving labour." Such pre-vocational and trade-preparatory work, they continued, "in no way" hindered "progress in general education of a cultural sort." They recommended more "hand-and-eye" training, drawing, physical culture, nature study, experimental science, singing, supervised games and play, and manual training from kindergarten through to ages eleven or twelve. To make room for these studies in what they described as an already crowded time-table, they suggested that the "work of the school day be arranged less and less on subjects" and "more and more on occupations, projects and interests" as a centre "for the correlated study of general subjects such as reading, composition, number work, writing and drawing." To assist the provinces in reforming elementary education, the commissioners suggested that the federal government spend $350,000 per year over a ten-year period, as a "carrot," to encourage provinces to provide drawing, manual training, nature study, experimental science, pre-vocational work, and domestic science.[106]

The commissioners called for similar sorts of reforms in secondary education. They criticized high schools for their focus on college preparation. They proposed a much broader secondary curriculum, suggesting pre-vocational work, continuation programs for school "drop-outs," shop work, and home economics. "Making homes," they argued, was "much more than building houses and providing furniture, food, clothing and things." It was "creating a temple, not made with the hands, as a place of culture for the best in human life." For the development of secondary and post-secondary education the commission recommended what it called "a Dominion Development Fund" that would spend three million dollars a year for ten years to encourage the provinces to expand industrial, technical, and rural education, home economics, and vocational guidance. For both the elementary and secondary funds, the commissioners argued, the federal government had set itself an ample precedent in the Agricultural Education Act of 1913.[107]

Four years of war intervened before the federal government took any action on the report.[108] Ignoring all suggestions regarding elementary education, the Technical Education Act of 1919 allocated ten million dollars to be spent on a matching basis with provincial governments over ten years.[109] In most provinces, this money stimulated projects already under way and brought a number of new or expanded technical schools and vocational programs. Between 1919 and 1927, the number of day teachers in vocational schools in Canada increased from 384 to 1515, the number of day students from 8512 to 34,703, the number of evening teachers from 1423 to 2129, and the number of evening students from 51,827 to 60,313. Central Canada, and particularly Ontario, made most use of the legislation. In the fiscal year 1926–7, only Ontario took the full amount of funds available to it under the act.[110]

In retrospect, one can see that the central function that the royal commission served was an educational one. Its hearings and report helped the English-Canadian community to accept the ideas of the new education as desirable and reasonable goals for its schools. The progression of the commission across the nation was accompanied by wide publicity. In each city it visited its meetings were well attended and reported in detail in the local press. In many places, Robertson, already a well-known and persuasive speaker, was called upon to make an address and to tour the local schools with his fellow commissioners.

To those already experimenting with new dimensions of schooling, the commission's visit gave them the chance to tell their fellow citizens what they were doing and to exhort their communities to further efforts. To those looking for change in their schools, Robertson's speeches and the commission's *Report* provided both a new program and a coherent rationale as to why it should be implemented. Finally, the sessions and the *Report* of the commission were amongst the most important of the events which gradually shifted opinion in English-speaking Canada to the view that their new society demanded a new kind of education. Had Robertson been of an ironic turn of mind he might have been amused by the fact that the movement which he began to regenerate rural Canada had its major impact in the cities which he sometimes scorned.

NOTES

1. The quotation in the title of the chapter is from J.W. Robertson, "The Macdonald Fund," National Education Association, Report, 1909, reprinted in Canada, Royal Commission on Industrial Training and Technical Education, *Report of the Commissioners* (Ottawa: King's Printer, 1913) [hereafter RCITTE, Report], vol. 2, pp. 157–8.
2. Ibid., p. 154.
3. For an account of the life of Macdonald, see J.F. Snell, *Macdonald College of McGill University: A History from 1904–1955* (Montreal: McGill University Press for Macdonald

College, 1963), part 1, and Maurry H. Epstein, "Sir William Macdonald: A Biographical Sketch," *McGill Journal of Education* V (Spring 1971), pp. 53–61.

4. Dominion Educational Association, *Proceedings*, 1901, pp. 23, 84–93; ibid., 1917, pp. 12–14.

5. James W. Robertson, *The Macdonald Sloyd School Fund: Manual Training in Public Schools* (Ottawa: E.J. Reynolds, 1899), p. 7; RCITTE, Report, vol. 2, p. 153.

6. RCITTE, *Report*, vol. 2, p. 153.

7. Robertson, *The Macdonald Sloyd School Fund*, p. 27.

8. A.H. Leake, "Looking Backward," Industrial Arts Teachers of Ontario, *Bulletin* (March 1950).

9. Orville E. White, "The History of Practical Education Courses in Canadian Secondary Schools" (MA thesis, McGill University, 1951), p. 599.

10. Ontario, Department of Education, *Report*, 1907, pp. 638–874.

11. Ontario, Department of Education, *Education for Industrial Purposes*, A Report by John Seath, Superintendent of Education for Ontario (Toronto: King's Printer, 1911), p. 269.

12. RCITTE, *Report*, vol. 2, p. 154.

13. The best Canadian discussion of the whole range of practical education in the period is Albert H. Leake, *Industrial Education: Its Problems, Methods and Dangers* (Boston: Houghton Mifflin, 1913).

14. See, for example, Manitoba, Department of Education, *Report*, 1909, p. 28.

15. RCITTE, *Report*, vol. 1, p. 10.

16. Leake, *Industrial Education*, chap. 3.

17. Hughes, "The School of the Twentieth Century," *Methodist Magazine and Review*, XLV (1897), p. 349.

18. See, for example, British Columbia, Department of Education, *Courses of Study for the Public High and Normal Schools of British Columbia* (Victoria: King's Printer, 1920), pp. 28–31.

19. See, for example, Dominion Educational Association, *Proceedings*, 1913, pp. 73–86.

20. National Council of Women (NCW), *Yearbook*, 1902, p. 114.

21. Toronto *Globe*, 2 January 1910, p. 12; *B.C. Federationist*, 7 February 1913, pp. 1, 4.

22. Robertson, *The Macdonald Sloyd School Fund*, pp. 22–3.

23. "Practical Education," pp. 616–17; see also John Keith Foster, "Education and Working a Changing Society: British Columbia, 1870–1930 (MA thesis, University of British Columbia, 1970)," pp. 17–18.

24. Leake, *Industrial Education*, especially chaps 4 and 9.

25. British Columbia, *Survey of the School System*, p. 96.

26. R.H. Cowley, "The Macdonald School Gardens," *Queen's Quarterly*, XII (April 1905), pp. 416–18.

27. See, for example, H.B. Spotton, *The Elements of Structural Botany with Special Reference to the Study of Canadian Plants* (Toronto: W.J. Gage, 1886), p. 1.

28. Manitoba, Department of Education, *Report*, 1905, p. 3.

29. Belle C. Gibson, *Teacher-Builder* (Victoria: Morriss Printing Company, 1961), pp. 39–45.

30. RCITTE, *Report*, vol. 2, p. 155.

31. A.J. Madill, *History of Agricultural Education in Ontario* (Toronto, University of Toronto Press, 1930), pp. 104, 226; see also S.B. McCready, "Adventures of a Schoolmaster," *Western Ontario Historical Notes*, IX (December 1951), pp. 130–45.

32. Ontario, Department of Agriculture, *The Macdonald Institute in Relation to Nature Study in Our Public Schools: A Letter to the Schools* (Toronto: King's Printer, 1904).

33. RCITTE, *Report*, vol. 1, pp. 308–10.

34. Ibid., vol. 4, p. 2196.

35. James W. Robertson, *Conservation of Life in Rural Districts* (New York: Association Press, 1911), pp. 11–12.

36. To sample this growing interest, see the report of the New Brunswick Agricultural Commission of 1908, summarized in *Canadian Annual Review*, 1909, pp. 448–9; Canada, House of Commons, *Journals*, 1908, app. 2; John MacDougall, *Rural Life in Canada: Its Trend and Task* (Toronto: The Westminster Company, 1913); John Mac-Dougall, "The Rural Problem," *Social Service Congress, Ottawa, 1914: Report of Addresses and Proceedings*, pp. 147–57; Hugh Dobson, "The School and the Rural Problem," ibid., pp. 173–6; Canada, Commission of Conservation, *Report*, 1914, pp. 134–8; ibid., 1916, pp. 24–31; Christie, "The Presbyterian Church in Canada," pp. 39–42.

37. Canada, *Statutes*, 1912, c. 3.

38. Ibid., 1912–13, c. 5.

39. Canada, Commission of Conservation, *Report*, 1917, pp. 215–25.

40. White, "Practical Education," pp. 497–8. The summer school attracted 260 teachers in 1913 and 371 in 1914.

41. Provincial Archives of British Columbia, Department of Education Records; Gibson, *Teacher-Builder*, pp. 65–85.

42. Madill, *Agricultural Education in Ontario*, p. 103.

43. Saskatchewan, *A Survey of Education*, pp. 59–64; British Columbia, Department of Education, *Report*, 1917–18, pp. D52–64.

44. Quoted in Chalmers, *Schools of the Foothills Province*, p. 51.

45. Albert H. Miller, *Rural Schools in Canada: Their Organization, Administration and Supervision* (New York: Teacher's College, 1913), p. 80.

46. Charles G.D. Roberts and Arthur L. Turnell, ed., *A Standard Dictionary of Canadian Biography: The Canadian Who Was Who* (Toronto: Trans-Canada Press, 1934), pp. 275–6; Ruth Howes, "Adelaide Hunter Hoodless," in Mary Quayle Innis, ed., *The Clear Spirit: Twenty Canadian Women and Their Times* (Toronto: For the Canadian Federation of University Women by the University of Toronto Press, 1966), pp. 103–19.

47. NCW, *Yearbook*, 1902, p. 120.

48. Toronto *Globe*, 30 April 1900, p. 6.

49. See, for example, NCW, *Yearbook*, 1896, pp. 388–92; ibid., 1898, p. 271; RCITTE, *Report*, vol. 4, pp. 49–50.

50. NCW, *Yearbook*, 1901, pp. 117–18.

51. RCITTE, *Report*, vol. 1, pp. 53–4.

52. Manitoba Archives, Dora Dibney Papers.

53. *Public School Domestic Science* (Toronto: Copp Clark, 1898).

54. British Columbia, Department of Education, *Courses of Study*, 1920, pp. 31–3, 56–9; White, "Practical Education," p. 97. The figures are for 1918–19.

55. I am indebted to my former students Nan Cart, Kathy Read, Bill McNulty, and Steve Erickson for their help with this topic.

56. *Manual of Drill and Calisthenics* (Toronto: W.J. Gage, 1879), pp. 4–5.

57. Patricia Anne Vertinsky, "Education for Sexual Morality: Moral Reform and the Regulation of American Morality in the Nineteenth Century" (DED dissertation, University of British Columbia, 1975).

58. Canadian Conference of Charities and Correction, *Proceedings*, 1912, p. 23.

59. See Carl Berger, *The Sense of Power: Studies in the Ideas of Canadian Imperialism, 1867–1914* (Toronto: University of Toronto Press, 1970), especially chap. 10.

60. Saskatchewan Archives, Premier Walter Scott Papers, Borden to Scott, 29 January 1909.

61. Hughes, *Manual of Drill and Calisthenics*; John Millar, *School Management and the Principles and Practices of Teaching* (Toronto: William Briggs, 1987), pp. 18–32.

62. NCW, *Yearbook*, 1905, pp. 99–100; ibid., 1911, pp. 55–8. See MacLean, *A Statistical Review of Canadian Schools* (Ottawa: Canadian Council on Child Welfare, 1923), pp. 31–5, for a nation-wide survey of public playground activities in Canadian urban centres by 1921–2.

63. CAR, 1907, p. 618.
64. Quoted in British Columbia, Department of Education, *Report*, 1910, p. A60.
65. Saskatchewan Archives, Premier Walter Scott Papers, J. Duff to commissioner of Education, 12 January 1910.
66. Miss Cartwright, "Physical Education and its Place in the School; the Function of the Strathcona Trust; and the Training of Teachers," Dominion Educational Association, *Proceedings*, 1913, pp. 109–20.
67. Strathcona Trust, *Syllabus of Physical Exercises for Schools* (Toronto: Executive Council, Strathcona Trust, 1911), n.p.
68. *School and Teachers' Bulletin*, quoted in RCITTE, *Report*, vol. 2, pp. 310–13.
69. Henry J. Morgan and Laurence J. Burpee, *Canadian Life in Town and Country* (London: George Newnes, 1905), p. 173.
70. RCITTE, *Report*, vol. 2, p. 156–8; see also CAR, 1902, pp. 405–7.
71. H.B. MacLean, interview with the writer, 23 February 1966.
72. See, for example, CAR, 1906, p. 413.
73. RCITTE, *Report*, vol. 4, pp. 1760–2.
74. University of British Columbia Library, Special Collections, Robertson Papers, Jones to Robertson, 13 January 1906; CAR, 1906, p. 413; compilations in Miller, *Rural Schools in Canada*, p. 107.
75. Leake, *Agricultural Education*, pp. 92–8.
76. RCITTE, *Report*, vol. 4, pp. 1759–62; see also the tax records of the school in Miller, *Rural Schools in Canada*, pp. 106, 108.
77. The early history of the Macdonald Institute is outlined in Edith Child Rowles, *Home Economics in Canada: The Early History of Six College Programmes: Prologue to Change* (Saskatoon: University of Saskatchewan, n.d.), pp. 36–49; that of Macdonald College is summarized in Snell, *Macdonald College*; see also Edwin John Pavey, "James Wilson Robertson: Public Servant and Educator" (MEd thesis, University of British Columbia, 1971), chap. 3.
78. RCITTE, *Report*, vol. 2, p. 158.
79. Toronto *Globe*, 5 April 1900, p. 5.
80. University of Guelph Library, Hoodless Papers, James Mills, president, Ontario Agricultural College to Mrs Hoodless, 9 March 1900; ibid., Mrs Hoodless to Hon. Richard Harcourt, minister of education, 23 October 1901; ibid., Mills to Robertson, 31 October 1901; ibid., Robertson to Mills, 16 December 1901.
81. *The Farmer's Advocate*, 22 December 1904, p. 1778; CAR, 1904, p. 532.
82. NCW, *Yearbook*, 1908, p. 83.
83. Sherwood, "Children of the Land: the Story of the Macdonald Movement in Canada," *The Outlook* (23 April 1910), p. 901.
84. RCITTE, *Report*, vol. 2, pp. 157–8.
85. CAR, 1906, pp. 380–1.
86. John Calam, "McGill Trains Teachers: 1857–1964," *The Teacher's Magazine*, XLV (September 1965), pp. 24–5.
87. Snell, *Macdonald College*, pp. 56–9, 169–71.
88. Ontario Agricultural College, *Programme of Closing Exercises at Macdonald Institute Nature Study Department*, 1905.
89. Vancouver School Board, *Report*, 1905, p. 6.
90. Rowles, *Home Economics in Canada*, p. 82.
91. Interview with the writer, 23 February 1966.
92. RCITTE, *Report*, vol. 4, pp. 2093–2101, 2105–8.
93. CAR, 1902, pp. 458–9.
94. RCITTE, *Report*, vol. 4, pp. 2084–90.

95. Ontario, Department of Education, *Education and Industrial Efficiency: Report of Albert H. Leake, to the Minister of Education on Recent Developments in the Schools of the Eastern States* (Toronto: King's Printer, 1906).
96. NCW, *Yearbook*, 1907, pp. 54–7; ibid., 1908, pp. 93–6.
97. RCITTE, *Report*, vol. 4, pp. 1753–4.
98. Alberta, Department of Education, *Report*, 1912, p. 81.
99. Victoria *Colonist*, 14 July 1909, pp. 1–2; ibid., 15 July, pp. 1–2; ibid., 16 July, pp. 1–2.
100. Manitoba, *Sessional Papers*, 1912, no. 3, pp. 281–356.
101. Saskatchewan appointed a Commission on Agricultural and Industrial Education in 1912 which reported in 1913. CAR, 1913, p. 618.
102. RCITTE, *Report*, vol. 1, p. v.
103. Robert M. Stamp, "Technical Education, the National Policy, and Federal–Provincial Relations in Canadian Education, 1899–1919," CHR, LII (December 1971), pp. 404–15.
104. RCITTE, *Report*, vol. 1, pp. vi–xii.
105. RCITTE, *Report*, vol. 1, pp. 58–61.
106. RCITTE, *Report*, vol. 1, pp. 8–11.
107. Ibid., pp. 15–39.
108. Stamp, "Technical Education, the National Policy, and Federal–Provincial Relations in Canadian Education, 1899–1919," pp. 417–22.
109. Canada, *Statutes*, 1919, c. 19.
110. *Vocational Education*, 28 (August 1928), pp. 8–20.

TOPIC SEVEN
Newcomers

Government posters in Slavic and Scandinavian languages, issued around the turn of the century, beckon newcomers to a life of opportunity in the Canadian West.

Glowing advertisements, embellished portrayals by immigration agents, and un-favourable social or economic conditions in their various homelands attracted some 2.94 million people to Canada between the turn of the century and the Great War. A large proportion came from the British Isles, but conspicuous in this latest wave of immigrants were throngs of Italians, Jews, Central Europeans, and, particularly, Slavs. Multitudes used Canada as a way station en route to joining family or making their fortunes in the United States, but many remained, and over the first four decades of the twentieth century, the number of Canadians of non-British European descent rose from 2.1 to 3.5 million.[1]

Earlier historical accounts tended to focus on those "sturdy" farmers whose arrival was presented as fulfilling the promise of Canada's national policy by transforming the prairies into one of the world's great breadbaskets. To a large extent, this presentation was accurate. During the early twentieth century, Clifford Sifton's Department of the Interior concentrated on recruiting people from agricultural areas in the United States and Western Europe, believing that they would contribute a great deal economically and, just as important, assimilate easily. In 1910, for example, over 55 000 newcomers described farming as their intended occupation. But that figure included members of many less favoured racial groups, and moreover — since the country had economic needs other than agriculture — made up only about one-third of the total number of people arriving that year. Well over half of the newcomers to Canada in 1910 indicated backgrounds destining them for unskilled urban labour or employment in the thriving resource sector.[2] And while the lot of the prairie homesteaders was arduous, that of immigrant workers in these other sectors was likewise difficult, since they were all too often treated as an ignorant, cheap, and expendable *lumpenproletariat*.

With the exception of the social reformers — whose answer to the immigrant's plight, in any case, was usually to preach assimilation — few in the host society felt much empathy. Organized labour considered newcomers a threat to decent wages; the middle class bemoaned the social disorder such people allegedly imported; and pseudo-scientific theorists linked the arrival of Central and Southern Europeans with the degradation of the gene pool and the eventual demise of Canada as a superior, Anglo-Saxon nation. Negative developments associated with immigrants, such as urban slums, were rarely admitted to be an outgrowth of racism on the part of the host society, but rather were seized upon as proof of the newcomers' cultural inferiority. Scholars now writing in the field of immigration and ethnic history have catalogued a litany of statutory and extra-legal consequences of nativism. One example of government policy was a proactive approach to deportation that, between 1903 and 1920, targeted nearly 14 000 people, sometimes on racial grounds or on the grounds that the subjects harboured what were considered foreign and radical political views.[3]

Besides exploring the many indications and consequences of nativist xenophobia, ethnic history has branched out to examine complex and not always laudable aspects of minority culture. While Gregory Robinson's portrait in Article 13 of Ukrainians in Alberta statistically disproves once-prevalent assumptions that this group was especially prone to criminal behaviour, it also reveals some unique cultural practices and internal social divisions that furnished the negative stereotype with surface legitimacy. In Article 14, Ruth A. Frager shows that the experience of discrimination in Europe and in Toronto did not make Jews any more open than society at large to the idea of equality between men and women. The socialist and Jewish-run textile unions,

in which women made up the majority of the rank-and-file, subordinated women to class and ethnic interests.

One might say that the new immigration and ethnic history truly illustrates the shallow intellectual roots of Canadian pluralism. As is made evident in this section, certain broad and unequal divisions in Canada were determined by ideology and policies emanating not only from the host society, but from newcomers themselves. For along with the unity born of a common background or the experience of oppression, among many minorities there existed a variety of virulent inter- and intra-group cleavages relating to origin, religion, class, gender, and, one suspects, the degree to which, over generations, acculturation took place.

QUESTIONS TO CONSIDER

1. In what ways does Robinson confirm or reject stereotypes about Ukrainians?
2. Does Robinson support or refute the idea of ethnicity as buttressing class solidarity?
3. Why were Jews attracted to communism?
4. Explain the view that obtained among Jewish women regarding their oppression.
5. What constitutes an ethnic group, and how might a historian identify its members?

NOTES

1. M.C. Urquhart and K.A.H. Buckley, eds., *Historical Statistics on Canada* (Toronto: Macmillan, 1965), series A75–132, A254–72.
2. Urquhart and Buckley, *Historical Statistics*, series A284–99.
3. Urquhart and Buckley, *Historical Statistics*, series A342–47. See also Allan Sears, "Immigration Controls as Social Policy: The Case of Canadian Medical Inspection, 1900–1920," *Studies in Political Economy*, 33 (1990): 91–112.

SUGGESTED READINGS

Abella, Irving, and Harold Troper. *None Is Too Many*. Toronto: Lester and Orpen Dennys, 1983.

Avery, Donald. *Dangerous Foreigners: European Immigrant Workers and Labour Radicalism in Canada, 1896–1932*. Toronto: McClelland & Stewart, 1979.

Burnet, Jean, and Howard Palmer. *"Coming Canadians": An Introduction to the History of Canada's Peoples*. Toronto: McClelland & Stewart, 1988.

Frager, Ruth A. *Sweatshop Strife: Class, Ethnicity, and Gender in the Jewish Labour Movement of Toronto, 1900–1939*. Toronto: University of Toronto Press, 1992.

Knowles, Valarie. *Strangers at Our Gates: Canadian Immigration and Immigrant Policy, 1540–1990*. Toronto: Dundurn Press, 1992.

Lindstrom-Best, Varpu. *Defiant Sisters: A Social History of Finnish Immigrant Women in Canada*. Toronto: Multicultural History Society of Ontario, 1988.

Patrias, Carmela. *Patriots and Proletarians: Politicizing Hungarian Immigrants in Interwar Canada*. Montreal and Kingston: McGill-Queen's University Press, 1994.

Roberts, Barbara. *From Whence They Came: Deportations from Canada, 1900–1935*. Ottawa: University of Ottawa Press, 1988.

Swyripa, Frances. *Wedded to the Cause: Ukrainian Canadian Women and Ethnic Identity, 1891–1991*. Toronto: University of Toronto Press, 1991.

Tulchinsky, Gerald. *Immigration in Canada: Historical Perspectives*. Toronto: Copp Clark Longman, 1994.

Zucchi, John E. *Italians in Toronto: Development of a National Identity, 1875–1935*. Montreal and Kingston: McGill-Queen's University Press, 1988.

THIRTEEN

Rougher Than Any Other Nationality? Ukrainian Canadians and Crime in Alberta, 1915–1929

GREGORY ROBINSON

Alberta seems to be in most cases confronted with offenders of the Slav race and some of the worst cases imaginable, so far as Alberta is concerned, are charged to their account.

Canadian Police Gazette, 1928

We hear quite often that Ukrainians do not respect the laws of this country, that there are too many assaults and murders committed by them and that they are rougher than any other nationality.

Peter Svasich, Vegreville, 1931

In his 1937 study of the Ukrainian bloc in east-central Alberta, Timothy C. Byrne remarked: "It is true that the Ukrainians, in general, do not enjoy a reputation as law-abiding citizens."[1] His observation understates public opinion in early twentieth-century Alberta, which held that Ukrainians were a primitive people with extraordinary proclivities for crime and vice. This reputation was founded on the claims of prairie social reformers, politicians, and other activists who alleged that western Canada's Ukrainian immigrants committed far more crimes than their numbers warranted. In the eyes of concerned Anglo-Canadians, Ukrainian rural colonies and urban quarters alike were breeding grounds for lawlessness and immorality.

Source: Excerpted from "Rougher Than Any Other Nationality? Ukrainian Canadians and Crime in Alberta, 1915–29," *Journal of Ukrainian Studies*, 16, 1–2 (1991): 147–80. Reprinted by permission of *Journal of Ukrainian Studies*.

UKRAINIANS' CRIMINAL REPUTATION

Over six decades after 1930, such claims remain virtually unchallenged. In fact, in recent years both mainstream and Ukrainian prairie historians have supported the old contentions that Ukrainian pioneer society suffered from a disproportionately high rate of crime.[2] The historical source cited most often by scholars to prove the high rate of crime among Alberta's pre-1930 Ukrainians is a 1928 roster from the Fort Saskatchewan Provincial Gaol. The first researcher to interpret this data was Charles Young, in his 1931 study of Ukrainian Canadians and assimilation. He wrote:

> This Gaol table is significant for two or three reasons. No list of the inmates according to racial origin could be obtained. No Ukrainians are reported though 104 "Austrians" are, which along with the 54 Poles, Russians and Roumanians, gives a total of 158 Slavs. Yet, while no Ukrainians are reported, 92 of the total population are Greek Catholics. That is to say, in the above table well over half of the Slavs are Greek Catholics, or Ukrainians in other words, for the Greek Catholics in Alberta other than Ukrainians are a totally insignificant number.
>
> In view of the above evidence, there is nothing left for us but to assume that . . . the Ukrainians are really to be found numbered among the other Slavs. The "exceedingly high rate for the Austrians" is further evidence of this. To what extent the Ukrainians contribute to the Slav aggregate, it is impossible to say exactly, but . . . it is safe to presume that a very large percentage of the Slavs, especially those classified as "Austrians," are probably Ukrainians.[3]

It is quite reasonable to conclude, as Young did, that prison officials did list convicts of Ukrainian origin under other national groupings (Austrians, Russians, Romanians, Poles). But the fact that it is impossible to determine the precise number of hidden Ukrainians in the statistics failed to prevent Young from endorsing claims of a high Ukrainian Canadian crime rate. In his 1985 study of the bloc settlement in east-central Alberta, Ukrainian Canadian historian Orest Martynowych resurrected Young's argument. He attempted a rough estimate of the number of Ukrainian offenders hidden in the 1928 Fort Saskatchewan Gaol figures and used that number to calculate the relative criminality of Alberta's Ukrainian population during the late 1920s. "Of 967 inmates," he wrote, "104 were born in Austria, 27 in Poland, three in Rumania and 24 in Russia. Of these, the 92 Greek Catholics and five Greek Orthodox inmates were almost certainly Ukrainians. A few of the 292 Roman Catholics and 170 Presbyterians may have also been Ukrainians. Thus, at least 10 per cent of the Provincial Gaol's inmates were Ukrainians at a time when Ukrainians constituted less than 7.6 per cent of the provincial population."[4]

There are several problems with interpreting the Fort Saskatchewan prison table in the way that Young, Martynowych, and others have done. Of paramount importance is the fact that Fort Saskatchewan was not Alberta's only provincial prison in the 1920s, as Lethbridge handled offenders from areas south of Red Deer. The scholars who have used the Fort Saskatchewan statistics have ignored this fact and interpreted the figures as though they represent the entire provincial gaol population. Once this mistake is corrected, the figures which once reflected so badly on the Ukrainians actually seem to flatter them. In the 1920s over 90 per cent of Ukrainians in Alberta lived in the northern half of the province — in the big Vegreville bloc, in several smaller settlements in west-central and northwestern Alberta, and in the city of Edmonton. While they may have constituted only about 7.4 per cent of Alberta residents, they made up more than 15 per cent of the population of the area which sent prisoners to Fort Saskatchewan Gaol.[5] Thus, if their proportion of inmates in the Fort was about 10 per cent, they would have been considerably more law-abiding than other peoples of North America.

Furthermore, when one considers that a variety of factors tended to inflate the number of Ukrainians in western Canadian prisons in the pre-Depression era, the Slavic settlers seem almost paragons of virtue. Not all prisoners sent to Fort Saskatchewan Provincial Gaol were dispatched directly by the courts; a good number ended up there because they could not afford the modest cash penalty imposed as punishment. As Ukrainians constituted one of the province's most economically disadvantaged groups, a convicted Ukrainian offender was far more likely to go to prison for non-payment of a fine than the average Anglo-Canadian lawbreaker was.[6] Thus, a higher percentage of Slavs should have ended up at Fort Saskatchewan.

The discrimination Ukrainians suffered at the hands of Alberta's policemen and judicial officials may also have artificially increased the number of Ukrainian offenders on police and prison ledgers. So might differential law enforcement, particularly in communities where Ukrainians were in the minority (that is, outside the bloc or along its borders). In greater Alberta, because law enforcement officers tended to scrutinize the behaviour of "foreigners" more closely than that of other persons, it seems probable that a higher percentage of Ukrainian crimes would be detected and a higher percentage of Ukrainian offenders prosecuted. In 1919, F. Heap decried the fact that most Anglo-Canadians believed Ukrainian immigrants to be more prone to crime despite the lack of reliable supporting statistics. "It should be borne in mind," he pointed out, "that the very prevalence of this opinion or prejudice may itself be responsible for a good many convictions which otherwise would have never taken place. Lawyers have often observed that the rule of English law, as to giving the accused the benefit of all reasonable doubt does not seem by any means to be applied in our courts in favour of the 'foreigners' in actual practice."[7] His own research led Heap to reject that Ukrainian Canadians were disproportionately criminal.

A final factor which would have contributed to a high rate of crime among Ukrainians in Alberta before 1930 was a straightforward demographic one, in that males between the ages of sixteen and twenty-nine accounted for an inordinately large proportion of the province's Ukrainian population.[8] As this is the sex and age group which has always committed the bulk of crimes in Western cultures, a comparative abundance of young men could be expected to have guaranteed the Ukrainians a relatively high crime rate.

The statistical evidence explored thus far, however, suggests that a higher rate of crime among Ukrainian settlers did not exist. How, then, does one account for the numerous contemporary accounts testifying that Ukrainians constituted one of the worst criminal elements in the pre-Depression West? Some of these claims can certainly be dismissed as nativist calumnies. Others can be rejected as politically motivated slanders. For example, the first accusations of Ukrainian immigrant lawlessness came from the turn-of-the-century Tory press. There is little doubt that these newspapers, given their affiliation with the federal Conservatives, made such accusations for political purposes, hoping that by slandering the Galician and Bukovynian peasants pouring into the West they could discredit the Liberal administration responsible for their presence.[9]

What this paper argues is that the furore about Ukrainian Canadian crime in the first decades of the twentieth century probably had more to do with the peculiarity of Ukrainian offenses than with their rate or frequency. Taken at face value, the criminal statistics of the 1915–29 period do not reveal any unique patterns of criminal behaviour in the Ukrainian bloc in east-central Alberta. Rather the settlers appear to have committed the same crimes as other Albertans and in roughly the same measure.[10] However, in going beyond the figures to examine the particulars of police reports, criminal case files, and court transcripts, several distinct trends emerge. Ukrainians in east-central Alberta broke the same laws as other Albertans, but in different ways and for different reasons. Two of the most common types of crimes, theft and violent assault, probably best exemplify the differences in criminal behaviour within the Ukrainian bloc.

THEFT

The pattern of theft in east-central Alberta between 1915 and 1929 reflected the rural nature of life in the colony and its residents' relative poverty. In an impoverished environment, the temptation to steal was great, but the range of items that could be stolen was quite small. Theft as a result generally involved the everyday goods of an agricultural society: grain, implement parts, harnesses, hand tools, and the like.

Theft of grain became a common crime in Ukrainian districts from the time settlers entered the commercial stage of farming during the Great War. In the next decade and a half, with the construction of new railway branch lines and the erection of conveniently accessible grain elevators in the bloc, stolen grain could easily be converted into cash. Stealing a farmer's grain was not complicated. A horse-drawn vehicle pulled up to a granary in a farmyard or field in the middle of the night, and the seed was quickly shovelled into sacks or directly into the grain box.[11] The only clues that the police could hope for were wagon or sleigh tracks that carelessness forgot to conceal. Wise thieves carried out their raids in late fall or early winter, when the ground was frozen but before snowfall, to avoid leaving traceable wheel or runner marks. The purloining of grain proved difficult to prevent, and the police could only encourage farmers to mix coloured confetti with their wheat and oats to help with identification if stolen.

Livestock theft, although less common than the stealing of grain, also plagued the Ukrainian bloc. While it does not figure prominently in police records, anecdotal evidence indicates that the nocturnal rustling of poultry was the most common offense, as hunger drove settlers to steal birds for meat or the eggs they would produce. Horses and cattle, which were both critical for survival and expensive to purchase, also presented a temptation. The relative ease with which stolen animals could be identified and the severity with which the courts dealt with rustlers, however, made stealing livestock a crime that did not pay. Inspector J.S. Piper of "A" Division of the Alberta Provincial Police (APP) contended that thefts of farm animals in east-central Alberta were generally poorly planned crimes that occurred on the spur of the moment, and attributed them "in a great measure to the accused wanting some ready cash." Piper also observed that stolen horses could be easily traced because a horse thief usually sold them "at the nearest livery stable."[12] APP superintendent W.C. Bryan felt that investigating cattle thefts was somewhat more difficult, principally because rustlers often slaughtered cows, calves, and steers.[13] In an attempt to facilitate the identification of stolen livestock, bloc policemen recommended that settlers brand their animals — but most Ukrainian farmers neglected to do so.

Thieves in east-central Alberta sometimes targeted farm implements, especially equipment left sitting idle in a field or broken-down by the roadside. It was rare for an entire piece of machinery to be stolen, but criminals would strip implements for parts — nuts, bolts, a canvas, a chain, or anything detachable. It seems that a fair number of the bloc's inhabitants favoured such pilferage over the often long trek to the nearest implement dealership or hardware store.[14]

Although most Ukrainian houses did not have locks on the doors, theft from homes occurred relatively rarely. When a burglar did risk entering a neighbour's dwelling, he was usually after a potential cache of money. Ukrainians seldom used banks in the pre-1930 period, distrusting both the institutions and the Anglo-Canadians who managed them. Several attempts to establish branches in the town-sites of the bloc failed because they could not attract depositors.[15] The typical Slav kept his entire life savings at home, whether the sum involved a few coins or a few hundred dollars. But keeping one's money at home was sometimes a perilous business. In one incident, two armed Ukrainians entered a farmer's house at night, tied up the man, forced his daughter to divulge where his savings ($350) were hidden, then shut his family in the cellar and nailed the door shut.[16]

Generally speaking, a thief could anticipate more immediate reward by breaking into a shop or store under cover of darkness. Such raids netted money, food, clothing, and tools. If a burglar was after cash, the best time to strike was in the late fall or early winter, when businessmen carried extra money to cash farmers' grain cheques. Storekeepers rarely put their money under lock and key, and usually used flimsy tin containers when they did. Some shopkeepers did own safes but often neglected to lock them at night, not infrequently because they never bothered to learn combinations.[17] The police complained that stores in the bloc were "nothing but 'set ups' for petty pilferers" as there were "no substantial locks on the doors nor any fastenings on the windows."[18]

The types of theft described above could and did take place elsewhere in the West. What is unique about stealing in the Ukrainian bloc is the utter triviality of the items taken. That is, the material value and quality of stolen goods was much lower in the colony than in other communities. Policemen (and Anglo-Canadians in general) were amazed by the thorough pettiness of Ukrainian thefts. Only in the Ukrainian bloc, for instance, would thieves stoop to stealing rusty barbed wire right off the fence posts.[19] Outsiders, disregarding the poverty of the bloc settlers, could not understand the motivations behind such filching — it scarcely seemed worthwhile in terms of either monetary gain or the risk of a fine and/or imprisonment. Critics ultimately sought biological and psychological explanations, suggesting that kleptomania was a distinctive genetic or national trait of the Galicians and Bukovynians. Thus, Ukrainians earned their reputation as a pilfering race not because of a relatively high rate of theft in their communities, but because of the types of articles stolen.

ASSAULT

The crimes most responsible for Ukrainians' infamy were violent offenses. Common assault, aggravated assault, manslaughter, and murder in the bloc all attracted much attention from policemen, the press, social reformers, and concerned citizens. In the public imagination the Ukrainian colony was a barbarous place, much like the frontier American West, where random violence and brutal murders were everyday occurrences. The official ledger sheets of the APP and the Department of the Attorney General do not suggest that Ukrainians committed more violent crimes than other Albertans. Ukrainian suspects or defendants figured in more than their fair share of homicide cases in some years between 1915 and 1929, for example, but were underrepresented in others; no Ukrainians were hanged in the province during this period.[20] All in all, the official figures do not reveal unique patterns of violent crime in the pre-Depression Ukrainian bloc.

It is only when one studies individual assault, manslaughter, and murder case files that significant differences in the violent behaviour of Ukrainians and other Albertans become apparent. In the years before 1930 Ukrainian offenses differed primarily in circumstance, motivation, and technique. One tendency, above all, stands out: very little provocation was needed to elicit a violent response. In their confrontations with one another, Galicians and Bukovynians displayed hair-trigger tempers, and any public or private display of anger was prone to induce violence. Examples abound in the official records of criminal assaults precipitated by seemingly harmless quarrels that saw Ukrainian disputants resort to violence almost as an inevitability. Physical blows, beatings, and brawls seem to have been routine means of resolving conflicts in the Slavic community.

Alberta's Ukrainian assaults featured different weapons (and, in fact, were more apt to involve weapons) than non-Ukrainian assaults. The bloc settlers rarely used knives or firearms, choosing everyday objects grabbed in the heat of the moment: a stick, a piece of firewood, an iron bar, an axe handle, a coal shovel, a spade, a wagon bolt, a pitchfork, a neck yoke.[21] Even in premeditated assaults, Ukrainians wielded some bizarre instruments. It is revealing that the immigrant press frequently depicted fighting with sticks, axes, pitchforks, and the like. In perhaps the most famous case of assault in the history of the Ukrainian bloc in Alberta (the main event of the "Great Ruthenian School Revolt" of 1913–14), a group of women brained an Anglo-Canadian schoolteacher with an iron pot.[22] The predilection of Ukrainians to arm themselves in altercations confounded the local constabulary. Years later, the only explanation one veteran bloc policeman could offer was "that is what they were used to at that time."[23]

Evidence suggests that Ukrainians' violent behaviour was a legacy of their historical experience in Galicia and Bukovyna. Until the abolition of serfdom in the Austrian empire in 1848, the landed gentry used systematic violence to control the Ukrainian peasants labouring on its estates.[24] Corporal punishment, usually with whips or cudgels, could result in death. In post-emancipation Galicia and Bukovyna it remained acceptable for an employer to inflict pain on his employee as chastisement for substandard performance or as incitement to greater achievement. On the eve of the First World War manorial officials still used the knout on Ukrainian labourers hired to work in the fields of large estates.[25] According to historian Roman Rosdolsky, the corporal punishment meted out to the Ukrainian peasantry had a "fatal, destructive influence on the peasant psychology as well as on the entire 'character' of that class."[26] Victims of abuse, many Ukrainian villagers became abusers themselves. Husbands beat wives, wives assaulted husbands, parents thrashed children, older or stronger siblings picked on younger or weaker ones, neighbours brawled with neighbours.

Ukrainians immigrating to Canada between 1892 and 1914 carried the psychological scars of their violent past. In their homeland they had exhibited a "slavish submissiveness and resignation" to "the lashings and floggings administered by the landlords, stewards, and manorial bailiffs," attributing such abuses to the misfortune of having been born peasants.[27] In Canada, they endured violence from authority figures with the same acquiescence, to the astonishment of Anglo-Canadians like the immigration official charged with settling a party of Bukovynians:

> They arrived . . . in charge of a man whom Mr. McNutt describes as a "dandified Jew," a little runt of a man whom a stout boy could handle, and who had been sent up from Winnipeg in charge as interpreter. This man was armed with a whip, and big burly men meekly took chastisement from his whip as he ordered them around. Mr. McNutt cautioned him against this conduct, but he repeated the offence, and was again cautioned. He said it was the "only way to manage them and they were used to it."[28]

The Ukrainian settlers not only accepted violence from authorities as natural, but also displayed a casual attitude towards it in their family and intra-group relationships. As in turn-of-the-century Galicia, violence played a role in social amusements. One popular party game, played not only by children and adolescents but also by adults, involved striking a blindfolded person, who had to guess the identity of his attacker. If he guessed correctly, the administrator of the blow donned the blindfold and took his place.[29]

One of the more distinctive aspects of violence in the Ukrainian bloc concerned its unusual settings — wedding feasts, christening parties, funeral receptions — prompting Charles Young to redefine "assault" as "a polite term for fighting which frequently occurs at their [Ukrainians'] weddings and dances."[30] The most notorious crime scene, commented upon by both Ukrainians and non-Ukrainians, was indisputably the Ukrainian wedding, whose reputation for wildness and fights was firmly enshrined in prairie legend well before 1930.[31] "It is a fact," the Crown Prosecutor for a liquor case in 1915 stated, "that the people go to these weddings . . . drink for three or four days, and they usually murder somebody or stab somebody before they get through with it." Veteran bloc policeman Dennis Mighall described the Ukrainian weddings he attended as events "where excellent food would be served, and liquor from the local still" and where "invariably a fight would break out." Noting that festive violence was rampant in the Smoky Lake area prior to 1930, one Bukovynian old-timer summed up with "it was wild and crazy!"[32]

While it would be a gross exaggeration to suggest that Ukrainian weddings typically ended in murder, three homicides did take place at nuptial celebrations in the Alberta bloc in the period under consideration. The first occurred in 1914 in the Skaro district, when Nikola Kutt was killed during a fight over the dance music to be played.[33] Then in 1922 two Smoky Lake youths, Harry Droniuk and George Worasczuk, waylaid George Popowich on his way home from the reception and beat him to death with grub-hoe handles. The farmer had stood up to their general bullying — as they amused themselves by slapping guests, knocking their hats off, and stealing cigarettes out of their mouths — and paid the price.[34] In the third case George Elaschuk clubbed his half-brother to death in 1924 for stealing sugar from his wagon during a wedding dance at the Ukrainian hall in Smoky Lake.[35]

What aroused violent passions when Ukrainian settlers gathered together? Contemporary observers almost universally blamed an excessive consumption of alcohol. APP reports attributed violence in the bloc to the conspicuous consumption of moonshine, claiming that Ukrainians' home brew was "of the vilest kind" and that a draught or two of it "often set a man crazy."[36] In the 1980s Ukrainian oldtimers themselves equated liquor with disorder at their nuptial celebrations, telling one researcher that "an unfortunate aspect of Ukrainian weddings in the Smoky Lake area . . . was widespread 'piatyka/pianstvo' ('excessive drinking'), which more often than not resulted in violent arguments and fights at what was supposed to a joyous event."[37] The problem was more complex. Although there does appear to be a strong link between drunkenness and violence in the Ukraiian bloc, the emergence of two groups of Ukrainian Canadian rowdies probably played a more direct role in provoking confrontations at community gatherings.

THE *DZHEKY* OR JACKS

The group which arguably deserves the greatest share of the blame for violence was "the Jacks" (*dzheky*), who formed a distinct subculture of young itinerant labourers employed on farms, railway gangs, and construction projects, and in logging camps and mines. William Czumer, schoolteacher and chronicler of pioneer life in east-central Alberta, insisted on distinguishing between the nomadic *dzheky* and the older, *bidni vuiky* or "poor uncles," "farmers who temporarily worked as frontier labourers and then returned to their homesteads."[38] In contrast to the poor uncle, the Jack had no farm, no family, no permanent home, and no permanent job; he belonged to a "large body of floating labour" which drifted from frontier camp to frontier camp, in and out of cities, and back and forth across the harvest fields.[39] Converging on the bloc settlement each year in search of jobs on threshing gangs, many Jacks also wintered in the colony, working as hired hands on farms in exchange for food and lodgings.[40]

The *dzheky* displayed attributes of the classic deviant subculture. Writing in the 1940s, Vera Lysenko called them "the equivalent of today's zoot-suiters," young men who spoke "their own lingo" (a macaronic fusion of English words and Ukrainian grammatical endings), delighted "in stirring up riots," and pitted themselves "against the existing social order."[41] Their clothing visibly set them apart:

They wore a distinctive dress which distinguished them from the other immigrants — a pathetic imitation of what they imagined to be the gentleman's dress of the Canadian: wide trousers with huge cuffs, shoes with thick toes; red neckties with gaudy pins; fancy arm bands and wide-brimmed black hats with tattered brims, worn dashingly to one side.[42]

The Ukrainian pioneers referred to a "Jack movement" or *dzhekomakhiia*.[43] It possessed its own value system that prized individual freedom, comradeship, valour, virility, cunning, action, adventurousness, and revelry; attached great importance to brute strength and fighting prowess; and scorned formal education and religion. By all accounts, the Jacks had little regard for the future or for the consequences of their actions. "Don't worry" (*ne zhurys*) was their slogan, prompting other Ukrainians to label the Jack movement the "Don't Worry Party" (*partiia ne zhurys*).[44] The Jacks spent their free time and meagre savings on carousing and gambling at their favourite haunts: the bar, the bootleg joint, the billiard room, the dance hall, the brothel.

But it was their violence that made them notorious. "So common were drunken brawls among Ukrainian labourers," Orest Martynowych writes, "that an anecdote current in Alberta's Creighton Mine in 1918 had the Finns building the local reading hall, the Italians organizing the local orchestra and the 'Galicians' erecting the local courthouse (with the fines they regularly paid for drinking and fighting!)."[45] Like other Ukrainian immigrants, the Jacks often fought with weapons — spades, chains, iron rods, spikes. The knives and revolvers many of them carried came into play more rarely. The pistol, in fact, seems to have served as the final accessory in the Jack's ensemble more than anything else.

Scholars and contemporary observers have interpreted the violence of the Jacks as a natural reaction to brutal and exploitative conditions in mining towns and frontier camps. In these environments, as one early twentieth-century policeman noted, fisticuffs were "as common as beans, boils, and bacon" and fighting served as a "means of letting off steam."[46] Much of the venting of frustrations in the camps took the form of inter-ethnic clashes. Immigrant groups from central and southeastern Europe comprised a large proportion of the work force on the labouring frontier of western Canada, and reciprocal prejudices and antipathies often soured relations so that outbreaks of violence between workers of different nationalities were commonplace. Anglo-Canadian labourers treated all "foreigners" with contempt and heightened camp tensions with their abuses, while owners and bosses encouraged inter-ethnic conflicts as a simple means of forestalling strikes and unionization.[47]

On the labouring frontier, where the lone Galician or Bukovynian became a target for harassment and exploitation by non-Ukrainians, wisdom dictated that he link up with a pack of his countrymen for protection. In fact, the Jack movement appears to have been partially a response to violence and mistreatment in the frontier encampments. William Czumer contended that the *dzheky* "were organized to rescue" Ukrainian comrades who ran into trouble.[48] As a force to be reckoned with, they proved formidable, and in terms of ruggedness and fighting prowess ranked among the toughest men in the pioneer West. The *bidni vuiky* often feared the Jacks, who willingly fought with their own people as much as (or more than) anyone else, yet admired them for their brawniness and the protection they offered to the greater mass of Ukrainian labourers.

The Ukrainian settler's appreciation of the Jacks in the mine or camp, however, turned to resentment when he encountered them in the city or rural bloc. Here the *dzheky* turned from defenders into victimizers, importing the brawling and barbarity of the bunkhouse, and venting their violent tendencies upon one another and fellow Ukrainians. Simply put, the Jacks attended social events to provoke fights or to take part in any altercations that might arise. Numerous crime reports from points in east-central Alberta describe them arriving at weddings or dances "looking for trouble," "wanting to lick someone," or "wanting to fight everyone."[49] An Andrew-area pioneer later maintained that the *dzheky* did not go to a wedding to socialize, but "to get drunk and have a fight."[50] If the Jack found no takers for his challenges, he could usually manufacture a confrontation with insults, boorish behaviour, or an unprovoked attack.

Violence at public gatherings served as both diversion and bravado for the Jacks. They seem genuinely to have relished fisticuffs or the administration of a beating and revelled in hooliganism as sport and recreation. Yet they also used fights to prove themselves and win recognition in a community where, as landless and penniless hired hands, they had very low status. "Making one's mark" meant showing that one was the toughest man (or among the toughest) in a rural community.

Most bloc settlers learned to endure the raging of the Jacks as they did prairie thunderstorms or blizzards. Some even came to sympathize in spite of all the trouble they caused. One said that "you couldn't really blame them, because they didn't know any better."[51] Ultimately, the men of the *dzhekomakhiia* continued their rowdiness until advancing age mellowed them, the Ukrainian Canadian socialist movement absorbed them, or the great eras of railway construction, coal mining, and the hired hand came to an end.

THE *BUHAI* OR BULLS

Before its demise the *dzhekomakhiia* contributed to the rise of a new breed of rough-necks in the bloc settlement, "the Bulls" *(buhai)*. Rather than develop their own distinct subculture, these youths simply adopted the values and trappings of the Jacks: dressing like their heroes, carrying revolvers, engaging in vandalism and petty crime, brawling at weddings and dances. The Bulls emerged from a generation of Ukrainian farm boys who had grown up during the most desperate years of the pioneer struggle. As children they idolized the Jacks and tried to emulate their behaviour. The *dzheky*, says Vera Lysenko, exercised a "demoralizing influence on the sons of farmers, whom they fascinated with their yarns of adventure, their flashy costume, and their specious ideas of freedom and don't-worry-ism. . . ."[52]

The values and attitudes of the *dzheky* appealed to the young men of the bloc. Like the Jacks, the Bulls knew poverty intimately, had minimal formal education, and held little hope for the future. They had spent their childhoods performing endless chores around the homestead, living in crude dugouts or one-room hovels, eating with their hands out of communal bowls, and drinking out of tin cans. They had gone barefoot in summer, worn homemade shoes of gunny sacks and rags in winter, and had virtually no free time for play. During these austere years, as one contemporary commented, Ukrainian children "were growing up like barbarians."[53]

Given their childhood poverty and drudgery, the dreams of a prosperous North American lifestyle exerted a strong hold on Ukrainian farm boys in the 1920s. Inevitably, these impossible hopes became sources of frustration. "Marginal men" caught in a sociocultural limbo, neither the Jacks nor the Bulls were equipped for success or acceptance in the new land. It is not surprising that "don't-worryism" provided a ready philosophy of life and hell-raising an effective outlet for discontent.

The Bulls' behaviour at weddings and dances exposed the developmental scars suffered during their upbringing. Few could be described as good mixers, rarely conversing or dancing at public gatherings, preferring to stand around the periphery — intently puffing cigarettes and quaffing moonshine. At social events, the interactions of the Bulls consisted chiefly of jostling with machismo bravado, knocking each other's hats off, or swatting cigarettes out of each other's mouths.[54] Sometimes these actions were designed to precipitate a fight but the young men generally accepted them as good-natured amusement. As a celebration wore on, however, and as the young men imbibed more and more alcohol, the jovial slaps and pushes became less controlled and more likely to incite anger and confrontation.

Some Bulls, however, went to weddings and dances with no other intention than to create disturbances. For example, Ukrainian toughs Nick and John Chomaschuk showed up at a wedding at Sunland and "wanted to fight everyone."[55] Some Bulls even disrupted the weddings of their own siblings. One farmer in the Kahwin district had to lay charges against his own son for "making lots of trouble" at a family wedding and "wanting to fight everyone there."[56]

The Bulls sometimes organized themselves into bands resembling youth gangs. The capers of small packs of brothers, cousins, or neighbours gave certain localities in the bloc settlement notorious reputations. Typically, the members of such groups became repeat offenders — perpetrating crimes from vandalism and petty theft to aggravated assault. Charles Young credited them with both a disproportionate amount of Ukrainian crime and Ukrainians' "unfortunate reputation" that was "altogether out of keeping with the general and actual situation." He identified the Two Hills district as being the most crime-ridden area of the Alberta bloc and blamed young men from two families. One of their members had been up for conviction seventeen times.[57]

One of the bloc's most infamous Bulls during the late 1920s and 1930s was George Basaraba, "the cause of considerable trouble in the Vegreville and Mundare districts."[58] By the time Basaraba reached twenty-one years of age in 1931, he had been convicted of numerous crimes (several assaults causing grievous bodily harm, thefts, vagrancy, and driving a car while intoxicated) and had served two prison terms. Each time the Bull was released from jail, he would run wild until the police managed to capture him — evidently no easy matter. APP Inspector Hancock commented: "In addition to parents and a large number of other relations he had many friends scattered through the district, also there were many who provided him with shelter and board through fear, thus he was successful in evading the police."[59] Nevertheless, Basaraba went to jail for the third time in 1931 for five offenses: assaulting farmer Victor Koroliuk with an iron bar, striking Koroliuk's wife with a large stone, rustling a horse, stealing a harness, and purloining a rifle.

UNDERSTANDING THE JACKS AND THE BULLS

There was, however, one major difference between the violence of the Jacks and that of the Bulls. The wedding brawling of the latter had overtones of the youth gang protecting its home territory, for the confrontations often involved young men from a particular farming district confronting guests from other districts. Evidently, many Bulls would not tolerate the presence of strangers or outsiders at festivities in their rural community.[60] Such territorial confrontations were also common at wedding celebrations in the homeland. According to John-Paul Himka, "antagonism between villages, which often passed into brawls" was a feature of traditional peasant life in late nineteenth-century Galicia.[61]

Such territorial antagonisms seem to have survived the uprooting of migration, despite the abundance of land in the Canadian West. During the settlement period, peasants from a particular village in Galicia or Bukovyna not only often left en masse but also chose adjacent homesteads in Canada, so that most of the Ukrainian blocs were characterized by clusters of settlers bound by strong old-country kinship and village ties.[62] Unfortunately, this preservation of solidarity and cultural distinctiveness retained the attendant animosities for countrymen originating from other villages. The pattern of Ukrainian settlement in Canada may actually have exacerbated traditional frictions between different groups of Ukrainian peasants. In Galicia and Bukovyna conflicts had been between villages in close proximity to one another, and the clashes stemmed, in part, from marginal differences in dialect and folk culture. In Canada, however, Ukrainian immigrants from one village often settled beside immigrants from a completely different region. This resulted in greater dissimilarities in dialect and folk culture, and thus greater antipathies, between adjoining groups of Ukrainians than in the homeland.

There are many examples of old-country-style antagonisms among Ukrainian settlers in Canada. Initially, the most obvious conflicts pitted Greek Catholic Galicians against Orthodox Bukovynians, people who differed not only in religion but also in dialect and customs. Canadian immigration officials noted a fierce friction between the two groups and attempted to keep them separated during the colonization process. For their part, at least in east-central Alberta, Galicians and Bukovynians preferred to settle apart from one another. It was not always possible, however, and when circumstances forced them to share the same immediate living space, confrontations ensued.[63] But many marriages in Canada united men and women from not only different villages but also different districts or regions of origin and different religions. Given the Ukrainian intra-group antipathies of the era, it is no wonder that such unions produced fisticuffs and assaults at weddings feasts. Fights often escalated into full-blown donnybrooks because kinsmen and friends of the original combatants took sides and joined the fray.[64]

One of the most elemental traditions of the Ukrainian wedding feast encouraged fighting: the custom of inviting all members of the community to the celebration. Tradition obligated the host to welcome anyone who might appear. As far as APP veteran Ted Buchanan was concerned, this was a recipe for disaster. He felt that most fights at Ukrainian weddings stemmed from the fact that a host often invited or welcomed guests who were sworn enemies: "Two people who hadn't been together in years and were at loggerheads would meet at a wedding, get boozed up, and then there was an argument and sometimes there was a murder or manslaughter. They would go after one another with a neck yoke or an axe handle or something. Or sometimes one waylaid the other on the way home."[65] Even if families flouted the rules and chose not to invite local troublemakers, the individuals often showed up anyway, their appearance precipitating a row.[66] In the course of daily life enemies could easily avoid each other, and tended to do so, but a wedding was a special occasion that drew a community physically together. Two enemies ending up in the same place at the same time — each convinced of his right to be there, each adamantly opposed to the presence of the other — meant trouble.

The custom of the "open invitation" may not have been the only practice that encouraged violence at Ukrainian weddings in east-central Alberta. Another tradition, the "confrontation at the gate," where the groom and his supporters gained access to the bride's house only after negotiations and a "symbolic" struggle, may have contributed to the problem: evidently, the ritual confrontation sometimes got out of hand.[67] The prolonged duration and cramped conditions of rural weddings may have also encouraged disorder. In the pre-Depression bloc most nuptial feasts took place in farmhouses, not community halls, and guests would pack the home day and night for as long as the festivities lasted (three or more days). Dozens or even hundreds of people showed up to celebrate, and while some went home to sleep, many others bedded down each night at the farm of the host. People slept all over his house, in his barn and outbuildings, and under wagons in his farmyard. In most cases guests had to eat and sleep in shifts so that all could be accommodated. Pioneer accounts testify to the fact that the congestion of the Ukrainian rural wedding could become irritating, especially by the third or subsequent day of partying. Sparks of irritation would then explode into fights and brawls, particularly when fuelled by prodigious quantities of alcohol. "The weddings lasted far too long in my opinion," stated one pioneer.[68]

The criminological theory which may offer the greatest insight into violence in the pre-1930 Ukrainian bloc — the pervasiveness of assaults, the use of weapons in altercations, the brawling at weddings and public gatherings, and the aggressiveness of the Jack and Bull movements — is the "subculture of violence thesis" developed by sociologists Marvin Wolfgang and Franco Ferracuti.[69] This thesis maintains that violence is viewed as an everyday part of life in certain subsocieties, particularly those of working classes and/or underclasses. It becomes part of a lifestyle where members of the culture group use physical attacks as a routine means of conflict resolution. Toleration and the acceptance of assaultive behaviour appear to have been prominent cultural themes of early Ukrainian Canadian society. Possibly the conditions of life in Galicia and Bukovyna predisposed the Ukrainians who immigrated to east-central Alberta to use aggression to settle disputes.

How does the subculture of violence thesis help to explain the behaviour of the Jacks and Bulls specifically? First of all, it holds that "the subcultural ethos of violence" will be "most prominent in a limited age group, ranging from late adolescence to middle age,"[70] precisely the age group of both the Jacks and the Bulls. It also holds that young men in the subculture of violence share the violent tendencies of their larger subsociety, but unleash them with greater frequency and ferocity, which aptly describes the assaultive behaviour of the Ukrainian roughnecks. Thus, according to the criteria used by Wolfgang and Ferracuti, the Jacks and the Bulls qualified as two subcultures of violence within early Ukrainian Canadian society (which, itself, qualified as a subculture of violence within contemporary Canadian society).

Wolfgang and Ferracuti also give insight into Ukrainian wedding violence through the proposition that members of the subculture of violence often commit violent acts only in specific situations. Jacks and Bulls showed up at weddings and dances anticipating the possibility that a fight would break out, if not ready to provoke it themselves. In fact, the bloc settlers as a whole came to these festivities aware of the less-than-remote chance that some type of altercation would take place. The highly-charged atmosphere of the Ukrainian wedding, where all guests warily watched for the outbreak of trouble, itself increased the probability that confrontations would occur. Any number of factors — a misinterpreted look, remark, jostle, or motion — could unintentionally spark a fight.

THE ANGLO-CANADIAN REACTION

As Anglo-Canadians were not themselves caught up in the vortex of violence in the Ukrainian community, they could afford to observe it with dispassionate superiority. When she visited the Ukrainian colony east of Edmonton in 1916, Emily Murphy commented on the "tremendous fighting energy" of the Slavs with the detachment of a Roman patrician viewing a gladiatorial spectacle. "They are bonny fighters these Ruthenians from Galicia," she wrote, "and if they cannot 'have the law' on one another they may always have the consolation of fisticuffs. And what pray, are muscles hard for and skulls thick, except to fight. Riddle me that!"[71] Murphy was expressing her Anglo-Canadian contemporaries' expectation that Slavs could not be expected to behave in other than a barbarous fashion, yet with the self-assurance that such behaviour would not touch their world.

Why did unthreatened Anglo-Canadians become preoccupied with Ukrainian violence? The answer lies in the outlandishness and luridness of the violent crimes committed by Ukrainians in the bloc. One finds bizarre details that would appeal to the prejudices and curiosities of tabloid readers. In terms of novelty, a Ukrainian wedding donnybrook rated higher than the run-of-the-mill barroom brawl. A battle with pitchforks proved more intriguing than a routine back-alley stabbing. An axe murder made for more tantalizing and shocking reading than one committed with a gun. Over time, the sensational coverage of Slavic crimes in newspapers and the peculiar particulars of these offenses had the psychological effect of convincing both the police and the general public that Ukrainians were committing a far greater number of violent crimes than their numbers warranted. This belief held sway for decades — despite the fact that no reliable statistics existed to support it.

Ukrainian assaults also attracted attention because their circumstances violated established principles of behaviour in the West. For example, the Ukrainian tendency to grab for weapons in a scuffle went against the established British standard of "the fair fight." In his 1909 novel *The Foreigner*, Ralph Connor had his Anglo-Canadian hero reprimand a Galician for using a stake as a weapon during a brawl, telling him that "only a fool loses his temper, and only a cad uses a club or a knife when he fights. . . . We won't stand that in this country." After introducing the Galician to gentlemanly fisticuffs (and thrashing him in the process), the protagonist warns the immigrant that he "must learn to fight without club or knife" or he would end up (like so many other Galicians) "in prison or on the gallows."[72] In the eyes of Anglo-Canadians, this "uncivilized" behaviour proved the Slav a brute.

Finally, the settings of Ukrainian assaults challenged the values of Alberta's Anglo-Canadian Protestant majority. While Anglo-Canadians and Ukrainian Canadians both participated in drunken brawls, they chose different locations. The former tended to limit fracases to the bar or billiard hall. The latter let fists fly in a wider variety of settings — most disturbingly at weddings, christening parties, and funeral receptions. To Anglo-Canadians, such behaviour at celebrations of Christian rites and sacraments was an abomination. Making matters worse, these celebrations (including requisite drinking and optional violence) frequently took place on Sunday. The Ukrainian wedding, then, became a favourite illustration of Ukrainian criminality and barbarity, and served as an especially useful instrument for temperance crusaders, prohibitionists, and Sabbatarians in harnessing western Canadian nativists to support their respective causes.

NOTES

1. Timothy C. Byrne, "The Ukrainian Community in North-Central Alberta" (M.A. thesis, University of Alberta, 1937), 96.
2. See, for example, Orest Martynowych, *The Ukrainian Bloc Settlement in East Central Alberta, 1890–1930: A History* (Edmonton 1985), 288–93; and Gerald Friesen, *The Canadian Prairies: A History* (Toronto 1984), 266.
3. Charles Young, *The Ukrainian Canadians: A Study in Assimilation* (Toronto 1931), 264.
4. Martynowych, *Ukrainian Bloc Settlement in East Central Alberta*, 289.
5. *Census of the Prairie Provinces 1926* (Ottawa 1931), xi–xiv; Martynowych, *Ukrainian Bloc Settlement in East Central Alberta*, 61; *Census of Canada 1931*, vol. 2, 464–82; J.T. Borhek

   et al., *Persistence and Change: A Study of Ukrainians in Alberta* (Toronto 1968), 121–2; and
   James S. Woodsworth, "Ukrainian Rural Communities" (unpublished manuscript, 1917),
   4.

6. See Frances Swyripa, "The Ukrainians in Alberta," in Howard Palmer and Tamara
   Palmer, eds., *Peoples of Alberta: Portraits of Diversity* (Saskatoon 1985), 227–30;
   Woodsworth, "Ukrainian Rural Communities," 73–94; Martynowych, *Ukrainian Bloc
   Settlement in East Central Alberta*, 120, 136–42; and Young, *Ukrainian Canadians*, 275.

7. F. Heap, "Ukrainians in Canada: An Estimate of the Presence, Ideals, Religion,
   Tendencies and Citizenship of Perhaps Three Hundred Thousand Ukrainians in Canada,"
   Canadian Magazine of Politics, Science, Art and Literature 53 (May–October 1919): 42.

8. Martynowych, *Ukrainian Bloc Settlement in East Central Alberta*, 291; Young, *Ukrainian
   Canadians*, 45–6, 274; Wasyl Swystun, "The Shandro District," in Woodsworth,
   "Ukrainian Rural Communities," 77; Borhek, *Persistence and Change*, 108–19; and
   Stanley Rands, "The Individual Offender: A Study Based on Case Histories of One
   Hundred and Twenty-Nine Inmates of Fort Saskatchewan Gaol" (M.A. thesis, University
   of Alberta, 1933), 126.

9. Vladimir J. Kaye and Frances Swyripa, "Settlement and Colonization," in Manoly R.
   Lupul, ed., *A Heritage in Transition: Essays in the History of Ukrainians in Canada* (Toronto
   1982), 44; John Lehr, "The Government and the Immigrant: Perspectives on Ukrainian
   Block Settlement in the Canadian West," *Canadian Ethnic Studies* 9, no. 2 (1977): 44; and
   Michael H. Marunchak, *The Ukrainian Canadians: A History*, 2d ed. rev. (Winnipeg and
   Ottawa 1982), 15, 75–6.

10. See APP annual reports, 1918–29 (Provincial Archives of Alberta, Edmonton, PAA
    72.370).

11. For a typical incident of grain stealing in the bloc during the 1920s, see PAA 83.1/4206
    (middle series).

12. *APP "A" Division Annual Report 1921*, 31 (PAA 72.370/4a).

13. *APP Annual Report 1920*, 55 (PAA 72.370/3a).

14. Interview (Gregory Robinson) with E.E. Buchanan, APP/RCMP veteran, Edmonton,
    Alberta, 3 November 1989.

15. See Byrne, "Ukrainian Community in North-Central Alberta," 35; Radomir Bilash,
    "Banking in the Rural Town of the 1920's" (environment interpretation statement,
    Ukrainian Cultural Heritage Village, nd); and A. Hrynchuk, ed., *Memories: Redwater and
    District* (Calgary 1972), 23.

16. *APP "A" Division Annual Report 1920*, 13–14 (PAA 72.370/3a).

17. *Edmonton Journal*, 23 November 1929.

18. Ibid., 2 August 1929.

19. See PAA 75.126/950. Young, *Ukrainian Canadians*, 275, conceded that poverty was a
    major factor behind theft, especially of wheat, in Ukrainian colonies.

20. See APP annual reports, 1918–29; Criminal Case Files, 1915–29 (PAA 72.26 and 83.1);
    and list of executions at Lethbridge and Fort Saskatchewan Gaols, 1912–60 (PAA 80.10).

21. See, for example, Orest Martynowych, *Ukrainians in Canada: The Formative Years,
    1891–1924* (Edmonton 1991), 95–8; and the following random sampling of assaults in
    the Ukrainian bloc prior to 1930: PAA 72.26/1340, PAA 72.26/3608, PAA 72.26/6282,
    PAA 72.26/6390, PAA 72.370/11a (p 3), PAA 75.126/955, PAA 83.1/3516 (middle
    series).

22. Martynowych, *Ukrainians in Canada*, 354–6, 376; and Alberta, *Department of Education
    Annual Report 1914*, 68–9.

23. Interview (Robinson) with Buchanan.

24. John-Paul Himka, *Galician Villagers and the Ukrainian National Movement in the Nineteenth
    Century* (Edmonton 1988), 1–58.

25. Ibid., 147.

26. Cited in ibid., 16.

27. Rosdolsky, cited in ibid., 16.

28. John Hawkes, *The Story of Saskatchewan and Its People*, vol. 2 (Chicago and Regina 1924), 685.

29. Andriy Nahachewsky, "First Existence Folk Dance Forms among Ukrainians in Smoky Lake, Alberta, and Swan Plain, Saskatchewan" (M.A. thesis, University of Alberta, 1985), 109–10.

30. Young, *Ukrainian Canadians*, 267.

31. See, for example, Ralph Connor [Charles W. Gordon], *The Foreigner: A Tale of Saskatchewan* (Toronto 1909), 87–8, 93–4; George Chipman, "Winnipeg — The Melting Pot," *Canadian Magazine of Politics, Science, Art and Literature* 33 (September 1909): 409; J.S. Woodsworth, "Foreign Immigrants and Temperance," *Christian Guardian* (13 April 1910): 8; Robert England, *The Central European Immigrant in Canada* (Toronto 1929), 84; and Young, *Ukrainian Canadians*, 267, 279.

32. PAA 72.26/23c; interview (Elise Corbet) with John Moisey, Andrew, Alberta, 23 September 1984, and Dennis Mighall, Edmonton, Alberta, 30 August 1984; interview (Robinson) with Buchanan; and Demjan Hohol, "The Grekul House: Narrative History Report" (unpublished research report, Ukrainian Cultural Heritage Village, Alberta Historic Sites Service, 1986), 175–6.

33. *RNWMP Report 1915* (Ottawa 1916), 95; and PAA 83.1/4007 (old series).

34. PAA 72.26/4267c; PAA 83.1/2493 (middle series); *APP Annual Report 1922*, 4–6 (PAA 72.370/5a); and PAA 67.172/1599.

35. *APP Annual Report 1923*, 7–8 (PAA 72.370/6a); PAA 72.26/5454; PAA 83.1/3592 (middle series); and PAA 67.172/1800.

36. *APP Annual Report 1918*, 23 (PAA 72.370/1).

37. V.S. Paviuk, *Prypovidky* (Edmonton 1946), 76–7.

38. Vasyl Chumer, *Spomyny pro perezhyvannia pershykh pereselentsiv v Kanadi, 1892–1942* (Edmonton 1942), 88–9.

39. Woodsworth, "Ukrainian Rural Communities," 3.

40. Marunchak, *Ukrainian Canadians*, 90; and England, *Central European Immigrant in Canada*, 29.

41. Vera Lysenko, *Men in Sheepskin Coats: A Study in Assimilation* (Toronto 1947), 95.

42. Ibid., 96.

43. Chumer, *Spomyny*, 85–6.

44. Ibid., 85.

45. Martynowych, *Ukrainians in Canada*, 123.

46. James Emmott, "Policing the Rails," in M.L. Barlee, ed., *The Best of Canada West* (Langley BC 1980): 144–7.

47. See, for example, Alfred Fitzpatrick, "Out Navvying the Navvies," *Canadian Magazine of Politics, Science, Art and Literature* 47 (May–October 1916): 23–4; and Allen Seager, "The Pass Strike of 1932," *Alberta History* 25, no. 1 (Winter 1977): 2, 6–7, 10.

48. Chumer, *Spomyny*, 85.

49. Ibid.

50. Interview (Sylvalya Elchen) with John Kawyuk, Andrew, Alberta, 17 November 1982.

51. Halya Kuchmij, dir., *Laughter in My Soul* (National Film Board of Canada 1983), documentary on Jacob Maydanyk.

52. Lysenko, *Men in Sheepskin Coats*, 96, 97. See also Young, *Ukrainian Canadians*, 268; and interview (Elise Corbet) with Mrs Wilma (Moisey) Bazian, Edmonton, Alberta, 20 November 1984.

53. Maria Adamovska, "Beginnings in Canada," in Harry Piniuta, trans., *Land of Pain, Land of Promise: First-Person Accounts by Ukrainian Pioneers, 1891–1914* (Saskatoon 1978), 73.

54. See, for example, PAA 75.126/953, PAA 72.26/4267c, and PAA 67.172/1599.

55. "Crime Report re. Nick and John Chomaschuk — Vagrancy," Andrew Detachment, 14 August 1926 (PAA 75.126/852).

56. "Crime Report re. Nick Wispenskie — Vagrancy," Andrew Detachment, 30 July 1926 (PAA 75.126/1004).

57. Young, *Ukrainian Canadians*, 269. The following represent a random sampling of the hell-raising activities of the Bulls in east-central Alberta: PAA 72.26/3799c, PAA 72.26/8117, PAA 72.370/14, PAA 83.1/3770 (middle series), PAA 83.1/4475 (middle series), PAA 83.1/6490 (middle series).

58. *APP "A" Division Annual Report 1931*, 12 (PAA 72.370/14).

59. Ibid., 13.

60. Young, *Ukrainian Canadians*, 268; also, for example, PAA 83.1/3770 (middle series).

61. Himka, *Galician Villagers*, 82.

62. John Lehr, "Kinship and Society in the Ukrainian Pioneer Settlement of the West," *Canadian Geographer* 29, no. 3 (Fall 1985): 207–19; and Radomir Bilash, "The Colonial Development of East Central Alberta and its Effect on Ukrainian Settlement to 1930" (M.A. thesis, University of Manitoba, 1983), 111–13.

63. Thomas McNutt cited in Hawkes, *Story of Saskatchewan and Its People*, 731–2; Lehr, "Kinship and Society in the Ukrainian Pioneer Settlement of the Canadian West," 214–16; and James G. MacGregor, *Vilni Zemli/Free Lands: The Ukrainian Settlement of Alberta* (Toronto 1969), 240.

64. See, for example, PAA 72.26/6374–6376.

65. Interview (Robinson) with Buchanan, 17 October 1989. Buchanan's observation is substantiated by numerous cases, including PAA 83.1/2172 (old series) and PAA 72.26/6720.

66. See, for example, PAA 75.126/957; and Young, *Ukrainian Canadians*, 276.

67. Hohol, "Grekul House," 175–6; see also Z. Kuzela, "Folk Customs and Rites Related to Family Life," in Volodymyr Kubijovyc, ed., *Ukraine: A Concise Encyclopedia*, vol. 1 (Toronto 1963), 337.

68. Zonia Lazarowich, "A Lifetime of Change: Reminiscences of Mary Kruk," in Bohdan Shulakevych, ed., *Tini mynuloho/Shadows of the Past* (Edmonton 1986), 109. See also Nahachewsky, "First Existence Folk Dance Forms," 41–53; and Young, *Ukrainian Canadians*, 279.

69. Marvin E. Wolfgang and Franco Ferracuti, *The Subculture of Violence: Towards an Integrated Theory in Criminology* (London 1967), especially 154–61, 188–9, 258–60, 267, 298, 305–6, 314.

70. Ibid., 159, 314.

71. Janey Canuck [Emily Murphy], "Communing with Ruthenians," *Canadian Magazine of Politics, Science, Art and Literature* 40 (March 1913): 405–6.

72. Connor, *The Foreigner*, 216, 218.

FOURTEEN

Class and Ethnic Barriers to Feminist Perspectives in Toronto's Jewish Labour Movement, 1919–1939

RUTH A. FRAGER

The history of Toronto's Jewish labour movement provides a critical context for examining the relationship between feminist and socialist currents in Canada's past. It also illuminates the relationship between these currents and ethnic identity within a key section of the working class. In the 1920s and 1930s, Toronto's Jewish labour movement not only was militant but also had a strong radical cast: the Jewish unions were led primarily by socialists and contained a significant socialist component within their rank and file as well. Furthermore, as in the United States, the Jewish labour movement was concentrated in the garment industry, an industry with a highly unusual gender composition of labour. During most of the period under consideration, women constituted over half of Toronto's garment workers. A significant number of the Jewish women were active not only as trade-union militants but also as socialists. An examination of the Jewish labour movement in the interwar period thus provides an opportunity to study the historical interaction between class and gender in the context of both trade-union and socialist politics.[1]

This interaction was characterized by the systematic subordination of women's issues to class issues. Significantly, this subordination of the interests of female workers as *women* stands in marked contrast to the prominence which the Toronto Jewish labour movement accorded to Jewish workers' specific interest as *Jews*. Because the commitment to ethnic identity within the Jewish labour movement was not only powerful but also considered a *legitimate* characteristic of both trade-union politics and Jewish socialist ideology, it provides a counterpoint to the subordination of women's issues. In addition, the intensity of ethnic concerns provides part of the explanation for the subordination of women's issues. Within Toronto's Jewish labour movement, the emphasis on both class consciousness and ethnic identity inhibited the development of feminist perspectives.

While Jewish women were subordinated within their families, in the factories, in their unions, and within the Jewish left, there was hardly any awareness of this subordination and even less attempt to struggle against it. This was partly a product of deeply held assumptions about a woman's domestic responsibility and a man's responsibility as the primary breadwinner. These assumptions helped ensure that union

Source: Excerpted from "Class and Ethnic Barriers to Feminist Perspectives in Toronto's Jewish Labour Movement, 1919–1939," *Studies in Political Economy*, 30 (1989): 143–65. Reprinted by permission of *Studies in Political Economy* and the author.

activists did not fundamentally challenge discriminatory wage structures or the gender division of labour in the garment factories. At the same time, the nature of Jewish activists' class analysis meant that they generally focused on the common oppression of all workers and ignored the fact that female workers encountered special forms of oppression. Moreover, the Canadian women's movement, which was weak in these years and predominantly Anglo-Celtic and middle-class, did not ally with Jewish women workers and thus did not help these women develop feminist perspectives of their own experiences. Jewish women themselves stressed that which they held in common with Jewish men — their deep commitment to Jewish identity, and their experience of anti-Semitism — rather than interests they might have shared with non-Jewish women. For all these reasons, women's issues were systematically subordinated.

In the garment shops, Jewish workers often toiled side-by-side with non-Jews, and both groups frequently worked for Jewish manufacturers. The International Ladies' Garment Workers' Union, the Amalgamated Clothing Workers, the International Fur Workers' Union, and the United Cloth Hat, Cap, and Millinery Workers' International Union were known as the "Jewish unions." While non-Jews constituted a significant minority within these four unions, a majority of the members and most of the leaders were Jews.

Although the term "Jewish unions" was sometimes used as a racial epithet in this period (particularly by the anti-labour English-language press and others who sought to prevent the non-Jewish clothing workers from uniting with the Jews in these organizations), much of the significance of the term lies in its use by Jews themselves. Despite the fact that these unions included non-Jews and despite Jewish labour activists' need to appeal more successfully to their non-Jewish co-workers, the Jews themselves characterized these four unions as the "Jewish unions." The term reflects the distinctive stamp imparted to these particular unions, for Jewishness pervaded and shaped them in fundamental ways. Moreover, the activists commonly used the term "Jewish labour movement" to refer to the movement they forged largely through these garment unions and also through the related cultural institutions, particularly the Jewish socialist fraternal organizations (which did not include non-Jews) and the pro-labour Yiddish-language press (which, of course, non-Jews could not read).

The Jewish labour movement of Toronto, which emerged at the turn of the century and blossomed during the inter-war period, was broadly based in the immigrant community. These immigrants had fled to the New World in the early twentieth century to escape extreme poverty and virulent anti-Semitism in Eastern Europe. By 1931, there were over 45,000 Jews in Toronto, where their occupational concentration in the garment industry, combined with a high degree of residential concentration, helped create a cohesive community basis for the Jewish labour movement.[2]

Women's position within this community, particularly as defined by family roles, significantly shaped their position on the shop floor, in the unions, and in the Jewish left. Within the city's East European Jewish community, as within Canadian society more broadly, housework and childrearing were female responsibilities. Like so many others in this period, immigrant Jewish women and men considered the man to be the family's primary breadwinner and expected most women to leave the paid labour force upon marriage in order to concentrate on domestic tasks. It is significant, however, that women's domestic responsibilities within the family did not change in cases which did not fit this pattern. If the husband's income was not sufficient to support the family (and if there were no older children to help earn money), the married woman would go out to work, while continuing to shoulder the domestic responsibilities.[3] In extended family arrangements where men did not have wives to keep house for them, unmarried female relatives often assumed the double burden of wage-earning and housekeeping. Moreover, although the many Jewish men who worked in the highly seasonal garment industry had considerable free time during the slow seasons, they typically did not use this time to help with the housework.[4]

Within the East European Jewish community, women and men were bound together not only by family ties but also by deep cultural bonds. Even those who questioned certain aspects of Jewish tradition commonly shared the community's commitment to preserving Jewish identity and believed that the family played a central role in cultural preservation. In the context of significant anti-Semitism in Toronto as well as the more severe prejudice encountered before immigration, females and males within this community shared a sense of oppression as Jews. Because of the continuing threat of anti-Semitism and because of the positive valuation of Jewish identity, there was serious concern for the interest of the Jewish community as a whole.[5]

Jewish identity was based on a tradition that was fundamentally patriarchal. In traditional East European Jewish culture, religion, which permeated every aspect of life, assigned women a distinctly subordinate role. Education in particular (especially since it was so closely tied to religion) was a male preserve. Although the traditional way of life had been significantly transformed in other ways, women generally retained their "second-class" status within Toronto's immigrant Jewish community in the inter-war period.[6]

Jewish women were also at a significant disadvantage on the shop floor. In the needle trades, where so many immigrant women toiled, they were systematically confined to the lower-paying jobs, which were deemed to be less skilled.[7] Statistics available for the city's garment industry in 1921, for example, illustrate the sharp difference between female and male wages. At that time, the average adult female worker earned only 58 percent of what her male counterpart earned.[8] Fifteen years later, the average earnings for women in Toronto's needle trades were a scant 52 to 53 percent of the average earnings of men.[9] This differential is mainly attributable to the fact that the women were generally confined to low-paying female job ghettoes within the industry, but unequal pay for equal work was also a factor.

One of the main rationales for this discrepancy in wage rates rested on the view of the woman garment worker as unskilled and temporary. The skills which women brought to the job were generally based on their domestic sewing experience and were devalued not only because these were not scarce skills, but also because work done by women was generally devalued. Most needle trades women were young and single and were expected to leave the paid labour force upon marriage. The married women workers, who constituted a significant minority, were usually expected to leave the shop floor as soon as their husbands were no longer ill or unemployed or earning too little money. The woman worker's temporary status was a rationale for excluding her from training for the better jobs.[10]

In situations where women earned substantially less than men who did the exact same jobs, the perception of women as temporary workers usually meant that they were assumed to be less experienced on the job, so their work was presumably worth less. In the men's fine clothing industry in 1920, for example, there were cases where women and men did the same work and the women earned considerably less. These women did have significantly less work experience. Male button-hole-makers, for example, had an average of 19 years of experience and received an average wage of $36 per week, while female button-hole-makers had an average of only 7 years of experience and received an average wage of $22 per week, which amounted to 61 percent of the male wage for this job. In these shops, women who did basting (i.e. temporary stitching) and women who made collars and lapels found themselves in similar situations.[11]

It is a dubious assumption, however, that women's unequal pay was simply a product of fewer years of work experience. It is unlikely that these women were so much less skilled than their male counterparts as to merit such wide pay differentials. After all, one could learn to be an efficient button-hole-maker in far less than seven years. Indeed, according to a 1920 Ontario government publication on vocational opportunities in the needle trades, "the maximum speed on a single [sewing machine] operation will generally be attained in one or two years."[12]

A major rationale for the wage discrepancy was, of course, the expectation that male workers would be the primary breadwinners for their families. Women workers were not normally expected to fulfill this role. Instead they were expected to be dependent on men, and these expectations were married to necessity. In Toronto's needle trades, as in many other sectors in this period, low wages for female workers often meant that a woman could not support herself, let alone support children or aging parents.[13] By making economic independence impossible for most women, women's low wages reinforced, even as they reflected, the systematic subordination of women.

The conception that men were the family's primary breadwinners was so deeply ingrained in the thinking of the working-class Jewish community that little thought was given to the systematic super-exploitation of women. The cases of unequal pay mentioned above occurred in the *unionized* shops. There is no evidence that the union attempted to rectify these inequities. Although the garment unions may have sporadically and half-heartedly supported the equal-pay principle at some other points in time, the Jewish labour movement did not seriously criticise the discriminatory wage structure.

The unions actually reinforced women's subordination, for union policies frequently *increased* the differential between women's pay and men's pay. In a period when the average female garment worker's wage usually amounted to between one half and two thirds of the average male garment worker's wage, unions such as the International Ladies' Garment Workers' Union and the Amalgamated Clothing Workers often fought for an across-the-board percentage increase in wages for all workers.[14] This common formula meant that the dollar difference between the average woman's wage and the average man's wage would widen.

An examination of the Jewish unions' arrangement with respect to its own funds makes it clear that the unions were not simply forced to go along with the manufacturers' insistence on gender-based pay differentials. Union fees and strike-benefit payments constituted an area of policy where the unions were able to operate in relative freedom from the constraints imposed by the employers. If union activists had felt that it was unfair for women to earn so much less than men, they could have structured strike benefits so that female strikers received the same as male strikers. This seldom happened.[15] The rationale for lower strike-pay for women was that women earned so much less than men on the shop floor. However, this did not necessarily mean that women paid lower union fees. In many cases, they had to pay the same fees as the men.[16]

Women's subordination within the unions and on the shop floor was, of course, closely related to their subordination within the home. Significant household responsibilities on top of a full-time wage-earning job meant that the woman worker had less time and energy left over for union activities and shop-floor struggles. Even if the woman worker was single and not directly responsible for keeping house for male relatives, she often had to help her own mother with the housework, or if she had immigrated without her mother, she usually had to look after her own household needs. Moreover, in cases where the woman had been less well educated than her male siblings, she was at a disadvantage as a unionist, particularly if she was not literate in Yiddish. She faced further barriers if her father or husband disapproved of her activism.

Women's subordination within the Jewish labour movement was also a product of the male culture of the unions. Although the Jewish men used to drop by the union halls to chat with their friends, sip coffee, and play dominoes, Jewish women did not take part in such informal socializing. This was not just because the woman worker usually had to hurry home from work to make supper or do the laundry. According to interviews with retired male garment workers, this informal social network at the union halls was perceived as a male domain where women did not fit. Since the male culture of the union hall gave the men greater opportunity to know each other and to discuss union issues, it reinforced a male-centered solidarity.[17] The marginalization of women within Toronto's garment unions is also apparent in the fact that the overwhelming majority of the leaders of the different needle trades unions were men.

On the one hand, the unions reflected the dominant assumptions about gender roles: men "deserved" the better jobs and better pay because they were the primary breadwinners for their families, and women's responsibility for household labour remained unquestioned, shaping the women workers' position on the shop floor and in the unions in fundamental ways. The commonplace acceptance of these differences in gender roles helped to mask the discrimination against women. On the other hand, despite these fundamental assumptions about gender differences, union leaders did not distinguish between female and male workers at another level. The nature of the Jewish activists' class consciousness meant that they focused on what they saw as the common oppression of all workers, ignoring the fact that women workers faced special constraints. Thus when retired union activists were asked if the Jewish unions had had special policies to appeal to women workers, the question surprised them, for the notion of the special interests of women workers was foreign to their class analysis. Typically, the unions appealed to each person "just as a worker!," as one retired male union leader proudly exclaimed.[18]

The Canadian women's movement was unable to provide a significant feminist counter-force, for it seldom reached the women garment workers. This was partly because the women's movement was weak in the inter-war years, the key period in the development of the Jewish labour movement. In addition, the Canadian women's movement was predominantly Anglo-Celtic and middle-class and hence did not appeal to working-class immigrant women. Although very little historical work has been done yet concerning the attitudes within the Canadian women's movement towards the plight of working-class women, the movement as a whole seems to have exhibited little understanding of working-class women's problems.[19]

In the United States, in contrast, the Women's Trade Union League existed as an explicitly feminist organization, specifically concerned with the plight of female workers. Consisting of a cross-class alliance of women, the League sought to improve the conditions of American women workers, sometimes by organizing them into unions and sometimes by pushing for protective labour legislation. The League also tried to make the American women's movement more attractive to working-class women and to develop their awareness of feminist issues. Although the League's influence was limited, and although class and ethnic tensions emerged within the League itself, this organization had a significant impact on several exceptional Jewish women, who were among the few females to enter the leadership of the garment unions in New York. Their heightened awareness of women's issues stands in sharp contrast to the situation in Toronto and contrasts, as well, with the situation of the majority of immigrant Jewish women in the United States.[20]

Toronto's Jewish unions rarely used a woman organizer to recruit women workers, and the general absence of special policies to organize Toronto's female garment workers is striking. Although there were minor exceptions, the activists in Toronto's Jewish labour movement attempted to organize men and women using the same methods instead of developing special techniques for organizing women.[21]

The dearth of women-centered organizing strategies was not simply a product of the nature of the Canadian women's movement and the absence of a women's trade union league in Toronto. Perhaps because Toronto's Jewish women felt more beleaguered as *Jews* than did their counterparts in New York City, Toronto's female Jews may have been less inclined to develop gender-based alliances with Anglo-Celtic middle-class feminists or even with the non-Jewish women workers. Jewish women's close identification with Jewish men may have been heightened in Toronto not only because Toronto's Jewish population was so much smaller than New York's but also because, in contrast to the high proportion of non-British immigrants in the major American cities where Jews congregated, Toronto's population was so overwhelmingly Anglo-Celtic. Moreover, Jews had significant political power in New York City, unlike the situation in Toronto in this period. These demographic and political differences probably increased the feeling of insecurity in Toronto and reduced Jewish women's openness to alliances with non-Jewish women.[22]

In this period, Toronto's immigrant Jewish community faced pressing economic needs, and both the women and the men in the Jewish labour movement depended on class gains to improve their lot. Furthermore, while women faced gender-conditioned economic deprivations, this was obscured by the traditional emphasis on the welfare of the family as a whole. Instead of focusing on their own disadvantaged position in the paid labour force, women commonly focused on the family income, for they often benefited directly from the wages of their husbands and fathers. The authority and privileges of males, predicated on their role as primary breadwinner, were usually taken for granted, and these overlapped with and reinforced a male-centered class analysis.[23]

In contrast to the lack of concern for women's issues within Toronto's Jewish labour movement, there was serious concern about relations between Jewish and non-Jewish workers within the Jewish unions. Whereas women were generally not organized into separate locals, it was usually necessary to organize the Jews and the non-Jews into separate locals not only because of the language problem but also because of ethnocentrism and anti-Semitism. Because of "the Jew/Gentile problem," union leaders often made a point of using Jewish organizers to recruit the Jewish workers and non-Jewish organizers to recruit the non-Jews. Sometimes the leadership even found it necessary to set up a wholly separate office for mobilizing the non-Jewish garment workers. Furthermore, whereas there was little concern to include women within the union leadership, great care was taken to make sure that some non-Jews were included within the predominantly Jewish leadership of the Jewish unions. In Toronto's Amalgamated Clothing Workers, for example, it was common practice to have a Jewish business agent and a non-Jewish business agent; in contrast, the union lacked similar provisions to ensure that women would have ongoing representation in the leadership.[24]

Since members of Toronto's Jewish left played a key role in shaping union policies, it is particularly significant that their radicalism did not include a critique of conventional gender relations. Instead, they — like the other members of the immigrant Jewish community — viewed men as the primary breadwinners for the family and did not question the assignment of exclusive responsibility for housework and childcare to women. Even the female Jewish socialists shared these assumptions. There was very little awareness of the fact that Jewish women were subordinated within their homes, on the shop floor, within their unions, and also within the Jewish socialist organizations. There was even less attempt to struggle against this subordination.[25]

For the Jewish left, the central issues were class and ethnicity, not gender. Jewish radicalism had, in fact, a double dimension, for most of these Jewish socialists had been radicalized not only as workers but also specifically as Jews. In part, they were responding to the poverty and exploitation which working people experienced on both sides of the ocean. In addition, many had experienced harsh anti-Semitism before emigrating from Eastern Europe. Although less severe in Toronto, anti-Semitism was still significant: Toronto's Jews faced serious occupational, educational, recreational, and residential discrimination not only in the 1930s but in the earlier decades of the twentieth century as well. In both the Old World and the New, poverty and anti-Semitism were closely intertwined, since prejudice often played an important role in barring Jews from access to better jobs. Immigrant Jewish radicals were deeply committed to socialism not only as a way to end class oppression but also because they felt that only socialism would bring real freedom and equality for the Jews.[26]

Typically, one woman activist, who had worked as a Toronto cloakmaker, explained that she had become a member of the Communist Party not only in response to the hardships faced by working people but also in response to anti-Semitism. She stressed that she had been radicalized as a Jew:

> I joined [the Communist movement] for [the] reason that [at] that time, we thought that the best solution for the Jew is in the Soviet Union. That was right after the revolution. And I joined for that reason, that I wanted my *people* should be equal with every other people. And that was the slogan of the Communist Party, that in the Soviet Union, all the citizens are the same.[27]

Like many other Jewish socialists, her analysis of oppression was limited to class and ethnicity: it did not encompass an awareness of women's subordination.

This woman's descriptions of her own experiences as a female garment worker and female union member revealed significant differences from the experiences of her male counterparts: throughout her seventeen years in Toronto's needle trades, she remained in a typically female job which was considered unskilled, and she used to rush back and forth between paid labour, union labour, and household labour. Yet her class analysis focused on the common oppression of all workers and denied these gender-based differences at the ideological level, obscuring the discrimination against women.[28]

This courageous woman asserted herself not only as a worker and a Jew but also as a Communist who disagreed with the other political groupings within the Jewish left. During the 1920s and 1930s, the Jewish left was made up of a number of competing factions whose differences revolved around class and ethnic issues. In addition to Communist Party adherents, there were Trotskyists, Anarchists, and Labour Zionists (who sought to establish a Jewish socialist state in Palestine). There were also many Bundists, i.e. non-Zionists who wanted Jews to preserve their own culture within decentralized, multi-ethnic, socialist federations.[29] Whereas gender was deeply subordinated to class, the same was not true of ethnicity. Among these different factions of the Jewish left, an ongoing debate took place concerning the precise relationship between the class struggle and the struggle to end the oppression of Jews. In contrast to the rich complexity and intensity of this debate, there was no comparable debate about the relationship between women's rights and the class struggle. Gender was simply not considered an important issue.

To an important degree, the very class consciousness and intense ethnic identity of the Jewish socialists inhibited a strong recognition or analysis of women's subordination and hindered the development of feminism. Oriented toward class, they stressed the common interests of female and male workers, so that at the level of their articulated socialist ideology, there was little if any recognition that women workers faced special impediments. This point of view, taken to its logical extreme, was expressed by the Communist Party of Canada in 1931: "The women workers have no interests apart from those of the working class generally. There is no room for 'feminism' in our movement. There is only place for unity and solidarity on the basis of the joint struggle against capitalism."[30] "Exactly right!" exclaimed Joshua Gershman, the main leader of the Jewish Communist faction in the needle trades, when recently asked to comment on this quotation in the context of discussing his union activities in the inter-war years.[31]

Yet, for Gershman and so many others, while their class consciousness obstructed a strong awareness of women's oppression, it did not obstruct a forceful emphasis on anti-Semitism. As the quotation from the Communist press indicates, the critique of feminism, from a class point of view, was that an emphasis on women's rights would weaken the working class by dividing female and male workers. Furthermore, any vision of the common oppression of women, which transcended class, threatened to dilute the class struggle. But clearly the same argument could have been made about ethnicity. These socialists might have argued, but did not, that a focus on Jewish rights should be avoided because it would weaken the working class by dividing Jewish workers and non-Jewish workers. In fact, most Jewish socialists were intensely committed to Jewish rights, and they had a profound awareness of ethnic differences within the working class. To a certain extent, Jewish socialists did fear that an emphasis on the common oppression of Jews, which transcended class, threatened to dilute the class struggle.[32] Yet this did not stop them from being deeply committed to the fight against anti-Semitism — a fight which sometimes saw them allied with the Jewish garment manufacturers.[33]

While the socialists' emphasis on the common oppression of all workers, regardless of gender, undermined the development of a strong feminist perspective, the ethnic concerns of the Jewish activists also undermined such a development. Jewish working-class women were less apt to develop a clear critique of their position as women within the immigrant Jewish community because they shared a common sense of oppression with most of the men in this community, not only as fellow workers but also as fellow Jews. Moreover, since the family was seen as so central to the perpetuation of Jewish culture, a serious feminist challenge to the traditional norms and role structures of the Jewish family would have been seen as a dangerous cultural threat.

Yet this emphasis on the welfare of the Jewish community as a whole, this perceived need for Jews to pull together in the face of serious anti-Semitism, did not prevent Jewish workers from pursuing their own class interests in opposition to the Jewish manufacturers. Fierce conflicts often broke out in the Toronto garment industry between these two classes of Jews. Numerous strikes and lock-outs meant that there were bitter fights between fellow Jews who, while divided by their class interests, were often relatives, neighbours, and members of the same Jewish community organizations.[34]

The immigrant Jewish activists fought tenaciously for justice for working people and for Jews. Their dedication and courage were remarkable in a situation where such dissidence meant heightened vulnerability to repression. Many of these activists had a radical vision of a new kind of society which, they felt, would truly liberate them from class exploitation and anti-Semitism. Yet their deep two-fold commitment to egalitarianism did not encompass a commitment to women's rights. Both class and ethnicity were definitive in shaping the politics and the identity of Toronto's Jewish labour movement, despite the fact that class issues functioned divisively within the Jewish community and ethnic issues functioned divisively within the working class. In contrast, feminism did not emerge, perhaps partly because of its divisive potential both within the Jewish community and within the working class. Working-class Jewish women sacrificed their own potential for *full* equality to male-dominated, male-defined collectivities of family, nationality, and class.

NOTES

1. In 1921, 62 percent of Toronto's garment workers were women, and this proportion dropped to 55 percent in 1931. These calculations are based on the *Census of Canada*, 1921, Vol. IV, pp. 534–535, and 538; and 1931, Vol. VII, pp. 288–289.

2. *Census of Canada*, 1931, Vol. IV, pp. 268–271. On the high degree of occupational and residential concentration of Canada's Jews, see, for example, Irving Abella's introduction to Irving Abella, ed., "Portrait of a Jewish Professional Revolutionary: The Recollections of Joshua Gershman," *Labour/Le Travailleur*, Vol. 2 (1977) pp. 184–213.

3. This attitude was stressed, for example, in an interview with Moe Levin, 1984. (In order to protect the confidentiality of the interviewees, pseudonyms and minimal citations are used in reference to interviews throughout this article.)

4. This was apparent, for example, in the interviews with Bessie Kramer, 1984, and Sadie Hoffman, 1978 and 1985.

5. On anti-Semitism in Toronto in this period, see Stephen A. Speisman, *The Jews of Toronto: A History to 1937* (Toronto: 1979), pp. 119–122, 318–323, and 332–335; and Cyril H. Levitt and William Shaffir, *The Riot at Christie Pits* (Toronto: 1987) pp. 9–11 and 34–39.

6. On the patriarchal nature of traditional Judaism, see, for example, Susan Weidman Schneider, *Jewish and Female* (New York: 1984) pp. 33–41.

7. On the fact that women garment workers were commonly in the unskilled job categories, see, for example, International Ladies' Garment Workers' Union, *Handbook of Trade Union Methods* (New York: 1937) pp. 23–24.

8. This percentage is based on weekly wage statistics listed in Michael J. Piva, *The Condition of the Working Class in Toronto 1900–1921* (Ottawa: 1979) pp. 34 and 40.

9. Canada, Department of Trade and Commerce, *Weekly Earnings of Male and Female Wage-Earners Employed in the Manufacturing Industries of Canada, 1934–1936* (Ottawa: 1940) pp. 68 and 70.

10. In 1931, only one quarter of Toronto's women garment workers were married. This statistic is based on the Annual Report of the Ontario Minimum Wage Board, in the Ontario Legislative Assembly's *Sessional Papers*, 1933, part VI, paper #39, p. 16. However, the proportion of married women in the garment industry was higher than in many other sectors. A mere 10 percent of all women who were in the Canadian paid labour force in 1931 were married. On this, see Canada, Department of Labour, *Women at Work in Canada* (Ottawa: 1965) p. 21.

11. "Averages in the Toronto Market as in Jan. 1, 1920," Box B, File: "Assoc. Meetings??," Papers of the Associated Clothing Manufacturers, George Brown College Archives, Toronto.

12. The quotation is from Ontario, Department of Labour, *Vocational Opportunities in the Industries of Ontario: A Survey: Bulletin No. 4: Garment Making* (1920) p. 10.

13. Early evidence of women garment workers' inability to earn a living wage is provided by Mackenzie King's 1897 investigation of government clothing contracts in Toronto, Hamilton, and Montreal. See W.L. Mackenzie King, *Report to the Honourable the Postmaster General of the Methods Adopted in Canada in the Carrying Out of Government Clothing Contracts* (1900) p. 21.

14. Many examples could be cited to document this practice. For a few typical examples see: *Der Yiddisher Zhurnal*, 17 April 1919, p. 1; *Der Yiddisher Zhurnal*, 14 August 1919, p. 1; Minutes of the Associated Clothing Manufacturers (in the private collection at the organization's office in Toronto) 2 August 1933, 19 February 1935, and 27 April 1937; Canada, Department of Labour, *Labour Gazette*, August 1933, p. 767; and *Labour Gazette*, July 1934, pp. 625–626.

15. This is based, in part, on an analysis of the benefits which are recorded in the Minutes of the Toronto Joint Board, Amalgamated Clothing Workers Collection, Public Archives of Canada, Ottawa. It is also based on scattered material in a wide variety of other sources.

16. See, for example, *Der Yiddisher Zhurnal*, 31 March 1919, p. 1; 27 July 1920, p. 1; 1 August 1920, p. 8; 30 October 1922, p. 1; 7 November 1922, p. 5; and 17 October 1924, p. 1.

17. This is apparent, for example, in the interviews with Bessie Kramer, 1984; Ida and Sol Abel, 1983; and Abe Hertzman, 1984.

18. The quotation is from the interview with Moe Levin, 1984. Other relevant interviews include those with: Bessie Kramer, 1984; Joshua Gershman (not a pseudonym), 1984; Ed Hammerstein, 1984; and Molly Fineberg, 1984.

19. For a detailed discussion of the class and ethnic composition of the suffrage leaders, see Carol Lee Bacchi, *Liberation Deferred?: The Ideas of the English-Canadian Suffragists, 1877–1918* (Toronto: 1983) pp. 3–12. There has not yet been much work done on the feminists in the inter-war period, but see Veronica Strong-Boag, *The New Day Recalled: The Lives of Girls and Women in English Canada, 1919–1939* (Toronto: 1988) pp. 24 and 189–190, for relevant material on this period.

20. For an interesting study of the Women's Trade Union League, see Nancy Schrom Dye, *As Equals and As Sisters: Feminism, the Labor Movement, and the Women's Trade Union League of New York* (Columbia, Missouri: 1980).

21. This conclusion is based on a wide variety of sources, including the minutes, newspapers, and correspondence files of the various unions.
22. In 1921, immigrants from continental Europe constituted less than 6 percent of Toronto's population. (At that time, Toronto contained very few other immigrants who had come from outside Britain or the United States.) In a number of major American cities in 1920, the proportions of immigrants from continental Europe were significantly higher than in Toronto. In that year, those who had been born in continental Europe comprised 15 percent of Boston's population and 16 percent of Philadelphia's population. In Chicago, Cleveland, and New York City, at least one quarter of each city's total population had come from continental Europe. These statistics are drawn from the *Census of Canada, 1921*, Vol. II, pp. 364–365; and the *Fourteenth Census of the United States Taken in the Year 1920* (Washington: 1922) Vol. II, pp. 47 and 732–736.
23. These attitudes were apparent, for example, in the interviews with Bessie Kramer, 1984, and Sadie Hoffman, 1985.
24. The quotation is from H.D. Langer to D. Dubinsky, from Toronto, 6 July 1937, Box 88, File 1b, David Dubinsky Papers, International Ladies' Garment Workers' Union Collection, Labor–Management Documentation Center, M.P. Catherwood Library, Cornell University, Ithaca, New York.
25. The interview with Bessie Kramer (1984) is particularly interesting regarding these issues.
26. The double dimension of Jewish radicalism is examined in detail in Ruth A. Frager, "Radical Portraits: The Roots of Socialism in Toronto's Immigrant Jewish Community, 1900–1939," *Polyphony* (forthcoming).
27. Interview with Bessie Kramer, 1969.
28. Interviews with Bessie Kramer, 1969 and 1984.
29. For a detailed discussion of the Bund in the East European context, see Henry J. Tobias, *The Jewish Bund in Russia: From Its Origins to 1905* (Stanford, California: 1972). For a detailed treatment of the Labour Zionists in Canada, see S. Belkin, *Di Poale Zion Bavegung in Kanade, 1904–1920* [The Labour Zionist Movement in Canada, 1904–1920] (Montreal: 1956).
30. *Worker* (Toronto) 28 February 1931, p. 1.
31. Interview with Joshua Gershman, 1984.
32. This concern is apparent, for example, in the interview with Ed Tannenbaum, 1984. Tannenbaum grappled with this issue in his distinction between "bourgeois Zionism" and Labour Zionism.
33. See, for example, *Der Yiddisher Zhurnal*, 9 December 1919, p. 1; 29 March 1933, p. 1; and 31 March 1933, p. 1. Further evidence is provided in the interviews with Jacob Black, 1971 and 1984, and Ed Hammerstein, 1977.
34. See Ruth A. Frager, *Sweatshop Strife: Class, Ethnicity, and Gender in the Jewish Labour Movement of Toronto, 1900–1939* (Toronto: University of Toronto Press, 1992), pp. 55–76, for a detailed discussion of the relations between Jewish workers and Jewish manufacturers in Toronto's needle trades.

Law and Justice: The Case of Canada's Native People

The Six Nations Council, 1910. Many members of the Six Nations, believing themselves part of another sovereign nation, did not feel the need to become Canadian citizens.

By raising questions about the possible agendas behind certain statutes, social historians crossing into the realm of legal studies have sometimes challenged the soundness of Canadian democracy. While many scholars work within an intellectual framework linking law with attempts by governments to promote equity or effectively organize increasingly complex societies, that framework has been called into question by claims that a number of legal developments were aimed at strengthening the position of the economically or socially dominant. For example, some scholars have portrayed government welfare legislation as designed to co-opt a potentially disruptive lower class and avert the need to redress serious socio-economic divisions, and others have dwelt on a variety of statutes as reinforcing the patriarchal construction of society.

Both articles in this section uncover prejudices within Canada's legal system by focusing on the experiences of British Columbia Natives during the late nineteenth and early twentieth centuries. In Article 15, Tina Loo examines the state's attempts to ban the potlatch — the feast-*cum*-religious ceremony through which debts were paid and/or good fortune was shared — as demonstrating law concerned essentially with promoting assimilation and the hegemony of capitalism. Yet in order to retain legitimacy within society, Loo writes, the legal system had to project a sense of itself as promoting justice — something it did, in large part, through the formalities of written statutes, legal procedures, and the courtroom as theatre. Far from constraining British Columbia Natives, the system thereby provided them with a rhetorical opportunity — to frame their arguments against the anti-potlatch law in the terms of the very norms the statute was trying to promote.

In Article 16, R.M. Galois writes of the drive by governments in British Columbia during the early part of the twentieth century to encourage an economic growth that was principally for the benefit of white settlers and that had as consequence the Natives' being denied legal consideration when it came to the alienation of their property. But this consequence, argues Galois, sparked co-ordinated protest from various tribes, who proved themselves adept both at employing certain aspects of Canadian law and at finding allies within White society, and so achieved at least a measure of success.

These articles, and many others from a variety of historical subfields and other disciplines — including sociology, criminology, anthropology, and, of course, law — clearly demonstrate that high-sounding legal principles often not only failed to protect the vulnerable, but were used to support and promote norms that resulted in many people's being denied justice. By exploring the application of the law from a grass-roots perspective, one can come to a better understanding of present-day campaigns by some Native groups for self-government (including the right to live by tribal legal codes), and of the insistence by others that all groups must be protected by Canada's 1982 Charter of Rights and Freedoms, and that the Constitution's "notwithstanding clause," which permits governments to override the rights set forth in the Charter, must be eliminated.

QUESTIONS TO CONSIDER

1. In technical terms, what was wrong with the anti-potlatch laws?
2. From whom did Natives receive support for their right to hold the potlatch? Why? Did any arguments from these people match those put forward by Natives before the courts?
3. Can you think of other areas besides the treatment of Natives in which the support given by the law to social or economic norms has resulted in injustice?
4. What, if any, impact did the Indian Rights Association and the Nisga'a Land Committee have?
5. What were the strengths and weaknesses of the Native groups described by Galois, and are such factors still relevant in the campaigns conducted by Canada's aboriginal people?

SUGGESTED READINGS

Carter, Sarah. *Lost Harvests: Prairie Indian Reserve Farmers and Government Policy*. Montreal: McGill-Queen's University Press, 1990.

Chunn, Dorothy. *From Punishment to Doing Good: Family Courts and Socialized Justice in Ontario, 1880–1940*. Toronto: University of Toronto Press, 1992.

Dickason, Olive. *Canada's First Nations: A History of Founding Peoples from the Earliest Times*. Toronto: McClelland & Stewart, 1992.

Essays in the History of Canadian Law. 5 vols. Toronto: Osgoode Society, 1981–94.

Kaplan, William. *State and Salvation: The Jehovah's Witnesses and Their Fight for Civil Rights*. Toronto: University of Toronto Press, 1989.

Kealey, Gregory, and Reginald Whitaker, eds. *The R.C.M.P. Security Bulletins*. St. John's: Canadian Committee on Labour History, 1988– .

Loo, Tina, and Lorna R. McLean. eds. *Historical Perspectives on Law and Society in Canada*. Toronto: Copp Clark Longman, 1994.

Macleod, R.C., ed. *Lawful Authority: Readings on the History of Criminal Justice in Canada*. Toronto: Copp Clark Pitman, 1988.

Macleod, R.C., and David Schneiderman, eds. *Police Powers in Canada: The Evolution and Practice of Authority*. Toronto: University of Toronto Press, 1994.

Marquis, Greg. *Policing Canada's Century: A History of the Canadian Association of Chiefs of Police*. Toronto: University of Toronto Press, 1993.

Miller, J.R., *Skyscrapers Hide the Heavens: A History of Indian–White Relations in Canada*. Toronto: University of Toronto Press, 1991.

Smandych, R.C., C.J. Matthews, and S.J. Cox, comps. *Canadian Criminal Justice History: An Annotated Bibliography*. Toronto: University of Toronto Press, 1987.

Weinrich, Peter, comp. *Social Protest from the Left in Canada, 1870–1970: A Bibliography*. Toronto: University of Toronto Press, 1982.

FIFTEEN

Dan Cranmer's Potlatch: Law as Coercion, Symbol, and Rhetoric in British Columbia, 1884–1951

TINA LOO

For non-native historians, the criminalization of the potlatch, the resistance on the part of aboriginal peoples to the law's enforcement, and the recent renaissance of the practice illustrate the contact experience in microcosm.[1] For many white British Columbians in the late nineteenth and early twentieth centuries, the ritual was symbolic of the savagery and depravity of Indians. As a result, the potlatch became a lightning rod for the efforts of Christian missionaries bent on civilizing the province's native peoples. When they failed to convince Indians to give up their practice, both Protestant and Catholic clerics, sometimes supported by Indian converts, turned to the federal government, asking it to assist their efforts by outlawing the potlatch. The government complied, and in 1884 the apparatus of white domination was further reinforced when the Indian Act was amended to meet the wishes of British Columbia's missionaries. The efforts to suppress the potlatch were part of a larger attempt on the part of white society to use the law, as well as other institutions like schools, to assimilate native peoples into a Western, capitalist culture. For missionaries and Department of Indian Affairs administrators alike, moral improvement was not only necessary for the continued survival of Indians, but also the prerequisite to humanity. According to the Indian Act, an Indian was not considered a "person" until he or she demonstrated to the superintendent-general of Indian Affairs "the degree of civilization to which he or she has attained, and the character for integrity, morality and sobriety."[2] At that time, Indians could be enfranchised. When they were, however, they "ceased to be Indians."[3] Despite these invidious distinctions and the harm inflicted as a result, native peoples managed to resist the assimilationist efforts of white society to a degree and, in the case of the law against the potlatch, to witness the triumph of their own customary law (as they saw the potlatch) over the "Queen's law" in 1951, when the provision against potlatching was left out of the revised Indian Act.

Although it is impossible to separate issues relating to Indian–white relations from a study of the potlatch, I want to try to do so. Like scholars of native history, I also consider the potlatch "a site of struggle"; however, I am interested in this struggle less for what it can reveal about the relations between native and non-native peo-

Source: Excerpted from "Dan Cranmer's Potlatch: Law as Coercion, Symbol, and Rhetoric in British Columbia, 1884–1951," *Canadian Historical Review*, 73, 2 (1992): 125–65. Reprinted by permission of University of Toronto Press Incorporated.

ples per se, and more for what it can tell us about how the law works. For if nothing else, the potlatch provision of the Indian Act was a law, and its enforcement history can show us the nature of the power invested in statute law and the courts as well as the consequences of its exercise.

There has been considerable interest from scholars working in a variety of disciplines, including history, in exploring the nature of the law's power. The historical literature focuses on two particular aspects of the law's power: its coercive and its symbolic or ideological dimensions. Because the coercive power of the law flows from the monopoly the state has on the use of legitimate force, some historians contend that those whose interests are represented by the state have those interests reinforced by and through statute and common law. Thus, despite the law's pretensions to neutrality, it creates and imposes a certain kind of order: it represents and reinforces the interests of whites, Anglo-Saxons, heterosexuals, the propertied, the married, and men — or any combination of these groups. People who do not fit these categories are labelled "other," and are subject to legal regulation and sanctions aimed at reinforcing a particular social, economic, and political order.

Other historians have shifted the focus away from the interests upheld and furthered by the law to how the law manages to compromise its neutrality but still retain its legitimacy. These scholars, while acknowledging the coercive dimension of the law, point to its symbolic and ideological dimensions as the key to understanding the nature of its power. Douglas Hay and E.P. Thompson, two of the most influential writers taking this line, argue that the power of the law cannot rest on naked force because obedience to the law depends on a continued belief in its legitimacy.[4] People must believe that despite their condition they will be treated equally before the law, and that those who administer it as well as the laws they enforce are reasonably fair. Belief in the rule of law is achieved and maintained by the theatrical and ritualistic features of courtroom procedure that mask the interests upheld by the law. However, as Thompson points out, the rule of law cannot be a complete fiction: there has to be some substance to it. In fact, he argues, the ruling class in eighteenth-century England were forced to trade some of their power for the legitimacy that underpinned their continuing right to govern. Thus, though the law was biased, the fact that its power depended on maintaining a belief in its neutrality meant there were very real limits to its being used to further ruling-class interests. Ultimately, the law's ideological nature tempered its power and the potential for abuse.[5]

Coercion and ideology, however, do not completely explain the power of the law or how it works. Focusing on the law's coercive dimension can reduce those who are the subjects of regulation to mere objects or victims who possess little agency. What little they do have is limited to resistance: reacting to the actions and agenda of the powerful, whoever they may be. While it is important to take notice of resistance on the part of the so-called "powerless," it is also important to recognize that they have the capacity to act as well as react. Similarly, while it is necessary and important to acknowledge the symbolic and ideological dimensions of the law, we should not make too much of them. People do not have to believe in the rule of law to obey it or use it; nor should their obedience or willingness to participate in the legal process be interpreted as an indication of their belief in the rule of law and the legitimacy of the larger system of authority of which it is a part. How else can we explain why people who are oppressed by the law, like women for instance, or people for whom the common law is culturally alien, like Indians, use it?

False consciousness and Gramsci's concept of hegemony take us a certain distance in understanding why and how people can be the authors of their own oppression, but they do not explain why people participate in a system of law that is alien to them. Perhaps there may be a simpler answer to both questions: people obey and use the law because it is in their interest to do so. While this is hardly a revelation, it seems a point worth noting because it has been lost in the debate over the nature of the power of the law and how it works. Because an individual's interests shift constantly and are contingent on a set of equally shifting, immediate, and fairly narrow circumstances, it is possible for that person simultaneously to maintain a belief in something as fuzzy and abstract as the rule of law (or any other ideology for that matter, like democracy, socialism, or equality, for instance) while acting in a manner that is completely inconsistent with that belief. Thus, there can be a dichotomy between belief and action that is sustained and explained by interest.

I want to explore the nature of the law's power and how it works from a perspective different from those discussed, but which take them into account while, I hope, avoiding their shortcomings. Using the potlatch provision of the Indian Act as an example, I argue that although this statute had coercive as well as symbolic and ideological dimensions, its enforcement revealed that the law and the legal process can be profitably viewed as a system of rhetoric or a way of arguing. The potlatch law certainly was an attempt to impose a certain kind of order on native peoples, and the reaction to its problematic enforcement by the province's missionaries and Indian agents certainly revealed the law's symbolic and ideological dimensions. However, the manner in which both the prosecution and the prosecuted argued the cases arising from the law's enforcement illustrated that argument or rhetoric is central to an understanding of how the law works and the nature of its power.

To understand how the law is a way of arguing, we need first to understand what arguing is. Arguing is a way of organizing our experience; it is a way of understanding the world. More importantly, arguments are also made so that we can make a decision about our experience and act accordingly — or, more precisely, arguments are made to convince others to see things as we do and to act in certain ways. But how do we argue? What makes an argument effective? How do arguments motivate people to act? What, in short, gives an argument power?

In answering these questions, it is useful to make a distinction between arguing in life and in the law. In life, the arguments we find convincing are those in which the teller makes her point of view and actions seem commonsensical, natural, and rational. Strong arguments have the effect of resonating with the listener so that, if placed in the same situation, the listener would see the situation similarly and act similarly to the teller. But what is involved in making arguments resonate? Primarily, arguments are made; they are self-consciously created by the teller. Making an effective argument requires understanding the audience to which the argument will be presented and manipulating the story so that it evokes certain sensibilities in the audience that forge a connection between it and the teller. For instance, depending on my reading of the audience, depending on whom I am talking to, I emphasize different aspects of my work: I can tell my colleagues about my research using a certain kind of language and an implicit frame of reference, but when my friends' children ask me what I do, my story changes: I tell them I teach. In neither case am I being untruthful; but in both I have adjusted my story in accordance with what I think will resonate with them.

Arguments are central to the law, and in the law, as in life, powerful arguments depend on the teller's ability to play to members of the audience and to evoke certain sensibilities in them. But arguing in the law is different in one very important respect: in framing legal arguments, the teller has to abide by rules of legal rhetoric. Legal arguments involve using a particular language, working within a set of rules of evidence and procedure that determine what can be said and how and when it can be said, as well as determining what value and meaning can be placed on those facts that are put forward. Equally importantly, and the point I will focus on, legal arguments must address the issues raised by the laws that govern the actions in question: Do the actions of the defendant match the description of the behaviour outlined by the law? What was the defendant's state of mind when she committed the act in question? What did the defendant think she was doing? What was the intent? In addressing these questions, legal arguments implicitly accept the terms of debate imposed by the law. There is no discussion of whether the law in question is just — that is deemed a political question, and outside the realm of the law — nor does a discussion of the larger social, political, or economic injustice of the situation that led both parties to get into the situation before the court occupy a central place. Trial courts are courts of law, not courts of justice. To a certain extent, then, the rules of legal rhetoric (the rules that spell out how we must argue in the law) result in removing actions from their social context. Though decontextualizing the actions of the contesting parties is done to clarify the issues, it has other implications: it shapes the questions that are asked and, in so doing, shapes the picture of the relationship between the two parties and the possibilities for the resolution of their dispute.

The necessity of adhering to the rules of legal rhetoric — adopting legal conventions and addressing the questions the law deems relevant — involves adopting something classicist, linguist, and lawyer James Boyd White calls a "culture of argument."[6] This culture of argument, like any other culture, creates a particular way of seeing the world that makes certain choices for action appear reasonable and thus possible and others not. We usually call the way of seeing the world that emerges from the legal process the "truth," but given the conventions that shape it, it would appear that "truth" is constructed in the courtroom and is partial at best — just like my responses to the question of what I do. That, however, is the point: as sociologist Carol Smart notes, "the power of the law lies in its claim to the truth."[7] Even though the construction of events on which a legal decision is made is partial, we still label that construction as the "truth" and the means of reaching it (the rules of legal rhetoric) truth-finding rather than truth-making.

Because the power of argument is creative, because it is all about making a case, seeing the law in this way opens up the possibility that people who are the subject of legal regulation can act as well as react. As will be discussed, the potlatch law was certainly oppressive (it had a coercive dimension) and symbolized white values, but the Indians who practised the ritual not only had success at avoiding prosecution, but also were successful in arguing their cases before the court.

....

A potlatch is a ceremony given by a family or extended family to display its hereditary possessions such as dances, songs, and carvings. Potlatches are usually given on the occasion of a birth, marriage, or death, but because a social debt is incurred by the attending guests, potlatches can be given simply to fulfil a social obligation. Dan

Cranmer held his potlatch to celebrate Emma Cranmer's "repurchase." He distributed goods to his wife's family and her relatives.[8] During the ceremony, the hosts might relate the genealogy of their hereditary privileges, introducing members of their family in the process, and perhaps bestowing new names (the equivalent of social ranks) on them. The formal display of those privileges follows: dances are performed and songs sung. The affair ends with the host distributing gifts to the guests. Guests are important to the ceremony because they validate the rights to the privileges displayed by the hosts and, ultimately, to the status associated with those privileges.[9]

According to anthropologists, the ceremony is a mechanism for social integration.[10] It publicly identifies people as belonging to a certain social group and defines each of their positions within that group. As well, the social order of the guests is recognized as gifts are distributed in proportion to social status. The potlatch did not, however, create social status; it was simply a way of proving and acknowledging existing status and changes in status (the giving of names, births, marriages, and deaths).[11] No matter how many potlatches a person gave, he could not alter his status beyond what he acquired through marriage or inheritance.[12] Having acquired a certain social rank, however, a person was expected to behave in a manner commensurate with his position or to risk embarrassment. Thus, a person stood to lose, but not to gain rank through potlatching.

Of course, the ceremony did change as a result of European contact.[13] Because the potlatch was a social ceremony that relied on material goods, important modifications came about in response to new economic conditions. In the late eighteenth century, Northwest Coast Indians began to participate in a European commercial economy, and the Kwakiutl potlatch reflected this change. There was an influx of new consumer goods that largely replaced many of the traditional gifts that were given away in the pre-contact potlatch. Most notably, woollen blankets became a chief item of exchange. But in the early twentieth century things like sacks of flour, mass-produced bolts of fabric, outboard motors, and fishing skiffs were also commonly distributed.[14]

Not only did the kinds of goods change, but their volume increased.[15] The new economy that Northwest Coast natives participated in was resource-based: trapping, sealing, and fishing were the main occupations for both Indians and non-Indians alike. Though these tasks were tied to a larger commercial capitalist economy, and in that sense were quite different from what existed prior to European contact, trapping, sealing, and fishing were all fields of native expertise. So Indians prospered — at least initially.[16] Because of their economic success, they were able to buy more goods — more blankets, more bolts of cloth, more flour, and more canoes. The potlatch expanded.

It was this expanded version of the potlatch that caught the attention of missionaries, some Christianized Indians, and Indian agents, who lobbied the federal government in the 1880s to put an end to the ceremony. Though the federal government believed a proclamation "discountenancing the custom of 'potlaches' [sic]" would be sufficient, I.W. Powell, British Columbia's superintendent of Indian affairs, disagreed. Acquainting Christian Indians "with the 'Queen's objection' to the potlatch [sic] . . . no doubt had a good effect," he told his Ottawa superiors, "but this class forms a small part of the whole Indian population, and to be effective in reaching all, I think some legislative enactment preventing the practice of the 'potlach' [sic] will be necessary. Otherwise, the proclamation will, really, have little effect on putting a stop to the custom."[17] Gustave Donckele, the Roman Catholic missionary at Cowichan, agreed. "Stringent measures" were necessary to put an end to the "heathen practice."[18] His secular counterpart at Cowichan, Indian agent William Lomas, believed that while some of his native charges opposed the potlatch, without a law they lacked the "moral courage" to refuse to participate outright.[19]

Powell, Donckele, and Lomas each considered the law and its sanctions a prerequisite to the progress and civilization of the native population. Their comments resonated with the same Victorian faith in the transformative capacity of the law that underlay other social reform agendas. If their confidence in the law as an instrument of reform reflected part of the progressive spirit, so too was the object of their energies. What the province's missionaries and Indian agents found so reprehensible about the potlatch was its singular combination of profligacy, debauchery, and squalor. "Individuals . . . in accordance with the well-known custom of giving away absolutely all they happen to possess . . . reduce themselves to beggery [sic] and distress," wrote Methodist missionary Cornelius Bryant in 1884, "but beyond a mere impoverishment, and what is much worse, [are] the physical misery and evils resulting from exposure of the elements in travelling to and from these 'potlatches,' which they do in their canoes in all kinds of weather, and the debauchery produced by intoxication, in which they often indulge upon such occasions leaves no doubt as to the personal demoralization which follows these native feasts." "Hapless children and aged people" were denied the "comforts of convenient homes and wholesome food, owing to [the] reckless and spendthrift customs which are maintained at the potlatches," he concluded.[20]

Furthermore, native hosts often resorted to illegal means — either theft or prostitution — to procure the goods they could not afford. "A man will say to his wife," argued British Columbia reserve commissioner Gilbert Malcolm Sproat, "nay to his maiden daughter, that before the spring or other appointed time he must have so many dollars for his proposed 'Potlach' [sic] and they in this way, and I believe more than from licentious desire, are forced into prostitution."[21] Moreover, the large groups of Indians that participated in the ceremony were themselves a threat to order. There were about 300 guests at Dan Cranmer's potlatch, but figures four, five, and six times that number were not unheard of — numbers that could be greater than the surrounding white population. Missionaries like Bryant and agents like Lomas contended these potlatches quickly turned into drunken orgies that lasted for days, or riots in which valuable property was destroyed. There were even reports of cannibalism and of the participants biting the flesh of their all-too-alive fellows. All told, the potlatch was "the parent of numerous vices which eat out the heart of the people"[22] — a "worse than useless custom."[23]

The lobbying efforts of British Columbia's missionaries and Indian agents were successful. In 1884 the federal government passed an amendment to the Indian Act making the potlatch an indictable criminal offence. The relevant section read as follows: "Every Indian or other person who engages in or assists in celebrating the Indian festival known as the 'Potlatch' or the Indian dance known as the 'Tamanawas' is guilty of misdemeanour, and shall be liable to imprisonment of a term not more than six months nor less than two months in any gaol or place of confinement; and any Indian or other person who encourages, either directly or indirectly, an Indian or other Indians to get up such a festival or dance, or to celebrate the same, shall be guilty of a like offence, and shall be liable to the same punishment."[24]

Unfortunately, no one had bothered to define what a "potlatch" was. This ambiguity turned out to be the grounds for an appeal in 1889. Charged with potlatching by Kwawkewlth Agency agent Reginald Pidcock, Hemasak pleaded guilty and was sentenced to six months' imprisonment in August 1889. Matthew Baillie Begbie's Supreme Court quashed the conviction on appeal, however, citing the ambiguity in the statute as the reason. "A plea of guilty means guilty of the Act forbidden by the Statute," the chief justice reasoned. "It is by no means clear that it was fully explained to the defendant what the Statute forbids. It would seem that the Statute should set out what acts constitute the forbidden festival. Until a defendant knows what those forbidden Acts are, how can he say whether he committed them or not?"[25]

It was not until 1895 that the Indian Act was amended again to address Begbie's critique. It read: "Every Indian or other person who engages in, or assists in celebrating or encourages either directly or indirectly another to celebrate any Indian festival, dance or ceremony of which the giving away or paying back of money, goods or articles takes place before, at or after the celebration of the same, or who engages in or assists in any celebration or dance of which the wounding or mutilation of the dead or living body of any human being or animal forms a part or is a feature of is guilty of an indictable offence and is liable to imprisonment for a term not exceeding six months and not less than two months. Providing that nothing in this section shall be construed to prevent the holding of any agricultural show or exhibition or giving of prizes thereat."[26] The amended statute appeared straightforward enough. The illegal acts consisted of giving away goods or money in association with a festival, dance, or ceremony, or the wounding of the dead or living body of a human or other animal. As will be discussed, those charged with enforcing the act did not find the amended version any easier to administer.

There were two other amendments. The first, made in 1914, was an additional attempt to restrict potlatching by outlawing the wearing of aboriginal costume (unless expressly permitted by the superintendent of Indian affairs or his official representative) and by making dancing off an Indian's home reserve illegal.[27] The second and more significant attempt came four years later, in 1918, when wartime exigencies made Ottawa even more sensitive to what it considered the improvident aspects of the potlatch and the need to eliminate it. In a circular distributed to all agents in British Columbia, Duncan Campbell Scott reminded his field officers of "the urgent need for conservation in all directions . . . no wasteful practice or mode of life can be countenanced." To this end, the department expected its agents to exercise to the full the powers given to them under the newly amended act — powers that made potlatching a summary, instead of an indictable, offence. Each agent in his concurrent capacity as a justice of the peace could now try to convict Indians for violations of the potlatch provision instead of simply committing them for trial.[28]

Of the many troubling aspects of native culture, the potlatch seemed to offend European sensibilities most deeply. The ceremony provoked an astonishingly emotional and protracted response that filled thousands of pages of correspondence and was manifested in a series of restrictive laws that remained in force for more than half a century. This action reflected and was rooted in the deep play of anxieties about the essential order of things in white society that were brought to the surface by the close juxtaposition of another seemingly alien culture.

For whites, the ceremony united and challenged two central ideas around and through which they constituted themselves: economics and law. The argument presented by those who lobbied for legislation outlawing the potlatch was primarily an economic one, though in characteristic Victorian fashion economics and morality were intertwined and mutually reinforcing standards of behaviour. Potlatching appeared wasteful and excessive — the antithesis to the twin pillars of the Protestant work ethic: industry and sobriety.

But was it? It appears that few Indians were reduced to complete penury through their participation. In fact, the potlatch was a far more ambiguous ceremony than the self-confident Victorian language of the missionaries and agents would have us believe. If the ritual were as decadent, debilitating, and demoralizing as its opponents charged, it is hard to imagine the practice continuing for long, for in short order few could afford to participate. But the potlatch did continue and, even more significantly, among the Kwakiutl it expanded. The reasons for this lay, as I noted, in their successful participation in the province's resource economy. Indians prospered, and the increased accumulations of goods that preceded Kwakiutl potlatches were not a sign of savage profligacy but, in many ways, of their successful accommodation and embodiment of La-Violette's Protestant work ethic — or at least a capitalist one. The anthropologists certainly thought so. People like Edward Sapir, Harlan Smith, and Franz Boas protested against the potlatch provisions of the Indian Act. In their opinion, the law was flawed in part not because it was ethnocentric, but because its architects failed to appreciate the broad similarities between the potlatch and modern Western economic behaviour. If Indians were economic people just like whites and their potlatch was a central economic institution, then neither they nor their culture was in need of reform through the law. In fact, the law against the potlatch stood as an obstacle to the integration of native peoples into white society. Sapir referred to the potlatch as a "system of credit" and a "business transaction." "Bankruptcy" would be the result of enforcing the law. "The abolition of the potlatch and the consequent inability of the owner of a copper to utilize his wealth works the same sort of havoc that the wanton destruction of a white man's checks [and] drafts [would]," he told Duncan Campbell Scott.[29] Franz Boas, after some thirty years' observation of the southern Kwakiutl, echoed his colleagues' comments, describing the ceremony as "a return on an interest-bearing investment,"[30] and suggested that "a policy might be developed in which the values invested in the potlatch might be administered more efficiently and wisely by what might be called a tribal bank."[31] By drawing analogies between the potlatch and capitalist behaviour, these anthropologists offered a way to make sense of an alien ritual. But in choosing capitalist economic behaviour as constituting the familiar, they revealed the assumptions of their own culture; their sense of what was "natural" and hence powerful.

The problem with and the significance of the ceremony to white society lay in the distributive aspect of the ceremony. Accumulation was laudable, but the way Indians disposed of their goods stood as a radical counterpoint to the existing material order in white society. When Dan Cranmer handed out jewellery, blankets, sacks of flour, pool tables, and gas launches, or simply gave away hundreds of dollars in envelopes, he and countless others who did the same thing up and down the coast displayed an attitude towards material goods that was simultaneously familiar and alien to white society. Working to consume and accumulate was intelligible behaviour, but when Indians gave away or destroyed all they had worked for they debased the very commodity — property — around which white society was constructed. Little wonder Gilbert Malcolm Sproat called the potlatch a "huge incubus."[32]

Potlatching also provoked a reaction from white British Columbians because it was the subject of law. As the DIA and those directly involved in enforcing the law against the potlatch discovered, the law's power was double-edged, a characteristic that made it an unwieldy tool of control. By designating the potlatch illegal, the Indian Act sharpened an old and ongoing conflict between Europeans and Indians. Articulating the conflict between them in the form of law made it harder to ignore, live with, or resolve disputes informally. Bringing certain kinds of behaviour under the formal gaze of the law meant that violations could not be ignored, because if they were, the effectiveness of those who administered it would be undercut. The DIA and its officers had a law they had to enforce but were afraid to, because if enforcement did not result in convictions, Indians would lose all respect for them. If enforcement were not even attempted, however, the same thing would occur. Frustrated with the double-edged nature of the law, the Rev. Dr Sutherland, head of the Methodist missionary organization — whose missionaries had been among those who lobbied for the potlatch law in the first place — told the superintendent-general in 1897 that he would rather do without it. "I would be quite willing, so far as the Indians are concerned, to meet the evil of the Potlatch entirely by moral force and without asking any aid from legal enactments," he insisted, "but since the Government has seen fit to put a law upon the Statute Book prohibiting the Potlatch ceremony, the very existence of that law, when not in force, is a hindrance in our way, and the appeals and exhortations of the missionary are met by sneering reference to the fact, or what seemed to the Indian to be a fact, that the government is not really opposed to Potlatching."[33]

Sutherland's remarks were motivated by more than twenty years of ineffectual enforcement. In fact, with the exception of the burst of activity shortly before and after the Cranmer potlatch, neither the Department of Indian Affairs nor the province pursued the enforcement of the potlatch provision of the Indian Act particularly vigorously. Very little of the charged atmosphere of moral indignation that led to criminalization of the ceremony translated into real action. Between 1884 and 1895 it appears that only two people were tried for violating the potlatch law and only one was convicted. Even after the 1895 amendment, indictments do not appear to have increased very much. Seventeen people were indicted for potlatching from 1895 to 1918. It was not until 1918 (when the offence was made a summary one) that the act was enforced with any real effect. In the four years from 1918 to 1922, 135 individuals were charged with violations of the potlatch law. The crackdown reached its peak with the Village Island arrests and fell off again (from 1922 to 1935 only ten individuals were indicted), even though potlatching continued, and perhaps even enjoyed a renaissance.[34] The statute remained on the books until 1951.

Initially, a jurisdictional dispute between federal and provincial authorities over who was responsible for enforcement hindered the efforts of the department's agents in prosecuting offenders. Though Indians were wards of the federal government, the enforcement of criminal law was a provincial jurisdiction. With neither level of government willing to assume responsibility — that is, willing to underwrite the costs of enforcement — agents like Harry Guillod of Ucluelet on Vancouver Island's west coast felt their hands were tied. Without a lockup or a constable to aid him in 1886, Guillod found it difficult, if not impossible, to enforce the law. Ottawa told him to petition Victoria, and the province referred him back to Ottawa.[35]

There were, however, deeper problems. Even after the jurisdictional dispute was resolved, judges were reluctant to convict, and when they did convict they were reluctant to bring the full brunt of the law to bear on the guilty. County court judge W.W.F. MacInnes told Indian agent William Halliday "that a penalty for potlatching would not be popular . . . and he doubted very much if any judge in BC would do anything but give suspended sentences."[36] Fifteen years later Halliday was still complaining. "You are aware," he told BC superintendent of Indian affairs Ditchburn, "that our Judges are inclined to deal very leniently in affairs of this kind."[37]

The reluctance of the courts to convict and their leniency in dealing with offenders reflected a degree of popular sympathy towards the Indians and the potlatch that stemmed from the ceremony's ambiguous nature. The law seemed to be drawing distinctions where none existed. Like the anthropologists, many other British Columbians saw nothing wrong with a ceremony that was, in many ways, similar to some of their own rituals. "The Indian, who is always having the white man held up to him as a worthy example, argues that the white man calls his friends at Christmas time & feasts them & has Xmas trees & gives presents & he dresses up a man & calls him Father Xmas & says he brings presents, etc." West Coast Agency agent A.W. Neill pointed out to A.W. Vowell, BC's superintendent of Indian affairs, in 1904. "Where is the justice in forbidding them the same species of amusements?"[38]

In addition to sentiments like these that reflected a certain empathy towards the Indians, there was a great deal of resistance to enforcing the potlatch law from the non-native residents of the locales where the ceremony was practised — the people one might expect to be most opposed to the potlatch. Their opposition was rooted in a pragmatic concern with economy and order. Quite simply, the potlatch meant business for many local merchants. The blankets, bolts of cloth, sacks of flour, and other items that were given away had to be obtained somewhere, and, despite the accusations of the missionaries to the contrary, Indians usually purchased them at the local general store. In fact, missionaries and agents commonly complained, as Cornelius Bryant did, that "the good intentions of the Government, in seeking to suppress so pernicious a practice . . . [are] discouraged and opposed simply for the purpose of selling a few hundred dollars worth of goods."[39]

Other than this material consideration, non-native residents were also concerned with the issue of order. Their concept of order differed, however, from that of the missionaries who had spearheaded the campaign for the potlatch law. These people were not so much concerned about the moral degradation and the future progress of the Indians, and the threat this posed to creating a Christian social order; instead, they were preoccupied with avoiding violent conflict. If the potlatch law were enforced rigidly, they felt, there was a chance that the local Indians might rise up, and they would pay the consequences. The threat of violent resistance seemed much more tangible than the moral and ethical danger posed by allowing the potlatch to continue.

The sympathy towards the potlatch and the resistance to enforcement from those who stood to gain materially and in terms of safety made securing convictions uncertain and created problems for the Department of Indian Affairs. Amending the law would have little effect if the courts were reluctant to enforce it. In fact, changes could do more harm than good. The department was unwilling to undertake any amendments or to consider repeal. Any alteration, they thought, would be construed by the Indians as a sign of weakness and would thus undermine the authority of the "Queen's Law" as a whole. As Vowell told Ottawa, when it came to Indians and the law, "vacillation always produces disrespect and a thorough want of confidence in the source from which it emanates."[40] Acquittals were potentially even more damaging than any "vacillation" in enforcing the potlatch law. If convictions were not secured, the department informed a missionary who had complained about the lack of enforcement, "more harm than good [may] result from prosecution, as it would give the Indians more courage to go on with their practices."[41] Agent William Halliday reported that a quashed conviction gave Alert Bay "offenders great jubilation and a decided moral victory."[42]

In fact, it was this "moral victory" that disturbed whites the most. Not only did it lead Indians to think that the law was "as weak as a baby," as they told Napoleon Fitzstubbs, but it also raised doubts in white minds about the distinction the law had drawn between civilization and savagery — about the validity of the social boundaries that gave meaning and coherence to white society.[43] The potlatch provoked concern because it was a focal point of the law — the other cultural system that, along with economics, shapes the ways whites see. Though the two are conflated somewhat in this paper, the function of the law consists of more than direct control through punishments and sanctions: the law also plays an important symbolic role. Laws express the rules that limit and shape behaviour and expectations, but they are also expressions of ethical norms. Thus, not only are we ruled by law, but law also embodies and articulates the broad ideas around which we are constituted as a society. In an important sense, the function of the potlatch provision of the Indian Act can be considered separately from its coercive effects. This law was a public articulation by white society of its own social norms and boundaries. In this formulation, the act of legislation becomes a symbolic act of self-determination, not one of control.

This argument for the symbolic function of the law is particularly compelling in the context of British Columbia. In other societies, the job of setting out social boundaries — the job of defining a group identity — is done by religious and educational institutions, to name two, over a long period of time. But the province was still a young place in the late nineteenth and early twentieth centuries, very much on the frontier, experiencing rapid and telescoped growth, and possessed of a culturally diverse population ("white" obscures that diversity) and few established institutions that could claim to speak for and define this amorphous "European" group. In a context like this, it might be possible that the law — or perhaps the act of making law — played a central role in adumbrating the social and ethical boundaries of white British Columbia.

The symbolic aspect of the law is not completely independent of its coercive effect, however. Enforcement does matter, as the law against the potlatch so graphically shows. The ambiguity surrounding the ceremony was manifested in a reluctance to prosecute violations fully and, as a result, enforcement was problematic. This not only weakened the authority of the Indian Act and those charged with administering it, but also compromised the authority of the law as a whole and the social order it symbolized and upheld. Given this, Sproat's "huge incubus" appeared even more threatening.

Enforcing the law against the potlatch proved problematic not only because white British Columbians were divided in their attitudes about the ceremony, but also because of the way the law works. The power of the law rests in its ability to define issues, set the terms of the debate and resolution, and provide the measures for assessing the fairness of the outcome. Though some scholars consider that the law and the "legal method" — the way in which cases are decided — are closed systems that tend to perpetuate the status quo under the guise of real, objective enquiry and neutrality, this does not always have to be the case. Both prosecutor and prosecuted had to work on the same narrow terrain, and in the case of the potlatch trials it was those on the side of the prosecution — the so-called powerful — who found themselves at a disadvantage.

The potlatch prosecutions reveal how the power of the law lay in its capacity to set the terms of debate by selectively limiting the terrain of the inquiry. From 1884 on what was at issue in these cases was the interpretation of words like "potlatch," "participation," "festival," and "ceremony." What did these words mean and did the specific instance of behaviour under scrutiny by the court conform to the actions defined by these words?

If the original legislation had failed to specify just what sort of behaviour constituted a potlatch (in *Hemasak*), those charged with enforcing the law or defending Indians indicted for violations of it felt that the amended legislation was the opposite: it was too inclusive. "It would seem," wrote Dickie and DeBeck, the lawyers for the Alert Bay Kwakiutl in 1922, "that the word 'Indian' does not limit the dance, festival or other ceremony to something which is peculiarly Indian, but might include any ceremony participated in by Indians."

> The assumption is a direct inference from the last part of section 149, which excludes from the operation of the statute any "agricultural show or exhibition." An agricultural show or exhibition is not a ceremony which is peculiar to Indians[;] in fact it is not an Indian ceremony at all in the sense that if it was necessary to exclude it from the Act the only conclusion that can be drawn is that an agricultural show or exhibition, if participated in by Indians, would otherwise come within the section; consequently, any other ceremony would . . .
>
> It will thus be seen that the scope of the law is extremely wide and not only is it a complete prohibition to carry on any of their tribal customs, but also they are technically liable if they take part in any transaction of a ceremonious nature, whether the transaction is of Indian origin or not, should such transaction involve a gift or payment of kind.

"It is respectfully submitted," the solicitors concluded, "that no blue law was ever so wide in its scope, or so oppressive."[44] Dickie and DeBeck's interpretation was supported by Chief Justice Hunter of the provincial Supreme Court in *R. v. George Scow et al.*, another potlatching case originating in the Kwawkewlth Agency that was heard by the superior court on appeal. Though Hunter sustained the convictions of Scow and his four compatriots, he noted that "'dance' and 'festival' were not words describing a class which would limit 'ceremonies' to events of a like nature, but that 'other ceremonies' might include any ceremonies whatever."[45]

Equally troublesome was the ambiguity surrounding three words in the statute: "participation," "festival," and "ceremony." William Halliday considered the interpretation given to "participation" by the courts of central importance in putting down the potlatch, and asked Ottawa for a definition. "In our courts in British Columbia, unfortunately, we are overstocked with lawyers who are addicted to what is commonly called hair-splitting on the meaning of the word."

> I take it that the wording of the Act means that any Indian who is present at an Indian dance off his own reserve is guilty of an offense, but I also feel sure that if a conviction were entered that it would be upset on appeal, unless the offenders actually danced themselves . . .

> The Indians are taking subterfuge under the dance question for attending what I believe are potlatches, but I hesitate to have any prosecutions made in this section . . . If the word "participation" does not mean "is present at" may I humbly recommend that these words be added[?][46]

Halliday's successor, M.S. Todd, also considered the meaning of "participation" given by the courts an obstacle to enforcement. Several Indians he had convicted for potlatching retained a lawyer and filed for appeal on the interpretation of "participation." In Todd's opinion, however, "any Indian in a Community Indian dance hall with a blanket or regalia on is participating in that dance . . . It is not necessary to be dancing on the floor to be participating. The definition of community is participation and to be present in the [community] hall with regalia on must be participating."[47]

If "participation" was unclear, defining what comprised an illegal "festival" or "ceremony" was even more problematic, as Agent Neill pointed out. "Half a dozen men joined together and invited a few of a neighbouring band," he reported: "They came, spent a few days, got small presents, mostly in food, had dancing and feasting at night but went about their business in the day & in less than a week it was over. Had it been called . . . 'a few friends for Xmas' no one could have found much fault."[48] The problem Neill described was brought into sharp focus several years later in the Cariboo. When Chief Isadore and Thomas and Mary Ketlo were arrested and convicted for holding an "Easter potlatch" in May 1928, they appealed and were granted a *de novo* hearing before the Cariboo District County Court in June. Their counsel asked that the case be dismissed, arguing that the section of the Indian Act dealing with the potlatch criminalized an "'*Indian* festival,' an '*Indian* dance,' or 'other *Indian* ceremony,'" and that the crown had not established that what had occurred fell under any of these categories. For its part, the crown held that what Isadore and the Ketlos had staged could be designated an "other ceremony." H.E.A. Robertson did not clarify the act's wording, but ruled in the appellants' favour, noting that the Indians' "supper followed by a 'white man's dance' did not constitute a ceremony."[49]

In other cases, however, the debate was even narrower, and cases were decided on the basis of "technicalities." For instance, Begbie quashed the conviction in *Hemasak* because the accused was incarcerated on an improper warrant of committal.[50] Johnny Moon and his father Chief Harry had the charges against them dropped because of "informalities in the information and the warrant."[51] Six Indians of the Nakwakto band at Blunden Harbour had their convictions overturned on appeal because Agent Halliday had filled out the warrants of committal and conviction improperly, neglecting to state the jurisdiction of his court and the fact he was acting as a justice of the peace.[52]

In none of these cases did the legal debate revolve around the larger social issues of justice or equity. Because there was an implicit acceptance of the law as it was, trials centred on determining whether the action in question constituted the illegal behaviour outlined in the statute. Although the system of argument employed by the law narrowed the terms of debate, it did not determine the outcome of trials. The wording of statutes and legal "technicalities" had a strategic potential that could be exploited by Indians as well as whites. When Indians did appeal to the law in the case of the potlatch prosecutions, they were often successful in securing suspended sentences or in having their convictions overturned on appeal. They showed themselves to be skilled legal players: they employed counsel,[53] certainly were not over-awed by the law's magisterial qualities, and knew its subtleties well enough to take advantage of it.

In the fall of 1913 Halliday informed Ottawa that he expected "some difficulty shortly with regard to the Potlatch as the Indians have determined to put the matter to the test . . . [T]he man who is giving the potlatch stated at a meeting of the Indians that . . . someone must test the matter and he would be the Agent by which it would be tested."[54] Far from shying away from confrontation, the Indians involved — Johnny Bagwany and Ned Harris — sought to test the law on its own terms.[55] If the exchange between Halliday and one Kwakiutl is any indication, some native people had a well-developed sense of those terms. In relation to some recent arrests of Cape Mudge Indians for potlatching, Halliday wanted to know "what the chances would be if some of the most reputable men of the Cape Mudge Indians . . . should be called as witnesses . . . would they tell the truth?" The Indian's reply was highly suggestive. "I do not think they would lie. I think they would not tell anything at all," he said. "You know they would have a lawyer to defend them, and the lawyer would not allow anyone to ask them 'were you present at the dance given by this man, or did you receive anything from him?' This would be a leading question, and the lawyer for the defence would not allow it to be asked. They would be hostile witnesses, and it would be a matter of very great difficulty to get any of them to give evidence."[56] His familiarity with the legal process and its terminology ("leading question" and "hostile witness") demonstrates a degree of skill that could easily be used to resist the law. And it was.

Nowhere was this familiarity with the law put to better effect than in the wake of the Cranmer arrests. Apparently, on the advice of a Vancouver lawyer named W.R. Vaughan, the Alert Bay Indians broke the potlatch into two parts to avoid prosecution. They would have the dancing and ceremonial part publicly, as usual, but dispense the gifts later (sometimes six months later), privately, and often door-to-door. Harry Speck, or Spike, chief of the Klowitsis band, did just this when he held a potlatch on Turnour Island in 1931. "He told the Indians that acting on the advice of his lawyer he did not intend to give anything away for at least six months after the dance and then his lawyer advised him he would be free of prosecution."[57] The six-month period was in reference to the criminal code provision that prohibited prosecutions for summary offences if six months had elapsed after the commission of the illegal act.[58]

The "disjointed"[59] or "bootleg"[60] potlatch was one strategy Indians used to get around the law. Another technique that was employed on at least one occasion was to have the agent distribute the goods. One Billy McDuff presented himself before the agent and asked for permission to distribute some 300 sacks of flour he had purchased from the Sointula Co-operative Store to the Kingcome Inlet Indians. Indian agent Todd refused, at which time McDuff "stated he did not wish to have anything further to do with it and asked if I would not take the flour over and make distribution myself." Todd agreed. It was only later that he found out that McDuff "had already distributed to four other tribes and Kingcome was the last, which would have completed this part of the potlatch. In view of this, it appears that I would be placing myself in this position — I would complete the potlatch by distributing to these Indians . . . and by doing so would help him evade the penalty of the law yet fulfil his obligations."[61]

Though both the Department of Indian Affairs and the native people who were charged with violating the Indian Act by potlatching were forced to frame their arguments within the very circumscribed boundaries provided by the law, it was the prosecution who found themselves disadvantaged. In confining both sides to addressing very narrow issues — to addressing the meaning of words and "technicalities" — the system of argument used by the court removed the potlatch from much of the social context that gave it meaning. The rules of legal rhetoric resolved conflict by reducing disputes to their bare bones; by "skeletonizing" them. In the case of the potlatch prosecutions, the bare bones amounted to ascertaining whether a ceremony at which goods or money was distributed had occurred. However, those who opposed the practice did not base their opposition on a skeleton but on a complete body. The potlatch was not just a "ceremony" or a "festival" where goods and money were exchanged by the "participants": it was emblematic of all that white British Columbians were not. However, much of this larger meaning was lost in the course of the trials, pared away by a system of argument that resolved disputes by reducing them to a set of technical questions. Rather than ascertaining the meaning of what happened, which was embedded in the larger social relationship between the disputing parties, these questions were designed primarily to reconstruct what happened and to compare it to the illegal behaviour outlined in the statute. Reduced in this way to its skeleton, the potlatch and the Indians who practised it did not seem so alien and threatening, or worthy of prosecution.

Decontextualizing actions from their larger social context, as the system of argument used by the courts does, distorts the picture of the relationship between the disputing parties. However, the potlatch prosecutions show that the distortion created by narrowing the terms of debate and by removing actions from their context can empower those we traditionally think of as powerless. Skeletonizing disputes had the effect of making Indians and their ceremony less alien. Confronted with actions that were now recognizable and even familiar, the courts found it difficult to punish them.

Strong legal arguments do not depend only on successfully addressing the issues raised by the law and on being fluent in its language. Strong legal arguments also have to be strong arguments; that is, they, like other arguments, have to evoke in the audience certain sensibilities that make them see the accused's actions in a particular way. Many Indians tried for potlatching were successful in making arguments that resonated with both the judges and the British Columbia public. Those arguments reveal much about how the law works; but equally importantly they reveal which sensibilities had power, and shed light on what "made sense" to white British Columbians. More broadly, these arguments give us insight into how they saw the world.

There appear to be three "logics of dispute" at work in the hearings. The first involved invoking tradition, not as a defence of guilt or innocence, but as a way of saying that Indians and their culture were not justiciable; that, in fact, their actions, because they were time-honoured traditions, could not be prosecuted legitimately. The Kwakiutl considered the potlatch a customary practice, and as such it was one that was legitimate simply by virtue of its history.

Second, the Kwakiutl drew analogies between their ceremony and the ones Europeans practised. "A strict law bids us dance," they told Franz Boas. "It is a strict law that bids us distribute our property among our friends and neighbours. It is a good law. Let the White man observe his law, we shall observe ours."[62] To the Kwakiutl, the potlatch was law — a customary law, but a law nonetheless that was as binding and legitimate as the white man's. They also argued that the potlatch was the same as Christmas; both were social and spiritual ceremonies that linked the present with the past and marked that link with gift-giving. So why was one illegal and the other not? "We observe that white people have great feasts, Dances and giving away of presents annually or periodically," Charles Nowell wrote in 1915. "Why therefore should our Feasts, Dances and charity be treated as a crime while you teach us that the white race consider their acts ones [of] virtue[?]"[63] In evoking tradition and using the analogy with "white man's law" and Christmas, Indians attempted to make the alien familiar. Given that many white British Columbians used similar logic to protest the enforcement of the potlatch law, such an argument did have a certain amount of resonance and power.

The third logic of dispute was quite different. Rather than arguing that the potlatch was a traditional social ceremony and thus outside the ambit of the law, the Kwakiutl, through their lawyers, argued that it was an economic transaction and thus subject to law. The potlatch was an occasion for paying back debts or for consummating a contractual obligation; consequently, the law against the potlatch, to put this argument most baldly, interfered with and was in direct contradiction to the laws of obligation (specifically, the laws of contract and debt). This was an effective tactic. As Edward Sapir told Duncan Campbell Scott, "the economic argument is naturally the weightiest" for abolishing the potlatch provision of the Indian Act.[64] It also demonstrates how legal arguments are constructed and suggests what made them successful. In the potlatch prosecutions, lawyers played a central role in framing arguments. Their success lay, as James Boyd White argues, in their ability to "translate" their clients' stories into effective accounts — accounts that are intelligible to the court.[65] These accounts are intelligible and effective if they utilize idioms familiar to the people sitting in judgment. In the case of the potlatch prosecutions, that idiom was economic. The language and logic of economics and the law were so closely allied and reinforcing that a sound economic argument could very well be an effective legal one. The lawyers for the Kwakiutl, particularly Dickie and DeBeck, were able to take their clients' vernacular descriptions and rationales for potlatching and translate them into another more articulate (within the confines of the law) idiom. Thus, in the hands of a lawyer, Chief Lohah's assertion that "it cannot be wrong to pay back what we owe"[66] and George Scow's attempt "to make a pillow,"[67] or downpayment for the purchase of a copper, became "investments or loans to be returned with interest" and "the formal consummation of a contract for the sale and purchase of a copper."[68]

The lawyers for the Kwakiutl had managed to find and exploit the points of intersection between two cultures of argument: one rooted in a native social and economic organization that stressed mutuality and hierarchy in the context of an organic whole, and the other anchored in the possessive individualism of Western capitalism. Phrases like "pay back what I owe" and words like "debt" had resonance in both. The double meaning of these words bridged two cultures of argument and opened up new and potentially revolutionary possibilities for resistance. Like puns, the language Indians used to describe the potlatch had the potential to subvert the domination of the law.

The power the law represented — the power of argument — was thus a creative force, not simply a repressive one. The system of domination the law was part of did not just happen: prosecutors and the prosecuted had to make strong arguments in order to succeed, and in making those arguments both parties had to abide by rules of legal rhetoric that constrained and empowered each of them. Quite apart from resisting attempts to make them stop potlatching, some native people recognized that the law's power was creative and used it to further their own interests. There are suggestions that natives used the creative potential of the law against each other to resolve their own internal disputes and to subvert the constraints of their own culture. These were not a backward people constricted by their own primitive ways. In fact, they were as likely to defend their actions by invoking tradition as they were to use the "Queen's law" to escape the obligations imposed by tradition. Custom and law were matters of "strategy and choice."[69] Some Alert Bay natives supported the potlatch law and sought its sanction to avoid paying back the social debts they incurred as guests at other potlatches. After the arrests of Johnny Bagwany and Ned Harris, Halliday noted that few Kwakiutl were willing to hold potlatches. "Those who owe money in the potlatch are loathe to pay . . . as they think if the prosecutions hold good and the potlatch is stopped they will escape payment."[70] Certainly, one of the "inducements" held out to the province's Indians to convince them to join the church was "that they need not afterwards repay the amounts they have received in that way [through the potlatch]." The chief of the upper Nass complained to Powell that "many Indians joined the mission so they might repudiate their debts."[71]

Material considerations were not the only ones that motivated Indians to support the potlatch law. The agents' reports suggest that some Indians used the law to over-throw the entrenched hereditary system of rank and privilege that existed within some native communities. It was the younger members of a band or those who had converted to Christianity who tended to support enforcement, seeing the ceremony as the centrepiece of "the old 'Indian Chief' form of government."[72] The Nishga'a were among the most vocal supporters of the law against the potlatch. "Amongst us Nishkas more than two-thirds of all our people are against it and we want it ended," they told Minister of the Interior Clifford Sifton in an 1899 petition:

> We want to follow the Queen's Law and the Indian Act, but the potlatch law [the cus-
> toms surrounding the potlatch] will not agree to the Queens' Law.
>   The whiteman's law declares that when a man dies his house and property must go
> to his widow and children. But the potlatch law says no, but his brothers and nephews
> may take all . . . [T]he potlatch gives him the power. The white man's law says no man
> may be chief unless he bears good character, but the Potlatch law is that any bad man
> may become chief if he gives a big potlatch.[73]

For the Nishga'a, the "Queen's law" offered the possibility of an alternate social order. By refusing to participate and by using the law to buttress that refusal, those with less status could challenge the existing social structures and better their own position.

The creation and enforcement of the law against the potlatch reveal both the nature of the law's power and how it works. The statute embodied certain interests — mainly those of British Columbia's missionaries and some of its Indian agents — and was an attempt to impose a certain kind of moral order on the province's native peoples. As a law, however, the potlatch provision of the Indian Act also had an important sym-bolic dimension and served an ideological function. Though its passage was the man-ifestation of the efforts of a particular group of people, the potlatch law embodied broader interests. It was as much a statement of the social and ethical boundaries of white society — of what they were not — as it was an attempt at regulation and control. Thus, when enforcement proved problematic, questions were raised in the minds of many whites about the validity of the distinction the law had drawn between Indians and whites.

While the potlatch law had coercive and ideological dimensions, its enforcement also revealed that the law was a way of arguing, that it was a rhetorical system. Legal arguments had to follow rules of rhetoric that narrowed the terms of debate and required the person arguing a case to address the issues raised by the law. This ability to limit debate, to shape the questions asked and the line of inquiry that is pursued, is where the true power of the law lies. Strong legal arguments were still dependent, however, on the teller's ability to forge a connection with the audience to whom they were directed. Good arguments make the audience see things the teller's way; they make her alien world and experience familiar. Making arguments resonate in this way involves using analogy: the potlatch was like the white man's law; it was like Christmas. But they must do more than make the alien familiar: arguments must offer the audience a way of seeing the teller's actions as rational, natural, and normal. In the potlatch prosecutions this was accomplished by using economic language to describe the ceremony. Cast in those terms, the potlatch ceased to be the profligate practice its detractors thought it was, and instead was transformed into the embodiment of rational capitalist behaviour.

Looking at the law as a way of arguing reveals a level of complexity and ambiguity in the exercise of its power that is not as apparent when we focus on the law's coercive and ideological nature. Though the system of argument characterized by the law narrows debate, it does not determine its resolution: it simply creates certain possibilities. The power of argument is creative. People have to make arguments — they have a degree of agency — and in making them they can exploit the strategic potential embedded in the way the law works. As a way of arguing, the law not only allows the powerless to resist the oppression of the powerful, but also gives them a means to transform their own relationships.

NOTES

1. The law against the potlatch is treated in Forrest LaViolette, *The Struggle for Survival: Indian Cultures and the Protestant Ethic in British Columbia* (Toronto 1973); Robin Fisher, *Contact and Conflict: Indian–European Relations in British Columbia, 1770–1890* (Vancouver 1977).
2. An Act to amend and consolidate the laws respecting Indians (Indian Act), 39 Vic., c.18, s.12, 86 (1876).
3. Ibid., s.93.
4. Douglas Hay, "Property, Authority and the Criminal Law," in Douglas Hay et al., eds., *Albion's Fatal Tree: Crime and Society in Eighteenth Century England* (London, 1975), 17–63, and E.P. Thompson, *Whigs and Hunters: The Origins of the Black Act* (London 1975).
5. Thompson, *Whigs and Hunters*, "Conclusions and Consequences."
6. James Boyd White, *Heracles' Bow: Essays on the Rhetoric and Poetics of the Law* (Madison 1985), 98.
7. Carol Smart, *Feminism and the Power of Law* (London 1989), 9.
8. Douglas Cole and Ira Chaikin, *An Iron Hand upon the People: The Law against the Potlach on the Northwest Coast* (Vancouver 1990), 119.
9. Philip Drucker and Robert F. Heizer, *To Make My Name Good: A Re-examination of the Kwakiutl Potlatch* (Berkeley 1967), 8; and Helen Codere, *Fighting with Property: A Study of Kwakiutl Potlatching and Warfare, 1792–1930* (Seattle 1950), 63.
10. Homer Barnett, cited in Drucker and Heizer, *To Make My Name Good*, 8.
11. Drucker and Heizer, *To Make My Name Good*, 26. Franz Boas disagreed, contending that the potlatch was a means of "acquiring status." See his *Kwakiutl Ethnography* (Chicago 1966), edited by Helen Codere, 77.

12. Drucker and Heizer, *To Make My Name Good*, 133.

13. Codere, *Fighting with Property*, chap. 4, and Drucker and Heizer, *To Make My Name Good*, 35ff.

14. Codere, *Fighting with Property*, 94; Drucker and Heizer, *To Make My Name Good*, 13.

15. Codere, *Fighting with Property*, 94.

16. Codere, in *Fighting with Property*, notes that "British Columbia was undergoing an enormous industrial expansion in these years [1900–20, approximately] . . . It is not surprising, in view of the Kwakiutl occupational and financial situation, to see them benefitting from the expansion of the British Columbia economy as it became more and more integrated with the world monetary economy" (49). She also notes that the per capita income of the Kwakiutl quadrupled in twenty years (1903–21) from $54 to $244 (43).

17. Powell to Macdonald, 15 Aug. 1883. Canada, Department of Indian Affairs, National Archives of Canada, RG 10, Black (Western) Series, vol. 3628, f. 6244-1.

18. Donckele to Lomas, 2 Feb. 1884, RG 10, vol. 3628, f. 6244-1.

19. Lomas to Powell, 5 Feb. 1884, RG 10, vol. 3628, f. 6244-1.

20. Bryant to the superintendent-general of Indian affairs, 30 Jan. 1884, RG 10, vol. 3628, f. 6244-1.

21. Sproat to the superintendent-general of Indian affairs, 27 Oct. 1879, RG 10, vol. 3669, f. 10961.

22. Ibid.

23. Deputy superintendent-general of Indian affairs to the Privy Council, 19 June 1883, RG 10, vol. 3628, f. 6244-1, cited in Cole and Chaikin, *An Iron Hand upon the People*, 21.

24. 47 Vic., c.27, s.3 (1884).

25. Judgment of M.B. Begbie, judge in *R. v. Hemasak*, nd, included in Moffat to Vankoughnet, 30 Aug. 1889, RG 10, vol. 3628, f. 6244-1.

26. 58 & 59 Vic., c.35, s.6 (1895). The amendment was framed with prairie dancing principally in mind.

27. 4 & 5 Geo. V, c.35, s.8 (1914).

28. Circular to all Indian agents in British Columbia from Duncan Campbell Scott, 21 Oct. 1918, RG 10, vol. 3629, f. 6244-3. There was a final, unsuccessful attempt to amend the act in 1935–6; Todd to deputy superintendent-general of Indian affairs, 27 March 1935, RG 10, vol. 8481, f. 1/24-3 pt 1; Mackenzie to Perry, 4 May 1936, ibid.; Cole and Chaikin, *An Iron Hand upon the People*, 147–50.

29. Sapir to Scott, 11 Feb. 1915, RG 10, vol. 3629, f. 6244-3. A copper is literally a piece of copper, shaped like a shield, which represents a large amount of wealth. Coppers were given, bought, or broken as a sign of the giver's or the recipient's wealth.

30. Boas, *Kwakiutl Ethnography*, 77. Boas first visited the Kwakiutl in 1886 and did his final work in the fall and early winter of 1930, when he was seventy-two (xxiii).

31. Boas to Sapir, 18 Feb. 1915, RG 10, vol. 3629, f. 6244-3.

32. Sproat to the superintendent-general of Indian affairs, 27 Oct. 1879, RG 10, vol. 3669, f. 10961.

33. Sutherland to the superintendent-general of Indian affairs, 12 May 1897, RG 10, vol. 3628, f. 6244-1.

34. Cole and Chaikin, *An Iron Hand upon the People*, chap. 9.

35. Guillod to [Powell], 7 July 1886, RG 10, vol. 3628, f. 6244-1.

36. Halliday to McLean, 20 Feb. 1915, RG 10, vol. 3629, f. 6244-2.

37. Halliday to Ditchburn, 10 June 1930, RG 10, vol. 3631, f. 6244-5.

38. Neill to Vowell, 12 Feb. 1904, RG 10, vol. 3629, f. 6244-2.

39. Bryant to ?, 30 Jan. 1884, RG 10, vol. 3628, f. 6244-1; also see Donckele to Lomas, 2 Feb. 1884, ibid.; Lomas to Powell, 5 Feb. 1884, ibid.

40. Vowell to the deputy superintendent-general of Indian affairs, 1 June 1897, RG 10, vol. 3628, f. 6244-1; similar sentiments were expressed by the Privy Council after it investi-

gated the potlatch. See Extract from the Report of the Privy Council . . . 22 Feb. 1897, ibid.

41. McLean to Ross, 8 Oct. 1913, RG 10, vol. 3629, f. 6244-2.
42. Halliday to secretary, Department of Indian Affairs [DIA], 1 March 1921, RG 10, vol. 3630, f. 6244-4 pt 1.
43. Pocock to Fitzstubbs, 12 March 1890, RG 10, vol. 3628, f. 6244-1.
44. Petition from the Indians of BC by their Solicitors, Dickie and DeBeck, to Scott, 27 Feb. 1922, RG 10, vol. 3630, f. 6244-4.
45. Ibid.
46. Halliday to secretary, DIA, 1 March 1921, RG 10, vol. 3630, f. 6244-4.
47. Todd to the deputy superintendent-general of Indian affairs, nd, Monthly Report, Jan. 1935, RG 10, vol. 8482, f. 1/24-3 pt 1.
48. Neill to Vowell, 12 Feb. 1904, RG 10, vol. 3629, f. 6244-2.
49. Constable A.M. Brien, Prince George Detachment to "E" Division, RCMP, Vancouver, 26 June 1928, RG 10, vol. 3631, f. 6244-5.
50. Reasons for Judgment, *R. v. Hemasak*, Matthew Begbie, CJ, included in Moffat to Vankoughnet, 30 Aug. 1889, RG 10, vol. 3628, f. 6244-1.
51. Vowell to deputy superintendent-general of Indian affairs, 16 Jan. 1897, RG 10, vol. 3628, f. 6244-1.
52. Halliday to secretary, DIA, 14 April 1923, RG 10, vol. 3630, f. 6244-4 pt 2.
53. Indians almost always retained counsel and had some very good ones represent them. Joseph Martin, KC, and Mr Ellis of McTaggart and Ellis represented the people prosecuted as a result of Dan Cranmer's potlatch. Halliday to Scott, 1 March 1922, RG 10, vol. 3630, f. 6244-4 pt 2. J.A. Findlay appeared for Mrs Dick Mountain, an Alert Bay Indian charged with potlatching in February 1922. Angermann to "E" Division, RCMP, Vancouver, 19 April 1992, ibid.
54. Halliday to McLean, 30 Oct. 1913, RG 10, vol. 3629, f. 6244-2.
55. They got suspended sentences. See Maitland, Hunter & Maitland to [the superintendent-general of Indian affairs?], 8 May 1914, RG 10, vol. 3629, f. 6244-4.
56. Halliday to Scott, 26 Feb. 1931, RG 10, vol. 3631, f. 6244-5.
57. Halliday to Scott, 27 Feb. 1931, RG 10, vol. 3631, f. 6244-5.
58. Ditchburn to Scott, 2 April 1931, RG 10, vol. 3631, f. 6244-5. It was the opinion of the minister of justice that the six-month statutory limitation did not apply to the potlatch law. Edwards to Scott, 18 April 1931, ibid.
59. Ditchburn to Scott, 2 April 1931, RG 10, vol. 3631, f. 6244-5.
60. Halliday to Scott, 27 Feb. 1931, RG 10, vol. 3631, f. 6244-5.
61. Todd to secretary, DIA, 10 March 1934, RG 10, vol. 3631, f. 6244-5.
62. From the film *Potlatch! A Strict Law Bids Us Dance*, 16mm, 53 min, Alert Bay: U'mista Cultural Society, 1975.
63. Nowell to ?, nd, enclosed in Crichton to [secretary, DIA], 30 March 1915, RG 10, vol. 3629, f. 6244-3.
64. Sapir to Scott, 11 Feb. 1915, RG 10, vol. 3629, f. 6244-3.
65. James Boyd White, *Justice as Translation* (Chicago 1991).
66. Cowichan Chiefs in regard to the Potlatch Act to [Lomas], 8 April 1885, RG 10, vol. 3628, f. 6244-1.
67. Angermann to "E" Division, RCMP, Vancouver, 28 Dec. 1921, RG 10, vol. 3631, f. 6244-5.
68. Indians of BC by their Solicitors, Dickie and DeBeck, to Scott, 27 Feb. 1922, RG 10, vol. 3630, f. 6244-4 pt 2.
69. On this theme see Sally Falk Moore, "History and the Redefinition of Custom on Kilimanjaro," in June Starr and Jane F. Collier, eds., *History and Power in the Study of Law: New Directions in Legal Anthropology* (Ithaca, NY 1989).
70. Halliday to McLean, 16 Feb. 1914, RG 10, vol. 3629, f. 6244-2.

71. Fragment of a letter [Powell to the superintendent-general of Indian affairs?], nd, following superintendent-general of Indian affairs to Green, 18 June 1886, RG 10, vol. 3628, f. 6244-1.
72. Loring to Vowell, 16 July 1897, RG 10, vol. 3628, f. 6244-2.
73. Nishka chiefs to Sifton, 1 July 1899, RG 10, vol. 3629, f. 6244-2.

SIXTEEN

The Indian Rights Association, Native Protest Activity and the "Land Question" in British Columbia, 1903–1916

R.M. GALOIS

INTRODUCTION

Between the construction of the Canadian Pacific Railway, beginning in 1880, and the First World War British Columbia experienced a major transformation. Social, economic and environmental changes were propelled by the growth of an industrial economy based on resource extraction and the rapid influx of population. The period has been viewed as an era of settling the frontier and province-building, to the accompaniment of almost unbridled optimism. But these developments were not greeted with universal enthusiasm. The expansion of settlement and resource extraction carried other meanings for Native peoples: the loss of access to resources, economic marginalization and institutionalized racism. This paper examines the growth of organized Native responses to these developments. More precisely, the paper focuses on the Indian Rights Association (IRA), together with brief discussions of the Interior Tribes and the Nisga'a Land Committee.[1] The existing literature, including Tennant's important study, provides an incomplete and sometimes inaccurate picture of these organizations and their activities. As a result, their importance in the development of Native protest in British Columbia has been underestimated.[2]

ECONOMIC CONTEXT

In 1881 Native peoples were still in the majority in British Columbia; forty years later they represented less than five percent of the provincial population. During this period non-Native population increased from 23,798 to 524,582. Rapid economic

Source: "The Indian Rights Association, Native Protest Activity and the 'Land Question' in British Columbia, 1903–1916," *Native Studies Review*, 8, 2 (1992): 1–34. Reprinted by permission of *Native Studies Review* and the author.

growth, generated by industrial production and export of staple resources (lumber, minerals and fish), accompanied this demographic transformation. The value of mineral production, for example, increased from $3.5 million in 1891 to $30.3 million in 1913; fishery production expanded from $3 million to $13.9 million over the same period. Most of this growth was concentrated in the years after 1900.[3]

Staples production in a mountainous landscape was predicated on the availability of an effective transportation system, primarily railways. Thus, by 1914, three transcontinental railways crossed British Columbia and a network of branch lines had penetrated the principal valleys of the southern interior of the province. Equally significant for this economic transformation was the establishment of a legal and administrative apparatus to regulate access to the lands and resources of the province. The system implemented by the provincial government proved adequate to the task; nearly 31 million acres of Crown land had been alienated by the time of World War I.[4] In short, the non-Native economy in British Columbia had expanded dramatically.

POLITICAL CONTEXT

In 1871 British Columbia abandoned its status as a British colony in favour of membership in the Canadian confederation. The structure of the new political arrangements was spelled out in the "Terms of Union." Whatever its other merits, this agreement paid scant regard to the Native people of British Columbia. In a single clause the roles of the respective governments towards the Aboriginal peoples of the new province were outlined. The federal government was charged with the "trusteeship" of the Native peoples of British Columbia; the province was to provide "tracts of land" for the "use and benefit" of the "Indians." Needless to say, Native people were neither parties to the "Terms of Union," nor consulted about its contents.[5]

Located a continent away, and lacking adequate information, it took some time for the federal government to appreciate the "peculiar" situation of Native peoples in British Columbia. The formula of the Terms of Union served, initially, to mask two crucial issues: first, the parsimony of previous British Columbia governments in providing tracts of land for reserves; second, and far more important, the absence of treaties extinguishing Native claims to their territories. As federal officials soon realized, there was reason to believe that "aboriginal title" to the lands of British Columbia had not been extinguished.[6]

Over the following decades these two issues were at the core of a three-sided dispute involving the two governments and the Native peoples of British Columbia. After some early uncertainty the federal and provincial governments sought to limit the dispute to matters concerning the number and size of reserves. But even here problems arose. While constitutional arrangements dictated that the federal government was responsible for administering policy pertaining to Native peoples, the provincial government retained control over lands necessary for implementation of the policy.

Native claims, by emphasizing the question of title, stood in opposition to the positions of both levels of government. Duncan Campbell Scott, as head of the Department of Indian Affairs (DIA) bureaucracy, commented on the evolution of this pattern:

From the year 1875 until the present time [1927] there has been a definite claim, growing in clearness as years went by, gradually developing into an organized plan, to compel the Provincial and Dominion Governments, either or both, to acknowledge an Aboriginal title and to give compensation for it.[7]

GOVERNMENT ACTIONS

Building on colonial precedents, the federal government developed a structure to administer its responsibilities to Native peoples. In 1880 this assumed the form of the DIA. Incorporating British Columbia into the operations of this emerging bureaucracy involved recognizing the peculiar circumstances in the province; not the least of these peculiarities was the "land question." The administrative solution to this problem was the formation of an Indian Reserve Commission (IRC) charged with allotting and surveying reserves.

To function effectively the IRC Commissioner required the co-operation of both federal and provincial governments. With the economic boom and the expansion of settlement in the first decade of the 20th century this basic requirement gradually evaporated. An important stage in this process was reached early in 1907, when the provincial government, through a Minute-in-Council, gave official notice to the federal government of two areas of disagreement on the reserve issue. The province argued, first, that some Indian reserves were of excessive size and should be reduced; second, it claimed the reversionary interest in Indian reserves.[8]

The following year the province took two further steps to strengthen its position. First, it initiated a case in provincial courts to determine its rights, vis-à-vis the federal government, concerning existing reserves; any reference to the rights of Native people was excluded. Although abandoned prior to judgement, in favour of direct negotiations, the objective of the province was clear enough: to "get the reserves cut down."[9] Secondly, the province halted the process of establishing further reserves. Given the current "unsatisfactory state of affairs," the Chief Commissioner of Lands and Works said it was "inadvisable . . . to make further allotments." Henceforth only applications "for purchase" of land by the DIA or offers of "suitable exchanges" would be considered. According to IRC Commissioner A.W. Vowell, this meant that, apart from surveying, the work of the Reserve Commission would "remain in abeyance until these questions are settled."[10]

Whatever their merits as part of a negotiating stance, these measures did nothing to address the underlying issues. This much was clear to Vowell, Reserve Commissioner from 1898 to 1910. The final sentence of his final annual report stated:

> Meanwhile the country is being settled very rapidly, and lands all over the province are being occupied as homesteads, &c., by incoming settlers, interfering more or less with the hunting and fishing grounds of the Indians.[11]

As the consequences of this impasse became apparent, Native peoples brought pressure on the federal government. In response, the federal government opted for an alternative approach designed to produce a judicial decision on the question of Aboriginal title and other outstanding issues. Negotiations with the provincial government were initiated and, by the summer of 1910, senior officials had reached a provisional agreement. It consisted of a series of ten questions to be used as the basis for reference of a test case to the Supreme Court of Canada.[12] On learning of these developments, however, B.C. Premier Richard McBride refused to proceed. He insisted on the removal of the first three questions: those dealing with the issue of Aboriginal title. In Laurier's opinion these questions were "absolutely material" to the points at issue and he was perplexed by McBride's objections.[13]

Over the next two years the federal government took a series of measures designed to overcome provincial obstruction and place a case before the courts. An amendment to the *Indian Act* in 1910 proved inadequate to the task, necessitating a further amendment in 1911. This was followed by the passage of Order-in-Council PC 1081, stating that the federal government proposed to "institute proceedings in the Exchequer Court of Canada on behalf of the Indians a provincial grantee, or licensee, in the hope of obtaining a decision upon the questions involved as soon as a case arises in which the main points in difference can be properly or conveniently tried."[14] At this stage the order-in-council seems to have disappeared within the bureaucracy of the Department of Justice. That, at any rate, was the explanation subsequently offered by Duncan Campbell Scott. Despite drafting the "Memorandum to Council," Scott recalled, the DIA "was not advised of its passage, and was, therefore, ignorant of it until the above date, namely 18th of April 1912."

Owing to the election of a Conservative federal government in the fall of 1911 the delay had significant repercussions.[15] Robert Borden, the newly elected prime minister, opted for a different approach to the problems of Native peoples in British Columbia. He decided to open negotiations on all outstanding issues with the government of his fellow Conservative, Richard McBride. After initial discussions at the ministerial level the federal government appointed J.A.J. McKenna, a DIA official, to "investigate claims put forth by and on behalf of the Indians of British Columbia as to lands and rights, and all questions at issue between the Dominion and Provincial Governments and the Indians in respect thereto, and to represent the Government of Canada in negotiating with the Government of British Columbia a settlement to such questions."[16]

At this stage the possibility of a test case remained under active consideration. It disappeared from the agenda following McKenna's visit to British Columbia in the summer of 1912. McKenna travelled around the province, meeting a number of Native leaders, and negotiated with the provincial government. The process reached a conclusion with the McKenna-McBride Agreement of 24 September, establishing the conditions for a joint federal–provincial Royal Commission on Indian Affairs. A crucial feature of the agreement was that the Commission, through its terms of reference, be limited to consideration of matters concerning reserves: numbers, location, size and the reversionary interest. The question of Aboriginal title, as claimed by Native peoples, was excluded.[17]

After three years of labour and ninety-eight interim reports the McKenna-McBride Royal Commission completed its final report in 1916. In sum, it recommended that 482 new reserves, encompassing 87,291 acres, be established and a total of 47,058 acres be "cut-off" from existing reserves. Any proceeds from the sale of these "cut-off" lands were to be divided equally "between the Province and the Dominion, the latter being bound to use the proceeds for the benefit of the Indians of British Columbia."[18] Following agreement on the number and extent of reserves the

. . . lands were all to be conveyed by the province to the Dominion. The federal government was to have full power to deal with the lands in any manner, even to selling

them. The only interest to be retained by the province was in the case of a reserve unoccupied because the tribe had become extinct. The land in such a case was to revert to the
province.[19]

Thus, the issues of the extent of the reserves and the reversionary interest would
be resolved to the satisfaction of the two levels of government. As events transpired
the path from the publication of the findings of the Royal Commission to their final
enactment was long and tortuous, largely as a result of Native opposition.[20]

NATIVE PROTESTS

The Native peoples of British Columbia were important participants in the political
process leading to the establishment of the Royal Commission. They did far more than
simply respond to governmental initiatives. Their efforts brought a substantial elabo-
ration of the forms of protest and clarification of the issues in dispute.

Shortly after the turn of the century a number of southern tribes, both coastal
and interior, began to organize in response to "increased pressure of settlement of
whites and restrictions being imposed on them in hunting and fishing." This discontent may have contributed to the decision by two interior chiefs, accompanied by an
Oblate priest, to visit England and Italy in 1904. They reportedly failed to see Edward
VII, "so they went over to Rome to Pope Leo XIII, and they succeeded in an interview
with his Holiness."[21]

Little more is known about this effort, but two years later several Coast Salish and
interior tribes combined to send a delegation to England. The prime mover in this
undertaking on the coast was Chief Capilano of the Squamish tribe. Early in 1906 he
began to drum up support for the project by travelling around the lower mainland
and Vancouver Island and corresponding with interior chiefs. At this stage participation seems to have been limited to "Catholic" tribes. A petition was prepared, outlining various grievances and demonstrating a clear awareness of the anomalous
situation in British Columbia:

> In other parts of Canada the Indian title has been extinguished reserving sufficient land
> for the use of the Indians, but in British Columbia the Indian title has never been extin-
> guished, nor has significant land been allotted to our people for their maintenance.[22]

Addressed to King Edward VII, the petition was carried to England by a delegation of
three chiefs: Joe Capilano, Charley Isipaymilt of the Cowichan tribe and Basil David
of the Bonaparte tribe.[23]

Although they obtained an audience with the King, the chiefs did not formally
present the petition. Instead it was forwarded through the "Canadian office in the
usual way." In due course, after following correct procedures, the delegation was
informed that their complaints should be laid "before Ottawa."[24]

Despite this rejection, the trip to London was far from a failure. Its real significance lay in the realm of public relations, where it played, with considerable success,
to both Native and White audiences. There can be little doubt, for example, that the
delegation provided a focus for the expression of Native grievances; it also helped
legitimize such expressions. Most significant, though, was the stimulus it provided for
further organization.[25]

The chosen vehicle for these efforts took the form of two petitions submitted to Edward VII. More important than their content were the signatories: twenty-three Fraser River chiefs, twelve Squamish chiefs, seven Vancouver Island chiefs, seven "Upper Country" chiefs and fourteen northern chiefs. The petitions represented the first major attempt at co-ordinating Native protests from a significant portion of the province.[26]

This pattern of co-operation continued. After receiving written confirmation that their grievances should be directed towards the Canadian government, a conference to discuss future plans was held at North Vancouver in mid-December 1907. The delegates were united on the principal issue confronting them: their opposition to the consequences of the "increasing development of the country." And, despite disagreements between "northern" and "southern" groups about the details, there was also agreement on the most appropriate response — a delegation to Ottawa.

In the summer of 1908, with construction of the Grand Trunk Pacific Railway underway along the Skeena river and discontent rising among the "northern Indians," a delegation of twenty-five "chiefs" made their way to Ottawa.[27] A meeting with Prime Minister Laurier was secured on 11 June, during which at least two petitions were presented. Laurier promised to forward them, through appropriate channels, to the King.[28] On returning to Vancouver the delegation was optimistic that "all matters pertaining to their rights in British Columbia" would be "amicably settled." Laurier had assured them that the land question "would be settled as soon as possible, and their rights protected."[29]

THE COWICHAN PETITION AND THE INDIAN RIGHTS ASSOCIATION

Although the hopes raised by the trip to Ottawa were not fulfilled, the urgency that had created the delegation was carried forward. The most significant new initiative was the Cowichan Petition of March 1909. Much remains uncertain about the precise origins of the petition, but two White supporters, Rev. C.M. Tate and Rev. A.E. O'Meara, were important in helping give Native discontent this form. Tate, a Methodist missionary, had been stationed at Duncan, in the heart of Cowichan territory, since 1899. O'Meara was an Ontario-trained lawyer who had become a missionary in 1906, serving in the mining communities of the Yukon. What brought these two men together is not known but they met on two occasions at the beginning of February 1909. Their discussions concerned "the conditions of the Indians and [the] planning [of] a course to ask for treaty."[30] By this time O'Meara was already aware of the Royal Proclamation of 1763 and its potential implications. He suggested obtaining the advice of J.M. Clark, a Toronto lawyer with "an expert knowledge of the matter of Indian Title."[31] The result was the Cowichan Petition.

In March O'Meara headed east and, after meeting with Clark, carried the petition to London. He presented a copy at the office of the Secretary of State for the Colonies, where it was promptly referred back to Canada for consideration.[32] Despite this rebuff the petition of 1909 was important for at least four reasons: it appears to have stimulated the federal government's pursuit of "discussions" with the provincial government concerning a test case; it invoked the Royal Proclamation of 1763 as the legal basis for recognition of Aboriginal title and sought a decision by the Judicial Committee of the Privy Council; it represented a closer interaction between Native people and White sympathizers and advisers; and it gave further impetus to Native organization.

The precise relationship between the formation of the Indian Rights Association (IRA) and the preparation and submission of the Cowichan Petition remains unclear. An informal organization, established to pursue the objectives expressed in the Cowichan Petition, seems to have evolved into the IRA. As early as May 1909, some form of organization had been established, and funds raised.[33] A meeting held in Vancouver at the end of September, attended by representatives of twenty coastal tribes, continued the process. Following the meeting a statement was issued indicating a desire that the question of Aboriginal title be taken "directly to the judicial committee of the Privy Council." Shortly thereafter a memorandum expressing these sentiments was forwarded to the Superintendent General of Indian Affairs by "their lawyer in Toronto," J.M. Clark.[34]

Further organizational steps were probably taken at the September meeting as, by the end of the year, the fledgling organization was using the title "Indian Rights Committee." With Tate as Secretary, the Committee actively sought funds for legal expenses. Although there was some opposition to these efforts, a thousand dollars was raised among coastal peoples and approaches were made to interior peoples for a similar sum.[35] As these fund-raising activities proceeded, counsel for the IRA presented a "Statement of Facts and Claims on behalf of the Indians of British Columbia" to the Superintendent General early in 1910. The objective was to have the "question of Indian title . . . submitted for Judicial adjudication."[36]

THE INTERIOR TRIBES

Interior peoples had participated in organized protest activities as early as the trip of Chiefs Chilihiza and Louis to England and Italy in 1904. About 1909, however, as the pace and complexity of the Native protests increased, James A. Teit was approached to help formalize further initiatives. An ethnographer married to a Thompson woman, Teit was recruited to attend the meetings and help "with their writing." This led to his assumption of the position of secretary-treasurer.[37]

Early in 1910, as information about the IRA spread, meetings were held by several interior peoples to discuss the implications. One notable result of this process was the publication in July of a declaration by a number of Thompson, Shushwap and Okanagan chiefs. They expressed agreement with the IRA program and pledged financial support for the cost of hiring legal counsel. Later that year the "Tahltan Tribe," of the Stikine valley in northern B.C., issued a comparable declaration. They claimed

> . . . the sovereign right to all the country of our tribe — this country of ours which we have held intact from the encroachments of other tribes from time immemorial, at the cost of our own blood. We have done this because our lives depended on our country. To lose it meant we would lose our means of living, and therefore our lives. . . . We deny the B.C. Government has any title or right of ownership in our country. We have never treated with them nor given them any such title.

Their solution to the current situation was that

> . . . all questions regarding our lands, hunting, fishing etc. and every matter concerning our welfare, be settled by treaty between us and the Dominion and B.C. governments.

These declarations seem to have provided the impetus for the emergence of the Interior Tribes as a rather loose coalition.[38]

Subsequently, according to Teit, the Interior Tribes worked in "unison" with the IRA and the Nisga'a "whenever they . . . thought it right to do so." Some bands went so far as to join the IRA and participate in some of their meetings; Teit himself, for a brief period, served on the executive of the IRA. Nonetheless, Teit claimed, the two organizations remained separate and the Interior Tribes "were not under the control of the Association in any way."[39]

THE NISGA'A LAND COMMITTEE

The Nisga'a had participated in a round of protest activity on the "land question" in the 1880s. Some form of organization may have been formed at that time but, if so, little is known of its activities.[40] By 1907, however, the land question had assumed a new urgency in the Nass valley. Two would-be settlers were turned back by the Nisga'a and, using an organizational model from Ontario Natives, the "Land Committee" was established. It is also probable that the Nisga'a were aware of developments among southern tribes and may have participated in the meetings held at North Vancouver in December 1907.[41]

By March 1908 the Land Committee had issued a petition, copies of which found their way to a Vancouver newspaper and the DIA. The petition included extensive quotations "from the Scriptures" and a claim to "land in the Nass Valley, about one hundred and forty miles in extent, [which] is all needed by themselves as hunting grounds, timber and fishing grounds." These claims were repeated to Vowell, who visited the Nass in his capacity as IRC Commissioner during May.[42]

Early in 1909, with discontent over the entry of White settlers into the Nass valley increasing, the Nisga'a learned of the Cowichan Petition from Rev. A.E. Green. He seems to have persuaded the Nisga'a to contribute to this initiative, at least to the extent of having "Mr. Clark present their complaints."[43] By summer the Nisga'a are reported to have raised $500 to obtain "the advice of counsel in the East" and sought the co-operation of the Tsimshian. Whether this action was taken on their own account or through the organization emerging from the Cowichan Petition is unclear. The latter seems more likely as Nisga'a representatives attended the September meetings in Vancouver that contributed to the evolution of the IRA.[44]

Nonetheless, the Nisga'a Land Committee continued to act independently. In the summer of 1910 the Committee combined an awareness of the legal basis of the claim for Aboriginal title with the traditional tactic of denying access to unwelcome visitors. Copies of a notice, claiming title to territory on the basis of the Royal Proclamation, were served to a number of White "landseekers" who were "turned back" from the Nass valley. The notice stated that

> . . . up to the present time our lands have not been ceded by us to the crown, nor in any way alienated from us by any agreement or settlement between the representatives of the crown and ourselves;

After noting that their case, presumably the Cowichan Petition, was before the Privy Council, it continued:

We do therefore, standing well within our constitutional rights, forbid you to stake off land in this valley and do hereby protest against your proceeding further into our country with that end in view, until such time as a satisfactory settlement be made between the representatives of the crown and ourselves.[45]

STRUCTURE AND ORGANIZATION

By 1910, then, there were three Native organizations in British Columbia directly concerned with the "land question." Information on the internal workings of these Native organizations is limited and often difficult to interpret. Although there was some overlap in membership, they differed in scale and structure. The Nisga'a Land Committee, based in a single cultural group, was both small and cohesive; the Interior Tribes appear to have had the least formal structure; the IRA fell somewhere between.

These organizations did reflect significant differences among Native peoples in British Columbia. The principal line of cleavage lay between north and central coast peoples on the one hand, and interior peoples on the other. This division expressed different cultural patterns, but it was also a product of the geography of missionary activity: Protestant among the former, Catholic among the latter. Notwithstanding these differences, and the independence of the three organizations, there was a clear sense of common purpose and, for a time, a pattern of common action. The principal objective was to obtain a judicial decision on their claims to Aboriginal title.

The Nisga'a Land Committee represented a compromise between traditional structures and the demands of new political circumstances. According to Tennant the creation of a formal committee "was clearly intended as something White politicians and the White public could readily understand and would take more seriously than they had been taking traditional chiefs in traditional roles." Traditional models, however, were reflected in committee membership, with representation on the basis of local clans and communities. But, as all traditional Nisga'a leaders were not fluent in English, delegations were accompanied by their own interpreter when meeting White politicians. Moreover, in 1911, they hired O'Meara as legal counsel.[46]

The structure of the IRA was more complex but it also owed a good deal to "White" models. At the centre was a small executive whose functions included fundraising, organizing conferences, circulating information to local representatives and maintaining links with legal counsel. Containing both White and Native members, with perhaps some form of regional responsibilities, the executive met in Vancouver at irregular intervals. Participation at this level required literacy and a familiarity with White culture.

Much less is known about the activities and membership of the IRA below the executive level. Some of the representatives who attended the various IRA meetings were hereditary chiefs; the status of others is not known. Not all representatives were fluent in English and, given the linguistic diversity in British Columbia, communication must have been a problem within the organization. One account of an IRA conference indicates that Chinook served as the lingua franca.[47]

Local operations are even less clear. Attempts were made to organize branches, at the community level, with their own officers. How successful this was and how it intersected with traditional authority structures is not known. C.M. Tate, the secretary, did visit local branches, primarily in 1915; presumably other executive members did likewise. Nonetheless, the suspicion exists that, at this level, much depended on the initiative and enthusiasm of individual delegates.

Continuity of involvement was another problem. There were fluctuations in participation; given the economic and linguistic barriers to communication, this is not surprising. Nonetheless the IRA raised and spent nearly $5000 between 1909 and 1914. Of this, nearly one half came from the Nisga'a and various Tsimshian (and possibly Gitksan) tribes.[48]

The Interior Tribes appear to have had the least formal structure, remaining closest to Indigenous models. When problems arose, meetings of chiefs seem to have sought consensus on appropriate actions. According to one account,

> All these chiefs used to get together. They'll sit and talk pretty near all night to see what's the best way to do it, which way to say it . . . They'll talk . . . and they'll travel to Ottawa or somewhere else.[49]

Many of the larger meetings were held at Spences Bridge, the home of James Teit, who, in his role as interpreter and secretary, played a crucial role in facilitating interaction with White political structures. Some of these larger meetings were also attended by Tate, presumably in an attempt to co-ordinate activities.[50]

THE ROUTE TO THE MCKENNA-MCBRIDE ROYAL COMMISSION

In the summer of 1910, with negotiations between the federal and provincial governments on "Indian issues" stalled, Prime Minister Laurier visited British Columbia. His itinerary included stops at Prince Rupert, Vancouver and Kamloops; at each location he received representations from Native delegations. Laurier's responses included reference to his government's policy of seeking to facilitate a judicial decision, at the highest level, on Native claims.[51] However, with the provincial government still firmly opposed, such a procedure remained impossible. In an attempt to eliminate this impasse Native peoples decided on a direct approach to Premier McBride.

The result was a meeting in Victoria on 3 March 1911, between Native representatives and McBride and four of his cabinet colleagues. "We have come here," the delegates informed McBride, "to tell you that our people are far from being satisfied, and are becoming more dissatisfied every day." Their objective was to have the question of Aboriginal title "submitted to the Courts." In reply, the Premier informed the Native representatives that there was "no proper case for submission" to the courts. This rejection was compounded by McBride's surrealistic comment that, in his opinion, Native people "were well satisfied with their position." The former point was repeated in a written reply to R.P. Kelly, who had made the Native presentation.[52]

Although unsuccessful in influencing the provincial government, the meeting represented a considerable organizational accomplishment. Measured in terms of participation it marked the high point of Native political activity in the pre-war period. Delegates from nearly sixty tribes, drawn from most parts of the province, made the trip to Victoria. Members of the IRA, the Interior Tribes and the Nisga'a were well represented.

The first important response to McBride's rejection of Native claims came from the Interior Tribes. In May 1911, after a meeting at Spences Bridge, they issued a "Memorial and Declaration." It reiterated the declaration of July 1910, protested the impact of railway construction and sought access to a judicial decision on claims to title.[53] About the same time a three-man delegation of Coast Salish tribes journeyed to Ottawa and London, apparently with a version of the 1908 petition, but achieved little.[54]

No further significant Native initiatives took place prior to the federal election of September 1911, which produced the Conservative government of Robert Borden. Early in 1912, though, a deputation of nine interior chiefs travelled to Ottawa. Accompanied by Teit and Clark, they met Borden and expressed their desire for "a legal settlement." In return the chiefs received assurances that their request would receive "careful consideration."[55] However, the real answer, to this and previous Native initiatives, came later in the year with the signing of the McKenna-McBride Agreement. The consequent Royal Commission posed new and complex problems for the Native peoples of British Columbia.

RESPONDING TO THE MCKENNA-MCBRIDE ROYAL COMMISSION

Native responses proceeded on two related fronts: first, a renewed quest for a judicial decision on the "title" issue, and second, opposition to the Royal Commission and its narrow terms of reference, which excluded consideration of the title issue. In developing these responses, however, differences emerged among the three Native organizations. Such differences, it should be emphasized, concerned the appropriateness of particular tactics rather than the basic objective of securing a just settlement.

On the judicial front the principal reaction was the Nisga'a Petition. With O'Meara as an adviser the Nisga'a had embarked on this course as early as August 1912, prior to the signing of the McKenna-McBride Agreement. A formal document was adopted in January 1913, and forwarded, through legal representatives in London, to the Privy Council on 21 May.[56] Like previous appeals to Imperial authorities, the Nisga'a Petition was quickly referred to the Canadian government for a response. According to O'Meara, however, a different explanation for not considering the petition was given to the London representatives of the Nisga'a. By this account the "reason for not immediately referring it to the Judicial Committee [was] the alleged fact that 'the whole matter raised by the Petition is at present under the consideration of a Royal Commission.'"[57]

The actions of the Nisga'a had three significant consequences. First, they helped provoke a further response from the federal government concerning the conditions for a judicial decision on the title question; these were spelled out by Order-in-Council PC 751. Second, O'Meara's version of events enabled him to sustain the belief that a direct appeal to the Privy Council was constitutionally possible. Third, the actions contributed to dissension between the different Native organizations.

Indications of dissension surfaced at an IRA meeting, held in Vancouver 10 and 11 December 1912. With about a hundred chiefs in attendance, two important resolutions were passed. The first opposed the terms of reference of the McKenna-McBride Agreement and asserted the need for a judicial decision on claims of Aboriginal title. The second urged the importance of unified action on this and related matters through the IRA. By this time, as noted earlier, O'Meara and the Nisga'a were busy preparing their own petition.[58]

Six months later the executive of the IRA grappled with the pragmatic question of how to deal with the hearings of the McKenna-McBride Royal Commission, which had just begun. A resolution was passed, and circulated, recommending that

. . . two or three members shall be selected by each tribe or band, — at least one of whom shall speak English, — whose duty it shall be to wait upon said Commission when it visits their particular locality, and request that the fundamental question of title first be settled before the question of re-arrangement of reserves be touched.[59]

About the same time the chiefs of the Interior Tribes published a statement that revealed the growing tactical disagreement among different organizations. The chiefs rejected the McKenna-McBride Agreement but expressed their support for the position of the Nisga'a.[60]

The next significant step took place at an IRA convention held in Vancouver in December 1913. A resolution instructing counsel, J.M. Clark, to take their troubles to the "Privy Council as soon as possible" was passed unanimously. To this end Clark travelled to England in the summer of 1914 to see the Secretary of State for the Colonies. The mission was no more successful than O'Meara's of the previous summer but the experience likely changed Clark's mind about future procedures.[61]

Even before his departure for England Clark had expressed disagreement with O'Meara over use of the Nisga'a Petition. He informed O'Meara that the IRA considered it "very prejudicial to the interests of the Indians that separate Petitions of various tribes not authorized by the said Association, should be presented to the authorities." This disagreement might have been of little significance but for two further actions taken by Clark. First, he informed the Superintendent General of Indian Affairs of the division within Indian ranks. Second, presumably accepting the constitutional difficulties of a direct petition to the Privy Council, he indicated that the IRA were prepared to support the terms of Order-in-Council PC 751.[62]

Passed on 14 July 1914, PC 751 was a federal response to the Nisga'a Petition. It stated the conditions under which the government would accept referral of the question of Aboriginal title to the Exchequer Court, "with the right to appeal to the Privy Council."[63] But PC 751 was rather less than it appeared. Native people were required to accept, in advance, the findings of the McKenna-McBride Royal Commission and to agree, if their case was successful, to surrender their title in return for benefits "in accordance with the past usage of the Crown in satisfying the Indian claim to unsurrendered territories." P.D. McTavish and Canon Tucker, on behalf of two White support groups, summed up the implications of the order: "what the Government proposes to the Indians is — If you will first surrender all your rights we will submit to the Courts the question of whether you ever had any rights."[64]

The Nisga'a, with O'Meara as legal counsel, were at the centre of Native opposition to this development. Support was quickly secured from a number of "northern tribes" and, early in 1915, a Nisga'a delegation travelled to Ottawa for a round of discussions with ministers and officials.[65] During a break in these discussions, two of the Nisga'a delegates returned to British Columbia to attend a meeting of the Interior Tribes at Spences Bridge. This produced a formal statement expressing opposition to the conditions of PC 751 and support for a series of counter-proposals the Nisga'a had presented to the federal government. These proposals, embracing procedures for reaching a settlement after a judicial verdict, were rejected by the federal government through a new Order-in-Council, PC 1422, on 19 June 1915.[66]

This setback to Native protest activity proved to be temporary. As the Royal Commission approached its conclusion in the spring of 1916, delegations representing the Interior Tribes and the Nisga'a spent about six weeks in Ottawa lobbying the federal government.[67] Their main objective, as expressed by a Nisga'a delegate, was to seek a delay in the implementation of the report of the Royal Commission until such time as the Nisga'a Petition had been "decided by the Judicial Committee."[68] This represented a clear rejection of the various orders-in-council pertaining to the Royal Commission and the conditions for any judicial decision.[69]

One of the responses to these arguments by the Superintendent General of Indian Affairs was to remind the delegates that not all Native organizations supported such a stance. More specifically, the IRA, as represented by J.M. Clark, "were prepared to accept the Order-in-Council [of June 1915]."[70] A prompt objection, that Clark's views were not in accord with those of his clients, was entered but the issue was too important to be brushed aside.[71] Hence, shortly after the delegations returned from Ottawa, a conference was organized to confront this difference of opinion. Held in Vancouver between 20 and 22 June 1916, these meetings brought together a wide spectrum of Indian representatives and marked the beginnings of a new organization: the Allied Tribes of British Columbia.[72]

Two significant results emerged from the Vancouver conference. The more important was to remove any uncertainty about Native perceptions of the orders-in-council (PC 751 and PC 1422). After some discussion, the conference passed a formal resolution rejecting the position taken by the IRA counsel. A secondary aspect of this decision, but one that grew in significance over the years, was that it opened the way for A.E. O'Meara to become legal counsel for the Allied Tribes as well as the Nisga'a. Thus O'Meara became the single most important adviser to the Native protest movement in British Columbia, a position he occupied until his death in 1928.[73] The Vancouver meetings also established an executive committee charged with responsibility for formulating plans for further action. One of the first decisions of the committee, perhaps reflecting O'Meara's influence, was to "recognize the Nisga'a petition as a test case for the land claims of all the tribes."[74]

The delegates to the conference also spent one day in discussions with Duncan Campbell Scott, who urged them to await the report of the Royal Commission before making any decisions on a course of action. The report would soon be completed, Scott observed, and he suggested that it might "meet their demands." In response some of the delegates signified their willingness to wait for a time, but not for "two or three years." Such a time period, they were assured, would not be required as Scott was "anxious that their claims should be fully and quickly considered, and that they should receive justice." In the light of subsequent events Scott's comments can be described, at best, as wishful thinking.[75]

CONCLUSION

Native peoples of British Columbia faced daunting challenges in the first two decades of this century. The rapid expansion of settler society during these years was predicated on ready access to land and resources. As a result Native peoples were increasingly, if unevenly, marginalized. That they were unable to stem the forces arrayed against them is not surprising. What is significant is that Native people were not swept away by the tide of changes.

In difficult circumstances, the range and diversity of organized Native protest activity is impressive: eloquent testimony to their persistence in seeking redress for grievances. Equally impressive was the geographical reach of the movement. It was pan-regional and even, at its height, provincial in scope; only the Athapaskan speakers north and east of Prince George, apart from the Tahltan, remained aloof. This was no small accomplishment.

Viewed from today's perspective at the end of the 20th century, the IRA was clearly a transitional organization in the history of Native protests. However, it embodied a transition of great importance: from the expression of particular grievances towards a generalized, legally rooted protest movement. The Interior Tribes and the Nisga'a Land Committee, although operating somewhat differently, contributed to this process.

In forging this transition Native people took their protest activities beyond the narrow, bureaucratic channels of the DIA. Native people sought access to the centres of political power in White society: imperial, federal and provincial governments. These endeavours involved the use of forms of protest that were readily intelligible to White politicians (letters, petitions, delegations). They also required extensive and expensive journeys. In the process two basic strategic alternatives for resolving the "land question" were defined: a negotiated settlement or a court decision. These alternatives remain fundamental to the present day.

Sympathetic Whites were important in helping to articulate Native discontent, but they did not create it. The escalating contest over access to land and resources produced grievances aplenty. Nonetheless, guidance in obtaining access to White political institutions was invaluable. Out of this interaction came knowledge about the legal basis of Native claims to title in British Columbia. The widespread dissemination of this information helped to sustain protest activity.

Reliance on White expertise, although unavoidable, had its costs. It facilitated the dismissal of Native protests as the work of "outside agitators." Although not new, such racist denials had a considerable currency in British Columbia. At the same time, antipathies among Whites — perhaps personal, perhaps denominational — were imported into Native struggles. There is even evidence that the DIA sought to promote such differences. Given the other difficulties confronting the creation and maintenance of Native unity, these were not insignificant issues.[76]

Native societies were by no means static, but political interaction with the White world required skills many traditional leaders lacked. All Native organizations grappled with this problem and one of their major legacies was the training provided for a new generation of leaders. These were men who could operate in both White and Native worlds: men such as Peter Kelly, Andrew Paull and Arthur Calder. They were also central figures in handing on the tradition of protest to another generation. Their efforts deserve to be remembered, by non-Natives as well as Natives.

NOTES

1. Nisga'a is the currently preferred orthography, replacing the more familiar Nishga or Niska.
2. See P. Tennant, *Aboriginal Peoples and Politics: The Indian Land Question in British Columbia, 1849–1989* (Vancouver: UBC Press, 1990), ch. 7. Other accounts include: G. Shankel, "The Development of Indian Policy in British Columbia" (Ph.D. thesis, University of Washington, 1945); D. Raunet, *Without Surrender, Without Consent: A History of the Nishga*

Land Claims (Vancouver: Douglas & McIntyre, 1984); E. May, "The Nishga Land Claim, 1873–1973" (M.A. thesis, Simon Fraser University, 1979).

3. British Columbia, Ministry of Mines, *Annual Reports*, 1886–1913; and Canada, Department of Fisheries, *Annual Reports*, 1886–1913.

4. See R.E. Cail, *Land, Man and the Law: the Disposal of Crown Land in British Columbia, 1871–1913* (Vancouver: UBC Press, 1974), p. 244.

5. The full text of clause 13 is contained in Cail, *Land, Man and the Law*, pp. 185–86.

6. Between 1850 and 1854 a total of fourteen treaties had been signed, covering portions of the former colony of Vancouver Island. Subsequently, Treaty 8 covered the north-east portion of the province; see W. Duff, "The Fort Victoria Treaties," *BC Studies*, no. 3 (1969), pp. 3–57; and D. Madill, "British Columbia Indian Treaties in Historical Perspective" (Ottawa: Research Branch, Corporate Policy, Indian and Northern Affairs, 1981).

7. These remarks were made in testimony before a joint committee of the House and Senate (Canada, Houses of Parliament, Senate, Special Joint Committee of the Senate and House of Commons Appointed to Inquire into the Claims of the Allied Tribes of British Columbia, as set forth in their Petition Submitted to Parliament in 1926, *Report and Evidence*, Appendix to the Journals of the Senate of Canada, First Session of the Sixteenth Parliament, 1926–1927, p. 6; hereafter, SJC, *Report and Evidence*).

8. McBride and Fulton to Lieutenant Governor, 26 Feb. 1907, British Columbia Dept. of Lands, file 37905/12.

9. The phrase is from the report of a speech by Attorney General Bowser: Venn to Pedly, 4 Sept. 1908, and Bowser to Vowell, 28 Oct. 1908, Public Archives of Canada (PAC), RG 10, vol. 27150-3-1.

10. Cited in Canada, Department of Indian Affairs, *Annual Report* (hereafter DIA *Annual Report*), 1908, p. 273.

11. DIA *Annual Report*, 1910, p. 252.

12. See Newcombe to Laurier, 16 June 1910, University of British Columbia (UBC), *Laurier Papers* (microfilm), pp. 17268–76.

13. See McBride to Laurier, 7 Jan. 1910, and Laurier to Newcombe, 21 June 1910, UBC, *Laurier Papers*, pp. 164831 and 172177; McBride to Rogers, 30 Nov. 1911, Dept. of Justice, Docket A599, pp. 418–20.

14. The Order, passed on 17 May 1911, is found in PAC, RG 2, vol. 1104.

15. SJC, *Report and Evidence*, p. 11.

16. The provincial Minister of Lands visited Ottawa in May 1912; see Friends of the Indians of British Columbia (FIBC), *The Nishga Petition to His Majesty's Privy Council: A Record of Interviews with the Government of Canada together with Related Documents* (n.p.: Conference of the Friends of the Indians of British Columbia, 1915; hereafter FIBC, *The Nishga Petition*), p. 80.

17. McTavish Memorial, 14 Nov. 1912, PAC, RG 10, vol. 7780, file 27150-3-1A; McKenna to McBride, 29 July 1912, PAC, RG 10, vol. 3822, file 59335-3.

18. See Cail, *Land, Man and the Law*, Table 10; D. Thompson, "A History of the Okanagan: Indians and Whites in the Settlement Era, 1860–1920" (Ph.D. thesis, University of British Columbia, 1985), p. 154.

19. Cail, *Land, Man and the Law*, p. 235.

20. See E.B. Titley, *A Narrow Vision: Duncan Campbell Scott and the Administration of Indian Affairs in Canada* (Vancouver: UBC Press, 1986), pp. 145–61; Tennant, *Aboriginal Peoples and Politics*, ch. 8.

21. See Attorney General of British Columbia, documents produced in *Delgamuukw et al. v. Attorney General of British Columbia* (AGBC), Document #1443; Teit statement July 1920, *Victoria Daily Colonist*, 15 Nov. 1904; *Vancouver News Advertiser*, 19 June 1908; UBC, *Borden Papers*, p. 16390.

22. The full text is contained in *Victoria Daily Colonist*, 6 July 1906.

23. See *Victoria Daily Colonist*, 6 and 13 July 1906; *London Times*, 14 Aug. 1906, pp. 7 and 8.

24. See *Victoria Daily Colonist*, 30 Aug. 1906.

25. See *Victoria Daily Colonist*, 16, 20 and 27 Mar. 1906; 2, 5, 6, 7, 13 and 17 July 1906; 1 and 14 Aug. 1906; 1 Sept. 1906.

26. Some of the organizational activity involved in these petitions is described in *Victoria Daily Colonist*, 8 May 1907.

27. See *Toronto Globe*, 6 June 1908; *Ottawa Journal*, 4 June 1908; and *Victoria Daily Colonist*, 24 May 1908.

28. One petition was on behalf of Coast Salish tribes from the Lower Mainland and Vancouver Island (Capilano et al. to Laurier, 11 June 1908, PAC, RG 10, vol. 7780, file 27150-3-1). A second petition came from the Coast Tsimshian. Laurier's response is indicated in Exhibit no. 2, PAC, RG 10, vol. 11019, file 506D.

29. *Vancouver News Advertiser*, 17 June 1908.

30. Tate Diary, 1 Feb., Public Archives of British Columbia (PABC), Add. Mss. 303.

31. See O'Meara to Stringer, 1 Dec. 1908, and O'Meara to Perrin, 15 Mar. 1909, PABC, K.R. Genn papers, vol. 141.

32. See Green to McLean, 29 Mar. 1910, PAC, RG 10, vol. 7780, file 27150-3-1.

33. Kelly et al., memorandum, 15 Apr. 1925, AGBC, #1579.

34. The Superintendent General of Indian Affairs (SGIA) was the political head of the DIA. See Tate diary, 2 Oct. 1909, PABC, Add. Mss. 303.

35. See Tate diary, 7 and 8 Dec. 1909, PABC, Add. Mss. 303; C.M. Tate, circular, 12 Jan. 1910, enclosure in Neill to Vowell, 29 Jan. 1910; Rev. Rohr to Pedley, 13 Mar. 1910; and Wedildahld to McLean, 19 Feb. 1910; PAC, RG 10, vol. 7780, file 27150-3-1.

36. Enclosure in Clark to SGIA, 27 Jan. 1910, PAC, RG 10, vol. 7780, file 27150-3-2.

37. J. Drake-Terry, *The Same as Yesterday: The Lillooet Chronicle the Theft of Their Lands and Resources* (Lillooet Tribal Council: Lillooet, BC, 1989), p. 231.

38. The Declarations and accompanying correspondence are found in PAC, RG 10, vol. 7780, file 27150-3-1. See also Drake-Terry, *The Same as Yesterday,* pp. 247–48, and Rohr to Pedley, 13 Mar. 1910, PAC, RG 10, vol. 7780, file 27150-3-1.

39. Tate circular, 12 Jan. 1910, enclosure in Neill to Vowell, 29 Jan. 1910, PAC, RG 10, vol. 7780, file 27150-3-1.

40. Raunet (*Without Surrender, Without Consent,* p. 132) states that the Land Committee was formed about 1890. However, E.P. Patterson ("A Decade of Change: Origins of the Nisga'a and Tsimshian Land Protests in the 1880's," *Journal of Canadian Studies* 18, no. 3, pp. 40–54), makes no mention of such a committee and Tennant (*Aboriginal Peoples and Politics,* p. 86) dates the establishment of the Land Committee to 1907.

41. Tennant (*Aboriginal Peoples and Politics,* p. 86) states that Charles Barton, after a trip to Ontario, and Arthur Calder were responsible for the formation of the Land Committee in 1907. On the opposition to settlers, see *Vancouver Province,* 28 Mar. 1908; PABC, GR 441, box 31, file 1, #44/08; and GR 429, box 15, file 5, #3949/08.

42. The full text of the petition was not included. See *Vancouver Province,* 28 Mar. 1908. See also PAC, RG 10, vol. 1283, p. 140.

43. Green to McLean, 29 Mar. 1910, PAC, RG 10, vol. 7780, file 27150-3-1.

44. See *Victoria Daily Colonist,* 25 June and 2 Oct. 1909.

45. The notice was issued by the Land Committee of the upper Nass at Aiyansh on 17 May 1910. A copy reached the Attorney General's office and the text was published in the *Victoria Daily Colonist* and the *Vancouver Province* (both of 3 June 1910).

46. Tennant, *Aboriginal Peoples and Politics,* p. 86; FIBC, *The Nishga Petition,* p. 21. O'Meara also became legal counsel to the Allied Tribes in 1916 "Notes of Interview with Honorable Doctor Roche," 17 Feb. 1915, PAC, RG 10, vol. 7781, file 27150-3-4; E.P. Patterson, "Arthur O'Meara, Friend of the Indians," *Pacific Northwest Quarterly* 58 (1967): 90–99.

47. On the IRA conference, see *Vancouver Province,* 10 Dec. 1912.

48. Tate reported in 1914 that branches had been established at Shushwap, Chase and Alexandria (circular, 27 Sept. 1915, PAC, RG 10, vol. 11047, file 33/general, pt. 6). A year later the Nisga'a stated that they had spent "upwards of $5000" on their own petition ("Notes of Interview with Honorable Doctor Roche," 17 Feb. 1915, PAC, RG 10, vol. 7781, file 27150-3-4).

49. Statement by Sam Mitchell, a Lillooet elder, quoted in Drake-Terry, *The Same as Yesterday*, p. 261.

50. For comments on Teit and his relationship with Interior peoples, see McKenna to Scott, 5 Feb. 1916, PAC, RG 10, vol. 59335-2.

51. At Prince Rupert Laurier met representatives from Port Simpson, Kitkatla, Metlakatla, Greenville and an unspecified Nisga'a village (*Vancouver News Advertiser*, 21 Aug. 1910, and *Vancouver Daily World*, 22 Aug. 1910). For a description of federal government policy during this period, see SJC, *Report and Evidence*, p. 11.

52. Peter Kelly, a Haida, was a Methodist missionary at Hartley Bay at this time. He went on to play a leading role in the Allied Tribes; see annexes L, M and N to PC 1081, PAC, RG 2, vol. 1104; and A. Morley, *Roar of the Breakers: A Biography of Peter Kelly* (Toronto: Ryerson, 1967).

53. See PAC, RG 10, vol. 7780, file 27150-3-1. A copy was sent to the SGIA. See Drake-Terry, *The Same as Yesterday*, pp. 257–60 and 268–70.

54. See undated letters (received 28 May 1911) from Matthias Capilano, Charley Tsilpaymilt and Simon Pierre, PAC, RG 10, vol. 7780, file 27150-3-1; and O'Meara, "An Historical Sketch," PAC, RG 10, vol. 7780, file 27150-3-2.

55. John Chilihitza and Basil David were in the deputation (*Ottawa Citizen*, 8 and 9 Jan. 1912).

56. The Nisga'a delegation to the meeting with McBride, in March 1911, apparently initiated O'Meara's involvement with their concerns. See Annex O to PC 1081, PAC, RG 2, vol. 1014; FIBC, *The British Columbia Indian Land Question from a Canadian Point of View* (n.p.: Conference of the Friends of the Indians of British Columbia, 1914), p. 11; and FIBC, *The Nishga Petition*, pp. 1–10.

57. See SJC, *Report and Evidence*, p. 12; and Memorandum for Government of Canada, 5 May 1914, AC, RG 10, vol. 7781, file 27150-3-4.

58. See Tate, circular, 16 Dec. 1912, PAC, RG 10, vol. 11023, file 662.

59. Paull and Tate, circular, 20 May 1913, PAC, RG 10, vol 11023, file 662. On the passage of the resolution see Tate [?] to McKenna-McBride Royal Commission, 21 May 1913, PAC, RG 10, vol. 11023, file 662.

60. UBC, *Borden Papers*, pp. 145248–49.

61. See *Vancouver News Advertiser* and *Vancouver Sun*, 13 Dec. 1913; Gibbons to Scott, 24 July 1914, PAC, RG 10, vol. 11023, file 662; Gibbons to Scott.

62. Clark to O'Meara, 29 Oct. 1914, and Clark to Roche, 8 and 9 Feb. 1915, PAC, RG 10, vol. 3822, file 59,335-2; and statement by Roche, 9 May 1916, UBC, *Borden Papers*, pp. 16423–24.

63. See SJC, *Report and Evidence*, p. 55.

64. Ibid.

65. The Nisga'a obtained the support of "nine other Tribes," including the Kitkatla, a Coast Tsimshian tribe, the Haida and the Gitksan. FIBC, *The Nishga Petition*, pp. 32 and 73; O'Meara to Minister of Justice, 18 Apr. 1913, UBC, *Borden Papers*, pp. 145237–39.

66. The Nisga'a proposals, the statement of the Interior Tribes and the Order-in-Council are all reprinted in FIBC, *The Nishga Petition*, pp. 23, 62–67 and 105–7.

67. Nisga'a delegates to Borden, 8 May 1916, UBC, *Borden Papers*, p. 16403.

68. See statement by Charles Barton in an interview with W.J. Roche on 9 May 1916, UBC, *Borden Papers*, p. 16414. The delegations also met with Prime Minister Borden on May 19; ibid., pp. 16427–34.

69. The clearest expression of this position is contained in the written statement of the Nisga'a and Interior delegates of 26 May 1916 (UBC, *Borden Papers*, pp. 16437–39).

70. Roche was aware of this split in February 1915 and raised the issue during his meeting with the Nisga'a delegates on the 17th of that month (FIBC, *The Nishga Petition*, p. 62).
71. See statement of Thomas Adolph, 26 May 1916, UBC, *Borden Papers*, pp. 16435–36.
72. See the statement of Andrew Paull, long-time secretary of the organization (SJC, *Report and Evidence*, p. 175).
73. O'Meara's rise to prominence was facilitated by the resignation during the Vancouver meetings of two White advisers to the IRA: J.E. Bird, a lawyer, and C.M. Tate, the General Secretary of the organization (*Victoria Times*, 3 Apr. 1928).
74. Allied Tribes, "Statement Issued by the Committee Appointed by the Conference, 28 June 1916" (n.p., 1916).
75. See *Vancouver Sun*, 23 June 1916. For an account of subsequent events, see Tennant, *Aboriginal Peoples and Politics*, and Titley, *A Narrow Vision*.
76. See Neill to Vowell, 29 Jan. 1910, PAC, RG 10, vol. 7780, file 27150-3-1; Keen to McKenna, 10 June 1913, PAC, RG 10, vol. 11023, file 662; Scott to Endicott, 7 Oct. 1914, PAC, RG 10, vol. 7780, file 27150-3-1A; Scott to McKenna, 14 Mar. 1916, PAC, RG 10, vol. 3822, file 59335-2.

TOPIC NINE

The Great War at Home and Abroad

Parade in Calgary celebrating
the Armistice and the end of
World War I, 11 November
1918.

Of Canada's 1914 population of 10 million, 600 000 donned khaki during the Great War, and of that figure 60 000 never returned from the front. On the home front, citizens, especially those from English Canada, who were eager to display loyalty to the mother country and determined to vanquish Kaiserism, rallied to the cause by buying Victory Bonds and making myriad war charity contributions, by embarking on food and fuel conservation, and by sending reams of supportive letters and ditty bags to their boys overseas. Over more than four years of struggle and sacrifice, the costs of the Great War to Canada, both human and material, were massive. But even after the conflict was over, multitudes continued to believe that a better world had been created, and that international respect, if not glory, had been attained by the Dominion. Newspapers told civilians that Johnny Canuck, through his stupendous battlefield accomplishments — at Ypres, at Vimy Ridge, and in several clashes during the last 100 days of the war, for instance — had forged a record of renown. His accomplishments, it was said, had proved a key factor in gaining for Canada by late 1917 a significant role in the making of military strategy as an equal member of the new Imperial War Cabinet, and in entitling the country, after the war ended, to affix its separate signature to the Treaty of Versailles and to take its seat at the new League of Nations.

But underneath the politics and propaganda, the wartime story seems far less heroic. The expansion of government to harness the nation for combat brought not only new regulation of the economy, but also unprecedented measures to maintain internal security, morale, and Canada's commitment to the war. Some developments are familiar, such as the implementation of conscription in 1917, which created deep cleavages between French and English as well as bitterness within significant portions of organized labour and the agricultural sector.[1] In Article 17, Gregory S. Kealey argues that in the pursuit of saving democracy overseas, Canada's federal government acted with brazen disregard for freedom at home. Long-established nativism fuelled by ultra-patriotism and an initial wartime labour surplus gave rise to an unjustified internment program applied against so-called enemy aliens. During the war's final stages, rising labour militancy, especially in the wake of the Russian Revolution, prompted the passage of comprehensive legislation denying free speech, expression, and association. Kealey demonstrates that "rough justice" was not simply an unfortunate and unavoidable by-product of wartime passions: civil liberties continued to be trampled on after the cessation of hostilities, as Ottawa sought to counteract the "red menace" — a campaign during the course of which it persisted in applying wartime emergency legislation and laid the groundwork for a permanent peacetime security service.

Overseas, Canadian soldiers often displayed great valour, but the day-to-day realities of trench warfare were far from uplifting. Young men who had been anxious to see action before the war ended, soon wondered if the shooting and death would ever stop. In Article 18, Sandra Gwyn, constructing her narrative from the accounts of members of the Princess Patricia's Canadian Light Infantry, tells a tale of sorrow — a tale that would grow even darker for her subjects, at Ypres for instance, where 6000 Canadians perished, many slowly suffocating in the poison gas utilized by German forces. Some soldiers, such as Agar Adamson in Gwyn's narrative, communicated blood-curdling details and their own personal disillusionment to those at home, but others, wary of military censors, or perhaps choosing to self-censor their correspondence in order to allay anxiety at home or keep up a manly image, provided far more cheery and sanitized accounts. Correspondence of this latter sort, one might speculate, when combined with home-front controls over opinion and Canada's dis-

tance from the carnage, ultimately added to the misery of the Great War experience for many soldiers. For eventually these men were reunited with civilians expecting the return of gallant heroes, and not of mere mortals who in many cases had been damaged by their experience of what proved nothing less than an earthly hell.

QUESTIONS TO CONSIDER

1. Did censorship and other controls become more extreme as the war went on? If so, can you cite evidence?
2. What domestic and international factors convinced authorities of the existence of a major postwar threat from the left?
3. Was the Canadian state at all justified in its wartime or postwar suppression of civil liberties?
4. In what way, if any, did the attitude of soldiers change during the war? To what extent was this change in attitude shared with those at home?
5. Should the military authorities have censored soldiers' correspondence? If so, what type of information should have been excised?

NOTES

1. On the French–English division, see Elizabeth Armstrong, *The Crisis of Quebec, 1914–1918* (New York: Columbia University Press, 1938); on labour, see Martin Robin, "Registration, Conscription, and Independent Labour Politics, 1916–1917," in Carl Berger, ed., *Conscription, 1917* (Toronto: University of Toronto Press, 1969), 60–77; and on agriculture, see W.R. Young, "Conscription, Rural Depopulation, and the Farmers of Ontario, 1917–1919," *Canadian Historical Review*, 53, 3 (1972): 289–320.

SUGGESTED READINGS

Berton, Pierre. *Vimy*. Toronto: McClelland & Stewart, 1986.
Brown, Robert Craig. *Robert Laird Borden: A Biography*. Vol. 2. Toronto: University of Toronto Press, 1980.
Granatstein, J.L., and J.M. Hitsman. *Broken Promises: A History of Conscription in Canada*. Toronto: Oxford University Press, 1977.
Harrison, Charles Yale. *Generals Die in Bed*. Owen Sound: Richardson, Bond and Wright, 1976.
Hyatt, A.M.J. "Military Studies in Canada: An Overview." *Revue internationale d'histoire militaire*, 54 (1984): 328–50.
Keshen, Jeffrey. *Propaganda and Censorship during Canada's Great War*. Edmonton: University of Alberta Press, 1996.
Morton, Desmond. *When Your Number's Up: The Canadian Soldier in the First World War*. Toronto: Random House, 1993.
Morton, Desmond, and J.L. Granatstein. *Marching to Armageddon: Canadians and the Great War, 1914–1919*. Toronto: Lester & Orpen Dennys, 1989.
Morton, Desmond, and Glenn Wright. *Winning the Second Battle: Canadian Veterans and the Return to Civilian Life, 1915–1930*. Toronto: University of Toronto Press, 1987.

Rawling, Bill. *Surviving Trench Warfare: Technology and the Canadian Corps, 1914–1918*. Toronto: University of Toronto Press, 1992.

Roy, Reginald, ed. *The Journal of Private Fraser*. Victoria: Sono Nis Press, 1985.

Socknat, Thomas. *Witness against War: Pacifism in Canada, 1900–1945*. Toronto: University of Toronto Press, 1987.

Thompson, John Herd. *The Harvests of War: The Prairie West, 1914–1918*. Toronto: McClelland & Stewart, 1982.

Thompson, John Herd, and Frances Swyripa, eds. *Loyalties in Conflict: Ukrainians in Canada during the Great War*. Edmonton: Canadian Institute of Ukrainian Studies, 1982.

SEVENTEEN

State Repression of Labour and the Left in Canada, 1914–1920: The Impact of the First World War

GREGORY S. KEALEY

For the Canadian working class, as for workers the world over, the experience of the First World War proved momentous. Not surprisingly, the Canadian bourgeoisie also learned important lessons from the process of organizing for war, not least of which was the potential power of the state apparatus to respond to serious threats from within as well as from without its borders. The Canadian labour revolt of 1917–20, which joined the international proletarian upsurge of those years, represented the first significant nationwide working-class challenge to bourgeois rule.[1] It met with a stern response, which established the parameters for state repression in the interwar years and set the pattern as well for the return to war in 1939. The Canadian state found itself unprepared initially to deal with labour radicalism in the late years of the First World War, but the solutions it devised, building on the mechanisms of repression developed for other purposes early in the war and on the similar experience of other Allied countries, proved successful and durable. When similar crises arose later during the Great Depression and the Second World War, the state would turn again to measures initiated in the years 1914–20 and to the institutions, such as the Royal Canadian Mounted Police, founded in the aftermath of the war.

Source: Excerpted from "State Repression of Labour and the Left in Canada, 1914–20: The Impact of the First World War," *Canadian Historical Review*, 73, 3 (1992): 281–314. Reprinted by permission of University of Toronto Press, Incorporated.

The Canadian state faced twin crises in those years. First came the obvious necessity of orchestrating the grim organization of the nation for war. Far less appreciated was the second challenge of these years: the defence of the country's capitalist system against the connected threats of labour militancy and socialism. This paper will not document in any detail the contours of the labour revolt that have been well described elsewhere. Table 17.1, however, illustrates its magnitude and emphasizes the decline of prewar labour militancy during the economic downturn that continued through 1915. A return to job actions came in 1916 and increased rapidly thereafter, peaking in 1919 with the Amherst, Toronto, and Winnipeg general strikes and the national wave of sympathy strikes that followed the arrest of the Winnipeg leaders.

For organizational purposes, these years can be divided into three distinct stages — 1914 to 1917, 1917 to mid 1919, and mid 1919 to 1920. Organizing for war characterized the first period; fighting on two fronts — domestic and overseas — the second; and pacification, the third. By tracing five overlapping issues through these three periods, we shall see how closely intertwined were the two crises facing the Borden government. "Enemy aliens," censorship, national security, labour policy, and recruitment for the armed forces represented significant problems from the war's outset and constituted the terrain on which this two-front war was fought.

ORGANIZING FOR WAR

In May 1914, with war clouds on the horizon, the Borden government gave an early indication of its future directions. Its British Nationality, Naturalization, and Aliens Act radically changed Canadian naturalization practice. Until the passage of this act a sworn affidavit testifying to three years' residence in Canada had sufficed to gain immigrants their naturalization. After its passage, immigrants were required to prove both five years' residence and an adequate knowledge of English or French to a supe-

TABLE 17.1 *Strike Activity in Canada, 1912–1921*

Year	Number of strikes	Number of strikes with complete data	Number of workers involved (000s)	Days lost (000s)
1912	242	190	43	1136
1913	234	164	41	1037
1914	99	67	10	491
1915	86	69	11	95
1916	166	131	27	241
1917	218	163	50	1124
1918	305	239	83	657
1919	427	350	149	3402
1920	457	335	77	814
1921	208	172	28	1050

Source: All strike data in this paper are drawn from recalculations of the general Canadian statistical series in Donald Kerr and Deryck W. Holdsworth, eds., *Historical Atlas of Canada*, vol. 3 (Toronto 1990).

rior court judge. In addition, the secretary of state received absolute discretionary power to deny naturalization to any individual deemed a threat to the "public good."[2] In light of what was to come, this act was but a mild initiative.

Among the first actions of the Borden government after the declaration of war, the War Measures Act gave the executive almost unlimited powers: "The Governor in Council shall have power to do and authorize such acts and things, and to make from time to time such orders and regulations, as he may by reason of the existence of real or apprehended war, invasion or insurrection deem necessary for the security, defence, peace, order, and welfare of Canada." Unprecedented in the annals of parliamentary government, the act went even further and specified, inter alia: "a) censorship and the control and suppression of publications, writings, maps, plans, photographs, communications and means of communication, b) arrest, detention, exclusion, and deportation."

The government wasted little time in exercising this remarkable power. Even before the War Measures Act's passage through parliament, it had issued an order in council to regulate the flow of "enemy aliens" (its phrase for citizens of enemy countries resident in Canada during the war) out of the country. It simultaneously assured these "foreign aliens" that their property and businesses were indeed safe, and then the very next day by order in council demanded that they surrender all fire arms and explosives.[3]

In late October the government took a far more dramatic step, demanding that all "enemy aliens" appear for registration and examination. Special registrars were appointed in major centres, while elsewhere police authorities were empowered; all this came under the mandate of Sir Percy Sherwood, the chief commissioner of the Dominion Police. On registration and examination, "foreign aliens" regarded as nonthreatening were either allowed to leave Canada or to remain free under condition that they report monthly to the registrar; those considered dangerous were interned as prisoners of war. Their compatriots who either failed to register or refused the examination soon joined them.[4] To supervise the anticipated flood of internees, the government appointed retired Canadian general Sir William Otter as director of internment operations. In an initial wave of enthusiasm, some 6000 aliens found themselves interned, most of whom were Ukrainians, not Germans. The fact that most Canadian Ukrainians passionately hated the Austro-Hungarian Empire made no difference. While most of these internees were released in 1916 when the Canadian economy recovered and a general labour shortage developed, the entire experience understandably embittered Canadian Ukrainians.

The second major problem facing the Canadian government at war involved censorship. Initially censorship was divided between the military, with responsibility for cables, and the press and the post office, with authority over the mails. Canada's deputy chief censor, Lieutenant-Colonel C.F. Hamilton, handled both cables and the press until June 1915, when the government created the office of chief press censor, to which it appointed Major Ernest J. Chambers in July.[5] Since Chambers's office reported to the secretary of state, it created a confusing departmental censorship triumvirate.

Press censorship, while handled by Hamilton, remained ineffectual. The appointment of Chambers, however, changed that. In his first years of operation Chambers depended largely on personal contact to establish his authority and to exercise as much influence as possible on foreign-language editors, to whom he devoted most of his attention. His lack of power to order a paper's closure largely dictated this style of operation. Only his minister, the secretary of state, possessed the power of closure and, much to Chambers's chagrin, the minister was reluctant to use this power. On frequent occasions, Chambers expressed dissatisfaction with the cabinet's caution and indicated clearly that, if allowed, he would have shut down the entire foreign-language press. In the one area where the censor's hands were not tied, bans were invoked vigorously and, by 17 August 1918, some 184 non-Canadian, almost all American, publications had been proscribed. The list included sixty-five books or pamphlets and 119 serials. Of the serials, forty-nine were in the English language, while seventy were not. Only three Canadian publications had met the censor's veto — an obscure book published in Toronto, *The Parasite*; an English-language paper, *The Week*, from Victoria, BC; and Toronto's *Zemla i Wola*, a Ukrainian paper edited by Ivan Stefanitsky.[6] The ever-increasing pace of Chambers's censorship can also be traced. In 1914 only two items were banned. This increased in 1915 to sixteen, but then leaped ahead under Chambers to fifty-two in 1916, fifty-eight in 1917, and fifty-nine in the first eight months of 1918.[7] This increase, however, derived as much from changing definitions of objectionable matter as from Chambers's growing zeal. The original orders in council of 1914 primarily restricted materials directly harmful to the war effort. The Consolidated Orders Respecting Censorship of 1917 both specified examples of materials harmful to the war effort and extended the ban to include hostility to conscription. Finally, in May 1918 the rules were yet again extended to cover the government's conduct of the war and, more pointedly, to include anything that might spread discontent or weaken the people's unanimity behind the war effort.[8]

Translation represented a major, albeit often amusing, difficulty that the chief press censor encountered in his zealous pursuit of the foreign-language press. While the historian of the Finnish press assumes that this problem was unique to his community's newspapers, the difficulty actually cropped up frequently. For example, Frederick Livesay, the press censor for Western Canada, resorted to using Pavlo Krat as his Ukrainian translator while Krat not only belonged to the Ukrainian Social Democratic party but also still edited *Robotchyi Narod*, the organization's newspaper.[9]

In the related field of national security almost as much confusion prevailed. While the Dominion Police had traditionally held responsibility in this area, their efforts had been amateurish and extremely limited at best. In effect, they lacked adequate resources and personnel to fulfil their mandate, especially as their duties multiplied in wartime conditions. The Dominion Police had traditionally functioned through cooperation with the existing municipal and provincial police forces and, when necessary, by hiring private detectives from standard United States agencies such as Pinkerton and Thiel. This latter method proved blatantly inappropriate under war conditions, although that did not prevent its continued use. The Royal North-West Mounted Police (RNWMP) received their initial security work in 1914 simply as the provincial police force of Alberta and Saskatchewan, working under Dominion Police supervision. In addition to the Dominion Police under the minister of justice, the minister of militia and defence had a military intelligence apparatus, which grew rapidly during the war, and the Immigration Department had developed a security operation, especially in British Columbia. Meanwhile, information from British and empire intelligence agencies was supplied through the offices of the governor general. Thus, Canadian security depended on extremely decentralized operations that were collectively held responsible for the gathering of domestic intelligence through the early years of the war.[10]

The government basically had no general labour policy in the early years of the war. Owing to the deep depression Canada had entered in 1913, the economy remained stalled for 1914 and much of 1915. Rampant unemployment both helped military enlistment and, as we have seen, provided a rationale for extensive internment. With economic recovery, however, new problems quickly manifested themselves. Built initially on the munitions industry, the boom started in central Canada but soon spread to the whole country. The flooded labour markets of 1914 suddenly dried up and the country faced a significant shortage of workers. In this new context, "foreign aliens" found themselves freed from internment. More important in the long run than the labour shortage, however, the Borden government failed in two significant areas to supervise the war economy. Its sole focus on financing and supplying the war effort led to run-away inflation, which it did almost nothing to check.[11] In addition, it refused to bring munitions production under its own fair-wages policy.[12] The combination of rampant inflation, ineffectual and apparently insincere labour policy, and the growing perception of massive corruption and war profiteering would all return to haunt the government in the war's next phase.

In the early months of the war, recruitment for the armed forces posed few problems. With the economy in a serious recession and with extremely high unemployment rates, many workers, especially British immigrants, joined the army in an initial wave of war enthusiasm. Nevertheless, as early as the summer of 1915, even before the economy had fully recovered, recruiters began to complain bitterly of difficulties in attracting adequate numbers of soldiers. By 1916, as the war wore on relentlessly and the horrible costs of trench warfare became ever more apparent, the government faced mounting difficulties in attempting to meet its manpower commitments to the British imperial forces. Under heavy pressure from various bourgeois patriotic groups, the Borden government in August 1916 passed an order in council creating a National Service Board (NSB) and appointing a director-general of National Service. In October the new NSB announced its intention to take a national inventory of manpower, which it initially proposed as a compulsory registration program. The Borden government, sensitive to working-class opposition in this realm, instead mandated a voluntary scheme, to be carried out by means of a postal survey. In the face of considerable labour criticism of even this voluntary scheme, Borden issued assurances that the national service schemes "are not connected with Conscription. Rather the idea was to make an appeal for voluntary National Service which would render unnecessary any resort to compulsion."[13] The Trades and Labour Council (TLC) leadership accepted these vague assurances and recommended compliance to their members. This apparent surrender of the labour movement's purely voluntarist stance led to renewed opposition to the TLC leaders, especially in Quebec and the west, but also in Ontario. The leaders' abandonment of their renewed anti-conscription mandate, which they had sought and received in August 1916, brought to the fore the deepening split in the labour movement about the progress of the war.[14]

A WAR ON TWO FRONTS

In the years 1917 to 1919, the war came home with a vengeance. War at home certainly did not await the return of the Canadian troops after the November 1918 armistice. Indeed, their return simply added waves to an already turbulent sea of unrest that swept across the country in the wake of the Bolshevik Revolution and the fall 1917 election of a new Union government, which united pro-conscription Liberals with the Tories in a prowar coalition government. Without doubt the Bolshevik Revolution and the subsequent tide of revolts across Europe stimulated Canadian socialists. Equally it aroused the fears of the Canadian government and set off a Canadian Red Scare of significant proportions.[15]

Internment, which had been used less and less in 1915 and 1916, made an instant recovery. Now the "enemy" was not only German but also Bolshevik. Although there had been some harassment of socialist and pacifist opponents of the war in its early years, these efforts grew massively in 1918. "Foreign aliens" charged with anything related to radical politics — possession of prohibited literature, attendance at illegal meetings, membership in an illegal group — found themselves whisked away to internment camps. Indeed, in February 1919, months after the war's end, the government had extended the camps' potential considerably by allowing any county or district court judge on summary complaint from a municipal authority or any reasonable citizen to intern on grounds no greater than "a feeling of public apprehension entertained by the community."[16] The "foreign alien" need not be present at the hearing and was explicitly denied the right to legal counsel. This proved quite convenient in dealing with radicals. Some thirty-three "aliens," for example, were interned at Kapuskasing in the aftermath of the Winnipeg General Strike.[17] Any expectation that the Armistice would bring a quick end to the camps proved sadly mistaken. The camps remained open until February 1920, fifteen months after the Armistice, and the Internment Operations Office formally closed only in June 1920.[18]

When finally closed, the camps had imprisoned 8579 men, 81 women, and 156 children. The men included 2009 Germans, 5954 "Austrians" (Ukrainians), 205 Turks, 99 Bulgarians, and 312 "miscellaneous." Of these, by Otter's own estimate, no more than 3179 could be considered even remotely as conventional prisoners of war. Some 80,000 other foreign-born Canadians had passed through the registration and examination procedures without being interned.

As dramatic as internment, however, was the drastic extension of censorship. We have already noted the growing mandate of the chief press censor, but in September 1918 his earlier wishes finally came true. PC 2381 of 25 September 1918 "respecting enemy publications" quite simply banned all "publications" in an "enemy language." Notable here was the inclusion of Finnish and Russian on the "enemy" list.[19] Contravention of this order ("prints, publishes, delivers, receives, or has in his possession") brought a fine of up to $5000 or imprisonment of up to five years, or both. Thus, at one fell swoop, Chambers's job became much simpler.

The debate that followed PC 2381 and its subsequent amendments made painfully clear that the intended target was socialism and had little to do with the war. While a case could perhaps be made for the inclusion of Russia and Ukraine given the intervention of Canadian troops in the Civil War in the Soviet Union on the side of the whites, this position was never even argued. Indeed, Canadian embarrassment about military involvement in the Soviet Union mounted quickly.[20] The Canadian intervention in Siberia met with considerable opposition from Canadian workers.

Thus in a series of amendments, which commenced even before the Armistice, the "enemy" language press was permitted to publish under strict guidelines. Initially this involved the parallel publication of an English translation of all stories for specific papers licensed by the chief press censor to reappear. In April 1919, restrictions were lifted against all but German, Turkish, Bulgarian, and Hungarian papers and, finally, in December 1919, they too became legal.[21]

All Finnish and Ukrainian papers, radical or not, were banned by PC 2381. The Finnish experience involved the suppression not only of the socialist Vapaus but also of the right-wing paper *Canadan Uutiset*. In the latter prohibition there was considerable poetic justice, since its editor, J.A. Mustonen, had played a major part in promoting the banning of *Vapaus*.[22] Mustonen had a cozy relationship with chief press censor Chambers and, from his paper's inception, he had issued reassurances that it would publish "in a thorough Canadian spirit."[23] So helpful was Mustonen that he supplied Chambers with one of his Finnish translators, Herman W. Niinimäki, as well as providing evidence in support of the suppression of the radical Finnish-American press.[24] Mustonen's activities proved doubly ironic because not only was his paper banned in October 1918, but also his earlier actions in eliminating the Finnish-American socialist papers had led the Finnish Socialist Organization of Canada (FSOC) to perceive far more urgently the need to replace *Työkansa*, the socialist paper that had failed in the summer of 1915, with a new Canadian socialist paper.

Canadan Uutiset, however, successfully played on its loyal image to become one of the first "enemy-language" papers to reappear under the modified orders in council. This involved gaining the special permission of the censor and publishing all articles in parallel translation. *Canadan Uutiset* reappeared in December 1918 and published in bilingual format until the ban was lifted in April 1919.

Vapaus, the paper of the FSOC, enjoyed no such privilege. Following the banning of the Finnish-American papers in 1917, the FSOC decided to publish a new paper. Considerable difficulty ensued, however, owing to its inability to find a printer willing to produce the paper. When none could be found in Port Arthur, the FSOC tried Sudbury, only to experience the same problem. Only after some months' negotiations, including sending a delegation to Ottawa to meet Chambers, was it able to gain his assent and a guarantee that the printer would not be liable.[25] With that agreement in place, the paper finally appeared on 6 November 1917.[26]

For the following year the paper attempted to stay clear of the censor, perceiving that being shut down would be no great achievement. Despite translator Niinimäki's best efforts, Chambers initially found little to object to, especially since his terms in late 1917 still involved only the war effort narrowly conceived. This attitude changed, however, in May 1918 with the extension of censorship to cover spreading internal unrest in Canada. Nevertheless, *Vapaus* kept publishing until all "enemy-language" papers fell under the censor's ban.[27] Unlike *Canadan Uutiset*, however, *Vapaus* did not receive a permit to publish before the lifting of the ban in April 1919. This refusal came despite the FSOC's efforts both to legitimate its organization, which had been banned by PC 2384, and to get permission to publish. Negotiations with C.H. Cahan, Borden's director of the Public Safety Branch of the Department of Justice, succeeded in gaining recognition of a new Finnish Organization of Canada (FOC), supposedly nonpolitical.[28] Their attempts, however, to convince Chambers to allow the FOC to publish a bilingual version of *Vapaus* failed totally.[29] No doubt *Canadan Uutiset's* continuous attacks on the Finnish socialists had hurt the quest for a permit, especially, for example, their critique of the new FOC as nothing but the old socialist society under a new name.[30]

The debates within the Ukrainian community took on additional complexity after the Russian Revolution. The clear left–right split, of course, intensified, and the events of the October Revolution and its aftermath increasingly led to the emergence of a left-wing nationalist position that favoured the Ukrainian Central Rada and opposed the Bolsheviks. Again the ideological niceties of such debate mattered little to the Canadian authorities, and all Ukrainian papers were prohibited under PC 2381. This ban shut down both the Ukrainian Social Democratic party's (USDP) *Robotchyi Narod*, which had become increasingly pro-Bolshevik, and *Robitnyche Slovo*, the Toronto paper of Ivan Stefanitsky and latterly of Pavlo Krat. While numerous right-wing Ukrainian papers received permission to publish under censor's permit, the left papers did not. Instead, a series of attempts in Toronto to issue successors to *Robitnyche Slovo* fell under the censor's ban.[31]

By mid 1919, then, the Canadian state had effectively suppressed the entire Canadian foreign-language radical press. Owing to a combination of mounting protest, the six-month hiatus after the Armistice, and some slight civil libertarian sentiment from Liberal elements of the Union Government, especially Newton Rowell and Thomas Crerar, it slowly started to re-emerge. It still existed at the whim of the censor, and he issued warnings to *Vapaus*, for example, on numerous occasions throughout 1919.[32]

More striking than even PC 2381 and its suppression of freedom of the press was the simultaneous PC 2384, which effectively banned freedom of association, assembly, and speech for a select group of Canadians, most of whom were foreign immigrants.[33] The confusing list of named societies and parties, replete with errors, soon had to be amended to add the FSOC and the Socialist Party of North America (SPNA), while deleting the Social Democratic party (SDP).[34]

PC 2384 did not simply ban these organizations. It also made it illegal to "sell, speak, write, or publish anything," "to become or continue to be a member," "or wear, carry or cause to be displayed . . . any badge, insignia, emblem, banner, motto, pennant, card, or any device whatsoever" indicating membership. Illegality, in effect, became retroactive, and in any prosecution "it shall be presumed in the absence of proof to the contrary" that the defendant was a member if, since the outbreak of the war, the person had "repeatedly" attended meetings, spoken publicly, or distributed literature. Further clauses outlawed possession of any prohibited literature or attendance at illegal meetings, which initially included any meeting except religious services held "at which the proceedings or any part thereof are conducted in the language of any country with which Canada is at war or . . . the languages of Russia, Ukraine, or Finland." All such offences were punishable by fines of up to $5000 and prison sentences of up to five years.[35]

No systematic study of the resultant repression exists. While vague in detail, it is clear that these efforts were orchestrated nationally. Ontario Provincial Police superintendent Joseph Rogers, for example, complained in February 1919 that federal efforts commencing in the fall of 1918 had not gone far enough. He wrote: "The Police of Canada are pretty familiar with the whole situation but it seems impossible to impress the authorities at Ottawa with the seriousness of the situation. The police brought great pressure to bear on the Government at Ottawa and I was one of three representatives who waited on the Minister of Justice last summer [1918], when we told them in no uncertain terms what was coming."[36] Claiming personal credit, he noted that PC 2381 and 2384 "practically gave us proper law to operate with." In their aftermath, he described a 6 October 1918 conference held in Dominion Police chief commissioner Percy Sherwood's Ottawa office intended "to formulate a general line of action." "At this meeting, it was decided that a systematic raid should be made by the police from the Atlantic to the Pacific." While he approved of the ensuing execution of this plan, he complained bitterly that it had not been carried further, for "the spirit of Bolshevism is strong among the aliens in this country and the Russians and the Finns are the class that requires the most attention."[37] Such police policy led to numerous arrests. A preliminary analysis of one major list entitled "Bolshevik Propaganda" includes 214 cases involving 199 men and six women between the fall of 1918 and June 1919.[38] The charges, primarily for possession of prohibited literature, also included eighteen for attending illegal meetings, thirty-one for membership in a prohibited group, four for general breach of orders in council, and one for creating discontent. The sentencing pattern is summarized in Table 17.2, which shows a wide range but demonstrates that many defendants received severe treatment.

The origins of PC 2381 and PC 2384 deserve our attention because they originated to some degree out of the Borden government's confusion as unrest increased throughout the country. The complete variance in reports received from the Dominion Police and from Military Intelligence in early 1918 had led to the commissioning of Montreal lawyer C.H. Cahan to draw up a report on left-wing activities in Canada. Cahan reported to the minister of justice in September confirming the government's worst fears about foreign agitators and Bolshevik agents. As a result, the government moved quickly and passed PC 2381 and 2384. There had been mounting veterans' pressure for foreign-language press censorship even before his report, but nativism was not the major cause here.[39] In addition, Cahan himself accepted a new position as director of the Public Safety Branch of the Department of Justice, with an ambiguous mandate to advise the government on security matters. He held this position only until January 1919, when he resigned, later complaining to Borden at the height of the Winnipeg crisis: "I tried in vain, after your departure [for the Paris Peace talks], to obtain a hearing from your colleagues; but they restated my representations with such contemptuous indifference, that there was for me no alternative but to retire quietly and await events."[40]

TABLE 17.2 *Sentences for "Bolshevik Propaganda" or Membership in Prohibited Organization*

Fines	144	Jail and fine	10
under $10	20	$500 + 1 month	1
$11–50	29	$500 + 6 months	2
$51–100	29	$500 + 2 years	2
$101–500	56	$500 + 3 years	1
over $500	10	$1000 + 3 months	1
Jail	35	$1000 + 3 years	2
interned	15	$4000 + 5 years	1
under 1 year	8	Suspended sentence	20
1–2 years	10	Dismissed	5
3–5 years	2	Total	214

Source: National Archives of Canada, RG 18, vol. 2380.

Cahan's career, no matter how brief, demonstrated the high profile that some government figures now gave to security and intelligence. The Winnipeg General Strike and the wave of sympathy strikes it inspired fully confirmed this position.[41] Moreover, while Cahan may not have been satisfied with the cabinet's response to his efforts, certainly the new security forces were hard at work in the early months of 1919. The Dominion Police's high-profile arrests were accompanied by extensive secret service work with the placing of agents in Sault Ste Marie, Toronto, Windsor, Montreal, Welland, and Hamilton. One Toronto agent was "in good with the foreign element — he is able to speak several of the foreign languages and only a few days ago was requested to make a speech in the Russian language at one of the meetings."[42] There was complete cooperation between company spies hired through American detective agencies, especially Thiels, and the various levels of police. In Hamilton, for example, a Thiel detective employed by Stelco provided reports that were passed on from the steel company to Hamilton local police, to Superintendent Joseph Rogers of the Ontario Provincial Police in Toronto, and selectively by him to the acting Dominion Police commissioner, A.J. Cawdron, in Ottawa.

A complete overview of the total Canadian internal security operation remains an important historical task. From the available RNWMP materials, however, one can construct clearly the birth of the modern Canadian security apparatus in 1919, which would be turned solely over to the Mounted Police under a new act of November 1919. This act gave the force complete jurisdiction in the area of federal law enforcement and national security, and explicitly banned trade-union rights to members of the force. The older Dominion Police force was quietly merged into the larger body.[43] The new Royal Canadian Mounted Police began its national role in February 1920.

A brief consideration of the 1918 working-class experience is not out of place here for it helps to re-emphasize that, while the rhetoric of the Red Scare may have been excessive, the underlying reality of working-class revolt presented the Canadian bourgeoisie with a significant challenge. The organization of the unorganized and the spread of trade unionism into previously unthinkable areas represented a major manifestation of this threat.

Two major strikes represent two distinct manifestations of this process. The first was the month-long Winnipeg civic workers' strike of May 1918, which ended only when Borden's minister of labour, Senator Gideon Robertson, hurried to Winnipeg to prevent the expansion of sympathy strikes into a threatened city-wide general sympathetic strike.[44] Such discussions were led by the Winnipeg TLC but were not confined to it. The Jewish immigrant left, for example, organized a late May Help the Strikers Conference that brought together all radical elements of the Jewish community — revolutionary Marxist, Socialist-Zionist, and anarchist.[45] To end the crisis and avoid a general strike, Robertson capitulated to almost all of the civic workers' demands. In the process, he helped to cement in Winnipeg and Canadian workers' minds the efficacy of the general-strike tactic. But Robertson's concession was not singular, and a similar threat by the Edmonton Trades and Labour Council led to the recognition of the firemen's union in that city. In general, there was a massive expansion throughout the country of civic employees' unionism, usually organized into federal labour unions (FLUs) directly chartered by the TLC.

Federal employees also expressed massive dissatisfaction with wartime conditions. The Civil Service Federation of Canada enjoyed major growth, but the story of its expansion and subsequent decline is too complicated to pursue here. Instead, let us consider the second major public sector strike of 1918 — the July 1918 national postal strike led by the Federal Association of Letter Carriers.[46] Commencing in Toronto on 22 July 1918, with at best half-hearted support from the union's national leader Alex McMordie, the strike spread across the country, involving at least twenty cities, and led to sympathetic walkouts by other postal workers. Supposedly settled on 25 July by McMordie, who ordered his workers to return to work for the promise of a cabinet investigation, the strike continued as rank-and-file letter carriers angrily rejected the settlement. A week later Borden cabinet ministers T.W. Crothers and Arthur Meighen arrived in Winnipeg to negotiate a new agreement with an ad hoc Joint Strike Committee, again in the face of a series of threatened general strikes in a number of western cities, including Winnipeg, Vancouver, and Victoria, and by United Mine Workers of America District 18. Among the terms of settlement were guarantees of nondiscrimination against the strikers, the dismissal of all scab labour, and, amazingly, pay for the strikers for the period of the walkout.

Perhaps most alarming of all to the Canadian bourgeoisie in 1918 was the emergence of police unionism. In ten major Canadian cities TLC-affiliated police activists organized unions that year. Only in Ottawa did civic officials quell the dissent by firing almost one-third of the force. In Toronto, Vancouver, Saint John, and Montreal serious struggles over the question of police unionism occurred, but trade-union rights won out. In Toronto, for example, police magistrate Denison remembered that during the 1886 street railway strike law and order prevailed only because "our police force was able to keep them down." "If they had been in a union," he concluded, "I don't suppose they would have been able to do such good work." Nevertheless, Toronto Police FLU no. 68 gained initial recognition after a successful strike to protest the firing of eleven union leaders.[47] Meanwhile, in Montreal a common front of some 1500 firemen and policemen struck in December. They gained victory in the aftermath of a night of rioting in which volunteer strike breakers were beaten and fire stations were occupied by crowds supporting the strikers.[48] In Vancouver the threat of a general strike after the firing of four police union leaders led to an ignominious surrender by the chief constable. But it was in Saint John, New Brunswick, that the degree of labour solidarity with these efforts found its most profound expression. The firing of half the force for joining a union led to a city-wide campaign organized by the labour movement to recall the police commissioners guilty of the victimization of the police unionists. The success of the recall campaign resulted in a new election in which the anti-union commissioners were defeated.

These 1918 public-sector successes did much to set the terms for the subsequent struggles of 1919. The extent of working-class support for public-sector workers stemmed from a combination of factors — a recognition of the generally blue-collar workers as labour, the strong First World War notion that the state was greatly indebted to the working class and should be a model employer, and, finally, the pervasiveness for all workers of the issues at stake in these strikes — the living wage and the recognition of the right to organize.

One other major element propelling Canadian labour forward into the labour revolt of 1919 was the Borden government's recourse to conscription despite all its previous assurances. In the aftermath of the TLC leadership's begrudging acceptance of national registration, a storm of protest arose from Canadian workers. In meeting after meeting throughout the early months of 1917 the Borden government's war plans were denounced, and resistance by any means, especially through the vehicle of the general strike, was discussed. Meanwhile, the government went through one final charade of voluntarism with an attempt to recruit a Canadian Defence Force to provide domestic defence and thus allow the Canadian army to be freed entirely for overseas duty. This force, which aimed to recruit 50,000 men, was allowed to disappear ignominiously when, after almost six weeks of recruiting, only 200 men had signed up.[49]

This final failure, combined with Borden's return from a meeting of the Imperial War Cabinet in England, led to a late May decision by the cabinet to proceed with conscription. A Military Service Act (MSA) was introduced into the House of Commons on 11 June 1917 and eventually became law on 27 August 1917. As soon as Borden made the official announcement on 18 May 1917, demonstrations commenced throughout Quebec denouncing conscription. For the entire summer the streets of Montreal, Quebec City, and numerous smaller centres were filled with demonstrations and, on occasion, riots as protesters clashed with police. Discussions of general strikes and even of revolution filled the air. The ensuing late 1917 election campaign saw similar clashes but ended in a convincing prowar Union Government victory, partially gained by electoral chicanery of a previously unheard of level in Canadian general elections.

For the mainstream labour movement, the conscription debate came to a head at the September 1917 TLC convention in Ottawa. The executive took the easy position that because the MSA was now law, labour could not afford to oppose it. The Resolutions Committee, however, brought to the floor a firmer statement: "This Congress is emphatically opposed to any development in the enforcement of any legislation that will make for industrial conscription, or the interference with the trade union movement in the taking care of the interests of the organized workers of the Dominion."[50] In the ensuing discussion a series of more radical motions was introduced, including a call for a general strike against conscription. In a fiery debate that lasted for many hours, general opposition to conscription of manpower prevailed, but fears of state repression and of radical action eventually led to the defeat of a motion that labour would oppose the conscription of manpower until wealth too was conscripted.[51]

While the national leadership had abdicated from the struggle against conscription, the fight did not end. Resistance to the MSA took many forms. The primary and easiest was simply to apply for an exemption and, of the first approximately 160,000 men called to report, fully 92 per cent did so. Indeed, by the end of 1917, of more than 400,000 men identified, 93.7 per cent had sought an exemption. By the end of 1917 some 73 per cent of those seeking exemptions had been successful and only 13 per cent had been denied. The others were either pending or under appeal. Further options, of course, existed outside the law and many took these steps as well, if they were actually ordered to report. In Montreal, for example, of the first 500 conscripts, 35 per cent of the English Canadians and 56 per cent of the French Canadians failed to report. By the end of the war almost 25,000 Canadians had succeeded in remaining "unapprehended defaulters" under the MSA.[52]

Perhaps two of the most serious responses to conscription can be used to illustrate the extent of Canadian working-class opposition. On the Easter weekend of 1918, Quebec City crowds rescued an arrested defaulter from the hands of Dominion Police officers and proceeded to wreck the offices of the city's two pro-Union Government newspapers, the *Chronicle* and *L'Événement*. The next night the crowd sacked the office of the registrar of the MSA, destroying his records and burning the building. The authorities, who had rushed troops from Toronto to help maintain order, turned them loose on the crowd with fixed bayonets. While the army restored order that night, the enraged citizenry rioted again on the following evening and, in the ensuing battle, at least four Quebec citizens were fatally wounded by machine gunfire. The riots were finally ended on 4 April when *habeas corpus* was suspended and all citizens were warned that any arrested rioters would be conscripted immediately.[53] While only limited studies of these riots exist, it is clear from the military authorities' discussions that the rioters involved were primarily young Quebec workers. The four dead were Honoré Bergeron, a member of the Carpenters Union, Alexandre Bussières, CNR machinist, Georges Demeule, a factory shoemaker, and Joseph-Édouard Tremblay, a student at l'École technique de Québec.[54]

The second event was Canada's first political general strike, held on 2 August 1918 in Vancouver to protest the Dominion Police murder of miners' leader and MSA defaulter Albert "Ginger" Goodwin. Goodwin, a Western Federation of Miners' leader, member of the SPC, and vice-president of the BC Federation of Labour, had initially been granted an exemption as unfit for military service, but while leading a strike in Trail he was suddenly reclassified as class A and called up for active service. He fled to Vancouver Island and took to the hills near Comox, where there was a colony of draft resisters. There, in late July, he was shot, allegedly in self-defence, by Dominion Police special constable Dan Campbell, who was eventually exonerated by a special inquiry. BC workers, however, believed Goodwin had been murdered. As a result the SPC-dominated Vancouver Trades and Labour Council declared a twenty-four-hour holiday as a protest, and on 2 August Vancouver workers shut the city down in an effective general strike.[55]

The Borden government had managed to impose compulsory military service over the heated objections of Canadian labour, but it had done so at considerable cost. To a large degree it had called the moderate leadership of the TLC into increasing disrepute and helped to pave the road to the massive labour revolt of 1919. The eventual defeat at Winnipeg in 1919, chronicled at length elsewhere, and the slow demise of the support strikes across the country signalled the beginning of the end of one major phase of Canadian working-class history.[56]

PACIFICATION

In the aftermath of the Winnipeg General Strike, there was much talk of the carrots as well as the far more evident sticks of state repression. Most of the conciliatory talk stemmed from the Royal Commission on Industrial Relations, that had had the dubious task of holding hearings across Canada during the worst "industrial relations" crisis in the country's history. The final report, with its enthusiastic endorsement of Whitley Council schemes, was carried forth by Borden's minister of labour, Senator Gideon Robertson, with an initial display of support. These schemes, however, ran into a frigid response from most elements of Canadian capital at the September 1919 National Industrial Conference, which had been intended as "a domestic peace conference." For all intents and purposes, significant state participation in such promotion then came to an end. In effect the slow-to-develop state wartime economic role, with its limited concession to the TLC, was being dismantled in general, and the massive victory of Canadian capital in 1919 speeded the process along.[57] After Winnipeg and in the subsequent economic downturn, capital would make no concessions and would instead try to retake ground lost in 1917–19.

Foreign immigrants of a radical leaning would need to live carefully for the next sixteen years because, under the spring 1919 pressures, the government had introduced significant amendments to the Immigration Act that allowed for the automatic deportation of anarchists and any other advocates of revolution. Further, under the direct pressure of the Winnipeg General Strike, the government had further amended the Naturalization Act to allow the revoking of the naturalization of anyone, even of British lineage, who fomented revolution. Amendments to the Criminal Code also made prosecution possible for anyone deemed to be promoting change outside of peaceful, parliamentary channels.[58]

In addition, the conviction and jailing of the Winnipeg strike leaders under basically trumped-up charges made only too clear the state's power. While such charges would not be used again so broadly until the prosecution of the Communist party leadership in 1931, the potential for such legal action remained. Moreover, the state's domestic intelligence ability grew far more sophisticated with the development of the RCMP security service.[59] For example, when the chief press censor's office was shut down, a summary of its activity was passed on to the RCMP with a clear indication of which papers the censor felt should be watched. This list included the *BC Federationist* ("incite[d] the public to violence and revolt against constituted authority"), *Calgary Searchlight* ("needs watching"), *Camp Workers* ("extremely revolutionary in tone"), *Labor* ("of a revolutionary socialist character"), *New Democracy* ("radical socialist"), *One Big Union Bulletin* ("revolutionary and opposed to constituted authority"), *Ukrainian Labor News* ("objectionable Bolshevist publication . . . worth watching closely"), *Vapaus* ("socialistic"), and *Western Labor News* ("created feeling of unrest and discontent").[60] In general, as Chambers's comments to the RCMP make clear, he continued to favour some form of censorship. Needless to say, the RCMP would continue the surveillance part of this work.[61]

This article has covered much ground in an attempt to review the interaction of the Canadian working class and the state in the fiery crucible of the First World War. The Canadian state initiated a whole new set of repressive measures and agencies during this war and in its immediate aftermath in response to the significant challenge mounted by Canadian workers. The state's position on the battlefield of class war, which had remained hidden to large segments of Canadian labour before 1914, now stood exposed. The economic climate of the 1920s, however, was to prove unpropitious for further labour gains. The state's new repressive apparatus, operating out of the Departments of Immigration and Justice and through Military Intelligence and the Royal Canadian Mounted Police, remained alert. These practices, initiated in the First World War and its aftermath and continued during the 1920s, would again come to the fore during the Great Depression, the next period of nationwide worker militancy.

NOTES

1. On the labour revolt see G.S. Kealey, "1919: The Canadian Labour Revolt," *Labour/Le Travail* 13 (1984): 11–44, and Allen Seager, "Nineteen Nineteen: Year of Revolt," *Journal of the West* 23, 4 (1984): 40–7.
2. For a discussion of this act see Orest Martynowych, "The Ukrainian Socialist Movement in Canada, 1900–1918," *Journal of Ukrainian Graduate Studies* 1 (1976): 27–44, and 2 (1977): 22–31, and Peter Melnycky, "The Internment of Ukrainians in Canada," in Frances Swyripa and John Herd Thompson, eds., *Loyalties in Conflict: Ukrainians in Canada during the Great War* (Edmonton 1985), 1–24.

3. Inter alia, see PC 2086, 7 Aug. 1914; PC 2128, 13 Aug. 1914; PC 2150, 15 Aug. 1914; and PC 2283, 3 Sept. 1914.

4. For details see Robert H. Coats, "The Alien Enemy in Canada: Internment Operations," in *Canada and the Great World War* (Toronto 1919), II, 144–61; Desmond Morton, "Sir William Otter and Internment Operations in Canada during the First World War," *Canadian Historical Review* 55 (1974): 32–58; Morton, *The Canadian General: Sir William Otter* (Toronto 1974), 315–68; Jean Laflamme, *Les Camps du Détention au Québec* (Montreal 1973); Melnycky, "Internment of Ukrainians," 2–3; Joseph A. Boudreau, "Western Canada's Enemy Aliens in World War I," *Alberta History* 12, 1 (1964): 1–9, and "The Enemy Alien Problem in Canada" (PhD dissertation, University of California at Los Angeles 1965).

5. On censorship see Allan L. Steinhart, *Civil Censorship in Canada during World War I* (Toronto 1986); Charles Hanburry-Williams, "The Censorship," in *Canada and the Great World War*, 238–41; Herbert Karl Kalbfleisch, *The History of the Pioneer German Language Press of Ontario, 1835–1918* (Toronto 1968), 105–6; Werner A. Bausenhart, "The Ontario German Language Press and Its Suppression by Order-in-Council in 1918," *Canadian Ethnic Studies* 4, 1–2 (1972): 35–48; W. Entz, "The Suppression of the German Language Press in September 1918," *Canadian Ethnic Studies* 8, 2 (1976): 56–70; and Arja Pilli, *The Finnish-Language Press in Canada, 1901–1939* (Turku 1982), 85–95. The key early order was PC 1330 (10 June 1915).

6. On these two papers see Peter Weinrich, *Social Protest from the Left in Canada, 1870–1970* (Toronto 1982), no. 5150 and no. 5218. *The Week's* strong pacifist and anti-conscription position as well as its general muckraking, pro-labour stance appalled the censor. When it began to republish on May Day 1920, its editor, W.E. Pierce, recalled the ban of two years before and his three-month jail sentence and $1000 fine. *Week*, 29 June 1918, 1 May 1920.

7. Ernest J. Chambers, *Revised List of Publications the Possession of Which in Canada Is Prohibited* (Ottawa, 19 Aug. 1918). National Archives of Canada (NA), RCMP Records, RG 18, vol. 2380. For an accessible but unaccountably incomplete list see Weinrich, *Social Protest*, 471–4.

8. See PC 2070 (6 Aug. 1914); PC 2821 (6 Nov. 1914); Consolidated Orders Respecting Censorship, 17 Jan. 1917; and PC 1241 (22 May 1918).

9. Pilli, *Finnish-Language Press in Canada*, 88; Nadia Kazymyra, "The Defiant Pavlo Krat and the Early Socialist Movement in Canada," *Canadian Ethnic Studies* 10, 2 (1978): 47.

10. S.W. Horrall, "The Royal North-West Mounted Police and Labour Unrest in Western Canada, 1919," *Canadian Historical Review* 61 (1980): 169–90, provides useful background. See also Carl Betke and S.W. Horrall, *Canada's Security Service: An Historical Outline* (Ottawa 1978). On British Columbia see Hugh Johnston, "The Surveillance of Indian Nationalists in North America, 1908–1918," *BC Studies* 78 (1988): 3–27.

11. R.T. Naylor, "The Canadian State, the Accumulation of Capital, and the Great War," *Revue d'études canadiennes* 16, 3 and 4 (1981): 26–55.

12. D.J. Bercuson, "Organized Labour and the Imperial Munitions Board," *Relations Industrielles* 28 (1974): 602–16; Peter Rider, "The Imperial Relations Board and Its Relationship to Government, Business, and Labour, 1914–1920" (PhD dissertation, University of Toronto 1974), esp. chap. 9.

13. Borden to Walters et al., 27 Dec. 1916, as quoted in J.L. Granatstein and J.M. Hitsman, *Broken Promises: A History of Conscription in Canada* (Toronto 1977), 45. See also Martin Robin, *Radical Politics and Canadian Labour* (Kingston 1968), 120ff, and A. Ross McCormack, *Reformers, Rebels and Revolutionaries* (Toronto 1977), 134ff.

14. Toronto Trades and Labour Council, Minutes, 4 May 1916, 4 Jan. 1917.

15. For a national view of the Red Scare see Theresa Baxter, "Selected Aspects of Canadian Public Opinion on the Russian Revolution and on Its Impact in Canada, 1917–1919" (MA thesis, University of Western Ontario 1973).

16. PC 332 (14 Feb. 1919).

17. Watson Kirckconnell, "Kapuskasing — An Historical Sketch," *Queen's Quarterly* 28 (1921): 273–4.

18. Morton, "Sir William Otter," 58.

19. For text see Swyripa and Thompson, eds., *Loyalties in Conflict*, 190–2.

20. John Swettenham, *Allied Intervention in Russia, 1918–1919, and the Part Played by Canada* (Toronto 1967), and Roy MacLaren, *Canadians in Russia, 1918–1919* (Toronto 1976), are the fullest accounts of this misguided mission.

21. PC 2521 (13 Oct. 1918); PC 2963 (13 Nov. 1918); PC 702 and 703 (2 April 1919); and PC 2465 (20 Dec. 1919).

22. Pilli, *Finnish-Language Press*, 111–17.

23. Ibid., 100, 105.

24. Ibid., 106.

25. Ibid., 113–18.

26. Ibid.

27. Ibid., 122–7.

28. See, among others, J. Donald Wilson, "The Finnish Organization of Canada, the 'Language Barrier,' and the Assimilation Process," *Canadian Ethnic Studies* 9, 2 (1977): 105–16, for a careful consideration of the negotiations with Cahan. On Cahan and the Public Safety Branch see my "The Surveillance State: The Origins of Domestic Intelligence and Counter-Subversion in Canada," *Intelligence and National Security* 7, 3 (1992): 179–210.

29. Pilli, *Finnish-Language Press*, 127–8.

30. *Canadan Uutiset*, 20 March 1919.

31. On the experience of the Ukrainian papers see Peter Krawchuk, *The Ukrainian Socialist Movement in Canada, 1907–1918* (Toronto 1979), 95–9; Martynowych, "The Ukrainian Socialist Movement in Canada, 1900–1918" (1976): 27–44; (1977): 26–30; Andrij Makuch, "Influence of the Ukrainian Revolution on Ukrainians in Canada, 1917–1922," *Journal of Ukrainian Graduate Studies* 6 (1979): 42–61; and John Kolasky, *The Shattered Illusion: The History of Ukrainian Pro-Communist Organizations in Canada* (Toronto 1979), 1–26.

32. Pilli, *Finnish-Language Press*, 129–32.

33. For the text of PC 2384 see Swyripa and Thompson, eds., *Loyalties in Conflict*, 193–6.

34. Edward W. Laine, "Finnish Canadian Radicalism and Canadian Politics: The First Forty Years, 1900–1940," in Jorgen Dahlie and Tissa Fernando, eds., *Ethnicity, Power and Politics in Canada* (Toronto 1981), 98–9, 107–8. Amended list is in PC 2786. The deletion of the SDP from the list was due to the efforts of Newton Rowell. See Margaret Prang, *N.W. Rowell: Ontario Nationalist* (Toronto 1975), 267–8.

35. Swyripa and Thompson, eds., *Loyalties in Conflict*, 193–6.

36. Major Joseph E. Rogers, superintendent, Ontario Provincial Police, to F.H. Whitton, general manager, Stelco, 24 Feb. 1919, Archives of Ontario, Ontario Provincial Police Papers, RG 23, E 30, file 1.6. On Rogers's career see D.D. Higley, *OPP* (Toronto 1984).

37. Rogers to Whitton, as in note 36 above.

38. W.H. Routledge to officer commanding, Regina, 16 Aug. 1919, CIB 104, "Bolsheviki Propaganda — List of Parties Prosecuted in connection with." NA, RG 18, vol. 2380.

39. This argument is frequently made. See, for example, Howard Palmer, *Patterns of Prejudice: A History of Nativism in Alberta* (Toronto 1982), 47–56.

40. C.H. Cahan to Sir Robert Borden, Montreal, 28 May 1919, NA, Borden Papers, MG 26, H, vol. 113, part 1, file OC564 (1) (A), 61631–2.

41. See Kealey, "1919," and Donald Kerr and Deryck W. Holdsworth, eds., *Historical Atlas of Canada*, vol. 3 (Toronto 1990), plate 39, for statistical evidence on the strike wave of that year.

42. Sergeant B.H. James to A.J. Cawdron, IWW Branch, Dominion Police, Ottawa, 24 March 1919, NA, RG 13, vol. 235, file 1013.

43. The most satisfactory account we have of the genesis of the RCMP and particularly its security responsibilities is Horrall, "The Royal North-West Mounted Police and Labour Unrest."

44. A. Ernest Johnson, "The Strikes in Winnipeg in May 1918. The Prelude to 1919?" (MA thesis, University of Manitoba 1978).

45. Roseline Usiskin, "Toward a Theoretical Reformulation of the Relationship between Political Ideology, Social Class, and Ethnicity: A Case Study of the Winnipeg Jewish Radical Community, 1905–1920" (MA thesis, University of Manitoba 1978), chap. 5, and her "The Winnipeg Jewish Radical Community: Its Early Formation, 1905–1918," in *Jewish Life and Times: A Collection of Essays* (Winnipeg 1983), 155–68.

46. William Doherty, *Slaves of the Lamp: A History of the Federal Civil Service Organizations, 1863–1924* (Victoria 1991), 193–238. See also NA, Post Office Papers, series 10, vol. 60, file 96853, "List of Offices Affected by the 1918 Postal Strike."

47. Jim Naylor, "Toronto 1919," Canadian Historical Association, *Historical Papers* (1986): 33–55. See also AO, Ontario, Royal Commission on Police Matters, 1919. For a useful discussion see Greg Marquis, "Police Unionism in Early Twentieth-Century Toronto," *Ontario History* 81 (1989): 109–28, esp. 113–20.

48. Geoff Ewen, "La contestation à Montréal en 1919," *Histoire des travailleurs québécois: Bulletin RCHTQ* 36 (1986): 37–62.

49. Granatstein and Hitsman, *Broken Promises*, 51ff, and Elizabeth Armstrong, *The Crisis of Quebec 1914–18* (New York 1937), chap. 7.

50. Trades and Labour Council, *Proceedings*, 1917, 141–2.

51. For varying versions of the debate see ibid., and Toronto *Globe*, 20–1 Sept. 1917.

52. Statistics are from Granatstein and Hitsman, *Broken Promises*, 64–96. Details on the "defaulters" have been lost to the historical record by the intentional postwar destruction of the pertinent files.

53. Accounts of these riots can be found in Jean Provencher, *Québec sons le loi des Mesures de Guerre 1918* (Montreal 1971); Mason Wade, *The French Canadians* (Toronto 1968), 764–9; Armstrong, *Crisis*, 228–37; and in NA, RG 24, C-5660, HQC 2358, "Disturbances in Quebec over the Enforcement of the Military Service Act, 1918."

54. See, for example, description by Douglas Kerr of the Dominion Police, who refers to "the tough young element" and notes that "no person of consequence" was involved. NA, RG 24, C-5660, HQC 2358, letter of 12 April 1918.

55. On Goodwin see Susan Mayse, *Ginger: The Life and Death of Albert Goodwin* (Madiera Park 1990).

56. David Jay Bercuson, *Confrontation at Winnipeg: Labour, Industrial Relations and the General Strike*, rev. ed. (Montreal 1990). For a periodization of Canadian working-class history see Gregory S. Kealey, "The Structure of Canadian Working-Class History," in W.J.C. Cherwinski and Gregory S. Kealey, eds., *Lectures in Canadian Labour and Working-Class History* (St John's 1985), 23–36.

57. Tom Traves, *The State and Enterprise: Canadian Manufacturers and the Federal Government, 1917–1931* (Toronto 1979). See also Myer Siemiatycki, "Labour Contained: The Defeat of a Rank and File Workers' Movement in Canada, 1914–1921" (PhD dissertation, York University 1987).

58. A good discussion of these issues is found in Barbara Roberts, *Whence They Came: Deportation from Canada, 1900–1935* (Ottawa 1988).

59. For a sketchy but useful overview see John Sawatsky, *Men in the Shadows: The RCMP Security Service* (Toronto 1980).

60. NA, Communist Party of Canada Papers, MG 28 IV 4, vol. 40, file 40-28. Chief Press Censor, Supplementary Report to RNWMP, 13 Jan. 1920.

61. See G.S. Kealey and R. Whitaker, eds., *RCMP Security Bulletins: The Early Years, 1919–1929* (St John's 1992).

EIGHTEEN

Fortunes of War

SANDRA GWYN

Instead of ending by Christmas, the war had ended in a "race to the sea" that itself had ended in a draw. The famed Schlieffen Plan, a strategy derived from Hannibal's victory at the Battle of Cannae, by which the Germans planned to crush the allied armies by a pincer-like assault, had failed — just — because there weren't quite enough Germans to bring it off and because the French had rushed reinforcements out of Paris in taxi-cabs. Barbed wire and the machine gun now ruled the battlefield. Nothing could get through them, nor, later, at Gallipoli, around them. Both sides, their generals weaned on Alexander, Caesar, Marlborough, Frederick the Great, Napoleon, still believed in the "the breakthrough." Both maintained their regiments of cavalry, ready to be unleashed in one glorious charge across open fields. To prepare for that day, both dug protectively into the earth, unfurled strands of barbed wire, and set up strongpoints for their machine guns. These were merely temporary bastions from which the breakthrough would be launched.

Trapped in a technological timewarp, the two armies settled into a war like none before or since. From just south of the mouth of the Yser, on the coast of Belgium, down to Beurnevisin on the Swiss frontier, stretched four hundred miles of twisting, looping, but roughly parallel lines of trenches. Into this immensely long but narrow space were compressed more men and more armaments than had ever been assembled before in even the widest of spaces. Three and a half years, and millions of dead young men, later, the lines followed almost exactly the same looping course between the mouth of the Yser and the hamlet of Beurnevisin. At times, as at Verdun or at Passchendaele, the line did shift a few miles eastwards or westwards. Later, it shifted back the same number of miles. "This isn't war," said Lord Kitchener early in 1915. He was right. It was mutual suicide.

"The idea of the trenches," writes Paul Fussell in his 1975 masterpiece, *The Great War and Modern Memory*, "has been assimilated so successfully in metaphor and myth that it is not easy now to recover a feeling for the actualities." A front-line trench could be as close as a few dozen yards from its enemy counterpart, although, quite randomly, the gap between them was sometimes as wide as a mile. In theory (as we shall discover shortly, practice was often quite different) a trench was about eight feet deep and four or five feet wide, thickly surrounded by barbed-wire entanglements, and the floors covered with wooden duckboards (in the damp soil of Flanders, these were often covered with a foot or more of sludgy water). To the front and rear were parapets of sandbags. Along the top of the parapet there were snipers' plates made of thick steel, with holes just large enough to accommodate a rifle barrel and the human eye. At the back of the trenches there was usually a row of dugouts, reached by dirt stairs

Source: Excerpted from *Tapestry of War: A Private View of Canadians in the Great War* (Toronto: HarperCollins, 1992), 133–48. Copyright © 1992 by Sandra Gwyn. Reprinted by permission of HarperCollins Publishers Ltd.

and used for officers' quarters. (Officers' meals were usually provided by a cook; other ranks did their own cooking, such as it was, sometimes using coal braziers and towards the end of the war, Primus stoves. Mostly, they simply opened tins of bully beef or the infamous meat-and-vegetable Maconochie stew.) A well-built trench did not run straight but zigzagged every few yards so that a shell or bomb that landed in it could kill only those in each "zig." With all these zigs, the allied front alone encompassed some twelve thousand miles of trenches. Communication trenches, running roughly at right angles to the front line, served to bring up supplies such as food and ammunition, and to bring back the dead and wounded. Behind these were more trenches parallel with the front line, to serve as a defence in depth for up to half a mile to the rear. Forward of the front line, shallow ditches known as "saps" thrust out into no man's land and served as posts for observation and grenade-throwing. In some instances, as at Vimy, as visitors can still see today, opposed "saps" might be less than twenty yards apart. A standard tour of duty in the front line was about four days. It was spent entirely head-down. To look up and out, other than through a periscope, was to die to a sniper or to a burst of machine-gun fire.

Within this "Troglodyte World," in Fussell's phrase, normal biorhythms were turned upside-down. His description of trench routine speaks for the Canadians as well as for the British. "During the day, men cleaned weapons and repaired those parts of the trench damaged during the night. Or they wrote letters, deloused themselves, or slept. The officers inspected, encouraged, and strolled around looking nonchalant to inspire the men. They censored the men's letters and dealt with the quantities of official inquiries brought to them by runner. . . . Daily 'returns' of the amount of ammunition and the quantities of trench stores had to be made. Reports of the nightly casualties had to be sent back. And letters of condolence, which as the war went on became form-letters of condolence, had to be written to the relatives of the killed and wounded." After evening stand-to, the real work began. No man's land came alive as small parties of men inched through the wire, scurrying from shell-hole to shell-hole, hugging the ground when a flare arched up, trying to pick up intelligence by listening to the enemy's whispered conversations, trying to snatch a prisoner, trying to demoralize the enemy with a sudden storm of hand grenades upon his trenches, or, as the textbooks demanded, just trying to keep up their own aggressive spirits. To relieve the tension and the monotony, almost everyone became a chain-smoker. Cigarettes were smoked behind cupped hands; no one, except newcomers, lit more than one from a single match. Only with the dawn could everyone begin to relax: its coming meant there would be no attack — except when it did come.

The first forty miles of the allied line of trenches, a mainly quiescent sector north of Ypres, was held by the Belgians. The next ninety miles, down to the river Ancre in northwest France, was held by the British and Colonial forces. The French manned the rest, to the south, their stronghold the fortress of Verdun on the River Meuse. The British and Colonial part of the line normally comprised some eight hundred battalions of about a thousand men each. They were concentrated in two main sectors: the Somme area in Picardy, which would take centre stage in 1916, and the Ypres Salient in Flanders. This latter was an untidy bulge, about nine miles long at its widest point and protruding about four miles eastward into the German lines. Vulnerable to attack on three sides, and under constant artillery fire on its exposed flanks, the Salient was a military insanity but a political necessity: it encompassed almost all of the little bit of Belgium that had been held onto at such an appalling cost, and therefore had to go on being held no matter how appalling the future cost. It was here that the Patricias first entered the line, on January 7, 1915, as part of the British 27th Division.

One of the best ways to recapture the *idea* of the trenches is to make a pilgrimage through the Ypres Salient. At first, the placid and prosperous Flemish farm country evokes little that's resonant. Only the occasional shell craters, now serving as waterholes for cattle and geese, or an unnatural wave in a field of cabbage or corn, serve as reminders of battles long ago. Even the daily sunset ceremony at the Menin Gate in Ypres, although moving, lacks a quality of immediacy. Then, when the suburbs of Ypres are still in the rear-view mirror, the road-signs marked "Passchendaele" flash into view. Suddenly, the tragic dimension of the war becomes recognizable as the pilgrim realizes how small was the battlefield over which so much blood was spilled. The description that best sets it in context for Canadians is that of Ralph Allen in *Ordeal By Fire*:

> During the three years between early 1915 and early 1918, the whole of the Canadian ground forces fought and died, and if fortunate, lived, in an area hardly bigger than three or four Saskatchewan townships. Their every value and perspective had to be adjusted accordingly. From one small piece of quagmire, another piece of quagmire fifty yards away could look as enticing as the towers of Cathay. The slightest bulge on the flat, sodden, dangerous plains became a hill or a mountain. On a reverse slope, a company or a battalion could buy respite from the incessant artillery barrages. On a forward slope, it could be wiped out. In the desperate lore of the front, hummocks not large enough to make a toboggan slide became as high and as famous as Everest or the Matterhorn.

The other quality of the Ypres Salient that soon intrudes upon a visitor is the ambience. Brooding and melancholy, it is that of a vast graveyard. Meticulously maintained cemeteries and memorials encroach everywhere upon the farmland: the huge British cemetery at Tyne Cot, close to Passchendaele; the giant statue of the "Brooding Soldier" at Vancouver Corner commemorating the 18,000 Canadians who faced the enemy nearby after the first German gas attacks in April 1915. As memorials go, the regimental cemetery of the Princess Patricia's at Voormezele, a village about four miles south of Ypres, is one of the smaller, mentioned in few of the official guidebooks. For us, though, because a number of our characters are now at rest there, it is a place filled with resonance.

....

Talbot Papineau and Charlie Stewart, recovered from the burns and accompanied by a detachment of forty men, caught up with the Patricias on February 1; Agar Adamson and his draft of two hundred arrived by way of Rouen three weeks later. They found the regiment near the village of St. Eloi, at the extreme southeast elbow of the Salient, engaged in a stubborn defence of a strongpoint that had been christened "The Mound" and that was just that, a hump of brickmakers' clay some twenty feet high and seventy feet long, standing beside the road at the southern approach to Ypres. Elsewhere in the area, the Germans held the high ground. "You never saw such a scene of utter desolation and destruction," was Papineau's first impression on arriving at regimental headquarters in the cellar of a ruined farmhouse that Colonel Farquhar had christened Shelley Farm, not in honour of the poet. "Every barn and house has been smashed to pieces. We passed a whole village smashed to ruins, church and all, not a stray dog or cat living. The Germans would throw up their famous lightning rockets and our whole party would throw themselves down flat in the mud til the darkness came again." Yet his first tour of front-line duty was an easy one, without casualties, and being young and full of mettle, he found it exhilarating. "It's like a game," he wrote his mother on February 5, "dodging and running and creeping and lying down. As it grows dusk we meet our guides and in the dark, in a single file, we are led silently across the fields. All about is the sharp crack of rifle fire. We follow hedgerows and avoid the open. Then we creep up to the opening of the trench, and one by one jump in. I wait until my men are all in and jump after. I have not been badly frightened yet. That will come, I suppose. This is so much like a *fête-de-nuit*, a thunderstorm and duck shooting, that I positively like it."

We can suspect that Papineau was being economical with the truth to spare Caroline's feelings. Soon — "I have faith in your courage" — he began telling her more. Yet he did not describe in detail the horrors that soon became routine, still less the black mood of hopelessness that after six weeks of fruitless fighting was starting to creep up on the regiment.

Adamson spared Mabel nothing. "At the present moment, the Germans have the best of it," he wrote within days of arriving. "Their bomb and mortar throwing is perfect, also their flares, and we are infants at it. Their trenches are beautifully made, they have their men do nothing else, and they are drained and all communicate with each other. Their sniping is organized, the snipers having fixed rifles with telescopic sights firing from about 300 yards. Their particular game is to enfilade the trenches. They fire all day, picking certain points where they know the men will be working, and at night keep up a steady fire about every 30 seconds, generally from both sides of the advance trenches."

The trenches inherited by the Patricias beggared description. Recently taken over from French troops, who had relied much more heavily upon their artillery than their infantry, they weren't trenches at all, only shallow ditches knee-deep in water, protected by a few sandbags and isolated from one another. Number 21, the most notorious death-trap of all, in which Adamson found himself in his first day in the line, "consisted of sandbags about 5 feet high and no trench whatever." Getting in and out involved crawling zigzag through half a mile or more of the mud, and was the most dangerous part. "We lose a lot of men in this way," he continued. "The routes have to be changed constantly as the Germans always find out, and the only way of knowing is by our number of casualties."

We can imagine Mabel shuddering as she read such reports by the dining room fire at Basil Street. Each letter she opened was grimmer. The putrefying stench of wet and decaying human and animal flesh, Agar told her, was incomparably worse than he'd anticipated, and far beyond the power of the smelling salts she'd sent him. "I counted seven dead horses just outside my trench yesterday," he wrote on March 3. "There is also a dead Frenchman there and has been for a long time. We got orders reading, 'Keep the Shelley Farm on your right, and pass between the broken tree and the dead Frenchman on your right,' so the poor fellow was being of some use in death. . . . One of the most disgusting sights was a couple of pigs deliberately feeding on the decomposed body of a soldier. You will be glad to hear it was their last meal, and they remain to add to the stench." A few days later, making improvements to a trench, his men dug into a mass grave. "We had to get the correct depth to give the living men shelter. The only thing to be done was to dig right on regardless of what we went through. The grave was some months old and it was a most horrible opera-tion, especially when the flares were turned on and you saw the awful sights you were digging and picking to pieces. It was too much for some men, who had to be relieved."

Almost as bad as the stench and the sights was the continual pounding of the artillery. "It affects the strongest of us," Agar went on. "The noise and the shaking of the earth gives us the most dreadful headaches and turns us deaf." Even on an uneventful day, the tension of being in the front lines was ever-present. "It gets on one's nerves, always having to be on the alert, as one never knows where or what they will do, and I think when you find they have not done anything, and you have really got out with the whole company safe, the relief is almost as bad as the strain."

....

Thus far, physical casualties to the Patricias had been relatively slight: seventy killed and wounded since early January. But the dreadful conditions produced much sick-ness — pneumonia, typhoid, rheumatism, a condition called "trench foot," a low-grade form of frostbite produced by standing for hours in cold water — so that by the time Adamson arrived, the regiment was nearly four hundred men under strength. "The suffering of the men is very great after they come out of the trenches," he reported. "Their hands and feet are all swelled up and a stiffening of the joints sets in." As damaging to morale in these early days was the large number of deaths that were caused by carelessness and inexperience. The first officer to be killed, Captain D.O.C. Newton, a former aide to the Governor General and great beau around Ottawa, lost his way at night in no man's land and was shot by one of his own sen-tries. A fortnight later, a Captain Fitzgerald jumped out of his trench in broad daylight to inspect a dead body and was instantly shot dead by a sniper. "He practically com-mitted suicide, so foolish was he," Papineau wrote home. On the same day, he con-tinued, "Lieutenant Price was killed. His guide led him incorrectly into the trenches, and he was shot in the chest." The moment when Talbot himself stopped thinking of the war as a *fête-de-nuit* came shortly before noon on March 3, when Captain J.S. Ward, the Okanangan fruit farmer who had become his close friend, jumped up too hastily to inspect the neighbouring trench. "He sank back in my arms," wrote Talbot. "He had been shot in the back of the head. He bled frightfully. The brain matter was easing out. I loved old Ward. He was one of the best fellows I know. It was terrible for me to see him like that so suddenly. He was conscious and could recognize me, although his mind wandered. He was in great pain, and I gave him a good deal of morphine. He would hold my hand sometimes. He said, 'Talbot, you're an angel.' He called for 'Alice, where's Alice?' A terrific snowstorm blew up. I never saw such dark-ness and such wind. Flocks of birds flew before it. Later there was thunder and light-ning. How long those hours were. It was not until 8:30 P.M. that the stretcher party came." Ward died a few days later.

Two other casualties not recorded in official regimental records dealt the Patricias another blow. On January 7, the first day the regiment was in the front line, two officers had broken under the strain. One was a Captain Smith, "accused of lying and cold feet," as Papineau reported. The other was Major J.W.H. McKinery, a big blustery man, Adamson's former company commander. "It appears that he 'blew up,'" Agar wrote Mabel. "He hid himself in the only safe place in the trench for 48 hours, curs-ing and swearing at his subalterns and NCOs all the time, and as soon as he got out bolted for the dressing station to have imaginary wounds attended to. The NCOs told the CO that if they were ordered to go into the trenches with him again, they would refuse and stand a courtmartial." As a cover story, it was put out that both men had been sent back to England on sick leave. Few people believed this — "It is surprising how men come back from the front just ill or tired out," Mabel noted skeptically in a letter to her mother — and the resulting gossip damaged the regiment's reputation. (Both men subsequently were struck "off strength" and reassigned to low-echelon staff duties.)

On February 27, Farquhar conceived of a way to hit at the enemy before being hit by him. He requested permission to make a sudden local attack on a new trench that the Germans were sapping directly in front of The Mound, and so less than twenty yards away from the Patricias' line. Described as a "reconnaissance in force," this was the first engagement fought by a Canadian regiment in Europe. It was also the first of the "trench raids" for which the Canadians were to become famous. Talbot Papineau was one of the ninety or so men chosen to take part. Nearly eight decades later, his private account, a sixteen-page letter to his mother scribbled hastily in pencil, remains the most riveting account of this singular Canadian military initiative.

"We have made an attack at last and I have led it," begins Papineau's letter. At midnight, he and the other raiders had assembled at Shelley Farm. Already, Hamilton Gault and another officer, Lieutenant Colquhoun, who unfortunately had been spotted by the enemy and taken prisoner, had reconnoitred the territory. They were divided into three groups. The first, led by Lieutenant C.E. Crabbe, consisted of about thirty snipers and riflemen, plus three grenade-throwers headed by Papineau. Their objective was to rush the German sap and clear it. The other two parties were to act as cover, and to break down the enemy parapet. "The moon was well down and dawn was coming," continued Papineau. "The colonel said, 'There are six snipers that will go ahead of you then you will go with your bomber-throwers. Crabbe will be behind you with his men. All right! Lead on!'"

I was pretty scared! My stomach seemed hollow. I called my men and we fell into line and began creeping forward flat on our bellies. I had a bomb ready in my hand. We lay for a moment exposed and then suddenly we were all up and rushing forward. My legs caught in barbed wire, but I stumbled through somehow. I set my fuse and hurled my bomb ahead of me. From that moment, all hell broke loose. I never thought there could be such noise. I had my revolver out. A German was silhouetted and I saw the flash of his rifle. I dropped on my knees and fired point blank. He disappeared. I said to myself, "I have shot him." I fired into the trench at whatever I thought was there. Then my revolver stopped. I lay flat and began to reload. I was against the German parapet. I looked behind me and could see only one man apparently wounded or dead near me. I thought, "The attack has failed. I am alone. I will never get out." A machine gun was going and the noise was awful.

Then I saw Crabbe coming. He knelt near me and fired over me with a rifle. I had got a cartridge home by this time and Crabbe and I went over the edge into the trench. It was deep and narrow, beautifully built, dried by a big pump, sides supported by planks, looked like a mine shaft. A German was lying in front of me. I pushed his head down to see if he was dead. He wasn't. I told a man to watch him. Then I began to pull down some of the parapet and sandbags. Three or four men were there too with shovels. The German machine guns were going like mad. It was beginning to grow light.

Presently we were told to evacuate the trench. I passed the order, then climbed out and made a run for our own line. Another man and I went over head first. The man that came after me was shot through the lungs. The next man got it in the stomach. They fell on me in the mud. I could not budge. Then over on top of us all came a German! He held up his hands and a couple of our men took him away. Gault was there and he worked pulling the wounded men off each other. One or two men came piling over with fixed bayonets and almost put our eyes out. I was finally pulled out of the mud. It was not quite light. I had to get back to my own trench. I beat it across the open expecting to get it any minute. I was so exhausted I wobbled from side to side in the mud. However, I reached home and dived for cover. I was tired but mostly glad to be back.

The stretcher bearers were carrying the wounded out past the back of my trench. The last party got halfway, then dropped their stretcher and ran. Gault crawled out to the man with a couple of volunteers and they dragged the stretcher into a ditch and then to a hedge. Gault was shot through the wrist. He will probably get the VC.

In practical terms, the raid achieved little, at a cost of twenty casualties. No ground was gained; the damage inflicted upon the German trench was slight; indeed, within minutes, as Papineau noted, the enemy was back in it throwing bombs. For the next three days, infuriated at having been outwitted even briefly, the Germans battered the regiment with mortar, rifle fire, and grenades and gave Adamson, now McKinery's replacement as commander of No. 2 Company, what he described as "the most awful day I ever put in."

"I could do nothing," he told Mabel. "There was only one rifle working owing to the mud and the debris knocked up by the bombs. We just lay there all day huddled together with constant fire pulling our breastwork down inch by inch. I lost 6 killed and 21 wounded." Nor was there any long-term gain; a fortnight later, after more severe fighting and many more casualties — including Charlie Stewart, badly hit in the stomach — the Germans captured The Mound and the first battle of St. Eloi was lost.

Yet within the context of early 1915, the raid was an important achievement. It demonstrated enterprise and daring. The Divisional Commander telegraphed "Well done PPCLI." Field Marshal Sir John French himself telegraphed "his great appreciation." Within the regiment itself, morale had been recouped and honour restored. Papineau and Crabbe both received the new decoration for junior officers, the Military Cross, and were the first Canadians to do so. Hamilton Gault won the first Canadian DSO for his gallant rescue of the wounded soldier. As mattered most of all, the newspapers having reported the affair, the future of the Patricias was secure at least for the time being.

This was to be "Fanny" Farquhar's last legacy to the Patricias. On March 19, shortly after receiving instructions to leave St. Eloi for the centre of the Salient, Farquhar was hit by a chance bullet while showing the commanding officer of the relieving battalion around. Adamson, leading his own company back to billets after a hard forty-eight hours in the trenches, learned what had happened when he stopped briefly at the dressing station. "I found the Colonel on the floor," he wrote Mabel. "The surgeon was dressing his wound. He was groaning and suffering a great deal. From the very first there was no hope." That same day, Adamson was also mourning the death of Sergeant Cork, his trusted emissary during the battle with Colonel James. "I had just spoken to him," he told Mabel. "He said he had received your remedy for chilblains and was going to write to thank you for it. He was shot through the spine a few minutes afterwards."

Two nights later the Patricias buried their colonel in the new regimental cemetery at Voormezele, a few yards away from Sergeant Cork's grave. "We all seem to think he would like to be with his men," Adamson wrote. "It was his own idea to rope off a separate piece of ground for them." Only forty officers and men were allowed to attend since the ground was continually raked by enemy fire. Nowadays, for the contemporary visitor, thanks to an eloquent letter that Papineau wrote Lady Evelyn, it requires no stretch of the imagination for the tidy rows of poplars around the cemetery and the well-tended rosebushes surrounding the graves, to dissolve into that long-ago muddy field just back of the front lines. "We paid our last respects to the Colonel. It was the first beautiful evening we had had. The lovely sunset still tinged the sky, a new moon and little stars were quiet and clear overhead. A warm stillness and peacefulness seemed with us as we stood by the grave, but just beyond there was the constant crackle of rifles, now and then the whine of a bullet or the loud explosion of a bomb. Peace upon one side, war upon the other . . ."

Papineau's letter went on to say all the right things. "As a Canadian, I feel a national debt of gratitude to him. An Imperial officer, who could have commanded the highest position in the British army, he accepted the task of creating as well as commanding a new and untried Canadian regiment. He knew how to combine the discipline and dignity of the regular British army with the easy independence and democracy of a volunteer Canadian regiment. . . . He himself is with us no longer but his influence and his memory will endure."

Yet, nearly eighty years on, Agar's stumbling description of his own feeling is the more telling. "We are all very much depressed but have to keep up an appearance of cheerfulness, and speak of it as if it were only the fortunes of war. . . . What really makes a real man is something very hard to fathom. I suppose it is a case of training, but I really think it is more than that. It must be a matter as difficult as the definition and reason for the production of a real genius."

....

On March 25, the Patricias marched to Poperinghe, a peaceful market town turned into a bustling transport centre and forward base. There they spent the next week luxuriating in hot baths and the first change of clothes in a month. (Adamson and the other officers had their baths in a hotel: the men splashed around in huge converted beer vats in the main square.) There was even a divisional race meeting with a steeplechase in which both Adamson and Papineau took part. Everyone roared with laughter at the regimental four-in-hand, a carriage painted yellow and black, with two men inside dressed up as a bride and bridegroom. A few moments later, recounted Adamson, "a very fat French nurse and a fatter priest turned up. General Plumer said it was the most perfect makeup job he had ever seen. He was quite upset when he found out it was a real woman and priest and that she was the. matron of the hospital at Poperinghe."

Soon the Second Battle of Ypres would begin. Compared to it, the desperate weeks at St. Eloi would seem like a militia manoeuvre.

TOPIC TEN
The Great Depression

A demonstration by strikers at Market Square on the eve of the Regina Riot on Dominion Day, 1935.

Debate continues to this day among both historians and economists over the precise causes of the 1929–39 Great Depression; little disagreement exists, however, over its devastating consequences. Between 1928 and 1933, for example, the average value of common shares sold on the Toronto and Montreal stock exchanges plummeted 71.5 percent; Canada's gross domestic product in manufacturing fell 48.3 percent; and retail sales plunged 43.7 percent. By 1933, unemployment was hovering around 30 percent. For those with work, the precarious state of many companies along with a desperately large pool of surplus labour meant falling salaries — a drop of approximately 20 percent over the first four years of the Depression for those working in the country's manufacturing sector. Much of the surplus labour resulted from rural-to-urban migration, as a combination of falling worldwide prices for many crops, and dust-bowl conditions in the Prairies made agricultural life untenable for many. In 1931 and 1932, the total net income realized by Canadian farmers amounted to $13.9 million in the red![1]

Compounding such suffering was a belief on the part of Ottawa and most provincial governments that it was crucial to avoid large-scale expenditures and significant public debt. Although the Liberal prime minister William Lyon Mackenzie King was defeated in 1930 largely for portraying the Great Depression as a temporary glitch in the business cycle, his Conservative successor Richard Bedford Bennett throughout most of his term stuck with such traditional, ineffective policies as raising tariffs — a measure that, rather than protecting Canadian jobs, actually worsened the economic situation by damaging the country's critical trading sector. Federal assistance to the provinces and municipalities to fight unemployment rose only marginally during most of the 1930s; Ottawa further justified its tight-fistedness on the grounds that such assistance was not a federal responsibility, and that its own frugality would force lower levels of government to ferret out and cut off assistance from those who, it was assumed, were abusing ill-managed make-work projects. But as Patrick H. Brennan contends in Article 19, basing his argument on case studies of Regina and Saskatoon, Ottawa's parsimonious approach undermined what were relatively effective programs to alleviate suffering. Moreover, stinginess on the part of the federal government actually forced more people onto the dole, because direct relief was cheaper than the public works projects that were approved by these cities, and which local residents preferred to cash payouts.

While a majority of historians dealing with the Depression have focussed on the suffering and protest of the era, José E. Igartua shows in Article 20 that even during this dark period a focus on common people could yield relatively positive results. Turning to demographic evidence derived from records of the Alcan Aluminum Company in the Saguenay region of Quebec, Igartua notes that the Depression, besides bringing great hardships, brought conditions in response to which the company formulated new personnel policies — policies that enabled it to draw together a relatively stable and committed workforce and to solidify its links with the surrounding community. Having thereby cut down on training costs and developed a more productive workforce, Alcan found itself well poised to respond to the soaring demand for aluminum during World War II.

QUESTIONS TO CONSIDER

1. Were there problems besides a lack of financial support from Ottawa besetting public works programs in Saskatchewan?
2. What, if any, role did the Saskatchewan provincial government play in alleviating unemployment? Was the federal government at all justified in holding back funds from Saskatoon and Regina?
3. On what evidence does Brennan rely in making his case that municipal make-work projects in Saskatoon and Regina were well planned and reasonably effective?
4. How did the Depression act as a stimulus to Alcan to improve its workforce?
5. Whom did Alcan's personnel department believe it best to hire? How did they reach their decision, and do subsequent statistics prove them to have been right?

NOTES

1. M.C. Urquhart and K.A.H. Buckley, eds., *Historical Statistics on Canada* (Toronto: Macmillan, 1965), series H631–50, L83–87, Q1–11, T25–34.

SUGGESTED READINGS

Broadfoot, Barry. *Ten Lost Years, 1929–1939*. Toronto: Doubleday, 1973.
Dumas, Evelyn. *The Bitter Thirties in Quebec*. Montreal: Black Rose, 1975.
Finkel, Alvin. *Business and Social Reform in the Thirties*. Toronto: James Lorimer, 1979.
Horn, Michiel, ed. *The Depression in Canada: Responses to Economic Crisis*. Toronto: Copp Clark Pitman, 1988.
MacDowell, Laurel Sefton. "Relief Camp Workers in Ontario during the Great Depression of the 1930s." *Canadian Historical Review*, 76, 2 (1995): 205–28.
Neatby, H. Blair. *The Politics of Chaos: Canada in the Thirties*. Toronto: Copp Clark Pitman, 1986.
Patrias, Carmela. *Relief Strike: Immigrant Workers and the Great Depression in Cowland, Ontario, 1930–1935*. Toronto: New Hogtown Press, 1990.
Pierson, Ruth Roach. "Gender and the Unemployment Debates in Canada, 1934–1940." *Labour/Le Travail*, 25 (1990): 77–103.
Struthers, James. *No Fault of Their Own: Unemployment and the Canadian Welfare State, 1914–1941*. Toronto: University of Toronto Press, 1983.
Thompson, John Herd, and Allen Seager. *Decades of Discord: Canada, 1922–1939*. Toronto: McClelland & Stewart, 1985.
Vigod, B.L. "The Quebec Government and Social Legislation during the 1930s: A Study in Political Self-Destruction." *Journal of Canadian Studies/Revue d'études canadiennes*, 14, 1 (1979): 59–69.

NINETEEN

"Thousands of Our Men Are Getting Practically Nothing at All to Do": Public Works Relief Programs in Regina and Saskatoon, 1929–1940

PATRICK H. BRENNAN

At the outset of the Depression, civic administrations and taxpayers alike in Saskatchewan shared the prevailing view that at least the married jobless should be provided with work, not "doles."[1] Regina and Saskatoon, the province's two largest urban centres, joined other Canadian cities in clamouring for financial assistance from the senior governments to provide as much work as possible. Although the resultant shared-cost public works programs proved costly, in Saskatchewan the projects constructed were useful and created badly-needed employment. Within two years, however, public works relief (or unemployment relief work — the terms were used interchangeably) on a national scale foundered on the twin shoals of "sound finance" and the constitutional doctrine of "local responsibility."[2] In its place, Ottawa fell back on the cheaper but unpopular system of "direct relief." Neither Saskatoon nor Regina ever willingly accepted this decision, and throughout the remainder of the 1930s both municipalities persisted in attempts to revive unemployment relief work. Unfortunately, financially strapped provincial authorities could offer little more than sympathy, and the federal government, for a variety of reasons beginning with cost, was uninterested. Only in the last year of the Depression would Ottawa, under the guise of "work and wages," once more make it possible for the two cities to undertake unemployment relief works on a significant scale.

Public works relief alone could never have eliminated the crushing burden of unemployment; in that assessment Ottawa was correct. However, the Saskatchewan experience with public works relief does not support the view that the approach was inherently inefficient and extravagant, and in the process, sheds light on the staggering administrative obstacles Canadian cities faced in trying to deal constructively with the unemployment crisis.

Although seasonal unemployment had been a fixture in Prairie cities throughout the 1920s, conditions during the winter of 1929–30 evoked widespread talk of a "crisis" and the need for "emergency measures." Both Regina and Saskatoon were prepared to carry out capital works to create winter employment, primarily for their res-

Source: Excerpted from "'Thousands of our men are getting practically nothing at all to do': Public Works Relief Programs in Regina and Saskatoon, 1920–1940," *Urban History Review*, 21, 1 (1992): 33–45. Reprinted by permission of *Urban History Review*.

ident married jobless, provided the senior governments agreed to cover any excess costs.[3] Ottawa refused, but with the offer of provincial assistance, both cities went ahead. The resultant programs generated $200,000 in wages, which proved enough to see most of their unemployed through the winter.

Choosing to emphasize productive work over the "dole" followed naturally from the prevailing attitude about the "demoralizing" effects of direct relief. At the same time, restricting the available work to resident married men and those single men with dependents reflected the conviction that the future prosperity of both communities depended on retaining this "settled" work force. Finally, an emergency program based on public works which were soon slated to be carried out anyway and could now be partially financed by the province made good economic sense to any municipality.

When spring brought no significant decline in unemployment levels, both Saskatoon and Regina launched ambitious public works programs and then pressed the senior governments for assistance in financing them.[4] Once again, the provincial government proved co-operative, authorizing Regina to proceed with the needed re-construction of the Albert Street bridge on a shared-cost basis.

Though the Anderson government's commitment was welcome, attention throughout the province was now rivetted on Ottawa. During the just completed federal election campaign, Conservative leader R.B. Bennett had relentlessly attacked the King government's inaction in the face of the growing unemployment crisis. As evidenced by the stunning, one-sided defeat suffered by Finance Minister (and former Premier) Charles Dunning in Regina, urban Saskatchewan had embraced Bennett's message enthusiastically. Like his Liberal predecessor, the new Prime Minister firmly believed that unemployment relief became a federal responsibility only when the burden threatened to overwhelm provinces and municipalities financially. Where they differed was in their assessment of the current situation: to his credit Bennett admitted it was a crisis and was prepared to act. To reinforce the point, his government promptly introduced the Unemployment Relief Act, with the bulk of its $20 million appropriation earmarked for the creation of "useful and suitable work for the unemployed." In the case of municipal public works, Ottawa agreed to match provincial grants up to 25 percent of approved costs. Leaving most of the administration in provincial hands preserved the facade of local responsibility.[5]

Word that Dominion funds would be forthcoming triggered a collective sigh of relief in Regina and Saskatoon, for by late summer all of their planned public works were rapidly nearing completion and there was no possibility of starting others without firm assurances of cost-sharing. The two cities quickly drew up plans for a total of $2.5 million in winter construction for inclusion under the federal initiative.[6] After brief scrutiny, the provincial cabinet's relief committee promptly forwarded these to Ottawa for final approval. The initial batch of projects authorized included a major (and badly needed) expansion of Regina's waterworks system, as well as an underpass and storm sewers in Saskatoon, well over $1 million of construction.

Unfortunately, delays in obtaining approval from Ottawa for Regina's full work relief program meant that by year's end the city was hard-pressed to provide jobs for 250 of the over 1,700 married and nearly 1,600 single men registered with its relief department. Privately, Mayor James Balfour, who like everyone else in the city's administration considered the "dole" a complete loss to the community, complained bitterly that "thousands of our married men are practically getting nothing at all to do and we are simply supplying them with . . . food supplies. . . ."[7]

As if the lack of work was not enough of a problem, controversy erupted between the city and its jobless over the running of the program. Unseemly squabbling with Ottawa over what constituted a fair wage for common labour in Regina was followed by Commissioner R.J. Westgate's heavy-handed order to investigate the qualifications of all tradesmen on relief in order to determine which of them were "less qualified and might be willing to accept a lower rate of wages."[8] Federal regulations required that contractors pay skilled workers at established rates; Westgate's goal was to maximize the amount of "common labour" on the city's various projects, and he had been attempting to ensure that unemployed skilled tradesmen would work for labourers' pay when the job in question called for it.

To "encourage" the co-operation of the unemployed, the city had begun striking men (though not their dependents) off the relief rolls if they refused any relief job offered them. Not surprisingly, both the unemployed and local trade unionists were strongly opposed, and as the winter dragged on, complaints steadily increased. All were investigated, many by committees which included trade union representatives or by the officials of the Department of Railways, Labour and Industries, the provincial department responsible for overseeing the Unemployment Relief Act in Saskatchewan urban centres. The evidence gathered in these inquiries indicates that while incompetence, understaffing, language problems, and "honest errors" persisted in the administration of the relief work projects, occurrences of favouritism and discrimination, along ethnic, religious or other lines, were infrequent. As one frustrated alderman pointed out:

> It seems to me that it is not thoroughly realized what a very difficult problem we have in dealing [with the unemployed] who are daily clamouring for work, work which we have not available at present. No authority, Federal, Provincial or Municipal could cope with such a situation without disappointment and in some cases unwarranted complaints.[9]

He was basically correct, of course, but resentment among the city's unemployed was understandable and not easily allayed.

By the end of October Ottawa had also confirmed a schedule of tripartite unemployment relief works for Saskatoon. The arrangements put in place by Saskatoon officials for allocating labour on these projects were even more ad hoc than Regina's. By December, under the pressure of 1,800 applicants, the system began to break down and with it, the patience of the city's unemployed.[10] Nevertheless, by year's end 450 men were toiling on the city's public works relief program, nearly a third of them on entirely municipal undertakings. During the remaining months of the winter, the city completed the greater part of its planned program, generating about $170,000 in wages, or almost six times the amount spent on direct relief over the same period.[11] Still, there was never enough work and by mid-winter a labour alderman was publicly complaining that some married men were receiving only a week's work in every eight or nine.[12]

During the summer of 1931 — the first year of general drought in Saskatchewan — conditions in the province were deteriorating at an alarming rate. Since the economies of both Regina and Saskatoon were almost totally dependent on the wheat economy, the impact of this disaster was immediate and devastating. With the volume of retail trade and construction plummeting, urban unemployment soared. Not surprisingly, in both cities there was almost universal support for a continuation of the unemployment relief works program; indeed, if possible on a considerably expanded scale. Apart from the perceived merit of work over direct relief, a belief which was quite sincerely held, self-interest was certainly a strong consideration. After all, unemployment relief work schemes of the tripartite variety meant cities could obtain useful public works at a fraction of their ordinary cost, and defer actual payment of their portion of the expenditure for up to thirty years. In contrast, Saskatchewan cities were still required to cover their share of direct relief out of current revenue, a bleak prospect indeed when one remembers that their share, if so-called administrative costs not subject to cost-sharing were included, now hovered around 50 percent. In a reference to such projects at their June meeting, delegates to the Union of Saskatchewan Municipalities (Urban Section) conference pointedly reminded Ottawa that "any expenditure to protect the social life of our people is productive and therefore economical." Newspaper editorials, too, regularly urged a start on the "many other useful works that could be performed by these [jobless] men with dignity to themselves [and] satisfaction to the community. . . ."[13] Furthermore, the unemployed themselves, while never more than loosely organized in either Regina or Saskatoon, were increasingly vocal in pressing their demands for work and the abolition of the "dole."[14] Given the alarming state of provincial and municipal finances in Saskatchewan, however, it was clear to everyone that any continuation of public works relief would depend entirely on decisions made in Ottawa. Local and provincial officials could only plan . . . and wait.

Frustrated with the Depression's intractability, Prime Minister Bennett had convinced himself that reports of desperate drought and unemployment conditions pouring in from civic and provincial officials in the West were greatly exaggerated. In June, to gather firsthand evidence on the true state of affairs, he despatched a delegation headed by Labour Minister Gideon Robertson. Officially, the jobless rate among males in both Regina and Saskatoon stood at 27 percent that month, and to make matters worse, during the preceding twelve months fully one-third of the male work force had been unemployed, the average period being a staggering 31 weeks.[15] Robertson was genuinely moved by what he saw and heard, and within days of his return the federal government dramatically announced plans to meet "the greatest national calamity that has ever overtaken this country."[16] The Unemployment and Farm Relief Act (1931), which followed within a month, possessed all the failings associated with the "temporary" and "emergency" aspects of its predecessor. Although it was clear that the major thrust would once again be jointly funded public works construction, regulations and particularly the size of the appropriation were kept purposefully vague. Bennett privately acknowledged that this was necessary to avoid unseemly squabbling among the provinces and thus prevent "prodigal" expenditures. Not unexpectedly, the federal government intended to exercise much tighter administrative control over its new relief work program.

Bennett's fears were not without justification, for Ottawa's announcement elicited a flood of submissions which soon surpassed the $200 million mark. Saskatoon and Regina were not outdone, quickly drawing up their own lists of projects easily adapted to relief work purposes, in other words those which minimized materials costs and maximized "pick and shovel" work.[17] The Department of Railways, Labour and Industries preferred smaller schemes on the grounds that they tended to create more labour per relief dollar expended, while cities still eyed large projects and most of their proposals reflected this. Formally, however, the province only required that projects be "sensible" (that is, legitimately useful on more than just work-creation grounds) and budget a minimum of 60 percent of their cost for labour; those which qualified they promptly forwarded to Ottawa.[18]

After such a promising beginning, however, interminable delays followed while the senior governments negotiated the financial terms so critical to the participation of Saskatchewan cities. One can readily appreciate the difficulty of dealing with day-to-day relief problems while trying to plan for the future without the benefit of any definite information on administrative regulations or financing. Efficient co-ordination under such circumstances was all but impossible and misunderstandings on the part of civic officials, who were often reduced to acting on rumour, were inevitable. Indeed, they risked Ottawa's wrath even in attempting to communicate directly with their federal counterparts because this would violate the sacred doctrine of "local responsibility." Yet an increasingly suspicious federal relief bureaucracy seized upon any failure to follow regulations as proof of municipal incompetence or worse.

On the assumption that Ottawa would eventually approve the project, a group of Regina aldermen had managed to persuade their colleagues to proceed with construction of a water reservoir to provide badly needed work.[19] Word that the province had "acquiesced" in this manoeuvre infuriated federal officials and Bennett in particular. For some time now, Premier Anderson's government had been compelled to seek federal assistance simply to meet its basic responsibilities, but these requests had only served to confirm the Prime Minister's suspicion "that money is being expended in [Saskatchewan] without a due regard to the fact that it is not easy to obtain it."[20] Unfair though the accusations were, Anderson soon had no choice but to comply with what amounted to a federal ultimatum that he replace his treasurer with someone who inspired more confidence in Ottawa.[21]

Within days of the August 18 passage of the Unemployment and Farm Relief Act, Ottawa confirmed that cities in the Western provinces would see their share of the costs of work relief projects reduced by half to 25 percent. In order to finance their portion, Regina and Saskatoon would "sell" their now all but unsaleable debentures to the provincial treasury. The funds to carry out this paper transaction, plus pay the province's own 25 percent share, ultimately had to come from the federal government, such "loans" being "secured" by the transfer of almost equally worthless Saskatchewan treasury bills. It was an elaborate charade carried out to satisfy Ottawa's demand that constitutional appearances be maintained.[22] Although it now seemed the way was open for an immediate start on the main program of relief work in Regina and Saskatoon, the two senior governments did not sign a formal relief accord until September 29, at which time the Premier revealed that the budget for municipal relief work programs in the province had been pared by 80 percent to a mere $1.5 million.

It was mid-October before Regina received notification from the Department of Railways, Labour and Industries that Ottawa had sanctioned a $600,000 expenditure, which the city was free to allocate on any of the works it had already submitted. Alarmed city officials quickly realized that the two projects already underway, the water reservoir and the dredging and beautification of Wascana Lake, would absorb most of these funds.[23] However, two weeks later the promise of an additional appropriation enabled the city to make a start on the pipeline supplying the reservoir, which they hoped would employ over 1,000 men for three months during the critical winter months. Ottawa's apparent lack of concern over which projects the city proceeded with seemed to indicate that the federal government's preoccupation was now simply the magnitude of its budgetary involvement. This conclusion was borne out during succeeding months by such financial pettiness as disallowing the $1000 purchase price of the land for the reservoir and several hundred dollars more for surveys and blueprints on the grounds that such expenditures did not directly create any work for the unemployed.[24] Cities, moreover, had to finance the entire cost of construction while awaiting federal reimbursement; time-consuming audits delayed this for months, and the resulting interest charges were a heavy burden on municipal finance.

The total public works relief appropriation authorized for Regina under the Unemployment and Farm Relief Act (1931) amounted to $1,171,080, of which the city actually spent slightly over $1 million during the fifteen months required to complete the reservoir, pipeline and lake schemes as well as various street improvements and storm sewer construction, in the process generating an impressive $680,000 in wages. Unfortunately, almost two-thirds of this came after the winter was over; the unpredictable and disjointed fashion in which the federal bureaucracy dealt with their overall schedule had stymied the city's best efforts to stagger the projects and thus ensure a reasonable regular flow of work.[25] Consequently, from December through March, when there were never fewer than 1,900 married men on Regina's relief rolls, there were usually eight or nine "reliefers" for every spot on a city work gang and all too frequently no work for these men at all. Spring brought a significant improvement and by the middle of June there were "only" 1,700 men vying for 700 jobs.[26] Average monthly earnings from September, 1931 through April, 1932 were a meagre $25. Although this figure doubled during the ensuing six months and certainly represented a marked improvement over the previous year, it was obviously inadequate to meet even the barest needs of Regina's jobless. Most men earned so little that they were back on relief as soon as the work was rotated; indeed, in recognition of this, the city had ceased discontinuing direct relief to those who were working. Instead, the men had been paid only 10 cents an hour in cash, with the relief department "retaining" the remainder.

Regulations governing eligibility for relief work, like direct relief, tightened considerably during the 1931–2 season. While Saskatoon continued to accept single men without dependents as long as they were taxpayers and not on relief, Regina increasingly began restricting its public works relief jobs to married "reliefers" with children, arguing that such men had been "checked out" and clearly had the strongest "claim" on a job. However, this policy virtually ensured that all married men with children who were laid off for any length of time would be driven onto the relief rolls.[27]

Rather unrealistically, both cities had intended to provide full-time work on public works projects for all "deserving" unemployed, but the very high levels of unemployment combined with drastic cutbacks in anticipated funding made this impossible. Instead, available work was rotated. Regina changed shifts weekly, with those considered "more needy" being recalled sooner than others, whereas Saskatoon used twelve-day shifts with every man theoretically receiving an equal amount of work. Administered by overworked relief departments, the rotation system frequently broke down and continued to be much criticized by the unemployed. Yet the fact that both cities managed to provide 90 percent of their able-bodied married "reliefers" with at least some employment during the fall and winter months attests to a considerable measure of fairness. That said, there is strong evidence that the obsession of some Regina officials with the threat of "communist subversion" led to the speedy dismissal of a handful of "politically active" reliefers from work crews. Saskatoon council was no friend of "rabble rousers" either but overall its willingness to co-operate with a grievance committee nominated by a newly formed married unemployed men's association produced a more harmonious atmosphere than had prevailed the previous year.[28]

One thing is certainly clear: the desire of the overwhelming majority of the able-bodied "reliefers" to work rather than suffer the indignities of the "dole" had not diminished. Engineering Department staff who were in daily contact with the men reported favourably on the willingness of frequently ill-clad and undernourished men to work under the most difficult conditions. Private contractors, too, seemed generally satisfied with the bulk of the workmen they were required to hire. While men in both cities continued to lose their relief eligibility if they refused assignments (a policy the unemployed married men's associations now endorsed), the opportunity to escape the boredom of joblessness, obtain some degree of economic independence, and maintain their dignity seems to have been more important.[29]

The bleak financial situation faced by both levels of government in Saskatchewan fed widespread rumours throughout the winter that a shift from public works to less costly direct relief was imminent. Despite the Prime Minister's New Year's optimism that the worst of the Depression was over, the financial implications of unemployment and drought relief were becoming an obsession in Ottawa. In February, federal officials ominously informed their Saskatchewan counterparts that the province's urban relief work effort should be scaled down. In fact, virtually the entire appropriation had already been committed. Regardless, by this time Prime Minister Bennett had already decided upon a new course; a Federal–Provincial relief conference called for April was merely a forum for presenting this *fait accompli* to the public as the product of a genuine consensus.

For the four Western premiers the proceedings must have been a grim ordeal, with Bennett sternly lecturing them on their collective failure to practice "fiscal prudence" and carry out their constitutional responsibilities to the unemployed. Upon his return, a chastened Premier Anderson cautioned a delegation of unemployed Saskatoon men that for the foreseeable future depression conditions made it "obviously impossible" to provide public work for everyone desiring it. Ottawa did make one concession: federal funds for projects already approved but not yet completed or, in some instances, even started, would not be cut off May 1 as had been feared.

From the federal government's perspective, public works relief, an initiative conceived two years earlier "as a system of stimulation to employment . . . [now] threatened to become a widespread and persistent [fixture]," and under the circumstances their concerns were valid. Moreover, Ottawa's conviction that Western cities were incapable of undertaking such programs without "widespread extravagance and inefficiency" was now unshakeable.[30] Yet the experience in Regina and Saskatoon, where the projects undertaken had produced useful assets within budgeted expenditures, clearly refuted the latter allegation. If the costs were somewhat "excessive" by pre-Depression standards, decisions to maximize manual labor and complete much of the work out of season, not "reckless" administration, were responsible. Nevertheless, as a method of delivering subsistence relief on the required scale, which is what public works relief had become in Saskatchewan cities, the program was proving a dubious solution, financially and otherwise. For officials in Regina and Saskatoon, however, the debate was academic; they had no choice but to accept Ottawa's verdict that

Canada could no longer afford to create employment through the construction of shared-cost public works.

The inevitable result of this policy was a dramatic rise in municipal direct relief costs — and short-term municipal debt in the form of the five-year debentures which cities in the province could now issue to cover the cost. It is hardly any wonder, then, that civic officials hoped 1933 would bring about a change of heart at Ottawa. But it was not to be; that year's Relief Act did provide some funds for shared-cost work relief projects, but under financial terms which made the participation of a poor province like Saskatchewan impossible. Speaking at the Regina Board of Trade that October, however, the Prime Minister had alluded to improved economic conditions justifying "moderate [soon altered to "extensive"] public works undertakings for relief" in 1934.[31] Unfortunately, what the federal government had in mind were purely federal public works, the need for which was limited in a recently settled province like Saskatchewan. Nevertheless, provincial and municipal officials were bitterly disappointed when they learned that Ottawa had authorized only one project for the province — a $460,000 federal building in Regina — and even work on that would be delayed until the following spring.[32]

In 1934, the Anderson government itself became a casualty of depression conditions when every member was defeated at the polls. During their five-year term, the Premier and his colleagues had worked tirelessly to ameliorate the unprecedented suffering being endured in urban and rural Saskatchewan, but the problems had simply overwhelmed them. The new Premier, Liberal James Gardiner, offered a delegation of city representatives sympathy but no concrete pledges of assistance for work-creation schemes; the desperate crisis in the drought area, he reminded them, must have first call on his government's extremely limited resources.[33] Nevertheless, a few months later, the province did agree to participate in a limited public works program proposed by the Regina council. The city's plan, which had the strong backing of the two local unemployed associations, was intended to provide married unemployed men with extra cash earnings equal to one-quarter of their normal direct relief allotment. Carried out in the autumn of 1934, the program generated $50,000 in wages, a figure which was dwarfed by the year's direct relief bill of almost $1,500,000, nearly half of which fell on the weary shoulders of Regina taxpayers.[34]

Ottawa's only "concession" to municipal public works relief during 1935 was to permit cities and provinces to use part of their monthly direct relief grants to cover the labour costs of any such projects they wished to undertake.[35] In Saskatchewan, where these grants were not even large enough to cover their intended purpose, this option was of only theoretical interest. Consequently, with one exception, no unemployment relief work projects were undertaken in the province during 1935. That exception involved a provincially approved plan to "pay" married "reliefers" in Regina the prevailing fair wage for any required trade but withhold all earnings. Each man would work enough to "earn" his monthly direct relief quota plus 10 percent to cover other needs. From the outset, the thousand or so men taken on resented what was, after all, little more than the "dole" with a work test, and within a month made their point by going on strike. Council agreed to hear their complaints and by agreeing to suspend the program defused the confrontation.[36]

Five years earlier, R.B. Bennett had rashly promised that there would be work for all and that no man would have to suffer the humiliation of the "dole." Performance, unfortunately, had fallen considerably short of expectation, and nowhere more than in Saskatchewan. Now his government faced the cheerless prospect of an election. As one of the embattled Prime Minister's Saskatchewan back-benchers had warned some months earlier: "An idle machine does not go on the dole and doesn't vote, but an idle man does. . . ."[37] In Saskatchewan as elsewhere, the outcome of the 1935 federal poll was a foregone conclusion. There was little reason, however, for the province's hard-pressed cities to expect innovation from the new Liberal government. Both Mackenzie King and his trusted finance minister, Charles Dunning, were fiscal conservatives who shared Bennett's suspicion that municipal administration of relief had been and continued to be chronically wasteful and hence a prime target for financial economies.[38]

During 1936, an average of one-quarter of Regina's male work force was unemployed and expenditures on direct relief reached a new peak.[39] City council, now dominated by a coalition of labour aldermen and benefitting from the vigorous leadership of Mayor A.C. Ellison, another labour man, was determined to replace the "dole" with a suitable "work and wages" program. That spring, Ellison travelled to Ottawa to press for a $400,000 loan the city intended to use to build municipally-owned rental housing. All of the labour would be recruited from among the city's unemployed construction workers. Unfortunately, while the scheme's self-liquidating aspect impressed Labour Minister Norman Rogers, his fear that its approval would spark an avalanche of similar requests from other cities doomed the proposal.[40]

Not surprisingly, when Regina tried to obtain federal financing for a still more ambitious "work and wages" housing scheme in the spring of 1937, it was turned down flat. For Ellison and his labour colleagues, the apparent equanimity with which the federal government seemed to accept direct relief as an indefinite solution to unemployment was incomprehensible. Thus, the following spring, after consulting with the union of the married unemployed men, council authorized its own small-scale program of relief work. Participation was made voluntary and workers, now with collective bargaining rights, would be paid 10 cents per hour in cash in addition to their normal direct relief. But the first shift of 250 men had hardly begun their two-week stint when they began complaining that the bulk of the work was useless. Most of the projects certainly lacked "glamour" and council sympathized with the men's frustration, but with almost no money to buy materials, Engineering Department officials could hardly be blamed for selecting the projects they had. Work continued on them throughout the summer of 1938.[41]

That autumn, Regina attained the dubious distinction of having spent a total of $10 million on direct relief. For disillusioned civic officials and taxpayers alike, the milestone served as a bitter reminder of the futility of passive relief which had seen such an enormous sum expended to no lasting purpose.[42]

Yet 1938 had also brought some good news. The passage of the Municipal Improvements Assistance Act heralded a welcome change in the federal attitude toward public works relief. Officially the legislation was intended "to create employment . . . by providing funds to municipalities at a low rate of interest to assist them in constructing or making extensions or improvements to, or renewals of . . . any . . . self-liquidating project for which there is urgent need and which will assist in the relief of unemployment."[43] Reaction in Saskatoon and Regina was generally favourable, although there was some grumbling over what amounted to a $200,000 loan "ceiling" for smaller cities and the limited amount of employment suitable projects (which would inevitably require large expenditures on materials) were bound to generate. Still, as Mayor Ellison was quick to point out, at least the King government had finally accepted the principle of subsidizing municipal borrowing for relief work purposes.[44] Their reservations aside, city and provincial officials both agreed that everything must be done to ensure projects were approved and work started before the onset of winter.

Regina quickly decided to apply for a $140,000 loan to purchase and install new generating equipment for its electrical utility, while Saskatoon, after several false starts (a swimming pool and transit buses were rejected by Ottawa as "frills," albeit self-liquidating ones), decided on a $190,000 program of sewer and water main construction and street improvements. Strictly speaking, neither of the latter projects was "self-liquidating," but at the province's urging Ottawa had agreed to interpret the term more liberally for Saskatchewan centres. Provincial officials had simply pointed out the obvious: after six years of virtually complete neglect, the need for such essential maintenance could not be put off any longer.[45] Unhappily, when it came to approving loan applications, the federal bureaucracy moved at its usual glacial pace with a predictable result: neither city was able to start work on its projects before the following spring.[46]

While the Municipal Improvements Assistance Act, despite its failings, was welcome, what the cities really sought was a revival of shared-cost public works relief along the lines of the 1930 and 1931 programs, and their hopes were soon to be at least partially answered. In the Speech from the Throne delivered in January 1939, direct relief, for nearly seven years the mainstay of public unemployment assistance, was dismissed as "ineffective." Accordingly, it would give way to ". . . the acceptance of responsibility by the Federal authority for a program of public works that will nourish useful expenditure in the Provincial and Municipal sphere as well as Federal purposes."[47] Within a matter of days, Labour Minister Rogers announced the Civic Improvements Plan, a scheme whereby the senior governments would absorb the entire labour cost of any additional municipal public works beyond those ordinarily planned by cities and towns and which were being specifically undertaken as an alternative to direct relief.

In Saskatchewan, however, initial reaction to the "Rogers Works Plan" (as it was promptly dubbed) was decidedly negative. Once again, Ottawa had ignored the impossible financial predicament of the province's cities. Where would money for materials come from, disbelieving civic officials wondered aloud?[48] Consultations between the two senior governments and between the province and its urban municipalities proceeded intermittently through the spring. For the latter, the whole procedure assumed an all too familiar pattern, and by June, municipal patience had run out.[49] As one Saskatchewan Liberal MP lamented, delays in implementing relief work legislation would once again guarantee "that work that should have started in July [will get] going about the same time Santa Claus comes down the chimney."[50]

When a formal agreement to implement the Civic Improvements Plan in Saskatchewan was finally signed on June 30, it became clear that the Patterson government's straitened finances would limit the program to an overall expenditure of $1,250,000. When broken down, the shares of Regina and Saskatoon were $300,000 and $200,000, respectively. In this last summer of the Depression, the two cities still had over one-sixth of their residents on the "dole."[51] Regina immediately submitted dozens of different projects for provincial approval, from parks and recreational facilities to roadwork and general maintenance, with 80 percent of the expenditure earmarked for wages, and Saskatoon quickly followed suit. As usual, the province acted expeditiously, but this time the authorization process in Ottawa, too, moved swiftly and by mid-August, a mere six weeks after the Dominion–provincial agreement had been struck, "work and wages" programs were actually underway.[52]

Both city administrations, whether out of habit or from wishful thinking, assumed married "reliefers" would have priority on Civic Improvements Plan schemes and that they would rotate labour in the traditional way. However, federal authorities rejected both practices as contrary to the spirit of "work and wages." To avoid any "misunderstandings," the province ordered city officials to ensure that no compulsion was used in hiring, that all men were taken on full-time for the duration of the project, and that every man received the prevailing wage for the work done in cash. As well, at least one-third of the work force had to be drawn from unemployed men who were *not* on relief.[53]

Among the jobless in Regina and Saskatoon, there was overwhelming support for "work and wages." Work rotation, which gave one no sense of real independence from the "dole," had lost its attraction early in the Depression, and the desire to earn a full salary had never been in question. When work began on a $250,000 flood control weir in Saskatoon (city council had finally convinced Ottawa to finance this separate "work and wages" project under the Prairie Farm Rehabilitation Administration), 700 men applied for the 200 openings even though the wages of those with large families were actually going to be lower than their direct relief over the six-month duration of the job.[54]

Both cities continued to submit projects for inclusion under the Civic Improvements Plan, the great majority of them inexpensive and labour intensive. In Regina's case, the final total reached seventy-four and ran the gamut from street gravelling, grading, and paving to tree planting, the painting and re-roofing of public buildings, incinerator improvements, a plant nursery, and the construction of sewer and water lines and sidewalks.[55] By the late summer of 1939, largely as a result of the Civic Improvements Plan, some 500 unemployed men were working on public works relief projects in Regina and a further 350 in Saskatoon.

Although the immediate prospects for work in Saskatchewan would remain bleak, the outbreak of war in early September was bound to have a significant impact on the need for work-creation programs nationally. On September 9, Ottawa had confidentially informed the various provincial governments that it was considering an early termination of the Civic Improvements Plan. An alarmed Patterson government forcefully reminded Dominion authorities that Saskatchewan's unemployment rate remained very high and it was unlikely (to say the least) that any of the works approved, with their minimal demands on construction materials or skilled labour, would interfere with the war effort.[56] This prompt action at least saved all of the projects already authorized, but making further submissions was pointless, as municipalities were soon instructed. Regardless of the justifications advanced, in Saskatchewan the abrupt reduction in the scale of the "work and wages" program was not well received. Municipal governments, business and labour groups, the unemployed, and the public at large had all strongly supported the Civic Improvements Plan. In all respects, the performance of the program had fulfilled expectations, with the effort put forward by the workers being specifically singled out.[57] In Regina, the thirty projects undertaken employed nearly 600 men, paying them an average of $200, and the earnings of the nearly 500 men who worked on Saskatoon's twelve projects were comparable.[58] By 1939, the federal government seemed to have concluded that shared-cost "work and wages" programs should form part of a balanced approach to dealing with the chronic unemployment of able-bodied workers, especially in the construction trades, which, in the case of Saskatchewan, constituted the largest group of unemployed throughout the 1930s. As it was, by 1940 the war would all but eliminate unemployment, even in Saskatchewan cities, and with it the need for public works relief.

At the outset of the Great Depression, three premises shaped thinking on unemployment. Firstly, joblessness and its relief were essentially emergency problems. Secondly, the responsibility for dealing with the socio-economic consequences of joblessness was (and should continue to be) primarily municipal and provincial. And thirdly, "active" measures to relieve unemployment — that is, work creation — were superior to passive assistance.[59] Developments during the 1930s cast serious doubts on all these assumptions. As the Saskatchewan experience with public works relief revealed all too vividly, the "local responsibility" doctrine crippled the formation of either effective long-term unemployment policies or the administration of such short-term policies as were developed. And urban municipalities, the level of government which in effect delivered the "service," had virtually no input into policy-making at all. Certainly, the provision of unemployment relief work on a large enough scale to meet the needs of even the married "elite" of the unemployed was financially impossible, and one might reasonably say of questionable wisdom, too.

But at the same time the shared-cost programs undertaken in Saskatchewan cities were not "boondoggles." With rare exception, the projects were efficiently carried out and at least modestly effective in meeting their employment and other objectives. Unfortunately, for much of the period financial constraints transformed "unemployment relief work" into little more than a means of distributing direct relief without as great a stigma of failure attached to the recipient and in a way that produced some permanent assets for the community as a whole. Proper "work and wages" programs, which the cities and certainly the unemployed would have preferred, were seldom possible.

Had unemployment not reached (and remained at) such unprecedented levels in Saskatchewan during the Depression, the verdict on public works relief, and particularly the Bennett programs, would have been a much more favourable one. But even considering the circumstances which prevailed, it is hard to believe more could not have been done, especially in the areas of housing and essential municipal capital improvements and maintenance. What was lacking at the local and provincial level was not the will but the resources. Only the federal government could act. Unfortunately, in Saskatchewan, city governments, taxpayers, and the unemployed bore the burden. As Regina Commissioner R.J. Westgate lamented in 1939: "There can be no doubt about the effect that the lack of employment, during recent years, has had upon the greatest asset of [our] community — its people."[60]

NOTES

1. Harry M. Cassidy, "An Unemployment Policy — Some Proposals," in *Canada's Problems as Seen by Twenty Outstanding Men of Canada* (Toronto: Oxford University Press, 1933), 58–9.
2. James S. Struthers, *No Fault of Their Own: Unemployment and the Canadian Welfare State, 1914–1941* (Toronto: University of Toronto Press, 1983), 60.

3. Saskatoon *Star-Phoenix*, 14 and 29 Nov. 1929. Such an agreement had been struck dur-ing the winter of 1921–2. James S. Struthers, "Prelude to Depression: The Federal Government and Unemployment, 1918–29," *Canadian Historical Review*, 58, 3 (Sept. 1977), 277–8. Saskatoon *Star-Phoenix*, 14 and 29 Nov. 1929 and Saskatoon Council Minutes [SCM], 16 June 1930.

4. Regina, Finance (file 31) 1930, McAra to Mayor Davidson of Calgary, 28 May 1930.

5. National Archives of Canada [NAC], MG26K, R.B. Bennett Papers, Unemployment Relief Act.

6. Regina *Daily Star*, 3 Oct. 1930; Regina, Finance (file 31) 1930, Redhead memorandum, 15 Oct. 1930; and SCM, 13 Oct. 1930.

7. Regina, Parks and Public Properties (file 705) 1931. Balfour to Coleman, 15 Jan. 1931.

8. Regina (file 382a, Part 1), Archives of Saskatchewan [AS], Westgate to White, 12 Feb. 1931. Ibid., Department of Labour to Westgate, 16 Feb. and Westgate to council, 20 Jan. 1931.

9. Regina, Finance (file 31) 1930, England to Merkley, 11 Nov. 1930. Regina (file 382a, Part 1) [AS], Westgate to Heseltine, 14 Mar. and Heseltine to council, 25 Mar. 1931.

10. Saskatoon *Star Phoenix*, 13 Nov. and 13 Dec. 1930 and 25 Feb. and 19 Mar. 1931.

11. SCM, various monthly unemployment relief committee reports for 1931.

12. Saskatoon *Star Phoenix*, 20 Jan. and 21 Feb. 1931 and SCM, 30 Mar. 1931.

13. Regina *Daily Star*, 15 May 1931, Union of Saskatchewan Municipalities, *Saskatchewan Municipal Record*, July 1931, 6.

14. Regina, Finance (file 31a) 1931, Redhead to council, 17 June 1931.

15. Dominion Bureau of Statistics, *Census of Canada, 1931*, Vol. 6, 66–73, 1268–70, 1280 and 1284; Regina *Daily Star*, 26 June 1931; and SCM, 29 June 1931.

16. Department of Labour, *Labour Gazette*, August 1931, 903.

17. Bennett Papers, regulations of the Unemployment and Farm Relief Act, 477251–2 and Cassidy, *Unemployment Relief in Ontario, 1929–32*, 64–8.

18. Bennett Papers, Anderson to Bennett, 18 July 1931, 477161–2; [AS], Department of Railways, Labour and Industries [RLI], Relief Records (Roll 28), Molloy memorandum, 19 June 1931; and Saskatoon *Star-Phoenix*, 14 and 17 July 1931.

19. Regina, Finance (file 31b) 1931, unemployment relief committee report, 29 July 1931 and Regina *Leader-Post*, 24 July 1931.

20. Bennett Papers, Bennett to McConnell, 11 Sept. 1931, 351023. Saskatoon *Star-Phoenix*, 2 Nov. 1931. Bennett Papers, MacPherson to Bennett, 5 Sept. 1931, 477610–11 and Bennett to Anderson, 3 Sept. 1931, 489033–4; and RLI, Relief Records (Roll 28), Robertson to Stewart, 8 Sept. 1931.

21. Bennett Papers, Anderson to Bennett, 30 Sept. 1931, 351030–4 and Saskatoon *Star-Phoenix*, 2 Nov. 1931.

22. Regina, Finance (file 31b) 1931, Westgate memorandum to department heads, 30 Oct. 1931 and (file 31) 1932, Westgate to council, 21 Jan. 1932 and SCM, 13 Oct. 1931.

23. Regina *Leader-Post*, 15 Oct. 1931 and Regina, Finance (file 31b) 1931, Westgate memo-randum to council, 14 Oct. 1931.

24. Regina, Finance (file 31a) 1932, Farrell to Beach, 19 Oct. 1932.

25. Bennett Papers, summary of unemployment relief work projects undertaken in Regina through 30 June 1932, 478735–60; RLI, *Unemployment Relief Report, 1929–32*, 56 and *Unemployment Relief Report, 1933–4*, 9; and Treasury Department, *Public Accounts, 1931–2*, 225.

26. Regina *Daily Star*, 11 Dec. 1931 and 21 Jan., 26 Apr., 28 June and 4 Oct. 1932.

27. Regina, Finance (file 31b) 1931, Preece to council, 22 Sept. 1931; Saskatoon *Star-Phoenix*, 15 Sept. and 22 Dec. 1931 and 5 Jan. 1932; and Fred V. Stone, "Unemployment and Unemployment Relief in Western Canada," unpublished M.A. thesis (McGill, 1933), 118.

28. Regina, Finance (file 31) 1932, Farrell to Redhead, undated; Regina *Daily Star*, 4 May, 17 June and 19 July 1932; RLI, *Unemployment Relief Report, 1929–32*, 56 and 59–60; Saskatoon *Star-Phoenix*, 9 Oct. 1931 and 19 Apr. and 10 May 1932; and Stone, 127–9.

29. [AS], Local Government Board [LGB] (Saskatoon file, 1932), Archibald as quoted in Phillips to Hume, 23 May 1932; Regina, Finance (file 31) 1932, Farrell to Redhead, undated; and Saskatoon *Star-Phoenix*, 25 Feb. and 14 Mar. 1932.

30. Bennett Papers, report on unemployment relief in Western Canada, undated (summer 1932), 478125.

31. Regina *Leader-Post*, 20 Oct. 1933. Bennett Papers, Bennett to White, 11 Sept. 1933, 354427.

32. Ibid., Regina Trades and Labour Council to Bennett, 25 June 1934, 498270 and Turnbull to Bennett, 26 Apr. 1934, 497670–2 and Regina *Leader-Post*, 22 June and 16 July 1934.

33. Regina, Finance (file 31) 1934, account of meeting between Gardiner and city representatives, undated (Aug. 1934).

34. Ibid., Boeckler to council, 18 Sept. 1934 and report of the relief works committee, 12 Sept. 1934.

35. Ibid., (file 31a) 1935, Gardiner to Westgate, 15 May 1935.

36. Regina *Leader-Post*, 10 Aug., 10 Sept., and 8 and 31 Oct. 1935 and Regina, Finance (file 31c) 1935, Mikkelson to council, 19 Aug. 1935 and (file 31d), Westgate memo, 8 Oct. and Molloy to Westgate, 22 Oct. 1935.

37. Unidentified MP to Finlayson, 10 Nov. 1934, as quoted in Michiel Horn, ed., *The Dirty Thirties* (Toronto, 1972), 292.

38. H. Blair Neatby, "The Liberal Way: Fiscal and Monetary Policy in the 1930's," in Victor Hoar, ed., *The Great Depression: Essays and Memoirs from Canada and the United States* (Toronto, 1969), 100–3.

39. Dominion Bureau of Statistics, *Census of the Prairie Provinces*, 1936, Vol. 2, 606–9 and 654–9.

40. Regina, Finance (file 31) 1936, report by Ellison, undated (April 1936).

41. Regina, Finance (file 31) 1938, submission of the Regina Union of Unemployed to council, 15 Feb. 1938 and Catholic Union of Unemployed to council, 22 June 1938 and Regina *Leader-Post*, 23 Apr., 28 May and 18 June 1938.

42. Regina *Leader-Post*, 25 Oct. 1938.

43. [AS], W.J. Patterson Papers, file 1, memo on the Municipal Improvements Assistance Act, undated (1938). LGB (Regina), 1938, Ilsley to Patterson, 20 July 1938.

44. Regina *Leader-Post*, 8 June 1938. SCM, 18 July 1938.

45. LGB (Regina) 1938, Grosch to Patterson, 16 and 19 Aug. 1938 and LGB (Saskatoon) 1938, Grosch to Tomlinson, 16 Sept. and 3 Oct. 1938.

46. [AS], Bureau of Labour and Public Welfare [BLPW], Relief Records, file 38, summary of loans made under the Municipal Improvements Assistance Act through 30 Dec. 1939, undated (1940) and Saskatoon *Star-Phoenix*, 5 Jan. 1939.

47. Regina *Leader-Post*, 14 Jan. 1939.

48. Ibid., 25 Jan. 1939.

49. BLPW, Relief Records, file 32, Rogers to Parker, 2 Feb. and Parker to Rogers, 26 Feb. 1939 and Regina, Finance (file 31) 1939, Ellison to Rogers, 6 Feb. and Ellison to Parker, 9 Mar. 1939.

50. Patterson Papers, file 3, Ross to Patterson, 2 June 1939. BLPW, Relief Records (file 32), Johnstone to Leslie, 17 Apr. 1939.

51. BLPW, *Annual Report, 1939–40*, 66 and Relief Records (file 38), list of tentative Civic Improvements Plans grants in Saskatchewan, undated.

52. Ibid., Johnstone to Hereford, 10 Aug. 1939 and schedule of projects approved under the Civic Improvements Plan by the Government of Saskatchewan through 31 Aug. 1939, undated.

53. Ibid., Johnstone to Hereford, 10 Aug. 1939; Regina, Finance (file 31a) 1939, Ellison to Butterfield, 21 Sept. 1939; and SCM, 14 Aug. 1939.

54. Saskatoon *Star-Phoenix*, 24 Mar. 1939. Ibid., 27 Jan., 21 Apr. and 4 May 1939.

55. BLPW, Relief Records (file 38), disposition of Regina's Civic Improvements Plan applications, undated (spring 1940) and SCM, 14 Aug. and 10 Oct. 1939.

56. Patterson Papers, file 1, Rogers to Parker, 9 Sept. and Parker to Rogers, 19 Sept. 1939 and SCM, Johnstone to Leslie (quoted), 13 Oct. and 6 Nov. 1939.

57. BLPW, Relief Records (file 38), report on Civic Improvements Plan, undated, and Regina, Finance (file 31a) 1939, Craven to Beach, 11 Oct. 1939.

58. BLPW, *Annual Report, 1939–40*, 67–71.

59. Cassidy, *Unemployment Relief in Ontario, 1929–32*, 275–6.

60. LGB (Regina) 1939, memorandum to council, 9 Jan. 1939.

TWENTY

Worker Persistence, Hiring Policies and the Depression in the Aluminium Sector: The Saguenay Region, Québec, 1925–1940

JOSÉ E. IGARTUA

INTRODUCTION

The turnover of labour constituted one of the most remarkable features of industrial production in North America at the turn of the century. The practice was characteristic of the early phases of industrialization; bosses laid off workers or reduced wages when demand slackened, and workers frequently quit to take up other jobs in the same city or elsewhere. The labour market was still considered to be made up of face-to-face dealings between employer and worker. Increasingly, however, larger firms recognized the costs associated with this practice: the hiring and training of new workers detracted from the efficiency of the firm and constituted a particularly heavy burden in times of expansion, when labour was scarcer, thus driving costs even higher.

Source: Excerpted from "Worker Persistence, Hiring Policies and the Depression in the Aluminium Sector: The Saguenay Region, Québec, 1925–1940," *Histoire sociale/Social History*, 22, 43 (1989): 9–33. Reprinted by permission of *Histoire sociale/Social History*.

The problem was particularly acute in heavy industries, such as steelmaking, metal-working and refining, where working conditions were harsh. Heat exhaustion, noise and chemical contamination made work in these industries particularly unpleasant. Employers resorted to various kinds of measures to reduce this turnover; collectively, these measures became known as "welfare capitalism."[1] They included a more systematic hiring policy, implemented by professionals rather than by foremen, as well as pension plans, bonuses linked to persistence and amenities outside the work area, such as libraries and playgrounds. The town of Pullman was a leading example of this experiment.[2]

The welfare capitalism movement spread unevenly across the industrial landscape. Generally, it was more prominently featured in the larger concerns, where the size of the manpower made its implementation practical. In the US, the steel industry was on the forefront of the movement.[3] Canadian steel producers adopted the practices of their American counterparts and put in place an impressive array of measures, the success of which remains debatable, in view of a replacement rate of 91 percent in the 1920s.[4]

Little is known about another North American heavy industry, aluminium. Yet aluminium was an emerging industry with a remarkable growth record. US output went from less than 6 million pounds in 1901 to 138 million pounds in 1920 and 229 million pounds in 1930. In Canada, production began in 1902, reached 10 million pounds in 1912, 22 million pounds in 1920 and peaked at close to 83 million pounds in 1927. At that time, Canadian production was half the US level. The expansion of capacity in the twenties more than doubled Canadian output.[5]

Manpower management in the industry was shaped both by its monopolistic character and by locational imperatives. Before World War II, the aluminium sector was made up of one firm: the Aluminum Company of America (Alcoa).[6] Its Canadian affiliate, Alcan, was the only producer north of the boundary.[7] Production methods were therefore very likely the same in the two countries: most of the personnel who set up the Canadian plants and ran them came from the US. Recruitment conditions, however, were different. In the US, the Alcoa plants were located at Niagara Falls (NY), Massena (NY) and East St. Louis (IL), areas where the potential labour pool was large. In Canada, aluminium smelters were located near hydro-electric power developments in remote regions of the province of Québec, where the potential labour pool appears at first glance to have been much smaller.

This study examines some of the determinants of worker persistence in the Canadian aluminium industry in the pre–World War II period. It focuses on the Arvida works in the Saguenay region of Québec, which accounted for 25 percent of total North American production by 1939. The study seeks to unravel the company's changing manpower practices and the workers' shifting persistence patterns from the chaotic early years through the Depression and the recovery of the late thirties by an examination of some of the personal and professional characteristics of the workers. The study ends with World War II, which opened a different chapter in the history of Arvida, as the gearing up of production and the construction of new power dams transformed the scale of Alcan's operations.

The sources for this study are both qualitative and quantitative. The qualitative evidence is scarce: it consists of a diary of the company's activity in the region, memoirs written by company managers, and a few newspaper accounts. But these few traditional sources are compensated to a degree by the availability of the company's personnel records. The personnel records of the Arvida works provide fairly extensive data on workers' background as well as information on job assignment, wage levels and reasons for the termination of employment. For the period from 1925 to 1940, the personnel records appear to be quite complete. A quantitative analysis of these records can shed some light on turnover and on evolving recruitment practices.

ALCAN'S ACTIVITIES IN ARVIDA, 1925–1940

Technical constraints rather than manpower considerations dictated the location of the Arvida plant. These technical constraints have to do with the production process itself, access to raw materials and access to shipping facilities. Aluminium is produced by electrolysis of alumina. The electrolytic process consumes large amounts of electric power, the cost of which becomes therefore a prime component of the total cost of production. In the 1920s, when techniques for the long-distance transportation of electricity were still primitive, aluminium plants were located close to their power source.

The availability of hydro power was a major factor in Alcoa's decision to expand its activities into Canada. It came to the St. Maurice region of Québec in 1899 because of the development of the hydro potential of the St. Maurice River. The Saguenay works were built in 1925 as a result of a merger between Alcoa and the large hydro interests held in the region by James B. Duke, the US tobacco king.[8] The 1925 merger brought under Alcoa's control the enormous hydro potential of the Saguenay River, which far surpassed what it could use in the foreseeable future.

The Saguenay River also provided Alcan with a deep sea port at Baie-des-Ha!-Ha!. Besides the shipping of aluminium for export, this Saguenay River port allowed the importation of bauxite, the ore from which alumina is derived, from deposits in the West Indies. Access to ocean shipping therefore made it possible to operate an ore reduction plant as well as a smelter in Arvida. A third plant was also built to produce the large quantities of carbon electrodes required in the electrolytic process. Thus the Saguenay works comprised three main plants, as well as lesser facilities.

The works were located close to an undeveloped hydro site on the Saguenay River, about half way between the cities of Chicoutimi and Jonquière. Alcoa intended to develop this site, known as Chute-à-Caron, to supply the works' power; construction of a power dam began at once.[9] Alcoa erected a small town next to the works to house its workers. Thus was born, in 1925, the community of Arvida, named after Alcoa's president, Arthur Vining Davis. Construction of the plant and of the town proceeded at once, and aluminium production started in 1926. The first phase of the town plan was completed by 1928, the year Alcan was set up as a separate entity to take over Alcoa's Canadian operations.[10]

The recruitment of manpower was not an issue when location of the Saguenay works was determined. The Alcoa engineer, who first surveyed the area to locate a plant site and to provide a rough estimate of input costs, spent a single sentence of his report on the issue, believing that "plant labour on an operating basis would be plentiful and cheap."[11] Other large projects in the area seemed to find manpower readily enough. The construction of a large dam and power house at Île Maligne, at the head of the Saguenay, from 1923 to 1924, had drawn large numbers of migrant construction workers.[12] Pulp mills in Kenogami and Jonquière obtained most of their manpower from the local population. But operating the plants at Arvida by hiring anyone who showed up at the plant gate would not be very efficient: in the first years, turnover was considerable.

The availability of work is one of the prime determinants of turnover.[13] It is therefore necessary to give a brief outline of the evolution of Alcan's activities from the first days of 1925 to the outbreak of World War II. These fifteen years comprise three different phases. The first is the construction period, from 1925 until September 1928, when the new corporate entity, Alcan, took over the works, cancelled all construction work not yet underway and started to reduce manpower to the level required for production only. During this period, four potrooms were built, the last of which began production in 1927. Besides the potrooms, the alumina plant, and the electrode plant, a wire plant, a remelt plant, a boiler plant, sheds, warehouses, offices and the plant rail lines were also built.[14] Work also continued on the town site to provide houses, roads and services.

During the second phase, from 1928 to 1935, the level of activity fluctuated noticeably. Production began to decline even before the Depression. Shortages in power forced the closing of one potroom in 1928. A second potroom was closed for six months in 1929, but both were back in service by the end of 1930. The Depression brought a reduction in the level of production in the four potrooms as well as a reduction in the duration of each shift from eight to six hours, to stretch out available work. The ore plant was closed, as the "dry ore" process of making alumina was not economically viable; alumina was then imported from Alcoa's East St. Louis plant. The carbon plant was also closed. In the spring of 1932, production levels hit their lowest mark. Three of the four potrooms were closed. The workforce was estimated at less than 300 workers. The signature of a contract with Japan for 3.5 million pounds of aluminium, in September 1932, brought about a brief upswing in production. Two potrooms were put back in service and the carbon plant resumed production. Shifts were brought back to eight hours. But further curtailments of production were imposed in early 1933 in order to keep within the production allotments established by the international aluminium cartel. Only two potrooms remained open, and they produced at a reduced capacity.

The last phase, from 1935 to 1940, was marked by recovery and by some expansion of the Arvida facilities. The conversion of the alumina plant to the Bayer process (chemical and heat purification) was undertaken in 1935 and gave work to up to 300 men. The refurbished plant was expanded and brought on line in 1937, at which time all four potrooms were operating at capacity. Two new potrooms as well as a small fluoride plant were built and put into operation by June 1938.

The size of the workforce fluctuated with the level of work production. Hiring for construction and production produced a peak in 1926, when close to 3,000 workers were hired. In 1927, more people left than were hired, and in 1928, twice as many workers left as were hired. Altogether, the first three years account for two thirds of all hirings and close to 60 percent of departures between 1925 and 1940. Hirings and departures had slowed to a trickle by 1933, and then resumed to reach new peaks in 1937 and 1938, respectively. From 1934 on, hirings were more numerous than departures, except for 1938, when the second phase of construction ended. This resulted in a total manpower that declined steadily from 1926 to 1933, and then increased markedly in 1935, 1937 and 1939.

THE FIRST WAVE OF WORKERS, 1925-1928

No accounts have been found of how hiring was conducted during the first years of the Arvida operation. According to case histories of workers who stayed with the company twenty-five years, some came as part of a family, while others were migrant workers who came to Arvida upon learning of the opening of the construction site.[15] No traces of specific recruitment efforts have been found. Employee records can, however, shed some light on how the company chose its workers. These records indicate that little attention was paid to what kind of worker was hired.

The personnel officers did not bother to record previous employment or the name of the previous employer on over 90 percent of the job application forms filled between 1925 and 1927. The occupations that were recorded range from "works foreman" to "on relief," and only a handful of occupations accounted for more than ten mentions. Similarly, most workers received an "A" on physical rating, apparently without any physical examination.

The ethnic origin of workers was reported under the heading of "nationality." The data appear quite reliable. The personnel officers sometimes listed as French Canadians persons whose surname had other ethnic roots, but additional information in the personnel record indicates that they were indeed born or raised as French Canadians.

French Canadians made up barely half of all workers hired between 1925 and the end of 1927. The next largest group were other Canadians, with 16 percent. Thus Canadian citizens made up two thirds of the manpower. Foreign-born workers from Western Europe and from Eastern Europe account for 18 percent and 13 percent respectively. Half of the Western Europeans were Finnish. The next largest group were the Czechs, with close to 5 percent of the total. Polish, Irish and Italian workers were each less than 2 percent of the workforce. Altogether, apart from the Canadians (French and English), there were 36 nationalities represented in Arvida during the early years.

Within the French-Canadian contingent, the low proportion of Saguenay workers is striking: they numbered only 41 percent of the French Canadians hired during those years.[16] Overall, Saguenay workers represented less than 20 percent of all workers hired. This seems quite surprising, given the ethnic homogeneity of the Saguenay region (over 95 percent French-Canadian) and the remoteness of the region from the main migration routes. Foreign workers had been in the region, working on construction sites, for a few years. Raoul Blanchard, the French geographer who visited the Saguenay in 1932 as part of the field work for his pioneering study of the economic geography of French Canada, reported that large numbers of itinerant workers of foreign origin came to work at Arvida after working at the Île Maligne power dam and the Price Brothers Riverbend paper plant, which were built between 1923 and 1925.[17]

Given the overwhelmingly French-Canadian character of Saguenay society, the presence of a large contingent of non-French-Canadian workers at Arvida made ethnicity a particularly noticeable attribute. In the local context, non-French-Canadian workers would be perceived as "foreign" by Saguenay residents. Since these "foreign" workers were apparently drawn to the Saguenay as "floaters," one would expect that they would differ from French-Canadian workers in terms of marital status. It is therefore striking that there were few differences of marital status between French-Canadian workers and the others. Each group was evenly split between single workers and married ones. Only among the few widowers (3 percent of the total) were the French Canadians over-represented. The fact that half the French-Canadian workers were single is an indication that a good portion of the workforce had a fairly high potential for mobility.

Ethnicity and marital status were the two most obvious characteristics of workers upon which the employer might have based a selection. But there were also slight differences in the type of work being offered to French-Canadian workers and workers of other ethnic origins. Forty-six percent of the French-Canadian workers were assigned to construction or maintenance work, against only 33 percent of foreign workers. The ratios are inverted for common labourers, with over half of the foreign workers being assigned such work against 37 percent for French Canadians. Overall, over 80 percent of both groups wound up in construction or day labour: there was, therefore, little difference between the two ethnic categories in those areas which accounted for the bulk of the hirings.

French-Canadian workers were, however, over-represented in aluminium production, support staff and transport work areas. In aluminium production, where French Canadians were the most numerous in relative terms, over a third of the workers were foreigners, still a large proportion given the local context. French Canadians were least numerous in the administrative group, largely made up of English-speaking Canadians and Americans from other Alcoa plants. These figures are only a rough indication of the propensity of each ethnic category to be assigned work in particular areas, since workers were frequently assigned to other tasks after they were hired.

The breakdown of marital status by work sector reveals that married workers were a majority in the construction and maintenance sector and in the raw material transformation sector, with close to 60 percent of all workers in these categories. Inversely, single workers made up about the same proportion of labourers. This probably indicates that fewer labourers had the means to support a family than the tradesmen in construction and maintenance. The strongest proportion of single workers was found among the administrative and support staff workers. This was where female workers were concentrated: in these categories, only 2 female workers — a charwoman and a stenographer — were married, against 31 single females.

These breakdowns indicate that the company did little to select a homogeneous workforce. The major feature is the over-representation of foreign workers as day labourers and that of French Canadians in construction and maintenance work. But since both of these categories were bound to suffer a quick decline in importance after construction was ended, these distinctions tell very little about the selection of workers for production work. A look at some of the determinants of persistence will provide a clearer picture.

DETERMINANTS OF PERSISTENCE

A multiple classification analysis of the measurable determinants of persistence available in the personnel records — ethnicity, marital status and area of work assigned at hiring — shows that these characteristics account for a small but statistically significant amount of the total variance in persistence. But multiple classification analysis also gives an indication of the specific effect of each factor, statistically eliminating interference from the others, and ranks factors in order of relative importance. This allows for a clearer analysis of measurable factors.

Of the three determinants used in the analysis, marital status was the strongest. Average duration of work was slightly less than three years, but close to two thirds of all workers hired were gone in less than a year. Married workers stayed on the job about twice as long as single workers. Next in importance was the type of work assigned upon hiring. Construction and maintenance workers tended to stay with the company a bit longer than the general mean of slightly less than three years, while the day labourers' stay was a little shorter. Larger variations are evidenced in the production, administrative and support staff categories: in the first two categories, workers tended to stay with Alcan about six years, while the support staff left after two.

Ethnicity as such made almost no difference in the duration of employment. This is surprising, as one would expect French-Canadian workers, more at ease in the social milieu of the Saguenay, to feel fewer pressures to leave. Geographic origin was more a determinant: workers from the Saguenay exhibited a higher than average persistence, followed by non–French Canadians and then by French Canadians from other regions than the Saguenay.

A multiple classification analysis focusing on the determinants of persistence among French-Canadian workers shows that geographic origin was the most important determinant. Workers from the Saguenay stayed at Alcan for an average of four years, compared to an overall mean of 2.75 years. Workers from Montréal (20 percent) or Quebec City (3 percent) lasted less than a year. Workers from other areas also left more quickly than the average.

Type of employment and marital status also affected the persistence of French-Canadian workers. Those in administrative functions and in aluminium production, with the better paid jobs, stayed the longest, with averages of six and four and a half years. Married workers stayed on about twice as long as single ones, or three and a half years against 21 months.

WORKERS WHO LEFT

Three quarters of all workers hired between 1925 and the end of 1927 left the company within two years. If we shift the analysis from the whole cohort of workers hired between 1925 and 1928 to only those who left within two years, we obtain some indications of the nature of the turnover problem, indications which are corroborated by the motives for separation recorded on employee files. On average, workers who left within two years lasted only about six months. This high rate of turnover would appear at first glance to reflect the relative importance of construction workers in the cohort. Construction and maintenance workers accounted for 39 percent of hirings; common labourers, who were most probably assigned construction duties, account for another 44 percent. Thus over 80 percent of the manpower hired may have been assigned to construction work. But in fact, construction workers were not over-represented among the workers who left within two years; rather, their proportion among those who were hired (82.9 percent) was very close to their proportion among those who left within two years (84.7 percent). Put another way, 79 percent of those who were hired as construction workers or common labourers left within two years. But support staff workers, a category which includes the cooks, waiters and dishwashers working in the temporary camps that housed the workforce, left even more quickly: 83 percent of them left within two years. Workers in other areas were only slightly slower to leave. Seventy-eight percent of workers in transportation and shipping left within two years; for workers in raw material transformation, the rate was 64 percent; for those in aluminium production, the rate was 63 percent; even in administration, 56 percent left within two years. The high rate of turnover that affected all areas of work at the Arvida works is silent testimony, among other things, to the absence of efficient manpower recruitment practices during these early years.

When workers who left within two years are grouped by area of work at the time of their departure, rather than at the time of their hiring, much the same picture emerges. But the internal mobility of labour — the frequency of transfers among different work areas — also becomes apparent. Common labourers, who made up 47 percent of those hired in the early years, only account for 37 percent of the separations. Close to 300 of the workers hired as common labourers and who left within two years were transferred to other sectors before leaving. Of course, the sector which receives the largest number of transfers is that of aluminium production, since few workers were assigned to it immediately upon hiring. While 106 workers were assigned to aluminium production upon hiring, 189 were in that area when they left. More than two thirds of the 116 workers who left within two years as potmen were originally hired as common workers or as construction and maintenance workers. But there were also numerous transfers from aluminium production to other sectors. Of the 82 workers hired as potmen (whose primary task was to oversee the electrolysis of aluminium in the pots), 47 left within two years and only 32 of them were still potmen at the time of their separation. These figures indicate that an internal high turnover rate was also in evidence for jobs related to aluminium production; they provide a rough indication of the workers' distaste for those jobs.

As has been seen earlier, marital status and ethnicity on the whole had little effect on shaping the group of departing workers. These were slightly more likely to be single (54 percent as against 49 percent of all those hired). They were also evenly divided between French Canadians and others, as they were on hiring. In fact, among those who left within two years, the average stay of French Canadians was shorter than for other workers (0.43 years versus 0.50 years). However, in some work areas, ethnic differences were more pronounced. French Canadians made up 51 percent of those hired in aluminium production, but they accounted for 65 percent of those in that type of work when they left. Similarly, French Canadians made up a greater proportion of workers in support staff positions at separation than at hiring (40 versus 60 percent). French Canadians thus did not seem to tolerate that type of work as well as workers from other ethnic origins. It may also have been easier for them to find employment alternatives in the region or in the province.

Reasons invoked at separation are also indicative of the lack of a well-defined employment strategy on Alcan's part. When workers left Alcan, the personnel office wrote a final entry on their service record, indicating whether the worker was fired, laid off, or whether he quit. As well, in a third of the separations taking place in 1926, 1927 and 1928, the worker's service record reports a reason for the separation. These data offer some indications of the circumstances of worker separation. The group of workers for which this information is available shared to a remarkable degree the characteristics of the whole group of transient workers: it had a slight over-representation of French Canadians (54 percent against 50 percent for the whole group), of married persons (45 percent against 42), and of workers in aluminium production (11 versus 6 percent), but was otherwise similar to the whole group. The evidence drawn from this segment of the whole group would thus seem representative.

In over half (57 percent) of the separations for which motives are given, workers quit by choice. This was a widespread phenomenon in the US as well as in Canada.[18] Company-initiated separations represent another 28 percent of departures, while 15 percent are due to miscellaneous reasons, such as sickness in the family. Those workers who left by choice (with or without prior notice) usually departed without giving a reason. Very few left citing the work they were asked to do at Alcan as the reason for leaving, and fewer still mentioned a new job. Most of those who gave the nature of work done at Alcan as a reason for leaving (14 out of 23) were in aluminium production, where conditions were especially harsh. Company-initiated dismissals, in 1926 and 1927, were primarily for disciplinary reasons (45 percent), then for lack of work (29 percent) or for reasons related to the worker's capacity to do the work (22 percent). In 1928, with the end of construction, curtailment of operations was the most frequently cited reason.[19]

During Arvida's first years of operation, Alcan did not exhibit any preferences in the type of worker it hired. Foreign workers were taken on almost as often as French-Canadian workers. Most of its manpower went to construction work, and workers in that area were mostly gone by the end of 1928. But workers in other areas of work also exhibited a high degree of transiency. Workers in aluminium production, especially, had high internal mobility. This is understandable given the very harsh nature of the work involved. Yet, overall, transiency was widespread among all ethnic groups and marital categories. The most significant aspect of transiency at Arvida was that it was a decision made by the worker, who obviously did not find the kind of work place he had envisioned. A much smaller number of workers were dismissed because the company found them unacceptable.

Thus a dual process of self-selection and company-initiated filtering winnowed the ranks of the workforce from the 4,600 workers who had been hired to the 1,000 remaining at the beginning of 1929. Alcan suffered from a common ailment of large-scale industry. Slichter reported that "the steel industry, power plants, forge shops, aluminium reduction, the enameled ware industry, all have numerous jobs in which exposure to great heat is inevitable and report difficulty in holding help on that account."[20] But, as has been seen, high turnover affected all areas of operations, not just the potrooms. It resulted from a lack of attention in the selection of workers. But the situation soon changed.

CHANGES IN HIRING POLICY, 1928–1940

With hindsight and statistics, one can see that married French-Canadian workers from the Saguenay had the most likelihood of long employment. Alcan's personnel managers came to perceive the same thing, for hiring became more selective from 1928 on. Increases in the proportions of French Canadians, in the proportions of workers from the Saguenay, and in the proportion of married workers hired during those years attest to the change in policy.

The proportion of Saguenay workers among all those hired rose rapidly, from a third in 1929 to a peak of three quarters in 1935, from which their proportion fell gradually to 1939. They comprised a growing proportion of French-Canadian workers hired during those years, who themselves made up two thirds of all workers hired. The preference given to French-Canadian workers, and to Saguenay workers in particular, is noticeably stronger from 1934 onwards, even during the construction periods of 1935 and 1937. This preference resulted in an increase in the proportion of French Canadians in the Alcan workforce from 53 percent on 1 January 1929 to 71 percent ten years later.

Pressures to be more selective in the recruitment of workers came both from the region and from upper management. As early as 1928, a letter to the regional newspaper complained of preference being given to "foreigners" (by which was meant non-French Canadians) in hiring in the region.[21] During the Depression, the Saguenay was one of the worst hit areas in the province of Québec. Raoul Blanchard, the French geographer, noted during his visit in 1932 that the "counties of Lake St. John and of Chicoutimi are, with Montréal, the most suffering in the province, those where unemployment is the highest."[22] In 1935, an estimated two thirds of the population of Chicoutimi, the regional centre, were receiving some form of relief from welfare agencies.[23] Thus, throughout the thirties, the region implicitly applied pressure on Alcan to hire local workers.

Even Alcan head office managers found the results of the lack of selection during the previous years puzzling. At the end of 1930, the company estimated that only 54 percent of the employees at the Arvida works were French-Canadian. This compared with 91 percent at their Shawinigan plant and 93 percent at their Saguenay railway and shipping subsidiaries. When asked to account for the difference, the local works manager explained that "hardly any Lake St. John residents would work in the Carbon Plant, and that many would still not go into the potrooms." "It took a number of years," wrote the company archivist, "to coax [French Canadians] off the farms in any large numbers to work indoors, particularly in the potrooms and carbon plant."[24]

With the Depression, Alcan's hiring policy increasingly favoured workers from the Saguenay. In 1932, the regional newspaper announced a resumption of production at Arvida with the warning that it was useless for people from outside the region to come look for work at Arvida without prior agreement from the company.[25] The company also gave preference to former workers.[26] The same warnings were given when the fourth potroom was reopened in January 1937. The company newspaper printed a statement from the General Manager that workers from Arvida and surrounding localities would have priority; he also warned its employees not to send for relatives or friends.[27] In April 1937, the regional newspaper reported that Alcan's newly hired workers from Chicoutimi had to provide a certificate from the city's mayor that they had resided in Chicoutimi for at least a year; this was the result of an arrangement between the company and the city to give preference to local workers.[28]

The policy worked. At the end of 1936, the company noted in its log of activities at Arvida that French Canadians made up 71 percent of its workforce; the following year, after hiring over 500 workers, the company noted that "with the exception of engineers, technical men, and a few skilled workers, all the increase in the number of employees was recruited from the District."[29] The results of the new policy were obviously worth entering into the record.

Marital status also became a criterion for recruiting. In the thirties, the company increasingly hired married workers, a practice that was common among employers during the period. The practice recognized the heavier burdens that married workers, principally those with children, had to shoulder, but it also selected workers who would be less mobile precisely because of their family obligations. In so doing, it implicitly called for a reciprocal bond of service on the workers' part.

This preference was evident among the French Canadians Alcan hired: two thirds of them were married, and this proportion rose to 71 percent among workers from the Saguenay region. Foreign workers, on the other hand, were evenly divided between married and single workers; it was probably more difficult to find foreign workers who were married. In any event, the foreign workers were also selected with some care, since they worked on average longer than the French Canadians (7.1 years versus 6.7 years).

Yet the most obvious predictor of stability was regional origin. The differences in duration of employment between French-Canadian workers who came from the Saguenay and those who came from elsewhere are remarkable. Married French Canadians from the Saguenay (N=639) stayed an average of seven years with the company, while married French-Canadian workers from other areas (N=70) stayed only about three years. Among single French-Canadian workers, those from the Saguenay (N=237) stayed on average six years, while the others (N=71) lasted only twenty months.

The improvement in selection methods was also apparent in the reversal of the ratio of voluntary to involuntary dismissals. During the early years, most separations had been initiated by workers. From 1929 to the end of 1939, separations were most frequently initiated by the company: 47 percent of the separations fell into that category, against 40 percent of worker-initiated separations. The company parted with personnel essentially because of reductions in operations, with disciplinary reasons accounting for between 10 and 20 percent of the causes in various years. The Depression obviously pressured workers to keep their jobs; at the same time, the company did what it could to keep as much of its manpower as possible on company rolls, by reducing wages and the duration of shifts. This was partly as a relief measure, but it also spared the company the expense of training new workers when production resumed.

THE CORE GROUP

Only about 10 percent of the workers hired before 1928 remained with Alcan at Arvida until 1 January 1940. But their importance lies in their absolute numbers (N=393) and in the slow pace of hirings throughout the thirties. These workers made up more than half the workforce during the first half of the thirties and still represented over a quarter of all employees by the end of 1939. They were the stable core of the workforce at Arvida and deserve closer scrutiny.

This core group was much more homogeneous than the cohort from which it came. Ethnically, 61 percent of its members were French Canadians; another 22 percent were English-speaking Canadians. The rest were a diverse lot of 18 different nationalities, none of which accounted for more than 8 workers. Most of the French Canadians in the core group were from the Saguenay region, whereas the region accounted for only 40 percent of all hirings from 1925 through 1927. Saguenay workers made up between a third and half of the core group, depending on how strict the criteria for defining geographic origin are.[30] Inversely, the core group retained only 6 of the 374 workers who came from Montréal during the first years.

Homogeneity in the core group is also reflected in marital status. Less than one worker in four was single at hiring. Among Saguenay workers, the proportion was even smaller (20 percent). The high proportion of married workers helped preserve the core group, since during the Depression the company tried to lay off single workers before married ones, a practice quite common during the Depression.

The stability of the core group was in part forced upon the workers by the number of dependents for which they were responsible. Almost all married workers, as well as a few single ones, had dependents when they were hired. Among the married and widowed workers, the average number of dependents was 3.4. One worker in five had six or more dependents. The number of dependents must have increased for most married workers, as they had in all likelihood more children in the years after they were hired.

The core group also differed from its cohort in the types of jobs its members were assigned upon hiring. Slightly more of them went into construction and maintenance than the whole 1925–1927 cohort (45 percent against 39 percent). As well, they were over-represented in aluminium production (9.4 percent against 4 percent). The core group included fewer common labourers as well (28 percent against 44 percent). This over-representation in some areas was even more pronounced among French Canadians.

THE WORKFORCE AT THE END OF THE THIRTIES

By the end of the thirties, Alcan's workforce in the Saguenay was considerably more homogeneous than during the first years of Arvida. Seventy-one percent of its workers were now French Canadians, and 74 percent of French Canadians came from the Saguenay. Saguenay workers, therefore, made up more than half the workforce. Two thirds of the workers were married, the ratio being slightly higher among French Canadians, and higher still among Saguenay workers, three quarters of whom were married.

By this time, non-French-Canadian workers had even become more stable than the French Canadians. On 1 January 1940, single workers who were not French-Canadian had been with Alcan an average of 6.4 years, whereas the French-Canadian single workers had done only 5.1 years. Among married workers, the French Canadians averaged 6.1 years, while the other married workers had done 8.6 years. These averages, however, hide the distribution of workers according to length of service. A majority of workers had been hired since 1935, but a quarter had been with the company since 1927 or earlier. Still, recently hired workers (less than two years) only made up 17.5 percent of the total. On the whole, therefore, Alcan could count on an experienced workforce at the beginning of World War II. The war brought a sudden expansion of the plant and of the workforce, and with it new challenges in labour relations.

CONCLUSION

Alcan had managed to keep a core group of workers at its Arvida plants throughout the thirties. It seemingly had understood, as early as 1928, that a *laisser-faire* attitude in the selection of workers led to high turnover. Most workers had chosen to move on and seek other employment, and a few had to be dismissed for unsatisfactory performance.

The new manpower policy, which focused on local workers, and preferably married ones, was put into effect before the Depression started. However, because of the

Depression, it took some time for it to show results in the composition of the work-force. The Depression added incentive to pursue selective hiring practices, and this too helped reduce turnover: half the workers hired from 1931 through 1934 were still at Alcan at the end of 1939.[31]

Alcan's personnel policies bore fruit in areas other than persistence. There were no strikes at Alcan from 1925 until a war-time wildcat strike in 1941. To be sure, the Depression years were not conducive to worker militancy. But Alcan also took positive steps to avoid trouble. The preference given to local labour, which was clearly expressed by the company, accorded with regional values of local solidarity. Alcan would portray itself as a local company in tune with local values. When hiring resumed on a large scale in 1937, it was already publishing a company paper, ostensibly concerned primarily with plant safety. But the company pursued larger goals: according to the paper, it aimed to "share common ideals" with its workers and to "consolidate in a co-operative and harmonious way the fraternal bonds" which linked the company and the workers' families.[32] Alcan workers had already formed a union in 1936,[33] which signed a collective agreement with the company the following year. The union was part of the Catholic union movement born in the Saguenay at the beginning of the century.[34] From the start, the aluminium workers' union adopted the co-operative attitude common to Catholic unions, to which the company responded in kind. This was wise for the company, since by accepting local institutions it forestalled, at least for a time, more militant forms of unionism.[35]

NOTES

1. See Stuart D. Brandes, *American Welfare Capitalism* (Chicago, 1976).
2. See Stanley Buder, *Pullman: An Experiment in Industrial Order and Community Planning* (New York, 1967).
3. Katherine Stone, "The origins of job structures in the steel industry," *Review of Radical Political Economics*, 6 (1974), pp. 113–173.
4. Craig Heron, *Working in Steel: The Early Years in Canada* (Toronto, 1988), pp. 99–111.
5. George W. Stocking and Myron W. Watkins, *Cartels in Action: Case Studies in International Business Diplomacy* (New York, 1946), pp. 236–237.
6. See Donald H. Wallace, *Market Control in the Aluminum Industry* (Cambridge, 1937). For a history of Alcoa, see Charles C. Carr, *ALCOA: An American Enterprise* (New York, 1952).
7. On the early years of Alcan, see Duncan Campbell, *Mission mondiale: histoire d'Alcan*, vol. 1 (n.p., 1985).
8. See José E. Igartua, "'Corporate' strategy and locational decision-making: the Duke-Price Alcoa Merger, 1925," *Journal of Canadian Studies/Revue d'études canadiennes*, 20, 3 (Autumn 1985), pp. 82–101.
9. The aluminium plant was completed before the dam, and power was obtained from the Île Maligne power plant, about fifteen miles upriver. The plant belonged to the Duke-Price Power Company, which was absorbed into Alcoa in 1926, after Duke's death.
10. Campbell, *Mission mondiale*, pp. 233–237.
11. The report is reproduced in United States District Court, Southern District of New York, Equity no. 85-73, United States vs. Aluminum Company of America et al., Exhibit 258, p. 1830. (This is the 1937 Alcoa anti-trust suit; page numbers refer to the printed volumes, not to the stenographic pages.)
12. Raoul Blanchard, *L'Est du Canada français: "Province de Québec"* (Montréal, 1935), pp. 100–106.

13. See James L. Price, *The Study of Turnover* (Ames, Iowa, 1977), p. 29.
14. The details are taken from a chronology of operations kept by the company. See Société historique du Saguenay, Fonds Alcan, "Newspaper Items," which contains the chronology.
15. See *Le lingot*, the Arvida plant newspaper, 1950–1952, passim.
16. For most French Canadians, one can infer geographic origin from information given on home address and the address of the person to notify in case of sickness or injury.
17. Blanchard, *L'Est du Canada français*, pp. 105–106.
18. Paul Frederick Brissenden and Emil Frankel, *Labor Turnover in Industry: A Statistical Analysis* (New York, 1922), p. 79; Heron, *Working in Steel*, pp. 78–82.
19. See José E. Igartua, "La mobilité professionelle des travailleurs de l'aluminium à Arvida, 1925–1940," *Labour/Le travail*, 20 (1987), pp. 33–60.
20. Sumner Huber Slichter, *The Turnover of Factory Labor* (New York, 1919), p. 74.
21. *Le Progrès du Saguenay*, 27 January 1928.
22. Blanchard, *L'Est du Canada français*, p. 111.
23. Martin Ringuette, "Des lendemains incertains. Les conditions de vie à Chicoutimi entre 1925 et 1940," *Saguenayensia*, 22 (1980), pp. 149–154.
24. T.L. Brock, "Alcan in the Saguenay: The Early Years," typescript, II: 25, 26. The author was company archivist.
25. *Le Progrès du Saguenay*, 29 September 1932.
26. Alcan chronology, 118.
27. *La sentinelle*, 8 January 1937.
28. *Le Progrès du Saguenay*, 29 August 1927.
29. Alcan chronology, 181, 184.
30. The lower proportion only excludes those who gave "Arvida" as home address and the higher one includes them as Saguenay workers.
31. Sanford M. Jacoby, *Employing Bureaucracy: Managers, Unions, and the Tranformation of Work in American Industry, 1900–1945* (New York, 1985) discusses the fluctuating manpower practices of American industries during the Depression.
32. *La Sentinelle*, 4 December 1936.
33. Le Syndicat national des employés de l'aluminium d'Arvida, "15 ans de lutte, 15 ans de progrès," undated.
34. Jacques Rouillard, *Les syndicats nationaux au Québec de 1900 à 1930* (Québec, 1979), pp. 187–190.
35. The wildcat strike of 1941 constitutes a special chapter in the history of Arvida that the author is currently writing.

World War II and the Promise of Change

A woman engaged in "men's work" at a shipbuilding yard in Pictou, Nova Scotia, in 1943.

Many scholars see Canada as becoming a truly independent, economically mature nation during the 1939–45 struggle to vanquish Nazism. Basking in the accomplishment of having supplied a million men in uniform, the third-largest Allied air force and navy, and an extraordinary amount of food and other materiel to the war effort, by 1945 those in the Dominion had finally shed lingering colonial attitudes and were talking enthusiastically about meeting international obligations as an independent "middle power." Change during the war years was not confined to the political and diplomatic realms. In being far more mechanized than the 1914–18 struggle, World War II witnessed the massive capitalization of industry; the creation of a better-funded central government through the levying of substantial corporate and income taxes (as justified by the 1940 Royal Commission Report on Dominion–Provincial Relations); and the start of a planned economy administered by a virtual army of new federal civil servants, whose numbers, between 1939 and 1945, spiralled from 46 106 to 115 908.[1]

Complaints emanated from some quarters about over-regulation and excessive taxation, but throughout the war, the general consensus favoured large-scale state intervention, not only because it seemed called for by wartime exigencies, but because it appeared to produce positive results. For instance, with wage and price controls in effect, full employment had been achieved with marginal inflation. Indeed, as noted in several historical accounts, there emerged, certainly by 1942, the widespread conviction that after hostilities ceased, Canada should refrain from reverting to a laissez-faire policy, for in the minds of many, such a policy had played a role in bringing about the Great Depression and/or exacerbating it. Opinion polls, federal by-elections, and several political contests at the provincial level, all of which yielded a strong showing for the Co-operative Commonwealth Federation, revealed to Prime Minister King that support for significant social welfare was mounting. Whether the change was born of political expediency, the progressive and Christian impulses King had expressed during his younger years (in his book *Industry and Humanity*, for example), or the desire to minimize the impact of an expected postwar economic downturn, Canada's federal government emerged from World War II committed to interventionist Keynesian economic theory and a social welfare system that included unemployment insurance, universal family allowances, generous veterans' benefits, and the promise of a national health care scheme in the near future.

But assessing the degree to which Canada moved forward during the war years now requires that one also take into account the work of several social historians. Scholars interested in ethnic minorities or civil liberties, for example, have written about a domestic repression every bit as extreme as that during the 1914–18 conflict. Much work has also appeared investigating the degree to which attitudes towards women altered as women were recruited into the paid employment market to take the place of men. With female labour participation climbing from 25 to 33.5 percent between 1939 and 1944 and women demonstrating that they could hold certain "male" jobs, there developed, some scholars have noted, a growing self-confidence in women and, as a result, demands such as for equal pay.[2] Counterbalancing this theme in social history, however, is a more dominant one, stressing the widespread concern over women's loss of femininity and of attachment to the family. Along with positive imaging of women's contribution in helping to "back the attack" was a profusion of propaganda underlining the idea that women laboured solely out of patriotism and looked forward to the day when they could trade in their factory overalls for a kitchen apron.

Social unease over working women is a theme in both articles in this section. At Cornwall's main textile mills, writes Ellen Scheinberg in Article 21, men, even those poorly qualified, continued to be hired for the most prized positions, and an unequal pay structure based on gender was maintained within single job categories. Simply put, for most women in this sector, the war brought little or no change. Jeffrey Keshen contends in Article 22 that pervasive wartime anxiety over family stability nourished a statistically unsupported assumption that working mothers were a factor in rising juvenile delinquency — a criminal trend that Keshen contends had more to do with such demographic anomalies as the absence from Canada of most of its 18- to 30-year-old males. Working women thus found themselves scapegoats for a non-existent crisis. But Keshen also argues that the "crisis" precipitated certain progressive initiatives adopted to address what an increasing number of people recognized as long-standing deficiencies in the treatment of youth.

Over six years of collective effort and sacrifice, Canada did grow into a nation more "modern" in many respects. Proud of its battlefield accomplishments, its citizens finally discarded the remnants of the colonial mentality that in part had driven the nation to war. Having served as a major supplier of men and materiel, Canada emerged in 1945 as a far more respected international player and a noteworthy economic power. And having moved both philosophically and concretely towards "big government," Canada had set the stage for its adoption of Keynesian economic planning and the flowering of the social service state. Yet in terms of the criteria established by some social historians — one such criterion being the degree to which gender-based inequities were narrowed or eliminated — these years were much less clearly a watershed. Indeed, as the following two articles suggest, for many ordinary Canadians the sense of having entered a new, more modern age would have to wait for at least another generation.

QUESTIONS TO CONSIDER

1. Describe the means by which textile employers in Cornwall maintained a gendered division of labour.
2. What type of resistance, says Scheinberg, did women fashion against on-the-job discrimination and/or exploitation?
3. What were the consequences, according to Keshen, of wartime concern over delinquency?
4. Besides the employment of women, what factors associated with the war placed strains on or gave rise to concerns about family life and morality?
5. What evidence might a historian use to suggest that the war had a liberating effect on women, not only during the conflict, but in the years that followed?

NOTES

1. M.C. Urquhart and K.A.H. Buckley, eds., *Historical Statistics on Canada* (Toronto: Macmillan, 1965), series W177–213.
2. See Carolyn Gossage, *Great Coats and Glamour Boots: Canadian Women at War (1939–1945)* (Toronto: Dundurn Press, 1991), and Gail Cuthbert Brandt, "'Pigeon-Holed and Forgotten': The Work of the Subcommittee on the Post-War Problems of Women, 1943." *Histoire sociale/Social History*, 15, 29 (1982): 239–59.

SUGGESTED READINGS

Broadfoot, Barry. *Six War Years, 1939–1945*. Toronto: Doubleday, 1974.

Doll, Maurice, ed. *For King and Country: Alberta and the Second World War*. Edmonton: Provincial Museum of Alberta, 1995.

Granatstein, J.L. *Canada's War: The Politics of the Mackenzie King Government, 1939–1945*. Toronto: Oxford University Press, 1975.

Granatstein, J.L., and Peter Neary, eds. *The Good Fight: Canadians and the Second World War*. Toronto: Copp Clark Longman, 1995.

Guest, Dennis. *The Emergence of Social Security in Canada*. Vancouver: University of British Columbia Press, 1985.

Hillmer, Norman, ed. *On Guard for Thee: War, Ethnicity, and the Canadian State, 1939–45*. Ottawa: Canadian Committee for the History of the Second World War, 1988.

MacDowell, Laurel Sefton. *"Remember Kirkland Lake": The History and Effects of the Kirkland Lake Gold Miners' Strike, 1941–42*. Toronto: University of Toronto Press, 1983.

Morton, Desmond, and J.L. Granatstein. *Victory, 1945: The Birth of Modern Canada*. Toronto: HarperCollins 1995.

Pierson, Ruth Roach. *"They're Still Women After All": Canadian Women and the Second World War*. Toronto: McClelland & Stewart, 1986.

Records of the Second World War at the National Archives of Canada. Ottawa: National Archives of Canada, 1993.

TWENTY-ONE

The Tale of Tessie the Textile Worker: Female Textile Workers in Cornwall during World War II

ELLEN SCHEINBERG

The typical image of North American women during World War II is that of an attractive, smiling, confident, independent woman clad in overalls, with a wrench, blowtorch, or gun in her hand. This stereotype, often referred to as "Rosie the Riveter" in the United States or the "Bren Girl" in Canada, was created and used

Source: Excerpted from "The Tale of Tessie the Textile Worker: Female Textile Workers in Cornwall during World War II," *Labour/Le Travail*, 33 (Spring 1994): 153–81. © Committee on Canadian Labour History. Reprinted by permission of the editor of *Labour/Le Travail*.

by the media during the war to help recruit large numbers of women into the labour-starved war industries.

Since the 1970s, liberal historians have perpetuated such images in depicting North American women during the war. The first liberal scholars who addressed the issue of women's wartime experiences included Americans such as Richard Polenberg, Chester Gregory, and William Chafe, who wrote during the early 1970s.[1] These early scholars argued that the war stimulated new social and economic opportunities for women, due to changes in societal attitudes concerning women's "proper place." This change in public opinion, they contend, enabled women to leave the home and work in high-paid occupations traditionally restricted to men. While all three scholars view these changes as having permanently and positively affected American women's role in society, Gregory and Polenberg assert that the war brought about a type of second emancipation for women, one which promoted "a fully American egalitarianism by democratizing labor."[2] Adopting a less optimistic stance, Chafe argued that although the war did not bring about an equality of the sexes, it did open up a new era of potential activity for women.[3]

During the late 1970s and early 1980s, a new group of liberal revisionists addressed the same issue, providing a less optimistic appraisal of the war's impact on North American women. Although scholars from this school such as Karen Anderson, Alan Clive, and Susan Hartmann accepted the argument that the war enhanced women's economic and social opportunities, they diverged from the first school in stressing the temporary and limited nature of such change.[4] Ruth Roach Pierson's *"They're Still Women After All": The Second World War and Canadian Women* adopted the same type of approach as the second school, but moved the focus from the workplace to the state by investigating Canadian government influence upon women's changing role in war industries, as well as in wartime military and volunteer organizations.[5] Like her revisionist American counterparts, Pierson challenged the notion that the war liberated women, arguing instead that "the massive recruitment of women into jobs outside of the home was intended to be only for the duration of the war and represented no concession of the principle of women's right to work."[6] The introduction of new tax incentives and daycare services, she argued, were simply short-term initiatives aimed at providing temporary relief to women employed in war industries, for once the war ended, the government immediately rescinded such programs.[7] The state, therefore, simply promoted measures aimed at solving the particular labour and military imperatives of the day. Once the war ended, so too did the government's support for the programs and policies that momentarily enabled women to enter areas in the workforce that were once a male domain.

While liberal feminist scholars focused on attitudinal change among North American men and women as the reason for women's new role in the workforce, Pierson emphasized the role of the state as a patriarchal structure which produced and sustained an "egalitarian rhetoric" that encouraged women to enter the workforce, thereby aiding the war effort by temporarily legitimizing the work that the women were engaged in during the war. Although the "liberationist" and "revisionist" schools have diverged in their assessment of the over-all effects and longevity of the changes that took place, I would argue that both have considerably underestimated the impact which material conditions had on women's lives during the war.

While Canadian middle-class women may have had the luxury to work during the war for patriotic reasons or in order to escape the confines of the home, as the early feminists argued, their working-class counterparts enjoyed no such choice, for individuals' choices are shaped by market forces. It was therefore economic necessity, rather than a change in attitudes, domestic ideology, or egalitarian rhetoric at the state level that dictated the occupational decisions of most women who worked during this period.

The literature on women and the war has focused on those who worked in the war industries, military, or large manufacturing plants located in North American urban centres, neglecting the significant number of North American, and particularly Canadian, women who toiled in the traditional female manufacturing sectors located in small communities during the war years. Although one American scholar, Marc Miller, has produced a study on the textile workers in wartime Lowell, Massachusetts, the two Canadian historians who have written influential studies on the textile industry in Canada during this period — Joy Parr and Gail Cuthbert Brandt — did not address the question of how and to what extent the war served in changing women's experiences in the textile industry.[8] This study will attempt to redress this imbalance by assessing the impact that the war had on working-class women's lives in the textile town of Cornwall, Ontario.

Using a dual structural analysis, this study will argue that rather than experiencing new job opportunities and increased mobility within the factories, Cornwall's 15 female textile workers remained segregated in the same traditionally "female" jobs that they had occupied before the war. The gender-typed structure of the textile industry, it will be argued, rather than eroding during the war years, was maintained due to the often-concerted efforts of management, male unionists, and, to a lesser extent, the state. All of these forces participated in preserving the patriarchal order, albeit in different ways.

....

The city of Cornwall was known during the late-19th and early-20th centuries as one of Canada's major centres of textile production. Ever since the first cotton mills were erected during the 1870s, the town's identity and economic fortunes remained intimately tied to its three cotton mills. Although there were many other types of industries in Cornwall, it was the textile mills that produced the most capital and provided the most jobs to the city's labouring citizens.[9] In 1927, British entrepreneur Samuel Courtaulds set up a branch plant of his rayon company in Cornwall. While the cotton mills had to compete with many other cotton companies across Canada, Courtaulds enjoyed a monopolistic reign over Canada's viscose-rayon market up until the 1940s. As a result, Cornwall was a magnet to immigrants and labour from rural areas, and even during the tumultuous depression years it sustained the Cornwall economy.

While Courtaulds and the three cotton mills in Cornwall produced different types of products and utilized different manufacturing processes, all relied heavily on female workers. Traditionally, women represented as much as half of the workforce at the cotton mills during the pre-depression years.[10] During the 1930s, however, their numbers began to decline due to two factors: technological innovations that made many female jobs obsolete; and secondly, the policy of the employers to give preference to male workers during the depression years. This latter trend was predicated on the prevailing notion that the men were the "breadwinners" of the family and as such were in greater need of jobs. By 1937, both industries began to implement massive layoffs of both men and women but women's proportion in the mills plummeted to 22 per cent of the workforce in the cotton industry and 40 per cent at Courtaulds.[11]

Married women became one of the main targets at Courtaulds following the signing of an agreement between the union and company in 1937, which was introduced and promoted by the union. It stipulated that married women would be laid off before single girls in the mills.[12] Although the company was somewhat reluctant to discharge these women, since many of them possessed more experience than the younger single girls, by 1939 the company felt that it had no choice but to capitulate to the union in order to gain labour cooperation in a massive layoff scheme involving 148 men, 147 girls, and 6 boys.[13]

Although the decline of female workers was a temporary trend in the textile mills, occupational segregation by sex was a permanent fixture that had endured since the establishment of the first mill during the 1870s. Each job in the mill was assigned to a specific sex. The men in the mill were usually placed in the supervisory positions or jobs that required greater skill or strength such as loom-fixing, dyeing, and bleaching in the cotton mills, or doffing, fixing, and engineering in the rayon mills. The women, in contrast, were relegated to the semi-skilled and unskilled jobs, which usually involved work on the machines or in the finishing room.[14] These occupational divisions within the mills had existed for so long and had remained such an intrinsic part of the textile industry that they were rarely questioned and were viewed, in fact, as quite natural by employers and workers alike.

One of the direct results of this gender-based structure was the creation of significant wage differentials between the male and female textile workers. These gaps were especially pronounced in the rayon industry, where men earned as much as 50 per cent more than women. The average weekly salary for men in the rayon industry in Ontario was $23.24 in 1934, while women earned a meagre average weekly income of $12.60. In the cotton industry, the men earned a significantly lower salary than their rayon-industry counterparts, making $17.26 a week on average. The female cotton workers, in turn, earned an average of $13.13 a week.[15] While these paltry female salaries were clearly inadequate to support a woman at that time, wage levels were based on the assumption that all the women working in the mills were dependents, and as such had their husbands and families to support them and therefore only needed enough for "pin money."

....

The war years did not alter or improve the situation of female textile workers significantly. If anything, the war produced new emotional and psychological hardships for these women. During the first two years of the war, a large segment of the workers at the mills left, either to serve their country abroad by joining the military, or in search of brighter occupational prospects in the war industries of large industrial centres like Toronto, Hamilton, and Montréal.

While the single female workers were able to spend some discretionary time engaged in organized sports and dances during the war, the married women were suddenly thrust into the role of being both single parent and provider. Although many husbands remitted to their wives weekly military pay cheques, these salaries often were very small. One married rayon worker, Rose Booth, received about ten dollars a week, approximately half the salary that her husband had received before the war at Courtaulds.[16] The sudden loss of income had the effect of increasing the need for the wives to work, in order to support their families during the war. For most women this was an arduous task: with the rising cost of living and a salary that remained fixed at thirteen dollars a week, it was often difficult for most of these women to make their monthly rent and furniture payments.[17]

The wartime financial burdens of married women were compounded by the problem of finding proper housing and daycare services for their children while they worked in the mills during the day. The local paper noted the scarcity of low-rental homes in Cornwall in 1943. The woman they interviewed, Miss Margaret Conliffe, Family Welfare Bureau assistant secretary, stated:

> The housing situation has become serious. There are a few low rent houses in Cornwall and when one is available most owners refuse to take a family with children and some bluntly say that they do not want a soldier's wife in their house. There may be some jus-tification for that attitude in certain cases but there are many worthy soldier's wives and families who are having great difficulty to find a home and get along on a small income.[18]

Although the government had funded daycare facilities for working women with chil-dren during the war, they were intended for those women who were employed by the war industries, and as such, were located in Ontario industrial cities such as Hamil-ton, Toronto and its suburbs.[19] Unable to take advantage of these subsidized daycare facilities, Cornwall's female textile workers were forced to rely on the services of fam-ily, friends, and babysitters instead, which in the latter two cases, often took a significant bite out of their incomes.

In addition to the financial strains that these women faced, wartime conditions were an emotionally stressful time. One woman who worked at Canadian Cottons, Lucille Duschesne Jarrett, recalled tearful goodbyes to the men going off to war.[20] Although married women in particular feared for the fate of their husbands, most other workers had a family member or close friend who was fighting in the war. Throughout this period, the atmosphere within the mills was much more grave and sombre than it had been during the 1930s. There was a pervasive fear among workers that they would be called into the manager's office and presented with the fateful telegram, informing them of the loss of a spouse or child. Lucille Jarrett described the scene, stating that "they were coming with papers that their husbands got killed. Everyday there was a note to someone who went to see the boss and he was looking at you and you knew there was something wrong there."[21]

Although the departure of the men who left to join the armed forces took a last-ing emotional toll on those women who stayed behind, it had the positive effect of creating vacancies in the mills, many of which were filled by the women who had been laid off during the depression years. Following the establishment of a war con-tract agreement between the textile companies and the government, the demand for labour was considerably heightened. Throughout the war years, the cotton and rayon mills were engaged in producing a wide variety of war goods. Courtaulds had altered many of its machines in the spinning room to accommodate the production of mater-ial for parachute and tire yarn. The cotton mills, in turn, manufactured tacking for the army, flannelette for the auxiliary forces, khaki drill for fatigue uniforms, and blankets for the men. These war contracts made up a considerable portion of the cotton com-panies' total production, representing 33–35 per cent of their output in 1943.[22] As the production demands at the mills increased during this period, so too did the pressure to hire more workers to keep up with war orders.

Throughout the war, employment in Canada was handled by the National Selective Service (NSS). The NSS was established on 21 March 1942 and was administered by the Minister of Labour. Its mandate was to direct the civilian labour supply toward meeting the requirements of war and essential services.[23] In order to hire any workers, the textile mills were required to go through the NSS. The problem, however, was that the government had given the war production companies priority over the consumer industries in drawing from the labour pool. While the textile companies in Cornwall were indeed producing materials to be used in the war, they were initially assigned a "C" rating on a scale from A to D in terms of necessary war production.[24] As a result, the local NSS was required to send most of Cornwall's eligible and mobile workers to war industries located in some of the larger industrial cities, leaving only a small number to work in the mills.[25]

Considering Cornwall's resulting labour scarcity, especially at the textile mills, one would imagine that the women would have found all types of employment opportunities due to the severe and pervasive shortage of men. Indeed, Marc Miller's *The Irony of Victory: World War Two and Lowell, Massachusetts* has stressed the considerable employment opportunities that women were afforded during the war in Lowell, the famous American cotton mill town. Miller asserts that the presence of war industries in Lowell and nearby Boston allowed women to leave the textile mills and secure higher-paid jobs in war industries. This exodus from the mills, in turn, prodded textile mill owners to increase the salaries of their workers, in order to remain competitive with the war industries. As a result, he contends, in addition to earning higher salaries, female workers experienced greater freedom and more choices than ever before.[26]

Unlike Lowell, however, Cornwall possessed only one war industry, which employed mostly men. The opportunities for war work were in the larger industrial cities, and thus available only to the mobile portion of the workforce. Many women, in fact, remained in Cornwall and continued to toil in the mills, preferring to accept the poor pay and work conditions rather than relocating, which would force them to leave friends and family. This reluctance on the part of Cornwall's women to leave their families and homes was noted in an article published in the *Standard-Freeholder*. The writer stated that while the registration of female workers was increasing, "frequently, it is found that applicants prefer to remain at home or in the nearby district."[27] While some single girls moved, most married women were not as mobile, and consequently had to remain in Cornwall and continue to work in the mills in order to support their children and to wait for their husbands to return.

In addition to emphasizing the new outside employment opportunities that women encountered during the war, most liberal historians have argued that women gained considerable occupational mobility within industries during the war. They contend that following the exodus of male workers, the women were granted the unprecedented opportunity of entering those higher-paying "male" jobs that had been restricted to men before the war. During the early war period, much of Cornwall's adult male population began to enlist or search for work in some of the war plants outside of town. This large exodus of men created severe labour shortages in the mills.[28] It was the cotton mills, however, that suffered the worst, due to the companies' lower pay structure for its male workers. As a result, those men who remained in town often chose to work in the other industries in Cornwall including Courtaulds, which offered considerably higher wages to males. Although the cotton mills hired more women, they continued to remain segregated in the traditionally "female" occupations. The only exception to this rule occurred in the weaving room, where management was forced to engage an increased number of women as weavers, an occupation that while never designated a "male" job, was, in fact, preponderantly a male preserve before the war. Rather than going out into the community and hiring men who had no experience at jobs at these levels, Canadian Cottons began to promote those women who had assisted in the weaving process as battery fillers before the war. Although the women were pushed up in the ranks in the weaving rooms, their salaries did not truly reflect this promotion. For instead of paying these women the same wages as male weavers, the company continued to pay them salaries that were only a little higher, but consistent with women's salaries elsewhere in the mill.[29]

The situation at Courtaulds remained even more strictly segregated as the union men there had always held firm to segregation by sex, due to the greater wage differentials involved. The rayon company attempted to fill its unoccupied positions by offering women more machines to tend at slightly higher pay, but the hard work and stress involved far outweighed the financial benefits. Women also were permitted to take over the "boys'" jobs that could be described as "gophering" type positions, requiring great speed and strength. While the girls in those jobs enjoyed the change of work, they found once again that the meagre financial benefits did not compensate for the more strenuous work.[30] Although the company and the union were willing to allow women to take on a heavier work load or move into the "boys'" jobs, they were unwilling to promote them to the more lucrative "male" jobs such as loom fixing, spinning, dyeing, and bleaching, despite wartime labour shortages.

Considering the firm position taken by the company concerning job segregation by sex, one would imagine that it would encounter problems keeping up production during the war, especially in the men's departments. Surprisingly, the mills were able to recruit enough men to keep the companies functioning at their required levels. One company representative, Jack Mills, asserted that "they didn't have trouble getting labour at Courtaulds, I can assure you, everybody was glad to work there at that time."[31]

Most of the male recruits came from outlying rural towns. Another group of men who helped fill the empty ranks in the men's departments were those individuals who were either too young, too old, or unfit physically to go off to war.[32] While many of these men, who were labelled 4F by the military, simply had minor physical problems or ailments, the companies, during this time, were accepting any male capable of operating a machine. One worker, Joe Vaillancourt, recalled that the company even hired handicapped men to fill in for those who had left. He stated that "the company hired people who were not hired before because of an artificial leg or a small arm or something like that. They even hired a blind man, who was responsible for nailing plywood boxes together to pack the yarn."[33] Clearly, this was not an enlightened policy toward the handicapped but rather an effort to maintain gender divisions within the mills. The last group of men that was brought in to alleviate the labour shortages in the men's departments were immigrants from Poland, Hungary, and Italy, who had arrived in Cornwall during the depression years and did not serve in the war.

Although the two companies found enough men to keep production going, they never secured enough to replace all the male employees who had left. They could have moved some women into these jobs, but they decided instead to leave such positions vacant, losing profits in the process. During the years after 1943, however, the emergence of severe labour shortages and growing absenteeism among male mill workers temporarily forced the companies to reconsider their segregation policies.

Throughout 1942–43, the two companies began to suffer from chronic absenteeism, which slowed production and exacerbated the companies' labour-shortage problems. With the exodus of many of the town's men to the military and the lure of higher-paid jobs in war industries in and outside of Cornwall during this time, the mills found themselves unable to maintain enough workers in the traditionally male jobs. One main factor that led to the exodus was the NSS autumn 1943 ceiling on the wages paid to those employed in non-war industries.[34] This meant that the textile companies could not increase the salaries of their workers without the NSS' permission. Since this process took some time, the mills ended up losing a large number of their workers to the more lucrative war industries. Mrs. Rex Eaton, NSS associate director, noted this trend, asserting that "the wage rate for beginners now paid in some cotton mills understandably is one handicap in making referrals of suitable applicants."[35]

In addition to the departures, the mills also suffered from a high level of turnover and absenteeism in the "men's" jobs. In January 1943 alone, Courtaulds experienced a 37 per cent turnover in the spinning room.[36] Competition eventually took its toll on the mills, for in just one year, the production rates of both companies began to decline by 10 per cent and 15 per cent in the cotton and rayon mills respectively.[37] In order to enlarge their labour pool, the companies began to hire back those employees who had been laid off during the 1930s, and temporarily rescinded the 1937 policy regarding married women.[38]

In addition to rehiring former employees and hiring married women, the companies attempted to solve their severe shortage of male workers by seeking a higher priority-rating from the NSS, which would enable them to acquire extra male workers in order to fill in the serious gaps.[39] When this request failed to elicit an immediate response from the NSS, Courtaulds felt that it had no recourse but to pursue a different and more radical course of action. Faced with growing war orders and a declining male workforce, it chose to abandon temporarily the old gender-segregation policy in favour of higher productivity and profits.

On 16 April 1943, Courtaulds broached the subject of allowing women to fill the empty "male" jobs for the duration of the war. Motivated more by economic necessity than any type of altruistic or feminist spirit, the Courtaulds manager Edward Hazeley attempted to demonstrate to the union how all the other attempted solutions had failed to create an adequate labour pool and so there was no other option but that of allowing the women to work in some of the "men's" jobs. Hazeley proposed this controversial change at a joint meeting of company and union representatives. He asserted:

> There are quite a number of jobs that can be done by girls. That does not mean I am asking to get rid of these men. We have quite a number of cases where they actually refused to do the job and because I wanted manpower I have not fired them.

The union members seemed to be a little surprised and unclear about the proposition that Hazeley was making and asked him to elaborate on it. Hazeley continued:

> One or two of the spindle motor men have to go into other jobs. I will have to replace them. There is a definite case of where we could get husky girls who could do the job.[40]

Rather than readily accepting the request, the union representatives inquired as to whether the women on these jobs would receive the same salaries as men. Hazeley responded by explaining that:

> If a girl takes a man's job she gets that man's rate providing one girl can do one man's job. If I get girls in the spinning who can doff they will get fifty cents an hour. I am not objecting to the wages for any girl replacing a man. If she can do the job she should get a man's rate. We have to get the spindle situation better so that we can get going without criticism.[41]

Even after the company agreed to meet this request as well as that of supplying work clothing for the women, the union remained reluctant to accept the placement of women in "male" jobs. It is apparent that while the company was finally willing to waive temporarily the job barriers that had excluded women from the "men's" jobs and pay them wages equal to the men's, it was the union that proved reluctant to adopt this new scheme. Throughout the war, the union waged its own internal conflict within the mills, one aimed at protecting job barriers that had in the past protected them from competition with the women and from the possible erosion of their higher wages.

When explaining the union's attitude, one active union member, Gordon Jarrett, argued that there were a number of factors behind the union men's reluctance to consider letting women work in the "male" jobs. The factors he cited included: the women's lack of physical strength to take on the more strenuous male jobs; the lack of suitable washrooms and changing rooms for the women in the men's departments; and finally, the possibility of weakening the union's organizational strength should the women enter the male departments. Jarrett expanded upon this final point, stating that "I think one of the things that might have bothered the men was the fact that the union was not as strong in the women's departments as it was in the men's and that there might be the possibility of a loss of some concessions down the line."[42] While perhaps some of the men truly were convinced of the validity and weight of these potential problems, for most these were excuses which simply served to mask their fear of female competition. One male worker revealed the men's sentiments, stating that "at that time there was no such thing as getting women to work in men's jobs. In those days there were laws and the protective mood of the men that they didn't want the women to cut in on their job."[43]

While the company appeared willing — even eager — to set aside the existing job barriers for the women, they made no effort to try to improve the job conditions or wages of their female workers. Conditions and pay, in fact, differed little from those that existed before the war. The companies continued to pay men by the hour, but used a piecework quota system within the women's workrooms. Whereas the men at the mills were able to earn as much as 77 cents an hour during this time, women's wage ceilings were set at 31 cents an hour at Courtaulds.[44] In order to earn this salary, however, the women had to meet the established quota for a three-week period of time. If they failed to sustain their production during this interval, their salaries would be cut from 28 to 25 cents an hour and they would face the prospect of severe chastisement from their managers.[45] In order to earn the top salary of 31 cents again, the women would have to meet the quota for three consecutive weeks.[46] Since the quotas were often set too high for the women to reach, a number of them would arrive at work before the factory opened in order to get a head start on their work. They were not remunerated for this extra time. Those employees who not only met but surpassed the quotas also found themselves unrewarded, for the company refused to pay a salary above the ceiling of 31 cents.

In November 1943, the female workers and the union representatives addressed and questioned this system, arguing that it was unfair for the women to work on their machines even after they had satisfied their quotas. Hazeley responded to this complaint, asserting that:

> The girl has to work the full eight hours of the shift. Nobody has ever said that 250 cakes is all we expect of a girl. We know that more cakes can be coned than that. The 250 cakes is only the minimum number of cakes that we expect for 31 cents an hour. If she falls below 250 then she doesn't get 31 cents. A good many girls do more than 250, and we expect more than 250 from any girl being paid 31 cents.[47]

While the natural tendency on the part of the women was to slow down or actually stop their machines after they met their quota, the company enforced its unpopular policy by empowering their staff with the right to use almost any type of tactic, including coercion, to see that the "girls" not only made their production but worked at their machines until the end of the day.

....

Unlike the men, who enjoyed a great deal of protection and privilege in the mills during the war years, the women constantly faced the threat of being dismissed if they failed to meet their quotas. Rather than remaining passive victims, the women at Courtaulds adopted a security scheme based on mutual cooperation. The practice was for older and more skilled women to use their extra time at the end of the day to help those who were struggling to meet quotas. One coning machine operator at Courtaulds, Jean Beaks O'Brian, explained that "if they said that I was faster than another girl, I would take some of her cakes and help her get done. If I was done ahead, we would help one another."[48]

In addition to the problems with wartime wages and the quota system, the women also received poor and occasionally coercive treatment by their foremen and floor ladies in the workrooms. Although the majority of the women who worked in Ontario's textile mills were between ages 20 and 34, they were treated like little girls, incapable of behaving properly without the watchful eye of the floor lady and the strict policies of the company. In addition to having to respond to the piercing sound of the whistle that blew at three different intervals during the day, they also had to face the indignity of asking their floor lady's permission to use the washroom.[49] While the men could come and go at will and visit the washroom whenever it suited them, the company felt that the "girls" would abuse this type of freedom by arriving late and chatting in the washrooms with their friends. To prevent this, the company posted a woman in the washrooms who was responsible for recording the name of each "girl" who came in and for ensuring that nobody spent too much time there. When the union and the women raised this grievance at one of the joint meetings with the company representative, Mr. Giles, he demonstrated his reluctance to alter this policy, stating that "you have to have some plan and system about it. You couldn't have a broad ruling that any girl could go any place without permission." One of the women attending the meeting illustrated her frustration and distaste for this practice, arguing "that is school days."[50]

Another practice that the women found intolerable was that of the floor ladies inspecting and cutting the female workers' fingernails if they were deemed too long. While the company argued that this was a safety measure against having the women get their nails stuck in the machines, their real concern was the quality of the yarn and the possibility that the women might accidentally rip or damage the product. It is evident that the company promoted these types of degrading and patriarchal practices, as a method of establishing a system of shopfloor control over the "girls" in order to insure higher production and profit, at the expense of the workers' sense of freedom and pride.[51]

The final and most serious problem that the female workers were exposed to during the war was that which we refer to today as "sexual harassment" by their foremen. While many of these foremen were married men in their mid-thirties or forties, and supposedly respectable individuals, there were a number at the mills who took advantage of their powerful position by verbally and physically harassing their female workers. Many of these cases went unreported, since the young women often were too frightened to report such incidents to the management or union for fear that they would not believe them, or, even worse, punish them. One woman who was herself the victim of this type of harassment brought no charge because she feared that the company would probably dismiss the accusation and insinuate that it was she who was responsible for leading on the foreman, thereby damaging her reputation in the workroom and the mill.[52] Two cases, in fact, were brought up at a joint meeting and immediately dismissed by the company. One exception to this failure to acknowledge harassment cases arose in 1940, following a strike involving all 1700 workers at Courtaulds. The union charged a company foreman, Louis Cinquini, with assault and improper moral behaviour in his department. Since the company was unwilling to dismiss Cinquini, the state was asked to intervene and mediate the case under the *Industrial Disputes Investigation Act*. Albert Constantineau, the judge for the County Court of Prescott and Russell, was appointed commissioner of the inquiry. The proceedings reveal that the union initiated the charges in response to an assault made by Cinquini with a two-by-four against a young boy in his department. The additional charges of sexual impropriety were meant to support the union's case for Cinquini's dismissal. Regardless of the motives involved, it became clear throughout the hearing that the company and the judge gave no more attention to these types of cases than the union did.

On 21 September 1940, six young women, ranging in age from 17 to 24 years, testified that foreman Cinquini had "indulged in vulgar stories or used words of a double meaning." They also revealed his physical violations of their privacy, divulging how he had pinched them or engaged in "other acts which they did not approve of."[53] While these female workers obviously did not elaborate on abuses out of shyness or fear of being too explicit, the numbers involved should have illustrated that something was awry. Following the trial, the judge ruled in favour of Cinquini, dismissing the testimony of the six women. Constantineau provided an explanation for his ruling and decision to ignore the "girls'" testimonies, stating that "even if the story told by the six girls who testified against him is true in every detail, the acts of impropriety imputed him are of such trivial character that they do not warrant his reputation being seriously besmirched on that account."[54]

Following this judgement, the union responded by writing to Judge Constantineau, explaining certain factors that they hoped might alter his decision. The union argued that the young women who testified had "a certain hesitancy in having to reveal in detail things of this nature." They also placed some of the blame on themselves, "in not having given a greater measure of consideration to the girls of the plant" and adding that "until the past few weeks, the girls had no machinery for the adjustment and consideration of their grievances, being an unorganized department." The union concluded with the statement that "it is obvious that in an unorganized department, there is the ever-present fear of discrimination and victimization when unorganized workers take it upon themselves to protest against existing conditions."[55] Since the union at that time operated under a closed-shop agreement, "unorganized department" must have meant that grievance procedures had not been elaborated for that particular workroom, which indicates the union's failure to supply adequate support for their female members. While the union appeared to show great sympathy for these women's situation, their concern lasted for only as long as this specific case was in progress. Following its completion, the union's interest in the issue disappeared entirely, even though harassment continued in many of the women's departments.

These harassment cases were only one of the many women's issues to which the union gave insufficient attention during this period. Throughout the war, the union tended to place the female workers' grievances on a back burner, giving precedence to those of the men. Considering the increased numbers of female union members during the war, one might assume that their problems would have received greater attention from their union. This situation has to be attributed, in part, to the women's lack of representation at the senior levels of the union leadership. During the war, men occupied all of the executive positions as well as those on the negotiating committees and delegation parties.[56] The only higher positions that the women occupied at this time were those as shop stewards. While stewards had the authority to act as intermediaries between company staff members and the female workers, their opinions and complaints were not taken very seriously or given much consideration by the union men. One women who served as a shop steward during this time described the union meetings as being "mostly about the men."[57] While the men occasionally listened to some of the women's minor problems at the meetings, the one subject that weighed heaviest on the female workers' minds and received little or no consideration by their union brothers was that of wages. During the war years, women were excluded from participating in the annual contract-renewal negotiations with the company. While the men usually did secure raises for the women, these were negligible, usually half the sum that the men received, and hardly kept up with the inflation rate. The justification that the men usually gave for demanding a higher raise than the women each year, and subsequently the existence of huge wage differentials between the two sexes, was that as dependents, women did not need more money. As a result, O'Brian stated, "the women got so much and the men got the most, because the men were seen as the breadwinners of the family."[58]

In 1944, the women once again came under attack by the union, whose leadership ostensibly was concerned about the prospects of returning veterans. The union men suggested to Courtaulds that the firm should prepare for the return of veterans by designating the married women as temporary workers so that they would be prepared to be the first to leave in deference to former servicemen's job needs. Leo Tessier, the president of the union at this time, presented the following suggestion to the company at one of their joint meetings:

> All married women are considered temporarily employed. On a lay off they should be the first to get laid off and if a girl becomes a married woman while she's working she shall go to the bottom of the line.

He continued his statement with the additional comment:

> I think the girls should have the preference in any promotion and if there is a lay off I think the married women should be laid off first and the married women should go to the bottom of the line.[59]

Although the union men may have honestly been concerned about the fate of veterans and single women, it appears that their real anxieties lay in the status of married women after the war. While the men believed that wartime imperatives demanded that married women work during this period, they apparently hoped that the postwar years would bring a return to domesticity and the re-establishment of traditional gender hierarchies both at work and at home.

The company, however, was reluctant to consider this type of proposition during a period of economic prosperity. Giles responded to Tessier, asserting that:

> After all, if we were in a period of serious unemployment there would be an entirely different problem involved in the processing, for instance, we can't get enough girls. When the time comes when there are not enough jobs the single women will be given preference. I don't think there is any real grievance to be discussed.[60]

It is apparent that timing played a significant role in determining the company's reluctance to support the union's demand regarding married women in this case. While the company was perfectly willing to collude in this type of scheme during the depression years, when it was plagued by severe unemployment problems, it was less enthusiastic to cooperate when the economy was as strong as it was during the war years. Evidently, then, economic reasons played a far greater role than values or attitudes in determining corporate policies affecting female workers.

....

The Cornwall example provides ample evidence of the synergism between capital and patriarchy within the mills. While some dual structuralists promote the argument that these two structures are so interdependent that they essentially operate as a single entity, or are separate structures that coexist in harmony, such theories tend to blur the intricacies and inherent tension that exists within this type of relationship. The Cornwall case demonstrates that although patriarchy and capitalism reinforce one another in terms of their support of a sex-segregated workforce, the commitment and motives of the two structures involved varied significantly. Both the union men and the managers were allied in supporting the patriarchal ideology of "woman's place" and the maintenance of a gender-based hierarchy at work that favoured men. The companies' commitment occasionally wavered only in response to economic and labour market fluctuations. In contrast, although the union men could be sympathetic to female grievances regarding work conditions, they remained unyielding in their support of a segmented workforce and "family wages" for the men, since this type of system provided them with a monopoly on the more skilled and higher-paid positions in the mills. The "family wage," in fact, was a seemingly benign concept that masked men's attempts to keep their wives at home and maintain a segmented workforce. The cotton and rayon mill owners and managers were therefore more willing to abandon, at least temporarily, the gender-based work structure when economic conditions rendered it a less than profitable option.

Although the women were subjected to discrimination by both of these bodies, they often were able to protect themselves through the use of strategies based on mutual cooperation, or simply by concealing their marital status from the company and the union when their jobs were on the line. While members normally would expect to receive support and protection from their union, the women were often left to fend for themselves. Rather than remaining passive victims, however, these independent women displayed a great deal of strength and ingenuity when defending themselves against the state-sanctioned discriminatory policies foisted upon them by both company and union. Although no amount of ingenuity could alter the well-entrenched sex-segregated job structure within the mills, the women's initiatives enabled them to secure for themselves a sense of collectivity, pride and self-esteem.

In addition to illustrating the predominant role that these two structures played in influencing the female textile workers' lives, the Cornwall case offers a marked contrast to the war industries during this period. Unlike the women employed in the war industries, who were earning higher wages and experiencing greater occupational mobility within the workforce, Cornwall's female textile workers, on the whole, remained relegated to the same low-paying unskilled jobs that they had occupied before the war. Rather than being treated with the type of respect and status afforded to the female workers in the war industries, Cornwall's female textile workers endured the same deplorable and discriminatory practices that had existed during the pre-war years. Continuity, then, rather than change, characterized Cornwall's female textile workers' experiences during the war.

Although women in the Canadian textile mills only comprised approximately seven per cent of the workforce, the Cornwall case provides another answer to the question of what type of impact World War II had on women's lives.[61] Thus, it illustrates the importance of examining the lives of women employed in areas outside the war industries, in order to establish a more complete picture of women's experiences during this period. In the future, I hope historians will venture beyond this realm, exploring women's experiences in occupational areas such as the clerical, service, and professional fields. Although these professions were not as visible or glamorous as the military or war industries, they employed approximately 69 per cent of all Canadian women during the war.[62] This figure alone should indicate the need to delve into these long-neglected areas if we hope to understand more fully the nature and scope of women's experiences during the war. Evidently, while Rosie and the Bren Girl worked and flourished in the war industries, their less famous and less fortunate sister Tessie toiled in the textile mills.

NOTES

1. Richard Polenberg, *War and Society: The United States, 1941–1945* (London 1972); William Chafe, *The American Woman: Her Changing Social, Economic and Political Roles, 1920–1970* (New York 1972); Chester Gregory, *Women in Defense Work During World War II: An Analysis of the Labor Problems and Women's Rights* (Philadelphia 1972).

2. Chester Gregory, *Women in Defense Work*, xi–xii.

3. William Chafe, *The American Woman*, 150.

4. Karen Anderson, *Wartime Women: Sex Roles, Family Relations, and the Status of Women During World War II* (Westport 1981); Alan Clive, "Women Workers in World War Two: Michigan as a Test Case," *Labor History*, 20 (Winter 1979); and Susan M. Hartmann, *The Home Front and Beyond: American Women in the 1940s* (Boston 1982).

5. Ruth Roach Pierson, *"They're Still Women After All": The Second World War and Canadian Women* (Toronto 1986). Also see her earlier work *Canadian Women and the Second World War* (Ottawa 1983).

6. Ruth Roach Pierson, *"They're Still Women After All,"* 11.

7. Ibid., 11–12.

8. Marc Miller, *The Irony of Victory: World War II and Lowell, Massachusetts* (Urbana 1988); Joy Parr, *The Gender of Breadwinners: Women, Men and Change in Two Industrial Towns, 1880–1950* (Toronto 1990); and Gail Cuthbert Brandt, "Weaving it Together: Life Cycle and the Industrial Experience of Female Cotton Workers in Quebec, 1910–1950," *Labour/Le Travailleur*, 7 (Spring 1981), 113–25.

9. J.F. Pringle, *Lunenburgh, or the Old Eastern District, its Settlement and Early Progress* (Cornwall 1890), 294 and *Cornwall: City of Opportunity* (Cornwall 1950), 24.

10. In 1925, women comprised 43.8 per cent of the cotton industry and 64.4 per cent of the silk and artificial silk industry in Canada. *Report of the Royal Commission into the Textile Industry* (hereafter RRCTI) (Ottawa 1938), 149.

11. *Standard-Freeholder*, 5 February 1937, 1.

12. At the time, it was felt that the married women should be laid off before the single women, since they had husbands to support them. It was not uncommon, however, for married women to conceal their marital status from the union and companies in order to protect their jobs. National Archives of Canada (hereafter NAC), Greater Cornwall Textile Joint Board Records (hereafter GCTJB), MG 28 I 219, Vol. 96, file #4, 4, Minutes from meeting held on 28 April 1939.

13. Ibid., Minutes from meeting held on 8 March 1939.

14. Gail Cuthbert Brandt notes that "many of the traits of the accomplished weaver were those traditionally associated with women: nimble fingers; long slender hands; and a careful attention to detail. By contrast, not even the most intelligent female weavers were considered potential candidates for the position of loom fixer." "The Transformation of Women's Work in the Quebec Cotton Industry, 1920–1950," in Bryan D. Palmer, ed., *The Character of Class Struggle* (Toronto: 1986), 120.

15. RRCTI, Exhibit #1289, 290.

16. Interview with Rose Booth, 2 October 1989.

17. Ibid.

18. *Standard-Freeholder*, 7 April 1943, 3.

19. Within Ontario, 13 of the 18 nurseries that were established and funded by the government during the war were located in industrial Toronto; the rest were situated in Brantford, St. Catharines, Hamilton, Galt, and Oshawa. See "Ontario Day Nurseries Meet Wartime Emergency," *Standard-Freeholder*, 26 February 1944, 9.

20. Interview with Lucille Duschesne Jarrett, 20 September 1989.

21. Ibid.

22. *Brief of Courtaulds Ltd.*, presented to the Trade Tariff Committee (Ottawa 1945), 3; and *Standard-Freeholder*, 30 January 1943, 7.

23. *Canada Year Book* 1944, 9.

24. *Canadian Textile Journal*, 60, 19 (September 1943), 17.

25. This information was extracted from the article "Desperate Need for Women to Aid in War Production," published in the *Standard-Freeholder*, 30 July 1942, 3.

26. Marc Miller, *The Irony of Victory: World War II and Lowell, Massachusetts*, 56.

27. "War Plants Call for Female Help," *Standard-Freeholder*, 24 July 1942, 1.

28. The 1941 *Census* indicated that 719 men from Cornwall left to serve in the armed forces during the early years of the war. They comprised approximately 24 per cent of the existing male workforce in 1941. Canadian *Census*, 1941, Vol. VI, 14–15 and Vol. VII, 244.

29. Interview with Lucille Duschesne Jarrett.

30. The boys' salaries ranged from about 28 to 40 cents an hour, a marginal increase from the women's salaries. Interview with Mrs. Jean Beaks O'Brian, 23 September 1989.

31. Interview with Jack Mills, 25 September 1989.

32. *Cornwall: City of Opportunity*, 24.

33. Interview with Joe Vaillancourt, 20 September 1989.

34. NAC, Records of the Wartime Prices and Trade Board, RG 64, Vol. 45, "Report on the Canadian Textile Industry," June 1944, 45.

35. NAC, Records of the Department of Labour, RG 27, Vol. 666, file #6-5-21-1, Memorandum written by Mrs. Rex Eaton, 13 September 1945, 1–2. The male learners at the mills were earning $.285–.414 an hour and their female counterparts earned $.235–.3175 an hour at the time. Many of the war industries, in contrast, were paying salaries that were close to one dollar an hour for men and more than 50 cents for women. NAC, RG 27, Vol. 1518, File #R-3, pt. 3, Memorandum from Primary Textiles Institute to Donald Gordon, Chairman of the National Textiles and Leather Requirements Committee, 21 June 1943, 5.

36. NAC, GCTJB, Vol. 96, file #7, Minutes from meeting held on 20 January 1942, 1.

37. NAC, RG 27, Vol. 1518, file #R-3(5), "Proposals for Standardizing Production and Releasing Manpower in the Textile Industry," November 1942, Tables IV and VI.

38. NAC, GCTJB, Vol. 100, file #1, Letter from Textile Workers Union of Canada, local 3, to E. Hazeley, 25 April 1942.

39. NAC, RG 27, Vol. 1518, file #R-3-1, Letter from V.W. Boyd, Canadian Cotton Co., to the National Selective Services, 21 May 1943.

40. NAC, GCTJB, Vol. 96, file #7, Minutes from meeting held on 16 April 1943, 7.

41. Ibid.

42. Interview with Mr. Gordon Jarrett, 11 September 1989.

43. Interview with Joe Vaillancourt.

44. NAC, RG 27, Vol. 1518, file #R-3-4, "Textile Report," 19 March 1945, 2.

45. NAC, GCTJB, Vol. 96, file #7, Minutes from joint meeting held on 14 October 1941, 9. Some of this information was also acquired during my interview with Jean Beaks O'Brian.

46. Ibid., 8.

47. Ibid., Vol. 96, file #7, 10 November 1943, 4.

48. Interview with Jean Beaks O'Brian.

49. Interview with Dorothy Chisamore, 24 September 1989.

50. NAC, GCTJB, Vol. 96, file #8, 16 June 1944, 7.

51. Interview with Dorothy Chisamore.

52. Interview with one of the women who worked at Courtaulds, September 1989. Due to the sensitive nature of this information, the woman's name will be withheld in order to protect her privacy.

53. NAC, GCTJB, Vol. 107, file #3, "Report of the Commissioner," 2.

54. Ibid., 4; Information about Judge Constantineau and the trial was extracted from the *Labour Gazette*, November 1940, 1137 and from the Strikes and Lockout Series, NAC, RG 27, Vol. 407, Strike #139, 99.

55. NAC, GCTJB, Vol. 107, file #3, Letter from the United Textile Workers Union to Judge A. Constantineau, 26 September 1940, 6.

56. An article in the *Standard-Freeholder* noted that a United Textile Workers of Canada meeting was held in Montréal and attended by the executive and eighteen delegates from Cornwall's rayon union, local no. 3. All of the individuals who were in attendance were male. 3 November 1942, 1.

57. Interview with Jean Beaks O'Brian.

58. Ibid.

59. NAC, GCTJB, Vol. 96, file #8, Minutes from joint meeting held on 16 June 1944, 8.

60. Ibid.

61. There were 57,366 women employed in the textile industry in Canada in 1941. This figure represents seven per cent of the total female workforce in Canada, which was 833,972 in 1941. *Census of Canada*, 1941, Vol. VII, 54.

62. Ibid.

TWENTY-TWO

Wartime Jitters over Juveniles: Canada's Delinquency Scare and Its Consequences, 1939–1945

JEFFREY KESHEN

Polls today show that numerous Canadians view their country as confronting a crisis with juvenile delinquency.[1] Juxtaposed with portrayals of aimless and alienated youth, or streetwise hooligans expertly exploiting the "liberal" provisions of the country's Young Offenders' Act, is a glowing image of bygone days when adolescents respected the law and their elders. One period given such a representation is that of World War II. According to both survivors of the era and contemporary newsreels, children and youth, rather than serving as a force for social disorder, performed a multitude of tasks to help vanquish Nazism. Across the land, schoolgirls knitted clothing for soldiers and refugees; over 40,000 boys constructed model aircraft for British Commonwealth Air Training Plan [BCATP] recognition classes;[2] and all young people, it seemed, collected old pots, pans, rain boots, toothpaste tubes, rags, and newspapers, and myriad other items, for salvage drives.

Source: Prepared for this volume.

Yet not only these and a multitude of other praiseworthy actions drew attention to the young during the period. Concern mounted over children who were supposedly going astray as a result of wartime conditions. The perception that young people were going bad had significant, and often contradictory, consequences. It was crucial, most Canadians concluded, to have working mothers return to domestic life as soon as hostilities ceased, not only to make room in the workplace for veterans and re-establish "natural" gender roles, but also to control juvenile behaviour more effectively. However, the belief that youth had become more deviant was met not only by this conservative response. In the face of what was perceived as a growing crisis with youth, there also emerged a greater proclivity to seek out and understand the opinions of the young, as well as to improve recreational, educational, and judicial services for young people.

The issue of wartime delinquency began to attract attention in Canada in 1941, when it was noted that the disruption or literal destruction of family life in Britain had produced a number of directionless youth, who were turning to such deviant behaviour as roaming city streets during blackouts to loot shops and homes demolished by enemy bombs.[3] Within months of the United States declaration of war, furthermore, journalistic accounts were describing young people who, with their lives dramatically disrupted by moves to the centres of war production, had become aberrant in behaviour as their working parents grew unable to provide adequate supervision.[4]

Certainly by 1942, many Canadians had concluded that the war was exerting a negative influence on the behaviour of their young people. Juvenile arrests rose from 9497 in 1939 to 13 802 three years later. The rates were highest where war industry congregated; over that four-year span, the increases in juvenile arrests in Toronto and Hamilton were 47.5 and 64.1 percent respectively.[5] Reinforcing the sense of crisis were more and more newspaper headlines referring to "child burglars" and "wayward youth." According to the *Canadian Periodical Index*, press accounts of delinquency increased by approximately 125 percent from 1929–39 to 1939–46.[6]

Several child welfare workers and psychologists warned parents that war conditions held out the potential to exacerbate the "new urges and self-doubt" that came naturally with adolescence. With more employment and money about, people constantly on the move, and "death in the air," a greater proportion of society, it was said, would develop a "devil may care" attitude.[7] As well, though most adolescent males remained determined to perform their duty, some, who had absorbed the lurid tales of Great War veterans or the anti-war works of Lost Generation writers, believed they should indulge themselves while they had the chance.[8]

Commentators worried that rather than receiving guidance and care from their elders, children were having to cope with a home life confronting unprecedented challenges, many of which derived from the new economic opportunities created by the war. While helping to solidify the monetary situation of numerous families who had suffered during the Great Depression, new jobs translated into huge numbers of personal upheavals, as approximately 300 000 Canadians relocated from the countryside to the urban centres between 1940 and 1943.[9]

In the cities, many faced the problem of securing adequate accommodation. In Toronto, for example, by 1941, before the war economy hit full stride, 12.4 percent of homes had been classified as "overcrowded."[10] To alleviate the crisis, on 24 February 1941 the federal government created Wartime Housing Incorporated, to build prefabricated temporary structures for servicemen's families and relocated war workers. But with free market–minded bureaucrats like W. Clifford Clark, the deputy minister of finance, playing a key role in directing this crown corporation, it failed miserably in satisfying national needs. Clark convinced the finance minister, J.L. Ilsley, that private realty interests would be unable to play their critical role in the eventual postwar recovery if government-assisted housing emerged as a major competitor. Consequently, while estimates of housing shortages ran into the hundreds of thousands, by May 1945 this government enterprise had completed only 18 300 structures.[11]

Numerous Canadians were forced to accept pitiful living conditions. A 1943 investigation in Montreal discovered tenants living in warehouses, garages, huts, factories, sheds, and five-foot-high cellars. To make matters worse, several landlords excluded children from their premises, considering them noisy and destructive. Numerous parents were forced to place their offspring in shelters, orphanages, or foster homes while searching for accommodation.[12] Assessing the situation in her keynote address to commemorate the fiftieth anniversary of the National Council of Women of Canada, Lady Althone, the wife of the governor general, identified "bad housing" as being "at the root of nearly all our social ills." *The Ottawa Citizen*, reporting on the speech, blamed shortages of decent living space for the "rise in juvenile delinquency."[13] The Big Brothers organization reported that many youngsters were kept away from home not only by depressing living conditions, but also by a poisoned emotional atmosphere, as congestion engendered an increase in family bickering.[14] Charlotte Whitton, the past president of the Canadian Welfare Council [CWC], claimed that overcrowded homes — especially those in which the parents worked and desired some rest and relaxation during their time off — meant that children were pushed outside to play, where, without proper guidance, they turned to "street dawdling," or, if in their teens, to the "cheap dance hall, hamburger joint, or seedy café." Compounding the situation, claimed Whitton, was that whereas in previous years neighbours often knew the local children and their parents, the radical demographic transformations experienced in several areas had eliminated this informal control mechanism.[15]

In response to this state of affairs, several communities began rigorously to enforce curfew by-laws designed to manage ungoverned youth.[16] Many perceived that an expanding number of neglected boys were forming gangs, from which, it was said, they obtained a sense of family.[17] Some older teenagers became "zoot suiters," with their wide-shouldered long coats, baggy trousers, and huge bow-ties showing what was seen as brazen disrespect for government restrictions to save cloth.[18] Newspapers highlighted both their obsession with jitterbugging and their frequent clashes with soldiers, who regarded them as slackers.[19] In the eyes of the Big Brothers, so serious was the likelihood that neglected youth would turn to gang activity that in the summer of 1943, the organization hired two Toronto secondary-school teachers to conduct a city-wide survey of the problem. Although it found that the members of several "associations" had banded together solely for the purpose of play and had existed before the war, the survey identified 26 other "groupings," in some of which the members ran floating crap games, engaged in petty theft, or intimidated other children into giving up their lunch money.[20]

When it came to young girls, anxiety revolved around the threat of moral corruption. In 1944, from La Ligue de la jeunesse féminine came the charge that teenage girls were primarily responsible for rising venereal disease rates.[21] Most commentators did not go that far, but they believed there was reason for concern, and with some justification. In Manitoba in 1942, the provincial Department of Health reported 56 girls between the ages of 14 and 17 as having contracted V.D., a number that was approximately double that of the immediate prewar years.[22] Moreover, between 1939 and 1945, the illegitimacy rate in Canada rose from 3.95 to 4.48 percent of total births. In illegitimate births to women under age 20, the aggregate increase was from 2866 to 3573, certainly a cause for concern. One must bear in mind, however, that illegitimate births to women under 20 as a percentage of total illegitimacy actually decreased, from 28.02 to 27.62 percent; it seems older Canadian women were proving more promiscuous than formerly.[23]

Still, the perception of teenage promiscuity prompted a steady flow of outraged commentary that too many girls wore "clingy" sweaters or nourished unhealthy obsessions with sex symbols such as Frank Sinatra.[24] With parents often occupied by war work, such girls, many assumed, headed for the streets, where troops milled about and excitement was in the air.[25] In consequence, police forces regularly swept through popular teen hangouts after dark; ordered the management of bars and dance halls to insist on proof of age or risk losing their licences; and asked members of the Provost Corps to pick up girls aged 16 and under who were hanging around military bases so that they could be returned to their parents.[26] As a result, between 1939 and 1943, the number of juvenile girls brought before Canadian courts climbed from 983 to 1430, with the majority of charges — breaking curfew, loitering, and drinking alcohol[27] — clearly indicating a focus on reducing the incidence of what was called "sex delinquency."

Parents too were warned to maintain close surveillance over their children, because an increasing number were cutting classes to assume "dead end" jobs. Ever since child labour had become an issue in Canada, during the late nineteenth century, protective legislation had proved weak owing to statutory loopholes and a dearth of government inspectors.[28] The war highlighted the issue as men vacated jobs to don khaki, and adolescents, recalling the extreme want of the Great Depression, abandoned the classroom in order to make money while they had the chance. Aside from the special age requirements for certain jobs such as mining, at the outset of the war the legal school-leaving age was 14 in New Brunswick and Manitoba; 15 in Prince Edward Island, Saskatchewan, Alberta, and British Columbia; and 16 in Nova Scotia and Ontario. In Quebec, public education was not compulsory.[29] Many teenagers were pulled out of school legally, as provincial education laws allowed parents who demonstrated economic need to obtain a permit allowing their child to seek full-time employment at age 14. Between 1939 and 1942, the number of such permits granted in Ontario rose from 2146 to 12 792, as mothers left on their own found it difficult to survive financially on military dependents' allowances, or as parents who had been without work during the Depression years found themselves ill-equipped to meet the rigours of employment in the war economy.[30] Surveying the situation after four years of war, *Saturday Night* magazine claimed, "Canada has almost reached the stage where . . . another Charles Dickens is needed to rouse the nation out of a wholesale reversion to child labour."[31]

While those who sought work permits for their children were frequently denounced for exploiting their offspring, equally condemned were parents who, supposedly utterly absorbed with making money, worked so many hours that they were unaware their underage children were not attending school or were holding down late-night jobs — often, it was said, at sleazy establishments like billiard halls and bowling alleys, where foul language abounded. One account carried by newspapers in London, Ontario, told of a 13-year-old lad working after school and on weekends as a pin setter for 48.5 hours a week.[32] *Maclean's* reported on girls baby-sitting up to 40 hours a week for working parents. The classified pages of newspapers revealed new opportunities in domestic service. "If you are under 16 and have a school leaving permit," advertised Toronto's George Weston Agency, "we will be glad to have you" — though it was common knowledge that many employers did not bother to inquire about age or permits.[33] In the minds of many, worst of all were the waitressing positions assumed by an increasing number of young girls: according to *Chatelaine*, this kind of work often exposed the "innocent" to forward male conduct.[34]

Some justification existed for apprehension, but as with the issue of "sex delinquency," there was embellishment of the problem. In Ontario, total absenteeism in public schools stood at 8.403 million days during the 1939–40 academic year, climbed to 9.962 million in 1942–43, and dipped to 8.151 million three years later. The factor that most accounted for the initial rise was an increase in "physical obstacles" (accounting for from 4.75 to 8.14 percent of absences), as a combination of hefty snowstorms and the introduction of gasoline and tire rationing in 1942 made it more difficult for many children, particularly in outlying areas, to attend class. By contrast, the number of children whom school officials identified as absent because of parental neglect and/or truancy went from 7.3 to 7.8 percent.[35]

Yet even if truancy was not as serious as some suspected, student employment constituted a problem. In 1944, in what was certainly the most exhaustive wartime study done on the subject, school administrators in London, Ontario, sent questionnaires to 4513 pupils aged 13 to 18. Just over half (52.7 percent) had jobs, and of that figure, 291 (12.2 percent) admitted that they worked in excess of the legal maximum of eighteen hours per week.[36] Although the study did not correlate employment with grade averages, another analysis by the Ontario Department of Education (based on an unspecified number of students) claimed that those who worked more than two hours after school on a regular basis had lower examination scores.[37]

In response, several school boards, wartime labour shortages notwithstanding, managed to appoint additional attendance officers, whose responsibility, besides tracking down truants, was to warn businesses of the possibility of heavy fines and/or loss of their operating licences should they "knowingly" hire minors.[38] Wartime increases in youth employment also no doubt played a part in finally convincing the Quebec government, in 1943, to pass a law providing for compulsory education to age 14.[39] Moreover, Ottawa's introduction of the Family Allowance Act in 1944, though primarily designed to shore up spending levels during what many foresaw would be an initial postwar economic downturn and to help the federal Liberal party undercut support for the socialistic Co-operative Commonwealth Federation, also seemed intended as a corrective to underage employment: in order to receive the benefit, which continued until the child reached age 16, parents had to ensure that the child was not "improperly absent from school."[40]

A majority of Canadians concurred that better housing and the stronger enforcement of curfews and compulsory school attendance laws were important steps in correcting the behaviour of youth. But they also clearly believed that these or any other reforms would be ineffectual unless the structures basic to family life were put solidly in place. In this respect, a fundamental dilemma arose when on 24 March 1942, Ottawa, faced with shortages of industrial labour and the need to recruit more men into uniform, began soliciting married women and mothers into the workforce and providing them with tax breaks and state-run day care. The result was a rise in labour force participation among women from 24.4 percent in 1939 to a peak of 33.5 percent in 1944.[41]

By and large, Canadians accepted this recruitment of women into the workforce as an emergency measure, but many worried that in taking over traditionally male roles, in the industrial sector, for example, women would lose their femininity and, having been enticed by relatively high pay, permanently discard their family responsibilities. To allay consternation, government propaganda and a multitude of press editorials represented such female participation as a patriotic attempt to "back the attack," thereby bolstering the idea that as soon as the shooting stopped, those with families would return to the hearth and concentrate on creating a tranquil haven after all the commotion. But even while the war raged, it was clear that many viewed the widespread phenomenon of working mothers as too high a price to pay for victory. Much damage, it was contended, was already being done as a result of servicemen's leaving behind housewives who were incapable of disciplining their children effectively.[42] Reasoning of this sort led *The Toronto Star* to quip that if the father was away, delinquency "increased," but if the mother also worked outside the home, it "doubled." Newspapers regularly bemoaned the so-called latchkey child, who returned at lunchtime or after school to "an empty house and cold meal."[43] In an article typifying the general national mood, *Chatelaine* columnist Adele Saunders cited the case of 9-year-old Jimmy, whose father was overseas and whose mother was away during the day in a munitions plant. While admitting that patriotism had guided the mother's decision to work, Saunders made clear that the eventual resumption of traditional gender roles was essential: with only strangers in the community to watch over him during the late afternoons, Jimmy fell in with a gang whose members were arrested for robbing homes.[44]

The determination that mothers not be distanced by their new jobs from familial duties is plainly evident in the way governments managed services such as day nurseries, after-school care, and school lunch programs. In establishing all-day facilities for those between the ages of 2 and 6 as well as afternoon supervision for youngsters not yet in high school under a June 1942 50-50 shared-cost agreement with interested provinces, Ottawa stipulated that 75 percent of the spaces be reserved for the children of "war workers."[45] Notwithstanding its promises to interpret the definition of "war workers" liberally, the federal government clearly intended to send the message that the employment of mothers was regarded as a temporary measure strictly related to the prevailing crisis.

In no jurisdiction were facilities made commensurate with need. In Ontario, where the concentration of war industry saw 28 day-care centres open, the 1135 spaces therein equalled approximately one-quarter of the number of eligible children of war workers. Meanwhile, severe opposition from Quebec's powerful Catholic church played a seminal role in keeping the number of day-care facilities in that province at just six.[46] But compared to mothers in other provinces, those in central Canada were fortunate. With increased naval construction, a 1943 estimate placed the number of working mothers in British Columbia at 15 000. That autumn, a Day Nursery Committee was formed, but it was unable to satisfy the provincial government that enough mothers worked in industries directly connected with the war effort as distinct from the surrounding service sector, and so the province was kept out of the 1942 day-care program. Perhaps indicative of the attitude of British Columbia's Conservative Coalition government was a statement by its Vancouver–Point Grey representative, Tilly Rolston, who denounced government-run child care as an "attack on . . . the Canadian home."[47]

Outside Ontario and Quebec, only Alberta considered acting in concert with Ottawa on the day-care front, after a number of war jobs were created by the BCATP, the Alaska Highway, and the Canol oil project. Pressure mounted from working women through 1942, but the Social Credit government proved cagey, demanding that municipalities, which it realized were still reeling financially from efforts to administer relief during the Depression, cover 25 percent of costs. Some businesses that depended on women workers came to support day care, such as Edmonton's Great Western Garment Corporation (which made uniforms), whose president reported that from May to July 1943, his female staff fell from 470 to 377 owing to an inability of mothers to find acceptable child-care services.[48] That September, the provincial government actually signed the federal day-care legislation but, as part of its ongoing investigation into Alberta's needs, said it would proceed with the program only if there were an adequate response to a newspaper campaign asking people to indicate that they favoured such a service. Supporters of state-run facilities in Alberta pointed out that many women workers read only Ukrainian and, as devout Catholics, were reluctant to admit to difficulties in caring for their children. The advertisements, moreover, failed to mention what the fees at government-supported facilities would be after subsidies and suggested that only the children of those directly involved with war work would qualify, thereby guaranteeing a less than overwhelming response and sealing the demise of day care in Alberta.[49]

An identical approach guided Ottawa's school lunch program. Principals were permitted to select needy children as long as 75 percent of them had mothers in industries directly connected to the war effort. If satisfied with a particular school's application, the federal government would pay for the necessary food and staff. Rejections were common, however, and some schools (in Edmonton and Calgary, for instance), convinced of their need though they had failed to qualify, used Home Economics facilities to start their own programs.[50] Others, lacking the necessary equipment or finances, sent home with their pupils information on nutrition, or even came to depend on local charities, a case being Toronto's Alexander Muir School, where during the noon hour nearly 100 pupils were directed to a nearby Salvation Army Hall.[51]

The sad and circular irony for women was that while the determination to protect the "traditional" family played a key role in limiting and, by April 1946, scuttling federal government support for child-care programs, that move towards traditionalism also drew strength from the consequences of the government's parsimonious approach to state-supported child care — a growing number of youngsters who, Canadians were constantly reminded, were too often left without adequate supervision. Typical was *Chatelaine's* exposé concerning "car babies" abandoned all day in parking lots while their mothers worked, or of a 4-year-old boy locked in a room at home with only a few pieces of bread to gnaw on and a gas stove within reach.[52] Although these situations were anomalies, they garnered massive attention owing to societal apprehension over women's relinquishing their "proper sphere," and the prominence given them created an unfounded assumption linking working mothers with child neglect. In fact, while charges for "non-support of family and neglecting children" rose from 1547 in 1938 to 2546 in 1941 (which rise government authorities accepted was primarily due to fathers' abandoning their dependents for military service or for new jobs away from home once the Depression ended), during the large-scale employment of women the next year the figure dipped to 2403.[53] As Ottawa discovered from the high absentee rates in war industry during the few months that elapsed between the recruitment of mothers and the creation of day care, most women would sooner have foregone a pay cheque than risk their children's safety.[54] In many cases of working mothers, the father, who perhaps worked an evening or night shift, was at home with the children. Grandparents too were called into action; older brothers and sisters pitched in; privately run crèches were utilized to the maximum; and some women banded together to hire baby-sitters.[55] An October 1942 survey in London, Ontario, of 218 working mothers with 118 preschool children showed that 38.4 percent of the youngsters stayed with fathers, siblings, or grandparents; 29.7 percent were in day care; 15 percent had formal supervision from neighbours; 13.3 were with relatives; and 3.6 percent were in families that enjoyed the services of a paid housekeeper.[56]

The issue of wartime delinquency, while not dismissible, likewise seems to have been surrounded more by assumption and hyperbole than by reasoned analysis. Few commentators mentioned or bothered to notice that from 1943 to 1945, while mothers were still employed in record numbers, juvenile arrests followed a downward pattern, of 12 225, then 11 554 and finally 9756 arrests per year.[57] Moreover, though wartime delinquency rates were regularly compared with those of the late 1930s, when the number of arrests hit a trough, it was rarely noted that throughout much of the 1920s and early 1930s, when most mothers were at home, juvenile offences stood well above wartime levels.[58] This is not to dismiss the argument that the constant presence of one parent at home would have helped keep some children on the straight and narrow during these often difficult years; but statistical patterns also make clear that behind changing delinquency rates were a number of more significant and less readily noticeable demographic factors.

Authorities should have expected a delinquency peak by the early 1940s, since the mid- to late 1920s was a time of heavy migration into Canada, including that of thousands of young couples whose children would have become teenagers by that time.[59] (Similarly, the boom migration of the early twentieth century helps explain the high delinquency rates during the 1920s through to the mid-1930s, and the trough in youth crime later that decade derived in part from there having been fewer newcomers and a lower birth rate during the Great War, and strict immigration controls until the mid-1920s.)[60] In accounting for the decreases in delinquency during the mid- to late 1940s, one must note, besides the return of many working mothers to the home and the reappearance of fathers after military service, the drastic cuts to immigration and the declining birth rate during the Depression.[61] Large-scale rural-to-urban migration during the war, moreover, was probably the most significant factor in the dramatic rise in juvenile crime recorded in a number of cities. By contrast, in agricultural districts where the population decreased, juvenile crime followed suit — in the Ontario counties of Essex, Grey, and Haldimand for instance, which saw aggregate arrests of minors drop by 22.1, 44.2, and 33.3 percent respectively in the three years from 1939 to 1942.[62]

Equally important in explaining national increases in wartime delinquency was the changing pattern in the nature of the violations committed. While some serious crimes, such as assault and willful damage, showed upward trends, most of the total rise came from the prosecution of more non-indictable offences, such as breaking curfew or disobeying traffic regulations while on a bicycle. For despite a reduction in the number of policemen during the war, from 1.30 officers per 1000 citizens in 1940 to 1.11 officers in 1944,[63] the fact that law enforcement authorities no longer had to concern themselves as much with 18- to 30-year-old males (the most crime-prone demographic group)[64] meant that their focus could expand to include less serious matters — a trend encouraged by the conviction that in the current emergency little tolerance ought to be shown to those who did not behave responsibly. Between 1939 and 1942, indictable offences among all Canadians dropped 18.3 percent, and non-indictable offences climbed 35.6 percent; among youth, between 1941 and 1943, minor offences increased at a rate slightly double that of major violations.[65] Revealing as well is that in 1944, when total youth crime began decreasing, the number of indictable offences within the population as a whole resumed an upward trend (an increase by 13.7 percent over 1943), a fact possibly attributable to the repatriation of wounded soldiers and the inauguration of a home leave system for the country's longest-serving troops. In 1945, total crime in Canada grew by 5 percent, with violations such as assault and burglary leading the way; among juveniles, non-indictable infractions dipped to 35.8 percent lower than the 1942 total, but serious offences (those that would have merited the vigilance of the police) declined by only 15.3 percent.[66]

It appears, therefore, that social attitudes about the proper role for mothers shaped conclusions as to the causes of and the best solutions for wartime delinquency. But the jitters over juveniles did not reverberate only towards conservative ends. It was during World War II, for example, that unprecedented efforts were launched to understand what young people thought, why some behaved themselves during this tumultuous time, and what might be done in addition to the reconstitution of family life to bring the rest around.

Such was the aim of the Canadian Youth Commission [CYC], which was established by the Young Men's Christian Association [YMCA] in November 1940 but by the end of the war had been brought by its director, R.E.G. Davis, under the purview of the secular CWC so that it might solicit more widespread participation and funding. During its seven-year life span, it attracted 54 commissioners, 35 of whom were listed in Canada's *Who's Who*; it boasted an executive that included the likes of University of Toronto President Sidney Smith and diplomat Hugh Keenleyside; and it received advice from prominent figures such as Leonard Marsh and Harry Cassidy, both of whom were pioneers in developing Canada's modern social security system.[67] Although it would be stretching matters to suggest that the opinions expressed by CYC participants played a key role in shaping government policy, still, the fact that approximately 800 youth study groups were formed and prompted the Canadian Broadcasting Corporation to produce a fifteen-minute weekly radio segment summarizing their views clearly demonstrates the growing importance attached to the concerns and expectations of minors — a trend no doubt bolstered by worries over rising delinquency.[68] The CYC executive noted that "ill-governed" and "disgruntled" youth had played a significant role in the social troubles of 1919 and the supposed promiscuity of the 1920s, and thus worked their way to the conclusion that it was "worthwhile to see that [youth] were properly understood . . . advised and helped."[69]

From CYC participants came strong views on issues such as recreation, employment, family life, education, health, religion, and citizenship. CYC study groups also demonstrated considerable concern over postwar economic prospects, pointing out that during the Depression, the young, because they had had little previous work experience, found themselves with higher than average unemployment rates. This concern led to an emphasis on education, as several CYC reports blamed schools for failing to prepare youth to meet the demands of the "real world" — an especially pertinent problem, it was stressed, for the 95 percent of students who did not go on to university.[70] In order to keep children in school, numerous CYC study groups maintained, it was essential to introduce or enhance technical classes and vocational guidance services, as well as better life-skills training, including sex education. Study groups with a connection to organized religion, particularly in Quebec, opposed this last proposal, but a majority of delegates to the 1943 Ontario and Halifax CYC conferences passed resolutions favouring the addition of sex education classes to the high-school curriculum, not simply as a means of satisfying youthful curiosity, but as a way of "directing young people into having a successful marriage and good family life."[71]

Suggestions such as these came to the minds of CYC participants probably not only as a result of their day-to-day experiences, but also because rising juvenile delinquency rates had attracted more attention to the issue in Canadian society as a whole. From 1942 onwards, for example, more activity was evident in providing organized leisure for youth, something that during the Depression had received little attention, and, of course, scant funding. Telling was the fact that whereas in 1940 only four municipal recreation councils existed in Canada, a decade later the number had reached approximately 100.[72]

Leading the way in this crusade were a number of social service groups such as the Big Brothers, the YMCA, and the Canadian Girls in Training, who had long worked with youth and who stressed the need for supervised recreation as a way of offsetting the supposedly debilitating physical and moral aspects of the urban environment. During the war, activists such as the Big Brothers' Toronto director Kenneth Rogers had stepped up efforts to involve more citizens in its work by citing the unprecedented demand placed on social service groups by the arrival of thousands of children in the cities, the apparent inability of working parents to offer adequate supervision, and the fact that a number of youth organizations had lost supervisory personnel to the military.[73] Vigorously, though unsuccessfully, Rogers and several others in the child welfare field attempted to persuade the federal government not to enlist recreational workers, stressing their relatively small numbers, their importance to young people, and Britain's adoption of such a policy.[74]

Such pleas, against the background of rising youth crime, prompted a higher level of voluntarism among citizens. Among the many who responded were the Calgary Rotarians, who in late 1942 donated for boys a building containing a lathe, an electric jig saw, a car motor, work benches, vices, ping-pong tables, and basketballs.[75] Two years later in Montreal, the Junior League, "aware of the tremendous increase in juvenile delinquency," purchased an eleven-room house and therein established its new Jabberwocky Club, where teens, for an annual fee of 25 cents, could meet, read, do crafts, and on some evenings have dances — an initiative that saw 600 sign up within weeks and an equal number place their names on a waiting list.[76]

Grass-roots pressure also increased on schools to remain open during evenings, on weekends, and over the summer for recreational activity. Attempting to build support for such a program, Stuart K. Jaffray, the director of the University of Toronto's School of Social Work, noted that whereas Chicago had lost $150 000 in 1941 in school windows broken by children with nothing to do, Milwaukee, by contrast, where educational institutions were open year round in the evenings at a similar cost, had suffered virtually no damage — bringing an overall savings to the community when one factored in the charges on the legal system.[77] Still, a number of Canadian schools resisted. Some with industrial arts facilities pointed out that after regular classroom hours, their premises were occupied by students being prepared to work in military production under Ottawa's War Emergency Training Programme. Most, however, cited tight budgets that would be strained past the breaking point by the addition of extra heating charges or janitors' overtime wages. A number of parent associations took the initiative, therefore, and covered the costs by charging children a nominal membership fee.[78] According to a report from Toronto's chief inspector of public buildings, over the final two years of the war several city schools became not just places of books and blackboards, but also "centres of social life and recreation," providing everything from drama classes to Saturday night soirees.[79]

As the war lengthened and the financial situation of many municipalities improved, this recreational movement received further encouragement. By the end of 1943, councillors in North Bay, Kingston, and Toronto had increased budget allotments for playgrounds.[80] The same year, following council debates on juvenile delinquency, Toronto's government sent its commissioner of public welfare to the Tremount district of Cleveland and to the Children's Bureau Area Projects in Chicago and Detroit so that ideas on organized leisure might be gathered for the Regent Park district, where, soon after the war, Toronto's first public housing project was constructed.[81] The result of the trip was a mid-1944 nomination of a steering committee, whose recommendation for a $5000 expenditure was approved by city council to enable local welfare workers, in concert with 49 service community groups in Regent Park, to develop a comprehensive recreational plan. One product was the placement of volunteers in two neighbourhood schools on weekends to direct a series of activities, which by May had attracted 4200 young people.[82] The apparent success in Regent Park prompted several community groups in Toronto's Beach district successfully to initiate a similar program the next year, in co-operation with city council. Soon, some councillors began talking about dividing Toronto into twelve zones and implementing a recreational project in each.[83]

By war's end, much work remained to be done in creating organized leisure for youth. Across the country, by mid-1945 only 24 percent of schools had ever utilized their premises for after-hours recreational activity.[84] None the less, much had been accomplished since the prewar period. Surveying the situation on New Year's Day in 1945, *Maclean's* concluded that "one of the healthy developments of recent years has been the renewed recognition . . . that society has been at fault in not providing enough recreational services at which the youngsters can divert their energies into socially-useful channels."[85]

The challenge with respect to wartime youth, however, was perceived not simply as one of keeping children constructively occupied outside regular school hours. Underage employment was evidence that greater efforts were required to keep young people in school. An increasing number of Canadians seem to have concluded that success in this area would demand more than tougher compulsory school attendance laws, curfews, and the condemnation of parental neglect. That is not to deny that some changes in the school system were conservative in nature. Convinced that rising delinquency demonstrated students' need for enhanced moral direction, in 1944 Ontario premier George Drew made Christian-oriented religious education, which had become optional during the interwar period, compulsory once again. A reaction also took place against the tenets of progressive education, which, by de-emphasizing pedagogical methods such as testing and rote learning, had sought to develop more adaptive and creative individuals. As wartime delinquency emerged as a pertinent issue, the progressive approach, which had become fairly widespread in English Canada by the mid-1930s, was increasingly denounced and rejected on the ground that it fostered a lack of discipline among youth.[86]

But it would oversimplify matters to characterize the new emphases in education as reflecting solely a renewed traditionalism. Equally significant was a campaign — justified to a notable extent on the basis that achievement of its goals would make institutions more useful to both young people and the nation — to consolidate school districts so that they might be better able to support larger and more modern facilities offering a wider range of services, particularly in areas like vocational training. This strategy had been proposed at the very outset of Canadian industrialization, yet by World War II, as several educators pointed out, courses such as industrial arts and commerce still were usually available only at urban-based technical collegiates. Moreover, in large parts of rural Canada, students who wished to proceed beyond Grade 8, especially in technically related fields, had to board in nearby towns or cities where, farmers complained, they were detached from their roots in institutions that rarely offered such relevant courses as agricultural science.[87] The goal for the postwar period, therefore, was to provide all students not simply with a more solid grounding in morality and the three R's, but also with access to composite institutions in which they might try both academic and vocational paths. The fruit, it was anticipated, would be fewer truants and ill-prepared drop-outs, and a better-trained and more content workforce.[88]

The process of educational reform was bolstered by wartime conditions that exposed deficiencies within the school system that many saw as contributing to rising drop-out and delinquency rates. At the outset of hostilities, public education in Canada was still overwhelmingly financed through local property taxes. With relatively little help from provincial governments, many school districts, primarily but not exclusively those in underpopulated rural areas, were continually starved for funds.[89] One resulting problem was teacher salaries, which, as patterns established during World War II revealed, were so meagre as to encourage little loyalty to their profession among instructors. In 1940, when the average yearly salary for an industrial worker in Canada was hovering around $1300, the mean for teachers stood at $860, and as late as 1944, some instructors in one-room rural schoolhouses were bringing home, after taxes, $58 monthly.[90]

Male teachers in the military not only received equivalent (and often better) pay, but in many cases were awarded officer status on the basis of their education. For instructors of both genders, who had often been held in their posts by a scarcity of other opportunities during the Depression, there now awaited better-paying jobs in war industry, particularly if they possessed some knowledge of physics, math, or industrial arts.[91] By the end of 1943, a year in which Ottawa froze teachers in their jobs except for military service, the exodus of instructors was being blamed for the closure of 449 Alberta and 295 Ontario schools — which closures, mostly in agricultural districts, forced children to travel to school long distances by bus, to board with relatives or other families, or, as in parts of the Prairies, to make do with a series of six-week school terms conducted out of railway cars that travelled between communities.[92]

Fewer teachers, along with rural-to-urban migration, also meant a preponderance of overcrowded classrooms and less opportunity for teachers to identify and deal with problem children. By September 1942, 120 of 204 rooms assigned to Calgary students in Grades 1 through 6 had 35 or more children despite a board policy limiting the number to 30.[93] Worry also abounded over the quality of the instruction provided, as school boards found themselves under tremendous pressure to hire replacements quickly. On the positive side, this state of affairs prompted some jurisdictions formally to rescind provisions forcing women to resign upon marriage.[94] But shortages also meant that boards had to call back into service a number of retirees not physically up to the task, or place in classrooms candidates who had not yet completed the prescribed course of study. During the 1942–43 academic year, Nova Scotia had in its education system 300 teachers with only a high-school diploma, and another 400 being hurried through a six-week summer course rather than the customary one year's normal-school training.[95]

Combined with prevailing anxieties over truancy, youth employment, and delinquency, the wartime teacher crisis helped focus more attention on the need for improvements. In 1945, after surveying several magazines and newspapers across the land, the Canada and Newfoundland Education Association [CNEA] remarked on "a surge of interest"[96] in schooling.

Consolidation in larger and more comprehensive institutions, which had proceeded slowly during the interwar years, had become something of a rage by 1945. As the war wound down, there was not only a greater availability of building supplies for construction, and of technical equipment for cut-rate purchase from Ottawa's War Assets Corporation, but also, most significant of all, more money to pursue the program of consolidation. Most provincial governments, in an effort to modernize their school systems to meet the needs both of children and of the presumably more complex postwar economy, became more active in funding education. Between 1939 and 1946, across the nation the provincial input into school financing grew from 15.9 to 29.1 percent.[97] Small school districts, most provincial education officials agreed, could support only one-room, often decrepit schoolhouses with inadequate equipment, and poorly paid teachers attempting to cover too many subjects and grade levels; and too often the small districts injected local idiosyncrasies into the curriculum. The result, according to a 1944 Alberta study, was students who dropped out earlier, had higher absentee rates, and scored about 10 percent lower on standardized math, social studies, language, and science tests compared to students in urban schools.[98] In Ontario and Saskatchewan, the yearly rate of school district consolidation grew between 1940 and 1945 to approximately ten times what it had been in the 1930s.[99] And by 1945, governments in Manitoba, Alberta, New Brunswick, Nova Scotia, and British Columbia had committed themselves to building new consolidated high schools or to making additions to existing institutions[100] so that each could provide adequate vocational and academic training (including agricultural science, where appropriate), as well as physical education and options such as art and music.[101]

This goal of establishing more dynamic and functional educational facilities is further manifest in the large-scale emergence of vocational guidance services, whose purpose was to help high-school students discover career paths for which they were suited; inform them whether jobs would likely exist in their fields; and, ideally, link them with prospective employers. Before the war, such programs existed in the United States, Australia, South Africa, England, Scotland, and Russia, but according to *Vocational Guidance throughout the World*, Canadian schools, as a whole, had yet to establish anything noteworthy.[102] A rudimentary service was inaugurated in Calgary's Western High School in 1934, but not until the 1941–42 academic year did it begin expanding, thereby precipitating a process that by 1945 saw both Calgary and Edmonton appoint guidance directors for their school systems and the provincial university establish a short course for teachers interested in branching out into this field.[103] Moreover, in 1943, vocational guidance programs began expanding throughout the Saskatchewan and British Columbia secondary-school systems, and within two years provincial directors had been named. Experimentation in 1938 at one Winnipeg academy grew over the next seven years to the point where guidance offices were established in Brandon, Flin Flon, and Dauphin. Pioneering projects inaugurated in Ontario during the interwar period, such as at London's Technical School,[104] evolved, over the course of the war, into the creation of a Grade 9 "occupations course" and the general spread of counselling services to academic high schools and collegiates. A few test programs were activated during the war for pupils in Montreal by the Protestant School Board. And guidance offices appeared between 1943 and 1945 at high schools in Halifax, Fredericton, and Saint John.[105]

Also to prepare students more effectively for life's challenges, a number of school boards endorsed a program of sex education. Prior to the war, treatment of this subject, except for consideration of such matters as the physical and mental dangers posed by masturbation, had rarely moved beyond the study of plant reproduction in biology class.[106] In 1943, however, one poll, no doubt influenced by wartime "sex delinquency" statistics, revealed that 76 percent of Canadian adults favoured some type of instruction on the subject in high schools, and 93 percent supported lectures on how to avoid V.D. for "senior level secondary students."[107] Still, with citizens being far from certain about what they considered a morally appropriate treatment of the subject in the classroom, sex education remained an explosive issue. Representing the views of many people was a minister from Devon, Alberta, who portrayed any initiative in this area as bound to transform the school "from a temple of learning into a den of iniquity."[108] Yet between 1943 and 1945, on the understanding that it would serve as tonic against immorality and a preparation for family life, sex education was added to the curricula of several high schools in at least Winnipeg, Vancouver, Victoria, London, and Toronto.[109] The courses usually were given such inoffensive titles as "Social Hygiene" or "Health and Human Relations"; generally consisted of only a few lectures, often delivered by school board medical personnel; invariably were sex-segregated; were available only to those in Grade 10 and higher; dealt with anatomy from a purely technical perspective;[110] and, at several junctures during the lessons, injected a heavy dose of morality so that students would be channelled into a life of "good parenting and family living."[111]

Finally, to ensure that the comprehensive schools of the future would function most effectively, efforts were escalated by war's end to attract high-calibre people into the teaching profession. By 1945, the Alberta, Ontario, Saskatchewan, Manitoba, and Nova Scotia governments had promised minimum salaries in the near future ranging from $1000 to $1200.[112] As well, several provincial governments, with support from organizations such as the CNEA, made greater strides in encouraging professionalization, which was seen as something that would serve everyone connected with the education system by making it more effective and creating a teaching corps with a stronger case for higher pay. Admittedly, the process proceeded rather slowly for more than a generation, largely because an exploding postwar school population continued to force administrators to accept less competent instructors. Nevertheless, by 1945, provincial governments were underwriting costs for a record number of summer upgrading courses for teachers, and in the case of Alberta, a December 1944 order-in-council required that training for teachers of Grades 11 and 12 take place at the provincial university.[113]

Almost all Canadians realized that, notwithstanding success in efforts to improve schools and recreational services and to push mothers back into the home, some young people would still go astray. Such individuals had come to be regarded as a greater threat during the war. Accordingly, more attention was focussed on the shortcomings of Canada's juvenile justice system.

In 1908, Ottawa had passed the Juvenile Delinquents' Act setting down age guidelines (ages 7 to 16 inclusive, unless stipulated differently by a province) and the services municipalities were required to establish before applying for a youth court (namely, a separate pre-trial detention facility for minors, a "suitable judge," and an "adequate staff of probation officers").[114] By 1914, Winnipeg, Halifax, Charlottetown, Montreal, Ottawa, Toronto, Vancouver, and Victoria had established juvenile courts, and three years later Alberta came on board, technically applying the federal legislation throughout the entire province. Soon after the Great War, Nova Scotia created two courts, Prince Edward Island one, Quebec one, Ontario thirteen, Manitoba two, and British Columbia three; and Saskatchewan adopted the Alberta model.[115] Yet by the mid-1920s, this trend had dissipated, as the "progressive" impulse which had proved so seminal in motivating various reformers gave way to postwar disillusionment; and during the Depression, with municipalities strapped for funds, only one new juvenile court appeared in Ontario (York County).[116] For all intents and purposes, in 1939 only Canada's larger urban centres had separate youth courts; 45 percent of minors were thus technically left to be tried and possibly punished as adults.[117]

Even where it was in force, the Juvenile Delinquents' Act frequently meant little in concrete terms. Standards as to what constituted a separate pre-trial detention facility were slipshod; in Edmonton, Calgary, Moncton, Regina, and Saskatoon, for instance, the separate facility was one section of the adult jail cordoned off.[118] As well, often it appeared that appointment to the juvenile court bench was a patronage perk: several judges were leading business figures or clergymen without legal training, let alone grounding in child psychology. Worse yet, perhaps, was that in several jurisdictions no effort was made to secure a separate juvenile judge, the duties being assumed on a part-time basis by a regular magistrate. This was, according to legal historian Dorothy Chunn, a "problematic" situation since the two judicial systems took radically different approaches to rehabilitation, requiring an intellectual shift not all judges were capable of making quickly.[119] Moreover, in almost all juvenile courts, psychologists were, at best, used sparingly; parole officers were too few in number, poorly paid, and inadequately trained; and co-ordination with local welfare agencies left much to be desired. At reformatories across the land, harsh physical punishment was common, professional staff was in short supply, and conditions frequently proved unhygienic.[120]

These conditions worsened as a result of the unusual circumstances created by the war. During the war, an increasing number of young people who were arrested were fined, paroled, or given suspended sentences (such sentences climbed from 59.2 to 79.1 percent of sentences between 1941 and 1943),[121] not only because a greater proportion of crimes were minor, but also because there was a shortage of space in foster homes, other private institutions, and publicly run reformatories. In Ontario, a crisis of sorts occurred in 1942, when the federal government, confronted with few appropriate places in which to house German prisoners of war, took over a major boys' reformatory in Bowmanville. To accommodate the juveniles thereby displaced, the province purchased some smaller buildings in the vicinity, and also attempted to enlist more people who would serve as foster parents. This, however, proved to be no solution, because potential spaces had already been occupied by nearly a thousand British child refugees, and because the rate of remuneration paid by the province to foster parents had not kept pace with early wartime inflation and so failed to bring enough extra participants into the program.[122] Another solution saw more young offenders placed on farms, the belief being that the physical labour there would serve as a valuable teaching tool. But in some cases, stories filtered back about child labour exploitation, or, conversely, about "incorrigibles who would not obey and had to be sent back."[123] Moreover, across Canada, church-run refuges and organizations such as the Children's Aid Society, to whom provinces had frequently turned in the past to help house delinquents, experienced a wartime space deficit as a result of efforts to deal with greater numbers of illegitimate and neglected children, the offspring of mothers who could not cope with youngsters on their own, and of young people who had to be cared for temporarily while their parents searched for urban accommodation. In several juvenile courts, therefore, there developed the unwritten rule that unless the crime committed was "serious," judges would not consider institutionalization until the second or, often, the third offence — a state of affairs that gave rise to rumblings about youth developing "contempt for the law."[124]

From some quarters came rather direct and inexpensive solutions. A group in Guelph recommended to Ontario's attorney general, Leslie Blackwell, "comparatively short terms in the local adult gaol and . . . a strapping."[125] Most of those who dealt with minors on a professional basis, however, and who presumably had more influence over policy formation, lobbied for the expansion of what Toronto police chief Dennis Draper called "humane, intelligent, and scientific strategies to fight crime," namely, "more juvenile courts . . . presided over by broad and socially-minded judges, supplied with an efficient staff of probation officers, a paediatrician-psychiatrist, and proper detention facilities."[126]

While wartime increases in delinquency triggered no immediate overhaul of Canada's juvenile court system, they do appear to have reinvigorated campaigns for quantitative and qualitative improvements. In mid-1943, Alberta's Social Credit government established a committee to improve the province's juvenile justice system. After hearing from 35 individuals/groups working with children, the committee released its formal recommendations, which included the following: encouragement and financial aid to communities to increase the number of juvenile courts; the appointment of judges clearly familiar with current psychological theories about deviant youth; the creation of separate pre-trial detention facilities where children might be examined by a psychologist or social worker; more effective training (perhaps at universities) for parole officers, and their appointment on the basis of one per 5000 people; greater efforts to co-ordinate courts with social welfare agencies to better monitor problem youth; and the establishment of state-run reformatories stressing rehabilitation and job training over punishment.[127] Within three years, part-time psychologists had been assigned to youth courts in Edmonton and Calgary; the Alberta and Edmonton governments had contributed a total of $40 000 for a new South Side pre-trial detention facility; and a new provincial Child Welfare Act had established committees to organize the inspection of foster homes as well as to select parole officers and child welfare workers.[128] In Ontario between 1943 and 1945, new juvenile courts were created in Cornwall, Dufferin County, and the Lakehead region,[129] and during the first half-decade following the war, youth courts were created to serve two more counties in Prince Edward Island, three in New Brunswick, two in Nova Scotia, three in Ontario, and two in Manitoba.[130]

Historians assessing the initial postwar years often present an era typified by conservatism, one that in many ways represented a backlash against the disconcerting social discontinuities created by World War II.[131] With regard to the family unit and the treatment of young people, in certain respects this presentation rings true. For many in Canada, the rise in delinquency in 1942 confirmed that wartime changes in gender roles had to be reversed as soon as possible, not only so that males would be re-established in their natural breadwinner role, but also so that the type of family stability that would prevent children from going astray would be reconstituted. To that end (and also to give itself a better chance of delivering on recent election promises to retain low unemployment in the initial postwar period), the governing Liberals, almost immediately after the conflict, withdrew the limited federal financial support for day care as well as tax breaks for married women who worked. Partially as a result of these actions, the female labour participation rate fell from 33.5 to 25 percent between 1944 and 1946.[132]

True, after years of loneliness and labouring at two jobs, many women happily retreated to the hearth. But also true is that strong conservative pressures shaped the initial postwar decade, a decade whose most enduring social images perhaps remain the "baby boom" and the migration of families to suburban "tranquillity." During this period, if a mother worked at all, usually she worked only after the children reached school age, and often on a part-time basis — the prevailing assumption being that her aim was the socially acceptable one of supplementing the family income and not pursuit of a career. Young people too were expected to conform to specific and rather straight-laced standards: for a boy, good grades and getting ahead were essential; and for a girl, physical appearance and purity were critical, so that she would attract the right type of boyfriend and future husband.[133]

Yet much of the wartime concern over youth, which helped produce such an emphasis on discipline and traditionalism during the 1950s, was clearly overblown. Not only were the histrionics about mothers neglecting their children statistically unsupported, but rising levels of delinquency among adolescents related less to working women and the so-called breakdown of the nuclear family than to demographic determinants such as earlier migration waves into Canada and the dispatching overseas of 18- to 30-year-old males.

In one respect, therefore, the wartime jitters over juveniles amounted to much ado about nothing. But such a characterization applies only if one confines oneself to the discrepancy between public pronouncements on the threat posed by youth crime and the actual statistics. On an ideological and social level, the consequences of the wartime jitters were indeed substantial. For married women, outraged commentary about aggregate delinquency levels helped confirm that their large-scale migration outside the home and into the workplace would wait yet another generation. Conversely, the view that significant problems prevailed among minors caused more than just a drift towards traditionalism. The resulting concern no doubt helped to legitimize and bolster pioneering efforts by the CYC to solicit opinions from youth. Furthermore, many of the hopes and expectations revealed through CYC study groups and surveys perhaps buttressed campaigns already under way to correct deficiencies that had been exposed by wartime conditions and that were viewed as contributing to delinquency — among them campaigns to improve recreational, educational, and judicial services for youth.

Thus, for families and young people just as in several other areas of Canadian history, World War II emerges as a watershed period. However, whereas with the development of a stronger national spirit, the flowering of the federal bureaucracy, the growth of the planned economy, and the emergence of the social security state, the movement was generally forward,[134] here there were multiple eddies and currents that sometimes flowed back upon themselves. For the wartime anxieties over adolescents not only helped usher in the conservatism of the 1950s, but also, it seems, played a role in bringing to fruition several campaigns whose roots lie in the ideas of turn-of-the-century progressives.

NOTES

1. See Gallup Canada Inc., *Public Opinion Polls*, 1 May 1989, 2 Jan. 1992.
2. *Saturday Night*, 19 Dec. 1942, 4–5.
3. National Archives of Canada [NAC], MG28 I 441, Canadian Association of Social Workers papers, vol. 10, file 10, Unidentified newspaper clipping, 6 April 1941. For discussion of the British experience with wartime juvenile delinquency, see John Costello, *Love, Sex, and War: Changing Values, 1939–1945* (London: Collins, 1985).
4. Richard R. Lingeman, "The Home Front during World War II," in John H. Carey, Julius Weinberg, and Thomas Hartshorne, eds., *The Social Fabric*, vol. 2 (Boston: Little, Brown, 1987), 260; John McCarthy, "The Individual Child and His Problems," unpublished bachelor of pedagogy thesis, University of Toronto, 1944, 1. For more information on the U.S. experience with wartime delinquency, see William M. Tuttle Jr., *"Daddy's Gone to War": The Second World War in the Lives of America's Children* (New York: Oxford University Press, 1993).
5. *Canada Year Book*, 1945, 1116. *Saturday Night*, 14 Nov. 1942, 24.
6. Toronto *Telegram*, 28 Jan. 1944, 2; *Canadian Periodical Index*, 1930–48.
7. Ernest Groves and Gladys Groves, "The Social Background of Wartime Adolescents," *American Academy of Political and Social Science*, 236 (1944): 27–28; *The School* (secondary ed.), 32, 1 (1943): 6.
8. See Richard M. Ugland, "Viewpoints and Morale of Urban High School Students during World War II — Indianapolis as a Case Study," *Indiana Magazine of History*, 77 (1981): 173–74.
9. *Canadian Affairs*, 15 Feb. 1944, 10.
10. Jill Wade, "Wartime Housing Limited, 1941–1947: Canadian Housing Policy at the Crossroads," *Urban History Review*, 15, 1 (June 1986): 43.

11. John Bacher, *Keeping to the Marketplace: The Evolution of Canadian Housing Policy* (Montreal and Kingston: McGill-Queen's University Press, 1993), 136; NAC, RG36, Boards, Offices and Committees, series 31, War Information Board, vol. 17, file 9-6-2-5, Post-War Planning Information, 15 Sept. 1945.

12. NAC, MG28 I 10, Canadian Council on Social Development papers [CCSD], vol. 54, file 1942–46, Excerpt from Montreal *Herald*, n.d.; *Canadian Welfare*, Oct. 1945, 11.

13. NAC, MG28 I 25, National Council of Women of Canada papers, vol. 84, file 16, Clipping from *The Ottawa Citizen*, 17 June 1943.

14. Archives of Ontario [AO], RG29, Department of Public Welfare records [PW], series 1–99, container 3, First Report of the Older Boys' Department, Big Brother Organization of Ontario, 1 June 1940.

15. NAC, MG30 E256, Charlotte Whitton papers [CW], vol. 82, Address entitled "Threats to the Home Base," n.d.

16. See Metropolitan Toronto Archives [MTA], RG5.1, Department of Social Services records [SS], vol. 3, file 73.1, General Manager of Social Problems Committee, Toronto Board of Trade to the Mayor, 23 Nov. 1944; City of Calgary Archives [CA], RG26, City Clerk records [CC], file 2239, Chief Constable J. Downey to J.M. Miller, 24 Oct. 1942; AO, RG4, Attorney-General records [AG], series 32, file 740/1942, Unidentified newspaper clipping; CCSD, vol. 87, file 1856, Agnes Collier to Joseph Laycock, 2 Jan. 1942; *Canadian School Journal*, 20, 10 (1942): 323; *Maclean's*, 15 June 1942, 46, 15 March 1943, 50.

17. Kenneth H. Rogers, *Street Gangs in Toronto: A Study of the Forgotten Boy* (Toronto: Ryerson Press, 1945), 11–20.

18. Clothing regulations introduced in April 1942 prohibited, among other things, the production of double-breasted suits, or pants with cuffs or pleats. J.L. Granatstein and Desmond Morton, *A Nation Forged in Fire: Canadians and the Second World War, 1939–1945* (Toronto: Lester and Orpen Dennys, 1989), 40.

19. AO, AG, series 32, file 1008/1942, Police Report (#6 Division), 1 June 1943.

20. Rogers, *Street Gangs in Toronto*, 1–2, 42–53.

21. NAC, CCSD, vol. 87, file 1856, Advertisement by Junior League of Montreal, La Ligue de la jeunesse féminine, and Jewish Welfare League for the Delinquency Prevention Week, 12–18 March 1944.

22. *New Advance*, Dec. 1943, 2.

23. *Canada Year Book*, 1946, 150.

24. Toronto *Globe & Mail*, 14 Sept. 1944, 7.

25. Archives of Alberta [AA], accession # 83.192/754, Department of Social Services records [SS], Mrs. R.J. Wilson to A.A. Miller, 10 July 1943.

26. NAC, CCSD, vol. 88, file 1856A-1942-43, Judge Helen Gregory MacGill to Joseph Laycock, 4 May 1942; CA, CC, note 16.

27. *Canada Year Book*, 1945, 1116; McCarthy, "Individual Child and His Problems," 5.

28. See John Bullen, "Child Labour and the Family Economy in Late Nineteenth-Century Urban Ontario," *Labour/Le Travail*, 18 (1986): 163–87, and Patricia T. Rooke and R.L. Schnell, *Discarding the Asylum: From Child Rescue to the Welfare State in English-Canada (1850–1950)* (New York: University Press of America, 1983), 354–360.

29. NAC, RG27, Department of Labour records, vol. 988, file 1-11-4, Untitled chart.

30. Robert Stamp, *The Schools of Ontario, 1876–1976* (Toronto: University of Toronto Press, 1982), 172; Kenneth Rogers, *Boys Are Worth It* (Toronto: Ryerson Press, 1944), 5–6.

31. NAC, CCSD, vol. 82, file 594-2, Report by the Labour Youth Federation of Canada entitled "Physical Fitness, Minimum Wage Laws," n.d.; *Saturday Night*, 23 Jan. 1943, 5.

32. AO, AG, series 2, file 19.23, Report of the London Council of Social Agencies to Leslie Blackwell, 29 Sept. 1944.

33. *Maclean's*, 15 April 1943, 15.

34. NAC, CW, vol. 80, file "Cdn Youth Comm.," Clipping from *Chatelaine*, Jan. 1945.

35. Ontario Department of Education, *Annual Report, 1943*, 62; *Annual Report, 1946*, 52.
36. See note 32.
37. NAC, MG28 I 11, Canadian Youth Commission papers [CYC], vol. 31, file 5(3a), "Proposals with Respect to School Attendance," 1944.
38. See Toronto Board of Education Archives [TBE], file II-I-180-b, Recommendation of the Special Committee re Truancy, 1943–44; AA, accession # 79.334/87, SS, Minutes of Executive Council, Canada and Newfoundland Education Association, 29–30 Oct. 1943; City of Vancouver Archives [CV], RG75 E1, Board of Police Commissioner Records [BPC], vol. 28-B-7, file "Juv Del," 1945 Report of the Committee on Juvenile Delinquency.
39. *Canadian Forum*, April 1943, 4.
40. Neil Sutherland, "'We Always Had Things to Do': The Paid and Unpaid Work of Anglophone Children between the 1920s and 1960s," *Labour*, 22 (1990) 135.
41. Ruth Roach Pierson, *"They're Still Women After All": Canadian Women and the Second World War* (Toronto: McClelland & Stewart Ltd., 1988), 48–49, 215; Ramona Rose, "'Keepers of Morale': The Vancouver Council of Women, 1939–1945," unpublished M.A. thesis, University of British Columbia, 1992, 70.
42. James Pitsula, *Let the Family Flourish: A History of the Family Service Bureau of Regina, 1913–1982* (Regina: Centrax, 1982), 67–68.
43. Diane G. Forestell, "The Victorian Legacy: Historical Perspectives on the Canadian Women's Army Corps," unpublished Ph.D. thesis, York University, 1986, 164; *New Advance*, Feb. 1943, 16.
44. *Chatelaine*, June 1943, 8–9.
45. *Canadian Welfare*, July 1942, 11.
46. AO, PW, series 1, file 1-872, Survey of Dominion–Provincial Wartime Day Nursery Programme, September 1942 to September 1945; Pierson, *"They're Still Women After All,"* 53.
47. Rose, "Keepers of Morale," 77–78; *Canadian Forum*, April 1943, 2.
48. City of Edmonton Archives [CE], RG11, City Clerk records [CC], class 32, file 7, Brief submitted to City Council from the Council of Social Agencies, Summer 1943; Ibid., F.D. Sutcliffe to Council of Social Agencies, 21 Sept. 1943.
49. Ibid., Information Regarding the Wartime Day Nursery Situation in Edmonton Presented to the City Council of Edmonton by the Day Care Committee of the Edmonton Council of Social Agencies, 12 June 1944; Pierson, *"They're Still Women After All,"* 51.
50. NAC, RG29, National Health and Welfare records [NHW], vol. 930, file 386-3-10, pt. 1, Report entitled "School Lunches in Alberta," n.d.; Edmonton Public School Board [EPSB], Board Minutes, 10 May 1943.
51. NAC, CCSD, vol. 55, file "Daycare 1941–7," Excerpt from Toronto *Globe & Mail*, 18 Feb. 1943.
52. *Chatelaine*, June 1943, 8.
53. Charges for "non-support and neglecting children" stood at 2099 in 1943 and 2442 in 1944. *Canada Year Book*, 1942, 913; Ibid., 1943, 984; Ibid., 1946, 1113; Ibid., 1947, 283.
54. Pierson, *"They're Still Women After All,"* 50–51.
55. *Canadian Affairs*, 1 Oct. 1943, 5; Interview with Bert Collins, Montgomery Legion Branch, Edmonton, Alberta, 22 Sept. 1992.
56. *Canadian Welfare*, Oct. 1942, 15.
57. *Canada Year Book*, 1946, 247.
58. In Toronto, for example, juvenile delinquency hit a peak of 1852 charges in 1942. However, in 1927, the figure was 2808, and during 1930, the first full year of the Depression, it stood at 2122. In 1938, the year to which wartime comparisons were often made, 1367 juveniles were arrested. AO, AG, series 2, file 24.3, 1945 Report of the Toronto Family Court.

59. In the five years from 1925 to 1929, migration to Canada stood at 84 907, 135 982, 158 886, 166 783, and 164 993 respectively. M.C. Urquhart and K.A.H. Buckley, eds., *Historical Statistics on Canada* (Toronto: Macmillan, 1965), series A254–72. Although the census does not break down age categories to the teenage years, between 1931 and 1941 the number of Canadians between ages 10 and 19 grew from 2.11 to 2.22 million. *Canada Year Book*, 1945, 101.

60. Whereas immigration to Canada averaged 309 061 per annum from 1910 to 1914, over the next four years the average was 51 599. Urquhart and Buckley, *Historical Statistics on Canada*, Series A254–72. Birth rates averaged 25.25 between 1910 and 1914 and over the next four years dropped to an average of 24.42. *Canada Year Book*, 1927–28, 109–10.

61. For example, between 1930 and 1931, immigration to Canada went from 104 806 to 27 530. Moreover, between 1929 and 1931, total births decreased from 242 246 to 228 296. Urquhart and Buckley, *Historical Statistics on Canada*, series A254–72, B1–14.

62. AO, AG, series 32, file 1217/1942, County Reports on Juvenile Delinquency, 1942.

63. *Canada Year Book*, 1942, 920; Ibid., 1946, 1121.

64. See Albert H. Burrows, "The Problem of Juvenile Delinquency," *Journal of Educational Psychology*, 19, 6 (1946): 384–85.

65. NAC, CCSD, vol. 87, file 1856, Excerpt from *Weekly Bulletin*, 13 Nov. 1943; Dominion Bureau of Statistics, *Daily Bulletin*, 13, 125 (23 June 1944).

66. *Canada Year Book*, 1946, 236, 261; *Canadian Welfare*, June 1946, 27.

67. Linda McGuire Ambrose, "The Canadian Youth Commission: Planning for Youth and Social Welfare in the Post-War Era," unpublished Ph.D. thesis, University of Waterloo, 72–74, 79–80.

68. NAC, CYC, series (c) 2, vol. 32, file 6(3a), Report entitled "The Voice of Youth," 1945.

69. Ambrose, "The Canadian Youth Commission," 33–34, 55; NAC, MG28 I 95, Young Men's Christian Association papers, vol. 84, file 7, Goodwin Watson to Murray J. Ross, 22 March 1945.

70. NAC, CCSD, vol. 83, file 594-1942-44, Results of CYC Questionnaire, 1944.

71. NAC, CYC, series (c) 7, vol. 42, file 7(3g), Report of the Halifax Regional Youth Conference, 22 Oct. 1944; NAC, CCSD, vol. 82, file 1939–44, Report of the Ontario Youth Conference, 1944.

72. Ambrose, "The Canadian Youth Commission," 293.

73. *Canadian Forum*, Sept. 1942, 171–72.

74. NAC, CCSD, vol. 87, file 1856, Edgar Brown to George Davidson, 29 July 1943.

75. Glenbow Institute [GI], M5841, Calgary Local Council of Women papers [CLCW], file 21, 1942 *Year Book*, 45–46.

76. *Canadian Welfare*, April 1945, 19.

77. *Canadian School Journal*, 20, 6 (1942): 178–79.

78. *Educational Courier*, vol. 14, no. 4 (1944): 10; EPSB, Board Minutes, 25 Feb. 1943.

79. MTA, SS, vol. 2, file 73.1, Submission from Chief Inspector of Public Buildings, 23 Nov. 1945; Ibid., W.A. Turner to R.J. Moris, 25 Nov. 1944.

80. Ibid., vol. 3, file 73.1, Memorandum on Recreational Programmes and Youth Services for the Committee on Public Welfare, March 1945.

81. Kenneth Rogers, *Boys Are Worth It*, 34; MTA, SS, vol. 1, file 73, "A Plan for the Reduction of Juvenile Delinquency in Toronto," submitted by the Welfare Council of Toronto & District, 15 Nov. 1943.

82. Ibid., vol. 2, file 73.1, A.W. Laver to Alderman William Collings, 2 March 1945; Ibid., William Turnbull to the Commissioner of Public Welfare, 15 Nov. 1945.

83. Ibid., City Council Memorandum, July 1945.

84. NAC, CYC, series (c) 5, vol. 38, file 7(3e), Summary of the Interim Report of the Recreation Committee, n.d.

85. *Maclean's*, 1 Jan. 1945, 39.

86. Stamp, *Schools of Ontario*, 178–81.
87. AA, accession # 79.334/89, Department of Education records [DE], CNEA Memorandum, 20 Dec. 1945. For early efforts at school consolidation, see Neil Sutherland, *Children in English-Speaking Society: Framing the Twentieth-Century Consensus* (Toronto: University of Toronto Press, 1976), 193–94.
88. J. Donald Wilson, Robert Stamp, and Louis-Philippe Audet, *Canadian Education: A History* (Scarborough: Prentice-Hall, 1970), 386.
89. For example, in 1941, whereas Winnipeg spent $88 on the education of each pupil, the figure in rural Prince Edward Island was $15.60. GI, CLCW, file 21, *1941 Year Book*, 26.
90. F.H. Leacy, ed., *Historical Statistics on Canada*, 2d ed. (Ottawa: Supply and Services, 1983), series E41–48; NAC, CW, vol. 104, file "Survey on Education in Canada," Dominion Bureau of Statistics' Survey, n.d.; *A.T.A. Magazine*, Feb. 1944, 12–13.
91. *A.T.A. Magazine*, Sept. 1942, 36; NAC, MG28 I 102, Canadian Teachers' Federation papers [CTF], vol. 28, file 328, Memorandum re 1942 CNEA Conference, 16 Oct. 1942.
92. *A.T.A. Magazine*, Jan. 1944, 8; Ontario Department of Education, *Annual Report, 1943*, 4–6.
93. GI, CLCW, file 21, *1943 Year Book*, 31.
94. One case being the Edmonton school board in 1943. EPSB, Board Minutes, 5 Oct. 1943.
95. AA, accession # 79.334/86, DE, H.C. Newland to Dr. S.J. Willis, 26 March 1942.
96. *A.T.A. Magazine*, Jan. 1945, 4–5.
97. *Canada Year Book*, 1948–49, 316–17; Wilson et. al, *Canadian Education*, 450.
98. *A.T.A. Magazine*, Jan. 1945, 6.
99. Ontario Department of Education, *Annual Report, 1946*, 6; *Canada Year Book*, 1947–48, 310.
100. AA, accession # 79.334/87, DE, Deputy Minister of Education to Dr. F.E. Robbins, 20 May 1943; NAC, NHW, vol. 930, file 386-3-10, pt. 1, Memorandum entitled "Trends in Education in Nova Scotia, 1944–45"; Manitoba Department of Education, *Annual Report, 1945*, 16–18; Wilson, et. al., *Canadian Education*, 387.
101. *Report of the Royal Commission on Education in Ontario, 1950* (Toronto: Baptist Johnson, 1950), 131, 256.
102. NAC, RG76, Department of Immigration Records, vol. 58, file 527-17, Petition to William Lyon Mackenzie King from the Ontario Vocational Guidance Association, 9 Dec. 1940.
103. EPSB, *Annual Report, 1945*, 17–18; John Abram Ross Wilson, "The Counsellor in Canadian Secondary Schools," education doctorate, Oregon State College, 1951, 22–23.
104. NAC, CYC, series (c) 2, file 9(3a), "Your Job Is Your Life Pattern," supplement printed by *The London Free Press*, 1945; Ivor F. Goodson and Ian R. Dowbiggin, "Vocational Education and School Reform: The Case of the London (Canada) Technical School," *History of Education Review*, 20, 1 (1991): 55; Stamp, *Schools of Ontario*, 115–16.
105. Between 1939 and 1945, seven Toronto collegiates started guidance services. Wilson, "The Councillor," 13–18, 20–50; Ross L. Donald, "The Development of Guidance in the Secondary Schools of the Dominion of Canada," unpublished M.Ed. thesis, University of Manitoba, 1951, 25–26; Nova Scotia Department of Education, Superintendent's Report, 31 July 1945, 136–38; Stamp, *Schools of Ontario*, 197.
106. On the lack of pre–World War II sex education, see Jay Cassel, *The Secret Plague: Venereal Disease in Canada, 1838–1939* (Toronto: University of Toronto Press, 1987), 244.
107. *New Advance*, Oct. 1944, 19; *The School* (secondary ed.), 34, 4 (1945): 309–10.
108. NAC, CYC, series (c) 7, vol. 42, file 7(3g), Brief from Devon CYC Study Group to the Provincial Youth Commissioner, n.d.

109. *A.T.A. Magazine*, Dec. 1944, 17; *Canadian School Journal*, 3, 2 (1945): 51–53; TBE, Minutes of Special Committee Appointed to Consider and Report on the Matter of Sex Education in the Schools, 1948.

110. CV, BPC, vol. 58-B-5, file 7, Board of School Trustees, Subcommittee #4 Report, 1 May 1945; NAC, MG28 I 63, Dominion Council of Health papers, reel C-9816, Report of the General Meeting, 29 Nov. to 1 Dec. 1945.

111. NAC, CTF, vol. 28, file 103, National Film Board — Special Convention Service for National Conference of Agencies Serving Youth, 30 Nov. 1946.

112. Manitoba Department of Education, *Annual Report, 1945*, 23–24; NAC, CTF, vol. 28, file 331, Memorandum to the Provincial Secretaries of the Canadian Teachers' Federation, 14 March 1945; *Chatelaine*, March 1944, 16.

113. *A.T.A. Magazine*, May 1944, 33–34, Jan. 1945, 15; Jean Linse Dixon, "The Prestige and Professional Growth of Canadian Teachers," unpublished M.A. thesis, University of Alberta, 1949, 5–11.

114. NAC, CW, vol. 80, file "Montreal School," Paper entitled "Juvenile Delinquency," n.d.

115. Sutherland, *Children in English-Speaking Society*, 125–26.

116. Dorothy E. Chunn, *From Punishment to Doing Good: Family Courts and Socialized Justice in Ontario, 1880–1940* (Toronto: University of Toronto Press, 1992), 98.

117. AO, AG, series 2, file 24.4, T.W. Laidlaw to Leslie Blackwell, 26 Sept. 1944.

118. NAC, CCSD, vol. 87, file 1855, Report to Miss Charlotte Whitton, 27 May 1941; AA, accession # 83.192/754, SS, Dorothy Begg to J. Miller, 31 Aug. 1943.

119. Chunn, *From Punishment to Doing Good*, 167–68.

120. For example, in Ontario, only Toronto's juvenile court enjoyed the services of a full-time psychiatrist. See note 118, Report to Whitton.

121. *Canada Year Book*, 1952–53, 315.

122. *Canadian Welfare*, June 1942, 17; MTA, SS, file 73.1, City Council Memorandum, July 1945. Between August 1939 and October 1941, before wage and price controls were implemented by Ottawa, total inflation amounted to 17.8 percent. Granatstein and Morton, *A Nation Forged in Fire*, 36.

123. AO, RG20, Department of Correctional Services records, series C-2, file 3.7, F.W. Armstrong to Premier G. Drew, 20 Aug. 1943.

124. Ibid., C.F. Neelands to C. Dunbar, 1 Sept. 1944; AA, accession # 83.192/754, SS, E.A. Bell to A.H. Miller, 17 Sept. 1943.

125. AO, AG, series 32, file 1033/1945, C.L. Snyder to F.P. Varco, n.d.

126. McCarthy, "The Individual Child and His Problems," 9–10.

127. AA, accession # 70.414/2147, SS, Report of the Child Welfare Committee as Appointed by Orders in Council Nos. 913/43 and 1256/43.

128. CE, CC, class 32, file 9, Mayor Fry to City Council, 12 March 1945; AA, accession # 70.414/2245, SS, Department of Public Welfare, *Annual Report, 1945*, 49–50.

129. NAC, CCSD, vol. 88, file 1856A, P.C. Bergeron to Joseph Laycock, 20 April 1943; AO, AG, series 32, file 24.14, T.H. Woolfe to C.L. Snyder, 11 Sept. 1943.

130. Dominion Bureau of Statistics, *Report on Delinquency*, 1950, 1951, n.p.

131. See, for example, Eileen Tyler May, *Homeward Bound: American Families in the Cold War* (New York: Basic Books, 1988), especially chap. 3.

132. Alison Prentice, Paula Bourne, Gail Cuthbert Brandt, Beth Light, Wendy Mitchinson, and Naomi Black, *Canadian Women: A History* (Toronto: Harcourt Brace Jovanovich, 1988), 311.

133. Wini Breines, *Young, White, and Miserable: Growing Up Female in the Fifties* (New York: Beacon Press, 1992), 131.

134. See J.L. Granatstein, *Canada's War: The Politics of the Mackenzie King Government* (Toronto: Oxford University Press, 1975) and *The Ottawa Men: The Civil Service Mandarins, 1935–1957* (Toronto: Oxford University Press, 1982).

Photo Credits

TOPIC ONE
City of Toronto Archives/RG-8-32-187.

TOPIC TWO
Glenbow Archives/NA-1831-1.

TOPIC THREE
David Miller Collection/National Archives of Canada/C-33392.

TOPIC FOUR
Canadian Football Hall of Fame and Museum.

TOPIC FIVE
Provincial Archives of Manitoba/Events 173/3 (N9905).

TOPIC SIX
Beaton Institute, University College of Cape Breton.

TOPIC SEVEN
National Archives of Canada/C-6196, C-89536, and C-89542.

TOPIC EIGHT
Department of Indian Affairs and Northern Development Collection/National
Archives of Canada/C-33643.

TOPIC NINE
Glenbow Archives/NA-431-5.

TOPIC TEN
Dick and Ada Bird Collection/Saskatchewan Archives Board/R-A27560-1.

TOPIC ELEVEN
National Film Board of Canada Collection/National Archives of Canada/PA-116153.

READER REPLY CARD

We are interested in your reaction to *Age of Contention: Readings in Canadian Social History, 1900–1945*, by Jeffrey Keshen. You can help us to improve this book in future editions by completing this questionnaire.

1. What was your reason for using this book?

   ❑ university course   ❑ continuing education course   ❑ personal interest

   ❑ college course   ❑ professional development   ❑ other _____

2. If you are a student, please identify your school and the course in which you used this book.

3. Which chapters or parts of this book did you use? Which did you omit?

4. What did you like best about this book?

5. What did you like least about this book?

6. Please identify any topics you think should be added to future editions.

7. Please add any comments or suggestions.

8. May we contact you for further information?

Name: _____

Address: _____

Phone: _____

(fold here and tape shut)

MAIL ➤ POSTE

Canada Post Corporation / Société canadienne des postes

Postage paid
If mailed in Canada

Port payé
si posté au Canada

**Business
Reply**

**Réponse
d'affaires**

0116870399   01

0116870399-M8Z4X6-BR01

Heather McWhinney
Director of Product Development, College Division
HARCOURT BRACE & COMPANY, CANADA
55 HORNER AVENUE
TORONTO, ONTARIO
M8Z 9Z9